Economists in Cambridge

Economists in Cambridge explores the notion of a distinctive 'Cambridge approach' to economics taken by authors working in Cambridge (UK) between 1921 and 1946. The study utilises unpublished as well as previously published material in order to examine the dynamic of this pioneering group and to delineate the characteristics of a distinctive 'Cambridge' approach.

Leading economists featured include John Maynard Keynes, Piero Sraffa and Joan Robinson as well as their major opponents.

The wealth of previously unpublished material contained within this volume will ensure that this book will be indispensable to all those studying the history of economic thought, interested in the development of economic ideas and in the cultural history of that period.

Routledge studies in the history of economics

1 **Economics as Literature**
Willie Henderson

2 **Socialism and Marginalism in Economics 1870–1930**
Edited by Ian Steedman

3 **Hayek's Political Economy**
The socio-economics of order
Steve Fleetwood

4 **On the Origins of Classical Economics**
Distribution and value from William Petty to Adam Smith
Tony Aspromourgos

5 **The Economics of Joan Robinson**
Edited by Maria Cristina Marcuzzo, Luigi Pasinetti and Alessandro Roncaglia

6 **The Evolutionist Economics of Léon Walras**
Albert Jolink

7 **Keynes and the 'Classics'**
A study in language, epistemology and mistaken identities
Michel Verdon

8 **The History of Game Theory, Vol 1**
From the beginnings to 1945
Robert W. Dimand and Mary Ann Dimand

9 **The Economics of W.S. Jevons**
Sandra Peart

10 **Gandhi's Economic Thought**
Ajit K. Dasgupta

11 **Equilibrium and Economic Theory**
Edited by Giovanni Caravale

12 **Austrian Economics in Debate**
Edited by Willem Keizer, Bert Tieben and Rudy van Zijp

13 **Ancient Economic Thought**
Edited by B.B. Price

14 **The Political Economy of Social Credit and Guild Socialism**
Frances Hutchinson and Brian Burkitt

15 **Economic Careers**
Economics and economists in Britain 1930–1970
Keith Tribe

16 **Understanding 'Classical' Economics**
Studies in the long-period theory
Heinz Kurz and Neri Salvadori

17 **History of Environmental Economic Thought**
E. Kula

18 **Economic Thought in Communist and Post-Communist Europe**
Edited by Hans-Jürgen Wagener

19 **Studies in the History of French Political Economy**
From Bodin to Walras
Edited by Gilbert Faccarello

20 **The Economics of John Rae**
Edited by O.F. Hamouda, C. Lee and D. Mair

21 **Keynes and the Neoclassical Synthesis**
Einsteinian versus Newtonian macroeconomics
Teodoro Dario Togati

22 **Historical Perspectives on Macroeconomics**
Sixty years after the 'General Theory'
Edited by Philippe Fontaine and Albert Jolink

23 **The Founding of Institutional Economics**
The leisure class and sovereignty
Edited by Warren J. Samuels

24 **Evolution of Austrian Economics**
From Menger to Lachmann
Sandye Gloria

25 **Marx's Concept of Money: the God of Commodities**
Anitra Nelson

26 **The Economics of James Steuart**
Edited by Ramón Tortajada

27 **The Development of Economics in Europe since 1945**
Edited by A.W. Bob Coats

28 **The Canon in the History of Economics**
Critical essays
Edited by Michalis Psalidopoulos

29 **Money and Growth**
Selected papers of Allyn Abbott Young
Edited by Perry G. Mehrling and Roger J. Sandilands

30 **The Social Economics of Jean-Baptiste Say**
Markets and virtue
Evelyn L. Forget

31 **The Foundations of Laissez-Faire**
The economics of Pierre de Boisguilbert
Gilbert Faccarello

32 **John Ruskin's Political Economy**
Willie Henderson

33 **Contributions to the History of Economic Thought**
Essays in honour of R.D.C. Black
Edited by Antoin E. Murphy and Renee Prendergast

34 **Towards an Unknown Marx**
A commentary on the manuscripts of 1861–63
Enrique Dussel

35 **Economics and Interdisciplinary Exchange**
Edited by Guido Erreygers

36 **Economics as the Art of Thought**
Essays in memory of G.L.S. Shackle
Edited by Stephen F. Frowen and Peter Earl

37 **The Decline of Ricardian Economics**
Politics and economics in post-Ricardian theory
Susan Pashkoff

38 **Piero Sraffa**
His life, thought and cultural heritage
Alessandro Roncaglia

39 **Equilibrium and Disequilibrium in Economic Theory**
The Marshall-Walras divide
Michel de Vroey

40 **The German Historical School**
The historical and ethical approach to economics
Edited by Yuichi Shionoya

41 **Reflections on the Classical Canon in Economics**
Essays in honor of Samuel Hollander
Edited by Sandra Peart and Evelyn Forget

42 **Piero Sraffa's Political Economy**
A centenary estimate
Edited by Terenzio Cozzi and Roberto Marchionatti

43 **The Contribution of Joseph Schumpeter to Economics**
Economic development and institutional change
Richard Arena and Cecile Dangel

44 **On the Development of Long-run Neo-Classical Theory**
Tom Kompas

45 **F.A. Hayek as a Political Economist**
Economic analysis and values
Edited by Jack Birner, Pierre Garrouste and Thierry Aimar

46 **Pareto, Economics and Society**
The mechanical analogy
Michael McLure

47 **The Cambridge Controversies in Capital Theory**
A study in the logic of theory development
Jack Birner

48 **Economics Broadly Considered**
Essays in honor of Warren J Samuels
Edited by Steven G. Medema, Jeff Biddle and John B. Davis

49 **Physicians and Political Economy**
Six studies of the work of doctor-economists
Edited by Peter Groenewegen

50 **The Spread of Political Economy and the Professionalisation of Economists**
Economic societies in Europe, America and Japan in the nineteenth century
Massimo Augello and Marco Guidi

51 **Historians of Economics and Economic Thought**
The construction of disciplinary memory
Steven G. Medema and Warren J. Samuels

52 **Competing Economic Theories**
Essays in memory of Giovanni Caravale
Sergio Nisticò and Domenico Tosato

53 **Economic Thought and Policy in Less Developed Europe**
The 19th Century
Edited by Michalis Psalidopoulos and Maria-Eugenia Almedia Mata

54 **Family Fictions and Family Facts**
Harriet Martineau, Adolphe Quetelet and the population question in England 1798–1859
Brian Cooper

55 **Eighteenth-Century Economics**
Peter Groenewegen

56 **The Rise of Political Economy in the Scottish Enlightenment**
Edited by Tatsuya Sakamoto and Hideo Tanaka

57 **Classics and Moderns in Economics Volume I**
Essays on nineteenth and twentieth century economic thought
Peter Groenewegen

58 **Classics and Moderns in Economics Volume II**
Essays on nineteenth and twentieth century economic thought
Peter Groenewegen

59 **Marshall's Evolutionary Economics**
Tiziano Raffaelli

60 **Money, Time and Rationality in Max Weber**
Austrian connections
Stephen D. Parsons

61 **Classical Macroeconomics**
Some modern variations and distortions
James C.W. Ahiakpor

62 **The Historical School of Economics in England and Japan**
Tamotsu Nishizawa

63 **Classical Economics and Modern Theory**
Studies in long-period analysis
Heinz D. Kurz and Neri Salvadori

64 **A Bibliography of Female Economic Thought to 1940**
Kirsten K. Madden, Janet A. Sietz and Michele Pujol

65 **Economics, Economists and Expectations**
From microfoundations to macroeconomics
Warren Young, Robert Leeson and William Darity Jnr.

66 **The Political Economy of Public Finance in Britain, 1767–1873**
Takuo Dome

67 **Essays in the History of Economics**
Warren J. Samuels, Willie Henderson, Kirk D. Johnson and Marianne Johnson

68 **History and Political Economy**
Essays in honour of P.D. Groenewegen
Edited by Tony Aspromourgos and John Lodewijks

69 **The Tradition of Free Trade**
Lars Magnusson

70 **Evolution of the Market Process**
Austrian and Swedish economics
Edited by Michel Bellet, Sandye Gloria-Palermo and Abdallah Zouache

71 **Consumption as an Investment**
The fear of goods from Hesiod to Adam Smith
Cosimo Perrotta

72 **Jean-Baptiste Say and the Classical Canon in Economics**
The British connection in French classicism
Samuel Hollander

73 **Knut Wicksell on Poverty**
No place is too exalted
Knut Wicksell

74 **Economists in Cambridge**
A study through their correspondence 1907–1946
Edited by M.C. Marcuzzo and A. Rosselli

Economists in Cambridge

A study through their correspondence, 1907–1946

Edited by Maria Cristina Marcuzzo and Annalisa Rosselli

Routledge
Taylor & Francis Group
LONDON AND NEW YORK

First published 2005
by Routledge
2 Park Square, Milton Park, Abingdon, Oxon OX14 4RN

Simultaneously published in the USA and Canada
by Routledge
270 Madison Ave, New York, NY 10016

Routledge is an imprint of the Taylor & Francis Group

Transferred to Digital Printing 2005

Typeset in Baskerville by Wearset Ltd, Boldon, Tyne and Wear

British Library Cataloguing in Publication Data
A catalogue record for this book is available from the British Library

Library of Congress Cataloging in Publication Data
A catalog record for this book has been requested

ISBN 0–415–34023–3

Contents

Tables

Contributors

Daniele Besomi is an independent researcher in the History of Economic Thought, based in Switzerland.

Pascal Bridel is Professor of Economics at the University of Lausanne, Switzerland.

Anna Carabelli is Professor of Economics at the University of Piemonte Orientale, Novara, Italy.

Bruna Ingrao is Professor of Economics at the University of Rome 'La Sapienza', Italy.

Maria Cristina Marcuzzo is Professor of History of Economic Thought at the University of Rome 'La Sapienza', Italy.

Nerio Naldi is Associate Professor of Economics at the University of Rome 'La Sapienza', Italy.

Fabio Ranchetti is Professor of Economics at the University of Pisa, Italy.

Annalisa Rosselli is Professor of Economics at the University of Rome 'Tor Vergata', Italy.

Eleonora Sanfilippo is Research Fellow in the History of Economic Thought at the University of Rome 'La Sapienza', Italy.

Claudio Sardoni is Professor of Economics at the University of Rome 'La Sapienza', Italy.

Acknowledgements

The spirit binding the group of economists dealt with in this book seems to have affected the authors of the individual chapters, too, enhancing collaboration throughout all the stages of research, from reports on the letters tracked down in the various archives to discussion, verbal or virtual, of the successive drafts of chapters and the introduction through to the final version. This volume may therefore be seen as much more the fruit of a collective effort than is normally the case for a book by various authors.

Specific acknowledgements are included at the beginning of each chapter. Here we wish to thank all those who, in their various capacities, assisted us in our research: Katia Caldari, Alessandra Caretta, Claudia Cicconi, Maureen Donegan, Maria Teresa Duda, Christian Galassi, Monica Gentile, Martina Mosco, Cristina Saggioro, Iolanda Sanfilippo, Emiliano Venditelli, Luca Zamparelli and in particular Nadia Marzullo who patiently kept track of a database that never stopped growing.

We are grateful to the Archive and Library Staff of the Bank of Italy and in particular the Head Librarian, Dr Maria Teresa Pandolfi; to the Librarian of the Department of Economics, Università di Roma, 'La Sapienza', Angela Masci; to the former Archivists of King's College, Cambridge (Jacky Cox and Rosalind Maud), to the Archivist of Trinity College, Cambridge (Jonathan Smith), to the Archivist of the Department of Special Collections and Western Manuscripts, Bodleian Library, Oxford (Steven Tomlinson) and finally to our editor for the English language, Graham Sells.

We are indebted to Alexandra Saunders, Jacky Cox and Simon Richardson for invaluable help in deciphering and transcribing letters by Pigou and Shove.

We are also particularly grateful for copyright permission granted by Pierangelo Garegnani (Sraffa papers), David Papineau (Kahn papers), the Provost and the Fellow of King's College, Cambridge (Keynes, J. Robinson papers), Anthony Thirlwall (Kaldor papers), Bruce Caldwell (Hayek papers), Judith Brown (Robertson papers) and by the publishers Elgar (Harrod 2003) and Macmillan (*The Collected Writings of J.M. Keynes*).

Introduction

Maria Cristina Marcuzzo and Annalisa Rosselli

More than kisses, letters mingle souls

John Donne, 'To Sir Henry Wootton'

Scope and purpose

In many fields of research the concentration of eminent scholars in Cambridge, which remained, until the Second World War, the intellectual centre of a country at the centre of the world, gave rise to a proliferation of ideas. In the field of economics, too, positive 'scientific revolutions' were set off by theoretical innovations, conditioning the way theory was conceived over the following years. J.M. Keynes, P. Sraffa, R.F. Kahn and J. Robinson were the leading figures in these theoretical revolutions, sparked off by internal debate and confrontation with their major opponents and interlocutors.

We have many studies on individual Cambridge economists of this period – Keynes and Sraffa in the first place – but wanting still is an overview able to bring out the points in common and differences both within the Cambridge tradition and *vis-à-vis* other schools of thought. Moreover, we have no comprehensive study of the context from which the contributions of that group of economists emerged, triumphed and eventually assumed minority status in the profession.

This book is a step forward in that direction, being an inquiry into the work of a group rather than an individual author. The method adopted is that of studying relations between authors, using published and unpublished material, mainly correspondence. The reason for specific study of the correspondence between these authors is in fact twofold, lying in the importance and characteristics of the group under scrutiny and the sheer volume of the correspondence itself (see Table A), most of which unpublished (see Table B).

Our main interest lay in tracing the links between various theoretical developments, exploring the circumstances and motivations orienting the positions taken up by the protagonists, and thus reconstructing the referential context from which certain concepts and ideas emerged. By referential context we mean the common language evolving from the professional and personal relationships established within that group, and self-validated when exposed to external influences. Since language and style germinate and grow in a network of intellectual and personal relations, the material to draw upon to this end consists not only in published works but also, in particular, in the correspondence and related texts.

In Cambridge, academic life was bound up with the college structure, with supervision as the staple didactic method, and with the personal and intellectual interactions of an elite sharing a set of values and lifestyles. Letter-writing played a fundamental role for communication in a world where systematic use of the telephone had yet to come, but where – thanks to the internal post system functioning within the college structure – a lunch invitation could be sent at breakfast time and answered in good time. Moreover, the Royal Mail was famous for its speed and efficiency, delivering and collecting post thrice daily (Johnson and Johnson 1978: 93), necessary also to keep the machinery of the British Empire running.

Publications then had a role they no longer have. Access to the *Economic Journal* – among the two or three leading economic journals of the period – was a fairly simple matter for anyone belonging to the circle of Keynes, who had a very keen sense of his role as editor, seeking references only when he found himself on uncertain ground or when the article had to do with controversial issues in which he was directly involved. Nevertheless, publication was quantitatively limited since there were few journals, and what did get published therefore received great attention, standing more as a goal than a stage in a process. The process itself consisted precisely in discussion, oral and written, on what was about to be or had just been published, and it was here that the academic community knit together, in agreement or in dispute. Reviews of their books were often commissioned from other members of the group, which saw continual internal restructuring through the exchange of roles.

The correspondence examined

Our study extends to 2,855 letters, written or received by John Maynard Keynes (JMK), Richard Kahn (RFK), Joan Robinson (JVR), Roy Harrod (RFH), Dennis Robertson (DHR), Piero Sraffa (PS), Arthur Cecil Pigou (ACP), Nicholas Kaldor (NK), Gerald Shove (GFS) and Friederich Hayek (FAH) over a time span between 1905 (date of the oldest extant letter) and 1946, the year of Keynes's death. Our aim was to examine all the extant correspondence between each pair of authors, but we are well aware that we may have fallen short of this goal. Although we painstakingly sifted through the personal papers of the economists involved,[1] we have knowledge of letters that survived their authors' death but can no longer be tracked down – mislaid, perhaps, or removed, or even destroyed.[2] We have moreover delved into the archives of various likely interlocutors (Maurice Dobb, John Hicks, James Meade, Austin Robinson, Richard Stone)[3] since, given the rate of intellectual exchange in the Cambridge of the 1930s, before the age of photocopies, letters would quite often be sent to third parties for comment (so it was that we found many letters addressed to Joan Robinson among Kahn's papers). Again, however, it is quite possible that something may have escaped our attention. A more serious shortcoming is that we made no systematic research in the archives of the public institutions where many of the economists we consider held posts, although we did research the Treasury papers of Lord Keynes at the Public Record Office at Kew (UK).

Table C shows the number of letters traced for each pair of correspondents. It is hard to tell just how closely the letters available to us reflect the actual correspondence, although we can at least console ourselves with the thought that the letters kept safe are often also the most significant. In determining the number of letters that came down to us chance clearly had an important role (missing, for example, are the letters Joan Robinson wrote between 1942 and 1945 to Kahn, who never threw anything away; they may have been swept away in the vicissitudes of wartime; while, unexpectedly, fifty-two letters from Keynes to Sraffa turned up in summer 2004) but so did the different habits and personal style of our correspondents. Keynes dictated a vast number of letters and kept carbon copies of them. Thus, if the original is not extant in the recipient's archive, the carbon copy is most likely to be found in Keynes's Archive. Robertson himself destroyed many of his professional papers; Shove left instructions that all his papers should be destroyed after his death and oral tradition in Cambridge has it that Pigou did the same. While Keynes, Kahn, Harrod and Sraffa typically kept all their letters and lived most of their life in the same places, Joan Robinson's is quite a different case: she was at one and the same time a great destroyer and a great traveller, which took a heavy toll on the number of extant letters sent to her. Few of the letters by Kahn to J. Robinson in this period are extant but, on the evidence of the letters written by J. Robinson to him during the same time period, they should not have come short of 400. The last line in Table C, giving the difference between letters received and sent, identifies 'destroyers' (Pigou, Robertson, J. Robinson and Shove) and 'keepers' (Harrod, Hayek, Kahn, Kaldor, Keynes and Sraffa).

Just over 65 per cent of the letters examined are from exchanges with Keynes. The largest number of letters exchanged is between Kahn and Keynes (611) and Kahn and J. Robinson (518), the latter two sets of correspondence alone accounting for approximately 40 per cent of the total. We may consider the volume of correspondence as an indicator of closeness – intellectual and affective – but one to be taken gingerly.

Problems arise regarding the interpretation and utility of the material. Few of the letters examined were typed, and the handwriting of some –

Kahn and Pigou in particular – created at times insuperable difficulties of decipherment. Then there is the frequent use of abbreviations, nicknames and expressions belonging to the private jargon used among people who would meet practically every day and while away their evenings together in the Common Room. To make matters worse, for many exchanges of correspondence we have only one side, and what the other wrote can only be reconstructed or conjectured on the basis of allusions in the answers or accounts given to others. Nor is dating always an easy matter, especially in the case of J. Robinson and Pigou, who were never in the habit of dating their letters as a matter of course.[4]

The significant data on each letter (and on notes and memoranda, if any) are given in tables at the end of each chapter, where archival references (of originals and copies, if any) are given.

The choice of period and authors

The period under consideration coincides with a process that saw political economy emerging as an independent academic discipline. The process had its formal origin in the institution of the Tripos engineered by Marshall in 1903 and found culmination in the 1930s, thanks to the *éclat* achieved by the writings of Keynes.

To date the beginning of each exchange of correspondence examined we took the year of the first letter available to us, while 1946, the year of Keynes's death, was taken as the final date, given the need to limit the field of research. Indeed, the death of Keynes – indisputably the leading figure in pre-war Cambridge – clearly marked, even more than the break brought about by the war itself, the 'before' and 'after' of public and scientific debate at Cambridge. However, it is a choice that cuts out the following decades, when Cambridge took on the features that would, above all in shared opposition to neo-classical theory, make it an international pole of attraction in the 1950s and 1960s, as the figures of the old generation made their exit and the play of alliances and contrasts saw radical shake-up. Thus the picture emerging from this book of the relations between the various pairs of correspondents proves fairly complete in a number of cases while constituting no more than an antefact for the younger figures involved.

A few words should also be spent on the choice of authors we decided to include. Constraints of space meant limiting the number (each author added to the group of n meant increasing the exchanges of correspondence to analyse by n), and we therefore had to choose between criteria of completeness and relevance. Since our aim was, as we have said, to identify the characteristics of a group, we thought it worthwhile to take into consideration also those authors who frequented the Cambridge of those times fairly intensively and kept sufficiently well-informed about how the new ideas were developing to make the debate possible. Three authors in particular were chosen for their decidedly different characteristics: Harrod, who was both directly involved in the debate on imperfect competition and one of the recipients of the proofs of the *General Theory*; Kaldor, who shifted from the pro-Austrian positions of the London School to convert to Keynesianism, and to become a leading light of post-war Cambridge; and Hayek, who, although he spent the wartime in Cambridge, remained unbending in his opposition.

This choice bore a cost, with the exclusion of two first-rate Cambridge economists – Maurice Dobb and Austin Robinson – and of various other figures involved in discussion with the Cambridge economists such as Ralph Hawtrey, John Hicks, James Meade and Lionel Robbins. Given his Marxism Dobb, as he himself admitted (Dobb 1978: 119), kept a rather low profile until the post-war years, maintaining relations of real friendship and sincere intellectual exchange with Sraffa alone in all probability. Such was not the case with Austin Robinson, a member of the Circus, Secretary of the Faculty of Economics as from 1929 and review editor of the *Economic Journal* from 1934 on; the inaccessibility of his papers, which were being catalogued while our research was underway, justifies his exclusion but makes it no less painful. In the case of the other authors, either the extant letters are not relevant to our purpose or would have required another volume.

The importance of this correspondence

What does this vast number of letters have to tell us that we could not have known or understood well without them? Here we must make a distinction between two aspects: first, the importance of the correspondence *vis-à-vis* purely scientific work (whether published or unpublished) and, second, the more general question of the importance of exploring archives rather than relying on published material alone.

Much could be said, and indeed has been said, on the latter issue, especially by historians of ideas, but we would like to offer a few observations on the former aspect, which is more relevant here.

In the first place, correspondence is the material upon which biographers build their narrative, providing clues to facts, circumstances and above all motives. Many (but few relative to the total amount) of these letters are quoted by the authors of two recent biographies of Keynes (Moggridge 1992 and Skidelsky 1983, 1992, 2000), Hayek (Ebenstein 2001), Robertson (Fletcher 2000), Sraffa (Potier 1991) and Kaldor (Thirlwall 1987). Few have been drawn upon in the case of Kahn, J. Robinson, Shove and Pigou whose full biographies are yet to be written, while Harrod's has been partly reconstructed by Besomi (Harrod 2003).

Second, correspondence helps us place ideas in time and context, and thus leads the historian of ideas to ask questions which would probably not have been asked in the same terms. Some answers to these questions are provided in the chapters of this book, offering interpretations and solutions which can better be supplied on the evidence of the letters. A few examples will suffice.

1 When and how did Keynes start worrying that the Fundamental Equations apparatus as set out in the *Treatise* might not be quite as watertight as he believed it to be at the time of publication? (Chs 1, 4);
2 Did the initiators of the 'imperfect competition revolution', namely Sraffa, Kahn and Robinson, agree on its purpose and implications? (Chs 11, 12);
3 Did Sraffa have any role in the transition from the *Treatise* to the *General Theory*? (Ch. 4);
4 When and why did the rupture between Robertson and Keynes actually take place? (Ch. 2);
5 What made it difficult for Hayek and Keynes to understand each other's points of view? (Ch. 9);
6 What was the nature of the collaboration between Kahn and J. Robinson in the making of *The Economics of Imperfect Competition*? (Ch. 10);
7 What were the reactions of the old Marshallian guard (Pigou, Robertson and Shove) to *The Economics of Imperfect Competition* and to the *General Theory*? (Chs 7, 14, 15);
8 Was Harrod really involved in the development of the *General Theory*? (Ch. 3);
9 Did Keynes misinterpret and misunderstand Pigou? (Ch. 5);
10 What was the nature of the misunderstanding between Hayek and the Keynesians? (Ch. 16);
11 Why did J. Robinson, Kahn and Keynes disagree so vehemently with Kalecki's results from the Cambridge Research Project? (Chs 1, 6);
12 What brought Kaldor to be attuned to Keynes's ideas during the Second World War? (Ch. 8).

It is difficult to summarise here the interpretations provided in the relevant chapters; rather, we can offer to the reader the main results of our inquiry into the characteristics of these economists as a group.

Cambridge economics was built on intellectual partnerships, some more successful and lasting than others. That between Keynes and Kahn certainly achieved the highest score on both accounts, especially after relations between Keynes and Robertson and Sraffa, albeit for different reasons, were severed precisely because of the change in Keynes's method and language after the *Treatise.*

The road to the *General Theory*, which was undoubtedly the major event in Cambridge economics in the period we have examined, was not exactly a solitary path, but few set foot on it. Initially, Keynes was exposed to the critical contribution coming from the Circus members, in particular Sraffa and Kahn, who were instrumental in persuading him that the *Treatise* approach had severe limitations, forcing him onto a new track. Interestingly enough, criticism from 'outside' – such as observations by Hayek or Robertson – did not get the same hearing, since it was not attuned with Keynes's attack to 'previously held views'. As close a follower and admirer as Harrod had trouble in understanding the 'new' relationship between saving and investment as late as 1934, and in 1935 was still defending the 'classical' theory of interest rate.

The other major event in Cambridge economics in the inter-war period – the imperfect competition revolution – is also marked by success in communication as in the case of Kahn and Robinson, and by lack of it, as in the case of Kahn and Sraffa. The collaboration between Kahn and J. Robinson on the economics of imperfect competition is another example of shared intellectual ground determining which questions can be raised and where answers should be sought. At the outset, this ground lay in the Marshallian framework, enriched by Kahn's extensions and insights into the economics of the short period and by J. Robinson's generalisation of the marginal cost – marginal revenue equality. Subsequently, it was Keynes's undermining of certain established relationships that provided the common ground, where a full appreciation of Sraffa's agenda in the 1920s and 1930s was lacking. Kahn and J. Robinson attended Sraffa's lectures, but little seems to have rubbed off on them. Not only did they fail to take in the implications of overthrowing Marshall orthodoxy, namely a return to the classical approach, but, rather, they set about rebuilding it, making 'perfect competition' a special case. (In the post-war years, however, J. Robinson changed her mind, championing Sraffa's point of view alongside with Keynes's.) This may explain why Sraffa estranged himself from both the Cambridge 'revolutions'.

Our conclusion is that sharing some common ground was a necessary, although not sufficient, condition for communication to be possible, for acceptance of criticism and to allow scope for genuine interaction; thus Cambridge economics was built as much on dissent, and 'impossibility' of communication, as shown in the case of Pigou, Robertson and Hayek *vis-à-vis* Keynes and the Keynesians, and of Keynes and the Keynesians *vis-à-vis* Sraffa.

The structure of the book

At this point we owe readers an account of how we have structured this volume and its division into three parts.

Although we approached research by studying the authors of the correspondence in pairs, and in an earlier version of the book had dedicated one chapter to each pair of correspondents,[5] proceeding to the subsequent draft we felt the need to overhaul our organisation of the work.

The three parts composing the book reflect the conviction that grew upon us as research proceeded that the correspondence actually shows three 'types' of exchange. The first type is with Keynes, involving those economists – both close to and removed from his theoretical framework – with whom Keynes kept up intensive exchange. The reason for this grouping is the 'centrality' of Keynes within the Cambridge set; we shall shortly be returning to this point. In Part I the order of chapters reflects the relative volume of extant exchanges, beginning with the substantial Keynes–Kahn correspondence and concluding with the letters exchanged with Hayek.

The second type of exchange consists of correspondence between and from the two staunchest defenders of Keynesian thought, Kahn and J. Robinson. Through the letters they exchanged we set out to reconstruct their relations, which were profound at both the personal and intellectual level, but also the relations they had with economists close to them such as Sraffa, Harrod and Kaldor – close in their common acceptance of a good part of Keynesian ideas, close in the contacts among themselves and exchange of ideas even though not all lived in Cambridge, and close also in belonging to the same broad age bracket. As we shall see, in content and style these exchanges are very different from the correspondence in Part I, where it is the impact of Keynes's personality and not only his ideas that largely conditions the dialogue.

In Part III we selected four interlocutors of Keynes (Hayek, Pigou, Robertson and Shove) who had taken a certain distance from him at the theoretical level in defence of the tradition, and with three of whom he had fairly sharp differences. These were the economists who had not shared in the enthusiasm aroused by the critique of Marshall's theory of prices launched by Sraffa or the innovations of the *General Theory*, such as Pigou, Robertson and Shove, or were decidedly averse, like Hayek, whose collection of essays was significantly entitled '*Contra* Cambridge' (Hayek 1995). These we took in relation to the entire set of sympathisers with Keynesian thought, whether faithful followers (Kahn and J. Robinson) or relatively independent (Kaldor and Sraffa, leaving out Harrod for lack of letters).

The centrality of Keynes

It is no mere chance that Keynes was both the major sender and recipient in this correspondence but, rather, shows just how important 'criticism and conversation' were for him. Let us recall a well-known passage in the Preface to the *General Theory*: 'It is astonishing what foolish things one can temporarily believe if one thinks too long *alone*, particularly in economics (along with the other moral sciences), where it is often impossible to bring one's ideas to a conclusive test either formal or experimental' (CWK VII: xxiii, italics added).

These letters show how Keynes gave form and finish to his ideas by submitting them to others, far more than do Keynes's contributions to the work of others. Even when his correspondents are pupils of his, such as Kahn, Shove and Robertson, Keynes never takes on the tone of master to student, and their relations rapidly shed any such form. In general Keynes approaches his correspondents as equals, regardless of academic hierarchy, gender, nationality or age, but when discussing economic theory he is discriminating and demanding. His interlocutors must be attuned to his thinking, or show a critical but sympathetic attitude. Dialogue on points of theory with people who had a different theoretical framework held no interest for him – as his early exchange with Kaldor shows – or bored him, as emerges from his terminological discussion with Hayek.

Keynes's greatness also emerges in his ability to exploit the individual capacities of his interlocutors to the full, drawing, for example, upon the philosophical bent of Harrod, the fastidiousness of Kahn, the remorseless logic of Sraffa, the professional expertise of Kaldor or the combative spirit of J. Robinson.

For Keynes, however, dialogue yielded the desired results only if it ran along the lines he traced out. Apart from the occasional comments and consultation, it was hard to draw him out on other grounds – like the theory of value – or induce him to accept some particularly highly formalised analysis (as practised by Pigou, Kahn and J. Robinson in the theory of imperfect competition) or dependent on *ad hoc* assumptions (as in Kalecki's analysis).

Nevertheless, it is not easy to define the characteristics of the group of people that Keynes accepted as his 'interlocutors'. Neither sharing the same point of view in terms of economic theory nor intellectual brilliance seem to have constituted a sufficient condition for acceptance, as shown by the distance Keynes took from Kalecki, who achieved results extraordinarily close to his own at the level of macroeconomic theory. Nor, however, were they necessary conditions; Shove, whose level of performance – at least as far as can be judged from his letters and publications – would class him as an underachiever, was a fully accredited member of the 'group'.

Thus the group of Keynes's correspondents examined in this volume seems to have been an extended community, membership of which depended not so much or not only on academic performance as on the capacity to encapsulate and convey understanding through discussion. Such characteristics define a group very different from any traditional 'school'.

Within the group, discussion of economic policy took second place to questions of theory outside wartime, and indeed there is scant correspondence on more general matters of politics. Approval of specific measures in economic policy would at times become a dividing issue. For example, 1932 saw the Cambridge group split on undersigning (Keynes, Kahn, Austin and J. Robinson) or not (Sraffa and Dobb) the letter drafted by Harrod and Meade in support of public works (Harrod 2003: 1242–4). However, the pattern changed during the Second World War, which saw many of them playing an active part in running economic affairs; priorities now changed, since the wrong ideas or measures could have dramatic and even catastrophic consequences. Internal conflict died down as *esprit de corps* waxed strong.

The war also opened up the field of discussion to matters of more general import, as demonstrated by confrontation with Hayek on whether or not it was expedient to entrust a body of enlightened civil servants with the conduct of economic affairs, favoured by Keynes but opposed by Hayek for fear that individual liberties might suffer. In this case Keynes proved far more open and tolerant than he had been on matters of economic theory: it is indeed revealing to compare his correspondence with Hayek in 1931 and 1939, on the one hand, and in 1944 on the other.

Pairs and group

The second part of the book is organised around two economists who played an essential role in disseminating and winning approval for the ideas of Keynes. Relations between Kahn and J. Robinson have a whole chapter dedicated to them, not only in virtue of the quantity of letters but also on account of the importance their relationship held for the two correspondents themselves and indeed for Cambridge more generally. From the post-war period until the end of the 1970s both had fundamental roles in shaping the Cambridge that attracted students and scholars in great number from all over the world.

The relationship between J. Robinson and Kahn epitomises the kind of intellectual collaboration that we described as typical of Cambridge. In the first place it was a sharing of time and spaces, which also entailed a sharing of knowledge and the habit of exchanging rather than possessing ideas. Intellectual and scientific activity were perceived as a 'social art that pervades one's life' – as Kahn wrote, remarking the difference to the United States – and as commitment to the search for truth, a sort of 'moral seriousness' in the words of a student who had J. Robinson as supervisor (Waterman 2003: 594).

There is something intellectually symbiotic in the Kahn–Robinson pair. Aggregation and alliances between the components of the Cambridge group changed as the scientific debate developed but – at least until the end of the 1950s – understanding between the two remained firm, cemented also by a common crusading spirit. In the correspondence of the 1930s they evoke the Middle Ages, a 'filthy kind of bilge' and 'abysmal darkness' in which the rest of the world is immersed, and from which it must be saved, which explains why Robertson spoke of them as a 'sect'. It was only Sraffa's message emerging with *Production of Commodities by Means of Commodities* – to some extent anticipated in his Introduction to Ricardo's *Principles* – that instilled an element of distinction in their positions bound by intellectual sodality (Marcuzzo 2005).

Apart from the Kahn–Robinson and Kahn–Keynes pairs, where Kahn's personality and strong ties with both play a decisive part, and apart also from the Robertson–Keynes pair in the 1920s, where the personal dependence between the two authors was still at play, the forms of collaboration and communication show lesser and varied gradations.

In this context it is not always a clear or simple task to ascertain the paternity (or maternity) of an idea. The referee report by Keynes to Macmillan on *The Economics of Imperfect Competition* is exemplary from this point of view: 'It [the book] appears to me to be predominantly a discussion of the development of ideas which have been started by others and which are now widely current, not only for learned articles, but in oral discussion at Cambridge and Oxford. She is, in a sense, taking the cream off a new movement which has not yet found its own expositor in print' (CWK XII: 866). The same comment might equally well have referred to the development of ideas that found their way into the *General Theory*, as indeed has been remarked – Schumpeter (1954: 1172) actually used the term co-authorship referring to Kahn. Unlike Robinson's book, however, the *General Theory* would never have needed a referee report to be published by Macmillan, and there would have been no one as authoritative as Keynes himself to provide it.

Interesting, too, is individual comparison of J. Robinson and Kahn with the others in the group, which forms the subject matter of the other two chapters in Part II. A characteristic feature of both is how enthusiastically they took to the questioning of received views, as indeed one might expect of a younger generation. In the case of imperfect competition, the project was revision, with more rigorous formulation of accepted concepts. This explains their adherence to the marginal method, and the interest they showed in Kaldor, who represented another 'variant' of the marginalist tradition.

As for the dissemination of Keynesian ideas, Kahn and J. Robinson launched a campaign of 'tutorage', either because requested to do so (as in the case of Kahn with Harrod) or out of proselytising passion (in the case of Robinson with Kaldor). We may well wonder how aware they were of the difficulties that authors weaned on a different theoretical framework might find in accepting the change in object and method of analysis imposed by Keynes: trade cycle no longer, but a permanent state of unemployment; the difference between saving and investment no longer identified – as it had also been by the Keynes of the *Treatise* – as cause of the cyclic trend in the economy, but equality between saving and investment indicated as the basis determining the equilibrium level of income.

Sraffa was indeed involved in all the intellectually important happenings at Cambridge, but found no company along his solitary path in quest of an alternative to the marginalist tradition, Marshallian or Austrian as it might be (Rosselli 2004). However, exactly why he dissented from the paths followed by others at Cambridge – the theory of imperfect competition and the theory of effective demand – he never explicitly made clear: we find some evidence on the former in his exchanges with Robinson and Kahn, but hardly anything on the latter.

It was characteristic of Keynes to make abrupt switches in strategy as he approached problems – while following a main line many consider constant – and this, together with the fascination of his proselytising art and flair for creating consensus, resulted in a sense of exclusion experienced by all deprived of contiguity, simply by not being at Cambridge. All sought special relations with Keynes, and this meant being in constant contact with his ideas. Kahn was every bit as piqued at the very idea of losing these relations – as when he complained that Kaldor had been chosen by Keynes to reply to Pigou's 1938 article – as Robertson had been on actually losing them.

Such emotional involvement was not limited to relations with Keynes, however: the entire group was aquiver with emotional tensions and powerful interpersonal dynamics, love, hatred and jealousy playing their part. On this plane J. Robinson, the only woman in the group, brought a touch of novelty, her intellectual vitality, temperament and looks attracting attention unknown to the tradition of Cambridge economists. Marshall's wife, who died four years before women were officially accepted in the University of Cambridge in 1948, offered the model of the woman economist who remained a wife in the shade of her husband. While Robinson expressed those unconventional attitudes and social criticism that had Cambridge overlapping with Bloomsbury (although this was very much the reserve of King's and Trinity men) rejection of conformism lapsing into eccentricity. Although no specifically feminist positions emerged, her behaviour in itself represented defiance of conventions. A gender stand, as we would call it today, rarely appeared in her correspondence, one exception possibly being the discussion with Harrod on population, where she countered his concern about the extinction of the British race with her own concern about freedom for women in relation to abortion, contraception and maternity.

Defending tradition

In Part III we find the entire *dramatis personae* of the group assembled to bring out the contrast between the old and new generations of economists active in Cambridge. To some extent this division also coincides with the line-up of defenders of orthodoxy, whether Marshallian or Austrian (Pigou, Shove, Robertson and Hayek) on the one hand, and the critics, who – apart from Sraffa – identified with the Keynesian position, on the other.

In order to appreciate the details of this new pattern traced out in the correspondence it is worthwhile to consider the style of discussion displayed by each of the protagonists of this section. Pigou appears more detached than Robertson and Shove, but at the same time more readily disposed to reappraise his own conceptual frameworks and results. More, perhaps, than a temperamental trait, this characteristic may have reflected his status of academic superiority as Marshall's appointed successor and the only Professor of the Faculty, until 1944, although these aspects were perhaps less evident when Pigou's theory of employment came under heavy fire from Keynes, Kahn and J. Robinson. An attitude manifestly striking in the correspondence about *The Economics of Imperfect Competition* is his amenable approach and wholehearted efforts to formulate certain issues as well as possible in his dealings with a young economist like J. Robinson, tackling her first book just six years after passing Tripos.

This common style of discussion – *Cambridge-y*, according to Robertson's definition – would fall away if the correspondent was perceived as sectarian and ideological, as J. Robinson must have appeared to the eyes of Pigou and Robertson in the aftermath of the *General Theory*. It is quite clearly in the correspondence from and to J. Robinson with all four of these authors that the tone sounds particularly heavy, with a note of intolerance. Just how much this is due to Robinson's temperament, how much to her partisan defence of Keynesianism, how much to misogyny – hardly even disguised in the case of Pigou and Robertson – or, rather, how much it was inspired by honest dissent *vis-à-vis* Keynes's thought it is clearly hard to tell. Shove is quite evidently a case apart; with J. Robinson he reveals all the insecurity of one who feels he cannot match up to the means she deploys (moreover, she had Kahn behind her) or compete with equally prompt action. At the same time, Shove perceived – rightly – that the way Robinson framed her theory of imperfect competition distorted, perhaps even betrayed, the framework created by Marshall, whose heir and continuator he felt he was. This may explain why Shove is on the whole seen as the 'least distant' from the younger generation, although his endorsement of the *General Theory* looks more like a necessary, token expression of respect for Keynes than true conviction.

Robertson is the most awkward correspondent of the older generation, apparently only at ease with Sraffa in theoretical dispute. Hayek took a very different attitude to Kaldor from Kahn and J. Robinson, as one might expect in relations with a person one feels betrayed by; he accepted intellectual challenge but would not suffer direct attack or lack of consideration for his own point of view.

Going on, now, to consider the attitude displayed by the younger generation, it must be noted that Sraffa occupied a position all of his own. Sraffa's relations appear always cordial and civilised, even with people – Hayek and Robertson, for example – he clashed with quite severely on the theoretical plane. Again, how much this reflects an attitude approaching, almost, double-dealing, or how much the capacity to share interests and enthusiasm in other areas, like the love of antique manuscripts shared with Hayek, of mountaineering with Pigou, and the camaraderie with

Robertson (possibly due to a common dislike of the *General Theory*) it is hard to tell. With these interlocutors, too, the odd thing is Sraffa's unwillingness to involve others in the construction of his ideas, ever ready to assume the position of one who comments on or interprets the positions of others when so requested. Given his extraordinary logical capacities he was particularly apt for this critical function, which he would be called upon to exercise but also feared for.

By contrast, J. Robinson was always ready to bicker, squabble or argue with almost all her correspondents, and on a number of occasions Keynes had to step in to save the situation with Shove and Robertson. Kahn was an extremely obliging correspondent, although here again we cannot rule out a touch of opportunism, given his self-appointed task of winning over academic acceptance for J. Robinson while extending and consolidating consensus around Keynesianism. He was careful not to arouse negative reactions, but at the same time sincerely more open than Robinson to criticism or doubt on those concepts and definitions, for which he had urged greater clarity from Keynes himself.

Kaldor's style of correspondence with Hayek was decidedly polemic and somewhat aggressive; unfortunately the paucity of his letters to Pigou, Shove and Robertson makes it hard to say anything about his style in correspondence with them (there are only two letters to Robertson and none to Pigou).

Pigou, Shove, Robertson and Hayek represent the Marshallian or Austrian tradition shoring up against the encroaching new wave. The new approach, for its part, often took on a style of argumentation that saw 'models' being trundled out, complete with simplifying hypotheses and limited applicability, designed to achieve certain results. Robertson's irritation with 'your [i.e. Kahn's and Keynes's] short-period method' was no less than Pigou's with the 'machinery' of curves in *The Economics of Imperfect Competition*, or Shove's with the failure to take account of time in discussion of costs with Sraffa, or Hayek's with *ceteris paribus*.

Conclusions

The distinction we feel is important is that between 'group' and 'school'; the former term – unlike the latter – does not necessarily denote adhesion to a common body of doctrine, although it does convey the idea both of cohesion and of sharing. Thus, following this weaker version of connotation of the Cambridge economists – as group rather than school – we have seen the elements working at the level of both cohesion and division to endow these various economists with identity as a group. In other words, we believe there is not a common denominator – in terms of theory – enabling us to define a Cambridge approach. Rather, we have identified those controversial issues about which the internal discussion developed, considering the reasons that led these economists to pit their wits together, and how understanding intersected between the various components. We might take intersecting circles as an appropriate image to represent the overall pattern, consisting of various links between various individuals.

As we see it, the elements of division in the period considered are precisely those traditionally recognised as characteristic of the Cambridge approach, namely the Marshallian representation of the market (and the associated method of determining equilibrium of the firm and of the industry) and the relation of saving to investment (with the associated determination of the rate of interest on the money market, on the basis of the theory of liquidity preference). These are two much debated points, which were objects of discussion within the group and also formed its connective tissue, as it were. As in all conversations, the distance between positions may well reflect misunderstandings, at time lack of a common language, at time adhesion to contrasting points of view. Nevertheless, discussion can only take place in the context of a certain sharing in knowledge and in seeking out solutions to problems considered common. In this respect, the Marshallian representation of market functioning and the relation of saving to investment are objects of discussion that both drew together and divided the Cambridge group.

More than in a shared theory, the identity of this group is rooted in motivations, values and habits: perhaps it is common lifestyles and work styles that most aptly and tellingly express these aspects. By work styles we mean the importance attached to correspondence and oral discussion in the process of forming ideas and drawing up texts – authoritativeness and authority founded on an internal hierarchy that does not necessarily reflect seniority in terms of age or academic qualification. By lifestyles we mean the importance ascribed to personal relations, affording a framework for scientific intercourse, which explains how so many theoretical divisions left ample safe ground for reciprocal respect and affection.

A system of values, a shared knowledge and an urge to connect mingled these Cambridge economists together, leaving us a precious inheritance.

Notes

1 JMK papers, JVR papers, RFK papers and NK papers in the Modern Archives of King's College, Cambridge; Treasury papers of Lord Keynes, Public Record Office at Kew (UK); DHR papers and PS papers in the Wren Library, Trinity College, Cambridge; RFH papers at Chiba, Nagoya and Tokyo Universities (Japan) and British Library, London; FAH papers at Stanford University (USA).

2 For example, we have transcriptions of three letters by J. Robinson to Keynes, made by one of the authors of this book before cataloguing of the JVR papers, but no longer to be found. Kahn (Kahn 1989: xv) refers to an important letter by Sraffa to Keynes, now impossible to locate.

3 Maurice Dobb papers in the Wren Library, Trinity College, Cambridge; John Hicks papers at the University of Hyogo, Kobe, Japan; James Meade papers in the British Library of Political and Economic Science, London; Austin Robinson

papers in the Marshall Library, Cambridge; Richard Stone papers in the Modern Archives of King's College, Cambridge.

4 We have in all cases pointed out when the date suggested by the archivist filing the papers appeared unconvincing. Moreover, in quotation from the letters, we corrected spelling mistakes and substituted abbreviated words and symbols (e.g. and for &, +, etc.).

5 The early draft of the book, whose number of correspondents was however restricted to seven, was published as Marcuzzo (ed.) (2001a).

Table A Total correspondence

	JMK	*RFK*	*JVR*	*DHR*	*RFH*	*PS*	*ACP*	*NK*	*GFS*	*FAH*
JMK										
RFK	611									
JVR	140	518								
DHR	303	19	7							
RFH	233	25	40	109						
PS	230	20	25	15	1					
ACP	140	10	14	12	1	7				
NK	77	2	24	18	18	2	2			
GFS	85	4	27	6	0	4	0	1		
FAH	66	2	9	0	1	18	0	9	0	
Total										2,855

JMK = J.M. Keynes, ACP = A.C. Pigou, RFK = R.F. Kahn, JVR = J.V. Robinson, DHR = D.H. Robertson, RFH = R.F. Harrod, PS = P. Sraffa, FAH = F.A. Hayek, NK = N. Kaldor, GFS = G.F. Shove.

Table B Number of letters published and unpublished

Correspondence	*Published*			*Unpublished*	*Total*
	Total	*Full*	*Excerpt*		
Keynes–Kahn	96	2	94	515	611
Robinson–Kahn	6	0	6	512	518
Keynes–Robertson	146	105	41	157	303
Keynes–Harrod	143	103	40	90	233
Keynes–Sraffa	50	7	43	180	230
Keynes–Pigou	45	21	24	95	140
Keynes–Robinson	82	76	6	58	140
Harrod–Robertson	89	80	9	20	109
Keynes–Shove	12	8	4	73	85
Keynes–Kaldor	18	14	4	59	77
Keynes–Hayek	16	14	2	50	66
Robinson–Harrod	39	37	2	1	40
Shove–Robinson	0	0	0	27	27
Kahn–Harrod	24	11	13	1	25
Sraffa–Robinson	6	0	6	19	25
Robinson–Kaldor	0	0	0	24	24
Kahn–Sraffa	2	1	1	18	20
Robertson–Kahn	0	0	0	19	19
Harrod–Kaldor	18	13	5	0	18
Hayek–Sraffa	0	0	0	18	18
Robertson–Kaldor	0	0	0	18	18
Robertson–Sraffa	1	0	1	14	15
Pigou–Robinson	0	0	0	14	14
Pigou–Robertson	2	0	2	10	12
Pigou–Kahn	0	0	0	10	10
Hayek–Robinson	0	0	0	9	9
Kaldor–Hayek	0	0	0	9	9
Pigou–Sraffa	3	1	2	4	7
Robertson–Robinson	0	0	0	7	7
Robertson–Shove	0	0	0	6	6
Shove–Sraffa	1	0	1	3	4
Shove–Kahn	0	0	0	4	4
Pigou–Kaldor	0	0	0	2	2
Kaldor–Sraffa	0	0	0	2	2
Kahn–Kaldor	0	0	0	2	2
Kahn–Hayek	0	0	0	2	2
Shove–Kaldor	0	0	0	1	1
Hayek–Harrod	0	0	0	1	1
Harrod–Pigou	1	0	1	0	1
Sraffa–Harrod	0	0	0	1	1
Total	800	493	307	2,055	2,855

Table C Correspondence by sender and recipient

Recipient \ *Sender*	*JMK*	*RFK*	*JVR*	*DHR*	*RFH*	*PS*	*ACP*	*NK*	*GFS*	*FAH*	*Total letters received*
JMK	–	304	66	176	93	89	92	34	70	22	946
RFK	307	–	461	10	7	7	10	0	3	0	805
JVR	74	57	–	5	17	16	14	9	21	9	222
DHR	127	9	2	–	39	3	9	3	5	0	197
RFH	140	18	23	70	–	1	1	8	0	1	262
PS	141	13	9	12	0	–	5	1	2	12	195
ACP	48	0	0	3	0	2	–	0	0	0	53
NK	43	2	15	15	10	1	2	–	1	4	93
GFS	15	1	6	1	0	2	0	0	–	0	25
FAH	44	2	0	0	0	6	0	5	0	–	57
Total letters sent	939	406	582	292	166	127	133	60	102	48	2,855
Letters exchanged	1,885	1,211	804	489	428	322	186	153	127	105	
Received – sent	7	399	−360	−95	96	68	−80	33	−77	9	

JMK = J.M. Keynes, ACP = A.C. Pigou, RFK = R.F. Kahn, JVR = J.V. Robinson, DHR = D.H. Robertson, RFH = R.F. Harrod, PS = P. Sraffa, FAH = F.A. Hayek, NK = N. Kaldor, GFS = G.F. Shove.

Part I

Keynes's correspondents

1 Keynes and his favourite pupil

The correspondence between Keynes and Kahn

Maria Cristina Marcuzzo

Introduction

The correspondence between Maynard Keynes and Richard Kahn, as we have it at present, consists of 611 letters, only 68 of which are published in the *Collected Writings* of J.M. Keynes (see Table 1.1). In presenting this material I focus on those aspects which may help to clarify the nature and scope of their friendship and collaboration. Inevitably, most biographical elements relate to Kahn rather than Keynes, on whom a vast literature is extant (see Moggridge 1992; Skidelsky 1983, 1992, 2000). It is in fact hoped that this work may also serve as a preliminary study of Richard F. Kahn, 'that elusive figure who hides in the preface of Cambridge books', as Samuelson put it (JVR papers, i/8/1).[1]

Kahn's Tripos and fellowship

We know that Keynes was impressed by Kahn's qualities from the outset,[2] when Kahn was a Tripos student and had Keynes as supervisor at King's.

The correspondence between them begins with a letter Keynes sent to Kahn immediately after the Tripos results were known: 'My dear Kahn, very warm congratulations that all was, after all, well in the Examination – though, as you know, I expected it' (letter 242, 15 June 1928). To which we have the reply:

> Dear Mr. Keynes, [. . .] the result was certainly a surprise, but I now recognise that I personally was but a minor factor involved in achieving it; and I should like to take this opportunity of thanking you from the bottom of my heart for your part as a major factor.
>
> (letter 240, 17 June 1928)

When, under the influence of Shove and Sraffa, whose lectures he attended together with Joan Robinson, Kahn came to write his Fellowship dissertation, the chosen topic fell outside Keynes's immediate field of interest.[3] In fact, until December 1929 the correspondence with Keynes contains no discussion of topics in the dissertation, but is rather concerned with issues raised by Keynes's own work, namely the final stage of the writing of the *Treatise of Money*, which was in the early proof stage.

The Dissertation was submitted in December 1929 and the Fellowship duly awarded on 15 March 1930. The next day, Keynes wrote to him: 'My dear Kahn, [. . . .] the election went through with ease and certainty, everyone recognising that it was an exceptionally distinguished thesis [. . .] I have permission to show you the reports on the dissertation' (letter 233, 16 March 1930).

Kahn reacted with characteristic modesty and equally unflagging gratitude towards Keynes, to whom he replied: 'Some strong stimulus must have been at work, and I suspect that this originated in the contact which your proofs provided me with the working of your own mind' (letter 269, 16 March 1930).

Drafting the *Treatise*

According to Kahn's later recollections, it was only after the Dissertation was submitted that he was asked by Keynes to help with the *Treatise*.[4] However, the correspondence shows that since July 1929 he had been assisting Keynes with various matters related to it. In September, he wrote: 'I have read the proofs and I have not much to say; but it would take some time to set it out' (letter 236, 29 September 1929, CWK XXIX: 4).[5] In fact, two months later, when he was just finishing his Dissertation, he managed to send Keynes a list of six general 'points' to discuss. We are told by no less an authority than J. Robinson that 'Kahn put in a good deal of work in the last stages of Keynes's *Treatise of Money*', although she added 'it can be seen from the correspondence that they were both in a great muddle' (JVR papers, i/8/1–2). The discrepancy between Kahn's later statement and the documents at our disposal can easily be accounted for with Kahn's different assessment of the importance of the kind of help he had given Keynes before and after completing work on the Dissertation. Moggridge came up with a very different interpretation: '[Kahn] deliberately (and mistakenly) distanced himself too much from the *Treatise* and thus overly highlighted his own role in the new ideas that were later to emerge' (Moggridge 1992: 532n).

What, it seems to me, does emerge from the correspondence prior to publication of the *Treatise* – much of which Keynes rewrote in 1929 and which was published on 31 October 1930 – is that *before* completion of the Dissertation Keynes engaged Kahn in discussion of problems of monetary theory rather than problems more closely concerning Kahn's work (letter 237, 13 December 1928). It was only *after* completion of the Dissertation that Kahn began to give Keynes suggestions as to how he might develop the theory in other directions (letter 379, 17 December 1929, CWK XIII: 120–1). Thus, it was in 'arguing out' rather than drafting the *Treatise* that Kahn was most influential (Marcuzzo 2002).

The transition from the *Treatise* to the *General Theory*

As is well known, the Circus was a discussion group consisting of James Meade, Joan and Austin Robinson, Piero Sraffa and Richard Kahn; a seminar was also held to which particularly good students were invited. They met from Michaelmas Term 1930 to May 1931. Much has been written about the influence of the Circus in bringing about the transition from the *Treatise* to the *General Theory*, but there is no consensus in the literature.

One of the crucial elements in the transition – adoption of the theory of aggregate demand and aggregate supply to determine the short period level of prices – was attributed by Keynes to the approach taken by Kahn in his 'multiplier article' (CWK VII: 400n), where the level of price is determined by the same forces as the level of output and not by the Quantity of Money. Kahn has argued that Keynes's long struggle to escape from the Quantity Theory won through only in the transition from the *Treatise* to the *General Theory*, claiming for himself (and the Circus) an important role.[6]

The point stressed by Keynes in the *Treatise* was that determination of the price level of consumption goods is entirely independent of determination of the price level of investment goods. This point was contested by Kahn in a set of letters in 1931 (letter 405, 5 April 1931, CWK XIII: 203–6; letter 380, 17 April 1931, CWK XIII: 206–7; letter 271, 7 May 1931, CWK XIII: 212–13; letter 265, 15 August 1931, CWK XIII: 218–19), when he sought to persuade Keynes to accept the criticism raised also by Robertson, Pigou and Sraffa. Shortly after Kahn's last letter on the subject, Keynes surrendered (CWK XIII: 225).

Keynes made an important step forward from the *Treatise* in the Harris Foundation lectures given in June 1931. There he adopted a new conception, the aggregate supply curve, which he explicitly attributed to Kahn. The supply curve, Keynes said, 'tells you that for a given level of prime profit [i.e. the difference between gross receipts and prime costs] there will be a given level of output' (CWK XIII: 368). The Harris Foundation lectures show Keynes shifting the emphasis from the *Treatise* analysis of aggregate profits as the difference between investment and saving, affecting the level of prices, to Kahn's short period analysis of aggregate profits as the difference between gross receipts and prime costs, affecting the level of output.

By the end of the summer of 1931 it had become clear to Keynes that the 'fundamental equations' approach needed revision and, as a result of various difficulties, he decided to postpone the lectures he was to give in the autumn. When he resumed them in spring 1932, he was able to present a 'new' argument:

> fluctuations of output and employment for a given community over the short period [...] depend almost entirely on the amount of

> current investment. This [...] is the result of taking account of the probable effect on saving of a *change* in the amount of investment.
>
> (CWK XXIX: 41)

These lectures were attended by Kahn, Austin and Joan Robinson, who presented Keynes with an 'alternative' to his proof of the positive relationship between variation in investment and variation in output based on the 'method of supply and demand', as they called it. Keynes's proof was as follows: an increase in output is equal to an increase in sales receipts (=income); an increase in investment is equal to an increase in sales receipts (=income) *minus* expenditure on consumption; consumption and income are positively correlated, and therefore changes in investment and changes in output have the same sign. The alternative proof was based on the argument that an autonomous increase in investment leads to an increase in the demand for consumption goods. Since by assumption supply conditions are independent of changes in demand, determination of consumption and therefore of income $(= C + I)$ is straightforward.[7]

The *General Theory* had begun to take shape.

The 'American' correspondence

Kahn sailed to the United States on the R.M.S. 'Majestic' on 21 December 1932, on a Rockefeller Fellowship (see Chs 10: 263–4 and 11: 302). Cambridge life was not entirely forgotten since he was busy working on the proofs of another major *opus, The Economics of Imperfect Competition,* which J. Robinson had been writing since mid-1930 in close consultation with Kahn (see 260).

The correspondence with Keynes shows no traces of his intense involvement with J. Robinson's book but is entirely occupied with consideration of the American way of life, the academic circles and the influence of the Quantity Theory of Money on the economic reasoning of most American economists (see letter 259, 7 March 1933).

From the University of Chicago, where he stayed for four weeks, Kahn went on to Toronto and Montreal to give a talk on 'Need depression last forever?' and then to Harvard, where he stayed with Schumpeter, and then on again to New York and Washington. 'The *Treatise* plays an enormously prominent role wherever I go' he wrote to Keynes (letter 260, 16 February 1933).

Keynes seemed to have missed his presence in Cambridge a great deal. In March, when he was writing the four articles in *The Times* later published as *The Means to Prosperity*,[8] worried that Kahn would not be able to read it in advance he wrote to him:

> I am now engaged in trying to write out for *The Times* [...] a really detailed, but nevertheless popular, account of the relation between

> primary and secondary employment. I hope I don't make any bloomers,- I wish you were here to look over my shoulder.
> (letter 276, 24 March 1933, CWK XIII: 413)

Then, after the first article was published, he complained: 'I was frightfully annoyed about the slip in the first article, which I had to correct in the second – one which would never have occurred if you had been in the neighbourhood' (letter 251, 16 March 1933).

The Keynesian revolution

When Kahn came back in April 1933, Keynes was well into the process of writing his new book. Unfortunately, the correspondence of 1933 contains no comments by Kahn on Keynes's autumn 1933 lectures, nor on the fragments of versions of the *General Theory* that came to light in Tilton's 'laundry hamper' (CWK XXIX: 63–110), on the basis of which most commentators date the conception of the new theory, with enunciation of the principle of effective demand. The role of profits had changed, since the level of output is now made to depend on prospective rather than actual magnitude; moreover the adjusting mechanism is dressed in a particular form: 'output is [. . .] pushed to the point at which the prospective selling price no longer exceeds the marginal variable cost' (CWK XXIX: 98). Keynes's use of marginal analysis – totally absent in the *Treatise* – is another instance of Kahn's influence in presentation of Keynes's new ideas. In accepting the 'method' of supply and demand suggested by Kahn, Keynes was progressively driven towards the marginal approach, which indeed is the language in which important parts of the *General Theory* are written (Marcuzzo 2001c).

By the end of 1933, Kahn's role now seems more that of a mentor than a pupil, as the following passage from a letter by Keynes to Lydia dated 15 October 1933 reveals: 'Alexander [the name Lydia gave Kahn to distinguish him from another Fellow of King's, Richard Braithwaite] has just been to give his criticism on the latest version of my three chapters – I got off much lighter than usual' (CWK XXIX: 62).

The collaboration continued steady during the early months of 1934. On February 1934 he wrote to Lydia: 'Alexander has proved to me that "my important discovery" last week is all a mistake' (CWK XXIX: 120). Again, on 20 March, Kahn spotted another blunder (CWK XXIX: 120). However, after 'a stiff week's supervision' from Kahn, Keynes reported enthusiastically: 'He is a marvellous critic and suggester and improver – there never was anyone in the history of the world to whom it was so helpful to submit one's stuff' (letter 1788 from JMK to JVR, 29 March 1934).[9]

Eventually, Keynes was able to send Kahn '[the] beautiful and important (I think) precise definition of what is meant by effective demand' (letter 249, 13 April 1934, CWK XIII: 422).[10]

By that summer of 1934, when Kahn spent most of his time at Tilton, 'the main lines of the *General Theory of Employment Interest and Money* had become clear' (Robinson 1979b: 185). Unfortunately, not many letters survive for this period, but the following passage from a letter by Keynes to Kahn, is revealing: 'I am getting towards the end of the re-writing which you led me into [. . .]' (letter 224, 27 September 1934, CWK XIII: 485).

More material is available for 1935, mainly related to the discussion of user cost (letter 221, 28 March 1935). Finally we have the letters, mostly published, relating to the proof reading of the *General Theory*. One in particular is interesting, where Kahn insists upon clarity on the conceptual framework employed:

> I do not like you saying that saving and investment are 'different names for the same thing'. They are *different* things (that is the whole point) – they are certainly different acts – but they are equal in *magnitude*. I still hold that the simple-minded proof that saving = investment, appropriate for those who cannot grapple with user cost, etc. is called for – not only for the sake of the simple minded, but to prevent the obvious retort that all your stuff depends on your peculiar definitions. What is wrong with saying that *however* income is defined,
>
> income = value of output = consumption + investment
>
> also income = consumption + saving
>
> ∴ saving = investment
>
> This truth is far too important (and far too seldom recognised) to be concealed in a mist of subtle definition.
>
> (letter 388, October 1935, CWK XIII: 637)

Keynes duly accepted his advice (compare *General Theory*, CWK VII: 63 with the third proof, CWK XIV: 424) and Kahn's formulation entered the final version of the book.

Finances

In the spring of 1937 Keynes fell seriously ill and for months all matters – especially College finances and University business – had to be handed over to Kahn. Kahn had already assisted Keynes in his capacity as First Bursar of King's;[11] during Keynes's illness matters related to College finances and their own financial investments were dealt with by mail. In fact, almost half of the surviving letters are from 1937 and 1938,[12] the bulk of them consisting of discussion of personal and College finances. Investment activities for the College consisted of farming, property transactions, securities, currencies and commodities. Keynes's personal investments covered the same range of assets, but on a smaller scale and in a different composition.

It is difficult to give a full account of their dealings, but we can consider a few aspects. On each issue they exchanged detailed information, comparing their respective evaluation and assessment. Although the final decision usually rested with Keynes, he invariably sought Kahn's approval. He taught Kahn – who was in any case by nature so inclined – to keep updated with detailed knowledge of every aspect of the matter in hand. For instance, he wrote to him with regard to commodities speculation:

> I feel ashamed to have given you so much trouble over commodities. But, as you are discovering, it is a business which needs hard work; and it does not turn out right over a period of years unless one attends to the details, which, cumulatively, add up to quite a lot.
>
> (letter 377, 14 July 1937)

Keynes's dealings in commodities involved speculating on spot and futures markets mainly for copper, wheat, cotton, oil and lard, with mixed success. However, he thought that uncertainty about the outcomes was in the nature of speculative activity, as he explained to Kahn:

> [. . .] it is safer to be a speculator than an investor in the sense that [. . .] a speculator is one who runs risks of which he is aware and an investor is one who runs risks of which he is unaware.
>
> (CWK XII: 109)

Keynes's investment policy as far as securities were concerned consisted in holding a restricted number of them, which in his personal case consisted of car company shares, gold, American utilities and, later, aircraft firms. In fact, he explained to Kahn:

> My [. . .] policy [. . .] assumes the ability to pick specialities which have, on the average, prospects of raising enormously more than an index of market leaders [. . .] It is largely the fluctuations which throw up the bargains and the uncertainty due to fluctuations which prevents other people from taking advantage of them.
>
> (letter 2078, 5 May 1938, CWK XII: 100–1)

Throughout the 1937–38 Stock Exchange crisis, Keynes believed (with some wishful thinking) that his philosophy helped in keeping the value of College investment and his own relatively stable. He wrote to Kahn:

> the indexes of ordinary shares, both in London and New York, are back almost exactly to the figures of January 1, 1935 [. . .] in the three

> years' swing, which has brought back prices to about where they were before, we shall have retained something approaching one-third of the appreciation as reported in 1936, which was not very far from the top point. If this is correct, it is a great deal better than most other people have done.
>
> (letter 2069, 28 February 1938)

The running of College finances was a sensitive issue between them, as can be seen from an exchange in December 1943, when peace was seen as imminent and both were planning to return from government duties to the academic life. Kahn wrote to Keynes:

> I am very much hoping that as soon as I am released from Whitehall you will allow me to relieve you to the fullest extent that you feel justifiable of the burden of bursial duties [...] The question, therefore, that is bothering me is not so much one of the College interest [...] as of my intense desire to relieve you of unnecessary work (having failed completely to do it during the war).
>
> (letter 25, 6 December 1943)

To which Keynes replied:

> I, too, have no intention of staying in Government service any longer than I can. There is much of College business which I actually enjoy and would miss, if I were without it. It does not put on me any burden which is unduly heavy, even in the present circumstances, and at what one hopes may be a fairly early date I shall be trying to disentangle myself from anything like whole time in Whitehall.
>
> (letter 24, 8 December 1943)

Keynes had helped Kahn with a loan of £500 in January 1934, when he was in financial difficulties arising from family problems and unlucky speculation in the German market. Four years later, Kahn was able to write to Keynes:

> I think you would like to know that my net assets, after deducting all loans, including yours, are still (just) positive [...] It has, of course, been touch and go, and without your great kindness I should by now have been done for.
>
> (letter 163, 27 March 1938)[13]

University

The other issue that occupied the correspondence during the time when Keynes's illness prevented him from attending to his normal occupations was University business. Two problems in particular needed careful handling. The first was the question of giving J. Robinson a full-time lectureship in 1938. Some members of the Board opposed it, but Kahn succeeded in the end thanks also to Pigou's stand in her favour. Keynes wrote to Kahn:

> I am extremely relieved that the matter of Joan's lectureship looks like being settled. For, if it had fallen through, it really would have been a case for armed insurrection. I am very glad that Pigou took the right line. Indeed, I expected him to do so. But how the other wretches can have failed to recognise that outside Cambridge she is unquestionably one of the most distinguished members of the staff, without the slightest doubt within the first half dozen, I cannot imagine. I wish I had been there to support you.
>
> (letter 171, 19 February 1938)[14]

The second episode concerns Kalecki. He had arrived in England in 1936 and had spent the academic year 1936–37 mostly at the London School of Economics; at the end of 1937 he moved to Cambridge. In January 1938, Kahn told Keynes about the difficult situation Kalecki found himself in. He wrote:

> Every time that I meet him I become more impressed by his absolutely terrific abilities. As you are aware, some of us would regard it as a terrible blot on economics and economists if towards the end of the summer he had to return to Warsaw with the idea of picking up a living by writing newspaper articles and possibly getting some minor commercial job. That is the alternative with which he is faced.
>
> (letter 177, 27 January 1938)

Keynes gave his help, although he had mixed feelings about Kalecki's approach. He wrote to Kahn:

> I have been greatly interested by his article in the latest *Econometrica.* I am not clear that he is perfectly right or that he has exploited his idea to the greatest possible advantage. But the idea itself seems to me an extraordinarily interesting and pregnant one. I am considering writing a comment on and development of what he has done. (I only wish he would not adopt such an appalling method of exposition. His Mathematics seems to be largely devoted to covering up the premises and making it extremely difficult to bring one's intuition to bear).
>
> (letter 157, 30 April 1938)

In the *Econometrica* article Kalecki showed that by assuming imperfect competition he was able to explain the stability of the wage rate in the cycle (Kalecki 1938). Thus it was Kalecki who challenged both the assumption of perfect competition and rising marginal costs and, consequently, his version of the theory of effective demand – unlike Keynes's – did not require the real wage to rise with employment. His result, however, was based on the assumption that the degree of monopoly varied inversely with the level of economic activity. Keynes did not like it, because Kalecki's answer to the question of the constancy of real wages depended on the 'coincidence' of the degree of monopoly having exactly the right magnitude to produce the desired outcome.

At the end of 1938, 'The Cambridge Research Scheme of the National Institute of Economic and Social Research into Prime Costs, Proceeds and Output' was set up and provided Kalecki with a job in Cambridge. The members of the Board were Austin Robinson, Kahn, Kalecki, Champernowne and Sraffa, while Keynes was Chairman. After one year, Kalecki presented the main results of his research on the degree of monopoly in the form of an 'Interim Report' (see Marcuzzo 1996a), which received very critical comments from J. Robinson and R. Kahn. Soon afterwards, Kalecki resigned and left Cambridge.[15]

War

Great Britain declared war on 3 September 1939. Keynes was anxious to secure Kahn a post as wartime Civil Servant in the Treasury, but initially there was opposition because he was 'so clearly associated with Keynes, who at this time was still regarded with suspicion' (Kahn 1988: 28).

Eventually a post was found for Kahn at the Board of Trade, under the Chairmanship of Oliver Lyttelton, and he started working there in December 1939, reporting to Keynes in a gloomy mood (letter 93, 17 December 1939). In May 1940 they corresponded on the issue of exchange control; Keynes sent him a draft of the report on the issue he was writing for the Treasury (CWK XII: 163–71) and got from Kahn 'as usual, most valuable criticism' (letter 84, 26 May 1940).

A few months later Kahn discovered that: 'The Treasury (in the shape of an official of the establishment Department – not Sir Horace Wilson) agreed to my appointment only on condition that I had nothing to do with currency questions!' (letter 77, 30 June 1940). Keynes took this information light-heartedly: 'Either all questions are currency questions, or none are. So I suggest you adopt the latter interpretation' (letter 75, 3 July 1940).

The Board of Trade covered a very wide administrative field. It was responsible for trade at home and for exporting abroad. Since at the outbreak of the war only 10 per cent of all goods required for consumption were produced within Britain, the first task of the Board of Trade was to find a consistent policy to reduce the consumer goods available on the market. The reduction in consumption was necessary to conserve shipping space, materials and manpower for war purposes, to free foreign exchange for vital purchases of war materials and civilian necessities abroad and to assure the fair distribution of limited resources. Within a year after the outbreak of the War, it had become clear that in order to reduce consumption sufficiently the Government had to resort to direct rationing for food and clothing. In this area Kahn gave an important contribution (see Kahn 1988: 36–7).

Initially, he felt that he did not have complete support from Keynes on the need to create unemployment, by releasing labour from civilian occupations in order to make it available to war production, and he complained to Keynes, who immediately reacted:

> I am not at all against your policy of creating unemployment. Far from it. It is a question of pace; and also I was talking in the context of creating unemployment to the detriment of exports, which is rather a different thing from home consumption. I am all for your policy, so far as the home consumer is concerned.
>
> (letter 81, 2 June 1940)

A month later, Kahn forcibly reaffirmed his position:

> To my mind the real moral to be drawn from our present difficulties lies in the overwhelming importance of strenuous measures to restrict home consumption. These will do everything that is required – release labour, reduce imports, increase exports.
>
> (letter 76, 2 July 1940)

Another issue arose a few weeks later over priorities, following a broadcast made by Keynes on 'British finances after the War' (CWK XXII: 240–5), to which Kahn strongly reacted:

> Your statement about the adequacy of existing measures might have been made equally well any time in the last three years. If it is a fact that the negligible sacrifices now imposed on us are adequate to deal with the existing scale of expenditure, is it not nothing less than criminal that we are not making more intense efforts to bring the war to a successful end? [. . . .] This brings me to the real issue between us. You still think of fiscal measures as required purely and simply to avoid a rise of prices. As the scale of war effort is enlarged further fiscal measures are necessary to achieve this end but only as and when. My own view is that all this emphasis on the danger of inflation is most retrograde and that what we ought really to be considering is how far fiscal and other measures are capable of speeding things up. I hold the view more strongly than ever that the immobilisation of labour for the purposes of home consumption is the main obstacle to

> an enlargement of the personnel and equipment of the fighting forces.
>
> (letter 72, 25 September 1940)

In the Middle East

At the outbreak of the War, the British wanted to be able to safeguard communications with India and the Far East and to keep open the Red Sea, the Suez canal and the Mediterranean for ocean shipping. With the intervention of Italy in June 1940 the Mediterranean was closed to sea transport, and supplies to the Middle East had to be shipped around the Cape of Good Hope. After the Italian invasion of Greece in October 1940 – which resulted in British support to the Greeks – the demand on shipping for supplies of all kinds (military and civilian) became extremely acute.

In London a proposal was drawn up for what was to be called a Middle East Supply Centre to co-ordinate procurement and shipping programmes for the area. In addition to Egypt, Sudan, Palestine, Malta and Cyprus, the area of the responsibility included – after the German invasion of the Balkans in June 1941 – Syria and Lebanon; between March and December 1942, Iraq, Persia, Saudi Arabia and the Persian Gulf Sheikhdoms were added to the area and in November 1942, Cyrenaica and Tripolitania were included.

Oliver Lyttelton was appointed Minister of State in the Middle East in 1941. Kahn wrote to Keynes:

> Oliver [Lyttelton] before leaving, sent a message that he would probably want me. You were not available for consultation and I gave way without hesitation to my natural instincts and said I would love it [. . .] I feel rather bad about you and the College. I have done practically nothing for either for a long time but I suppose having me in the background is some slight safeguard.
>
> (letter 64, 21 August 1941)

Keynes acquiesced with some doubts;[16] at least he wanted to make sure that Kahn was given 'a more substantial job than the particular thing, which Oliver proposes to invent for you' (letter 62, 24 August 1941). Shortly afterwards, Keynes asked Kahn, 'as my traditional first class critic' (letter 61, 9 September 1941), for his comments on the proposal of an international currency union, and received a very favourable response.

Kahn came to Cairo in October 1941; he was made Economic Adviser and from January 1942 he acted as Deputy Director General of the Centre. The Centre was concerned with the collection of information, recommendations on the priority of imports, and co-ordination of the executive acts of the governments of the Middle East. It required dealings with

20 or more different governments with separate administrations and independent monetary systems (see Kahn 1988: 42–5). The Middle East Supply Centre has been described as 'one of the most ambitious and successful of the British War time experiments' (Beherens 1955: 227).

Keynes continued to consult Kahn on various matters, such as post-war currency policy (letter 61, 9 September 1941) and College accounts (letter 58, 31 October 1941). For his part, Kahn turned to Keynes for advice and consultation on Middle East affairs, such as the finances of Palestine (letter 52, 30 March 1942) and Persia (letter 32, 1 November 1942).

However, Kahn soon grew dissatisfied with his position and the way matters were being handled between London and Cairo, and asked Keynes's help to be sent back home (letter 42, 16 August 1942). Keynes was supportive:

> I expect you are taking much too dark a view of the position and that you will feel differently after a change and a holiday. All the same, I expect you have done all that is possible to do there, and I am strongly of your opinion that it would be a good idea to come home, where you are badly wanted.
>
> (letter 41, 28 August 1942)

Approval from London was held up for a while, but eventually granted.

Last years

When Kahn returned to London, in January 1943,[17] he spent one year with the Ministry of Supply, where he was concerned with the post-war situation of raw materials (copper, steel, wool, tin), both their production and their prospective prices. He then joined the Ministry of Production for a while and consequently returned to the Board of Trade. Once again collaboration with Keynes was close, and both worked on buffer stocks and the post-war problems of the sterling area.

The correspondence of the last two years of Keynes's life is very scant. In April 1944, Keynes was urging Kahn – 'very much in the interest of the College and of economics at Cambridge' (letter 12, 24 April 1944) – to return to academic life.[18] In November 1945, once negotiations in the US were over, Keynes himself longed to be back in King's. He wrote to Kahn:

> This has been the most harassing and exhausting negotiation you can imagine. All of us are stale and exhausted and have outstayed our welcome. There is nothing more to be said on either side [. . .] So if I can turn up back home in time for the Annual Congregation [on the 8th December], it will be a great happiness.
>
> (letter 5, 23 November 1945)

He did not make it after all, as we know, since he embarked on the Queen Elizabeth, in New York, on 11 December and arrived in Southampton on 17 December (Moggridge 1992: 815).

The last letter to Kahn is from Savannah, where Keynes had travelled on March 1946 to christen the IMF and the World Bank, and shows all his disappointment:

> The Americans have no idea of how to make these institutions into operating international concerns, and in almost every direction their ideas are bad. Yet they plainly intend to force their own conceptions through regardless of the rest of us.
>
> (letter 1, 13 March 1946, CWK XXVI: 217)

We do not have Kahn's reply to this letter, but we do have an article that he wrote in 1976, entitled *Historical Origins of the International Monetary Fund*, in which he meticulously reconstructed Keynes's ideas, his commitment to building a new monetary order and the anguish of the last weeks of his life (Kahn 1976).

Kahn returned to Cambridge only in September 1946, a few months after Keynes's death, in the April of that year. He succeeded Keynes as First Bursar of the College, was in charge of winding up his estate and looking after the finances of his wife, Lydia, and acted as Keynes's literary executor.

Notes

1 This sentence can be found in the 'Introduction' by J. Robinson to the Italian edition of R.F. Kahn's *Essays on Employment and Growth* (Kahn 1972) which was published in Italian but not in English. This original is in JVR papers, XI/8.

2 For instance, Keynes pencilled an essay by Kahn, dated 4 November 1927, with the comment: 'I think you have a real aptitude for Economics' (RFK papers, XI/3). A few months later, on 27 April 1928, he marked another essay with the following words: 'Very good – almost a perfect answer'(RFK papers, XI/3). Again, a couple of days later, he wrote to his wife: 'Yesterday my favourite pupil Kahn wrote me one of the best answers I ever had from a pupil – he *must* get a first class' (JMK papers, PP/45/190/4/46).

3 'Under the influence of Marshall's *Principles*, I chose *The Economics of the Short Period*. In making my choice I was encouraged by Shove and Piero Sraffa. Keynes happily acquiesced. Neither he nor I had the slightest idea that my work on the short period was later on going to influence the development of Keynes's own thought. But there are no traces of Keynesian thought in the dissertation itself' (Kahn 1989: x–xi). See Marcuzzo (1994).

4 'Keynes did not want to divert me from writing my Dissertation, and it was only after December 1929 that he started giving me for comments the proofs of the *Treatise*' (Patinkin and Leith 1977: 148). See also Kahn (1984: 175).

5 This partly contradicts what he recalled almost 50 years later.

6 Keynes cannot have entirely shared the idea of having been for such a long time a believer in the Quantity Theory, since many years afterwards he wrote to him: 'I enclose as a specimen the letter I wrote on Christmas Eve, 1917, which is interesting for two reasons – [...] (ii) the fact that even then I was

thinking in terms of supply and demand and not of the quantity theory of money!' (letter 83, 27 May 1940).

7 Keynes took up the alternative 'method' in his lectures the following autumn, where we find him using the expression 'demand as a whole relatively to supply as a whole' (CWK XXIX: 53; Rymes 1989: 55)

8 The American edition of the pamphlet [. . .] also incorporated material from Keynes's article 'The Multiplier' which appeared in the New Statesman of 1 April 1933' (Editorial note, CWK XIII: 412).

9 However, just two weeks before Kahn had written to Keynes: 'I am feeling very distressed that I have not found time to read very much of your book. I seem this term to have got myself completely bogged. It is a rotten way to treat you (and the subject which you, at least, are so anxious to "do full justice" to)' (letter 283, 14 March 1934).

10 'The fundamental assumption of the classical theory, "supply creates its own demand", is that $OW = OP$ [W = marginal prime cost of production when output is O; P = expected selling price of this output; OP = effective demand] *whatever* the level of O [. . .] On *my* theory, $OW \neq OP$, for *all* values of O, and entrepreneurs have to choose a value of O for which it *is* equal; – otherwise the equality of price and marginal prime cost is infringed. This is the real starting point of everything' (letter 249, 13 April 1934, CWK XIII: 422–3).

11 Keynes became Second Bursar in November 1919 and from 1924 until his death in 1946, First Bursar. Kahn was appointed Second Bursar in 1935. On Keynes's death Kahn succeeded him as First Bursar. Kahn's abilities were highly praised, as Keynes wrote to him: 'The following reaches me from the Estates Committee (don't confess I sent it you): 'It may interest (though not surprise) you to hear from outside that Kahn's handling of the Committee, with its immense agenda, was masterly, alike for lucidity, persuasiveness and speed; a very fine performance' (letter 296, 26 July 1937). In November 1937, Keynes wrote to Kahn with gratitude: 'now that Audit has come and the fulfilment of the worst part of your tasks, I must write to thank you for all your labours and for how well you have done them. Also I very much appreciated being kept in such close touch with everything, and only hope that this has not added too much to your work' (letter 411, November 1937).

12 From 18 June to 23 September 1937 Keynes stayed at the clinic at Ruthin Castle in Wales.

13 Half of the loan was repaid in October 1938 (letter 130, 7/12 October 1938).

14 This was not the first time that Keynes had to step in to prevent J. Robinson from being ostracised. It also happened in 1935, when her lectures on 'Money' met strong opposition from some members of the Faculty and Keynes had to send letters around to win her case. See Marcuzzo (1991 and 2003). See Chs 2 (69), 6 (176), 7 (208) and 13 (339).

15 See letters between Kahn and Kalecki in July 1939 (RFK papers, 5/1/146–7; 149–58; 159–62; 163–9).

16 'I expect you will greatly enjoy the trip, but whether the gain to the Middle East will be equal to the loss of the Board of Trade, I am not sure' (letter 62, 24 August 1941).

17 See letter 1727 from JMK to NK, 15 January 1943: 'Kahn is expected in London tomorrow – he is believed to have reached Lisbon.'

18 Keynes was at the time involved in the process of reshaping the post-war academic economic research and teaching in Cambridge, which he felt was badly needed. He wrote to Kahn: 'It is a great misfortune for an economist to have been brought up on economics, and I should like to return to the old custom of always selecting for Professorships those who had no previous acquaintance with the subject' (letter 16, 3 April 1944).

Table 1.1 Keynes–Kahn correspondence

From	*To*	*Year*	*Month*	*Day*	*Date*	*Archive*		*Published in*	*Item*
JMK	RFK	1928	June	15	Dated letter	Kahn–King's	RFK/13/57/1	Marcuzzo 1998: 4, (E)	242
RFK	JMK	1928	June	17	Dated letter	Keynes–King's	L/K/1–2		240
RFK	JMK	1928	October	10	Dated letter	Keynes–King's	UA/5/2/83		241
RFK	JMK	1928	December	13	Dated letter	Keynes–King's	L/K/3–7		237
RFK	JMK	1929	July	19	Dated letter	Keynes–King's	L/K/8–11		239
JMK	RFK	1929	July	29	Dated letter	Keynes–King's	L/K/12–16		238
RFK	JMK	1929	September	29	Dated letter	Keynes–King's	TM/1/2/42–3	CWK XXIX: 4, (E)	236
RFK	JMK	1929	December	17	Dated letter	Keynes–King's	L/K/17–20	CWK XIII: 120–1, (E)	379
RFK	JMK	1930	March		Attributed	Keynes–King's	EJ/1/3/183–5		231
RFK	JMK	1930	March		Attributed	Keynes–King's	L/K/21–2	CWK, XIII: 123–4, (E)	235
RFK	JMK	1930	March	12	Dated letter	Keynes–King's	L/K/23–4	CWK XIII: 124–5, (E)	395
JMK	RFK	1930	March	12	Dated letter	Kahn–King's	RFK/13/57/2		234
RFK	JMK	1930	March	16	Dated letter	Keynes–King's	L/K/27–30	Marcuzzo 1998: 6, (E)	269
JMK	RFK	1930	March	16	Dated letter	Kahn–King's	RFK/13/57/3–4	Marcuzzo 1998: 5, (E)	233
JMK	RFK	1930	March	18	Dated letter	Keynes–King's	L/K/25–6	CWK XIII: 125–6, (E)	232
JMK	RFK	1930	May	26	Dated letter	Kahn–King's	RFK/13/57/5–6		285
RFK	JMK	1930	August	17	Dated letter	Keynes–King's	EA/1/50		230
RFK	JMK	1930	August	26	Dated letter	Keynes–King's	EA/1/63		229
RFK	JMK	1930	September	17	Dated letter	Keynes–King's	L/K/31–2		244
RFK	JMK	1930	September	19	Dated letter	Keynes–King's	L/K/33–4		243
RFK	JMK	1931	March	25	Dated letter	Keynes–King's	TM/1/4/120A–D	CWK XXIX: 11–12, (E)	381
RFK	JMK	1931	April	5	Dated letter	Keynes–King's	TM/1/4/128–34	CWK XIII: 203–6, (E)	405
RFK	JMK	1931	April	17	Dated letter	Keynes–King's	TM/1/4/135–6	CWK XIII: 206–7, (E)	380
JMK	RFK	1931	April	20	Dated letter	Keynes–King's	GTE/1/1	CWK XXIX: 12–13, (E)	382
RFK	JMK	1931	May	7	Dated letter	Keynes–King's	TM/1/4/124–7	CWK XIII: 212–13, (E)	271
JMK	RFK	1931	May	29	Dated letter	Kahn–King's	RFK/13/57/7	CWK XX: 310, (E)	270
RFK	JMK	1931	July	28	Dated letter	Keynes–King's	EJ/7/11		268
JMK	RFK	1931	July	29	Dated letter	Kahn–King's	RFK/2/2/1–2		424

RFK	JMK	1931	July	31	Dated letter	Keynes–King's	L/31/99–103		267
JMK	RFK	1931	August	13	Dated letter	Kahn–King's	RFK/13/57/8	CWK XX: 594–5, (E)	266
RFK	JMK	1931	August	15	Dated letter	Keynes–King's	EJ/6/7/1–6	CWK XIII: 218–19, (E)	265
JMK	RFK	1931	September	20	Dated letter	Keynes–King's	GTE/1/20–2	CWK XIII: 373–5, (E)	396
RFK	JMK	1931	September	24	Dated letter	Keynes–King's	GTE/1/18–19	CWK XIII: 375, (E)	403
JMK	RFK	1932	February	1	Dated letter	Kahn–King's	RFK/13/57/9		264
RFK	JMK	1932	October	11	Dated letter	Keynes–King's	CAC/1/91		282
RFK	JMK	1932	October	11	Dated letter	Keynes–King's	TM/1/4/215–6		286
RFK	JMK	1932	October	14	Dated letter	Keynes–King's	GTE/1/89–92		316
RFK	JMK	1932	October	29	Dated letter	Keynes–King's	EJ/1/3/308		263
JMK	RFK	1932	December	12	Dated letter	Kahn–King's	RFK/13/57/10–3		262
RFK	JMK	1933	January	20	Dated letter	Keynes–King's	L/K/35–8	CWK XIII: 412–13, (E)	254
JMK	RFK	1933	January	29	Dated letter	Kahn–King's	RFK/13/57/14–5	CWK XIII: 413, (E)	261
RFK	JMK	1933	February	16	Dated letter	Keynes–King's	L/K/39–42	Marcuzzo 1998: 18, (E)	260
RFK	JMK	1933	March	7	Dated letter	Keynes–King's	L/K/43–4		259
RFK	JMK	1933	March	10	Dated letter	Keynes–King's	L/K/45		288
JMK	RFK	1933	March	10	Dated letter	Kahn–King's	RFK/13/57/16–7	Moggridge 1992: 590, (E)	250
JMK	RFK	1933	March	16	Dated letter	Kahn–King's Keynes–King's	RFK/13/57/18–9 L/K/48–9	CWK XXI: 168, (E)	251
RFK	JMK	1933	March	19	Dated letter	Keynes–King's	L/K/50–1		252
JMK	RFK	1933	March	20	Dated letter	Kahn–King's	RFK/13/57/20	CWK XXI: 168, (E)	253
JMK	RFK	1933	March	24	Dated letter	Kahn–King's	RFK/13/57/21	CWK XIII: 413, (E)	276
RFK	JMK	1933	March	30	Dated letter	Keynes–King's	L/K/52–5	CWK XIII: 414, (E)	274
JMK	RFK	1933	March	30	Dated letter	Kahn–King's	RFK/13/57/22	CWK XIII: 413–14, (E)	275
RFK	JMK	1933	April	5	Dated letter	Keynes–King's	L/K/56–9		273
RFK	JMK	1933	April	6	Dated letter	Keynes–King's	L/K/60–1		287
JMK	RFK	1933	April	7	Dated letter	Kahn–King's	RFK/13/57/23–4		272
RFK	JMK	1933	April	9	Dated letter	Keynes–King's	L/K/62–4		280
RFK	JMK	1933	April	14	Dated letter	Keynes–King's	L/K/65–6		255
RFK	JMK	1933	June	14	Dated letter	Kahn–King's	RFK/13/57/53–4		257
JMK	RFK	1934	January	11	Dated letter	Keynes–King's	UA/14/2/107		407
RFK	JMK	1934	January	16	Dated letter	Keynes–King's	L/K/73–4		258

Table 1.1 continued

From	*To*	*Year*	*Month*	*Day*	*Date*	*Archive*		*Published in*	*Item*
RFK	JMK	1934	January	24	Dated letter	Keynes–King's	UA/14/2/119		256
RFK	JMK	1934	March	14	Dated letter	Keynes–King's	PP/45/161/1–2	Marcuzzo 1998: 20, (E)	283
RFK	JMK	1934	March	20	Dated letter	Keynes–King's	GTE/1/191–5	CWK XXIX: 120–2, (E)	383
RFK	JMK	1934	March	21	Dated letter	Keynes–King's	GTE/1/196	CWK XXIX: 122, (E)	384
JMK	RFK	1934	April	13	Dated letter	Kahn–King's	RFK/13/57/46–7	CWK XIII: 422–3, (E)	249
JMK	RFK	1934	May	23	Postmark	Kahn–King's	RFK/13/57/48		392
JMK	RFK	1934	May	27	Dated letter	Kahn–King's	RFK/13/57/49–50		281
JMK	RFK	1934	June	25	Dated letter	Keynes–King's Sraffa–Trinity	UA/5/3/90 Add.ms.a.427/30		406
JMK	RFK	1934	August	1	Dated letter	Kahn–King's	RFK/13/57/57		247
RFK	JMK	1934	August	2	Dated letter	Keynes–King's	UA/5/3/100–1		248
RFK	JMK	1934	August	5	Dated letter	Keynes–King's	L/K/75		246
RFK	JMK	1934	August	9	Dated letter	Keynes–King's	L/K/76–7		245
JMK	RFK	1934	August	13	Dated letter	Kahn–King's	RFK/13/57/58–9		228
RFK	JMK	1934	September	16	Dated letter	Keynes–King's	L/K/78–9		227
JMK	RFK	1934	September	18	Dated letter	Kahn–King's	RFK/13/57/60–1	CWK XIII: 484–5, (E)	226
JMK	RFK	1934	September	27	Dated letter	Kahn–King's	RFK/13/57/62	CWK XIII: 485, (E)	224
JMK	RFK	1934	October	3	Dated letter	Kahn–King's	RFK/13/57/63		213
JMK	RFK	1934	December	15	Dated letter	Kahn–King's	RFK/13/57/112–3		212
JMK	RFK	1935	January	1	Dated letter	Kahn–King's	RFK/13/57/122		211
RFK	JMK	1935	January	9	Dated letter	Keynes–King's	L/K/80		225
RFK	JMK	1935	January	11	Dated letter	Keynes–King's	SE/1/2/1–2		284
JMK	RFK	1935	January	13	Dated letter	Kahn–King's	RFK/13/57/122		210
RFK	JMK	1935	January	14	Dated letter	Kahn–King's	RFK/13/57/123		201
JMK	RFK	1935	January	15	Dated letter	Kahn–King's	RFK/13/57/124–5	CWK XIII: 525, (E)	223
RFK	JMK	1935	March	22	Dated letter	Keynes–King's	L/K/81		202
RFK	JMK	1935	March	25	Dated letter	Keynes–King's	L/K/84		203
JMK	RFK	1935	March	26	Dated letter	Kahn–King's Keynes–King's	RFK/13/57/126–7 L/K/82–3	CWK XIII: 525, (E)	222

RFK	JMK	1935	March	28	Dated letter	Keynes–King's	L/K/85–6		221
JMK	RFK	1935	March	31	Dated letter	Kahn–King's	RFK/13/57/128–9		220
JMK	RFK	1935	July	29	Dated letter	Kahn–King's	RFK/13/57/130–1	CWK XIII: 634, (E)	277
JMK	RFK	1935	July	30	Dated letter	Kahn–King's	RFK/13/57/132–3	CWK XIII: 634, (E)	278
JMK	RFK	1935	August	27	Dated letter	Kahn–King's	RFK/13/57/134–6	CWK XIII: 634, (E)	219
JMK	RFK	1935	September		Attributed	Keynes–King's	GTE/1/337	CWK XIII: 635, (E)	387
RFK	JMK	1935	September		Attributed	Keynes–King's	GTE/1/338–9	CWK XIII: 635–6, (E)	386
RFK	JMK	1935	September	2	Dated letter	Keynes–King's	KC/5/5/191–2		320
JMK	RFK	1935	September	4	Dated letter	Keynes–King's Keynes–King's	GTE/1/350–1 GTE/1/347–8	CWK XIII: 634–5, (E)	391
RFK	JMK	1935	September	5	Dated letter	Keynes–King's	KC/5/5/193		321
JMK	RFK	1935	September	8	Dated letter	Kahn–King's	RFK/13/57/137–8		209
JMK	RFK	1935	September	15	Dated letter	Kahn–King's	RFK/13/57/139–40		208
RFK	JMK	1935	September	22	Dated letter	Keynes–King's	KC/5/5/194–6		413
RFK	JMK	1935	October		Attributed	Keynes–King's	GTE/1/343–5	CWK XIII: 637, (E)	388
JMK	RFK	1935	October	7	Dated letter	Keynes–King's	GTE/1/349	CWK XIII: 636, (E)	389
JMK	RFK	1935	October	24	Dated letter	Kahn–King's	RFK/13/57/141		218
RFK	JMK	1936	January	15	Dated letter	Keynes–King's	KC/5/5/197		322
RFK	JMK	1936	February	21	Dated letter	Keynes–King's	A/36/6		412
JMK	RFK	1936	March	10	Dated letter	Keynes–King's	GTE/2/4/255		207
RFK	JMK	1936	March	17	Dated letter	Keynes–King's	GTE/2/3/1–2		206
JMK	RFK	1936	March	26	Dated letter	Keynes–King's	GTE/2/3/3–4		217
RFK	JMK	1936	March	27	Dated letter	Keynes–King's	GTE/2/2/2–4		216
RFK	JMK	1936	June	2	Dated letter	Keynes–King's	UA/5/4/9		426
RFK	JMK	1936	July	20	Dated letter	Keynes–King's	KC/5/5/204		323
JMK	RFK	1936	July	22	Dated letter	Keynes–King's	KC/5/5/205–6		317
JMK	RFK	1936	August	27	Dated letter	Kahn–King's	RFK/13/57/142–3		215
JMK	RFK	1936	November	9	Dated letter	Keynes–King's	BM/2/405		318
RFK	JMK	1936	November	9	Dated letter	Keynes–King's	BM/2/405		2195
JMK	RFK	1936	November	9	Attributed	Keynes–King's	KC/5/5/212		414

Table 1.1 continued

From	*To*	*Year*	*Month*	*Day*	*Date*	*Archive*		*Published in*	*Item*
RFK	JMK	1936	November	9	Dated letter	Keynes–King's	KC/5/5/212		2196
RFK	JMK	1936	December	6	Dated letter	Keynes–King's	A/37/77–8		319
JMK	RFK	1936	December	10	Dated letter	Kahn–King's	RFK/13/57/144		204
RFK	JMK	1936	December	13	Dated letter	Keynes–King's	GTE/2/3/5	CWK XIV: 108, (E)	390
JMK	RFK	1936	December	13	Dated letter	Keynes–King's	UA/14/2/233–4		214
RFK	JMK	1936	December	17	Dated letter	Keynes–King's	KC/5/5/241		324
RFK	JMK	1936	December	17	Dated letter	Keynes–King's	UA/14/2/236–7		205
RFK	JMK	1936	December	18	Dated letter	Keynes–King's	KC/5/5/245–7		279
RFK	JMK	1936	December	24	Dated letter	Keynes–King's	KC/5/5/250		415
JMK	RFK	1937	March	25	Dated letter	Kahn–King's	RFK/13/57/145–6		408
JMK	RFK	1937	March	30	Dated letter	Kahn–King's	RFK/13/57/149–50		291
JMK	RFK	1937	April	19	Dated letter	Kahn–King's	RFK/13/57/151–2		357
RFK	JMK	1937	April	21	Dated letter	Keynes–King's	KC/5/5/244		358
RFK	JMK	1937	May	7	Dated letter	Keynes–King's	L/37/9		359
JMK	RFK	1937	June	20	Dated letter	Kahn–King's	RFK/13/57/157–9	Skidelsky 2000: 7, (E)	360
JMK	RFK	1937	June	23	Dated letter	Kahn–King's	RFK/13/57/162		361
JMK	RFK	1937	June	24	Dated letter	Kahn–King's	RFK/13/57/165–6		370
JMK	RFK	1937	June	25	Dated letter	Kahn–King's	RFK/13/57/167–8		371
JMK	RFK	1937	June	30	Dated letter	Kahn–King's	RFK/13/57/169–70	CWK XII: 22, (E)	372
JMK	RFK	1937	July	1	Dated letter	Kahn–King's	RFK/13/57/171–2		362
RFK	JMK	1937	July	2	Dated letter	Keynes–King's	KC/5/6/40–2		292
JMK	RFK	1937	July	2	Dated letter	Kahn–King's	RFK/13/57/173		363
JMK	RFK	1937	July	3	Dated letter	Kahn–King's	RFK/13/57/174–5		293
JMK	RFK	1937	July	6	Dated letter	Kahn–King's	RFK/13/57/176		2090
JMK	RFK	1937	July	6	Dated letter	Kahn–King's	RFK/13/57/177–8	Moggridge 1992: 608, (E)	364
JMK	RFK	1937	July	7	Dated letter	Kahn–King's	RFK/13/57/179	Moggridge 1992: 608 (E)	373
JMK	RFK	1937	July	8	Dated letter	Kahn–King's	RFK/13/57/180–1		374
JMK	RFK	1937	July	9	Dated letter	Kahn–King's	RFK/13/57/187		365

RFK	JMK	1937	July	11	Dated letter	Keynes–King's	KC/5/6/43–4		366
JMK	RFK	1937	July	11	Dated letter	Kahn–King's	RFK/13/57/182–4		294
JMK	RFK	1937	July	12	Dated letter	Kahn–King's	RFK/13/57/188–9	Skidelsky 2000: 32, (E)	295
JMK	RFK	1937	July	13	Dated letter	Kahn–King's	RFK/13/57/190		376
JMK	RFK	1937	July	13	Dated letter	Kahn–King's	RFK/13/57/191–2		375
JMK	RFK	1937	July	14	Dated letter	Kahn–King's	RFK/13/57/193–4		377
JMK	RFK	1937	July	15	Dated letter	Kahn–King's	RFK/13/57/195–6		378
JMK	RFK	1937	July	17	Dated letter	Kahn–King's	RFK/13/57/197–8		367
JMK	RFK	1937	July	17	Dated letter	Kahn–King's	RFK/13/57/199–200	CWK XII: 24, (E)	398
JMK	RFK	1937	July	17	Dated letter	Kahn–King's	RFK/13/57/201		351
RFK	JMK	1937	July	18	Dated letter	Keynes–King's	KC/5/6/60		356
RFK	JMK	1937	July	19	Dated letter	Keynes–King's	KC/5/6/61–3		290
JMK	RFK	1937	July	20	Dated letter	Kahn–King's	RFK/13/57/202–3		352
RFK	JMK	1937	July	21	Dated letter	Keynes–King's	KC/5/6/64		404
RFK	JMK	1937	July	22	Dated letter	Keynes–King's	KC/5/6/70–1		289
JMK	RFK	1937	July	22	Dated letter	Kahn–King's	RFK/13/57/204		353
JMK	RFK	1937	July	23	Dated letter	Keynes–King's	KC/5/6/72–3		312
RFK	JMK	1937	July	23	Dated letter	Keynes–King's	KC/5/6/74–5		313
JMK	RFK	1937	July	23	Dated letter	Keynes–King's	KC/5/6/76–9		315
JMK	RFK	1937	July	23	Dated letter	Keynes–King's	KC/5/6/80–2		314
JMK	RFK	1937	July	24	Dated letter	Kahn–King's	RFK/13/57/205	Skidelsky 2000: 28, (E)	354
JMK	RFK	1937	July	24	Dated letter	Kahn–King's	RFK/13/57/206–7		355
RFK	JMK	1937	July	26	Dated letter	Keynes–King's	KC/5/6/84		350
JMK	RFK	1937	July	26	Dated letter	Kahn–King's Keynes–King's	RFK/13/57/208–9 KC/5/6/85–6		296
RFK	JMK	1937	July	27	Dated letter	Keynes–King's	KC/5/6/87–8		297
JMK	RFK	1937	August		Attributed	Kahn–King's Keynes–King's	RFK/13/57/213–6 EJ/1/4/67–70	CWK XIV: 238–9, (E)	298
JMK	RFK	1937	August		Attributed	Kahn–King's	RFK/13/57/221		2052
JMK	RFK	1937	August	20	Dated letter	Kahn–King's	RFK/13/57/210–1		349

Table 1.1 continued

From	*To*	*Year*	*Month*	*Day*	*Date*	*Archive*		*Published in*	*Item*
JMK	RFK	1937	August	20	Postmark	Kahn–King's	RFK/13/57/212		397
JMK	RFK	1937	August	21	Dated letter	Kahn–King's	RFK/13/57/217–8		299
JMK	RFK	1937	August	22	Dated letter	Kahn–King's	RFK/13/57/219–20		343
RFK	JMK	1937	August	23	Dated letter	Keynes–King's	KC/5/6/106		418
RFK	JMK	1937	August	23	Dated letter	Kahn–King's	RFK/13/57/222		344
JMK	RFK	1937	August		Dated letter	Kahn–King's	RFK/13/57/222		452
JMK	RFK	1937	August	24	Dated letter	Kahn–King's	RFK/13/57/223–4		345
JMK	RFK	1937	August	25	Dated letter	Kahn–King's	RFK/13/57/225		347
RFK	JMK	1937	August	25	Dated letter	Kahn–King's	RFK/13/57/225		2197
JMK	RFK	1937	August	25	Dated letter	Kahn–King's	RFK/13/57/226		346
JMK	RFK	1937	August	26	Dated letter	Kahn–King's	RFK/13/57/225		2198
JMK	RFK	1937	August	26	Dated letter	Kahn–King's	RFK/13/57/227–8		348
RFK	JMK	1937	August	27	Dated letter	Keynes–King's	EJ/1/4/71–3		401
RFK	JMK	1937	August	28	Dated letter	Keynes–King's	KC/5/6/94–7		300
RFK	JMK	1937	August	29	Dated letter	Keynes–King's	KC/5/6/89–90		338
RFK	JMK	1937	August	29	Dated letter	Keynes–King's	KC/5/6/91		333
RFK	JMK	1937	August	29	Dated letter	Keynes–King's	KC/5/6/93		334
JMK	RFK	1937	August	29	Dated letter	Kahn–King's	RFK/13/57/229–30		339
JMK	RFK	1937	August	30	Dated letter	Keynes–King's	EJ/1/4/71		402
RFK	JMK	1937	August	30	Dated letter	Keynes–King's	KC/5/6/92		340
RFK	JMK	1937	August	31	Dated letter	Keynes–King's	EJ/1/4/81		342
RFK	JMK	1937	August	31	Dated letter	Keynes–King's	KC/5/6/98–101		341
JMK	RFK	1937	September	2	Dated letter	Kahn–King's	RFK/13/57/231–2	CWK XII: 24–5, (E)	301
JMK	RFK	1937	September	4	Dated letter	Kahn–King's	RFK/13/57/233–6		302
JMK	RFK	1937	September	5	Dated letter	Keynes–King's	KC/5/6/102–3		325
RFK	JMK	1937	September	8	Dated letter	Kahn–King's	RFK/13/57/244		369
JMK	RFK	1937	September	9	Dated letter	Kahn–King's	RFK/13/57/244		368
RFK	JMK	1937	September	12	Dated letter	Keynes–King's	KC/5/6/104		326

JMK	RFK	1937	September	13	Dated letter	Kahn–King's	RFK/13/57/245–6		335
JMK	RFK	1937	September	16	Dated letter	Kahn–King's	RFK/13/57/247–8		336
JMK	RFK	1937	September	20	Dated letter	Kahn–King's	RFK/13/57/249		337
RFK	JMK	1937	September	22	Dated letter	Keynes–King's	KC/5/6/107–8		327
RFK	JMK	1937	October	3	Dated letter	Keynes–King's	KC/5/6/110		329
RFK	JMK	1937	October	3	Dated letter	Keynes–King's	KC/5/6/115		330
JMK	RFK	1937	October	6	Dated letter	Keynes–King's	KC/5/6/116		331
JMK	RFK	1937	October	7	Dated letter	Kahn–King's	RFK/13/57/252–3	CWK XIV: 258, (E)	303
RFK	JMK	1937	October	8	Dated letter	Keynes–King's	PP/45/178/6		2192
JMK	RFK	1937	October	11	Dated letter	Keynes–King's	EJ/1/4/152		304
JMK	RFK	1937	October	11	Dated letter	Keynes–King's	KC/5/6/117–20		332
JMK	RFK	1937	October	11	Dated letter	Kahn–King's	RFK/13/57/254		308
RFK	JMK	1937	October	13	Dated letter	Keynes–King's	KC/5/6/109		328
RFK	JMK	1937	October	14	Dated letter	Keynes–King's	KC/5/6/130–1		419
RFK	JMK	1937	October	15	Dated letter	Keynes–King's	KC/5/6/122–3		305
RFK	JMK	1937	October	18	Dated letter	Keynes–King's	EJ/1/4/176	CWK XIV: 259, (E)	400
RFK	JMK	1937	October	18	Dated letter	Keynes–King's	EJ/1/4/177	CWK XIV: 258, (E)	399
RFK	JMK	1937	October	20	Dated letter	Keynes–King's	EJ/1/4/178	CWK XIV: 260, (E)	394
JMK	RFK	1937	October	20	Dated letter	Kahn–King's Keynes–King's	RFK/13/57/257 EJ/1/4/185	CWK XIV: 259	306
RFK	JMK	1937	October	22	Dated letter	Keynes–King's	EJ/1/4/186–7	CWK XIV: 260, (E)	393
JMK	RFK	1937	October	25	Dated letter	Keynes–King's	EJ/1/4/201–3	CWK XIV: 260–2, (E)	307
JMK	RFK	1937	October	25	Dated letter	Keynes–King's	KC/5/6/37		416
JMK	RFK	1937	October	26	Dated letter	Keynes–King's	PP/45/178/6		2193
JMK	RFK	1937	October	26	Dated letter	Kahn–King's	RFK/13/57/258–9	CWK XII: 22–3, (E)	309
RFK	JMK	1937	October	27	Dated letter	Keynes–King's Keynes–King's	KC/5/6/132–3 KC/5/6/38–9		310
RFK	JMK	1937	October	27	Dated letter	Keynes–King's	PP/45/178/6		2194
RFK	JMK	1937	October	28	Dated letter	Kahn–King's	RFK/13/57/258		2199
JMK	RFK	1937	October	28	Dated letter	Kahn–King's Keynes–King's	RFK/13/57/260–1 KC/5/6/260–1		311

Table 1.1 continued

From	*To*	*Year*	*Month*	*Day*	*Date*	*Archive*		*Published in*	*Item*
RFK	JMK	1937	October	29	Dated letter	Kahn–King's	RFK/13/57/256	CWK XII: 24, (E)	385
JMK	RFK	1937	November		Attributed	Kahn–King's	RFK/13/57/262–3		411
JMK	RFK	1937	November	1	Dated letter	Keynes–King's	KC/5/6/136–8		428
JMK	RFK	1937	November	4	Dated letter	Keynes–King's	KC/5/6/140–2		423
RFK	JMK	1937	November	7	Dated letter	Keynes–King's	KC/5/6/143		422
JMK	RFK	1937	November	7	Dated letter	Keynes–King's	KC/5/6/149–50		421
RFK	JMK	1937	November	10	Attributed	Keynes–King's	KC/5/6/139		425
JMK	RFK	1937	November	14	Dated letter	Keynes–King's	KC/5/6/144		200
JMK	RFK	1937	November	17	Dated letter	Keynes–King's	KC/5/6/151–5		199
RFK	JMK	1937	November	17	Dated letter	Keynes–King's	KC/5/6/176–7		439
RFK	JMK	1937	November	17	Dated letter	Keynes–King's	L/K/87–8		437
JMK	RFK	1937	November	22	Dated letter	Keynes–King's	KC/5/6/188–9		196
RFK	JMK	1937	November	22	Dated letter	Keynes–King's	KC/5/6/190–1		442
RFK	JMK	1937	November	23	Dated letter	Keynes–King's	KC/5/6/192–4		444
RFK	JMK	1937	November	24	Dated letter	Keynes–King's	KC/5/6/203		446
RFK	JMK	1937	November	25	Dated letter	Keynes–King's	KC/5/6/204		192
RFK	JMK	1937	November	25	Dated letter	Keynes–King's	KC/5/6/213–4		191
RFK	JMK	1937	November	26	Dated letter	Keynes–King's	KC/5/6/205–6		449
JMK	RFK	1937	November	27	Dated letter	Keynes–King's	KC/5/6/195–202		188
JMK	RFK	1937	November	27	Dated letter	Keynes–King's	KC/5/6/207–8		189
RFK	JMK	1937	November	28	Dated letter	Keynes–King's	KC/5/6/209		187
RFK	JMK	1937	December	1	Dated letter	Keynes–King's	KC/5/6/235		186
JMK	RFK	1937	December	2	Dated letter	Keynes–King's	KC/5/6/244–5		453
RFK	JMK	1937	December	19	Dated letter	Keynes–King's	EJ/1/4/234–5	CWK XIV: 265–6, (E)	184
JMK	RFK	1937	December	23	Dated letter	Kahn–King's	RFK/13/57/270–2		183
RFK	JMK	1937	December	26	Dated letter	Keynes–King's	EJ/1/4/239–40		182
JMK	RFK	1937	December	29	Dated letter	Kahn–King's Keynes–King's	RFK/13/57/274–6 EJ/1/4/236–8	CWK XIV: 266–7, (E)	181

RFK	JMK	1938	January	5	Dated letter	Keynes–King's	KC/5/9/2		2051
RFK	JMK	1938	January	6	Dated letter	Keynes–King's	KC/5/7/17–25		2055
JMK	RFK	1938	January	7	Dated letter	Keynes–King's	KC/5/7/27		2056
RFK	JMK	1938	January	15	Dated letter	Keynes–King's	KC/5/6/210		180
JMK	RFK	1938	January	16	Dated letter	Kahn–King's	RFK/13/57/277–8	CWK XII: 28, (E)	179
RFK	JMK	1938	January	17	Dated letter	Keynes–King's	KC/5/7/38		2057
RFK	JMK	1938	January	18	Dated letter	Keynes–King's	KC/5/7/39		2058
RFK	JMK	1938	January	18	Dated letter	Kahn–King's	RFK/13/57/277–8		2200
RFK	JMK	1938	January	24	Dated letter	Keynes–King's	KC/5/7/40–1		2059
JMK	RFK	1938	January	26	Dated letter	Kahn–King's	RFK/13/57/279		178
RFK	JMK	1938	January	27	Dated letter	Kahn–King's	RFK/13/57/383–4		177
JMK	RFK	1938	January	29	Dated letter	Kahn–King's	RFK/13/57/295		445
RFK	JMK	1938	January	30	Dated letter	Keynes–King's	EJ/1/5/3–5		2208
JMK	RFK	1938	January	30	Dated letter	Kahn–King's	RFK/13/57/284		443
JMK	RFK	1938	January	30	Dated letter	Kahn–King's	RFK/13/57/381		176
RFK	JMK	1938	January	31	Dated letter	Keynes–King's	CO/11/311		175
RFK	JMK	1938	January	31	Dated letter	Keynes–King's	KC/5/7/42–4		2060
RFK	JMK	1938	January	31	Dated letter	Kahn–King's	RFK/13/57/284		2201
RFK	JMK	1938	January	31	Dated letter	Kahn–King's	RFK/13/57/381		2202
RFK	JMK	1938	February	1	Dated letter	Keynes–King's	KC/5/7/45		2061
RFK	JMK	1938	February	1	Dated letter	Keynes–King's	KC/5/7/46		2062
RFK	JMK	1938	February	4	Dated letter	Keynes–King's	KC/5/7/47–8		2063
JMK	RFK	1938	February	4	Dated letter	Kahn–King's	RFK/13/57/285		174
JMK	RFK	1938	February	10	Dated letter	Keynes–King's	KC/5/7/58		2064
RFK	JMK	1938	February	14–18	Dated letter	Keynes–King's	L/K/89–93		172
RFK	JMK	1938	February	16	Dated letter	Keynes–King's	KC/5/7/69–71		2053
JMK	RFK	1938	February	16	Dated letter	Kahn–King's	RFK/13/57/286–7		173
JMK	RFK	1938	February	19	Dated letter	Keynes–King's	L/K/94–6	Moggridge 1992: 602 (E)	171
JMK	RFK	1938	February	21	Dated letter	Keynes–King's	KC/5/7/72–5		2065
RFK	JMK	1938	February	21	Dated letter	Keynes–King's	KC/5/7/79		2070

Table 1.1 continued

From	*To*	*Year*	*Month*	*Day*	*Date*	*Archive*		*Published in*	*Item*
RFK	JMK	1938	February	24	Dated letter	Keynes–King's	KC/5/7/90		2071
JMK	RFK	1938	February	26	Dated letter	Keynes–King's	KC/5/7/88–9		2066
JMK	RFK	1938	February	26	Dated letter	Keynes–King's	KC/5/7/94–5		2067
RFK	JMK	1938	February	27	Dated letter	Keynes–King's	KC/5/7/102–3		2068
JMK	RFK	1938	February	28	Dated letter	Keynes–King's	KC/5/7/104		2072
JMK	RFK	1938	February	28	Dated letter	Keynes–King's	KC/5/7/91–3		2069
JMK	RFK	1938	March	3	Dated letter	Kahn–King's	RFK/13/57/288		170
JMK	RFK	1938	March	5	Dated letter	Kahn–King's	RFK/13/57/289		168
JMK	RFK	1938	March	5	Dated letter	Kahn–King's	RFK/13/57/290	Skidelsky 2000: 18, (E)	166
JMK	RFK	1938	March	7	Dated letter	Keynes–King's	KC/5/7/106–17		2073
RFK	JMK	1938	March	8	Dated letter	Kahn–King's	RFK/13/57/289		169
JMK	RFK	1938	March	9	Dated letter	Kahn–King's	RFK/13/57/289		167
JMK	RFK	1938	March	16	Dated letter	Keynes–King's	KC/5/7/118–19		2074
JMK	RFK	1938	March	16	Dated letter	Kahn–King's Keynes–King's	RFK/13/57/291 KC/5/7/120–1		165
JMK	RFK	1938	March	22	Dated letter	Kahn–King's	RFK/13/57/379		441
RFK	JMK	1938	March	24	Dated letter	Keynes–King's	KC/5/7/122–3		2206
RFK	JMK	1938	March	24	Dated letter	Keynes–King's	KC/5/7/124–6		2207
RFK	JMK	1938	March	25	Dated letter	Keynes–King's	NS/1/4/166		164
RFK	JMK	1938	March	27	Dated letter	Keynes–King's	L/K/97		163
JMK	RFK	1938	March	29	Dated letter	Kahn–King's	RFK/13/57/292–3	CWK XII: 28–9, (E)	162
JMK	RFK	1938	April	9	Dated letter	Kahn–King's	RFK/13/57/371		161
JMK	RFK	1938	April	13	Dated letter	Kahn–King's	RFK/13/57/294		160
JMK	RFK	1938	April	15	Dated letter	Keynes–King's	KC/5/7/137		2075
RFK	JMK	1938	April	19	Dated letter	Keynes–King's	KC/5/7/137		2076
JMK	RFK	1938	April	23	Dated letter	Kahn–King's	RFK/13/57/300–1		159
JMK	RFK	1938	April	29	Dated letter	Keynes–King's	EJ/1/5/112–13		158
JMK	RFK	1938	April	30	Dated letter	Keynes–King's	KC/5/7/138–9		2077

JMK	RFK	1938	April	30	Dated letter	Kahn–King's	RFK/13/57/365–6		157
JMK	RFK	1938	May		Attributed	Kahn–King's	RFK/13/57/302		448
JMK	RFK	1938	May		Attributed	Kahn–King's	RFK/13/57/364		451
RFK	JMK	1938	May	3	Dated letter	Kahn–King's	RFK/13/57/363		155
JMK	RFK	1938	May	3	Attributed	Kahn–King's	RFK/13/57/363		156
JMK	RFK	1938	May	5	Dated letter	Not found in the archives		CWK XII: 100–1, (E)	154
JMK	RFK	1938	May	5	Dated letter	Keynes–King's	KC/5/7/140–1		2078
RFK	JMK	1938	May	5	Dated letter	Keynes–King's	KC/5/7/142–3		2079
JMK	RFK	1938	May	5	Dated letter	Keynes–King's	KC/5/7/144		2211
RFK	JMK	1938	May	8	Dated letter	Keynes–King's	KC/5/7/218		2080
RFK	JMK	1938	May	8	Dated letter	Keynes–King's	KC/5/7/219–24		2081
RFK	JMK	1938	May	9	Dated letter	Keynes–King's	KC/5/7/144		2210
RFK	JMK	1938	May	12	Dated letter	Keynes–King's	KC/5/7/158		2082
JMK	RFK	1938	May	12	Dated letter	Keynes–King's	KC/5/7/159		193
JMK	RFK	1938	May	12	Dated letter	Keynes–King's	KC/5/7/180–1		2083
JMK	RFK	1938	May	13	Dated letter	Kahn–King's	RFK/13/57/304	CWK XII: 29, (E)	153
RFK	JMK	1938	May	18	Dated letter	Keynes–King's	KC/5/7/182–3		2084
RFK	JMK	1938	May	19	Dated letter	Keynes–King's	KC/5/7/182		2085
RFK	JMK	1938	May	29	Dated letter	Keynes–King's	EJ/1/5/138–40		152
RFK	JMK	1938	June	9	Dated letter	Keynes–King's	KC/6/28–9		2086
RFK	JMK	1938	June	13	Dated letter	Keynes–King's Keynes–King's	KC/6/25–7 KC/6/18–20		2087
JMK	RFK	1938	June	14	Dated letter	Keynes–King's	KC/6/30		2088
JMK	RFK	1938	June	21	Dated letter	Keynes–King's Keynes–King's	KC/6/50–6 KC/6/35–40		2089
JMK	RFK	1938	June	25	Dated letter	Kahn–King's	RFK/13/57/307–8		151
RFK	JMK	1938	June	27	Dated letter	Keynes–King's	KC/5/8/3–4		2092
RFK	JMK	1938	June	27	Dated letter	Keynes–King's Keynes–King's	KC/6/42–3 KC/6/33–4		2091
JMK	RFK	1938	June	27	Dated letter	Kahn–King's	RFK/13/57/351		150
							KC/6/57–8		2093
JMK	RFK	1938	June	28	Dated letter	Keynes–King's Keynes–King's	KC/6/59–60 KC/6/61–2		

Table 1.1 continued

From	*To*	*Year*	*Month*	*Day*	*Date*	*Archive*	*Published in*	*Item*
RFK	JMK	1938	June	30	Dated letter	Keynes–King's KC/6/57		2094
RFK	JMK	1938	July		Attributed	Keynes–King's EJ/1/5/226–7		450
RFK	JMK	1938	July	4	Dated letter	Keynes–King's GTE/2/4/180		149
RFK	JMK	1938	July	14	Dated letter	Keynes–King's UA/14/2/252 Kahn–King's RFK/13/57/346		148
RFK	JMK	1938	July	15	Dated letter	Keynes–King's KC/5/8/34		2095
RFK	JMK	1938	July	16	Dated letter	Keynes–King's KC/5/8/32		2096
RFK	JMK	1938	July	16	Dated letter	Keynes–King's KC/5/8/33		2097
JMK	RFK	1938	July	16	Dated letter	Kahn–King's RFK/13/57/345		147
JMK	RFK	1938	July	25	Dated letter	Kahn–King's RFK/13/57/310–11		146
RFK	JMK	1938	August	1	Dated letter	Keynes–King's KC/5/8/36–7		2098
JMK	RFK	1938	August	4	Dated letter	Keynes–King's KC/5/8/38		2099
JMK	RFK	1938	August	11	Dated letter	Keynes–King's KC/5/8/39–41		2100
JMK	RFK	1938	August	11	Dated letter	Keynes–King's KC/5/8/42		2101
JMK	RFK	1938	August	11	Dated letter	Keynes–King's KC/5/8/52–3		2102
JMK	RFK	1938	August	16	Dated letter	Keynes–King's GTE/2/3/180		438
JMK	RFK	1938	August	16	Dated letter	Keynes–King's KC/5/8/54		2103
RFK	JMK	1938	August	17	Dated letter	Keynes–King's KC/5/6/211		440
RFK	JMK	1938	August	17	Dated letter	Keynes–King's KC/5/8/55–6		2104
RFK	JMK	1938	August	18	Dated letter	Keynes–King's GTE/2/3/180		436
RFK	JMK	1938	August	18	Dated letter	Keynes–King's KC/5/8/61		2105
RFK	JMK	1938	August	18	Dated letter	Keynes–King's KC/5/8/76		2106
RFK	JMK	1938	August	18	Dated letter	Keynes–King's KC/6/70–1		2107
RFK	JMK	1938	August	19	Dated letter	Keynes–King's KC/5/8/57–8		2108
RFK	JMK	1938	August	21	Dated letter	Keynes–King's UA/5/4/158–9		145
JMK	RFK	1938	August	22	Dated letter	Keynes–King's KC/5/6/212		144
JMK	RFK	1938	August	22	Dated letter	Keynes–King's KC/5/8/62–5		2109
JMK	RFK	1938	August	22	Dated letter	Keynes–King's KC/5/8/77–8		2110

JMK	RFK	1938	August	22	Dated letter	Keynes–King's	KC/5/8/79–80		2111
JMK	RFK	1938	August	22	Dated letter	Keynes–King's	KC/6/69		2112
JMK	RFK	1938	August	23	Inferred from other sources	Keynes–King's	CO/11/301	CWK XIV: 289, (E)	143
JMK	RFK	1938	August	23	Dated letter	Keynes–King's	KC/5/8/59–60		2113
JMK	RFK	1938	August	23	Dated letter	Keynes–King's	KC/5/8/81–2		2114
JMK	RFK	1938	August	23	Dated letter	Kahn–King's	RFK/13/57/316–17		142
RFK	JMK	1938	August	24	Dated letter	Keynes–King's	CO/11/309–10		141
RFK	JMK	1938	August	24	Dated letter	Kahn–King's	RFK/13/57/337		140
JMK	RFK	1938	August	27	Dated letter	Kahn–King's	RFK/13/57/318–19		139
JMK	RFK	1938	August	27	Dated letter	Kahn–King's	RFK/13/57/337		2203
RFK	JMK	1938	August	28	Dated letter	Keynes–King's	KC/5/8/83		2115
JMK	RFK	1938	August	31	Dated letter	Kahn–King's	RFK/13/57/320–1		138
RFK	JMK	1938	September	2	Dated letter	Keynes–King's	KC/5/8/48–9		2117
RFK	JMK	1938	September	2	Dated letter	Keynes–King's	KC/5/8/66–70		2116
JMK	RFK	1938	September	3	Dated letter	Kahn–King's	RFK/13/57/322–3		137
RFK	JMK	1938	September	4	Dated letter	Keynes–King's	KC/5/8/93		2118
JMK	RFK	1938	September	5	Dated letter	Keynes–King's	KC/5/8/50–1		2119
JMK	RFK	1938	September	5	Dated letter	Keynes–King's	KC/5/8/71–5		2120
JMK	RFK	1938	September	5	Dated letter	Keynes–King's	KC/5/8/91–2		2121
RFK	JMK	1938	September	5	Dated letter	Keynes–King's	KC/5/8/94		2122
RFK	JMK	1938	September	5	Dated letter	Keynes–King's	KC/5/8/97		2123
JMK	RFK	1938	September	5	Dated letter	Kahn–King's	RFK/13/57/324		136
RFK	JMK	1938	September	6	Dated letter	Keynes–King's	KC/5/8/100		2124
RFK	JMK	1938	September	6	Dated letter	Keynes–King's	KC/5/8/101–2		2125
RFK	JMK	1938	September	7	Dated letter	Keynes–King's	KC/5/8/103		2126
JMK	RFK	1938	September	20	Dated letter	Kahn–King's	RFK/13/57/328		135
RFK	JMK	1938	September	22	Dated letter	Keynes–King's	KC/5/8/106–7		2127
JMK	RFK	1938	September	26	Dated letter	Kahn–King's	RFK/13/57/326–7		134
JMK	RFK	1938	September	30	Dated letter	Keynes–King's	KC/5/8/124		2128
JMK	RFK	1938	September	30	Dated letter	Keynes–King's	KC/5/8/125		2131
JMK	RFK	1938	September	30	Dated letter	Kahn–King's	RFK/13/57/331–2		133

Table 1.1 continued

From	*To*	*Year*	*Month*	*Day*	*Date*	*Archive*		*Published in*	*Item*
JMK	RFK	1938	October	1	Dated letter	Kahn–King's	RFK/13/57/333		132
RFK	JMK	1938	October	2	Dated letter	Keynes–King's	KC/5/8/124		2129
RFK	JMK	1938	October	3	Dated letter	Keynes–King's	L/K/98–9		131
JMK	RFK	1938	October	4	Dated letter	Kahn–King's	RFK/13/90/3/101–2	2209	
RFK	JMK	1938	October	7–12	Dated letter	Keynes–King's	L/K/106–7		130
JMK	RFK	1938	October	11	Dated letter	Kahn–King's	RFK/13/57/334		129
RFK	JMK	1938	October	23	Dated letter	Keynes–King's	KC/5/8/132–3		2130
RFK	JMK	1938	November		Attributed	Keynes–King's	KC/5/8/95–6		2054
JMK	RFK	1938	November	10	Dated letter	Keynes–King's	KC/5/8/134		2132
RFK	JMK	1938	November	14	Dated letter	Keynes–King's	KC/5/8/137		2134
JMK	RFK	1938	November	21	Dated letter	Keynes–King's	KC/5/8/138–9		2135
RFK	JMK	1938	November	26	Dated letter	Keynes–King's	KC/5/8/134		2133
RFK	JMK	1938	November	26	Dated letter	Keynes–King's	KC/5/8/136		2136
JMK	RFK	1938	December	3	Dated letter	Keynes–King's	KC/5/8/155		2137
RFK	JMK	1938	December	13	Dated letter	Keynes–King's	KC/5/8/150–2		2138
JMK	RFK	1938	December	14	Dated letter	Keynes–King's	KC/5/8/153–4		2139
JMK	RFK	1938	December	17	Dated letter	Keynes–King's	SE/2/7/101–4		128
JMK	RFK	1938	December	19	Dated letter	Keynes–King's	SE/2/7/112		127
JMK	RFK	1939	January	12	Dated letter	Keynes–King's	KC/5/9/11		2140
JMK	RFK	1939	January	12	Dated letter	Keynes–King's	KC/5/9/28		2143
RFK	JMK	1939	January	12	Dated letter	Keynes–King's	KC/5/9/29–30		2142
RFK	JMK	1939	January	13	Dated letter	Keynes–King's	KC/5/9/11		2141
RFK	JMK	1939	January	15	Dated letter	Keynes–King's	KC/5/9/28		2144
RFK	JMK	1939	January	16	Dated letter	Keynes–King's	KC/5/9/34–6		2215
JMK	RFK	1939	January	18	Dated letter	Keynes–King's	KC/5/9/31–3		2145
RFK	JMK	1939	January	19	Dated letter	Keynes–King's	KC/5/8/156		2146
JMK	RFK	1939	January	23	Dated letter	Keynes–King's	KC/5/8/157–8		2147
JMK	RFK	1939	January	23	Dated letter	Keynes–King's	KC/5/8/159–61		2148

RFK	JMK	1939	January	27	Dated letter	Keynes–King's	KC/5/9/39		2149
JMK	RFK	1939	February	21	Dated letter	Keynes–King's	BM/3/86–7		126
JMK	RFK	1939	March	6	Dated letter	Kahn–King's	RFK/13/57/401–2		125
JMK	RFK	1939	March	14	Dated letter	Kahn–King's	RFK/13/57/403–5		124
JMK	RFK	1939	March	15	Dated letter	Keynes–King's	L/K/108–9		123
JMK	RFK	1939	March	23	Dated letter	Kahn–King's	RFK/13/57/406–7		122
JMK	RFK	1939	March	25	Dated letter	Kahn–King's	RFK/13/57/408–9	Moggridge 1992: 617, (E)	121
JMK	RFK	1939	April	6	Dated letter	Keynes–King's	PP/45/255/11–12		120
JMK	RFK	1939	April	11	Dated letter	Kahn–King's Keynes–King's	RFK/13/57/410–12 L/K/110–12	Moggridge 1992: 553, (E)	119
RFK	JMK	1939	April	17	Dated letter	Keynes–King's	PP/45/255/10		118
RFK	JMK	1939	April	18	Dated letter	Keynes–King's	KC/5/9/69–70		2150
JMK	RFK	1939	April	20	Dated letter	Keynes–King's	KC/5/9/71–3		2151
JMK	RFK	1939	April	20	Dated letter	Keynes–King's	PP/45/255/22		435
RFK	JMK	1939	April	21	Dated letter	Keynes–King's	KC/5/9/74–5		190
JMK	RFK	1939	April	22	Dated letter	Keynes–King's	KC/5/9/76		2152
RFK	JMK	1939	May	12	Dated letter	Keynes–King's	KC/5/9/86		2153
RFK	JMK	1939	May	18	Dated letter	Keynes–King's	KC/5/9/87–8		2154
JMK	RFK	1939	May	22	Dated letter	Kahn–King's	RFK/5/1/109–11		2217
JMK	RFK	1939	May	23	Dated letter	Kahn–King's	RFK/13/57/415		117
RFK	JMK	1939	May	29	Dated letter	Keynes–King's	A/39/85		433
JMK	RFK	1939	May	29	Dated letter	Keynes–King's	A/39/85		434
JMK	RFK	1939	June	17	Dated letter	Keynes–King's	UA/5/4/319		114
RFK	JMK	1939	June	20	Dated letter	Keynes–King's	KC/5/9/116		2155
RFK	JMK	1939	June	27	Dated letter	Keynes–King's	UA/5/4/386–7		116
JMK	RFK	1939	June	30	Dated letter	Keynes–King's	KC/5/9/125		2156
JMK	RFK	1939	June	30	Dated letter	Keynes–King's	KC/5/9/126–7		2157
JMK	RFK	1939	June	30	Dated letter	Keynes–King's	KC/5/9/128–9		2158
JMK	RFK	1939	June	30	Dated letter	Kahn–King's	RFK/13/57/416		115
JMK	RFK	1939	July		Attributed	Kahn–King's	RFK/5/1/142–4		2218

Table 1.1 continued

From	*To*	*Year*	*Month*	*Day*	*Date*	*Archive*		*Published in*	*Item*
RFK	JMK	1939	July	2	Dated letter	Kahn–King's	RFK/13/57/416		2204
JMK	RFK	1939	July	4	Dated letter	Keynes–King's	KC/5/9/117		2159
RFK	JMK	1939	July	6	Dated letter	Keynes–King's	UA/5/4/319		113
RFK	JMK	1939	July	10	Dated letter	Keynes–King's	KC/5/9/130		2160
RFK	JMK	1939	July	10	Dated letter	Keynes–King's	KC/5/9/131		2161
JMK	RFK	1939	July	11	Dated letter	Keynes–King's	SE/2/7/122		112
JMK	RFK	1939	July	12	Dated letter	Kahn–King's	RFK/13/57/417–18		111
RFK	JMK	1939	July	13	Dated letter	Keynes–King's	KC/5/9/134–5		2162
RFK	JMK	1939	July	13	Dated letter	Keynes–King's	SE/2/7/121		110
RFK	JMK	1939	July	17	Dated letter	Keynes–King's	KC/5/9/136–7		2163
RFK	JMK	1939	July	17	Dated letter	Keynes–King's	KC/5/9/144–5		2164
RFK	JMK	1939	July	18	Dated letter	Keynes–King's	KC/5/9/146–51		2165
RFK	JMK	1939	July	18	Dated letter	Keynes–King's	KC/5/9/152–3		2166
JMK	RFK	1939	July	20	Dated letter	Kahn–King's	RFK/13/57/416		2205
JMK	RFK	1939	July	22	Dated letter	Keynes–King's	KC/5/9/142–3		2167
JMK	RFK	1939	July	27	Dated letter	Kahn–King's Keynes–King's	RFK/13/57/419–20 CO/11/408–9	Moggridge 1992: 621, (E)	109
RFK	JMK	1939	July	28	Dated letter	Keynes–King's	CO/11/410–11		107
RFK	JMK	1939	July	28	Dated letter	Keynes–King's	KC/5/9/154–6		2168
JMK	RFK	1939	July	28	Dated letter	Kahn–King's	RFK/13/57/421–2		108
JMK	RFK	1939	July	30	Dated letter	Keynes–King's	KC/5/9/158–61		2169
RFK	JMK	1939	August	3	Dated letter	Keynes–King's	KC/5/9/157		2170
JMK	RFK	1939	August	4	Dated letter	Keynes–King's	CO/11/412–28		106
JMK	RFK	1939	August	4	Dated letter	Kahn–King's	RFK/13/57/423–4		105
RFK	JMK	1939	August	6	Dated letter	Keynes–King's	CO/11/429		104
RFK	JMK	1939	August	7	Dated letter	Keynes–King's	KC/5/9/164–5		2171
RFK	JMK	1939	August	9	Dated letter	Keynes–King's	KC/5/9/170		2172
RFK	JMK	1939	August	10	Dated letter	Keynes–King's	CO/11/430		103

RFK	JMK	1939	August	10	Dated letter	Keynes–King's	L/K/115		102
RFK	JMK	1939	August	10	Dated letter	Kahn–King's	RFK/13/57/425–6		101
JMK	RFK	1939	August	11	Dated letter	Keynes–King's	KC/5/9/166–9		2173
JMK	RFK	1939	August	11	Dated letter	Keynes–King's	KC/5/9/17[illegible]		2174
JMK	RFK	1939	August	11	Dated letter	Kahn–King's	RFK/13/57/427–9		100
RFK	JMK	1939	August	13	Dated letter	Keynes–King's	L/K/116–17		99
JMK	RFK	1939	August	14	Dated letter	Keynes–King's	L/K/118–20	CWK XXII: 3, (E)	432
					Dated letter	Kahn–King's	RFK/13/57/430–2		
RFK	JMK	1939	August	15	Dated letter	Keynes–King's	KC/5/9/178–9		2175
RFK	JMK	1939	August	25	Dated letter	Keynes–King's	KC/5/9/185		2177
RFK	JMK	1939	August	25	Dated letter	Keynes–King's	KC/5/9/186–7		2176
RFK	JMK	1939	August	25	Dated letter	Keynes–King's	L/K/121		96
JMK	RFK	1939	August	25	Dated letter	Kahn–King's	RFK/13/57/433		97
RFK	JMK	1939	September		Attributed	Keynes–King's	KC/5/9/202		2212
JMK	RFK	1939	September	1	Dated letter	Kahn–King's	RFK/13/57/434	Skidelsky 2000: 47, (E)	95
RFK	JMK	1939	September	6	Dated letter	Keynes–King's	KC/6/73		2178
RFK	JMK	1939	September	7	Dated letter	Keynes–King's	KC/5/9/200		2179
JMK	RFK	1939	September	15	Dated letter	Kahn–King's	RFK/13/57/435		94
JMK	RFK	1939	October	3	Attributed	Keynes–King's	KC/5/9/202		2213
RFK	JMK	1939	October	18	Dated letter	Keynes–King's	KC/5/9/205		2180
RFK	JMK	1939	November	5	Dated letter	Keynes–King's	KC/5/9/206		2181
RFK	JMK	1939	November	15	Dated letter	Keynes–King's	KC/5/9/217		2182
RFK	JMK	1939	November	15	Dated letter	Keynes–King's	KC/5/9/219		2050
RFK	JMK	1939	November	16	Dated letter	Keynes–King's	KC/5/9/218		2183
RFK	JMK	1939	November	19	Dated letter	Keynes–King's	KC/5/9/238–9		2184
JMK	RFK	1939	November	19	Dated letter	Keynes–King's	KC/5/9/240		2185
RFK	JMK	1939	November	19	Dated letter	Keynes–King's	KC/5/9/241		2186
RFK	JMK	1939	November	30	Dated letter	Keynes–King's	HP/2/20		431
RFK	JMK	1939	December	17	Dated letter	Keynes–King's	L/K/122–4		93
RFK	JMK	1939	December	24	Dated letter	Keynes–King's	KC/5/9/291		2187
RFK	JMK	1940	March	14	Dated letter	Keynes–King's	W/3/56		92

Table 1.1 continued

From	*To*	*Year*	*Month*	*Day*	*Date*	*Archive*		*Published in*	*Item*
JMK	RFK	1940	March	16	Dated letter	Kahn–King's Keynes–King's	RFK/13/57/436–8 W/3/57–9	CWK XXII: 157–8, (E)	91
JMK	RFK	1940	April	10	Dated letter	Kahn–King's	RFK/13/57/439–40		90
JMK	RFK	1940	May	9	Dated letter	Kahn–King's Keynes–King's	RFK/13/57/441–2 UA/14/2/293–4	Skidelsky 2000: 76, (E)	89
RFK	JMK	1940	May	10	Dated letter	Keynes–King's	UA/14/2/ 296–7		88
RFK	JMK	1940	May	20	Dated letter	Keynes–King's	W/3/182		87
JMK	RFK	1940	May	22	Dated letter	Kahn–King's Keynes–King's	RFK/13/57/443–44 W/3/231–2		86
RFK	JMK	1940	May	24	Dated letter	Keynes–King's	W/3/246–8		85
JMK	RFK	1940	May	26	Dated letter	Kahn–King's Keynes–King's	RFK /13/57/457–9 W/3/255–7		84
JMK	RFK	1940	May	27	Dated letter	Kahn–King's Keynes–King's	RFK/13/57/460–1 L/K/125–6	Marcuzzo 1998: 8, (E)	83
RFK	JMK	1940	May	30	Dated letter	Keynes–King's	A/40/9		82
JMK	RFK	1940	June	2	Dated letter	Kahn–King's Keynes–King's	RFK/13/57/462–4 A/40/10–12	Skidelsky 2000: 76, (E)	81
RFK	JMK	1940	June	3	Dated letter	Keynes–King's	A/40/13–14		80
RFK	JMK	1940	June	28	Dated letter	Keynes–King's	W/3/299–301		79
JMK	RFK	1940	June	29	Dated letter	Kahn–King's	RFK/13/57/465–6		78
RFK	JMK	1940	June	30	Dated letter	Keynes–King's	W/3/302–3		77
RFK	JMK	1940	July	2	Dated letter	Keynes–King's	W/3/309		76
JMK	RFK	1940	July	3	Dated letter	Kahn–King's Keynes–King's	RFK/13/57/467–8 W/3/310–11		75
RFK	JMK	1940	July	9	Dated letter	Keynes–King's	UA/14/2/306		74
JMK	RFK	1940	July	11	Dated letter	Kahn–King's	RFK/13/57/469–70		73
RFK	JMK	1940	September	25	Dated letter	Keynes–King's	L/K/127–8		72

RFK	JMK	1940	November	4	Dated letter	Keynes–King's	L/K/129	CWK XXII: 327–8, (E)	71
JMK	RFK	1941	March	4	Dated letter	Kahn–King's	RFK/13/57/471		70
JMK	RFK	1941	April	21	Dated letter	Keynes–King's	L/K/130A–B		69
RFK	JMK	1941	April	22	Dated letter	Keynes–King's	L/K/131		68
JMK	RFK	1941	April	24	Dated letter	Keynes–King's	L/K/132–4		67
RFK	JMK	1941	August	15	Dated letter	Keynes–King's	KC/5/10/33–9		2188
RFK	JMK	1941	August	19	Dated letter	Keynes–King's	L/K/135	Skidelsky 2000: 202, (E)	66
RFK	JMK	1941	August	19	Dated letter	Keynes–King's	L/K/136–7		65
JMK	RFK	1941	August	21	Dated letter	Keynes–King's	L/K/138–9	CWK XXV: 20, (E)	63
RFK	JMK	1941	August	21	Dated letter	Keynes–King's	L/K/140–1		64
JMK	RFK	1941	August	24	Dated letter	Keynes–King's	L/K/142–3		62
JMK	RFK	1941	September	9	Dated letter	Kahn–King's	RFK/13/57/472–3	Skidelsky 2000: 203, (E)	61
RFK	JMK	1941	September	15	Dated letter	Keynes–King's	L/K/144–6		60
JMK	RFK	1941	October	31	Dated letter	Keynes–King's	L/K/147–57	CWK XXIII: 317–18, (E)	59
JMK	RFK	1941	October	31	Dated letter	Keynes–King's	L/K/158–9		58
JMK	RFK	1941	December	2	Dated letter	Kahn–King's Keynes–King's	RFK/13/57/474 L/K/160		57
RFK	JMK	1941	December	15	Dated letter	Not found in the archives		CWK XXIII: 318	185
RFK	JMK	1941	December	17	Dated letter	Keynes–King's	L/K/161–2		56
RFK	JMK	1942	January	10	Dated letter	Keynes–King's	L/K/170		55
JMK	RFK	1942	January	12	Dated letter	Keynes–King's	L/K/163–7	Skidelsky 2000: 164, (E)	54
JMK	RFK	1942	January	21	Dated letter	Keynes–King's	L/K/168		429
RFK	JMK	1942	February	17	Dated letter	Keynes–King's	L/K/171		53
RFK	JMK	1942	March	30	Dated letter	Keynes–King's	L/K/174–6		52
RFK	JMK	1942	April	9	Dated letter	Keynes–King's	L/K/177		51
JMK	RFK	1942	May	11	Dated letter	Keynes–King's	L/K/178–83	CWK XXIII: 319–20, (E)	50
JMK	RFK	1942	May	11	Dated letter	Keynes–King's	L/K/184–7	CWK XXV: 143–4, (E)	49
JMK	RFK	1942	May	15	Dated letter	Keynes–King's	L/42/69		48
RFK	JMK	1942	May	29	Dated letter	Keynes–King's	L/K/188–90		47
JMK	RFK	1942	June	16	Dated letter	Keynes–King's	L/K/191–2		46

Table 1.1 continued

From	*To*	*Year*	*Month*	*Day*	*Date*	*Archive*		*Published in*	*Item*
JMK	RFK	1942	June	16	Dated letter	Keynes–King's	L/K/193–5		45
JMK	RFK	1942	June	19	Dated letter	Keynes–King's	L/K/196–7		44
JMK	RFK	1942	June	19	Dated letter	Keynes–King's	L/K/198–201		43
RFK	JMK	1942	August	16	Dated letter	Keynes–King's	L/K/202	Skidelsky 2000: 150, (E)	42
JMK	RFK	1942	August	28	Dated letter	Keynes–King's	L/K/203–8	Skidelsky 2000: 247, (E)	41
RFK	JMK	1942	September	14	Dated letter	Keynes–King's	L/K/209–12		40
RFK	JMK	1942	September	15	Dated letter	Keynes–King's	L/K/213–14		39
RFK	JMK	1942	September	17	Dated letter	Keynes–King's	L/K/215		38
JMK	RFK	1942	September	22	Dated letter	Keynes–King's	L/K/216–18		37
RFK	JMK	1942	September	23	Dated letter	Keynes–King's	L/K/219–20		36
RFK	JMK	1942	October	13	Dated letter	Keynes–King's	L/K/221–2		35
JMK	RFK	1942	October	16	Dated letter	Keynes–King's	L/K/223–5		34
RFK	JMK	1942	October	28	Dated letter	Keynes–King's	L/K/226–8		33
RFK	JMK	1942	November	1	Dated letter	Keynes–King's	L/K/229–34		32
RFK	JMK	1942	November	7	Dated letter	Keynes–King's	L/K/235–6	Skidelsky 2000: 164, (E)	31
JMK	RFK	1942	November	13	Dated letter	Keynes–King's	L/K/237–40	Skidelsky 2000: 248, (E)	30
RFK	JMK	1942	November	30	Dated letter	Keynes–King's	L/K/241–2		29
JMK	RFK	1943	April	7	Dated letter	Kahn–King's	RFK/13/57/477–8		28
RFK	JMK	1943	May	13	Dated letter	Keynes–King's	L/K/243–5		27
RFK	JMK	1943	June	1	Attributed	Keynes–King's	PC/1/9/49–50		26
JMK	RFK	1943	June	3	Dated letter	Keynes–King's	PC/1/9/55		427
RFK	JMK	1943	December	6	Dated letter	Keynes–King's	L/K/265–8		25
JMK	RFK	1943	December	8	Dated letter	Kahn–King's Keynes–King's	RFK/13/57/479 L/K/269	Skidelsky 2000: 159, (E)	24
RFK	JMK	1943	December	31	Dated letter	Keynes–King's	KC/5/10/70		2216
JMK	RFK	1944	January	10	Dated letter	Kahn–King's	RFK/13/57/480–1		23
JMK	RFK	1944	January	13	Dated letter	Not found in archives		CWK XXVI: 283–4, (E)	22

RFK	JMK	1944	February	12	Dated letter	Keynes–King's Kahn–King's	L/K/270–2 RFK/13/57/482		21
RFK	JMK	1944	February	21	Dated letter	Keynes–King's	L/K/273–4		20
JMK	RFK	1944	February	22	Dated letter	Keynes–King's	L/K/275–7		19
RFK	JMK	1944	March	7	Dated letter	Keynes–King's	L/K/278		18
JMK	RFK	1944	March	9	Dated letter	Kahn–King's Keynes–King's	RFK/13/57/485 L/K/279		17
JMK	RFK	1944	April	3	Dated letter	Kahn–King's	RFK/13/57/483–4		16
RFK	JMK	1944	April	12	Dated letter	Keynes–King's Kahn–King's	L/K/280–310 RFK/13/57/486–7		15
JMK	RFK	1944	April	15	Dated letter	Kahn–King's	RFK/13/57/495–6		14
JMK	RFK	1944	April	17	Dated letter	Kahn–King's Keynes–King's	RFK/13/57/488–9 L/K/312–13		13
JMK	RFK	1944	April	24	Dated letter	Kahn–King's	RFK/13/57/490–1		12
RFK	JMK	1944	April	25	Dated letter	Kahn–King's	RFK/13/57/492–4		11
RFK	JMK	1944	May	31	Dated letter	Keynes–King's Kahn–King's	L/K/314–15 RFK/13/57/500–1		10
JMK	RFK	1944	June	1	Dated letter	Kahn–King's Keynes–King's	RFK/13/57/498–9 L/K/316–17		9
RFK	JMK	1944	June	2	Dated letter	Kahn–King's	RFK/13/57/497		8
RFK	JMK	1944	November	9	Dated letter	Keynes–King's	L/K/318–19		7
RFK	JMK	1945	February	27	Dated letter	Keynes–King's	KC/5/10/88–90		2214
RFK	JMK	1945	May	24	Dated letter	Keynes–King's	KC/5/10/91–2		2189
RFK	JMK	1945	May	24	Dated letter	Keynes–King's	KC/5/10/93–4		2190
JMK	RFK	1945	May	27	Dated letter	Keynes–King's	KC/5/10/95–7		2191
JMK	RFK	1945	November	2	Dated letter	Kahn–King's	RFK/13/57/516–7		6
JMK	RFK	1945	November	23	Dated letter	Kahn–King's	RFK/13/57/518–9	Skidelsky 2000: 437, (E)	5
RFK	JMK	1945	December	31	Dated letter	Keynes–King's	L/K/320		4
JMK	RFK	1946	February	2	Dated letter	Keynes–King's Keynes–King's	L/K/324–5 KC/5/10/147–8		3
RFK	JMK	1946	February	24	Dated letter	Keynes–King's	L/K/326–7		2
JMK	RFK	1946	March	13	Dated letter	Keynes–King's	L/K/328–9	CWK XXVI: 217, (E)	1

2 Keynes's valuable opponent and collaborator

The correspondence between Keynes and Robertson

Eleonora Sanfilippo

The correspondence between Robertson and Keynes consists of at least 303 items[1] – 176 of which from Robertson to Keynes – dating from 1912 to 1946 (see Table 2.1). The exchanges are not evenly distributed over time: most of the letters belong to the periods 1925–33 (72 items) and 1935–38 (67 items), before and after the publication of their main works, and 1941–45 (138 items), when, both working at the Treasury, they collaborated on international monetary agreements and various other subjects like national income accounting, public corporations and international trade policy.

Although a significant number of letters (146) are published – in full or excerpts – in the *Collected Writings* of J.M. Keynes, and in Keynes's or Robertson's biographies (Moggridge 1992; Skidelsky 1992, 2000; Fletcher 2000), comprehensive analysis of this correspondence is still lacking.

The Robertson–Keynes relationship: what we know and what the correspondence can tell us

The relationship between Dennis Robertson and Maynard Keynes has been widely examined in the literature (see, for example, Samuelson 1963; Hicks 1964; Dennison 1968; Patinkin and Leith 1977; Johnson and Johnson 1978; Presley 1978, 1992b). Its evolution from the intensive collaboration in the 1920s to their drift apart subsequent to the writing and publication of the *General Theory*, and then on to the rupture in 1938 (when Robertson left Cambridge for the LSE) and later rapprochement in the 1940s – has been fully reconstructed.

All commentators agree on the significance of their scientific partnership during the 1920s. Hicks (1964: 309) considers their respective works of this period as 'separate publications, but a series that belongs together'.[2] According to Mizen, Moggridge and Presley (1997: 576) 'from 1920 onward Robertson was increasingly Keynes's intellectual confidant, with a major input into each other's research'. The correspondence confirms that their reciprocal theoretical influence started long before, in 1913, to be precise, when Keynes read Robertson's dissertation on business fluctuations. As scientific co-operation developed, so did a solid friendship based on common interests – literature, theatre, music and arts, besides economics and politics – and educational background (they were both students at Eton, although at different times), as well as affection and esteem.

On when and why their relationship begun to deteriorate there is no agreement in the literature. Moggridge (1992: 599) traces their rift to 1935, during the gestation of the *General Theory*, ascribing it not only to their keen theoretical contrast but also to the increasing role of the younger generation of Cambridge Circus economists along with the difficult psychological state Robertson fell into after the death of his mother (in January 1935). Aslanbeigui and Oakes (2002: 23) date the trouble between them to 1936, after the publication of the *General Theory*, and associate it with the stormy relations that had been developing in Cambridge between Keynesians and Keynes's opponents. Skidelsky (1992: 272) sees the origin of their split in 1931, when discussion of Keynes's *Treatise* brought to light a substantial theoretical disagreement between them. Fletcher (2000: 140–1) finds the first signs of their rift in the role played by Robertson's personality and dates it as from 1926–27, when Robertson – just after the publication of his *Banking Policy and the Price Level* (1926) – went to Asia 'to escape Keynes's great influence'.

Perusal of the entire correspondence suggests a balanced line of interpretation, in which personal and psychological motives – while highly relevant – are not disjoint from consideration of the fundamental theoretical divergences between them, which openly emerged in 1931. These were grounded on their opposite explanations for the cycle (over-investment for Robertson, under-investment for Keynes), their different approaches in terms of stocks and flows to macroeconomic analysis, and the different role they attributed to the banking system in economic fluctuations. The correspondence also leads us to attribute some importance at least to three other circumstances in exacerbating feelings on either side: (1) the sense of exclusion Robertson felt once the *Treatise* had come out, and he realised Keynes's preference for Circus economists in scientific collaboration; (2) the fact that the debate became public with publication of Robertson's critical article on Keynes's work in the *Economic Journal* (Robertson 1931a); (3) the awkward relations between Robertson and Keynes's young disciples (especially J. Robinson).

Although received opinion sees Keynes and Robertson above all as staunch opponents (as indeed they were for a period of time), the image the correspondence reflects as a whole is of two scholars belonging to the same generation, sharing the same cultural values and sympathising with each other (see A. Robinson 1975: 12–14).

Keynes consistently showed Robertson respect and affection: recognising in him great analytical capacities in understanding economics, he seems to have taken serious account of all his objections and criticism.

Widespread opinion has it that their discussions eventually became sterile, revolving on terminological questions and technical details. By contrast, the energy and commitment they put into their debate – amply witnessed by the volume of their exchanges – show just how much importance they both attributed to definition of the economic variables, revealing here their common Marshallian background.

It was in the first place at the personal level that they were able to heal their relations at the end of the 1930s. Subsequently – from 1941 onward – setting aside their theoretical controversy, they collaborated fruitfully on policy and international economic affairs, retaining great estimation of each other's intellectual capacities to the end.

Robertson's dissertation and its publication as *A Study of Industrial Fluctuation* (1915)

The first letter attesting to the scientific co-operation between Robertson and Keynes is very early, dating to 28 September 1913 (letter 3057, CWK XIII: 1), and contains Keynes's comments on Robertson's Fellowship dissertation. This was an empirical work on output fluctuations in different industrial sectors in pre-war Britain, with a final part suggesting quite a novel (for the time) theory of business cycles grounded on real phenomena. The fundamental thesis contained in the *Study* is that the cycle is mainly due to the new investment opportunities offered by inventions or an exceptionally good harvest, followed by excess accumulation of fixed capital deriving from the difficulty entrepreneurs experience (because of the long gestation of investment) in correctly estimating the optimal quantity of capital to immobilise. The result is a condition of over-investment, which leads to the downturn in the cycle. Robertson's theory was in sharp contrast with Fisher's and Hawtrey's monetary explanations for the cycle, and close to Schumpeter's analysis, although Robertson was at that time totally unaware of Schumpeter's work (Robertson [1915] 1948: ix). That same year the dissertation was unsuccessfully submitted to Trinity, but Keynes was nevertheless much impressed.[3]

The influence of Robertson's dissertation on Keynes's work – according to Moggridge (CWK XIII: 1) – clearly appears in a paper Keynes presented to the Political Economy Club meeting of 3 December 1913 (in London), where for the first time he addressed the subject of business fluctuations, taking specific account of Robertson's explanation for the cycle (CWK XIII: 1–14).

In May 1915 – when Robertson had already left Cambridge for London as a volunteer in the Army – Keynes read the redraft of the dissertation (successfully submitted in 1914) for possible publication by Macmillan. Having renewed his positive judgement of Robertson's work, which he recommended should be published 'without hesitation' as 'a most brilliant and important contribution to the subject', Keynes criticised the style

Robertson adopted in writing about economics[4] and considered the first chapter 'weak and dull and but a poor introduction to the rest of the book' (letter 3062, 30 May 1915, CWK XIII: fn2).

Replying from the 11th Battalion of London Regiment Robertson wrote to Keynes he had promised to Macmillan 'to make required alterations' if possible, suggesting that:

> if the book is worth publishing at all, it is probably worth publishing quickly, as the problems it deals with are just those which are likely to become acute towards and after the end of the war, and it might be useful to the experts who will have to deal with them.
>
> (letter 3063, 6 June 1915)

Driven by this sense of urgency while realising he had no chance of revising his dissertation, Robertson contacted another publisher, P.S. King, who published the work soon after in the unaltered version. The book eventually appeared at the end of 1915.

Robertson's dependence on Keynes's judgement and the need he felt for recognition of his work on a theoretical ground are also testified in a letter Robertson wrote to Keynes soon after his enlistment:

> I don't know whether the study of pre-war economics is still carried on at Cambridge, but it occurred to me that if it is, my Dissertation [...] or its pictures [...] might be of some use for someone to lecture on next term.
>
> (letter 3059, 19 November 1914)

In the same letter he asked Keynes about some common friends and life in Cambridge. In his reply, Keynes delicately informed Robertson of the death of one of their friends on the front, gave him news about Cambridge academic life, and on the dissertation wrote: 'If we have to improvise any lectures for Part II, I'll seize your documents' (letter 3060, 22 November 1914).

From April to August 1916, while Robertson was with his Battalion in Egypt, we have few letters between the two correspondents containing extensive discussion of some poetry books and novels Keynes sent to Robertson.[5] The tone was on both sides always agreeable and affectionate (letters 3066–3068). The particular circumstance of Robertson being on the front favoured a special climate of closeness and reciprocal support between them. What seems interesting is Keynes's attitude: he spent most of his time in Tribunal 'testifying to the sincerity, virtue and truthfulness' of his friends who were conscientious objectors (like Gerald Shove or Bertrand Russell) – as he wrote to Robertson (letter 3067, 18 June 1916); but he showed a sincere feeling of respect towards Robertson, a young man of the same generation who, notwithstanding his pacifist position before the outbreak of the War,[6] decided to enlist as a volunteer in the Army.

The 1920s: fruitful scientific collaboration

After the War, in 1919, Robertson was able to take up his appointment at Trinity. One year later he wrote a very appreciative and indeed acute review[7] (Robertson 1920) of Keynes's *The Economic Consequences of the Peace* ([1919] in CWK II), thereby gaining great consideration from Keynes. A new phase opened in their relationship. Robertson became one of the best readers of Keynes's work for an entire decade.

In letter 3070, 22 September 1921, Robertson made some comments on five articles by Keynes published in the *Sunday Times* (August–September) under the heading of *Europe's Economic Outlook*, about the question of German reparations and other related matters. In these comments Robertson moved no objection to the political position assumed by Keynes – which was courageous and very provocative, as is well known; but he questioned, not without some grounds, Keynes's explanation for the unexpected rise in wage earnings during the War (see CWK XVII: 240–79).

These early theoretical exchanges contributed to Keynes's positive opinion of Robertson as a scholar. Soon after, as editor of the *Cambridge Economic Handbooks* Keynes chose him as the author of *Money* (Robertson 1922) and, subsequently, the *Control of Industry* (Robertson 1923). The two books earned Robertson high repute as a leading Cambridge economist.

In 1924, when Keynes started work on what some years later would become the *Treatise on Money*, Robertson was working on *Banking Policy and the Price Level*. It was Robertson who first gave finished shape to his ideas and suggested a pioneering theory of economic fluctuations in which real and monetary phenomena are interrelated. In his book Robertson focused on the difference between saving (in its different forms) and investment in explaining the cycle. He also introduced a crucial role for the banking system and credit conditions in amplifying business fluctuations arousing Schumpeter's admiration.[8]

A group of letters in 1925 (letters 3074–3080, all published in CWK XIII: 30–41) contain discussions of the proofs of Robertson's *Banking Policy and the Price Level*. Keynes initially expressed very negative judgement, discouraging him from publishing it (letter 3074, May 1925, Sunday). After much revision, Robertson gained his final approval (letter 3080, 10 November 1925). Just how much this acceptance depended on the changes Robertson made to meet Keynes's criticisms or simply on Keynes's anxiety not to discountenance Robertson, and how much it would have come about anyway in due course, none can tell. What seems clear is the main point of opposition: Keynes considered hardly relevant – and fundamentally wrong – the distinction Robertson made between 'Hoarding' and 'Forced Effective Short Lacking', the latter being the part of resources that holders of money are 'forced to save' because of an act of inflation by the Government producing as an effect that people cannot buy the same amount of goods as they could before the rise in prices. According to Robertson this is the real source of new investment in working capital: absence of the 'Short Lacking' could spell the end of boom or crisis. Keynes thought that inflation – in the case of constant hoarding – was simply a situation in which money is transferred from some holders of money to others, without any real effect on investment decisions as a whole or decisions on current consumption and expenditures. The consequence is that in the absence of an independent act of new hoarding on the part of some people, it is impossible to have new resources for investment. In Keynes's words: 'If there is no increased hoarding, [. . .] there is no increased short lacking' (letter 3076, 28 May 1925, CWK XIII: 34). Thus Robertson's distinction loses part of its importance. In June 1925 (letter 3078, CWK XIII: 39) Robertson seemed to accept Keynes's criticism but, at the same time, still appeared reluctant to abandon the distinction he had made, and all the more as it represented the keystone on which the original part of his work was built. In fact, in the following years they frequently returned to the question of defining saving and investment and the effect of inequalities between them on the entire production. One of the main sources of disagreement on this point seems to lie on the different temporal frameworks they had in mind. Keynes (after the *Treatise*) seems to reason in terms of current values of the main aggregates at a definite moment, in contrast with Robertson, who adopts a 'step-by-step' method of an inter-temporal kind on the basis of which saving and investment are not only different concepts but also separate in time, money (and credit conditions) being the link between the two (Robertson 1940: 39).

In a letter of 10 November 1925, Keynes eventually accepted the book: 'I think that your revised chapter V[9] is splendid – most new and important. I think it is substantially right and at last I have no material criticism. It is the kernel and real essence of the book' (letter 3080, CWK XIII: 40).

In the light of the following theoretical developments, Robertson appears somewhat more Keynesian than Keynes himself, in the sense that he first allowed for a substantial separation between the act of hoarding (or saving) and the act of investment in working capital, while Keynes reaffirms the traditional view of saving (hoarding) as a necessary prerequisite of investment. This debate had some part in the main ideas Keynes developed in the *General Theory*, as he recognised some years later in a letter to Robertson: 'I certainly date all my emancipation from the discussions between us which preceded your *Banking Policy and the Price Level*' (letter 3157, 13 December 1936, CWK XIV: 94). This element shows that in the 1920s their exchange represented a real cross-fertilisation of ideas and not a one way influence of Keynes on Robertson.[10]

The Asian tour (August 1926 to April 1927)

After the publication of his book – and the period of intense collaboration with Keynes – Robertson decided to leave Cambridge for an eight-month tour of Asia (including China, Japan and the Laccadive Islands). During his travels he wrote some particularly evocative letters (letters 3081–3083) to Keynes, describing his impressions of the customs, ways of living and landscapes, and sharing emotions and reflections with him. We may conjecture that Keynes greatly missed Robertson's intellectual stimulus since he worked very little on his *Treatise* from Michaelmas term 1926 to Vacation 1927 (more or less the period of Robertson's absence). (See also Moggridge 1992: 441).

The *Treatise* and the public debate on saving and investment definitions

In late 1928 and in 1929 Keynes got down to hard work on the *Treatise* once again, submitting his proofs to Robertson to read. At the same time Robertson was growing increasingly involved in Keynes's activities. He became the second editor of the *Cambridge Economic Handbooks*, and in this capacity sent to Keynes some comments on Dobb's book on *Wages* (1928):

> I think it's very regrettable if the theoretical part has to be merely descriptive of what various people have said, for people will look to a Cambridge book for analysis: and I'm hoping that he may be able to glorify marginal productivity a *little* more! He clings tenaciously to 'exploitation', saying that no ethical judgement is involved in saying that it means 'to treat selfishly as mere material', which may be a virtuous thing to do! But I insisted that if used it must be precisely defined, and I think in the end he may drop it. I think that even so, we might find that in the general preface we want to guard ourselves a little more against implying that his is *the* Cambridge doctrine.
>
> (letter 3085, 27 July 1928)

This unpublished letter[11] is very interesting because Robertson clearly refers to the leading role for economic analysis of the Cambridge tradition as a whole – notwithstanding important theoretical differences between scholars. He seems preoccupied primarily with the high analytical standard required of a book coming out of Cambridge, and second with defence of the Marshallian orthodoxy against heretical doctrines. A peculiarity of his system of thought lies precisely in his being something of a stickler for tradition in microeconomic analysis (he defends Marshall against Sraffa – see the *Symposium* in the *Economic Journal*, 1930 – on the theory of perfect competition, Pigou against Keynes on the theory of wages) but very innovative in macroeconomics, for example in his theory of business fluctuations.

Almost all the 1929–33 correspondence concerning the *Treatise* has been published (CWK XIII: 201–2, 211–12, 219–37, 271–321 and XXIX: 3, 16–29). The points of opposition emerging between Robertson and Keynes regard (1) the cause of the crisis and depression, which was insufficient saving (hoarding) for Robertson and excess of saving for Keynes; (2) the aim of the economic policy, which was 'reasonable' fluctuations for Robertson and stabilisation for Keynes; (3) the role of the banking system, which was to ensure equality between 'Short Lacking' and investment for Robertson, and between saving and investment for Keynes (who never accepted Robertson's different and complex definitions of savings); (4) the unreliability (according to Robertson) of the mechanism of forced saving (or inflation) in restoring equilibrium in the economic system; (5) the question of protectionism (Keynes was in favour, Robertson against). (See, for example, Bridel 1987; Fletcher 1987; Tsiang 1990; Dennison and Presley 1992; Skidelsky 1992; Laidler 1995; Costabile 1997).

In September 1931 their divergences became public with the appearance of Robertson's article 'Mr. Keynes's Theory of Money' in the *Economic Journal* and Keynes's Rejoinder. It is not surprising that Robertson, author of the famous *Cambridge Handbook* on *Money* (1922, 1928a), wrote a commentary on Keynes's *Treatise*: what does set us wondering is the fact that the article appeared almost a year after the publication of the *Treatise*, in a period when their private correspondence on these themes was also very intensive. Robertson's intention to publish his objections to the *Treatise* was already clear in a letter of 7 January 1931, even though overshadowed by his usual insecurity: 'If I can make my difficulties explicit, I shall try to put them into an article eventually: but I may not be able to' (letter 3096, CWK XIII: 202).

When, in May 1931, having submitted to Keynes his 'document' – as Robertson called it – and having recognised that for some of the points raised he was evidently running into misunderstanding of Keynes's words, he decided to leave it mostly unchanged for publication, he offered Keynes this justification:

> I think it is probable that if I am muddled other people are more so: and that it would be to the advantage of students to have the thing available, as a running commentary, more or less in its present form, even if there turn out to be *other* points on which, as a result of long conversations supplementing the written word, we could more or less reach agreement.
>
> (letter 3099, 2 May 1931, CWK XIII: 211–12)

Robertson hoped that the criticisms contained in his article might 'throw a little more light on what remains a field of appalling intellectual difficulty', and – most importantly – 'assist the author himself towards giving to his fertile and penetrating ideas that harmonious synthesis of which he seems conscious that they still stand in need'(Robertson 1931a: 395). Therefore, if the latter motive could equally well be satisfied with private correspondence, the former (as well as the motive of helping students in understanding the *Treatise*) could be met only with public discussion.

There is also another element to consider: it was in fact precisely from November 1930 to May 1931 that the Cambridge Circus were arguing out the *Treatise* (Kahn 1984; A. Robinson 1985). Robertson was not involved in the Circus activities (we do not know whether from his own choice), and by publishing his article he may well have decided to give a signal – not only to Keynes – that he too was working on scrutiny and revision of some of the ideas contained in the book. Robertson must have realised at this point that his influence on Keynes's opinion was on the wane, and that his maestro was beginning to prefer Kahn's and J. Robinson's judgement to his own. As from Spring–Summer 1931[12] Robertson felt that Keynes was in some way confining him to a secondary role in the work of constructing his theoretical framework, and this feeling did not bode well for their personal and professional relationship.

As is well known, the controversy between Robertson and Keynes overlaps with those engaged in by various other economists in Cambridge, including Pigou, Hayek, Hawtrey, Kahn, Sraffa, Kaldor, Joan and Austin Robinson and Meade. Robertson's criticism of the supposed independence between the price of consumption goods and the price of investment goods maintained by Keynes was also advanced by Pigou and considered fundamentally right by Kahn, Sraffa and Hawtrey (see Ch. 1: 23 and Ch. 4: 126–7). Robertson's argument (similar to that suggested by Hayek) on Keynes's ambiguity in the definitions of saving and investment (letter 3093, 4 March 1930, CWK XIII: 122–3) was fundamentally the same as the 'old' objections moved at the time of their discussions on *Banking Policy*, showing the crucial role this question had in their theoretical controversy.

One year and a half later – after many other exchanges in between – Keynes was able to explain very clearly the main points of opposition with Robertson (letter 3103, 6 October 1931, CWK XIII: 272–4). Unfortunately (and symptomatically) this letter was never sent, leaving the whole debate unsettled.

After October 1931 we have a gap of almost five months in the correspondence: the subsequent letter, with two long notes enclosed, is a further attempt by Keynes to smooth over the misunderstandings with Robertson. He wrote to him:

> I have been trying recently to avoid controversy and to get back to the beginning in restating the point of view which I seem to have put inadequately in Book Three of my *Treatise*. Here are two instalments

> for your inspection, which I would be rather grateful if you would look at.
>
> (letter 3104, 22 March 1932, CWK XIII: 275)

Their discussions continued until September 1932 on a series of detailed explanations about the definitions of Saving. In a letter of 2 September 1932, sending Keynes a further note, Robertson was also looking for some kind of reconciliation for their different positions: 'The enclosed is the product of a lot of reflection. It *may* still be a muddle! But if not, I hope you'll be able to regard it as one advance towards re-agreement in substance, if not in terminology' (letter 3117, CWK XIII: 301).

It is likely that this letter did not achieve its purpose since it was followed by another gap in the correspondence lasting until April 1933. When Robertson decided to submit another critical article ('Saving and Hoarding') for possible publication in the *Economic Journal*, he again felt the need to justify himself to Keynes (letter 3118, 1 April 1933, CWK XXIX: 16).

In fact their opposition was already quite keen. Some months later Robertson pointed out that if his article was published in the September issue of *Economic Journal* and Keynes's reply in the December one, Keynes would have the last word. He suggested that if so, he should have the chance of further defence in the same issue as Keynes's reply (letter 3127, 22 July 1933, CWK XXIX: 27) and Keynes accepted.

Before and after the *General Theory*: keen contrast

A further significant occasion for theoretical clash between Robertson and Keynes came with the appearance of Pigou's *The Theory of Unemployment* in the second half of 1933. Keynes's comments were very negative and cutting: he dismissed the whole book as 'nonsense'.[13] Robertson engaged in defending Pigou from Keynes's attacks by showing that Keynes had misunderstood Pigou's arguments and, worse, imputed Pigou with positions he had never maintained (letter 3130, 10 September 1933, CWK XXIX: 28). Keynes probably took a dim view of this obstinate defence of Pigou, especially as his ideas on unemployment, at that time, started to become clearer and in contrast to the traditional view. The result was that when Keynes began intensive work on the *General Theory* the rift between them was already accomplished.

Nevertheless, the beginning of 1935 saw Robertson and Keynes engaged in extensive discussion of the proofs. In letter 3147, 10 February 1935 (CWK XIII: 506), Robertson wrote:

> I'm afraid you'll feel the general tenor of my comments [...] rather hostile. And I'm the more sorry for that in that I don't think I'm unsympathetic to what I feel to be the newest and practically the most

> important thing which you are saying, – viz. that in the post-war world there have been certain long-term depressive influences at work of a kind which most critics hitherto have regarded as purely slump-phenomena [. . .]. I think it is early to judge whether it is going to be true in the future, i.e. how far it is a strictly-post-war phase and how far a rich-20th-century phase. But I'm far from certain it isn't the latter: and if turns out to be, I may often be found agreeing with you in practice on the need for Govt work programmes [. . .]. On the other hand a large part of your theoretical structure is still to me almost complete mumbo-jumbo!

This letter seems to confirm that the trouble between them, apart from the psychological condition of exclusion Robertson felt from Keynes's whole intellectual and, perhaps, personal world, is not a question of misunderstanding of the *General Theory*'s central message about persistent unemployment, or disagreement with Keynes's conclusions on economic policy, but concerns the analytical structure of the book, which was 'complete mumbo-jumbo' for Robertson.

At the end of January 1935 Robertson suffered the death of his mother. Surprisingly enough, the letters of this period contain not a single word by Robertson or Keynes about this loss. Robertson was psychologically shaken by the event, in the following months revealing fragility of mind and intractability in his relations with other members of the Cambridge Faculty.

The debate continued until March 1935 when Robertson himself suggested a break in their correspondence (letter 3149, 11 March 1935, CWK XIII: 520). Keynes started his reply with these words:

> My dear Dennis, Yes, I think that we had better break off the discussion at this point [. . .]. What bothers me is not so much that I should have failed to convince you that it [the proposition saying that the rate of interest is the price of the use of loanable funds] is false, as that I should have apparently failed to convey to you that I deny it!
>
> (letter 3150, 14 March 1935, CWK XIII: 522–3)

This exchange marks a fundamental point of rupture between them.

The well known controversy about the *General Theory* revolves about three main points of substance. First of all, the question of method. Robertson was accustomed to reason in terms of a succession of periods, all of a definite length of time, which was, according to him the only way to address – from a theoretical point of view – the problems of economic fluctuations, cycle, depression and, generally speaking, dynamics. At the beginning of every period there is a given level of the main economic variables which is the result of the past levels and, more generally, of what happened in the previous periods. He found it hard, for example, to accept Keynes's approach where the current level of saving is a function of current income without any reference to the past level of savings; as indeed it was hard for him to imagine a theory of investment in which the latter was not linked to the saving decisions made in the previous periods. For the same reason he had some doubts about the mechanism of the multiplier of investment and, in general, the short-period method, both derived by Keynes from Kahn. He could not understand how the effect of the multiplier on income could be instantaneous. Nor could he see how Keynes could speak of differences between Effective Demand and Aggregate Demand without using any kind of (inter)temporal method.

Second, there was the question of the rate of interest. Robertson, despite Keynes's arguments to the contrary, continued (as from his article in the *Economic Journal*, 1931) to consider the rate of interest as the price bringing the demand and supply of loanable funds into equilibrium, and to consider money like every other good from the point of view of the determination of its price, pointing out that Keynes's theory of liquidity preference put undue emphasis on the speculative motive against the transaction motive for demanding money.

Third, we come to the – in some respects – most important point: the question of cycle versus long-term stagnation (see Tonveronachi 1983). In all their discussions Keynes was above all concerned with the problem of the tendency of contemporary capitalist economies towards a condition of persistent underemployment of resources, while Robertson, on the other hand, was always concerned with the 'old' question of business cycle. This seems to be the main reason for their failure to communicate: they were talking about different problems. Robertson was not able to understand why Keynes had so shifted his interest to a situation which might come about but might not, while Keynes failed to understand why Robertson, who was the first economist Keynes knew to have stressed the role of the inequalities between saving and investment in explaining depressions, refused to accept his message about the risk of persistent states of underemployment.

Between March 1935 and May 1936 we have only two letters of somewhat polemical content (letters 3151 and 3152, 10 and 11 October 1935, CWK XIII: 523–4), which shows just how deep their rift went. Meanwhile two noteworthy events took place: in March 1935 Robertson clashed with J. Robinson on the courses to be given at the Cambridge Faculty; in February 1936 the *General Theory* was published. The episode involving J. Robinson is accurately reconstructed by Moggridge (1992: 599–601) and revisited by Aslanbeigui and Oakes (2002: 24–5). In March 1935 J. Robinson proposed to the Faculty Board (which Robertson chaired at the time) to lecture a two-term course on money for second-year students, while Robertson gave the lectures to the third-year students on the same subject. Robertson firmly opposed Robinson's lecturing: he feared, not without grounds, being ridiculed by her before his own students. The problem arose again in 1936 when Robertson, eventually accepting the arrangement list of the courses (which contemplated Robinson's course for second-year students on a different subject) as 'the least bad in the circumstances', did not conceal his disappointment (letter 3154, 28 August 1936, Moggridge 1992: 600). (See Chs 6: 176; 7: 208; 13: 339). The feeling of growing hostility experienced by Robertson also emerges from a letter he sent to Hicks on the 20 May 1936 commenting on Hicks's review of the *General Theory* (Hicks 1936):

> It will be a comfort to find somebody who thinks there is a great deal in this book [the *General Theory*] and with whom nevertheless one can discuss – for *entre nous* my trouble is that with the author and his more whole-hearted disciples I can no longer discuss but only be made to feel obsolete and pig-headed for not having seen the light!
>
> (DHR papers, C4/1/7)

In the late summer of 1936 both Robertson and Keynes were eager for rapprochement, although perfectly aware of the difficulties that had arisen (letters 3154 and 3156, 28 August and 20 September 1936 respectively, CWK XXIX: 164 and XIV: 87–8). In the meantime, in November, Robertson published his highly critical review of the *General Theory* (Robertson 1936). It was exactly at that moment that they decided to rescue their personal relationship 'off Economics'. They both seemed sorry to have lost their better feelings through theoretical divergences. In the last two letters of 1936 (dated 13 and 29 December) their tone was more peaceful even though they did not eschew certain sarcastic quips about each other's personalities. Once again the keener conflict seems to have come much more from Keynes's disciples than from Keynes himself (letter 3158, 29 December 1936, CWK XIV: 95). In fact, the heavy climate between Keynes and Robertson was eventually cleared. In early 1937 (until March) they had several fruitful exchanges on Harrod's *Trade Cycle*, just published. (See Ch. 3: 100.)

Notwithstanding their personal rapprochement, in the summer of 1937 there were two more episodes of public theoretical debate: publication in the *Economic Journal* of Robertson's rejoinder to Keynes's 'Alternative Theories of the Rate of Interest' (Robertson 1937), and comments on Pigou's 'Real and Money Wage Rates in relation to Unemployment' (Keynes 1937d). In particular, in letter 3163, 31 August 1937 (CWK XIV: 250) Keynes, still recovering from his heart attack, sharply reproached Robertson for having 'committed the unforgivable sin' of letting Pigou publish that article. (See Chs 6: 177; 8: 219–20; 15: 378–82.)

Robertson's isolation and his abandonment of Cambridge for the LSE

According to Aslanbeigui and Oakes (2002: 28–32) Robertson's departure from Cambridge to join the LSE can be seen as the result of the 'fight' led by the Keynesian avant-garde (Kahn, Joan and Austin Robinson), with Keynes's approval, in order to affirm the 'Keynesian revolution'. They explain Robertson's decision to leave precisely in October 1938 referring to a specific episode in which Keynes's disciples plus Sraffa, Kalecki, Champernowne and Keynes himself were involved and in which Robertson once again felt he was being intentionally isolated by the others, Pigou playing a *super partes* role. The episode regarded a research project to be carried out in the Cambridge Faculty in co-operation with the National Institute of Economic and Social Research.

With the help of the correspondence Keynes's position can be brought into better focus. The details of the above project had been discussed between Robertson and Keynes since March 1938 (letter 3180, 23 March 1938). Until the end of May (letter 3185, 22 May 1938), Keynes did not seem to have any particular intention to exclude Robertson deliberately (see Johnson and Johnson 1978: 136–7; Moggridge 1992: 601–2).

This question overlapped with the matter of the publication of Robertson's critical article 'Mr. Keynes and Finance' and his 'sur-rejoinder' in reply to Keynes's rejoinder (letters 3187–3198, from May to August 1938, CWK XXIX: 171–84). Keynes submitted the matter to Pigou, who confirmed Keynes's doubts about the diminishing returns of this controversy. Eventually Keynes decided to publish both the article and the brief note by Robertson (Robertson 1938a, 1938b), but it is likely that renewed public opposition to his theory convinced him that it was impossible to work constructively with Robertson on a common research project. At the end of August Keynes settled the matter once and for all, writing to Pigou that co-operative work had to be done by people 'who are at ease among themselves' (letter 4208 JMK to ACP, 30 August 1938). (See Ch. 5: 153.)

When Robertson (letter 3199, 7 October 1938) communicated to Keynes his intention to leave Cambridge to take up the Cassel Chair at the LSE he had already taken his decision. Keynes, aware of the difficult climate for Robertson, did nothing to hold him back but clearly expressed his regret:

> It is a great wrench and loss that you have decided to go away. I can understand the conflict of motives which went to your decision. But I think it may be a right one. The post may be a good one and in many ways attractive. Here the state of struggle in the Faculty which has existed lately I have seen and hated. I don't know why it need have been.[14] But it seemed to be too deeply rooted in feelings to be easily composed by reasonableness. It is all a great pity.[15] [. . .] Well, Dennis, I trust that time and some measures of absence, which will only be partial I hope, will obliterate the miserable divisions of the last year or two.
>
> (letter 3200, 9 October 1938, Aslanbeigui and Oakes 2002: 32)

Robertson was also very much involved, as he replied:

> Yes it is a wrench in many ways: but I thought it over as carefully and calmly as I could, and I think it is a right decision. [. . .] As you say, there are many attractive things about the post, and (to me) about London residence. [. . .] Thank you again for writing, – and for much else over many years.
>
> (letter 3201, 11 October 1938)

This was the end of their long controversy, but not of their correspondence. After a break of three years,[16] they once again got down to working together fruitfully on various issues and, in particular, on post-war international monetary settlements.

Renewed collaboration on international affairs and Robertson's return to Cambridge

According to Moggridge (1992: 671), in September 1941 at Tilton Keynes was able in just a few days to write a plan (known afterwards as the 'Keynes's plan') for an International Currency Union to be implemented at the end of the War. In November 1941 Robertson[17] and Keynes discussed the plan and the difficult economic situation facing Great Britain – especially in its external position. In letter 3205, 10 November 1941, Robertson provided some insightful comments on the figures calculated by Sir Frederick Phillips (who, as joint second Secretary, represented the Treasury in the negotiations with the USA) on financial and commercial exchanges. He appeared quite doubtful (if not pessimistic) about the positive impact on the adverse balance of the Lend-Lease Bill which Great Britain was negotiating with her main ally.

At the end of the month, Keynes presented to the Treasury the second draft of his plan, which gained general approval in Whitehall. Robertson greeted Keynes's proposal with great enthusiasm declaring that 'the spirit of Burke and Adam Smith is on earth again [. . .]' (letter 3206, 27 November 1941, CWK XXV: 67).

Exchanges between them continued intensively during the whole of 1942 and touched upon many different subjects including Clearing Union drafts, national accounts, public expenditures and trade policy, testifying the prominent role Keynes attributed to Robertson as economic adviser. In March 1943, when Robertson was in Washington as Treasury delegate, they returned to analysis of international post-war settlements. From then until July their exchanges were very frequent, showing the key contribution Robertson gave with his comments on the 'Whines' plan, as Robertson called it from the fusion of 'Keynes's Plan' and 'White's Plan' (letter 3224, 13 July 1943, CWK XXV: 315). It is impossible here to give a full account of all the points raised. What we can say is that the general tone of the letters was very collaborative. Robertson constructively discussed each clause related to the Clearing Union and Stability Fund, supporting Keynes in careful analysis of the main consequences of each of them, obviously on the British side. Keynes found Robertson's collaboration in the preparatory work for the Bretton Woods Conference 'indispensable'[18] as he wrote to Sir Richard Hopkins[19] in July 1944 (Moggridge 1992: 742). In the same period, in a letter to his mother (Skidelsky 2000: 350), Keynes referred to him as a 'first-class brain'. We may well understand, therefore, why Keynes was so taken aback by events just after the closing of the Conference. In 'A Note on the International Monetary Fund' (sent to Keynes on 31 July 1944, letter 3259, CWK XXVI: 114–17) Robertson pointed out (when it was too late for any modification) a problem of interpretation of Article VIII, Section 2(a) and 4(a), about the obligations of each member regarding the convertibility of foreign held balances.[20] When Keynes realised that the question raised was a serious one and that interpretation of the clause in the sense which Robertson had shown could result in the impossibility for Great Britain (especially after the War) to honour its debts with other nations he asked the American Treasury in vain for clarification favourable to his own country.

Skidelsky (2000: 358) maintains that this episode shows that the reconciliation between Robertson and Keynes after their long controversy in the 1930s was not full. Keynes must have wondered why Robertson did not raise the question before. On the one hand, during Robertson's negotiations of this part of the document with the US and Canadian Delegations there was a real misunderstanding between them about Keynes's supposed agreement to it – as Lionel Robbins (CWK XXVI: 171) and Sir Wilfrid Eady[21] (CWK XXVI: 170) reminded Keynes in a subsequent reconstruction of this episode. On the other hand, it is not unlikely that Robertson fully realised all the implications of the two clauses on convertibility only after the end of the Conference, when he returned to further analysis of the Final Act. From August 1944 to January 1945 (letters 3324, 3343, 3298, 3299, 3232–3235, CWK XXVI: 159–63) they engaged in deeper examination of some doubtful aspects of the Stability Fund Agreement, which had just been signed, as well as the question of Article VIII (4a) and (2a). In letter 3260, 29 December 1944 (CWK XXVI: 148–49) Keynes, even complaining that his attention had not been drawn to this delicate point at Bretton Woods and that it was only sprung on him afterwards by Robertson,[22] seemed to consider the matter on the whole as a drafting error (due to the overworking conditions experienced by all participants at the Conference[23]) and not as a deliberate act by Robertson to damage him, or worse, the interests of Great Britain. Even when Robertson left his official position at the Treasury and came back to Cambridge, Keynes submitted to him all the confidential documents related to the question in hand and seemed to trust his careful reading, even more than before.

In the realm of academic affairs, at the beginning of 1944 Keynes favoured Robertson's election as Professor of Political Economy in the Cambridge Faculty as Pigou's successor. After some indecision (letter 3584 from DHR to RFK, 11 February 1944), he eventually accepted the post.

In the same period they collaborated on the annual elections of the British Academy members: they successfully supported Hicks' candidature in 1942 and – with Pigou's approval – Hayek's[24] in 1944 (letters 3210, 5 January 1942 and 3226–3228, 1, 9 and 26 February 1944) (see Ch. 5: 154–5). On the other hand, their opinion of Joan Robinson's scientific contribution remained to the end in sharp contrast. In 1946, when her candidature was renewed (her name having already been unsuccessfully proposed by Keynes in 1944), not surprisingly Robertson wrote to Keynes:

> *Mrs Robinson* and I are, as you know, somewhat allergic towards one another's work, which makes it difficult for me to form a reliable judgement on her claims. But for what my opinion is worth, I should find it hard to put her intellectual achievement above Harrod's: while [. . .] I should be inclined to rank *Shove* decidedly above both'.
>
> (letter 3245, 22 January 1946)[25]

The motivation put forward by Robertson to elect Shove – besides the 'high quality' of his very few publications – went that he was 'a scholar whose tongue is more fertile than his own pen, but has very manifestly contributed to fertilising the pens of others'.

Robertson's proposal – which reveals the central role he still granted the Marshallian orthodoxy in spite of the numerous attacks it had come under from 1925 until then – was not taken into account, with the result that Shove was never elected to the British Academy. Marshall's era, in fact, was definitely on the wane but this last episode seems to confirm what Keynes once wrote to Robertson: 'You are, so to speak, bent on creeping back into your mother's womb; whilst I am shaking myself like a dog on a dry land' (letter 3172, 6 December 1937, CWK XXIX: 165).

Acknowledgements

Besides all the contributors to this collective work, who helped me in many ways and circumstances and to whom I am extremely grateful, I would like to thank Mario Amendola, Gordon Fletcher, Toshiaki Hirai, Andrea Micocci, Paolo Sylos Labini and, in particular, Don Moggridge, for their precious comments and suggestions on previous drafts of this chapter. All remaining errors and misunderstandings are obviously mine.

Notes

1 Including letters, memoranda and notes. (See the forthcoming edition of

Robertson's correspondence edited by Moggridge.)

2 The series Hicks refers to is: Robertson, *Money* (1922), Keynes, *Tract on Monetary Reform*, ([1923] in CWK IV), Keynes, *Economic Consequences of Mr. Churchill* ([1925b] CWK XIX: 357–453), Robertson, *Banking Policy and the Price Level* (1926), Robertson, the new *Money* (1928a) together with the important lecture 'Theories of Banking Policy' (1928b), Keynes, *Treatise on Money* ([1930] in CWK V–VI).

3 The same draft of the dissertation won the Cobden Prize in 1913, when the examiners were Pigou, Ashley and Kay-Shuttleworth.

4 On the question of style in Robertson's production see Fletcher (2000: 126–50).

5 Robertson took a First in Part I in Classical Tripos (1910) and had a sincere passion for literature and theatre. He wrote poems and had a parallel career as a theatrical actor (quite well-known in the field).

6 On Robertson's decision to enlist – fundamentally due to his deep sense of duty – see Fletcher (2000: 71–82).

7 The only letter we have referring to this review is interesting for a literary detail. Robertson (letter 3069, 12 March 1920) wrote to Keynes that he realised he had made a 'gross historical mistake' in the first sentence of his review quoting from *Macbeth*. The error consists in considering Duncan (the King of Scotland) as Macbeth's host while the opposite was true. Asking Keynes if he was still in time to correct the error before publication, he feared for his reputation as a Shakespeare scholar. Unfortunately, it was too late and in the published version the error is still there (see Robertson 1920: 77).

8 In a letter dating 7 November 1926 about *Banking Policy and the Price Level* Schumpeter wrote to Robertson: 'I consider it a splendid and most original as well as frightful achievement and I have learnt a lot from it. Its main importance seems to me to lie in this: you are the first Englishman [. . .] to grasp the fundamental theoretic importance of credit *created* by banks and of the fact of forced saving (if I may use this expression) for the mechanism of the dynamics of capitalistic economic life which in fact cannot be understood without it, not even in the purest of pure theories' (DHR papers, C18/3).

9 The chapter is entitled 'The Kinds of Saving' and contains an explanation of the different forms of saving as well as their different roles in the economy.

10 On Robertson's influence on Keynes's analysis in the passage from the *Tract on Monetary Reform* to the *Treatise on Money* see Hirai (1997–99, Ch. 6).

11 Only a small excerpt is published in Fletcher (2000: 101).

12 In the same period Robertson worked with the group of LSE economists led by Robbins and Beveridge on an anti-protectionist project, in contrast with Keynes's proposals (Moggridge 1992: 598). In 1931 Robertson also published, together with Pigou, the book *Economic Essays and Addresses*.

13 See letters from September to November 1933 (CWK XIII: 310–21 and XXIX: 27–33).

14 'I do!' wrote Robertson on the margin.

15 'Yes' wrote Robertson on the margin.

16 There were two letters in March 1940 about Keynes's book *How to Pay for the War*. Robertson's comment was 'you won't be surprised to hear that at first blush I think it your best work since E.C.P. [Economic Consequences of the Peace]' (letter 3203, 6 March 1940).

17 Robertson was a civil servant at the Treasury from 1939 to 1944.

18 Keynes and Robertson both took part in the British Delegation to the Conference as well as the Atlantic City preparatory meetings, held in June 1944.

19 He was Permanent Secretary at the Treasury from 1942 to 1945.

20 For a detailed reconstruction of this episode see Pressnell (1987, I: 170 and ff.), Moggridge (1992: 748–53) and Skidelsky (2000: 357–8).

21 He was joint second secretary at the Treasury from 1942 to 1952 and member of the British Delegation to the Bretton Woods Conference.

22 This is why in letter 3234, 21 January 1945 Robertson wrote: '[. . .] I need not say I am very sorry for my share of responsibility for the misunderstanding which occurred at B.[retton] W.[oods]'.

23 Keynes himself (in the same letter) underlined how much pressure there was in the Conference: many participants were obliged to vote a text without having had the possibility to read it carefully beforehand.

24 Robertson seems to have been the first to draw Keynes's attention to Hayek's candidature as early as 1942 (letter 3210, 5 January).

25 Joan Robinson had to wait until 1958 to be elected while Harrod obtained his membership in 1947.

Table 2.1 Keynes–Robertson correspondence

From	*To*	*Year*	*Month*	*Day*	*Date*	*Archive*		*Published in*	*Item*
DHR	JMK	1912	July	23	Dated letter	Keynes–King's	L/R/1–2		3056
JMK	DHR	1913	September	28	Dated letter	Robertson–Trinity	C2/1/1	CWK XIII: 1, (E)	3057
DHR	JMK	1914	April	8	Dated letter	Keynes–King's	L/R/3–4		3058
DHR	JMK	1914	November	19	Dated letter	Keynes–King's	L/R/5–6	Fletcher 2000: 75, (E)	3059
JMK	DHR	1914	November	22	Dated letter	Robertson–Trinity	C2/1/3		3060
DHR	JMK	1915			Attributed	Keynes–King's	L/R/7		3061
JMK	DHR	1915	May	30	Dated letter	Robertson–Trinity Robertson–Trinity	C2/1/4 C2/1/8	CWK XIII: 1, fn. 2, (E)	3062
DHR	JMK	1915	June	6	Dated letter	Keynes–King's	L/R/3–9		3063
DHR	JMK	1916	January	13	Dated letter	Keynes–King's	L/R/10–11		3064
DHR	JMK	1916	February	7	Dated letter	Keynes–King's	L/R/12–13		3065
DHR	JMK	1916	April	7	Dated letter	Keynes–King's	L/R/14–15	Fletcher 2000: 77–8, (E)	3066
JMK	DHR	1916	June	18	Dated letter	Robertson–Trinity	C2/1/11	Moggridge 1992: 259, (E)	3067
DHR	JMK	1916	August	15	Dated letter	Keynes–King's	L/R/16–17	Fletcher 2000: 78, (E)	3068
DHR	JMK	1920	March	12	Dated letter	Keynes–King's	EJ/1/2/153–4		3069
DHR	JMK	1921	September	22	Dated letter	Keynes–King's	L/R/20–1	CWK XVII: 278–9	3070
DHR	JMK	1924	February	20	Postmark	Keynes–King's	L/24/1		3071
JMK	DHR	1924	September	14	Dated letter	Robertson–Trinity	C2/1/19	CWK XIII: 16	3072
DHR	JMK	1925	February	27	Dated letter	Keynes–King's Robertson–Trinity	TM/1/2/1–5 C2/1/23	CWK XIII: 24–6	3073
DHR	JMK	1925	May	Sunday	Dated letter	Keynes–King's Robertson–Trinity	TM/1/2/9–14 C2/1/13	CWK XIII: 30–3	3074
DHR	JMK	1925	May	Saturday	Attributed	Keynes–King's	TM/1/2/15	CWK XIII: 29	3075
JMK	DHR	1925	May	28	Dated letter	Keynes–King's	TM/1/2/18–20	CWK XIII: 34–6	3076
JMK	DHR	1925	May	31	Dated letter	Keynes–King's	TM/1/2/25–31	CWK XIII: 36–9	3077
DHR	JMK	1925	June		Attributed	Keynes–King's	TM/1/2/16–17	CWK XIII: 39	3078
JMK	DHR	1925	September	28	Dated letter	Not found in the archives		CWK XIII: 39–40	3079

Table 2.1 continued

From	*To*	*Year*	*Month*	*Day*	*Date*	*Archive*		*Published in*	*Item*
JMK	DHR	1925	November	10	Dated letter	Robertson–Trinity	C2/1/21	CWK XIII: 40–1	3080
DHR	JMK	1926	October	13	Dated letter	Keynes–King's	L/R/22–7	Fletcher 2000: 99, (E)	3081
JMK	DHR	1926	November	4	Dated letter	Robertson–Trinity	C2/1/22		3082
DHR	JMK	1927	January	15	Dated letter	Keynes–King's	L/R/39–44	Fletcher 2000: 99, (E)	3083
JMK	DHR	1927	September	22	Dated letter	Robertson–Trinity	C2/1/28		3084
DHR	JMK	1928	July	27	Dated letter	Keynes–King's	L/R/45–8	Fletcher 2000: 101, (E)	3085
DHR	JMK	1928	September	18	Dated letter	Robertson–Trinity	C2/2/1–2	CWK XIII: 65–6, (E)	3086
DHR	JMK	1928	December	21	Dated letter	Keynes–King's	PP/45/270/1–4		3087
JMK	DHR	1929	January	20	Dated letter	Keynes–King's	CEB/1/19		3088
DHR	JMK	1929	August	30	Dated letter	Keynes–King's	TM/1/2/33	CWK XXIX: 3, (E)	3089
DHR	JMK	1929	December	5	Dated letter	Keynes–King's	TM/1/2/34–5	CWK XIII: 118–19	3090
DHR	JMK	1930			Attributed	Keynes–King's	TM/1/2/36–7		3091
DHR	JMK	1930	January	8	Dated letter	Keynes–King's	TM/1/2/38–9	CWK XIII: 121–2	3092
DHR	JMK	1930	March	4	Dated letter	Keynes–King's	TM/1/2/40–1	CWK XIII: 122–3	3093
DHR	JMK	1930	June	15	Dated letter	Keynes–King's	L/R/49–51		3094
DHR	JMK	1930	July	2	Dated letter	Keynes–King's	L/R/52–3		3095
DHR	JMK	1931	January	7	Dated letter	Keynes–King's	TM/1/4/99–100	CWK XIII: 201–2	3096
DHR	JMK	1931	March	30	Dated letter	Keynes–King's	L/R/54–5		3097
JMK	DHR	1931	April	18	Dated letter	Robertson–Trinity	C2/2/13		3098
DHR	JMK	1931	May	2	Dated letter	Keynes–King's	CO/8/96	CWK XIII: 211–12	3099
JMK	DHR	1931	May	5	Dated letter	Robertson–Trinity	C2/2/15–24		3252
DHR	JMK	1931	May	13	Dated letter	Keynes–King's	CO/8/114–24	CWK XIII: 214	3100
JMK	DHR	1931	July	26	Dated letter	Robertson–Trinity	C2/2/26		3248
DHR	JMK	1931	July	26	Attributed	Robertson–Trinity	C2/2/26–7		3249
DHR	JMK	1931	September	5	Dated letter	Keynes–King's Robertson–Trinity	L/R/56–7 C2/2/28–9		3101
DHR	JMK	1931	October	4	Dated letter	Keynes–King's Robertson–Trinity	CO/8/136–7 C2/2/30–1	CWK XIII: 271–2	3102

JMK	DHR	1931	October	6	Dated letter	Keynes–King's	CO/8/133–5	CWK XIII: 272–4	3103
JMK	DHR	1932	March	22	Dated letter	Keynes–King's	CO/8/138–59	CWK XIII: 275–89	3104
DHR	JMK	1932	May		Attributed	Keynes–King's	CO/8/160–6	CWK XIII: 289–94	3105
DHR	JMK	1932	May		Attributed	Keynes–King's	CO/8/167–8	CWK XIII: 294–5	3106
JMK	DHR	1932	May	18	Dated letter	Keynes–King's	CO/8/169	CWK XIII: 295–6	3107
DHR	JMK	1932	May	18	Dated letter	Keynes–King's	CO/8/170–1	CWK XIII: 296–7	3108
JMK	DHR	1932	May	20	Dated letter	Keynes–King's	CO/8/173	CWK XIII: 297	3109
DHR	JMK	1932	May	21	Dated letter	Keynes–King's	CO/8/174–5	CWK XIII: 297–8	3110
JMK	DHR	1932	May	22	Dated letter	Keynes–King's Robertson–Trinity	CO/8/176–7 C2/3/32–3	CWK XIII: 298–9	3111
DHR	JMK	1932	May	after 22	Attributed	Keynes–King's Robertson–Trinity	CO/8/178 C2/3/14	CWK XIII: 299	3112
JMK	DHR	1932	May	29	Dated letter	Keynes–King's Robertson–Trinity	CO/8/179 C2/3/27	CWK XIII: 300	3113
DHR	JMK	1932	June	21	Dated letter	Keynes–King's	GTE/1/84 and CO/8/180–1	CWK XIII: 300–1	3114
DHR	JMK	1932	August	18	Dated letter	Keynes–King's	L/R/58–9		3115
DHR	JMK	1932	August	24	Dated letter	Keynes–King's	L/R/60		3116
DHR	JMK	1932	September	2	Dated letter	Keynes–King's	CO/8/182–90	CWK XIII: 301–6	3117
DHR	JMK	1933	April	1	Dated letter	Keynes–King's	L/R/61–2	CWK XXIX: 16–7, (E)	3118
DHR	JMK	1933	May		Attributed	Keynes–King's	CO/8/191	CWK XIII: 306–7	3119
JMK	DHR	1933	May	3	Dated letter	Not found in the archives		CWK XXIX: 17–19	3120
DHR	JMK	1933	May	4	Dated letter	Keynes–King's	GTE/1/115–16	CWK XXIX: 23, (E)	3121
JMK	DHR	1933	May	4	Dated letter	Keynes–King's	GTE/1/117–21	CWK XXIX: 19–23	3122
DHR	JMK	1933	May	19	Dated letter	Keynes–King's	GTE/1/122–6	CWK XXIX: 23–6	3123
JMK	DHR	1933	May	20	Dated letter	Keynes–King's Robertson–Trinity	CO/8/192–5 C2/3/29–32	CWK XIII: 307–8	3124
JMK	DHR	1933	May	20	Dated letter	Keynes–King's	GTE/1/127	CWK XXIX: 26	3125
DHR	JMK	1933	May	23	Dated letter	Keynes–King's	CO/8/196–7	CWK XIII: 308–9	3126
DHR	JMK	1933	July	22	Dated letter	Keynes–King's	L/R/63–4	CWK XXIX: 27, (E)	3127
JMK	DHR	1933	September	5	Dated letter	Robertson–Trinity	C2/3/51–4	CWK XIII: 310–13	3129
DHR	JMK	1933	September	10	Dated letter	Keynes–King's	GTE/1/129–32	CWK XXIX: 27–8, (E)	3130

Table 2.1 continued

From	To	Year	Month	Day	Date	Archive		Published in	Item
DHR	JMK	1933	September	15	Dated letter	Keynes–King's	GTE/1/134–7	CWK XIII: 313–14, (E)	3131
DHR	JMK	1933	September	21	Dated letter	Keynes–King's	GTE/1/138–43	CWK XIII: 314–15, (E)	3132
DHR	JMK	1933	September	25	Dated letter	Keynes–King's	GTE/1/128	CWK XXIX: 28–9, (E)	3128
DHR	JMK	1933	October		Attributed	Keynes–King's	GTE/1/144–7	CWK XIII: 317–19	3133
DHR	JMK	1933	October		Attributed	Keynes–King's	GTE/1/148–9	CWK XXIX: 29–30	3134
JMK	DHR	1933	October	2	Dated letter	Keynes–King's	GTE/1/150	CWK XXIX: 29	3135
JMK	DHR	1933	October	19	Dated letter	Keynes–King's Keynes–King's	GTE/1/151–2 GTE/1/153–4	CWK XXIX: 30–2	3136
DHR	JMK	1933	October	22	Dated letter	Keynes–King's	GTE/1/155–7	CWK XXIX: 32–3, (E)	3137
JMK	DHR	1933	October	26	Dated letter	Keynes–King's	GTE/1/158–61	CWK XIII: 315–17, (E)	3139
DHR	JMK	1933	October	26	Dated letter	Robertson–Trinity	C2/3/46		3138
JMK	DHR	1933	November	1	Dated letter	Keynes–King's	GTE/1/171	CWK XIII: 320	3140
DHR	JMK	1933	November	after 1	Attributed	Keynes–King's	GTE/1/172	CWK XIII: 320–1	3141
DHR	JMK	1934	December	1	Dated letter	Keynes–King's	CEB/1/31–2		3142
DHR	JMK	1935	January		Attributed	Keynes–King's Robertson–Trinity	GTE/1/202 C2/4/17	CWK XIII: 493	3143
DHR	JMK	1935	January	26	Dated letter	Keynes–King's	UA/14/2/166		3144
JMK	DHR	1935	January	29	Dated letter	Keynes–King's Robertson–Trinity	GTE/1/197–201 C2/4/18–22	CWK XIII: 494–6	3145
DHR	JMK	1935	February	3	Dated letter	Keynes–King's Robertson–Trinity	L/R/65–79 C2/4/31–9	CWK XIII: 496–506	3146
DHR	JMK	1935	February	10	Dated letter	Keynes–King's Robertson–Trinity	L/R/80–9 C2/4/40–4	CWK XIII: 506–11	3147
JMK	DHR	1935	February	20	Dated letter	Keynes–King's Robertson–Trinity	L/R/90–103 C2/4/48–61	CWK XIII: 511–20	3148
DHR	JMK	1935	March		Attributed	Robertson–Trinity Keynes–King's	C2/3/15 L/R/108		3255
DHR	JMK	1935	March	11	Dated letter	Keynes–King's	L/R/104–7	CWK XIII: 520–2	3149

JMK	DHR	1935	March	14	Dated letter	Keynes–King's	L/R/109–10	CWK XIII: 522–3	3150
JMK	DHR	1935	October	10	Dated letter	Robertson–Trinity	C2/5/7–8	CWK XIII: 523–4	3151
DHR	JMK	1935	October	11	Dated letter	Keynes–King's	L/R/111–12	CWK XIII: 524	3152
JMK	DHR	1936	May		Attributed	Robertson–Trinity	C18/23/6–11		3253
DHR	JMK	1936	June	7	Dated letter	Keynes–King's Robertson–Trinity	UA/5/4/11–12 C2/5/11–12		3153
DHR	JMK	1936	August	28	Dated letter	Keynes–King's	L/R/117–8	CWK XXIX: 163–4, (E)	3154
JMK	DHR	1936	September	20	Dated letter	Robertson–Trinity	C2/5/13–17	CWK XIV: 87–8, (E)	3156
DHR	JMK	1936	November		Attributed	Keynes–King's	L/R/121–133		3262
JMK	DHR	1936	December	13	Dated letter	Keynes–King's	GTE/2/4/69–77	CWK XIV: 89–95	3157
DHR	JMK	1936	December	13	Dated letter	Keynes–King's	GTE/2/4/78–86		3261
DHR	JMK	1936	December	29	 Dated letter	Keynes–King's Robertson–Trinity	GTE/2/4/122–3 and 87–95 C2/7/1–9	 CWK XIV: 95–100	3158
JMK	DHR	1937			Attributed	Keynes–King's	CO/2/46		3051
DHR	JMK	1937			Attributed	Keynes–King's	CO/2/47		3052
DHR	JMK	1937			Attributed	Keynes–King's	CO/2/50		3053
DHR	JMK	1937			Attributed	Keynes–King's	CO/2/53		3054
DHR	JMK	1937	January	28	Dated letter	Keynes–King's	CO/2/44–5		3159
JMK	DHR	1937	March	19	Dated letter	Keynes–King's	CO/2/49		3160
JMK	DHR	1937	March	27	Dated letter	Keynes–King's Keynes–King's	CO/2/51 CO/2/52		3161
DHR	JMK	1937	August	17	Dated letter	Keynes–King's	L/R/134–5	Moggridge 1992: 601, (E)	3162
JMK	DHR	1937	August	31	Dated letter	Robertson–Trinity	C2/5/22	CWK XIV: 250, (E)	3163
DHR	JMK	1937	October	11	Dated letter	Keynes–King's	EJ/1/4/157–8	CWK XIV: 251, (E)	3164
JMK	DHR	1937	October	12	Dated letter	Keynes–King's	EJ/1/4/159–60	CWK XIV: 251–2	3165
DHR	JMK	1937	October	17	Dated letter	Keynes–King's Kaldor–King's	EJ/1/4/161–5 NK/3/30/179/7	CWK XIV: 252–4, (E)	3166
JMK	DHR	1937	October	20	Dated letter	Keynes–King's Robertson–Trinity	EJ/1/4/166–7 C2/5/31–2	CWK XIV: 254, (E)	3167
JMK	DHR	1937	October	25	Dated letter	Keynes–King's	EJ/1/4/168	CWK XIV: 255	3168
JMK	DHR	1937	November	1	Dated letter	Robertson–Trinity	C2/6/4–5		3169

Table 2.1 continued

From	*To*	*Year*	*Month*	*Day*	*Date*	*Archive*		*Published in*	*Item*
DHR	JMK	1937	November	28	Dated letter	Keynes–King's	GTE/2/4/124–7	CWK XXIX: 164, (E)	3170
JMK	DHR	1937	December	5	Dated letter	Robertson–Trinity	C2/6/6–9	CWK XIV: 223–6	3171
JMK	DHR	1937	December	6	Dated letter	Keynes–King's	GTE/2/4/128–32	CWK XXIX: 164–5, (E)	3172
DHR	JMK	1937	December	19	Dated letter	Keynes–King's	GTE/2/4/133–4	CWK XXIX: 165, (E)	3173
JMK	DHR	1937	December	22	Dated letter	Keynes–King's	GTE/2/4/138		3174
DHR	JMK	1937	December	31	Dated letter	Keynes–King's Kahn–King's	GTE/2/4/143–6 RFK/13/57/296–9	CWK XIV: 227–9	3176
DHR	JMK	1937	December	31	Dated letter	Keynes–King's	GTE/2/4/135–7	CWK XIV: 226–7	3175
DHR	JMK	1938			Attributed	Keynes–King's	L/R/143		3055
DHR	JMK	1938	January	1	Dated letter	Keynes–King's	GTE/2/4/139–42	CWK XXIX: 166–8	3177
JMK	DHR	1938	January	3	Dated letter	Keynes–King's	GTE/2/4/147	CWK XXIX: 168, (E)	3178
JMK	DHR	1938	March	22	Dated letter	Keynes–King's	UA/5/4/23–4		3179
DHR	JMK	1938	March	23	Dated letter	Keynes–King's	UA/5/4/25–6		3180
JMK	DHR	1938	March	25	Dated letter	Keynes–King's	UA/5/4/27–8		3181
JMK	DHR	1938	March	30	Dated letter	Keynes–King's	GTE/2/4/164–5		3182
DHR	JMK	1938	May	5	Dated letter	Keynes–King's	GTE/2/4/166–8	CWK XXIX: 170, (E)	3183
JMK	DHR	1938	May	22	Dated letter	Keynes–King's	GTE/2/4/169	CWK XXIX: 171	3184
JMK	DHR	1938	May	22	Dated letter	Keynes–King's Keynes–King's	GTE/2/4/170–1 MM/5/41–2		3185
DHR	JMK	1938	May	28	Dated letter	Keynes–King's	GTE/2/4/172–3	CWK XXIX: 171, (E)	3186
JMK	DHR	1938	May	30	Dated letter	Keynes–King's	GTE/2/4/174–5	CWK XXIX: 171–2, (E)	3187
DHR	JMK	1938	June	1	Dated letter	Keynes–King's	GTE/2/4/176–7	CWK XXIX: 172–3, (E)	3188
DHR	JMK	1938	June	25	Dated letter	Keynes–King's	GTE/2/4/178–9	CWK XXIX: 178–9	3189
JMK	DHR	1938	July	10	Dated letter	Keynes–King's	GTE/2/4/181	CWK XXIX: 179	3190
DHR	JMK	1938	July	22	Dated letter	Keynes–King's	GTE/2/4/184	CWK XXIX: 180	3191
JMK	DHR	1938	July	25	Dated letter	Keynes–King's	GTE/2/4/185	CWK XXIX: 180–1	3192
DHR	JMK	1938	July	27	Dated letter	Keynes–King's	GTE/2/4/186	CWK XXIX: 181	3193
JMK	DHR	1938	July	29	Dated letter	Keynes–King's	GTE/2/4/187	CWK XXIX: 181	3194

JMK	DHR	1938	August	3	Dated letter	Keynes–King's	GTE/2/4/193	CWK XXIX: 183	3195
DHR	JMK	1938	August	4	Dated letter	Keynes–King's	GTE/2/4/194	CWK XXIX: 183–4	3196
JMK	DHR	1938	August	9	Dated letter	Keynes–King's	GTE/2/4/196	CWK XXIX: 184	3197
DHR	JMK	1938	August	11	Dated letter	Keynes–King's	GTE/2/4/197	CWK XXIX: 184	3198
DHR	JMK	1938	October	7	Dated letter	Keynes–King's	L/R/137–8		3199
JMK	DHR	1938	October	9	Dated letter	Robertson–Trinity	C2/6/33	Aslanbeigui and Oakes 2002: 32, (E)	3200
DHR	JMK	1938	October	11	Dated letter	Keynes–King's	L/R/141–2		3201
DHR	JMK	1939	November	25	Dated letter	Keynes–King's	W/3/28		3202
DHR	JMK	1940	March	6	Dated letter	Keynes–King's	HP/4/114–15	Moggridge 1992: 633, (E)	3203
JMK	DHR	1940	March	12	Dated letter	Keynes–King's	HP/4/116–18		3204
JMK	DHR	1940	December	27	Dated letter	Public Record Office	T247/126		3351
JMK	DHR	1941	January	23	Dated letter	Public Record Office	T247/52		3288
DHR	JMK	1941	March	23	Dated letter	Public Record Office	T247/48	CWK XXII: 338–41	3277
JMK	DHR	1941	March	27	Dated letter	Not found in the archives		CWK XXII: 342	3264
DHR	JMK	1941	March	27	Dated letter	Public Record Office	T236/300	CWK XXII: 341	3274
JMK	DHR	1941	March	28	Dated letter	Not found in the archives		CWK XXII: 342	3265
DHR	JMK	1941	March	31	Dated letter	Public Record Office	T236/300	CWK XXII: 343–4	3266
JMK	DHR	1941	April	1	Dated letter	Not found in the archives		CWK XXII: 344–5	3267
DHR	JMK	1941	April	2	Dated letter	Not found in the archives		CWK XXII: 345	3268
JMK	DHR	1941	April	2	Dated letter	Not found in the archives		CWK XXII: 346	3269
DHR	JMK	1941	April	2	Dated letter	Public Record Office	T247/48	CWK XXII: 346–7	3270

Table 2.1 continued

From	*To*	*Year*	*Month*	*Day*	*Date*	*Archive*		*Published in*	*Item*
DHR	JMK	1941	April	3	Dated letter	Public Record Office	T236/300		3275
JMK	DHR	1941	April	3	Dated letter	Public Record Office	T247/48		3289
JMK	DHR	1941	April	4	Dated letter	Public Record Office	T236/300		3276
JMK	DHR	1941	August		Attributed	Public Record Office	T247/53		3295
DHR	JMK	1941	November	10	Dated letter	Keynes–King's	L/P/6–10		3205
DHR	JMK	1941	November	27	Dated letter	Public Record Office	T 247/33	CWK XXV: 67	3206
DHR	JMK	1941	November	29	Dated letter	Kahn–King's	RFK/13/57/475–6		3207
JMK	DHR	1941	December	10	Dated letter	Keynes–King's	L/P/23		3208
DHR	JMK	1941	December	10	Dated letter	Keynes–King's	L/P/23		3209
DHR	JMK	1941	December	22	Dated letter	Public Record Office	T247/116	Skidelsky 2000: 224, (E)	3278
JMK	DHR	1941	December	29	Dated letter	Public Record Office	T247/116	Skidelsky 2000: 224, (E)	3279
DHR	JMK	1941	December	30	Dated letter	Public Record Office	T247/116		3280
DHR	JMK	1942	January	5	Dated letter	Keynes–King's	BA/1/60–1		3210
JMK	DHR	1942	February	19	Dated letter	Public Record Office	T247/69		3290
JMK	DHR	1942	June	14	Dated letter	Keynes–King's	LLK/3/14/1		3211
DHR	JMK	1942	June	15	Dated letter	Keynes–King's	LLK/3/14/1		3212
DHR	JMK	1942	June	15	Dated letter	Keynes–King's	LLK/3/14/1		3213
JMK	DHR	1942	June	15	Dated letter	Keynes–King's	LLK/3/14/1		3214
DHR	JMK	1942	July	7	Dated letter	Public Record Office	T247/73		5111

JMK	DHR	1942	July	10	Dated letter	Public Record Office	T247/74	3325
JMK	DHR	1942	July	13	Dated letter	Public Record Office	T247/73	3291
DHR	JMK	1942	July	13	Attributed	Public Record Office	T247/73	3292
JMK	DHR	1942	July	14	Dated letter	Public Record Office	T247/74	3326
JMK	DHR	1942	July	15	Dated letter	Public Record Office	T247/73	3293
DHR	JMK	1942	July	15	Dated letter	Public Record Office	T247/74	3327
DHR	JMK	1942	July	16	Dated letter	Public Record Office	T247/73	3294
JMK	DHR	1942	July	16	Dated letter	Public Record Office	T247/74	3328
DHR	JMK	1942	July	17	Dated letter	Public Record Office	T247/74	3329
DHR	JMK	1942	July	18	Dated letter	Public Record Office	T247/74	3330
JMK	DHR	1942	July	20	Dated letter	Public Record Office	T247/74	3331
DHR	JMK	1942	July	21	Dated letter	Public Record Office	T247/74	3332
DHR	JMK	1942	July	23	Dated letter	Public Record Office	T247/74	3333
DHR	JMK	1942	July	23	Dated letter	Public Record Office	T247/74	3334
JMK	DHR	1942	July	27	Dated letter	Public Record Office	T247/74	3335
DHR	JMK	1942	July	30	Dated letter	Public Record Office	T247/74	3336

Table 2.1 continued

From	*To*	*Year*	*Month*	*Day*	*Date*	*Archive*		*Published in*	*Item*
JMK	DHR	1942	August	6	Dated letter	Public Record Office	T247/10		3348
DHR	JMK	1942	August	7	Dated letter	Public Record Office	T247/33		3307
JMK	DHR	1942	August	10	Dated letter	Public Record Office	T247/33		3308
DHR	JMK	1942	September	15	Dated letter	Public Record Office	T247/74		3337
DHR	JMK	1942	December	18	Dated letter	Public Record Office	T247/2		3344
DHR	JMK	1943	January	15	Dated letter	Public Record Office	T247/10		3349
DHR	JMK	1943	January	16	Dated letter	Public Record Office	T247/2		3345
JMK	DHR	1943	January	22	Dated letter	Public Record Office	T247/10		3350
JMK	DHR	1943	January	25	Dated letter	Public Record Office	T247/93		3309
DHR	JMK	1943	January	25	Dated letter	Public Record Office	T247/93		3310
JMK	DHR	1943	January	27	Dated letter	Public Record Office	T247/93		3311
DHR	JMK	1943	January	28	Dated letter	Public Record Office	T247/93		3312
JMK	DHR	1943	January	28	Dated letter	Public Record Office	T247/93		3313
DHR	JMK	1943	January	29	Dated letter	Public Record Office	T247/93		3314

JMK	DHR	1943	February	4	Dated letter	Keynes–King's	BA/1/114		3215
DHR	JMK	1943	February	6	Dated letter	Keynes–King's	BA/1/114		3216
JMK	DHR	1943	February	19	Dated letter	Public Record Office	T247/30C		3305
DHR	JMK	1943	February	19	Dated letter	Public Record Office	T247/2		3346
DHR	JMK	1943	March	3	Dated letter	Public Record Office	T247/30A	CWK XXV: 228–9	3217
DHR	JMK	1943	March	5	Dated letter	Public Record Office	T247/30A	CWK XXV: 231	3218
DHR	JMK	1943	March	20	Dated letter	Public Record Office	T247/126		3352
JMK	DHR	1943	March	24	Dated letter	Public Record Office	T247/126		3353
JMK	DHR	1943	March	26	Dated letter	Public Record Office	T247/126		3354
DHR	JMK	1943	May	24	Dated letter	Public Record Office	T247/30A	CWK XXV: 285–7	3219
JMK	DHR	1943	June	2	Dated letter	Public Record Office	T247/30A	CWK XXV: 287–9	3220
JMK	DHR	1943	June	11	Dated letter	Public Record Office	T247/30 A	CWK XXV: 296–9	3221
DHR	JMK	1943	June	14	Dated letter	Public Record Office	T247/30A	CWK XXV: 299–300	3222
DHR	JMK	1943	June	28	Dated letter	Public Record Office	T247/81	CWK XXV: 300–2	3223
JMK	DHR	1943	July	1	Dated letter	Public Record Office	T247/30B		3321
DHR	JMK	1943	July	5	Dated letter	Public Record Office	T247/81		3302
DHR	JMK	1943	July	13	Dated letter	Robertson–Trinity	C2/8/17–18	CWK XXV: 314–16	3224
DHR	JMK	1943	July	13	Dated letter	Robertson–Trinity	C2/8/15–16		3247

Table 2.1 continued

From	*To*	*Year*	*Month*	*Day*	*Date*	*Archive*		*Published in*	*Item*
JMK	DHR	1943	July	19	Dated letter	Public Record Office	T247/81	CWK XXV: 302–4	3225
DHR	JMK	1943	July	22	Dated letter	Public Record Office	T236/300		3300
DHR	JMK	1943	July	24	Dated letter	Robertson–Trinity	C2/8/19		3250
JMK	DHR	1943	August	10	Dated letter	Public Record Office	T236/300		3273
DHR	JMK	1943	September	17	Dated letter	Public Record Office	T247/82		3301
DHR	JMK	1943	September	30	Dated letter	Public Record Office	T247/82		5110
JMK	DHR	1943	December	6	Dated letter	Public Record Office	T247/93		3315
DHR	JMK	1943	December	6	Attributed	Public Record Office	T247/30B		3322
JMK	DHR	1943	December	10	Dated letter	Public Record Office	T247/34		3283
JMK	DHR	1943	December	30	Dated letter	Public Record Office	T247/7		3316
JMK	DHR	1944	January	4	Dated letter	Public Record Office	T247/34		3284
JMK	DHR	1944	January	7	Dated letter	Public Record Office	T247/34		3285
DHR	JMK	1944	January	11	Dated letter	Public Record Office	T247/7		3317
JMK	DHR	1944	January	11	Dated letter	Public Record Office	T247/7		3318
DHR	JMK	1944	January	12	Dated letter	Public Record Office	T247/7		3319

JMK	DHR	1944	January	17	Dated letter	Public Record Office	T247/75		3339
DHR	JMK	1944	January	20	Dated letter	Public Record Office	T247/75		3340
JMK	DHR	1944	January	20	Dated letter	Public Record Office	T247/75		3341
DHR	JMK	1944	January	24	Dated letter	Robertson–Trinity	C2/8/20–3		3251
JMK	DHR	1944	January	26	Attributed	Public Record Office	T247/30B		3323
JMK	DHR	1944	February	1	Dated letter	Keynes–King's	BA/1/128		3226
JMK	DHR	1944	February	1	Dated letter	Public Record Office	T247/7		3320
DHR	JMK	1944	February	9	Dated letter	Keynes–King's	BA/1/142–3		3227
JMK	DHR	1944	February	11	Dated letter	Public Record Office	T247/34		3286
DHR	JMK	1944	February	26	Dated letter	Keynes–King's	BA/1/149–50		3228
DHR	JMK	1944	March	3	Dated letter	Public Record Office	T247/75		3342
JMK	DHR	1944	March	12	Dated letter	Public Record Office	T247/8		3347
JMK	DHR	1944	April	24	Dated letter	Keynes–King's	T247/74		3338
DHR	JMK	1944	May	22	Dated letter	Public Record Office	T247/28	CWK XXVI: 23–4	3256
DHR	JMK	1944	May	22	Dated letter	Not found in the archives		CWK XXII: 458	3271
DHR	JMK	1944	May	27	Dated letter	Public Record Office	T247/28	CWK XXVI: 24–5	3257
						Public Record Office	T247/28	CWK XXVI: 25–6	3258
JMK	DHR	1944	May	31	Dated letter	Public Record Office	T247/35		

Table 2.1 continued

From	*To*	*Year*	*Month*	*Day*	*Date*	*Archive*		*Published in*	*Item*
DHR	JMK	1944	June	8	Dated letter	Public Record Office	T247/28		3272
JMK	DHR	1944	July	2	Dated letter	Public Record Office	T247/51		3303
JMK	DHR	1944	July	4	Dated letter	Public Record Office	T247/38		3296
JMK	DHR	1944	July	8	Dated letter	Public Record Office	T247/69		3306
DHR	JMK	1944	July	9	Dated letter	Public Record Office	T247/51		3304
JMK	DHR	1944	July	11	Dated letter	Public Record Office	T247/69		3287
DHR	JMK	1944	July	11	Dated letter	Public Record Office	T247/38		3297
DHR	JMK	1944	July	18	Dated letter	Public Record Office	T247/35		3281
JMK	DHR	1944	July	18	Dated letter	Public Record Office	T247/35		3282
DHR	JMK	1944	July	31	Dated letter	Public Record Office	T247/38	CWK XXVI: 114–17	3259
DHR	JMK	1944	August	4	Dated letter	Public Record Office	T247/64		3324
JMK	DHR	1944	August	7	Dated letter	Public Record Office	T247/75		3343
JMK	DHR	1944	August	9	Dated letter	Public Record Office	T247/38	CWK XXVI: 117–21	3229
JMK	DHR	1944	August	14	Dated letter	Public Record Office	T247/64	CWK XXVI: 122–4	3230

DHR	JMK	1944	August	29	Dated letter	Public Record Office	T247/38	CWK XXVI: 124–7	3231
DHR	JMK	1944	September	20	Dated letter	Public Record Office	T247/38		3298
DHR	JMK	1944	September	21	Dated letter	Public Record Office	T247/38		3299
JMK	DHR	1944	December	29	Dated letter	Public Record Office	T247/38	CWK XXVI: 146–59	3260
DHR	JMK	1945	January		Attributed	Public Record Office	T247/39	CWK XXVI: 159–61, (E)	3232
DHR	JMK	1945	January	4	Dated letter	Keynes–King's	UA/5/6/78–9		3233
DHR	JMK	1945	January	21	Dated letter	Keynes–King's	W/10/132–3	CWK XXVI: 162–3	3234
JMK	DHR	1945	January	23	Dated letter	Keynes–King's Public Record Office	W/10/134–5 T247/39	CWK XXVI: 163, (E)	3235
JMK	DHR	1945	February	7	Dated letter	Keynes–King's	BA/1/141		3236
DHR	JMK	1945	February	8	Dated letter	Keynes–King's	BA/1/141		3237
JMK	DHR	1945	February	8	Dated letter	Public Record Office	T247/39	CWK XXVI: 163–4	3238
DHR	JMK	1945	February	12	Dated letter	Public Record Office	T247/39	CWK XXVI: 164–5	3239
DHR	JMK	1945	February	17	Dated letter	Public Record Office	T247/39	CWK XXVI: 167	3241
JMK	DHR	1945	April	14	Dated letter	Public Record Office	T247/40	CWK XXVI: 166–7	3240
DHR	JMK	1945	June	14	Dated letter	Keynes–King's	RES/1/2/215–16		3242
JMK	DHR	1946	January	1	Dated letter	Keynes–King's	UA/5/6/73–4		3243
DHR	JMK	1946	January	4	Dated letter	Keynes–King's	UA/5/6/75–7		3244
DHR	JMK	1946	January	22	Dated letter	Keynes–King's	BA/1/192–3		3245
DHR	JMK	1946	February	11	Dated letter	Keynes–King's	BA/1/204		3246

3 A goodwilling outsider

The correspondence between Keynes and Harrod

Daniele Besomi

The extant correspondence between Harrod and Keynes consists of 233 letters, notes and postcards (145 of which sent in the inter-war years), dated between 1922 and 1946 (see Table 3.1).[1] The correspondence described below (94–106) is published in Keynes's CWK XIII and XIV.[2] The entire inter-war correspondence is published (or, at least, cited) in *The Collected Interwar Papers and Correspondence of Roy Harrod* (Harrod 2003).

What follows is a brief description of the themes taken up in the correspondence, with reference to the recent literature regarding these exchanges. It should be noted that most of these exchanges are occasional in origin: although Harrod and Keynes frequently commented upon their respective writings (Harrod's writings were often sent to Keynes as editor of the *Economic Journal* or the Cambridge Economic Handbooks), there lacks that systematic exchange of views and cross-checking which characterise, for instance, the correspondence between Keynes and Kahn, or Keynes and Robertson. Although Harrod, who was based in Christ Church, Oxford, was later identified as a member of the Cambridge group, probably because of an erroneous deduction based on his role as Keynes's official biographer (in this, scholars were encouraged by a number of rather bold remarks regarding Harrod's own role in the development of Keynes's thought, which are not supported by the extant evidence) and commentator upon the *General Theory*, close examination of the correspondence shows that at several crucial stages in the evolution of Keynes's thought Harrod was unaware of the developments taking place.

Harrod seems to have perceived that after the *Treatise on Money* something rather radical was going on in Cambridge, and in fact frequently inquired of Keynes himself and others (with Robertson occasionally throwing out hints).[3] The first (weak) evidence of Harrod's inquisitiveness dates from May 1933, when he invited Keynes to expound the sort of things he was writing about before the Luncheon Club; Keynes, however, declined in order to be able to be master of a reasonable proportion of his own time (letter 1192, 3 May 1933, Harrod 2003: 221). On 27 October 1933 (letter 1194, Harrod 2003: 229) Keynes promised that he would let

Harrod see his argument on Pigou's theory of unemployment, but on 30 December he explained that he found it 'impossible to make [his] points successfully without bringing in a quantity of [his] unpublished theorising, for which there would not be room, and which would be out of place in a brief note', and he abandoned the idea (letter 1195, Harrod 2003: 259; for context see below: 96–7). The matter seems to have remained at that, as a year later the correspondence with Kahn reveals that Harrod was completely in the dark as to the main developments of Keynes's thought, and was eager to learn. On 15 October 1934 he wrote to Kahn criticising Haberler's and Robertson's views on the saving-investment relationship, pointing out that the 'system of JMK' (referring to the *Treatise* definition of saving) was 'somewhat complicated' and explaining that he was 'very impatient to know his revised version' (letter 1357, in Harrod 2003: 299–301). Kahn, not having understood that Harrod was referring to the *Treatise*, was bewildered that Harrod did not appreciate the beauty and simplicity of the saving = investment truism to be incorporated in the *General Theory*. Kahn also explained that he and Keynes no longer thought in terms of prices (letter 1359, 22 October 1934, Harrod 2003: 309). In his reply Harrod again stated that he was impatient for Keynes's new book (letter 1360, 25 October 1934, Harrod 2003: 310), and, after Kahn had explained that talking of a difference between saving and investment makes no sense (letter 1361, 28 October 1934, Harrod 2003: 318), Harrod finally gathered that the old system was 'now thrown overboard', and again asked for something to be written soon (letter 1362, 29 October 1934, Harrod 2003: 320). On 1 November Kahn started 'tutoring' Harrod on the saving = investment truism (letter 1363), which Harrod found paradoxical and frightening (letter 1364, 2 November 1934, Harrod 2003: 324–5).

The exchange continued with Kahn writing that he fully agreed with the earlier part of Harrod's letter but adding – after realising that Harrod did not accept the statement that saving and investment cannot determine the rate of interest – that he 'was brought up with a damaging jar', and concluding that Harrod was 'one of the few economists in the whole world on whom Maynard can reckon' (letter 1366, 13 November 1934, Harrod 2003: 341–2). Harrod (probably quite flattered) replied by requesting that the new versions be 'expressed in terms which are used in marginal analysis, so that it can be fitted in to the corpus of economic theory such as it is' (letter 1367, 17 November 1934, Harrod 2003: 345–6), and Kahn assured him that Keynes was aware of the importance of this (letter 1368, 24 November 1934, Harrod 2003: 353).

Harrod's next recorded opportunity to glean a fragment of Keynes's ideas took place on 21 February 1935, when Keynes spoke to the Oxford economists on 'the marginal efficiency of capital and the rate of interest' (JMK to Meade, 10 January 1935, JMK papers, PS/6: 13; Keynes's engagement diary, 1935, JMK papers, PP/41): later, Harrod recollected that the saving = investment argument 'convinced no one' (letter 1210, 1 August 1935, CWK XII: 531).

The exchange with Kahn proves that Harrod was unaware of Keynes's argument, and remained unconvinced when tutored on it. It is not known whether Kahn informed Keynes, but the audience's reaction to Keynes's speech in Oxford is likely to have made Keynes aware of Harrod's doubts. Why, then, was Harrod sent the proofs of the *General Theory* for comments?

I do not think the fact they strongly agreed on policy (see below: 96) would be a sufficient reason. The explanation lies in part in the fact that Keynes undoubtedly had a high opinion on Harrod's intellectual capacities[4] and in part must be sought precisely in Harrod's partial sympathy only for Keynes's new ideas. Keynes relied on friends and sympathetic commentators when developing his views, but these could not also act as critics. For this role, Keynes needed goodwilling outsiders: Robertson was becoming hypercritical and was in any case no longer available at the final, crucial stage of revision, and Harrod surely was a good alternative candidate for the job. The conclusion of the correspondence with Keynes on the *General Theory* seems to confirm this interpretation: Keynes was content that *even Harrod* could not make the classical theory make sense (letter 1225, 25 September 1935, CWK XIII: 561; the passage is quoted below: 98).

Harrod's international economics

Harrod met Keynes in July 1922, attended his lectures during the following term and submitted his essays to him. At the time, Harrod was granted leave by Christ Church to catch up with (or, rather, get acquainted with) Economics. The episode is recalled in Harrod's *The Life of John Maynard Keynes* (1951: 317–25). Two letters from Keynes to Harrod are extant regarding this episode (letters 1151 and 1152, 21 July and 15 August 1922), and Keynes's diaries attest to five meetings to discuss Harrod's essays.

This acquaintance was enough to induce Keynes to accept Hubert Henderson's suggestion to invite Harrod to contribute a book on *International Economics* for the Cambridge Economic Handbooks series (letters 1162–1164, 27 January to 4 February 1927, Harrod 2003: 85–7). At the outset Harrod was unprepared to tackle the subject; then, in 1928, he suffered a nervous breakdown which prevented him from working on the book for several months. He resumed the project only towards the end of 1931. In March 1932 he read a paper on the 'Theory of Balance of Foreign Payments' before the Marshall Society, which stimulated some correspondence with Kahn in which Harrod apparently expounded the first version of his foreign trade multiplier (letters 1352 and 1353, 24 March and 18 April 1932, Harrod 2003: 144–6 and 153). By April 1932

Harrod was ready to submit an initial draft of the book to Robertson (Assistant Editor of the Series). In November he had a long exchange with James Meade on the foreign trade multiplier, and in December 1932–January 1933 discussed it with Keynes (letters 1182–1185, 26 December 1932 to 31 January 1933).[5]

This correspondence is interesting in that Keynes failed to understand the implications of Harrod's foreign trade multiplier. Keynes criticised Harrod's exposition of his 'self-regulating theory of the foreign balance' for appearing to be 'independent of the policy pursued by the Central Bank'. Keynes thought that Harrod's kind of analysis was 'very interesting in itself', but required the explicit introduction of a number of assumptions:

> You really have primarily in mind, I think, the abstract case when there is no banking and no foreign investment, where a loss of gold depletes private balances pari passu and where individuals 'automatically' reduce their spending in order to restore their balances. But this is quite unrealistic.
>
> (letter 1182, 26 December 1932, Harrod 2003: 194)[6]

After further discussion, both through correspondence and *viva voce*, Harrod introduced two sections in his chapter VI (and probably radically redrafted the remainder of it) where he analysed equilibrium and the transition in simplified conditions. These satisfied Keynes, who asked for further revision of the section on 'International Capital Movements' without, however, 'criticising the substance of [Harrod's] argument' (letter 1184, 25 January 1933, Harrod 2003: 199).

A similar situation arose in 1937, when Keynes again discussed the foreign trade multiplier with Robertson (see below: 100 and Besomi 2000b). However, Keynes approved of Harrod's exposition of the Comparative Costs doctrine.

Although no longer having any editorial responsibility for the CEH series, Keynes also commented on Harrod's 1939 second edition of the book (letter 1294, 20 October 1938, summarised in Harrod 2003: 891).

The invention of 'marginal revenue'

In July 1928, Harrod submitted to Keynes a short article for the *Economic Journal*, 'Notes on Monopoly and Quasi-Competition',[7] where the concept of the 'marginal revenue' was first presented. Keynes was favourably impressed by this part of the article and the corresponding diagram, but had some reservations about Harrod's discussion of the implication of his curve on cartels. Keynes then handed the paper to Ramsey, who also criticised Harrod's discussion of cartels while appreciating the diagrams themselves. The paper was rejected, but Keynes suggested that Harrod should elaborate on the notion of marginal revenue (letters 1168–1174, 7 July to 1 August 1928, Harrod 2003: 94–103). Harrod was prevented from doing so by the nervous breakdown mentioned above;[8] he took up the matter again several months later, replied to Ramsey's criticism, and the paper was eventually published as 'Notes on Supply' in the *Economic Journal* 1930 – too late for Harrod's claims to priority. Harrod's close account of the episode is given in *The Life of John Maynard Keynes* (Harrod 1951: 159 fn.)

Harrod goes public on policy

Between 1932 and 1934, Harrod wrote a number of letters on monetary policy to the Press and promoted a few collective letters to *The Times*. These were often discussed with Keynes, either as he was invited to sign them or in order to co-ordinate publication with Keynes's own writings (in particular with *The Means to Prosperity*). Keynes approved of Harrod's 'admirable' letter to *The Economist* on 'Monetary Policy' (Harrod 1932c), which expresses 'the *sense* of the matter' (letter 1178, 6 June 1932, Harrod 2003: 156), as also of his 'most excellent article' for *The Times* on 'The Dilemma in the Economy' (Harrod 1932a), where reflationary measures aimed at bringing prices back to the level of 1929 were advocated (letters 1180 and 1181, both dated 4 November 1932, Harrod 2003: 184–5) and of 'Trade of the World' (Harrod 1933b) (letter 1191, 23 April 1933). In February and March 1933 the exchanges regarded the publication of Keynes's *Means to Prosperity* and Harrod's collective letter 'More Money in Circulation', published respectively on 13 to 16 March and 10 March 1933 in *The Times* (letters 1187–1189, 25 and 28 February 1933, summarised in Harrod 2003: 204–5). Harrod and the other signatories suggested that reflation should be carried through by means of a division of the budget into expenditure on current account and expenditure on capital account, the former to be balanced out of income and the latter to be 'financed by borrowing and explicitly used as a means for injecting new credit into active circulation'.

Harrod's review of Pigou's *Theory of Unemployment*

In October 1933, Harrod submitted to Keynes a review article on Pigou's *Theory of Unemployment*. Keynes did not know what to do with it, as Macgregor had already commissioned a review from Beveridge, and Keynes planned to write something of his own on the subject. Beveridge eventually declined, and Keynes decided against expounding his criticism before making public the line of argument that was to become the *General Theory*; Harrod's article was thus revised on the basis of Keynes's critical remarks, and published in the *Economic Journal* in 1934 (for details on the negotiations see Young 1989: 42–6). Unfortunately, only Keynes's side of the correspondence is extant (letters 1193, 10 October 1933; 1194, 27

October 1933; 1198, 13 January 1934, all reproduced in Harrod 2003: 226–30 and 264), but it does have the particular interest that Keynes outlines his method of criticism of the classical theory (on which see Carabelli 1991):

> Perhaps I should myself have attributed rather more blame to him for so perpetually tacitly introducing assumptions which are neither realistic nor explicit. One knows with the Prof. that there is generally some hypothesis from which his conclusions follow. But he seldom tells one what it is, and I doubt whether he usually knows himself. And the job of working backwards to discover what the hypothesis must be is tiresome as well as difficult.
>
> (letter 1198, 13 January 1934, Harrod 2003: 264)

Keynes's *General Theory* and Harrod's 'Mr. Keynes and Traditional Theory'

The correspondence between Keynes and Harrod on the proofs of the *General Theory* is well known, being published in CWK XIII: 526–65 (letters 1205, 1209–1226, 26 June – misdated 5 June in CWK XIII – to 27 September 1935). Besides a number of remarks on specific passages, the main debate regarded Harrod's criticism of Keynes's attack on the traditional theory of interest. While Harrod appreciated the 'positive doctrine' of books III and IV, he did not endorse the violence or content of Keynes's attack on traditional theory: 'the view that I object to lies in the argument that because saving must always and necessarily equal net investment (which I accept) there is 'no sense' in the view that interest is a price which equates the demand for saving in the shape of investment to the supply which results from the community's propensity to save' (letter 1210, 1 August 1935, CWK XIII: 530).

Harrod contended that the classical theory of interest was not nonsense or, as he himself put it, 'inconsistent or confused on its own premises' (letter 1220, 22 August 1935, CWK XIII: 546) but, rather, simply erroneous, being founded on a false premise: 'the classical theory is invalid but not nonsense' (letter 1215, 12 August 1935, CWK XIII: 540). In fact Harrod agreed with Keynes that the orthodox theory implicitly assumed that income was constant. Harrod interpreted this hypothesis as one of the *ceteris paribus* clauses necessary to determine the equilibrium price level (in this case, interest) from demand and supply curves (namely, investment and saving). Keynes replied by specifying that the saving and investment functions are not independent (letter 1214, 9 August 1935, CWK XIII: 537–9), and that therefore there is no question of their intersecting and enabling one to find the rate of interest. He disagreed with Harrod's opinion that the traditional theory maintained its cogency if one assumed that the level of income was given: 'one can only invent a meaning for the classical ideas, if one assumes that income and employment cannot change' (letter 1216, 14 August 1935, CWK XIII: 541). In fact

> if either the propensity to save or the marginal efficiency curve changes, the level of income changes; so that the assumption of a given level of income involves us in assuming that neither of the classical theory's own chosen variables is capable of change, – unless there are changes in certain factors which happen by a miracle to be such as to leave income unchanged (and in this case it is the nature of the miracle which determines the rate of interest)
>
> (letter 1223, 14 September 1935, CWK XIII: 558)

Keynes's and Harrod's remarks concluding the exchange bear witness to the incompatibility of their viewpoints. Keynes sarcastically concluded: 'I am content! If the classical theory could not be made, even by you, to make more coherent sense than that, it does not deserve very many compliments' (letter 1225, 25 September 1935, CWK XIII: 561); Harrod, somewhat depressed, lamented: 'I deplore all the more attacks from ill-chosen ground' (letter 1226, 27 September 1935, CWK XIII: 562).

Looking back at this debate a few weeks later Harrod recorded that his attack on Keynes's criticism of the classical theory of saving and investment had 'only succeeded in getting the most offending chapter printed in smaller type as an appendix. I regret them, I feel they will raise unnecessary dust – but there it is, that is his way' (letter from RFH to DHR, 7 October 1935, Harrod 2003: 444–5).[9]

Even before the *General Theory* was published, Harrod was planning to write a 'posh piece' explaining the relationship of Keynes's book with the traditional theory, in particular Robertson's. Harrod first read his piece before the Oxford Political Economy Club in May 1936, and a revised version was read before the Econometric Society meeting in Oxford in September 1936. Keynes was sent a draft of the latter on 24 August 1936 (the draft is in JMK Papers, GTE/2/2: 41–63), and commented upon it in the subsequent exchange (letters 1235–1238, 24 August to 7 October 1936) – which is printed in CWK XIV: 83–6, with the exception of letter 1238 (Harrod 2003: 585).[10]

'Mr. Keynes and Traditional Theory' has been interpreted as providing the first rendition of the IS-LM model: Warren Young demonstrated that a preliminary draft of the paper was read by Hicks and Meade, and that there is a striking similarity between the corresponding equations. Both the paper itself and Harrod's previous correspondence with Keynes on the *General Theory* make the view untenable that Harrod interpreted the *General Theory* along the IS-LM lines. Harrod's 'equations', in fact, were not meant to express functional relationships between variables, to be solved as a system of equations, but only as a counter for the number of unknowns and the number of causal relationships. Harrod's purpose was to show that Keynes did not revolutionise economics, but only rearranged the 'pieces' of the traditional approach (Harrod 1937c: 85): he thus listed the variables to be determined, and the relationships to be used for that purpose, comparing Keynes's to the orthodox ones.

Even if interpreted as proper equations, however, the set proposed by Harrod should not be mistaken for an IS-LM model: the latter, in fact, is essentially a *simultaneous equations* model, where everything determines everything else. Harrod, on the contrary, interpreted the *General Theory* as a *causally structured* system:

> Your view, as I understand it is broadly this:
>
> | | |
> |---|---|
> | Volume of investment determined by | { marg. efficiency of cap. schedule
rate of interest |
> | Rate of interest determined by | { liquidity preference schedule
quantity of money |
> | Volume of employment determined by | { volume of investment
multiplier |
> | Value of multiplier determined by | propensity to save. |
>
> (letter 1222, 30 August 1935, CWK XIII: 553)

Of course, in a closed system where the number of equations equals the number of unknowns there is 'mutual dependency' (Harrod 1937c: 83). But this only means that changes in any variable, e.g. in money wages, would determine a chain of events which eventually involves the whole system, not that everything is determined at once. Actually some links are 'very indirect', and their ultimate effect depends on factors such as expectations and preferences rather than on the mechanical interplay of the endogenous variables (ibid.: 84).

Harrod on dynamics and method

The discussions between Harrod and Keynes regarding dynamics began in March 1935, when Harrod started experimenting with the acceleration principle. The extant one-sided correspondence with Keynes (letters 1202 and 1203, 21 and 28 March 1935, Harrod 2003: 389–90) and Kahn indicates that Harrod was seeking some connection between this principle and the Austrian notion of 'roundaboutness'. As for Keynes, it reveals that he had never 'been able to know exactly how roundaboutness was measured! I confess that I was assuming that when the volume of investment increased, roundaboutness increased, and I have never yet seen a definition of the latter which made it possible to distinguish between the two' (letter 1202, 21 March 1935). Keynes's interpretation that 'the Austrians, in so far as they have any precise ideas, have been disposed to measure roundaboutness by amount of capital per head; in which case, increased roundaboutness is necessarily the same as an increase in investment' derived from Hill (1933) and Gifford (1933) (letter 1203, 28 March 1935).

The matter was taken up again in 1937 (letters 1239–1241, 17–19 February 1937, Harrod 2003: 634–36), after Harrod had implicitly used his notion of technological progress in *The Trade Cycle*. It was also discussed with J. Robinson (see Ch. 12: 318–19) and Hawtrey, and taken up – albeit in a different context – with Kaldor in 1938.[11]

The Trade Cycle was written between January and May 1936 (see, for a chronology, Besomi 1999a, Ch. 3). In February Harrod announced to Keynes that he was writing it (letter 1233, 19 February 1936); the book was printed in September, but Keynes did not read it until early 1937. The first comments were not addressed to Harrod but to Robertson in February, when Keynes expressed some doubts about the foreign trade multiplier (see above: 95). At the end of March, Keynes sent some lecture notes and miscellaneous notes (attached to letter 1243, 31 March 1937, CWK XIV: 150–63), which were characterized by a major misunderstanding as he failed to realise that Harrod's trade cycle theory argument was based on deviations from a moving equilibrium, rather than fluctuations around a stationary state. Harrod explained this using arithmetical examples (letters 1244 and 1245, 6–7 April 1937, CWK XIV: 163–70). Keynes acknowledged his mistake in the following letter, and offered a formula summarising the equilibrium growth rate as $100/(MR-1)$, where M and R represent the multiplier and the acceleration coefficient (*Relation*, in Harrod's terminology) (letter 1246, 12 April 1937, CWK XIV: 170–3). This bears striking similarities to the 'fundamental equation' of Harrod's 'Essay in Dynamic Theory'. The letter spurred Harrod into action, and eventually led him to elaborate his theory into the 'Essay in Dynamic Theory'.

This exchange anticipates many of the misinterpretations of Harrod's cycles and growth theory in the post-war secondary literature. First, Harrod's insistence that his dynamic method requires thinking of continuous changes, as opposed to Keynes's emphasis on *once over* changes typical of economic statics (letter 1244, 6 April 1937, CWK XIV: 163–4), provides the background for Harrod's later stress on instantaneous dynamics. The moving equilibrium is characterised by continuous and harmonious growth of all the variables involved, and the appropriate method of analysis is to focus on the internal proportions at a point in time. But when these are disrupted the consequences are cumulative, and the focus is shifted to the instability of equilibrium:

> The essential point is that once the rate of increase of income slows down by more than a microscopic amount, the absolute amount of

> investment must fall: and this in turn leads to a decrease of income: and that to a fall of investment to zero aside from long period planning.
>
> (letter 1245, 7 April 1937, CWK XIV: 165)

And finally, Harrod looks into the causes and consequences of the rupture of equilibrium, both lying in the changes in the multiplier and the accelerator:

> I quite agree with what you say about the necessity of supposing that forces operate upon both the Relation and the Multiplier to distort them from normal in boom and slump. So far as the Multiplier is concerned, I have referred, as you recognize, to the shift to profit. But I have not assumed the Relation constant either. cf. p. 59 [of Harrod 1936b] where I have referred to 2 forces, viz. changes in interest rate, and changes in relative prices of goods (on which you lay stress in your paper) tending to alter the Relation. And I refer anyhow to the first of these in the subsequent argument.
>
> (letter 1245, 7 April 1937, CWK XIV: 165)

Harrod's approach, however, seems to have been somewhat distant from Keynes's, as in spite of Harrod's careful explanations Keynes failed to understand Harrod's point when reformulated a year later in the 'Essay in Dynamic Theory' (on which see below).[12]

Meanwhile, in December 1937 Harrod was elected President of Section F of the British Association. His presidential address on 'Scope and Method of Economics' was discussed with Keynes between July and September 1938. Keynes also added some methodological remarks concerning a draft of Tinbergen's League of Nations inquiry (Harrod was among those who attended some League of Nations preparatory meetings, in September 1937 in Geneva and in July 1938 in Cambridge). The correspondence (letters 1258, 1260–1263, 1265–1270, 1272, 1283, 1286, 1288 and 1290–1291, 24 January to 21 September 1938) is partly printed in CWK XIV: 295–305 (complete transcriptions in Harrod 2003), and is frequently referred to in the literature. On the relevance of this exchange to Harrod's thought see Besomi (1999a, Ch. 5).

This correspondence is of interest as it reflects the difference in Keynes's and Harrod's views on modelling in economics. Harrod seemed to attribute a twofold task to scientific models. On the one hand, they are called upon to 'bring order to the chaos' by organising the relevant concepts in a consistent framework. In other words, the model was conceived as an instrument of thought necessary for *interpretation* of the apparent heterogeneity of the immediately perceived experiences. Accordingly, Harrod saw the preliminary formulation of his dynamics as providing 'a method of thinking, a way of approach to certain problems' (Harrod 1939: 15). On the other hand, Harrod thought that between the model and the world there may be (as an ideal of knowledge, at least) a complete isomorphism; the model was therefore called upon to provide a *representation* of 'the external world' (title of Ch. 2 of *The Known and the Unknown*, 1940/41, unpublished manuscript, of which 14 chapters are extant in HP V–70 and HP V–71), and – as a corollary – to enable prediction (on the hermeneutic *vs.* the predictive views on models see for instance Borutti 1985, in particular section 4).

When Harrod's essay on 'Scope and Method' came into Keynes's hands, this ambiguity did not pass unnoticed. In fact, Keynes remarked that 'economics is a branch of logic, a way of thinking', and criticised Harrod for not having repelled 'sufficiently firmly attempts à la Schultz to turn it into a pseudo-natural science':

> it is of the essence of a model that one does *not* fill in real values for the variable functions. To do so would make it useless as a model. For as soon as this is done, the model loses its generality and its value as a mode of thought. [. . .] The object of statistical study is not so much to fill in missing variables with a view to prediction, as to test the relevance and validity of the model.
>
> (letter 1267, 4 July 1938, CWK XIV: 296)

Keynes, by his own process of thought, had at the time of reading Harrod's presidential address already fully developed the implications of the notion of models as 'an instrument of thought' (letter 1269, 10 July 1938, CWK XIV: 299, misdated 16 July), and had reached the conclusion that the heterogeneity through time of the object of economics and its lack of uniformity and regularity oppose the nature of economic thinking to that of 'the typical natural science' (letters 1267 and 1269 of 4 and 10 July, CWK XIV: 296 and 299). His criticism of Harrod did not therefore regard the heuristic quality of the model: accordingly, Keynes stressed that he did not expect Harrod to differ much from his own reflections (see CWK XIV: 297 and 299). What Keynes was criticising was the model's rigidity, derived from Harrod's belief that scientific handling of facts is possible only as far as these show some persistence, i.e. as far as nature reveals some uniformity, which implied that axioms and maxims could be fixed once and for all.

> One can make some quite worth while progress merely by using your axioms and maxims. But one cannot get very far except by devising new and improved models. This requires, as you say, 'a vigilant observation of the actual working of our system'. Progress in economics consists almost entirely in a progressive improvement in the choice of models. [. . .] Economics is a science of thinking in terms of models joined to the art of choosing models which are relevant to the contemporary world.
>
> (letter 1267, 4 July 1938, CWK XIV: 296)

Keynes therefore contrasted Harrod's interpretation of the empirical generalisations, in terms of axioms giving rise to qualitative equations with parameters to be filled in, with the *art* of choosing new and improved models. Both Harrod's and Keynes's starting point presupposed 'vigilant observation'. But while Harrod, like Tinbergen, aimed at establishing the general laws and afterwards at specifying their functional form, Keynes did not rely on induction merely as a procedure of empirical research. On the contrary, he interpreted it as providing the logical foundation for the scientific role of *analogy* (Carabelli 1988, Ch. 4). But analogy is a *selective* process, for it highlights certain features and neglects others. The difficulty lying in 'the art of choosing models which are relevant to the contemporary world' thus translates Keynes's awareness that the language (e.g. differential equations) used for asking questions to a specific object of analysis constrains the replies of the object within the limitations of that formalism. Keynes knew that a risk is incurred where judgements as to what is essential in the analogy point at the wrong properties, so that transferring a language from one domain to another may mutilate the object under consideration. Hence Keynes's insistence that 'The specialist in the manufacture of models will not be successful unless he is constantly correcting his judgement by intimate and messy acquaintance with the facts to which his model has to be applied' (letter 1269, 10 July 1938, CWK XIV: 300).

Despite Keynes's insistence, Harrod only conceded that the quantitative value of parameters needed re-estimating from time to time (letter 1268, 6 July 1938, CWK XIV: 297) and that the most important task is that of getting a suitable model (ibid.: 298). However, he glossed over Keynes's point that inserting figures destroys the heuristic value of the model. This suggests that Harrod did not appreciate Keynes's argument of the incompatibility of the two views of the cognitive role of models.

The correspondence does not enable us to ascertain whether Harrod later changed his mind, for the subject of the debate shifted from his methodological essay to Keynes's disagreement with Tinbergen. Harrod maintained that Keynes somewhat misdirected his attack, and suggested a different interpretation of Tinbergen's aim and procedure. However, he did not explicitly take a stand in favour of or against the econometricians' use of statistics. Nevertheless, some clues regarding Harrod's attitude on this problem can be found in 'Scope and Method of Economics', where he observed that the econometricians' lag theory of the cycle 'would be self-consistent and consistent with the generalisations of theory, and also subject to fairly approximate empirical verification at both ends' (Harrod 1938: 409). This comment suggests that, in spite of Keynes's criticism, Harrod remained faithful to the representative conceptions of models. As a matter of fact, he saw the filling in of the values of the parameters as a possible line of development of the framework of ideas outlined in his 'Essay in Economic Dynamics' (Oxford Economists' Research Group,

'Report of the meeting held on Monday 22nd May 1939 at Christ Church', in Andrews and Brunner papers:[13] 171).

Harrod incorporated his methodological reflections in his famous 'Essay in Dynamic Theory', written in July 1938 and submitted to Keynes early in August for publication (the draft is published as Harrod 1996). This gave rise to an intense exchange of correspondence (letters 1271, 1272, 1274, 1276–1278, 1281, 1282, 1285, 1287, 1289, 1292, 1293 and 1295–1297, 6 August 1938 to 18 March 1939), which is printed in CWK XIV: 321–50.

The main feature of this exchange consists in Harrod's and Keynes's incapacity to recognise the problems either were discussing. Harrod was arguing in terms of *instantaneous* growth rates, making a photograph of the simultaneous relationships characterising equilibrium at one moment in time: he acknowledged that his parameters changed as the cycle progressed, and indeed his cycle theory depended on this; but his limited understanding of mathematics did not allow him to express it in formal terms, and he had therefore to limit his range to an interval in which the parameters could be taken as constant: strictly speaking, an instant. Keynes did not appreciate Harrod's methodological point (which was indeed far from clear), and insisted on expectations and change, which imply the flow of time. Harrod, in turn, did not understand Keynes's point. As a result, Harrod dropped most of the sections where he described his trade cycle theory (they were condensed in a few paragraphs only), thereby giving the impression that the *Essay* was concerned with growth rather than cycles.

Albeit in a different form, the misunderstandings between Harrod and Keynes still concern the same points discussed a year earlier with respect to *The Trade Cycle*: 'dynamics at one point of time' (absurd as the concept may appear) reflects the methodological distinction of continuous *vs.* discrete variations; the changes in the multiplier and the accelerator are excluded from the 'first stage of dynamics' (concerning equilibrium and its stability), while Keynes insisted that the analysis of stability means inquiring into what happens to the parameters while the changes are taking place. As Keynes had the benefit of discussing Harrod's approach with its author and failed to accept it (and, to some extent, to understand it), it is not surprising that in the post-war years Harrod's dynamics was frequently misunderstood precisely on the points discussed here.

Besides the above-mentioned issues, Keynes also suggested a number of amendments, some of which were eventually introduced in the final version (see, for a comparison of the draft and the final version, the appendix to the draft: Harrod 1996).[14]

Wartime correspondence

Early in September 1939 Harrod solicited Hawtrey, Beveridge and Keynes to 'remember the existence of the still job-less Roy' (letter 1298, 4 September 1939; some passages transcribed in Harrod 2003: 904) in case the Treasury needed personnel for the war effort. Keynes took the matter to heart, and wrote to the Second Secretary to the Treasury suggesting that Harrod's name be included in the list they were preparing. Harrod himself transcribed (in his post-war handwriting) the passages regarding himself:

> There is one other man [viz. other than Kahn] I think it would be worth for Whale to put on your special list, namely Roy Harrod, of Christ Church, Oxford. His qualities are not quite the same as Kahn's, but he is another of the people I should pick out as of absolutely the right temperament & qualification for the Treasury. Harrod is an exceptionally good and rapid worker on paper and can get through quite a vast amount of things very quietly and efficiently. When the time comes that you want to stiffen up with people in the '30s of the right sort of experience and the kind of efficiency which would have got them in very near the top of the Class I Examination, Kahn & Harrod would be my pick.[15]

The position never materialised and Harrod joined Lindemann's S-branch.[16] This did not prevent him from being Keynes's 'most prolific correspondent' (Moggridge 1992: 676) at the time of the preparation of the Clearing Union and related proposals. During the war 60 letters were exchanged between Harrod and Keynes, a number of which accompanied memoranda becoming the subject of lengthy discussions between them. Harrod described himself as bombarding Keynes with 'memoranda in favour of co-operation with America, of a world bank, etc.' (Harrod 1951: 531), and these indeed constitute the main bulk of the correspondence.[17]

The two main themes were the Clearing Union (Keynes's 'Eutopia': letter 1332, 7 August 1942) and Buffer Stocks control. The discussion concerned technical aspects (the issues at stake are described by Skidelsky 2000, Ch. 6 §5 and Ch. 7 §1, respectively, where Keynes's important concessions to Harrod are detailed) but also diplomatic issues and the plans' philosophies. In particular, against Keynes's internationalism, Harrod insisted on favouring the Anglo-American relationship, on the grounds that while some desirable measures did require indeed some sort of international body, the intervention of individual governments should be co-ordinated by an Anglo-American Service which ought to be able to lay out a framework of action immediately, while other countries would join at a later stage (letter 1315, 4 May 1942). This attitude reflects Harrod's long-standing conviction that Britain should lead the world's economic policy (an article for the *Daily Telegraph* in 1933 was titled 'Britain's Lead in Currency Policy': Harrod 1933e; numerous other examples are to be found in Harrod 2003, vol. 3), and guides

Harrod's own narration of these events in his *Life of Keynes* (Harrod 1951: 531–4).

Conclusion

The occasional frequent exchanges of correspondence between Keynes and Harrod[18] offer precious material for the understanding of their respective positions on a number of issues. Harrod's ideas were more often subjected to criticism by Keynes than vice versa, especially in his capacity of Editor of the *Economic Journal*. Keynes also felt the need to submitting the proofs of the *General Theory* to Harrod's criticism, as sympathetic reader far enough from the Cambridge debates to be able to look at the book with the necessary detachment. In both cases, the results are illuminating, for both friends had inquisitive minds and were able to bring to light subtle problems lying behind the original formulations and were forced to make explicit a number of tacit assumptions and special viewpoints that characterise their thought. Not only would Harrod's and Keynes's writings have been different if these exchanges had not taken place, but our understanding of these issues would have been more difficult if the correspondence had not been preserved for future interpretation.

Notes

1 They are kept in part among the Keynes papers at King's College, Cambridge (henceforth JMK papers), and in part in the Harrod papers at Chiba University of Commerce, Ichikawa, Japan (HP), the Keynes and Harrod Letters and Memoranda, at Tokyo University (KHLM) and in the Harrod Papers at the British Library (HPBL).
2 This edition, however, bears the marks of having used as copy-text the carbon copies of Keynes's letters, included in the JMK papers, while the originals are in HP. There are therefore a number of discrepancies in the reproduction and dating of some items.
3 The correspondence between Harrod and Robertson is discussed in Besomi (2004), a section of which is dedicated to their relationship with Keynes.
4 He seems to have particularly appreciated Harrod's philosophical bent, as proved by the otherwise very rare correspondence on methodological issues: see 97 and 101–4; more generally, see Keynes's letter to Hopkins describing Harrod's capacities cited below: 105.
5 None of the drafts survives, but from the correspondence (Harrod's own letters are not extant, excepts those to Meade) it clearly emerged that it underwent several drastic changes; it originally comprised at least ten chapters, while the final version has only nine.
6 Harrod's side of the correspondence is not extant.
7 The original version is included in Harrod (2003: 1063–8).
8 Contrarily to what is suggested in Phelps Brown's otherwise fairly accurate 'Memoir' (1980: 9), the nervous breakdown was independent of the rejection of the paper (Harrod 2003, note 1 to p. 102).
9 For more detailed discussions see Kregel (1985) and Besomi (1997). Regard-

ing Harrod's later claim to have contributed the only diagram in Keynes's book (CWK VII: 180) see O'Donnell (1999a, 1999b), Ahiakpor (1999) and Besomi (2000a).

10 On the presentation of Harrod's paper before the Econometric Society see Young (1987a: Ch. 1); on the significance of the paper for Harrod's dynamics see Besomi (1999a: Ch. 7).

11 See, for discussion, Besomi (1999a); all this correspondence is included in Harrod (2003).

12 This correspondence (letters 1243–1248, 31 March to 20 April 1937) was published in CWK XIV: 151–79, and has been discussed in the literature (Kregel 1980; Besomi 1995, 1996b).

13 British Library of Political and Economic Science, Archives Division, London.

14 For a more detailed description of the circumstances see Besomi (1996a), for discussion of the implications of the correspondence see Kregel (1980) and Besomi (1995, 1996b).

15 In HP, folder of later acquisitions. A carbon copy of Keynes's letter to Richard Hopkins, dated 7 September 1939, of which Harrod's is a fairly accurate transcription, is in JMK papers, UA/14/2: 309–10.

16 The S-branch was originally founded in order to supply unofficially Churchill, then First Lord of the Admiralty, with relevant statistical information and elaboration. The branch retained its anomalous status even after Churchill became Prime Minister: see Harrod (1959: 186 ff.).

17 The memoranda include Harrod's 'Anglo-American collaboration. Buffer stock control', April 1942, and a paper on the Reconstruction Bank, March 1944; Keynes's 'Monetary and Financial Policy', dated 29 November 1941, 'International Control of Raw Materials', amended in February 1942, 'National Income and Expenditure after the War', 28 May 1942, amended 9 June 1942 and again by 23 June, following – among others – Harrod's suggestions in 'International Regulation of Primary Products', June 1942; Harrod's 'Classification of Measures of International Economic Classification', June 1942.

18 Besides the major topics listed above, Harrod and Keynes exchanged correspondence on a number of occasional subjects. As Editor of the *Economic Journal*, Keynes acknowledged receipt of, or commented upon, a number of Harrod's articles, or articles submitted by other authors on Harrod's suggestion. Among the latter, the exchange on Donald MacDougall's 'The Definition of Prime and Supplementary Costs' (1936) is of a certain interest given Keynes's remarks on the use of mathematics in economics: 'I feel increasingly that one cannot think as an economist unless one's method of thought is capable of handling material which is not completely clear-cut and which is, so to speak, symptomatic thinking, (I do not know if that quite expresses what I mean) rather than completely formal, water-tight thinking. What one hopes from people like Champernowne and MacDougall is that they may learn to be mathematicians and economists simultaneously, capable of keeping in their minds at the same time formal thinking and 'sifting' uncertain material. But it is a very difficult thing to do, and they are always in danger of producing something which is jejune, and of wasting a lot of time and space on stuff which they have to discard as soon as they get down to the real topic in hand' (letter 1234, 2 July 1936, Harrod 2003: 575). (Keynes's aversion to formalism has its counterpart in his view on the role of models, as illustrated above.)

Harrod's own articles for the *Economic Journal* submitted to Keynes included an 'admirable' critical review of '*Banking*, by W. Leaf' (Harrod 1927) – the Editor commented that it is a scandal that such books should be allowed to be written (letter 1161, 29 December 1926, summarised in Harrod 2003: 83); a

'Note on Collective Bargaining', which was withdrawn because it was superseded by Joan Robinson's *Economics of Imperfect Competition* (1933) and remained unpublished (but is included in Harrod 2003: 1083–6) (letter 1199, 6 April 1934, in Harrod 2003: 273; see also Harrod's letter 1115 to Joan Robinson, 6 October 1933, Harrod 2003: 226); a note on *Laissez-Faire* (Harrod 1936a); (letters 1230 and 1231, 16 and 23 October 1935, Harrod 2003: 453 and 455); and 'Lord Nuffield's Foundation in Oxford' (1937b) (letter 1254, 17 October 1937, in Harrod 2003: 726).

Among the extant documents we also have Harrod's description of Edgeworth's lectures (letter 1158, 25 March 1926, Harrod 2003: 56), some exchanges regarding his career (which Keynes seems to have taken to heart) (letters 1175 and 1176, 4 and 6 January 1931, Harrod 2003: 125–6, and 1249 and 1250, 30 April and 5 May 1937, Harrod 2003: 698–90), the Meeting of Economists organised by the Antwerp Chamber of Commerce in July 1935, to which Harrod seems to have been invited on Keynes's suggestion (letters 1204, 1206–1208, 18 June to 6 July 1935, summarised in Harrod 2003: 394 ff.) (Harrod's contribution is printed in the proceedings: Harrod 1935), Keynes's paper before the British Association 1938 meeting, held under Harrod's presidency (letters 1257–1259, 1272, 1273 and 1275, 20 January to 20 August 1938, reported in Harrod 2003: 756 ff.), and Keynes's advice regarding a speech on monetary policy Harrod was to deliver before the Monetary Parliamentary Committee in November 1938 (letter 1295, 26 October 1938, excerpt in Harrod 2003: 893). Three letters survive (1227–1229, 8 to 10 October 1935, Harrod 2003: 447–8 and 450–1) on Credit Creation (the exchange was stimulated by Harrod's correspondence on the subject with Robertson, in Harrod 2003: 439 ff.).

From 1945 onwards, the correspondence mainly concerned Harrod's editorship of the *Economic Journal*. The last exchange (letters 2016 to 2023) regards the publication of Keynes's last article (Keynes 1946) and the reasons for its deferment until after the Congressional debate on the loan (the story is narrated in Moggridge 2001).

Table 3.1 Keynes–Harrod correspondence

From	To	Year	Month	Day	Date	Archive		Published in	Item
JMK	RFH	1922	July	21	Dated letter	Harrod–Tokyo	2	Harrod 2003: 12 (E)	1151
JMK	RFH	1922	August	15	Dated letter	Harrod–Tokyo	3		1152
JMK	RFH	1922	December	14	Dated letter	Harrod–Tokyo	4	Harrod 2003: 18 (E)	1153
RFH	JMK	1923	April	9	Dated letter	Harrod–Chiba	II/147	Harrod 2003: 21, (E)	1154
JMK	RFH	1923	November	17	Dated letter	Harrod–Chiba	II/12		1155
JMK	RFH	1924	January	9	Dated letter	Harrod–Chiba	II/13	Harrod 2003: 24, (E)	1156
JMK	RFH	1924	May	11	Dated letter	Harrod–Chiba	II/14		1157
RFH	JMK	1926	March	25	Dated letter	Keynes–King's Harrod–Chiba	EJ/6/6/53 II/200	Harrod 2003: 56–7	1158
JMK	RFH	1926	March	26	Postmark	Harrod–Tokyo	6	Harrod 2003: 57	1159
JMK	RFH	1926	April	20	Dated letter	Harrod–Tokyo	7		1160
JMK	RFH	1926	December	29	Dated letter	Harrod–Chiba	II/15	Harrod 2003: 83, (E)	1161
JMK	RFH	1927	January	27	Dated letter	Keynes–King's Harrod–Chiba	CEB/1/7 II/200	Harrod 2003: 85	1162
RFH	JMK	1927	February	3	Dated letter	Keynes–King's Harrod–Chiba	CEB/1/8 II/200	Harrod 2003: 86	1163
JMK	RFH	1927	February	4	Dated letter	Harrod–Tokyo	8	Harrod 2003: 87	1164
JMK	RFH	1927	August	15	Dated letter	Harrod–Tokyo	9	Harrod 2003: 88–9, (E)	1165
JMK	RFH	1927	August	19	Dated letter	Harrod–Tokyo	10		1166
RFH	JMK	1927	August	22	Dated letter	Harrod–Tokyo	11		1167
RFH	JMK	1928	July	7	Dated letter	Keynes–King's Harrod–Chiba	EJ/1/3/83 II/200	Harrod 2003: 94–5	1168
JMK	RFH	1928	July	17	Dated letter	Harrod–Chiba Harrod–Chiba	II/16 II/200	Harrod 2003: 95–6	1169
RFH	JMK	1928	July	20	Dated letter	Keynes–King's Harrod–Chiba	EJ/1/3/86–8 II/200	Harrod 2003: 96–8	1170
RFH	JMK	1928	July	23	Dated letter	Keynes–King's Harrod–Chiba	EJ/1/3/89–90 II/200	Harrod 2003: 98–9	1171

Table 3.1 continued

From	*To*	*Year*	*Month*	*Day*	*Date*	*Archive*		*Published in*	*Item*
JMK	RFH	1928	July	24	Dated letter	Harrod–Chiba	II/17	Harrod 2003: 99	1172
RFH	JMK	1928	July	27	Dated letter	Keynes–King's Harrod–Chiba	EJ/1/3/91 II/200	Harrod 2003: 101	1173
JMK	RFH	1928	August	1	Dated letter	Harrod–Chiba Harrod–Chiba	II/18 II/200	Harrod 2003: 102–3	1174
RFH	JMK	1931	January	4	Dated letter	Harrod–Chiba	II/148	Harrod 2003: 125–6	1175
JMK	RFH	1931	January	6	Dated letter	Harrod–Tokyo	12	Harrod 2003: 126, (E)	1176
JMK	RFH	1931	July	22	Dated letter	Harrod–Tokyo	13	Harrod 2003: 136, (E)	1177
JMK	RFH	1932	June	6	Dated letter	Harrod–Chiba	II/22	Harrod 2003: 156	1178
JMK	RFH	1932	July	5	Dated letter	Harrod–Chiba	II/23	Harrod 2003: 166, (E)	1179
RFH	JMK	1932	November	4	Dated letter	Keynes–King's	CAC/1/106–7	Harrod 2003: 184	1180
JMK	RFH	1932	November	4	Dated letter	Harrod–Chiba	II/24	Harrod 2003: 185	1181
JMK	RFH	1932	December	26	Dated letter	Harrod–Chiba	II/25	Harrod 2003: 193–5	1182
JMK	RFH	1932	December	30	Dated letter	Harrod–Chiba	II/26	Harrod 2003: 196	1183
JMK	RFH	1933	January	25	Dated letter	Harrod–Chiba	II/27	Harrod 2003: 199–200	1184
JMK	RFH	1933	January	31	Dated letter	Harrod–Chiba	II/28	Harrod 2003: 200–2	1185
JMK	RFH	1933	February	16	Dated letter	Harrod–Chiba	II/29	Harrod 2003: 202–3	1186
JMK	RFH	1933	February	25	Dated letter	Harrod–Chiba Keynes–King's	II/30 A/33/1/127	Harrod 2003: 204, (E)	1187
RFH	JMK	1933	February	27	Dated letter	Keynes–King's	A/33/1/128	Harrod 2003: 205, (E)	1188
JMK	RFH	1933	February	28	Dated letter	Harrod–Chiba Keynes–King's	II/31 A/33/1/130		1189
JMK	RFH	1933	March	2	Dated letter	Harrod–Chiba Keynes–King's	II/32 A/33/1/135	Harrod 2003: 205–6, (E)	1190
JMK	RFH	1933	April	23	Dated letter	Harrod–Chiba	II/33	Harrod 2003: 218, (E)	1191
JMK	RFH	1933	May	3	Dated letter	Harrod–Tokyo	14	Harrod 2003: 221, (E)	1192
JMK	RFH	1933	October	10	Dated letter	Harrod–Chiba	II/34	Harrod 2003: 226–7	1193
JMK	RFH	1933	October	27	Dated letter	Harrod–Chiba	II/36	Harrod 2003: 229–30	1194

JMK	RFH	1933	December	30	Dated letter	Harrod–Chiba	II/37	Harrod 2003: 259	1195
JMK	RFH	1934	January	10	Dated letter	Harrod–Chiba	II/38		1196
JMK	RFH	1934	January	13	Dated letter	Harrod–Chiba	II/39	Harrod 2003: 264	1198
JMK	RFH	1934	February	8	Dated letter	Harrod–Tokyo	15		1197
JMK	RFH	1934	March	29	Dated letter	Harrod–Chiba	II/40	Harrod 2003: 272–3	2024
JMK	RFH	1934	April	6	Dated letter	Harrod–Chiba	II/41	Harrod 2003: 273	1199
RFH	JMK	1934	October	26	Dated letter	Harrod–Chiba	II/149	Harrod 2003: 315–17	2025
JMK	RFH	1934	October	28	Dated letter	Harrod–Chiba	II/43	Harrod 2003: 317	2026
JMK	RFH	1935	February	6	Dated letter	Harrod–Tokyo	16		1200
JMK	RFH	1935	February	28	Dated letter	Harrod–Tokyo	17		1201
RFH	JMK	1935	March	6	Dated letter	Keynes–King's	GTE/1/203–4	Harrod 2003: 387, (E)	2027
JMK	RFH	1935	March	10	Dated letter	Harrod–Tokyo	18	Harrod 2003: 389, (E)	2028
JMK	RFH	1935	March	21	Dated letter	Harrod–Chiba	II/44	Harrod 2003: 389, (E)	1202
JMK	RFH	1935	March	28	Dated letter	Harrod–Chiba	II/45	Harrod 2003: 390	1203
JMK	RFH	1935	June	18	Dated letter	Harrod–Chiba	II/46	Harrod 2003: 394–5, (E)	1204
JMK	RFH	1935	June	26	Dated letter	Harrod–Chiba	II/47	Harrod 2003: 396, (E)	1206
JMK	RFH	1935	June	26	Dated letter	Harrod–Chiba Keynes–King's	II/48 GTE/1/282	Harrod 2003: 395	1205
JMK	RFH	1935	July	1	Dated letter	Harrod–Chiba	II/50	Harrod 2003: 396 (E)	1207
JMK	RFH	1935	July	6	Dated letter	Harrod–Chiba	II/51	Harrod 2003: 397 (E)	1208
RFH	JMK	1935	July	31	Dated letter	Keynes–King's	GTE/1/283	CWK XIII: 527–30	1209
RFH	JMK	1935	August	1	Dated letter	Keynes–King's	GTE/1/290–5	CWK XIII: 530–3	1210
RFH	JMK	1935	August	1	Dated letter	Keynes–King's	GTE/1/296–7	CWK XIII: 533–4	1211
RFH	JMK	1935	August	3	Dated letter	Keynes–King's	GTE/1/298–9	CWK XIII: 534	1212
RFH	JMK	1935	August	6	Dated letter	Keynes–King's	GTE/1/300–4	CWK XIII: 535–7	1213
JMK	RFH	1935	August	9	Dated letter	Harrod–Chiba Keynes–King's	II/52 GTE/1/305–6	CWK XIII: 537–9	1214
RFH	JMK	1935	August	12	Dated letter	Keynes–King's	GTE/1/307–8	CWK XIII: 539–40	1215
JMK	RFH	1935	August	14	Dated letter	Harrod–Chiba Keynes–King's	II/53 GTE/1/309	CWK XIII: 540–2	1216
JMK	RFH	1935	August	17	Dated letter	Harrod–Chiba	II/54	CWK XIII: 542	1217
RFH	JMK	1935	August	19	Dated letter	Keynes–King's	GTE/1/310–13	CWK XIII: 542–4	1219

Table 3.1 continued

From	*To*	*Year*	*Month*	*Day*	*Date*	*Archive*		*Published in*	*Item*
RFH	JMK	1935	August	21	Dated letter	Keynes–King's	GTE/1/314–16	CWK XIII: 544–6	1218
RFH	JMK	1935	August	22	Dated letter	Keynes–King's	GTE/1/317–19	CWK XIII: 546–7	1220
JMK	RFH	1935	August	27	Dated letter	Harrod–Chiba Keynes–King's	II/55 GTE/1/320–19	CWK XIII: 547–53	1221
RFH	JMK	1935	August	30	Dated letter	Keynes–King's	GTE/1/330–15	CWK XIII: 553–6	1222
JMK	RFH	1935	September	14	Dated letter	Harrod–Chiba Keynes–King's	II/56 GTE/1/386–90	CWK XIII: 557–9	1223
RFH	JMK	1935	September	20	Dated letter	Keynes–King's	GTE/1/414–16	CWK XIII: 560–1	1224
JMK	RFH	1935	September	25	Dated letter	Harrod–Chiba Keynes–King's	II/57 GTE/1/391	CWK XIII: 561	1225
RFH	JMK	1935	September	27	Dated letter	Keynes–King's	GTE/1/392–6	CWK XIII: 562–3	1226
RFH	JMK	1935	October	8	Dated letter	Keynes–King's	GTE/1/409	CWK XIII: 564	1227
JMK	RFH	1935	October	9	Dated letter	Keynes–King's	GTE/1/410	CWK XIII: 564	1228
RFH	JMK	1935	October	10	Dated letter	Keynes–King's	GTE/1/411–12	CWK XIII: 564–5	1229
JMK	RFH	1935	October	16	Dated letter	Harrod–Chiba	II/58	Harrod 2003: 453	1230
JMK	RFH	1935	October	23	Dated letter	Harrod–Chiba	II/59	Harrod 2003: 455	1231
JMK	RFH	1935	November	27	Dated letter	Harrod–Chiba	II/60	Harrod 2003: 466	1232
JMK	RFH	1936	February	19	Dated letter	Harrod–Chiba	II/61	Harrod 2003: 507	1233
JMK	RFH	1936	July	2	Dated letter	Harrod–Chiba	II/62	Harrod 2003: 575–6	1234
RFH	JMK	1936	August	24	Dated letter	Keynes–King's	GTE/2/2/40	CWK XIV: 83–4	1235
JMK	RFH	1936	August	30	Dated letter	Harrod–Chiba	II/65	CWK XIV: 84–6	1236
RFH	JMK	1936	September	3	Dated letter	Keynes–King's	GTE/2/2/68–70	CWK XIV: 86	1237
JMK	RFH	1936	October	7	Dated letter	Harrod–Chiba	II/86	Harrod 2003: 585	1238
RFH	JMK	1937	February	17	Dated letter	Keynes–King's	GTE/2/2/71–5	Harrod 2003: 632–4	1239
JMK	RFH	1937	February	18	Dated letter	Harrod–Chiba Keynes–King's	II/67 CO/2/2/76–9	Harrod 2003: 634–5	1240
RFH	JMK	1937	February	19	Dated letter	Keynes–King's	GTE/2/2/78A	Harrod 2003: 635–6	1241
JMK	RFH	1937	February	21	Dated letter	Harrod–Chiba Keynes–King's	II/68 GTE/2/2/79–80	Harrod 2003: 637	1242

JMK	RFH	1937	March	31	Dated letter	Harrod–Chiba Keynes–King's	II/69 CO/3/54–5	CWK XIV: 150–63	1243
RFH	JMK	1937	April	6	Dated letter	Keynes–King's	CO/3/76–8	CWK XIV: 163–4	1244
RFH	JMK	1937	April	7	Dated letter	Keynes–King's	CO/3/73–5	CWK XIV: 164–70	1245
JMK	RFH	1937	April	12	Dated letter	Harrod–Chiba Keynes–King's	II/72 CO/3/86–92	CWK XIV: 170–4	1246
RFH	JMK	1937	April	15	Dated letter	Keynes–King's	CO/3/93–6	CWK XIV: 174–6	1247
JMK	RFH	1937	April	20	Dated letter	Harrod–Chiba Keynes–King's	II/73 CO/3/100–3	CWK XIV: 177–9	1248
RFH	JMK	1937	April	30	Dated letter	Harrod–Chiba	II/150	Harrod 2003: 689	1249
JMK	RFH	1937	May	5	Dated letter	Harrod–Chiba Harrod–Chiba	II/74 II/75	Harrod 2003: 690	1250
RFH	JMK	1937	May	9	Dated letter	Harrod–Chiba	II/151	Harrod 2003: 691–2	2029
JMK	RFH	1937	June	6	Postmark	Harrod–Chiba	II/64	Harrod 2003: 696	1251
JMK	RFH	1937	June	13	Dated letter	Harrod–Chiba	II/76	Harrod 2003: 700, (E)	1252
JMK	RFH	1937	August	25	Dated letter	Harrod–Chiba	II/77		1253
RFH	JMK	1937	October	17	Dated letter	Keynes–King's	EJ/1/4/169–71	Harrod 2003: 726–7	1254
JMK	RFH	1937	November	30	Dated letter	Harrod–British Library	71740/2	Harrod 2003: 735, (E)	1255
RFH	JMK	1938	January	19	Dated letter	Keynes–King's	EJ/1/5/30		1256
RFH	JMK	1938	January	20	Dated letter	Keynes–King's	EJ/1/5/31–2		1257
JMK	RFH	1938	January	22	Dated letter	Keynes–King's	EJ/1/5/33–4	Harrod 2003: 756, (E)	1259
RFH	JMK	1938	January	24	Dated letter	Keynes–King's	EJ/1/5/35–6	Harrod 2003: 756–7, (E)	1258
RFH	JMK	1938	January	25	Dated letter	Keynes–King's	RES/1/2/117–18		1260
JMK	RFH	1938	January	26	Dated letter	Harrod–Tokyo Keynes–King's	19 EJ/1/5/37	Harrod 2003: 759	1261
JMK	RFH	1938	February	13	Dated letter	Harrod–Tokyo	20	Harrod 2003: 761	1262
RFH	JMK	1938	June	13	Dated letter	Keynes–King's	RES/1/2/123–4	Harrod 2003: 785–6	1263
RFH	JMK	1938	June	14	Dated letter	Keynes–King's Harrod–Chiba	RES/1/2/125 II/200		1264
JMK	RFH	1938	June	15	Dated letter	Harrod–Chiba Keynes–King's	II/200 RES/1/2/126	Harrod 2003: 789, (E)	1265

Table 3.1 continued

From	*To*	*Year*	*Month*	*Day*	*Date*	*Archive*		*Published in*	*Item*
RFH	JMK	1938	June	16	Dated letter	Keynes–King's Harrod–Chiba	RES/1/2/127–8 II/200	Harrod 2003: 789, (E)	1266
JMK	RFH	1938	July	4	Dated letter	Harrod–Chiba Keynes–King's	II/78A EJ/1/5/218–20	CWK XIV: 295–7	1267
RFH	JMK	1938	July	6	Dated letter	Keynes–King's Harrod–Chiba	CO/11/269–76 II/200	CWK XIV: 297–9	1268
JMK	RFH	1938	July	10	Dated letter	Harrod–Chiba Keynes–King's	II/79 CO/11/277–80	CWK XIV: 299–301	1269
RFH	JMK	1938	August	3	Dated letter	Keynes–King's	EJ/1/5/221–4	CWK XIV: 301	1270
RFH	JMK	1938	August	6	Dated letter	Keynes–King's	EJ/1/5/271	Harrod 2003: 812	1271
JMK	RFH	1938	August	11	Dated letter	Harrod–Chiba Keynes–King's	II/83 EJ/1/5/272–3	CWK XIV: 302	1272
RFH	JMK	1938	August	16	Dated letter	Keynes–King's	EJ/1/5/274–5	Harrod 2003: 826–7	1273
JMK	RFH	1938	August	17	Dated letter	Harrod–Chiba Keynes–King's	II/84 EJ/1/5/295–304	CWK XIV: 321–7	1274
RFH	JMK	1938	August	20	Dated letter	Keynes–King's	PS/6/2/251–3	Harrod 2003: 833–4, (E)	1275
RFH	JMK	1938	August	21	Dated letter	Keynes–King's	EJ/1/5/305–8	CWK XIV: 328–9	1276
JMK	RFH	1938	August	23	Dated letter	Harrod–Chiba Keynes–King's	II/86 EJ/1/5/309–12	CWK XIV: 330–2	1277
RFH	JMK	1938	August	26	Dated letter	Keynes–King's Harrod–Chiba	RES/1/2/129–30 II/200		1279
RFH	JMK	1938	August		Attributed	Keynes–King's	EJ/1/5/316–17	CWK XIV: 332–3	1278
JMK	RFH	1938	August	29	Attributed	Harrod–Chiba Keynes–King's	II/87 EJ/1/5/313–15	CWK XIV: 333–5	1281
JMK	RFH	1938	August	29	Dated letter	Keynes–King's Harrod–Chiba	RES/1/2/131–2 II/200		1280
RFH	JMK	1938	September	6	Dated letter	Keynes–King's	EJ/1/5/318–19	CWK XIV: 335–6	1282
RFH	JMK	1938	September	7	Dated letter	Keynes–King's Harrod–Chiba	CO/11/281–4 II/200	CWK XIV: 303–4	1283

RFH	JMK	1938	September	7	Dated letter	Keynes–King's	EJ/1/5/320–1	CWK XIV: 336–7	1284
JMK	RFH	1938	September	9	Dated letter	Keynes–King's	EJ/1/5/322–3	CWK XIV: 337–8, (E)	1285
JMK	RFH	1938	September	13	Dated letter	Harrod–Chiba Keynes–King's	II/80 CO/11/285	CWK XIV: 304	1286
RFH	JMK	1938	September	14	Dated letter	Keynes–King's	EJ/1/5/324–5	CWK XIV: 338, (E)	1287
RFH	JMK	1938	September	18	Dated letter	Keynes–King's Harrod–Chiba	CO/11/286–9 II/200	CWK XIV: 304–5	1288
JMK	RFH	1938	September	19	Dated letter	Harrod–Chiba Keynes–King's	II/88 EJ/1/5/326–31	CWK XIV: 339–42	1289
JMK	RFH	1938	September	20	Attributed	Harrod–Chiba	II/81		1290
JMK	RFH	1938	September	21	Dated letter	Harrod–Chiba Keynes–King's	II/82 CO/11/290	CWK XIV: 305	1291
RFH	JMK	1938	September	22	Dated letter	Keynes–King's	EJ/1/5/332–6	CWK XIV: 342–5	1292
JMK	RFH	1938	September	26	Dated letter	Harrod–Chiba Keynes–King's	II/89 EJ/1/5/337–45	CWK XIV: 345–50	1293
JMK	RFH	1938	October	20	Dated letter	Harrod–Chiba	II/90	Harrod 2003: 891, (E)	1294
JMK	RFH	1938	October	26	Dated letter	Harrod–Chiba	II/91	Harrod 2003: 893, (E)	1295
RFH	JMK	1938	December	21	Dated letter	Keynes–King's	EJ/1/5/443	CWK XIV: 350	1296
JMK	RFH	1939	March	18	Dated letter	Harrod–Chiba	II/92	Harrod 2003: 921, (E)	1297
RFH	JMK	1939	September	4	Dated letter	Keynes–King's	UA/14/2/280		1298
JMK	RFH	1939	September	7	Dated letter	Harrod–Chiba Keynes–King's	II/95 UA/14/2/281–2		1299
RFH	JMK	1939	September	9	Dated letter	Keynes–King's	UA/14/2/283		1300
JMK	RFH	1940	September	5	Dated letter	Keynes–King's	W/1/86		1301
RFH	JMK	1940	September	6	Dated letter	Keynes–King's	W/1/87–8		1302
RFH	JMK	1941	January	13	Dated letter	Harrod–Tokyo	22		1303
RFH	JMK	1941	September	28	Dated letter	Harrod–Chiba	II/103c		1304
RFH	JMK	1941	November	12	Dated letter	Harrod–Chiba	II/103c		1306
RFH	JMK	1941	November	12	Dated letter	Keynes–King's	L/41/59		1305
JMK	RFH	1941	November	13	Dated letter	Keynes–King's	L/41/60–1		1307
JMK	RFH	1941	November	14	Dated letter	Harrod–Chiba	II/101		1308

Table 3.1 continued

From	*To*	*Year*	*Month*	*Day*	*Date*	*Archive*		*Published in*	*Item*
RFH	JMK	1941	November	17	Dated letter	Public Record Office	T247/121	Skidelsky 2000: 220–1, (E)	2032
JMK	RFH	1941	December	16	Dated letter	Not found in the archives		CWK XXV: 95–8	1309
RFH	JMK	1942	January	22	Dated letter	Harrod–Tokyo	23		1310
JMK	RFH	1942	February	10	Dated letter	Harrod–Chiba	II/108		1311
RFH	JMK	1942	February	12	Dated letter	Harrod–Tokyo	24		1312
RFH	JMK	1942	April		Attributed	Harrod–Tokyo Harrod–Tokyo	26 27		1313
RFH	JMK	1942	April	4	Dated letter	Public Record Office	T247/67	Skidelsky 2000: 220, (E)	2033
JMK	RFH	1942	April	27	Dated letter	Harrod–Tokyo	28	CWK XXV: 146–51	1314
RFH	JMK	1942	May	4	Dated letter	Harrod–Tokyo Harrod–Chiba	30 II/154		1315
RFH	JMK	1942	May	4	Dated letter	Harrod–Chiba	II/54		2030
JMK	RFH	1942	May	8	Dated letter	Harrod–Tokyo	31	CWK XXV, 151–2	1316
JMK	RFH	1942	May	26	Dated letter	Harrod–Tokyo	32		1317
JMK	RFH	1942	May	27	Dated letter	Harrod–Tokyo	33		1318
JMK	RFH	1942	May	29	Dated letter	Harrod–Tokyo	34		1319
RFH	JMK	1942	June	4	Dated letter	Harrod–Tokyo Harrod–Tokyo	38 37		1320
JMK	RFH	1942	June	5	Dated letter	Harrod–Tokyo	39		1321
JMK	RFH	1942	June	9	Dated letter	Harrod–Tokyo	40		1322
RFH	JMK	1942	June		Attributed	Harrod–Tokyo Harrod–Tokyo	41 41		1323
JMK	RFH	1942	June	18	Dated letter	Harrod–Tokyo	42		1324
JMK	RFH	1942	June	19	Dated letter	Harrod–Tokyo Harrod–Tokyo	43 44		1325

RFH	JMK	1942	July	2	Dated letter	Harrod–Tokyo	48		1326
JMK	RFH	1942	July	7	Dated letter	Harrod–Tokyo	49		1327
JMK	RFH	1942	July	9	Dated letter	Harrod–Tokyo	53		1328
JMK	RFH	1942	July	16	Dated letter	Harrod–Tokyo	54		1329
JMK	RFH	1942	July	22	Dated letter	Harrod–Tokyo	55		1330
RFH	JMK	1942	August	5	Dated letter	Harrod–Tokyo Harrod–Tokyo	56 56		1331
JMK	RFH	1942	August	7	Dated letter	Harrod–Tokyo	57		1332
RFH	JMK	1942	August	20	Dated letter	Harrod–Chiba	II/155		1333
JMK	RFH	1942	August	24	Dated letter	Harrod–Tokyo	59		1334
RFH	JMK	1942	August	26	Dated letter	Harrod–Chiba	II/156		1335
RFH	JMK	1942	August	26	Dated letter	Harrod–Chiba	II/157		1336
JMK	RFH	1942	August	31	Dated letter	Harrod–Chiba	II/115		1337
RFH	JMK	1942	September	1	Dated letter	Harrod–Chiba	II/158		1338
JMK	RFH	1942	September	2	Dated letter	Harrod–Chiba	II/116		1339
RFH	JMK	1942	September	7	Dated letter	Harrod–Chiba	II/159		1340
RFH	JMK	1942	September	9	Dated letter	Harrod–Chiba	II/160		1341
JMK	RFH	1942	September	15	Dated letter	Harrod–Chiba Keynes–King's	II/117 L/42/105–8	Skidelsky 2000: 252, (E)	1342
JMK	RFH	1942	October	7	Dated letter	Harrod–Tokyo	64		1343
JMK	RFH	1943	January	25	Dated letter	Harrod–Tokyo	66		1344
JMK	RFH	1943	February	2	Dated letter	Harrod–Tokyo	68		1345
RFH	JMK	1943	March	2	Dated letter	Harrod–Chiba Harrod–Chiba	II/161 II/161		1346
JMK	RFH	1943	March	4	Dated letter	Harrod–Chiba	II/118	CWK XXV: 229–30	1347
RFH	JMK	1943	March	6	Dated letter	Harrod–Chiba Harrod–Chiba	II/161 II/161		1348
JMK	RFH	1943	March	8	Dated letter	Harrod–Chiba	II/119	CWK XXV: 232	1349
JMK	RFH	1943	April	1	Dated letter	Harrod–Chiba	II/120		1350
RFH	JMK	1943	April	5	Dated letter	Harrod–Chiba	II/162		2001
JMK	RFH	1943	April	6	Dated letter	Harrod–Chiba	II/121		2002
RFH	JMK	1943	April	14	Dated letter	Keynes–King's	RES/1/2/211–14		2003

Table 3.1 continued

From	*To*	*Year*	*Month*	*Day*	*Date*	*Archive*		*Published in*	*Item*
JMK	RFH	1943	April	27	Dated letter	Keynes–King's	RES/1/2/213–4	CWK XXV: 268	2004
JMK	RFH	1943	July	14	Dated letter	Harrod–Chiba	II/122		2005
JMK	RFH	1944	March	20	Dated letter	Harrod–Chiba	II/125		2006
JMK	RFH	1945	February	16	Dated letter	Harrod–Chiba	II/130		2007
JMK	RFH	1945	February	25	Dated letter	Harrod–Chiba	II/131		2008
JMK	RFH	1945	July	24	Dated letter	Harrod–Chiba	II/132		2009
JMK	RFH	1945	August	2	Dated letter	Harrod–Chiba	II/133		2010
RFH	JMK	1945	August	2	Dated letter	Keynes–King's	UA/14/2/384–5		2011
JMK	RFH	1946	January	4	Dated letter	Harrod–Chiba	II/134		2012
JMK	RFH	1946	January	16	Dated letter	Harrod–Chiba	II/135		2013
RFH	JMK	1946	January	19	Dated letter	Keynes–King's	EJ/3/7		2014
RFH	JMK	1946	January	21	Dated letter	Keynes–King's	EJ/3/8–9		2015
JMK	RFH	1946	January	25	Dated letter	Harrod–Chiba	II/136		2016
RFH	JMK	1946	January	26	Dated letter	Keynes–King's	EJ/3/10		2017
JMK	RFH	1946	January	28	Dated letter	Harrod–Chiba Keynes–King's	II/137 EJ/3/11–14		2018
RFH	JMK	1946	January	29	Dated letter	Keynes–King's	EJ/3/15–16		2019
JMK	RFH	1946	February	6	Dated letter	Harrod–Chiba Keynes–King's	II/138 EJ/3/17		2020
RFH	JMK	1946	February	8	Dated letter	Keynes–King's			2031
JMK	RFH	1946	February	11	Dated letter	Harrod–Chiba	II/139		2021
JMK	RFH	1946	February	19	Dated letter	Harrod–Chiba	II/140		2022
JMK	RFH	1946	April	20	Dated letter	Harrod–Chiba	II/141		2023

4 Communication and intellectual integrity

The correspondence between Keynes and Sraffa

Fabio Ranchetti

> My dear Maynard,
>
> This is to introduce to you a great friend of the Salveminis, a young Signor Sraffa, who is now in London to study English political economy, and who of course longs to make your acquaintance. Prof. Salvemini thinks very well of him [. . .].
>
> (JMK papers, L/5/1–3)

Thus wrote Mary Berenson, wife of Bernard and sister of Alys, Bertrand Russell's first wife, on 15 July 1921. With this letter of introduction, the young and unknown Italian economist met the still quite young, but already highly respected and internationally celebrated British economist. Keynes was struck by Sraffa's brilliance of mind, particularly on discussing with him hedging in foreign exchange markets and the Italian Bank Crisis after the end of the First World War,[1] and immediately asked Sraffa to write an article on the latter topic. (The article – 'The Bank Crisis in Italy' – duly appeared in the June 1922 issue of the *Economic Journal*, then jointly edited by Keynes and Edgeworth, and made Sraffa internationally known.) This first encounter in the summer of 1921 saw a relationship and a friendship kindled which ended only with Keynes's death in 1946 – a very close and important relationship and friendship, probably among the most remarkable examples of loyalty and intellectual exchange between two great figures in the history of twentieth-century thought.[2] Sraffa's life, as well as his intellectual development, was to a great extent influenced by the relationship he had with Keynes. In fact, it is certain that without Keynes's invitation and constant support Sraffa would never had gone to Cambridge and stayed there, and it is difficult to conceive how he could possibly have devised his economic theory outside the cultural and scientific context of Cambridge. It is even harder, however, to ascertain the influence Sraffa exerted on Keynes's thought. Nevertheless, their extant correspondence makes a notable contribution towards an understanding of the precise nature of their relationship, and of how they were able (or unable) to influence each other's ideas and approach.

The extant correspondence consists of 230 documents, of which 89 are from Sraffa to Keynes and 141 from Keynes to Sraffa (see Table 4.1). The first document (letter 1049, 5 August 1921) is a short letter from Sraffa to Keynes in which Sraffa asks for the meeting mentioned above, the last a lively, humorous letter (letter 1038, 28 March 1946) from Keynes to Sraffa, written less than a month before Keynes's death (21 April). Most of the documents are dated. With just a few exceptions the correspondence has remained unpublished.

The correspondence can be conveniently arranged in five groups according to the subjects dealt with, which cover the many and various aspects of the relationship between Keynes and Sraffa. Within each group, we follow (with one exception) chronological order. The classification is: (1) economic theory *strictu sensu*; (2) the edition of David Ricardo's *Works and Correspondence* for the Royal Economic Society; (3) the edition of David Hume's *Abstract*; (4) the Italian and French editions of the *Tract* and the *General Theory*; and (5) academic and personal matters.

Economic theory

From the point of view of economic theory *strictu sensu*, the most relevant documents number about twenty-five. It is significant that, with one exception (which we shall see later), they are concentrated in two periods, 1926–30 and 1931–32, the former corresponding to Sraffa's first years at Cambridge and the debates on Marshallian economics, the latter to the years of the so-called Circus, the transition from the *Treatise* to the *General Theory*, and the triangular dispute between Keynes, Hayek, and Sraffa.

Critique of Marshall and the beginnings of the theory of imperfect competition

The first significant document, Sraffa's letter to Keynes (letter 1915, 6 June 1926), is of the utmost importance for economic theory, and is already known, having been published by Roncaglia (1975 in the Italian translation; 1978 in the original English text). It marks the transition from Sraffa's 1925 Italian article (Sraffa 1925) to his 1926 English article (Sraffa 1926).

In this four-page letter Sraffa summarises 'the substance' of his previous essay, and goes on to sketch out the lines along which he intended to write 'a sequel' to it, which was to become the famous article subsequently published in the December issue of the *Economic Journal*, from which it is customary to date the beginning of the theory of imperfect competition (at least in its British version). What is remarkable about this letter is the fact that Sraffa touches on a few points that were *not* to be pursued in the published article. In fact, in his letter to Keynes Sraffa indicates three possible lines along which to develop the theory of value: (1) elaboration of Marshallian partial equilibrium on the hypothesis of constant returns to scale; (2) elaboration of 'Pareto's point of view', and therefore of the general equilibrium approach; and (3) abandonment of the hypothesis of perfect competition, consequently extending the theory of monopoly to markets with many competitors. The theory of imperfect competition Sraffa outlined in that letter was not actually pursued by him but taken up by various other Cambridge economists, and in particular by Richard Kahn and J. Robinson. Sraffa soon lost interest in it, and became very critical of the developments it subsequently saw along Marshallian lines (see Roncaglia 1975, 1978; Ingrao and Ranchetti 1996).

In 1927 Sraffa had been appointed Lecturer in Economics at the University of Cambridge as from October, Keynes having acted as the main force behind Sraffa's appointment (see below). Sraffa therefore left Italy and moved to Cambridge – a move that, although at the time thought only to be provisional, was to become permanent and, indeed, changed his life for ever. A short exchange of letters between Keynes and Sraffa survives, which is important for an understanding of Sraffa's choice of subject and method for the lectures he was to deliver in the following academic years. It also shows how helpfully, and with what affectionate solicitude, Keynes took care of Sraffa's move to Cambridge.

The first letter, from Keynes, is long. Here we quote the most relevant part:

> My dear Sraffa,
>
> I am delighted to say that you were yesterday appointed a University Lecturer in Economics in the University of Cambridge, as from next October. This means that there are one or two things which we ought to try to settle as soon as possible. First of all as regards your lectures during the year 1927–28. Your obligation as University Lecturer is to give three courses during the year, each of 16 lectures. The most convenient way is to give one course in each term, that is to say, two lectures a week. Probably in the first year at any rate it would suit you best to give some advanced lectures, so as not to have to deal with too large a class [. . .] Will you let me know what subjects [. . .] you feel most inclined to give. It occurred to me that possibly a course on the Theory of Value, in which you would be free not to follow any text but to bring in your own notions, might make a course for one term; a similar course on Distribution for a second term; and a course on some realistic subject which you might like to choose for the third term. For example, as regards the third, a course on Problems of Public Finance as handled by Continental Economists, and with

> special reference to Continental practices. But what we really want is to get your own ideas of what you would like to do.
>
> (letter 1006, 31 May 1927)

In his answer Sraffa readily takes up Keynes's suggestions; he sets out clearly his teaching (and research) programme for the following academic year, as he had then planned it, and thus helps us to understand the precise stage in the development of his economic thought in what turned out to be probably its most crucial year. It is therefore worth quoting almost in its entirety:

> My dear Sir,
>
> I am happy to learn of my appointment as Lecturer at Cambridge, the more so that I know it is solely due to your goodwill; I refrain from expressing my gratitude, first because words would be insufficient, and also because I don't want to incur into your reproach. As to the things which remain to be settled, I entirely accept your suggestions. In regard to my lectures during the year 1927–28, I shall be very glad to give advanced lectures, so as I have to deal with a smaller class, and probably a more tolerant one as my faulty English.... I would much like the course on the Theory of Value upon the lines you suggest.
>
> (letter 1921, 5 June 1927)

Then we find a most important and revealing remark by Sraffa (let us recall the date of the letter 1921, 5 June 1927):

> But, as to the similar course on Distribution, I confess I have rather confused and fragmentary ideas on the subject: if I had to give a systematic course upon it, I could do little more than taking it ready-made from textbooks and delivering it without convincement.

Consequently, Sraffa proposes dropping the subject of distribution altogether and concentrating, instead, on the theory of value. Actually, Sraffa suggests extending the part devoted to the theory of value over two terms, dealing first with the supply side, and then with the demand side (the order is also revealing). As regards the third course Sraffa was supposed to give in the third term 'on a realistic subject', Sraffa suggests the topic of 'Relations of Banks to Industry on the Continent'.[3]

Sraffa's 1926 article in the *Economic Journal* was followed by heated debate on the questions of increasing returns and the Marshallian representative firm in the *Economic Journal*, to which Pigou, Gerald Shove, Lionel Robbins and Allyn Young contributed (Pigou 1927, 1928; Shove 1928; Robbins 1928; Young 1928). To take stock of the issues Keynes, as

Editor, decided to organise and then publish in the *Economic Journal* a *Symposium*, asking for contributions from Dennis Robertson, who offered 'a partial rehabilitation of Marshallian orthodoxy along conservative lines' (Keynes 1930b: 79), Sraffa, who advanced 'some negative and destructive criticism' (ibid.), and Shove, who offered 'some constructive suggestions' (ibid.). (See Marchionatti 2001; Rosselli 2004; and Ch. 14.)

It is within this context that we must understand the letter Sraffa sent to Keynes on January 28, during preparation of the *Symposium*:

> Dear Maynard,
>
> Here is my criticism of Dennis, with reply and rejoinder. But *please* do read it and, if possible, destroy it. As you will see it is a) silly, b) rude to Dennis, c) badly written. I didn't mean it to be any of these things, but good intentions will not help me.
>
> (letter 1922, 28 January 1930)

As we know, Keynes destroyed neither Sraffa's criticism of Robertson, nor his rejoinder. In fact, they were published in the *Economic Journal*, and in the published version they still contained some – if not rude – certainly quite pointed remarks by Sraffa.

In a way, the *Symposium* marked an end to a phase of Cambridge economics, at least for Keynes and Sraffa. In the winter of 1929–30 Keynes was busy reading and correcting the proofs of his *Treatise on Money* (which was to be published in October 1930); Sraffa was working on his new book (which was to be published in May 1960!) and, in February 1930, embarked on a new project, editing Ricardo's *Works and Correspondence*. Before we consider these new lines in research and debate, we must, however, note that in the late summer of 1941, in the middle of the Second World War, Sraffa and Keynes had a very important exchange (of seven letters) on Marshallian issues, and even conceived (at least Keynes) the possibility of a second, updated, *Symposium*.

The occasion for this reappraisal came by Sraffa with a proposal, in contrast with the negative advice of Austin Robinson, to publish an article in the *Economic Journal* on the topic of external economies by F. Zweig, a Polish economist then at Cambridge. Keynes was not impressed by Zweig's article – which 'makes no contribution to clearing up any problems whatever' (letter 2241, 22 August 1941) – and declared himself 'perplexed' to discover why Sraffa thought it worthy of publication. As one might imagine, Sraffa answered with a six-page letter – actually an extremely interesting document, since it gave him the opportunity 'to put my view of the matter' (letter 2242, 27 August 1941). In fact, Sraffa put forward a crucial distinction:

> a) Marshall introduced external economies as an essential part of his theory of value – to reconcile variation in cost as a function of output

> of an industry with competition; he defined them, as the problem in hand required, as a function of the quantity produced.
>
> b) Pigou took over the concept and used it in a totally different context – i.e. to explain the divergence between social and individual net products. But he took it over literally as Marshall had made it for a different purpose, without noticing that he (Pigou) was not in the least concerned with the quantity of output, and that he ought to have taken a wider definition. This is what Zweig supplies.
>
> (letter 2242, 27 August 1941)

Sraffa concludes:

> In fact, in the whole of Pigou's subject, the connection with the size of output is purely accidental. The matter has been forced into the frame of Marshall's definition for no good reason, except a historical one. Looking this over, I suspect that it may only make poor Zweig's obscurity still darker. In this case let us be damned together [. . .]
>
> (ibid.)

Keynes may not have been impressed by Zweig's article, but indeed he was by Sraffa's comments, to the point of answering him immediately: 'it is obvious from your letter that you could write a very good article on the subject. Why don't you?' (letter 2243, 28 August 1941).

Three more letters followed about the possibility of publishing something on the subject, Sraffa trying to back down – 'better still, someone else (who had not undertaken to finish Ricardo by the end of the war, or to finish the war by the end of the year) would no doubt develop his [i.e. Zweig's] point' (letter 2245, 15 September 1941) – and Keynes still insisting, indeed all the more since Sraffa continued – albeit incidentally – to add important comments, as the following:

> the problem in which Marshall and countless generations were passionately interested, and in the solution of which he used external economies, is now as dead as mutton: that is, the problem whether demand or supply or both determine values. Whereas the question to which Pigou applied external economies . . . is still alive, and of great interest to the present generation – that is, whether perfect competition and laissez faire maximize social welfare.
>
> (letter 2245, 15 September 1941)

In particular, Keynes thought of organising a new Symposium to bring together contributions by Zweig, Austin Robinson (who was critical of Zweig's approach), and, of course, Sraffa. Keynes, however, set a condition: 'the condition will be that your contribution should be at least as long as Zweig's' (letter 2246, 22 September 1941). A further condition he added was that 'this need not interfere with Ricardo, though I was hoping that that was finished by now' (ibid.). Knowing Sraffa, it is hardly surprising to see how readily he took the cue Keynes had given him:

> I am beginning to see some of the objections to the publication of Z[weig]'s article! In any case, before thinking of the Symposium (my contribution to which, if I undertook it, would occupy all my time from now till March) I must finish Ricardo, or give up trying to.
>
> (letter 2247, 29 September 1941)

This put an end to any project. But let us now resume our chronological narrative and go back to the early 1930s.

The Circus and the controversy with Hayek

As is well known, Keynes was far from satisfied with his *Treatise on Money*. As soon as it was published (end of October 1930), his closest circle of economist friends and colleagues started, on Sraffa's initiative, to meet and discuss Keynes's ideas in what was called the Circus – 'presumably not because it was a travelling show of performing animals, acrobats and clowns but because it met the alternative dictionary definition of a scene of lively action and a group of people engaged in common activity, in this case trying to understand and, later, to criticize the *Treatise*' (Moggridge 1992: 532). On the Circus we have J. Robinson's original testimony, especially important as it evidences Sraffa's role:

> In those days seminars were uncommon. Our circus, first proposed by Piero Sraffa, was organized as an unofficial venture. The main speakers were Kahn, James Meade, who was spending a year in Cambridge in order to transplant economics to Oxford, Sraffa (*who was secretly sceptical of the new ideas*), Austin Robinson and myself. Only students who were considered up to it were allowed to come.
>
> (J. Robinson 1978a: xii, emphasis added)

The Circus activities took place from November 1930 to May 1931.[4]

These were not only the years of the Circus and the difficult, complex transition from the *Treatise* to the *General Theory*, but also of the keen, even barbed controversy with Hayek. At that time, Sraffa was no longer the brilliant and promising young man of August 1921, but a well established Cambridge figure with a great intellectual reputation and authority, and not only among the economists (above all the Circus economists, among whom Sraffa was a senior member), as his relations with such formidable figures as Wittgenstein, Ramsey and Blackett testify: thus he was able to argue with Keynes on equal terms. Their correspondence reflects this change in their relationship: they were no longer addressing each other as 'My dear Sir' and 'My dear Sraffa', but as 'Dear Piero' and 'Dear Maynard'. As their correspondence attests, these were also the years that saw them coming closer and more interconnected in the development of their economic theory: they met every week to compare their respective conceptual frameworks and analytical tools, discussing them in detail and joining forces against Hayek's economic theory.

In this section, we shall deal first with the documents related to the Circus and Keynes's own theory, and second to the controversy, which saw Keynes and Sraffa opposed to Hayek.

On the basis of the extant evidence, Sraffa's role in the criticism of Keynes's *Treatise on Money* and in the transition towards the *General Theory* was important and effective in the period spanning from January 1930 to 1932. Besides the material already published in volumes XIII and XXIX of the *Collected Writings* of Keynes, among the Keynes and the Sraffa Papers we have some other very important unpublished documents by both Keynes and Sraffa. To the best of my knowledge, on this material (some of which, as we said, has been published – most recently twenty-five years ago!) the literature has practically next to nothing to offer.[5]

Sraffa's criticism is directed mainly at Chapter 10 ('The Fundamental Equations for the Value of Money') and Chapter 11 ('The Conditions of Equilibrium') of the *Treatise* – the very chapters, that is, which constituted the theoretical core of Keynes's economic analysis, and which were the major target of criticism by other economists, not only members of the Cambridge Circus but also 'opponents' from inside and outside Cambridge: Hawtrey, Robertson, Pigou, and Hayek. The two main objects of Sraffa's criticisms were (1) the nature (and the causes) of profits, and (2) the relationship between output and prices in the equilibrating process.

As we know, profits are at the centre of analysis in the *Treatise*. One of the most important features of Keynes's *Treatise* is in fact the detailed analysis of the channels and the causal links between monetary and financial phenomena, on the one hand, and real phenomena, on the other. In fact, by determining the terms of lending and therefore the money rate of interest, the banking system may affect the level of investment, and hence profits. One of Keynes's fundamental theses in the *Treatise* is the independence of the price-level of consumption-goods with regard to the price-level of investment-goods: 'the price level of consumption-goods is *solely* determined by the disposition of the public towards "savings"', whereas 'the price level of investment-goods (whether new or old) is *solely* determined by the disposition of the public towards "hoarding" money' (Keynes [1930a]: 144, in CWK V: 129–130, emphasis added). Hence follows the conclusion, that

> a fall in the price of consumption-goods due to an excess of saving over investment does not in itself – if it is unaccompanied by any

> change in the bearishness or bullishness of the public or in the volume of savings-deposits, or if there are compensating changes in these two factors – require any opposite change in the price of new investment-goods.
>
> (Keynes [1930a]: 145, in CWK V: 130)

To which statement, Keynes presciently added: 'I believe that this conclusion may be accepted by some readers with difficulty'. In fact, as we can infer from his unpublished papers, Sraffa pointed out at least two 'difficulties'.

The first difficulty regards the direct effect of a fall in the demand for consumption goods. According to Sraffa, the consumption-goods market being imperfect, the price of such goods will fall very little (when savings exceed investment, and therefore entrepreneurs incur losses): 'at first stocks will accumulate, or go to waste, and then the output will be reduced' (PS papers, D1/71/2). Conversely, the securities market being the typical instance of a perfect market, on this market

> the price of securities will, in the first instance, rise sharply; and if it rises in proportion to the increase of savings, firms as a whole, *if they go on issuing securities*, will receive a premium on new issues which is sufficient to finance their stocks, or to compensate their losses.
>
> (PS papers, D1/71/2, emphasis added)

This would be a position of equilibrium, in the sense that profits made by firms on the financial market will be equal to their losses on the goods market. But this is true only in theory; in fact, the firms producing consumption-goods and experiencing losses would be unwilling to issue new securities, but would instead reduce output. Sraffa's conclusion is the opposite of Keynes's: it is this reduction in output (and therefore in incomes) that will bring about the fall in the price-level, and not vice versa. Furthermore, and again contrary to Keynes's view, Sraffa concludes that there is a symmetry in the way prices, and hence profits (or losses), are determined: 'the price of investment-goods is determined in the same way as that of consumption goods, and a change in the demand for either may give rise (or fail to give rise) to profits and losses' (PS papers, D1/72/3).

The second difficulty raised by Sraffa regards Keynes's identification of machinery and securities 'under the ambiguous name of "new investment goods"' (PS papers, D1/71/1). According to Sraffa, 'these two price-levels have little in common', since in the short period the price of machines depends upon the demand of entrepreneurs and the price of securities upon the demand of investors, while in the long period the price of machines depends upon their cost of production and that of securities upon the money rate of interest.

Having thus briefly reconstructed Sraffa's argument, we are now better placed to appreciate the four documents Keynes and Sraffa exchanged in February 1931. The first document is a short handwritten note by Keynes, sent to Sraffa on 3 February. Keynes's note refers to page 145, second paragraph, of the *Treatise,* which is precisely the passage we have quoted above, and says:

> Please note the assumption that there is *no change in the volume of saving-deposits.* If the entrepreneur diminishes his output, less money is required for the Income and Business-Deposits. So that, in order to satisfy the above assumption and avoid a change in the volume of saving-deposits, the banks must sell securities. Thus in this contingency the securities necessary to satisfy the demand of savers will be forthcoming from the banks.
>
> (letter 1428, 3 February 1931)

In the evening of the same day, an unconvinced Sraffa immediately replied:

> I don't think your explanation affects my argument. However, before writing it down in extenso, I should like to be sure that I have not misunderstood you.
>
> If the entrepreneurs who are making losses require less Income and Business-Deposits, and the Banks sell securities in order to meet their requirement, all such securities must be purchased by those very entrepreneurs, who will pay for them out of their deposits. (These deposits were left intact by the losses, production, or rather 'input', having fallen in proportion to the fall in proceeds – or more.)
>
> Thus the same circumstance that brings about an additional supply of old securities, produces an equal additional demand for them; and no part of this supply remains available to meet the savers' demand for investments.
>
> (letter 1426, 3 February 1931)

The next day, Keynes, in his pencilled answer, objected:

> No. The entrepreneurs will have failed to get their deposits replenished in the ordinary way as the result of sales proceeds. Instead, the savers (or those from whom they have bought securities) will have extra Savings-deposits, which the banks must cancel by selling Consols to them. The result of the extra saving is that at the end of the production period savers or their nominees possess balances which other-

> wise the entrepreneurs would have had ready to meet their outgoings in the next production period.
>
> (letter 1427, 4 February 1931)

Still not convinced, two days later, Sraffa wrote a note (we do not, however, know if it was actually sent to Keynes):

> How can losses deplenish the entrepreneur's deposits, if he reduces input in proportion to the fall in price? If the outflow (total cost of production) falls with the inflow (sales' proceeds) deposits are not affected.
>
> I therefore conclude that you are withdrawing the concession which you seemed to be willing to make in your first note [letter 1428, quoted above, referring to page 145 of the *Treatise*] – i.e. that entrepreneurs reduce output when the sales' proceeds fall short of cost of production.
>
> (PS papers, D1/76/3)

And here Sraffa adds a most important remark, pointing out a matter that was to have enormous impact on the following discussions and interpretations of the *Treatise* within the Circus, namely the implicit assumption of a fixed output, which is related to Keynes's parable of the widow's cruse:

> It is necessary for you to assume that they [the entrepreneurs] do not reduce output *at all*. Because, if they reduced it to any extent, however small, their requirements for paying costs would fail to absorb (via sale of securities, etc.) the whole of the excess of savings over investments; the difference would represent a net increase in the demand for securities, and their price would rise in consequence.
>
> (ibidem)

For a couple of months we have no more correspondence between Keynes and Sraffa. However, it is likely that they went on arguing out the *Treatise viva voce*, since we know they met quite frequently. In the meanwhile, the Circus continued their meetings, and the 'hot' topic was precisely that section iii – 'The Price-level of New Investment-goods' – of Chapter 10 which was at issue in the February correspondence between Keynes and Sraffa cited above. In particular, two related questions were discussed: the so-called 'widow's cruse fallacy' – 'the most important issue discussed by the Circus', according to Kahn (Kahn 1984: 106) – and the asserted independence of the two price-levels (see Ch. 1: 23). On these questions there is a very important unpublished six-page note by Sraffa dated 15 April 1931 (PS papers, D1/81), in reply to a note – 'The price-level of investment-goods' – by Kahn of 5 April (CWK XIII: 203–6). (To Sraffa's criticism Kahn replied with a further note, also published in CWK XIII: 206–7.) As we shall be dealing with these documents later (in

Ch. 11), we need here only recall Sraffa's main argument in that note, since it reinforces and enlarges upon the criticism we have considered so far. Let us now look at the 'new' argument. According to Sraffa, profits are paid at the end of the production period, once the output has already been reduced (or increased). Therefore, the way in which entrepreneurs spend the profits (i.e. the case of the 'widow's cruse') or make up for the losses (i.e. the case of the 'Danaid jar') will affect the level of the output only in the following period, rather than, as Keynes stated in the *Treatise*, the price-level in the current period. It is worth noting that this criticism is peculiar to Sraffa, and does not seem to have been taken up by others within the Circus, despite the stress Sraffa placed on its importance.

As we have already seen, in June 1931 the Circus's activities came to an end, and so did the written discussion of the *Treatise* between Keynes and Sraffa. However, a new front of controversy opened up, fire coming, this time, from outside the Cambridge citadel.

The year 1931 saw the great controversy between Hayek and Keynes burst onto the scene (see Chs 9 and 16). In the August issue of the London School of Economics periodical, *Economica*, Hayek published a review-article of Keynes's *Treatise* (Hayek 1931a). Keynes replied with an article in the November issue of the same periodical (Keynes 1931a), to which Hayek added a Rejoinder (1931d). Hayek then published the second part of his review-article in February 1932 (Hayek 1932a), to which an exhausted Keynes decided not to reply. In the meanwhile, Keynes had asked Sraffa to join in the debate. As usual, Sraffa took the charge very seriously, and the closing months of 1931 saw him hard at work on it (indeed, the proofs of the forthcoming article were ready by December), as the impressive amount of unpublished notes and earlier drafts testify.[6] Out of this work, Sraffa produced an article as concise (only eleven pages long) as severe, published in the March 1932 issue of the *Economic Journal* (Sraffa 1932a). First and foremost it was an attack on Hayek's theory as presented in *Prices and Production*, but it also contained, albeit somewhat elusively, some new theoretical notions that were later to be exploited *both* by Keynes *and* by Sraffa. In particular, as is well known, in Chapter 17 of the *General Theory* Keynes introduced and utilized the notion of 'the own-rates of interest' which he attributed to Sraffa, referring precisely to the March 1932 article in the *Economic Journal*. (It is to be noted that that is the only place in the *General Theory* where Keynes cites Sraffa.[7])

Two letters from Keynes relate to Sraffa's article. In the first letter Keynes says that, having read the pages of the article, he has 'no substantial criticisms to add' and thinks 'it is excellent'. He writes:

> I have pencilled some small verbal changes, either for the sake of the English or for the sake of clearness. The only material point is the rewording which I suggest on page 16. But here I think I must be giving the meaning which you intend.
>
> (letter 1431, 18 December 1931)

But what was 'the material point' on page 16? And what was the meaning Sraffa intended? Actually, involved here was the fundamental question of the exact nature and the rigorous definition of the notion of the rate of interest. On that particular page[8] Sraffa was devising the notion of a 'natural or commodity rate of interest' as the ratio between the spot and the forward prices of a commodity, and he had proposed two substantially similar alternatives, the first of which (with some minor amendments) was the one eventually chosen and is therefore the one we find in the published article, where Sraffa suggested the following example:

> Loans are currently made in the present world in terms of every commodity for which there is a forward market. When a cotton spinner borrows a sum of money for three months and uses the proceeds to purchase spot a quantity of raw cotton which he simultaneously sells three months forward, he is actually 'borrowing cotton' for that period. The rate of interest which he pays, per hundred bales of cotton, is the number of bales that can be purchased with the following sum of money: the interest on the money required to buy spot 100 bales plus the excess (or minus the deficiency) of the spot over the forward prices of the 100 bales.
>
> (Sraffa 1932a: 49–50)

If the reader is still curious to know what Keynes's alternative definition of the rate of interest – rejected by Sraffa – actually was, we are now able to satisfy his or her curiosity. In fact, from the Sraffa unpublished papers, we know that Keynes had suggested the following 're-wording' of Sraffa's definition:

> The rate of interest which he pays, per hundred bales of cotton, is the number of forward bales that can be purchased with the interest on the money required to buy spot 100 bales, plus the excess over 100 (or minus the deficiency) of the number of forward bales which can be purchased for the same price as 100 spot bales.
>
> (PS papers, D3/7)

Furthermore, in his second letter, Keynes had returned to, and expanded on, the same question, putting forward the following most interesting argument:

> As regards the forward bales, I am sending the first of your alternatives to the printer, but will you in proof again consider my alternative, since I am not yet persuaded that it is wrong? It is a characteristic of interest to be payable in arrear, and not in advance. If it is payable in advance we call it discount. Thus it seems to me to be of the essence of the case that the amount of interest should be calculated in

> forward [Keynes's underlining] bales; that it is to say we have to find how many forward bales can be obtained by parting with a given number of spot bales.
>
> (letter 1432, 21 December 1931)

However, as we know, Sraffa remained unmoved by Keynes's argument, and insisted on having his own definition of the rate of interest printed.

What is really remarkable is the fact that when, five years later, in Chapter 17 of the *General Theory*, Keynes reconsidered the matter, he stated that the 'exact relationship' between the money rate of interest and the 'own-rate of interest' was 'first pointed out by Mr Sraffa' in his essay in the March 1932 issue of the *Economic Journal*.

What can we then conclude from this episode, which I find highly symptomatic of the nature of their relationship? On the one hand, we see that their relationship was very close and important: they sided together to rebut Hayek's attack, and Keynes's spared no pains even in helping Sraffa to improve his written style. On the other hand, and at the same time, it would be difficult to find two more independent intellectual figures: relatively speaking, Keynes emerges from the correspondence as the more accommodating of the two, Sraffa as the more inflexible. I would not say that theirs was 'a case of non-communication', as they did indeed communicate, and very intensely, at least in this period. However, their theoretical paths failed to converge fully, and theirs was an alliance against the common external enemy (Hayek in this instance, and more generally the orthodox theory), rather than an attempt to produce at least some shared material or tools as a prelude to a new, alternative economic theory. Actually, Joan Robinson was not too wide of the mark when she described Sraffa as 'secretly sceptical of the new [Keynesian] ideas'. In September 1931, Sraffa had written to Gramsci via Tania: 'Keynes, who involuntarily produced a critique of liberal, capitalist economy, concludes with an apology for the capitalist entrepreneur and a search for "remedies"' (Sraffa 1991: 34, letter from PS to Tania, 9 September 1931, my transl.). Sraffa always kept a sort of a cultural distance, if not aloofness, from his Cambridge friends, which, as the above observation shows, also had something to do with his political stance.

Other documents on economic theory

We group here some other documents on economic theory. First of all, we have two documents on Marxian matters. The first document (letter 1923, 11 November 1928) testifies to Keynes's reliance on Sraffa for Marxian matters. In fact, it concerns criticism of a paper on Marx by a certain Mr Ferrand, proposed for publication in the *Economic Journal*. Sraffa's advice was to reject the paper. (The paper was rejected.)

Evidencing Sraffa's attempts to interest Keynes in Marx's economic theory, we find a second document, a short letter, dated 5 April 1932, in which Keynes wrote the following very telling lines:

> I made a good try at the Marx volumes, but I swear that it absolutely beats me what you find in them, or what you expected me to find! I did not discover a single sentence of any conceivable interest to a rational human being.
>
> (letter 1433, 5 April 1932)

Despite this blunt remark, however, some elements of Marxian economic theory must have had a certain impact on Keynes's thinking in that period, since we find him relying quite heavily on the Marxian distinction between the *C-M-C'* and the *M-C-M'* circulation of commodity and money in one of the 1933 drafts of Chapter 2 of the *General Theory*. Sraffa's attempts cannot have been so unsuccessful after all, if Keynes was prompted to make the important distinction between a co-operative economy and an entrepreneur economy (see CWK XXIX: 76 ff.).

Then we have an important exchange of notes that can probably be dated to 1932. They were found in that famous 'laundry hamper' full of papers discovered only during the winter of 1975–76. Among other things, there is a file named by Keynes 'Discussion with Piero'. It contains three undated documents: a note with a diagram by Sraffa (letter 1047, in CWK XXIX: 157–8), followed by two longer notes by Keynes (letters 1001 and 1002, in CWK XXIX: 158–60). The subject of these notes is the consequences on profits and output of a reduction in wages: they have already been published, in CWK XXIX, and there is no need for us to dwell on them here.

With regard to economic theory, the extant correspondence between the two Cambridge economists does not include anything of interest until October 1937. In this month we have a batch of four letters, two from Keynes together with the two answers by Sraffa. They deal with questions Keynes suggested to Sraffa as suitable subjects to be discussed with his research students (see Marcuzzo 2004).

With the exception of the 1941 exchange on the question of external economies dealt with above, as from the end of 1937 no correspondence on the subject of economic theory survives.

Editing Ricardo

As from 1930 Sraffa was, as we well know, engaged in editing Ricardo's *Works and Correspondence*. It was Keynes who suggested Sraffa as the editor of this enterprise, which took forty-three years to carry to a successful conclusion. Sraffa and Keynes exchanged about sixty letters on the subject from 1930 to 1943. With very few exceptions the contents and the interest of this correspondence are essentially editorial or historical. From the point of view of their relationship, it emerges that Keynes's role was threefold: (1) to help Sraffa to find new documents, by introducing Sraffa to people and obtaining permits and passports during the war; (2) to press Sraffa to finish the editorial work, applying both kindness and firmness; and (3) to provide comment on Sraffa's introductions and notes, without interfering. Since the history of Sraffa's edition of Ricardo has already been related (Rosselli 2001) and the relevant unpublished correspondence examined in great detail (Gehrke 2003), we need not to dwell upon them here.

Hume's *Abstract*

It is often forgotten that Keynes and Sraffa were also joint editors of the new publication of Hume's *Abstract* of the *Treatise on Human Nature*, published in 1938 by the Cambridge University Press. In their Introduction, the two Cambridge scholars reveal for the first time the true identity of the author of the pamphlet (originally anonymously published in 1740), namely Hume himself, previously and mistakenly attributed to Adam Smith. The Introduction is significant, since Keynes and Sraffa point out the importance of the Humean notions of causality, custom, belief and probability in explaining human behaviour and social institutions; moreover, they are constant themes in both Keynes's and Sraffa's thought. Coming to Cambridge, Sraffa, whose education was mainly in the Continental tradition – closer to Kantian idealism, that is – had had long discussions with Keynes on Hume and British Empiricism. These discussions are reflected in about twenty letters Sraffa and Keynes exchanged, from January 1937 to January 1938, dealing with their common task of editing Hume. For Sraffa it was a difficult time, in Italy looking after his father, who was seriously ill. Eventually, on 15 December 1937, Sraffa wrote to Keynes: 'My father died a few days ago, peacefully and painlessly. I wish I could convey how intensely grateful he was to you to his last for all that you have done for me: his last happiness was to see my name next to yours on the proof of the Hume title-page' (letter 1947, 15 December 1937). In general, we can infer from these letters not only the importance both economists attached (to a fault, even, if fault there may be in such matters) to precise, rigorous historical and philological research, but also to Humean philosophy and analytical method as a possible foundation for a rigorous economic theory (see Fitzgibbons 1988; Ingrao and Ranchetti 1996; Ranchetti 1999).

The Italian and French editions of Keynes's works

It is a well-known fact that Sraffa translated Keynes's *Tract on Monetary Reform* into Italian (Keynes 1925); less well known is the circumstance that Sraffa acted as a sort of foreign editor and adviser for Keynes's *Treatise on*

Money and the *General Theory*. Fourteen letters, running from 1924 to 1946, document just how much Keynes relied upon Sraffa in these matters, and the care and trouble Sraffa took over making sure that the Italian and French editions of Keynes's works were accurate and free from error.

Academic and personal matters

Finally, I group here all the other extant letters, which deal with a variety of subjects. Particularly significant among them is the correspondence dealing first with Sraffa's appointment in 1927 as lecturer in the Cambridge Faculty of Economics and, later, with Sraffa's internment on the Isle of Man during the Second World War. This part of their correspondence again attests to the affection and efficiency Keynes showed in ensuring Sraffa the best possible conditions for living and studying in two especially hard periods of his life.[9]

With regard to Sraffa's appointment at Cambridge, we have Keynes's letter in which he says:

> Your article in the December *Journal* [Sraffa 1926] has been very much liked over here. Everyone I have spoken to agrees that it puts you in the front rank of the younger economists. Pigou is extremely interested, and has been looking up your Italian article. You may be interested to know that he feels he must, in the light of it, reconsider his whole position.
>
> (letter 1005, 25 January 1927)

There then ensued an offer of a Lectureship at Cambridge University. Very interesting, too, is Sraffa's reply (only partially published) dated 6 February 1927. Sraffa, then a young man of 28 but already a professor, holder of the chair of Political Economy at the University of Cagliari, was 'filled with joy' by Keynes's offer. However, in his characteristic way, Sraffa expressed some hesitation and doubts:

> If I were to rely only upon my own judgement, I would oscillate between the desire of coming to Cambridge and the fear of a fiasco – and would probably be unable to decide. But if I might assume that your having made the suggestion implies that you think that I could take the risk, I would entirely trust your judgement; and in this case, if an offer were made of an University-Lectureship in the University of Cambridge, I should be happy to accept.
>
> (letter 1916, 6 February 1927)

In the letter dated 5 June 1927, Sraffa again expresses his gratitude to Keynes, showing the kind of relationship he enjoyed with his great mentor in that period of his youth:

> You will easily imagine how happy I am in thinking that I am coming to Cambridge. As to the 'plunge into the unknown',[10] I rely upon the fact that I am taking it under your guidance and with the help of your benevolence for hoping not to be after all drowned.
>
> (letter 1921, 5 June 1927)

With regard to Sraffa's internment on the Isle of Man (see Ch. 12), it is remarkable that, notwithstanding the unfavourable conditions, Sraffa was still able to get some work done and keep up a sort of a scholarly correspondence with Keynes. From the Metropole Internment Camp, Home N.3, Isle of Man, Sraffa wrote to Keynes:

> I should be grateful [. . .] for permission for me to receive the *Economist* and other scientific periodicals. If I had these I think I could do some work, for in this camp (my fifth in a week) we have bedrooms, and although we are two men per bed and two beds per room, I may be able during a few hours to secure enough privacy for work.
>
> (letter 1960, 13 July 1940)

Conclusion

As I wrote at the beginning of this chapter, the last letter of the correspondence between Sraffa and Keynes is from Keynes. It is a short letter; Keynes had just returned from the United States. The last two sentences read:

> Lydia, and I too, sends her love to the Signora [Sraffa's mother, then living in Cambridge], for whom she has some spaghetti – and enough chocolate for you to make you sick. I travelled on the boat with Viner, and he was, I can tell you, much better company than one generally gets at the Captain's table.
>
> (letter 1038, 28 March 1946)

Affection and intellectual exchange: for twenty-five years, from 1921 to 1946, these were indeed the cement and the hallmark of the correspondence between Keynes and Sraffa, and of their personal relations.

Notes

1 So I was told in 1972 by Luigi Malagodi, a former Italian Prime Minister, and an acquaintance of Keynes since the 1920s.
2 For quite the contrary view, see Skidelsky, who defined the relationship between Sraffa and Keynes 'a case of non-communication' (Skidelsky 1986: 73). But see also Skidelsky (1992), where the importance of their intellectual and human relations cannot fail to emerge.
3 For a detailed account of Sraffa at the University of Cambridge see Marcuzzo (2004).

4 On the Circus, and on Sraffa's role in it, see also Moggridge (CWK XIII: 202 and 337–43), E.A.G. Robinson (1947, 1985), Patinkin and Leith (1977), Kahn (1984), Dimand (1988), Skidelsky (1992) and Marcuzzo (2001b).

5 The only attempts I am aware of, are Ranchetti (1998), Panico (2001) and Marcuzzo (2001b), although they are still somewhat incomplete.

6 See PS papers, files D3/9 and D3/10; to which should be added the annotations, both by Sraffa and by Keynes, on a copy of Hayek's *Prices and Production* conserved in the Wren Library among Sraffa's books.

7 Further details on the Hayek–Keynes–Sraffa controversy, and their impact on both Keynes's and Sraffa's thought, can be found in Hayek (1995), Ranchetti (2001), Ingrao and Ranchetti (1996: chapters on Sraffa and on Keynes) and Kurz (1995, 2000).

8 In fact, 'page 16' refers here to the pagination of the typescript kept among the PS papers, but it corresponds to page 50 of the published article (Sraffa 1932a), where we find the definition of the rate of interest.

9 More details on these two important periods of Sraffa's life can be found in the chapter on Sraffa in Ingrao and Ranchetti (1996).

10 In his previous letter (letter 1006, 31 May 1927), to which Sraffa is answering, Keynes had written: 'I am very much delighted to think that we are to have you at Cambridge, at any rate for a time. But I realise at the same time that it is something of a plunge into the unknown on your side'.

Table 4.1 Keynes–Sraffa correspondence

From	*To*	*Year*	*Month*	*Day*	*Date*	*Archive*		*Published in*	*Item*
PS	JMK					Keynes–King's	B/1/77		1046
PS	JMK					Keynes–King's	EJ/6/8/52		1048
JMK	PS					Sraffa–Trinity	Add.ms.a.427/1		5140
PS	JMK	1921	August	5	Dated letter	Keynes–King's	L/S/4		1049
JMK	PS	1921	December	3	Dated letter	Sraffa–Trinity	Add.ms.a.427/2		5113
JMK	PS	1922	March	13	Dated letter	Sraffa–Trinity	Add.ms.a.427/3		5114
JMK	PS	1922	March	14	Dated letter	Sraffa–Trinity	Add.ms.a.427/4		5115
PS	JMK	1922	April	15	Dated letter	Keynes–King's	EJ/1/2/197–8	Naldi 1998: 503, (E)	1050
JMK	PS	1922	October	9	Dated letter	Sraffa–Trinity	Add.ms.a.427/5		5141
PS	JMK	1922	December	25	Dated letter	Keynes–King's	L/S/5–6	Kaldor 1985: 618, (E)	1051
PS	JMK	1923	January	6	Dated letter	Keynes–King's	L/S/7–8		1052
PS	JMK	1923	January	13	Dated letter	Keynes–King's	L/S/9	Naldi 1998: 500, (E)	1908
PS	JMK	1923	January	22	Dated letter	Keynes–King's	L/S/10–11	Naldi 1998: 500, (E)	1909
JMK	PS	1923	January	24	Dated letter	Sraffa–Trinity	Add.ms.a.427/6		5116
PS	JMK	1923	January	26	Dated letter	Keynes–King's	L/S/12–13		1910
JMK	PS	1923	February	14	Dated letter	Sraffa–Trinity	Add.ms.a.427/7		5117
PS	JMK	1924	March	8	Dated letter	Keynes–King's	MR/1/1/83–4		1911
JMK	PS	1924	September	18	Dated letter	Sraffa–Trinity	Add.ms.a.427/8		5118
PS	JMK	1924	November	6	Dated letter	Keynes–King's	L/S/18–19	Naldi 2004: 90, fn. 12, (E)	1912
PS	JMK	1924	November	23	Dated letter	Keynes–King's	L/S/20	Naldi 1998: 498, (E)	1913
PS	JMK	1924	December	22	Dated letter	Keynes–King's	MR/1/1/85		1914
JMK	PS	1924	December	30	Dated letter	Keynes–King's	MR/1/1/86	CWK XIII: 22, (E)	1003
JMK	PS	1925	February	23	Dated letter	Sraffa–Trinity	Add.ms.a.427/9		5119
JMK	PS	1926	April	20	Dated letter	Sraffa–Trinity	Add.ms.a.427/10		5142
PS	JMK	1926	June	6	Dated letter	Keynes–King's	L/S/21–4	Roncaglia 1978: 11–13, (E)	1915
JMK	PS	1927	January	25	Dated letter	Keynes–King's	L/S/25	Kaldor 1985: 624–5	1005

PS	JMK	1927	February	6	Dated letter	Keynes–King's	L/S/26–7	Kaldor 1985: 626, (E)	1916
						Sraffa–Trinity	B9/1/4		
						Sraffa–Trinity	B9/1/5		
						Sraffa–Trinity	B9/1/6	Naldi 2004: 98, fn. 29, (E)	
PS	JMK	1927	February	16	Dated letter	Keynes–King's	L/S/28–9		1917
PS	JMK	1927	February	26	Dated letter	Keynes–King's	L/S/30–1	Naldi 1998: 501, (E)	1918
JMK	PS	1927	March	2	Dated letter	Sraffa–Trinity	Add.ms.a.427/11		5120
PS	JMK	1927	March	10	Dated letter	Keynes–King's	L/S/32		1919
JMK	PS	1927	May	4	Dated letter	Sraffa–Trinity	Add.ms.a.427/12		5121
PS	JMK	1927	May	9	Dated letter	Keynes–King's	L/S/33–6	Marcuzzo 2004: 124, fn. 6, (E)	1920
JMK	PS	1927	May	31	Dated letter	Sraffa–Trinity	Add.ms.a.427/13	Marcuzzo 2004: 125, fn. 7 and 9, (E)	1006
						Keynes–King's	L/S/37–9		
PS	JMK	1927	June		Attributed	Sraffa–Trinity	B9/1/7		2251
PS	JMK	1927	June	5	Dated letter	Keynes–King's	L/S/40–1	Naldi 2000b: 201, (E)	1921
JMK	PS	1927	August	12	Dated letter	Sraffa–Trinity	Add.ms.a.427/14		5123
JMK	PS	1927	September	19	Dated letter	Sraffa–Trinity	Add.ms.a.427/15		5144
JMK	PS	1928	March	14	Dated letter	Sraffa–Trinity	Add.ms.a.427/16		5145
JMK	PS	1928	November	5	Dated letter	Sraffa–Trinity	Add.ms.a.427/17		5146
PS	JMK	1928	November	11	Dated letter	Keynes–King's	EJ/1/3/117–8		1923
JMK	PS	1929	January	16	Dated letter	Sraffa–Trinity	Add.ms.a.427/18		5147
JMK	PS	1929	January	25	Dated letter	Sraffa–Trinity	Add.ms.a.427/19		5122
JMK	PS	1929	June	11	Dated letter	Sraffa–Trinity	Add.ms.a.427/20		5148
PS	JMK	1930	January	28	Dated letter	Keynes–King's	EJ/1/3/181	Marchionatti 2000: 79–80, (E)	1922
JMK	PS	1930	February	17	Dated letter	Sraffa–Trinity	Add.ms.a.427/21		5149
JMK	PS	1930	February	20	Dated letter	Sraffa–Trinity	Add.ms.a.427/22		5124
JMK	PS	1930	March		Attributed	Sraffa–Trinity	D3/11/65/48		1397
JMK	PS	1930	March	16	Dated letter	Sraffa–Trinity	D3/11/65/42		1398
PS	JMK	1930	March	17	Dated letter	Keynes–King's Sraffa–Trinity	L/S/42 D3/11/65/40	Gehrke and Kurz 2002: 646, (E)	1925

Table 4.1 continued

From	*To*	*Year*	*Month*	*Day*	*Date*	*Archive*		*Published in*	*Item*
JMK	PS	1930	March	21	Dated letter	Sraffa–Trinity	D3/11/65/43		2221
PS	JMK	1930	March	22	Dated letter	Keynes–King's Sraffa–Trinity	L/S/43–4 D3/11/65/41	Naldi 2004: 109, fn. 47, (E)	1926
JMK	PS	1930	March	24	Dated letter	Sraffa–Trinity	D3/11/65/45		1399
PS	JMK	1930	March	28	Dated letter	RES–British Library	RES/10/2/1	Naldi 2004: 109, fn. 47, (E)	2229
JMK	PS	1930	March	29	Dated letter	Sraffa–Trinity	D3/11/65/50		1422
PS	JMK	1930	April	7	Dated letter	Keynes–King's	L/S/48–9		1927
JMK	PS	1930	April	8	Dated letter	Sraffa–Trinity	D3/11/65/49		1400
PS	JMK	1930	April	14	Dated letter	Keynes–King's	RES/1/1/180–1	Gehrke and Kurz 2002: 649, (E)	1928
JMK	PS	1930	June	27	Dated letter	Sraffa–Trinity	D3/11/65/47		1419
JMK	PS	1930	June	30	Dated letter	Sraffa–Trinity	D3/11/65/59		1420
JMK	PS	1930	July	2	Dated letter	Sraffa–Trinity	D3/11/65/54		1421
PS	JMK	1930	July	2	Attributed	Keynes–King's	L/S/57		1924
PS	JMK	1930	July	3	Dated letter	Keynes–King's	L/S/54	Gehrke and Kurz 2002: 650, (E)	1929
PS	JMK	1930	July	21	Dated letter	Keynes–King's	L/S/55–6		1930
JMK	PS	1930	December	4	Dated letter	Sraffa–Trinity	D3/11/65/55	Naldi 2004: 109–10, (E)	1423
PS	JMK	1930	December	11	Dated letter	Keynes–King's	L/S/70–1		1931
JMK	PS	1930	December	25	Dated letter	Sraffa–Trinity	D3/11/65/46		1424
PS	JMK	1931	January	22	Dated letter	Sraffa–Trinity	D3/11/65/62	Gehrke and Kurz 2002: 651, (E)	1425
PS	JMK	1931	February	3	Dated letter	Sraffa–Trinity	D1/76/2		1426
JMK	PS	1931	February	3	Dated letter	Sraffa–Trinity	D1/76/4		1428
JMK	PS	1931	February	4	Dated letter	Sraffa–Trinity	D1/76/2		1427
PS	JMK	1931	May	9	Dated letter	Keynes–King's Kaldor–King's	L/S/72–5 NK/1/49/1/48–51	CWK XIII: 207–9	1932

JMK	PS	1931	May	15	Dated letter	Sraffa–Trinity Keynes–King's	D1/77/1–3 L/S/76–8	CWK XIII: 209–11	1007
PS	JMK	1931	September	8	Dated letter	RES–British Library	RES/10/2/1	Gehrke and Kurz 2002: 652, (E)	2230
JMK	PS	1931	November	7	Dated letter	Sraffa–Trinity	Add.ms.a.427/23		5150
JMK	PS	1931	December	2	Dated letter	Sraffa–Trinity	D3/11/67/7		1429
JMK	PS	1931	December	12	Dated letter	Sraffa–Trinity	D3/11/67/3		1430
JMK	PS	1931	December	18	Dated letter	Sraffa–Trinity	D3/11/65/56		1431
JMK	PS	1931	December	21	Dated letter	Sraffa–Trinity	D3/11/65/52		1432
JMK	PS	1932			Attributed	Keynes–King's	GTE/1/81	CWK XXIX: 158	1001
JMK	PS	1932			Attributed	Keynes–King's	GTE/1/75–8	CWK XXIX: 158–60	1002
PS	JMK	1932			Attributed	Keynes–King's	GTE/1/82–3	CWK XXIX: 157–8	1047
JMK	PS	1932	February	1	Dated letter	Kahn–King's	RFK/13/57/9	CWK XIII: 265	1008
JMK	PS	1932	April	5	Dated letter	Sraffa–Trinity	D3/11/65/53	De Vivo 2000: 274, fn. 39, (E)	1433
JMK	PS	1932	May	19	Dated letter	Sraffa–Trinity	D3/11/56/35		1434
JMK	PS	1932	December	9	Dated letter	Sraffa–Trinity	Add.ms.a.427/24		5151
JMK	PS	1932	December	15	Dated letter	Sraffa–Trinity	D3/11/65/57		1435
JMK	PS	1932	December	16	Attributed	Sraffa–Trinity	C155		2238
PS	JMK	1932	December	20	Dated letter	Keynes–King's	B/1/37–9		1933
JMK	PS	1932	December	25	Dated letter	Sraffa–Trinity	D3/11/65/51/1–2		1436
PS	JMK	1933	January	1	Dated letter	Keynes–King's	B/1/40–1		1934
JMK	PS	1933	January	6	Dated letter	Sraffa–Trinity	D3/11/65/60a		1437
JMK	PS	1933	January	10	Dated letter	Sraffa–Trinity	D3/11/65/58		1438
PS	JMK	1933	January	12	Dated letter	Keynes–King's	B/1/42–3		1935
JMK	PS	1933	January	18	Dated letter	Sraffa–Trinity	Add.ms.a.427/25		5152
PS	JMK	1933	February		Attributed	RES–British Library	RES/10/2/1		2237
JMK	PS	1933	March	8	Dated letter	Sraffa–Trinity	Add.ms.a.427/26		5153
JMK	PS	1933	September	14	Dated letter	Sraffa–Trinity	D3/11/65/65/1–2	Gehrke and Kurz 2002: 660, (E)	1439
JMK	PS	1933	December	3	Dated letter	Sraffa–Trinity	Add.ms.a.427/27		5154

Table 4.1 continued

From	*To*	*Year*	*Month*	*Day*	*Date*	*Archive*		*Published in*	*Item*
JMK	PS	1934	January	5	Dated letter	Sraffa–Trinity	D3/11/65/61		1440
PS	JMK	1934	January	From 5 to 24	Attributed	Sraffa–Trinity	D3/11/63/37/i–ii	Gehrke and Kurz 2002: 665, (E)	5112
JMK	PS	1934	March	22	Dated letter	Sraffa–Trinity Keynes–King's	Add.ms.a.427/28 UA/5/3/72		1009
PS	JMK	1934	March	29	Dated letter	Keynes–King's	UA/5/3/77–8	Naldi 2004: 110, fn. 48, (E)	1936
JMK	PS	1934	April	6	Dated letter	Sraffa–Trinity Keynes–King's	Add.ms.a.427/29 UA/5/3/79		1010
PS	JMK	1934	April	10	Dated letter	Keynes–King's	L/S/82		1937
JMK	PS	1934	August	1	Dated letter	Sraffa–Trinity Keynes–King's	Add.ms.a.427/31 UA/5/3/98		1011
JMK	PS	1934	August	9	Dated letter	Sraffa–Trinity	Add.ms.a.427/32		5157
JMK	PS	1934	September	13	Dated letter	Sraffa–Trinity	Add.ms.a.427/33		5158
PS	JMK	1934	September	18	Dated letter	Keynes–King's	L/S/83–4		1938
JMK	PS	1934	December	20	Dated letter	Sraffa–Trinity	Add.ms.a.427/34		5125
JMK	PS	1935	January	13	Dated letter	Sraffa–Trinity	Add.ms.a.427/35		5159
JMK	PS	1935	October	7	Dated letter	Sraffa–Trinity	Add.ms.a.427/36		5126
JMK	PS	1935	October	24	Dated letter	Sraffa–Trinity	Add.ms.a.427/37		5127
PS	JMK	1936	February		Attributed	Keynes–King's	A/36/6		1040
JMK	PS	1936	March	4	Dated letter	Sraffa–Trinity	D3/11/65/67		1441
PS	JMK	1936	March	21	Dated letter	Keynes–King's	RES/1/2/83		1939
JMK	PS	1936	August	31	Dated letter	Sraffa–Trinity	Add.ms.a.427/38		5160
JMK	PS	1936	September	20	Dated letter	Sraffa–Trinity	Add.ms.a.427/39		5161
JMK	PS	1936	September	21	Dated letter	Sraffa–Trinity	Add.ms.a.427/40		5128
JMK	PS	1937			Attributed	Sraffa–Trinity	C155/66		2220
JMK	PS	1937	January	18	Dated letter	Keynes–King's	UA/14/2/245–6		1442
JMK	PS	1937	August	22	Dated letter	Sraffa–Trinity Kahn–King's	D3/11/65/39 RFK/13/57/221		1012

JMK	PS	1937	September	5	Dated letter	Sraffa–Trinity RES–British Library	Add.ms.a.427/41 RES/10/2/1		2231
JMK	PS	1937	September	6	Dated letter	Sraffa–Trinity	Add.ms.a.427/42		5129
PS	JMK	1937	September	9	Dated letter	RES–British Library	RES/10/2/1		2232
PS	JMK	1937	October	13	Dated letter	Keynes–King's	PP/64/4–5		1940
PS	JMK	1937	October	13	Dated letter	Keynes–King's	PP/64/6–7		1941
JMK	PS	1937	October	18	Dated letter	Sraffa–Trinity Keynes–King's	Add.ms.a.427/43 UA/5/4/13–4	Marcuzzo 1993: 451, (E)	1013
JMK	PS	1937	October	18	Dated letter	Sraffa–Trinity	Add.ms.a.427/44		5130
PS	JMK	1937	October	20	Dated letter	Keynes–King's	PP/64/8–9	Marcuzzo 2004: 136, fn. 40, (E)	1942
JMK	PS	1937	October	25	Dated letter	Sraffa–Trinity	Add.ms.a.427/45	Marcuzzo 2004: 138, fn. 43, (E)	1014
JMK	PS	1937	October	26	Dated letter	Keynes–King's Sraffa–Trinity	EJ/1/4/204 D3/11/63/51ii	Marcuzzo 2004: 138, fn. 44, (E)	1443
PS	JMK	1937	October	26	Dated letter	Keynes–King's	EJ/1/4/205–6		1943
JMK	PS	1937	October	28	Dated letter	Sraffa–Trinity	Add.ms.a.427/46		5131
JMK	PS	1937	November	1	Dated letter	Sraffa–Trinity Keynes–King's	Add.ms.a.427/47 PP/64/27–8		1015
JMK	PS	1937	November	7	Dated letter	Sraffa–Trinity	Add.ms.a.427/48		5143
JMK	PS	1937	November	14	Dated letter	Sraffa–Trinity Keynes–King's	Add.ms.a.427/49 PP/64/29–37	Fitzgibbons 1988: 200, (E)	1016
PS	JMK	1937	November	20	Dated letter	Keynes–King's	PP/64/38–45		1944
JMK	PS	1937	November	27	Dated letter	Sraffa–Trinity Keynes–King's	Add.ms.a.427/50 PP/64/46–57	Fitzgibbons 1988: 200–1, (E)	1017
PS	JMK	1937	December	4	Dated letter	Keynes–King's	PP/64/58–63		1945
JMK	PS	1937	December	6	Dated letter	Sraffa–Trinity Keynes–King's	Add.ms.a.427/51 PP/64/64–7		1018
PS	JMK	1937	December	7	Dated letter	Keynes–King's	PP/64/68–9		1946

Table 4.1 continued

From	*To*	*Year*	*Month*	*Day*	*Date*	*Archive*		*Published in*	*Item*
PS	JMK	1937	December	15	Dated letter	Keynes–King's	PP/64/80–1		1947
JMK	PS	1937	December	29	Dated letter	Sraffa–Trinity Keynes–King's	Add.ms.a.427/52 PP/64/92–3		1019
PS	JMK	1938	January	4	Dated letter	Keynes–King's	PP/64/94–5		1948
JMK	PS	1938	January	7	Dated letter	Sraffa–Trinity Keynes–King's	D3/11/65/38/1–2 PP/64/96–7		1020
JMK	PS	1938	January	13	Dated letter	Sraffa–Trinity Keynes–King's	Add.ms.a.427/53 PP/64/98		1021
PS	JMK	1938	January	15	Dated letter	Keynes–King's	PP/64/99–100		1949
PS	JMK	1938	January	18	Dated letter	Keynes–King's	PP/64/101–2		1950
JMK	PS	1938	January	19	Dated letter	Sraffa–Trinity Keynes–King's	Add.ms.a.427/54 PP/64/103		1022
PS	JMK	1938	January	21	Dated letter	Keynes–King's	PP/64/104–6		1951
JMK	PS	1938	January	22	Dated letter	Sraffa–Trinity Keynes–King's	Add.ms.a.427/55 PP/64/107–9		1023
PS	JMK	1938	January	26	Dated letter	Keynes–King's	PP/64/110–11		1952
JMK	PS	1938	February	1	Dated letter	Sraffa–Trinity	Add.ms.a.427/56		5132
PS	JMK	1938	February	2	Dated letter	RES–British Library	RES/10/2/1		2233
JMK	PS	1938	February	7	Dated letter	Sraffa–Trinity RES–British Library	D3/11/65/37 RES/10/2/1–2	Rosselli 2001: 190, 205, (E)	1444
PS	JMK	1938	February	10	Dated letter	RES–British Library	RES/10/2/1		2234
JMK	PS	1938	February	20	Dated letter	Sraffa–Trinity	Add.ms.a.427/57		5133
JMK	PS	1938	February	23	Dated letter	Sraffa–Trinity	Add.ms.a.427/58		5134
JMK	PS	1938	March	26	Dated letter	Sraffa–Trinity	Add.ms.a.427/59		5135
JMK	PS	1938	April	25	Dated letter	Sraffa–Trinity	Add.ms.a.427/60		5136

JMK	PS	1938	April	29	Dated letter	Sraffa–Trinity	Add.ms.a.427/61		5162
JMK	PS	1938	May	10	Dated letter	Sraffa–Trinity Keynes–King's	Add.ms.a.427/62 GTE/3/79		1024
PS	JMK	1938	May	12	Dated letter	Keynes–King's	GTE/3/80–3		1953
JMK	PS	1938	July	5	Dated letter	Sraffa–Trinity	Add.ms.a.427/63		5137
JMK	PS	1938	July	10	Dated letter	Sraffa–Trinity	Add.ms.a.427/64		5138
PS	JMK	1938	July	18	Dated letter	Keynes–King's	GTE/3/247–8	Marcuzzo 2004: 143, fn. 67, (E)	1954
JMK	PS	1938	July	25	Dated letter	Sraffa–Trinity Keynes–King's	Add.ms.a.427/65 GTE/3/249		1025
JMK	PS	1938	July	30	Dated letter	Sraffa–Trinity	D3/11/67/47	Gehrke and Kurz 2002: 668, fn. 18, (E)	1445
JMK	PS	1938	August	22	Dated letter	Sraffa–Trinity	Add.ms.a.427/66		5163
PS	JMK	1938	September	15	Dated letter	Keynes–King's	GTE/3/250		1955
PS	JMK	1938	December	12	Dated letter	Keynes–King's	GTE/3/101–2		1956
JMK	PS	1938	December	22	Dated letter	Keynes–King's	GTE/3/106		1026
PS	JMK	1939	March	9	Dated letter	Keynes–King's	PP/64/132		1957
JMK	PS	1939	March	14	Dated letter	Sraffa–Trinity Keynes–King's	Add.ms.a.427/67 GTE/3/252		1027
PS	JMK	1939	March	15	Dated letter	Keynes–King's	GTE/3/254–5		1958
JMK	PS	1939	June	4	Dated letter	Keynes–King's	GTE/3/257		1446
JMK	PS	1939	June	23	Dated letter	Sraffa–Trinity Keynes–King's	D3/11/65/36/1–2 PP/64/133–4		1028
JMK	PS	1939	July	5	Dated letter	Sraffa–Trinity Keynes–King's	D3/11/65/29–30 L/S/88–94		1029
JMK	PS	1939	July	30	Dated letter	Sraffa–Trinity	D3/11/65/34		1448
JMK	PS	1939	August	4	Dated letter	Sraffa–Trinity	D3/11/65/31		1449
JMK	PS	1939	August	5	Dated letter	Sraffa–Trinity	D3/11/65/35		1039
JMK	PS	1939	August	5	Dated letter	Sraffa–Trinity	D3/11/65/28	Rosselli 2001: 191, (E)	1450
JMK	PS	1939	August	6	Dated letter	Sraffa–Trinity	D3/11/65/32		1045
JMK	PS	1939	October	28	Dated letter	Sraffa–Trinity	Add.ms.a.427/68		5139

Table 4.1 continued

From	*To*	*Year*	*Month*	*Day*	*Date*	*Archive*		*Published in*	*Item*
JMK	PS	1940	March	30	Dated letter	Sraffa–Trinity	D3/11/65/63		1044
PS	JMK	1940	April	11	Dated letter	Keynes–King's	HP/4/242		1959
JMK	PS	1940	June	15	Dated letter	Keynes–King's	UA/5/5/89–90		1030
JMK	PS	1940	June	15	Dated letter	Keynes–King's	UA/5/5/92–5		1031
JMK	PS	1940	June	15	Dated letter	Sraffa–Trinity	Add.ms.a.427/69		5164
JMK	PS	1940	June	18	Dated letter	Keynes–King's	PP/45/254/50		1032
JMK	PS	1940	June	20	Dated letter	Sraffa–Trinity	Add.ms.a.427/70		5165
PS	JMK	1940	July	13	Dated letter	Keynes–King's	UA/5/5/131–2	Naldi 2004: 116, fn. 57, (E)	1960
JMK	PS	1940	July	29	Dated letter	Sraffa–Trinity Keynes–King's	Add.ms.a.427/73 UA/5/5/175	 Naldi 2004: 116, fn. 57, (E)	1033
JMK	PS	1940	August	7	Dated letter	Sraffa–Trinity Keynes–King's	Add.ms.a.427/76 UA/5/5/133		1034
JMK	PS	1940	August	20	Dated letter	Sraffa–Trinity Keynes–King's	Add.ms.a.427/77 UA/5/5/228–30		1035
JMK	PS	1940	October	18	Dated letter	Sraffa–Trinity	D3/11/65/21		1004
JMK	PS	1941	February	24	Dated letter	Sraffa–Trinity RES–British Library	D3/11/65/24 RES/10/2/1	Naldi 2004: 110–11, fn. 48, (E)	1043
PS	JMK	1941	March	1	Dated letter	Sraffa–Trinity RES–British Library	D3/11/65/22 RES/10/2/1		1042
PS	JMK	1941	August	11	Dated letter	Keynes–King's	MM/4/63–4		2240
JMK	PS	1941	August	22	Dated letter	Sraffa–Trinity Keynes–King's	Add.ms.a.427/82 MM/5/61–2		2241
PS	JMK	1941	August	27	Dated letter	Keynes–King's	MM/4/279–84		2242
JMK	PS	1941	August	28	Dated letter	Keynes–King's	MM/4/278		2243
JMK	PS	1941	September	3	Dated letter	Keynes–King's	MM/4/271		2244
PS	JMK	1941	September	15	Dated letter	Keynes–King's	MM/4/272–4	Mongiovi 1996: 220, (E)	2245

JMK	PS	1941	September	22	Dated letter	Sraffa–Trinity	Add.ms.a.427/83		2246
						Keynes–King's	MM/4/270–1		
PS	JMK	1941	September	29	Dated letter	Keynes–King's	MM/4/275–6		2247
JMK	PS	1942	June	22	Dated letter	Sraffa–Trinity	Add.ms.a.427/84		5166
JMK	PS	1943	March	26	Dated letter	Sraffa–Trinity RES–British Library	D3/11/65/27 RES/10/2/1	Rosselli 2001: 191, (E)	1041
PS	JMK	1943	March	31	Dated letter	RES–British Library	RES/10/2/1		2222
						Sraffa–Trinity	D3/11/65/26/1–2		
JMK	PS	1943	April	2	Dated letter	Sraffa–Trinity RES–British Library	D3/11/65/18 RES/10/2/1	Rosselli 2001: 191, (E)	2223
PS	JMK	1943	April	6	Dated letter	RES–British Library	RES/10/2/1		2224
						Sraffa–Trinity	D3/11/65/19		
JMK	PS	1943	April	16	Dated letter	Sraffa–Trinity	D3/11/65/20		2225
JMK	PS	1943	April	25	Dated letter	Sraffa–Trinity RES–British Library	D3/11/65/17 RES/10/2/1		2226
PS	JMK	1943	July	1	Dated letter	RES–British Library	RES/10/2/1		2235
PS	JMK	1943	July	5	Dated letter	Keynes–King's	L/S/95–8	Porta 1986: 35, (E)	1961
PS	JMK	1943	July	12	Dated letter	Keynes–King's	L/S/105		1962
JMK	PS	1943	July	16	Dated letter	Sraffa–Trinity Keynes–King's	D3/11/67/67 L/S/107		1036
PS	JMK	1943	July	18	Dated letter	Keynes–King's	L/S/110–12		1963
PS	JMK	1943	July	19	Dated letter	Keynes–King's	L/S/113–14		1964
PS	JMK	1943	July	22	Dated letter	Keynes–King's	L/S/120		1965
JMK	PS	1943	July	23	Dated letter	Sraffa–Trinity	D3/11/67/75		2227
JMK	PS	1943	July	26	Dated letter	Sraffa–Trinity	D3/11/67/84		2228

Table 4.1 continued

From	*To*	*Year*	*Month*	*Day*	*Date*	*Archive*		*Published in*	*Item*
PS	JMK	1943	July	27	Dated letter	Keynes–King's	L/S/121–2		1966
PS	JMK	1943	August	5	Dated letter	Keynes–King's	L/S/126–7		1967
JMK	PS	1943	August	13	Dated letter	Sraffa–Trinity Keynes–King's	D3/11/67/88 L/S/128–9		1037
PS	JMK	1943	August	15	Dated letter	Keynes–King's	L/5/130–5		1968
PS	JMK	1943	September	4	Dated letter	RES–British Library	RES/10/2/1		2236
PS	JMK	1946	January	8	Dated letter	Keynes–King's	GTE/3/269–72		1969
JMK	PS	1946	March	28	Dated letter	Keynes–King's	L/46/96		1038

5 Managing Cambridge economics

The correspondence between Keynes and Pigou

Pascal Bridel and Bruna Ingrao

Keynes and Pigou: their personal relationship and correspondence

Pigou's intellectual biography remains to be written. Despite his influence on Cambridge economics, no comprehensive study is currently available. Apart from Collard's valuable essays (Collard 1981, 1996, 1999), Austin Robinson's entries in two encyclopaedia (A. Robinson 1968, 1971) and a few obituaries (Champernowne 1959; Johnson 1960; Saltmarsh and Wilkinson 1960), the main sources on the relationship between Pigou and Keynes are to be found in the writings of Keynes's scholars, focusing on their controversies during the 1930s and 1940s. Most authors seldom go further than considering Pigou as Keynes's archetypal neo-classical economist, 'a composite Aunt Sally of uncertain age' (Robertson 1937: 436).

Pigou was a subtle theorist who invented welfare economics, virtually single-handed, developed the first analysis of 'market failures', wrote – before Keynes's *General Theory* – the first theoretical treatise on systematic unemployment (Pigou 1913, 1933a), contributed an important book on trade cycles (Pigou 1927a) and laid down the real-balance effect as the stepping stone to the neo-classical synthesis. Probably the tip of an iceberg, their surviving correspondence offers interesting insights on the long-term relationship between Marshall's two favourite pupils.

Starting with their early intellectual collaboration at the beginning of the century, exchange on their ongoing research was constant between them. Keynes held Pigou's opinion in high esteem, even during the tense post-1936 episode, although in later years he tended to reply to Pigou's queries somewhat superciliously. Adepts of the Marshallian methodology, they were both interested in bridging the gap between economic theory and economic policy, but differed substantially on the connection between ethics and economics. They were jointly involved in the daily running of King's College and the Economics Tripos (including the all-important appointment committee).

In terms of economic theory, between 1907 and the early 1920s it was Pigou, not Keynes, who led the intellectual circle in Cambridge (Skidelsky

1983: 221). Their correspondence[1] reflects the progressive shift in their respective influence. In 1907 Pigou was instrumental in introducing Keynes to the London Political Economy Club, but by 1923 Pigou was 'only' the elder member of Keynes's own Political Economy Club. In 1908 Pigou reached into his own pocket to provide Keynes with the financial backing (on leaving the India Office) to take on his first lectureship. In the 1930s Keynes was the driving force behind most Cambridge appointments (e.g. Champernowne and Clark), asking for Pigou's support at the last committee stage. In 1924 Pigou was appointed full member of the Committee on the Currency and Bank of England Note Issues (the Chamberlain Committee), Keynes being one of the numerous witnesses to give evidence. In 1930, Keynes, as the most influential permanent member of the Macmillan Committee, 'was extremely sharp and close in his questioning of his professional colleagues, most notably Pigou' (Moggridge 1992: 493).

After the publication of the *General Theory*, Pigou judged Keynes's attack unfair to his own work on unemployment and to the Cambridge corpus of business cycle theory (Pigou 1936, [1950] 1999: 65). Despite Harrod's moderating influence, Keynes had chosen a strategy of all-out attack on the contemporary literature to underline the novelty of his own approach. In his books Pigou had indeed taken into account persistent unemployment phenomena, and even the idea of involuntary unemployment.[2] In *The Theory of Unemployment* he considered the welfare losses associated with 'enforced leisure', when unemployment continues over a long period hitting 'with tremendous force' a small group of people (Pigou 1933a: 14 ff.). In these conditions the 'would-be wage-earners' at the current wage rate, who are subjected to long spells of unemployment with heavy welfare losses, are clearly involuntary unemployed:

> Nobody can suppose that, with a distribution of this sort, the leisure associated with unemployment is an asset to be weighted against the loss of what work would have produced. It is an aggravation, not a mitigation of the subjective cost involved.
>
> (Pigou [1933a] 1999: 15)

As an aspect of fluctuations, persistent unemployment was a recognised phenomenon in pre-1936 business cycles theory. Much as for Robertson and Hayek (each along different lines), Pigou's core dissent was on Keynes's exclusive focus on under-employment equilibrium, combining Marshallian short-term analysis and stagnation. In terms of policy, Pigou never denied the importance of government intervention. In the early 1930s he signed with Keynes open letters in favour of government spending policies and as welfare theorist he studied corrections to market failures through fiscal policy. Keynesian themes in relation to market failures do indeed intersect with Pigouvian themes (limited rationality and the failure in optimal intertemporal decisions).

Despite various scholars' assertions to the contrary (Robbins 1971: 134; A. Robinson 1971), Pigou never completely recanted his criticism of Keynes's *General Theory*. His first reaction was to produce a severely critical review (Pigou 1936). In the late 1940s he moderated his judgement, showing appreciation of Keynes's insights, but never accepted Keynes's claim to have drafted a genuine *general* theory.[3] Pigou attempted to reabsorb Keynes's model in a wider analytical perspective, as a special case, qualifying the results, much as post-war neo-classical macroeconomics would later try to achieve (Pigou 1941, 1950). He anticipated many issues recurring in post-war criticism of Keynesianism, even pointing out the risk of 'progressive monetary inflation' as a result of full employment policies (Pigou [1944] 1999: 105).

From the mid-1930s onwards Pigou grew wary of the changed climate in Cambridge. He feared 'the school' at Cambridge – a preoccupation recurrent in his letters regarding the editorial policy of the *Economic Journal*, the Economic Tripos and new appointments. He joked ironically about 'certain priests' of the 'new economics', meaning Keynesianism (Pigou [1944] 1999: 100). However, he did not stop worrying about Keynes's health or seeking his advice. Keynes went on consulting him on scientific issues, even after their 1937–38 dispute over wage flexibility, when he privately considered Pigou's refutations as 'the work of a sick man'. In 1944, Pigou and Keynes together engineered Robertson's appointment at Cambridge and secured Hayek's election to the British Academy.

The correspondence includes 140 letters, written between 1905 and 1945, of which 92 by Pigou and 48 by Keynes, all to be found in JMK papers (see Table 5.1). A major problem arises because of Pigou's almost illegible handwriting and his habit of never dating his letters. The archivists suggest datings for certain items; a few postmarks are available. Some letters are published in Keynes's *Collected Writings*, partially reproduced in Keynes's biographies (Skidelsky 1983; Moggridge 1992), or in other sources (Aslanbegui and Oakes 2002). We suggest datings for most of the remaining letters.

Academic affairs

On retiring, Marshall supported Pigou's candidature as full professor of economics. In 1908, at barely thirty years old, Pigou was appointed to the Cambridge chair of Political Economy. He gave both curricular lecture courses and courses on subjects of his choice (Collard 1999: xxv). Pigou disliked administration and academic politics (Collard 1999: ix, xxv) but, as the only full professor of economics, he was responsible for the Economic Tripos and found himself deeply involved in the task. Over the years Pigou and Keynes discussed curricula, scholarships, appointments and other academic issues. Pigou looked to his younger, authoritative colleague for advice, while Keynes consulted 'the professor' on important issues and never failed to seek his support in academic decisions.

The early letters testify to their social relations. In 1907 Pigou invited Keynes to dinner 'en vêtements magnifiques' (letter 4160, 10 April 1907). Shortly after, he asked Keynes to dinner prior to Maynard's introductory meeting at the London Political Economy Club (letter 4232, late April 1907), to be held on 1 May 1907 (Moggridge 1992: 172). Early in 1908 he invited Keynes to visit his 'new palace' at King's: his repapered rooms, 'altogether glorious' (letter 4161, March–April 1908).

Well informed about Keynes's dissertation, he inquired about Keynes's discussion with W.E. Johnson (1858–1931) (Moggridge 1992: 175–6). Later that year, he invited Keynes to lecture on Money, Credit and Prices, specifying that he should treat the subject 'as realistically as possible' (letter 4162, 6 July 1908). These were Keynes's maiden lectures at Cambridge (Moggridge 1992: 198–9). A few years later they discussed Yule's appointment as University lecturer in Statistics (letter 4163, 1912).

In January 1915 Keynes duly informed Pigou that he had accepted for the duration of the War an appointment at the Treasury 'for special duty'. He advanced proposals for lectures at a time when teaching at Cambridge was in dire straits, the best men being absorbed by war duties. As Keynes commented, 'our lecture list, therefore, practically falls to the ground' (letter 4170, 9 January 1915).

No further correspondence exists on academic issues till the late 1920s, when the younger generation entered the scene. In June 1928 Keynes warmly supported Kahn's candidature for the Wrenbury studentship (letter 4179, 4 June 1928). In the following year Pigou pointed out to him that Kahn's dissertation 'on the whole' was '*extremely* good' (letter 4181, after 15 December 1929). The end of the 1930s found Keynes sharing with Pigou his worries about the prospects for the constitution of the Department of Applied Economics.[4] Fearing that Colin Clark might decide to leave, he supported Champernowne's appointment to a lectureship (letters 4196, 14 December 1937 and 4198, 5 March 1938). Later that year Champernowne was appointed Lecturer in Statistics. Pigou had prepared the motions to the Board (letter 4116, before 28 May 1938), which Keynes approved adding minor changes (letter 4199, 28 May 1938).[5]

Robertson's position in Cambridge was dealt with on a number of occasions. In 1925, Keynes discussed procedures to open a new lectureship in the context of the new statutes, approved but not yet in force, apparently referring to Robertson's course on money (letter 4171, 5 December 1925). In 1931 Pigou informed Keynes about 'confidential' academic business, concerning an appointment (letter 4235, 1931). Beveridge was involved, and Robertson was mentioned among other possible names (Clay, Gregory, Schumpeter). In 1937 Pigou supported Robertson's pupil, Stanley Dennison (letter 4135, 23 December 1937).

Relations between Robertson and Keynes had been deteriorating ever since the early 1930s. The crisis came to a head in August 1938 over the research project proposed by a committee including Austin Robinson,

Sraffa and Champernowne (Presley 1978; Bridel 1987; Aslanbegui and Oakes 2002). Devised to give Kalecki a position, the project aimed at investigating the depression and the following recovery with a statistical study of British industries during the first half of the 1930s. It was approved under the denomination *Cambridge Research Scheme of the National Institute of Economic and Social Research into Prime Costs, Proceeds and Output* (Marcuzzo 2002). Robertson was excluded and felt ostracised (see Ch. 2: 71). In a Faculty meeting misunderstandings and conflict erupted between him and some of the committee members (Aslanbegui and Oakes 2002: 29–33).

Pigou acted to smooth out their conflict, trying to protect Robertson whom he saw as psychologically fragile (letter 4207, 18 August 1938). Sensitive to Dennis's resentment at being left out and eager to assuage his distress, Pigou suggested an advisory committee to supervise the research, including Keynes, Robertson and himself (letter 4117, before 17 August 1938). In agreement with Austin Robinson, who had proposed diluting the committee by adding other members, Keynes raised polite but substantial objections (letter 4206, 17 August 1938). The true aim was to secure Keynes's supervision and to guarantee the group a substantial degree of autonomy. A subtle, but ruthless academic war was then declared to impede Robertson's interference in the project. Keynes outspokenly remarked to Pigou:

> It seems to me that, whatever formal arrangements are made, the cooperative research should be carried on by people who are at ease among themselves and have real authority to do what they want. It would be practically the first attempt in Cambridge at cooperative research, and I do feel that those who have initiated the matter and taken a lot of trouble about it should be allowed to have their way.
>
> (letter 4208, 30 August 1938)

Robertson could stomach no more. In October 1938 he accepted a chair at the LSE and left for London the following year (not to return to Cambridge until 1944). Privately informed in advance by Robertson, Pigou withdrew his proposal to include him in the committee (letters 4118, 31 August 1938; 4119, 6 September 1938).[6] He added humorously: 'If Austin wants a committee of reference as *real* machinery, there is no objection in my being on it, because I should be most unlikely to do anything' (letter 4118, 31 August 1938).

The rift with Robertson was exasperated by the clash between him and J. Robinson, which Keynes attributed to Dennis's aggressive attitude. He wrote:

> It is a great pity that everything becomes so political. What makes it all particularly morbid is that there is really no difference of opinion

> between myself and Dennis on the major points. We are on the same side of the fence as against past doctrine and as against many other economists, *e.g.* in America. But he seems to think it a duty to invent and to magnify differences.
>
> (letter 4206, 17 August 1938)

The Italian government's declaration of war in June 1940 had both Keynes and Pigou worried about the possibility of Sraffa being interned as an enemy alien (letter 4215, before 18 June 1940). While Sraffa was in Evelyn Hospital, seeking to delay his internment, Keynes suggested provisions for temporary closure of the Marshall library, which Sraffa had been in charge of since the early 1930s (letter 4217, 18 June 1940). In the same exchange Pigou discussed the Economic Tripos, and criticised the dogmatic teaching of Keynes's theory inflicted on the students.

> The chief bad thing we found was that a very large number of people had been stuffed like sausages into bits of your stuff in such a way that (1) they were quite incapable of applying their own intelligence to it, and (2) they perpetually dragged it in regardless of its relevance to the question.
>
> (letter 4214, June 1940)

Pigou attributed the 'parrot-like treatment' of Keynes's 'stuff' by the students to the 'lectures and supervision of the beautiful Mrs. R.' [J. Robinson], 'a magpie breeding innumerable parrots!' (Moggridge 1992: 599: see Ch. 13: 341). Keynes answered briefly.

> As regards the Tripos, at any rate I am glad that you found five men deserving of a First. If there can be a few of reasonable merit at the top, I do not so much mind what happens at the bottom.
>
> (letter 4217, 18 June 1940)

In 1942, in view of an election to the British Academy, Robertson mentioned Hayek as a qualified candidate although giving preference to Hicks, who was eventually elected that year (letter 3210 from DHR to JMK, 5 January 1942). Pigou twice communicated to Keynes his preference for Hayek over Hicks, Harrod, Robbins or Clark, although he feared opposition from 'patriots' to an Austrian born scholar (letters 4153 and 4152, February 1942). He wrote: 'I should myself put Hayek first for the B.A. Though he is sometimes woolly, he has written a great lot, and has much more of a position than any of the others' (letter 4152, February 1942).

In 1944, when Hayek was finally elected Fellow of the British Academy, Robertson warmly expressed his preference for him over J. Robinson and Cole (letter 3227 from DHR to JMK, 9 February 1944). Pigou, too, expressed his preference for Hayek, assessing the possible favourable votes (letters 4155 and 4157, 1944). He firmly denied his vote to J. Robinson (letter 4155, 1944),[7] while at the same time recognising that she was entitled to serious consideration (letter 4156, 1944). He wrote back to Keynes: 'As to Mrs. R. for next year, I'm in a weak position to have a view because her dogmatism and arrogance, when equipped with a pen, irritate me so much that I can't read her' (letter 4156, 1944). The issue was not private dislikes; Pigou openly decried the practice of disseminating Keynes's theories dogmatically.

In 1945 Pigou wrote a report to recommend Hayek for the Degree of D. Sc. (Econ.) at the LSE (letter 4120, 1945). Keynes, who arranged for Hayek's nomination, approved, although annoyed by the emphasis Hayek placed in his motivation letter on *The Pure Theory of Capital* (letter 4230, 3 March 1945): 'I wish Hayek had not laid so much strain on that particular book, which is not my favourite among his writings. In my opinion he loses himself in it and never reaches daylight.'

During the early 1940s a few passages reveal some heartfelt sentiments about the war. In Spring 1940 Pigou's mood was gloomy. 'It was impossible to avoid the bloody war, impossible to stop it, impossible to win it, and, if only by a miracle we do win it, impossible to do anything except make another rotten peace' (letter 4137, 1 April 1940).

'[...] if peace ever comes' he wrote in June 1940, adding a touch of human compassion: 'I suggested to Sraffa to write to your mother to keep a friendly eye on his mother when he gets pinched' (letter 4214, 12 June 1940). Keynes wrote back a dramatic letter about wartime Cambridge.

> Clapham reports that Cambridge is now an armed camp with official head-quarters in Gibbs, and the front court, I am told, is parked full of military motor-cars. All the same, the most probable expectation still seems to me to be something rather like 1917–18. What people should do about taking the trouble to prepare courses for such a situation is hard to say.
>
> (letter 4218, 3 July 1940)

He added: 'No news whatever about Piero'.

Pigou worried about the effects of air raid sirens on Keynes's rest at night; Keynes reported he had not lost his sleep, since the 'whole household' slept on the ground floor, with the shutters up (letters 4138, 2 September 1940; 4219, 5 September 1940). War did not destroy Pigou's sense of humour and appetite. In 1943 from his cottage at Buttermere (Lake District) he mentioned to Keynes: 'I've just seen a dozen enormous hams arranged around the kitchen of the farm here and have had eggs and bacon for breakfast' (letter 4222, 24 March 1943).

Scientific controversies

Albeit with varying intensity over the years, the correspondence testifies to continuous exchange on scientific subjects. The letters deal mainly with their own contributions, but also comment on papers submitted for publication or published contributions by other economists.

The earliest exchange is an undated comment Pigou wrote on a note by Keynes on index numbers, possibly a draft for the *Economic Journal* (letter 4101, 1905–09). In 1908 Pigou acknowledged Keynes's suggestions on index numbers and probability theory in revising various texts (letter 4161, March–April 1908). The young Keynes helped Pigou revise *Wealth and Welfare* (Pigou 1912: viii) and five letters in 1912–13 have to do with this collaboration (letters 4166, 30 June 1912; 4167, 13 August 1912; 4164, before September 1912; 4165, before September 1912; 4168, 1913).

In 1916 Pigou commented favourably, although with some reservations, on Robertson's *Industrial Fluctuation* (letter 4110, 1916). In early 1927 he expressed deep appreciation of a draft by Ramsey, probably the famous optimal taxation article (Ramsey 1927).

> Ramsey is writing out a paper on some results he got in the course of doings sums for me – with a marvellously simple generalised formula about taxes. Don't let him be too modest to produce it for the Journal.
>
> (letter 4127, before March 1927)

Pigou read Keynes's books and on various occasions congratulated him. In 1913 he discussed *Indian Currency and Finance* (letter 4169, 1913). In 1921 he expressed 'enormous interest' having read Keynes's *Treatise on Probability* (letter 4148, after August 1921), and announced that he was going to review it on Edgeworth's request. In 1924 he warmly welcomed Keynes's draft of Marshall's biographical essay (Keynes 1924).

As from the late 1920s an asymmetric attitude characterises their scientific exchange. Pigou often criticised Keynes's theses but was open to suggestions and sensitive to criticism. Keynes, still relying on Pigou's advice, often reacted brusquely in substance, if not in tone.

In the cost controversy, as Collard suggests, Pigou was on the 'wrong' side, since he did not accept Sraffa's critique of Marshall's original position.[8] An exchange of correspondence in 1928 shows how the idea of the representative firm was promptly put aside. Pigou submitted a text for the *Economic Journal*: 'this thing that Dennis made me write' (letter 4126, December 1927). The 'thing' was the draft of the article published under the title 'An Analysis of Supply' in June 1928 (Pigou 1928). Keynes reacted by adding handwritten notes to Pigou's letter; he then offered his comments in two longer letters (letters 4173, 2 January 1928, and 4176, 10 January 1928), which reveal his sceptical attitude towards the representative firm of Marshallian descent, even before Robbins's radical critique (Robbins 1928), with which he readily agreed (Aslanbeigui 1996: 281).

Keynes discarded the representative firm as a conception deliberately too vague to be expressed in rigorous mathematical language and, minimising its importance, noted that Marshall mentioned it only twice. He criticised Pigou's remarks, arguing that they pointed to 'conclusions both familiar and obvious', underlining Pigou's failure to give a clear definition of the representative firm, and complained that he examined the effects of an increase in demand on the rate of growth (or decay) of individual firms in a totally static world. Pigou never made clear 'the precise character of the abstract world in which [he is] moving [...]'. The reasoning seemed confined to an abstract model, 'so completely static as to be quite remote from anything in experience' (letter 4176, 10 January 1928).

Pigou defended in detailed notes 'the gist' of his paper (letter 4128, from 2 to 10 January 1928). However, stung by Keynes's and Ramsey's comments, he decided to cut 'badly worded' sections on the real supply price, 'added in bed', during his illness. On Ramsey's suggestion he focused his analysis on the money supply price.[9] In May 1928, after more comments by Ramsey, he promised the final version (letters 4130 and 4129, before 18 May 1928).

In 1931 Pigou reviewed *A Treatise on Money*, criticising Keynes's 'carping at "current economic theory" – whatever precisely that may be' as ungenerous to previous contributions (Pigou 1931: 544). The professor appreciated the book as an important contribution on short period, dynamic economics, but pointed out how theoretically Keynes built upon the conception of business fluctuations thoroughly investigated by Robertson. We may conjecture that Keynes was not overly pleased by Pigou's outspoken judgement of the fundamental equations as essentially an elaboration on Robertsonian foundations.

Pigou saw the focus of the book in 'the processes of change, on what precisely happens during the passage from one state of equilibrium towards another' (ibid.). The short review questioned the exclusive attention paid to business profits and losses as arising from differences between investment and saving in explaining the dynamics of business cycles. Pigou contended that in depression businessmen were affected by the low level of both aggregate returns and expected marginal returns; the 'whole situation', not just arbitrarily defined variables of current losses governed their behaviour. He supported his contention with reference to Fisher's analysis of deflation.

In correspondence only fragments survive from Pigou's reactions to Keynes's *Treatise on Money* (CWK XIII: 215–17). Keynes sent him drafts of various chapters as early as May 1925 (Moggridge 1992: 436) and, subsequently, galley proofs (from which Keynes lectured) during the autumn of 1929 (letter 4182, 15 December 1929). They discussed the *Treatise* again in May 1931. Writing in reaction to a note by Pigou (now lost), accompanied by a covering letter, Keynes suggested Pigou should write a shorter note on their disagreement for the *Economic Journal* (letter 4189, 15 May 1931). Pigou seemed convinced by Keynes's argument (letter 4187, before 15 May 1931), and gave up the idea of having his comments published. Tongue in cheek, he added the punch line: 'I don't think it would serve any purpose to print my thing. It would surely muddle people up more than they are muddled already'.

Apart from a few narrower points,[10] their discussion revolved around the conception of the quantity theory and the link between the fundamental equations and the Cambridge equation (the ultimate version of which had been offered by Pigou in 1917). Pigou got the impression that with his fundamental equations Keynes was trying to explain 'price changes that could not be revealed by the "Cambridge equation" ', and he was yet another victim of Keynes's definitions of saving and investment (letter 4102, May 1931). His initial reading of the fundamental equations was that the prices of consumption goods are determined in one way and the prices of production goods by an entirely different equation (letter 4187, before 15 May 1931); he correctly understood that P and P' were determined independently. Similar, more effectively articulated criticism by Kahn, Sraffa and Robertson, forced Keynes to revise his position in the *Rejoinder* (Keynes 1931b).

The thrust of Keynes's argument was to make it clear that the *Treatise* approach was in line with the Cambridge equation. The fundamental equations enabled him 'to distinguish the essentially different causes which affect P and P' respectively'. By distinguishing consumption and investment goods, he could show 'how changes in Q [total profits] are related to changes in I [investment] and S' [saving]'. He illustrated his disagreement with Pigou with a parable about the kitchen bill and the distribution of expenditure between meat (consumption) and vegetables (investment). The old-fashioned quantity-theory tutor [i.e. Pigou], who only looks at the quantity of the kitchen bills has, therefore, nothing to learn from the new theories about the causes of dyspepsia! (letter 4188, 11 May 1931). Summing up their debate, he was confident enough to write: 'The misunderstanding has been due, I think, to your supposing that I held my equations to be in some way inconsistent with the Cambridge equation' (letter 4189, 15 May 1931).

A major controversy arose after the publication of the *General Theory*, centring upon the effects of wage reductions (CWK XIV: 36–45, 40, 68, 234–8, 265–8). Pigou's article 'Real and Money Wage Rates in Relation to Unemployment' (Pigou 1937), was submitted for publication when Keynes had again fallen sick. Acting as surrogate editor, Robertson accepted it. Keynes and his closest circle found the article execrable, although on different grounds (Collard 1999: xxxvi). Keynes, having seen the proofs once his health had improved, wrote to Pigou that he had decided to comment on it (letter 4193, 12 October 1937). He announced also publication of a longer comment by Kaldor (Kaldor 1937; see Ch. 8).

The following correspondence in October 1937 (published in CWK XIV: 256–8) focused on the expediency of publishing two replies to Pigou's paper, and on the rejoinder Pigou finally wrote (letters 4131, 15 October 1937; 4132, 18 October 1937; 4194, 20 October 1937; 4133, 21 October 1937; 4195, 25 October 1937). Pigou invoked a misunderstanding by Keynes and credited Kaldor with correct interpretation (letter 4132, 18 October 1937). Later on, recognising a 'badly put' argument, he attributed a misinterpretation to Kaldor too (letter 4133, 21 October 1937). He firmly denied having assumed fixed money income in his argument.

> I don't assume or make any assumption which implies that money income is fixed. The argument was that, *if* a cut in wages leaves employment unchanged, money income has no ground for change; that, therefore, we cannot conclude that a wage-cut leaves employment unchanged without getting involved in a contradiction about money income.
>
> (letter 4132, 18 October 1937)

Keynes sharply replied that his criticism was precisely on what Pigou reaffirmed. '[. . .] I maintain that, if there is a cut in wages, unemployment being unchanged, there *is* a ground for a change in money income' (letter 4194, 20 October 1937).

What followed was mostly on editorial matters. Pigou announced a 10,000-word reply on money wages, sent to Champernowne for comments (letter 4134, 14 December 1937, CWK XIV: 265); Keynes confirmed he was ready to publish it (letter 4196, 14 December 1937). Having heard from Champernowne ('carefully briefed' by Kahn without Pigou's knowledge), Pigou reduced the text to a short note (letter 4135, 23 December 1937), finally published under the title 'Money Wages in Relation to Unemployment' (Pigou 1938). He was extremely worried about upsetting the sick Keynes, and tried to avoid confrontation. To Keynes the argument in Chapter 19 of the *General Theory* was crucial for the foundation of his theory and his recommendations in terms of policy. He closed the correspondence with a blunt reference to his Chapter 19 and the appendix on Pigou's theory (letter 4197, 3 January 1938), certain to have won Pigou's recantation.

Occasional discussions went on in 1937 and the following years. On 11 April 1937, Keynes asked Pigou to explain the labour supply schedule in his theory. The question was prompted by Keynes's reading of Hawtrey's *Capital and Employment* (Hawtrey 1937). Pigou clarified his position, outlining the diagram where labour supply is infinitely elastic at a given wage rate up to the full employment position, where it becomes vertical (letter 4151, May 1937, CWK XIV: 54). In 1938 Pigou inquired about Miss

Gilboy's interpretation of Keynes's assumptions on the propensity to consume, and suggested Keynes should write a reply (letters 4146, December 1938; 4211, 10 December 1938; 4145, after 10 December 1938).

In 1938 and 1939 they debated the editorial policy of the *Economic Journal* as far as controversy on Keynes's theory was concerned (letters 4202, 17 June 1938, in Lydia's handwriting; 4203, 27 June 1938; letter 4136, before 15 June 1939; 4212, 15 June 1939).

Keynes had asked for Pigou's evaluation of a polemical rejoinder Robertson had submitted for publication in the *Economic Journal* after an inconclusive round of their controversy (letter 4200, 3 June 1938). Acting as a go-between, Pigou criticised Keynes's aggressive tone and questioned his editorial policy (letters 4106, before 27 June 1938 and 4201, 10 June 1938). Seriously worried by the prospect of a dogmatic Keynesian 'school', suffocating alternative contributions and shrinking the traditional *Economic Journal* openness to various streams of theoretical thought, he favoured a policy of inviting contributions from scholars with a wider spectrum of opinions and scientific interests. Keynes maintained that the number of contributions dealing with his own theory resulted from genuine interest: the subjects were hotly debated in the profession and most papers submitted raised them again and again. A difference arose on debates on terminology, which Pigou dismissed as uninteresting, and Keynes thought essential to clarify controversial issues. In conclusion, Pigou softened his tone towards the editor; but the point had been raised sharply.

This exchange was an opportunity to comment on Harrod's growth theory (Harrod 1939); Pigou had suggested outright rejection of such a 'hopelessly muddled' article (letter 4136, before 15 June 1939). Keynes expressed a milder view: '[...] I do think that he has got hold of a very interesting point which, subject to the necessary qualifications, is of real importance' (letter 4212, 15 June 1939, CWK XIV: 320).

In 1940 Keynes involved Pigou in his debate with Tinbergen, whose essay (Tinbergen 1939) he had critically reviewed for the *Economic Journal* (Keynes 1939d; see Ch. 3). He asked for Pigou's advice on the advisability of further controversy, since Marschak and Lange had submitted a joint comment which he disliked (letter 4213, 29 March 1940) while he had appreciated Tinbergen's reply (Tinbergen 1940). He went as far as remarking disparagingly on both Marschak and Lange ('very poor opinion' of Marschak, 'moderately good' of Lange). Pigou did not encourage publication; he defined the draft by Marschak and Lange as 'pompous and boring' (letter 4137, 1 April 1940).

In private correspondence Keynes reiterated his criticism to Tinbergen, carefully considering the statistical questions involved, especially as regards linearity.

> I have, of course, never said anything to the effect that no business cycle theory can be tested statistically. I was dealing solely with Tinber-

> gen's very special method of analysis. The early part of the article is written on the assumption that I was disputing the validity of any conceivable statistical method. [. . .] Every single case to which Tinbergen has applied his method assumes that the same formula is valid over a long period of years. If this is never the case, then it is hardly worth while to bother about the details of this method.
>
> (letter 4213, 29 March 1940)

In August 1943 Pigou submitted an article contrasting Hansen's argument on full employment in *Fiscal Policy and Business Cycles* (Hansen 1941) (letter 4140, August 1943). The article was published as 'The Classical Stationary State' in the *Economic Journal* of December 1943 (Pigou 1943).

In the same letter Pigou mentioned a note about elasticity, which Keynes had left unpublished. Keynes, apologising, sent it back (letter 4229, 31 August 1943). This was the conclusion of an aborted series of revisions, which had involved Kaldor as a referee (see Ch. 8: 217). Keynes had read Pigou's original note during Christmas 1942, and was soon addressing outspoken criticism to the author (letter 4242, 13 January 1943). Pigou, acknowledging 'a slip' in his 'thing', produced an improved version. Keynes, overburdened with war duties, left it aside for Easter (letter 4223, 30 March 1943). In fact, he abandoned it to Kaldor's scathing criticism. In the coming months Keynes was 'badly overworked', his concentration getting lost 'after getting through official stuff'. He never read the last version properly: 'I have carried this round with me more week-ends than I can remember'. Politely, Keynes left it with Pigou to 'come to a conclusion' (letter 4229, 31 August 1943). Finally, Pigou decided to withdraw his note.

Of this exchange, only two letters are of theoretical interest, containing the original criticism by Keynes and Pigou's reply (letters 4242, 13 January 1943 and 4243, after 13 January 1943). Keynes suggested that the elasticity concept 'is useless except in the Marshallian framework of analysis, when one considered one tax at a time, all other taxes being given'. Pigou conjectured to distinguish first-order and second-order effects in cases of 'interrelativity of elasticitiy', but he left the conjecture open for further analysis.

Despite the controversies, there was some common ground. After reading Keynes's obituary of Mary Paley Marshall (Keynes 1944b) Pigou found it 'quite extraordinarily good and sympathetic'. He commented: 'Cannan once said to me that biography was really your métier. It certainly stands high on the list' (letter 4144, 1944).

Economic policy debate

With respect to economic policy questions, the surviving correspondence spans from 1917 to 1943. From the war years to the late 1920s, the brief comments that have survived deal with exchange rates and interest rate policy. During the 1930s, Pigou and Keynes had a number of opportunities to correspond and collaborate on economic policy to address recession. War finance and post-war reconstruction dominate in the letters during the final period.

After reading the *Economic Consequences of the Peace*, Pigou expressed his warm appreciation: an '*absolutely splendid* and quite unanswerable' argument (letter 4147, after 12 December 1919) (Skidelsky 1983: 394).

In the aftermath of the October 1917 revolution (Skidelsky 1992: 102–5) and during the disastrous British December offensive in Flanders, Pigou wrote to Keynes referring to an unidentified essay on the exchange rate, possibly one of Keynes's internal Treasury memoranda. Pigou argued that 'the effect of a change in the real ratio of international exchange' affects the purchasing power parity according to the particular index numbers applied for evaluation (letter 4111, 12 December 1917).

In 1922, apparently, Keynes incorporated the draft into his article 'The Theory of the Exchanges and "Purchasing Power Parity"' (Keynes 1922) published in the Reconstruction Supplements to the *Manchester Guardian Commercial* (to which, on Keynes's request, Pigou also contributed an article). After the publication of the *Tract on Monetary Reform* (December 1923), Pigou expressed a sympathetic judgement on Keynes's book, though with critical remarks.[11] In his letter, as a preliminary step towards restoring Britain's international credibility, he defended the necessity to go back to pre-war parity at 4.86 to the dollar (letter 4149, 1923).

In 1924, the British Government initiated a series of protracted moves that would eventually bring the pound back to this pre-war parity by 1928. Amongst the first steps taken, the Government set up a Committee on the Currency and Bank of England Note Issues chaired by Austen Chamberlain. Pigou sat as a full member of this Committee; Keynes only appeared to give evidence on various occasions, notably in July 1924. A brief exchange of correspondence survives around an extension of Keynes's evidence (letters 4122, before 17 May 1928; 4178, 17 May 1928). In May 1928 Pigou offered critical comments on a draft of what was to become Keynes's article in the *Economic Journal* (Keynes 1928). In his answer, Keynes was already showing worries about the influence of too rigid a ceiling to the issue of fiduciary notes on the rates of interest and, of course, on the level of domestic activity. Central to both the *Treatise* and the *General Theory*, Keynes's qualms on the inter-war British dilemma between exchange rate and interest rate policies were clearly already taking shape. During the early 1930s, the correspondence reflects both men's involvement in the crucial discussions around public works, the Treasury View, the crowding out hypothesis, and early versions of the Keynes–Kahn multiplier.

Early in 1930, Keynes reacted to a draft Pigou had sent him with the attached comment: 'Here at last is my theory about unemployment' (letter 4184, before 5 January 1930). The text, presumably theoretical in character had the ambition to be (in Keynes's words) a 'summing up of the controversy' (i.e. the debate about the Treasury view and the appropriate employment policy). Keynes's answer was entrenched in his *Treatise* framework. He was still suggesting the 'obvious common sense example', where government borrowing crowds out private borrowing. He wrote: 'For, in order to get my geometrical progression, I undoubtedly *am* assuming that the Government pays its way in the first instance by bringing into existence an additional quantity of money' (letter 4185, 5 January 1930).

Clearly, 'the possibility of government works causing' a rise in employment implies 'something which amounts to an act of inflation'. The 'geometrical progression' was a first version of the multiplier process, which here Keynes conceived as a process through time, the initial inflationary expenditure being later financed by reducing dole payments.[12]

> For the dose of extra employment directly produced will save half its gross expenditures out of the dole; the remaining half will be satisfied after the lapse of one production period out of the labour of newly employed persons producing consumption goods, which will have the effect of saving a half of that (i.e. a quarter of the original expenditure) out of the dole; and so on. I quite agree, of course, that if the Government tried to do the trick with no greater expansion of bank money than is required to finance the extra transactions which intervene when Government takes money from non-wages earners and hands it over to wage earners, then there would not be enough money to bring my series of repercussions into operation.
>
> (letter 4185, 5 January 1930)

Moreover, Keynes underlined the distinction between barter economy and monetary economy – a major theme in his theoretical work, and in his later criticism of Pigou's theory of unemployment. In his answer Pigou toyed with the preliminary idea of writing a book on unemployment, melting the draft sent to Keynes into the wider project (letter 4183, after 5 January 1930).

Late in the summer of 1930, Pigou, Robbins, Henderson and Stamp joined the Committee of Economists with Keynes acting as chairman (Skidelsky 1992: 363–78; Moggridge 1992: 497–507). Keynes contacted all the members to organise the various meetings (CWK XX: 402–3). Pigou answered Keynes's letter (sent at the end of August 1930) and mentioned the evidence he had just given before the Committee on Finance and Industry (letters 4103 before 1 September 1930; 4104 and 4105 before 11 September 1930).

In 1932, faced with an ever-deepening recession, Keynes began to doubt seriously whether cheap money would be enough to stimulate recovery. On various occasions he began using an argument for pump priming to raise the level of activity, or at least to alter investors' expectations. On 11 October 1932, *The Times* invited economists to state whether they agreed on the expediency of encouraging spending as a way out of the crisis. Keynes, Pigou, Stamp, A. Salter, W. Layton and D.H. MacGregor reacted by writing a joint letter to *The Times*, which was subsequently rebuffed by Gregory, Hayek, Plant and Robbins (Moggridge 1992: 545, CWK XX: 137–40). The letter, published on 17 October 1932, made clear that 'to spend less money than we should like to do is *not* patriotic'. On this occasion Pigou and Keynes exchanged correspondence from which it emerges that Pigou (not Keynes) wrote the published text. In fact, Pigou informed Keynes that he was ready to write a draft (letters 4108 and 4109, between 10 October and 13 October 1932). Keynes promised that he would have the draft circulated to collect the necessary signatures (letter 4190, 13 October 1932). He warmly approved of the text ('the letter is excellent'), and sent it unaltered to *The Times.*

During the war Keynes was 'in the machine' and the Professor thought it 'natural' to make him 'the wastepaper basket for bright ideas' (letter 4138, before 5 September 1940). In late August or early September 1940, he submitted to Keynes a draft paper containing proposals for wartime fiscal policy. Early in April 1943, once again trying to use the Keynes's connection to gain access to the Treasury, he sent Keynes suggestions for a plan about a post-war capital levy to repay war debts (letters 4224 and 4225, April 1943). Commenting on Pigou's suggestions for war taxation, Keynes appraised the situation of the country at the beginning of the war (letter 4219, 5 September 1940). He opposed Pigou's proposal to increase heavily the tax burden on higher incomes,[13] considering that the yield would be insufficient to meet the budget requirement, while the higher taxes would 'interfere [...] seriously with the ability of the rich to fulfil their contractual liabilities'. On the budget Keynes was moderately optimistic, provided wage increases could be prevented.[14] He encouraged Pigou to think about the 'employment position'. On the employment situation in Great Britain, the crucial problem was for Keynes the possibility of rapidly expanding munitions output. The letter closed with some extremely worried remarks on the condition of military supply at the end of the Battle of Britain: 'It is almost true to say that on 1 June we had no warlike equipment whatever'.

During the early war years Keynes was working himself to exhaustion at the Treasury on war finance issues. In 1942 he refused to write on Malthus and pointed out to Pigou: '[...] to prepare anything fresh would be absolutely beyond my present capacity. Work has almost reached saturation point' (letter 4239, 28 May 1942). Pigou remained at Cambridge trying, with a much-depleted staff, to keep the teaching of economics running. He often sought Keynes's help. Despite deteriorating health and the burden of his heavy responsibilities, Keynes always managed to answer, even when Pigou's queries concerned matters far removed from wartime pressures.

In 1941–42 Pigou worked on a memorandum for the 'Reconstruction People'; in view of post-war reconstruction, he was writing an historical survey of the post-First World War years covering 1918–25. The memorandum was published after the war as *Aspects of British Economic History* (Pigou 1947); but in 1942 Pigou complained to Keynes that government officials were delaying the printing.[15] Keynes patiently informed him that 'your stuff cannot be published' (letter 4221, 5 October 1942) and later tried again unsuccessfully to have it printed.

On April 25 1943, Keynes criticised the way Beveridge set up an office, as if claiming an official role he had not been attributed, pretending 'that he is a Royal Commission himself'. Pigou had already expressed his refusal to have anything to do with a Royal Commission on post-war unemployment (letter 4226, 11 or 18 April 1943).

On August 31 1943 Keynes told Pigou that he was leaving for the United States. He commented: 'Wish us reasonable luck. It is beyond human hopes to have a success in the U.S.A. The best one can expect is the avoidance of a fiasco!'

In January 1945 Keynes informed Pigou that his 'term of office as editor of the *Journal*' 'came to an end' (4244, 2 January 1945). A year later his life also came to an end.

After Maynard's untimely death, Pigou acknowledged his friend's contribution in intellectual honesty, smoothing over the sharper criticism. The Professor embarked on the task of dealing with Keynes's thorny conception of short period stagnation, and he managed to translate it into the analysis of a special case. While paying tribute to his friend's intellectual stature, he forced Keynesian analysis into the theoretical scaffolding of long-term macroeconomic equilibria built on Marshallian foundations. It was both honest recognition of Keynes's insights, and infidelity, since he denied Keynes's claim that he had got off the beaten track of classical theory.

Notes

1 The volume of which safely puts to rest Skidelsky's assertion that 'Keynes had little correspondence with Pigou [. . .]' (Skidelsky 1992: 586).

2 'For unemployment clearly does not include all the idleness of wage-earners, *but only that part of it which is, from their point of view and in their existing condition at the time, involuntary*' (Pigou [1913] 1999: 14). Pigou specified that the existing conditions include the current wage in a particular area or industry where the worker is usually employed. 'Pigou had allowed, at least since his book Unemployment (1913), that involuntary unemployment could exist so it would have been surprising if he had altogether ruled it out' (Collard 1999: xxxiv).

3 '[. . .] Keynes's analysis is, to my mind, very much more limited in scope and range than is often supposed'(Pigou [1950] 1999: 61). Pigou lamented that Keynes's analysis is 'a staccato one', unable to provide a coherent analysis of moving disequilibria and long-term dynamic tendencies (Pigou [1950] 1999: 64).

4 The Department of Applied Economics was eventually established in December 1939.
5 Meanwhile, in 1935 Keynes asked Pigou to give the address at the annual meeting of the Royal Economic Society, but Pigou declined (letters 4191, 14 January 1935 and 4141, 1935).
6 The correspondence is extensively quoted in Aslanbegui and Oakes (2002).
7 She was considered in part because the new member would have to replace Beatrice Webb, who had died in 1943.
8 'Pigou's (1928) contribution to the debate was to offer the concept of the "equilibrium firm" to replace Marshall's notion of the "representative firm" and to "save" competitive equilibrium by means of economies external to the firm but internal to the industry' (Collard 1999: xxvi).
9 Note 1 in the published paper refers to the change in terminology (from average and marginal costs to normal supply price) (Pigou 1928: 238).
10 Among which the most prominent are index numbers (*à la* Edgeworth-Jevons), elasticities, velocities of circulation and the *modus operandi* of the Bank rate (letters 4186 and 4102, May 1931; 4188, 11 May 1931).
11 The elasticity of demand Pigou refers to in the letter is discussed by Keynes in relation to the inflation tax (CWK IV: 42–3). In both Pigou's letter and Keynes's text, the reference appears to be to Cannan.
12 A geometrical progression involving income payments and consumption is introduced in the *Treatise* in a theoretical exercise to analyse the trade cycle (Keynes [1930a] CWK V: 274–92).
13 '[...] although social justice may require more taxes on the relatively rich, there is scarcely any money to be got except from the group with £700 a year or less' (letter 4219, 5 September 1940).
14 '[...] But I think that, if wages could be prevented from going up, the purely budgetary problem is distinctly manageable' (letter 4219, 5 September 1940).
15 In May 1946 Pigou wrote in the Preface: 'The Chancellor of the Exchequer now allows what I wrote to be published. [...] In war-time many of us had to do the best we could in jobs for which we were ill equipped' (Pigou 1947: vi).

Table 5.1 Keynes–Pigou correspondence

From	*To*	*Year*	*Month*	*Day*	*Date*	*Archive*		*Published in*	*Item*
ACP	JMK					Keynes–King's	GTE/1/88		4125
ACP	JMK	1905			Attributed	Keynes–King's	IN/1/18–21		4101
ACP	JMK	1907	Late April		Attributed	Keynes–King's	PP/45/254/6–7		4232
ACP	JMK	1907	April	10	Postmark	Keynes–King's	PP/45/254/1–2		4160
ACP	JMK	1908	March–April		Attributed	Keynes–King's	PP/45/254/4–5		4161
ACP	JMK	1908	July	6	Attributed	Keynes–King's	PP/45/254/3	Moggridge 1992: 199, (E)	4162
ACP	JMK	1912			Attributed	Keynes–King's	PP/45/254/8–9		4163
ACP	JMK	1912	June	30	Attributed	Keynes–King's	PP/45/254/14–15		4166
ACP	JMK	1912	August	13	Attributed	Keynes–King's	PP/45/254/16–17		4167
ACP	JMK	1912	Before September		Attributed	Keynes–King's	PP/45/254/10–11		4164
ACP	JMK	1912	Before September		Attributed	Keynes–King's	PP/45/254/12–13		4165
ACP	JMK	1913			Attributed	Keynes–King's	PP/45/254/18–19		4168
ACP	JMK	1913			Attributed	Keynes–King's	PP/45/254/20–1		4169
JMK	ACP	1915	January	9	Dated letter	Keynes–King's	UA/5/1/31–3		4170
ACP	JMK	1916			Attributed	Keynes–King's	L/R/18–19		4110
ACP	JMK	1917	December	12	Postmark	Keynes–King's	PP/45/254/22–4		4111
ACP	JMK	1919	December	After 12	Attributed	Keynes–King's	EC/2/1/67	Skidelsky 1983: 394, (E)	4147
ACP	JMK	1920			Attributed	Keynes–King's	PP/45/254/25	CWK XVII: 116–17	4112
ACP	JMK	1921	After August		Attributed	Keynes–King's	TP/1/1/48–9		4148
ACP	JMK	1923			Attributed	Keynes–King's	MR/1/2/1–2	Skidelsky 1992: 161, (E)	4149
ACP	JMK	1924	From 13 July to 24 October		Attributed	Keynes–King's	EJ/6/4/86–7		4142
ACP	JMK	1924	From 13 July to 24 October		Attributed	Keynes–King's	EJ/6/4/88–9		4143

Table 5.1 continued

From	*To*	*Year*	*Month*	*Day*	*Date*	*Archive*		*Published in*	*Item*
ACP	JMK	1925	May		Inferred from other sources	Not found in the archives		CWK XIII: 28	4234
JMK	ACP	1925	December	5	Dated letter	Keynes–King's	UA/5/2/61–2		4171
ACP	JMK	1927	Before March		Attributed	Keynes–King's	EJ/1/3/5–6		4127
ACP	JMK	1927	December		Attributed	Keynes–King's	EJ/1/3/1–2		4126
JMK	ACP	1928	January	2	Dated letter	Keynes–King's Kahn–King's	EJ/1/3/3–4 RFK/14/75/65–6		4173
JMK	ACP	1928	January	10	Dated letter	Keynes–King's Kahn–King's	EJ/1/3/7–8 RFK/14/75/60–1		4176
ACP	JMK	1928	January	From 2 to 10	Attributed	Keynes–King's Kahn–King's	EJ/1/3/9–11 RFK/14/75/62–4		4128
ACP	JMK	1928	May	Before 17	Attributed	Keynes–King's	PP/45/254/26–7		4122
ACP	JMK	1928	May	Before 17	Attributed	Keynes–King's	EJ/1/3/14–15		4130
JMK	ACP	1928	May	17	Dated letter	Keynes–King's	PP/45/254/28–9		4178
ACP	JMK	1928	May	Before 18	Attributed	Keynes–King's	EJ/1/3/12–13		4129
JMK	ACP	1928	June	4	Dated letter	Keynes–King's	PP/45/254/30		4179
ACP	JMK	1929	Autumn		Attributed	Keynes–King's	TM/1/2/46–53	CWK XXIX: 4–6, (E)	4159
ACP	JMK	1929	After September		Attributed	Keynes–King's	PP/45/254/31–2		4180
JMK	ACP	1929	December	15	Dated letter	Keynes–King's	TM/1/2/44		4182
ACP	JMK	1929	December	After 15	Attributed	Keynes–King's	TM/1/2/44–5		4181
ACP	JMK	1930	January	Before 5	Attributed	Keynes–King's	PP/45/254/33–6		4184

JMK	ACP	1930	January	5	Dated letter	Keynes–King's	PP/45/254/37–40		4185
ACP	JMK	1930	January	After 5	Attributed	Keynes–King's	PP/45/254/41		4183
ACP	JMK	1930	Before September		Attributed	Keynes–King's	EA/1/64–5		4103
ACP	JMK	1930	September	Before 11	Attributed	Keynes–King's	EA/1/66–7		4104
ACP	JMK	1930	September	Before 11	Attributed	Keynes–King's	EA/1/68–9		4105
ACP	JMK	1930	September	26	Attributed	Not found in the archives		CWK XX: 420–1	4245
ACP	JMK	1930	September	27	Attributed	Not found in the archives		CWK XX: 421	4246
JMK	ACP	1930	September	27	Dated letter	Not found in the archives		CWK XX: 422–3	4247
ACP	JMK	1931			Attributed	Keynes–King's	PP/45/254/42–43		4235
ACP	JMK	1931	May		Attributed	Keynes–King's	TM/1/2/54–5		4102
ACP	JMK	1931	May	Before 11	Attributed	Keynes–King's	CO/8/125	CWK XIII: 214–15	4186
JMK	ACP	1931	May	11	Dated letter	Keynes–King's	CO/8/126–9	CWK XIII: 215–16	4188
ACP	JMK	1931	May	Before 15	Attributed	Keynes–King's	CO/8/130–1	CWK XIII: 217	4187
JMK	ACP	1931	May	15	Dated letter	Keynes–King's	CO/8/132	CWK XIII: 217–18	4189
ACP	JMK	1932			Attributed	Keynes–King's	GTE/1/85		4123
JMK	ACP	1932	October	13	Dated letter	Keynes–King's	CAC/1/96		4190
ACP	JMK	1932	October	From 10 to 13	Attributed	Keynes–King's	CAC/1/92–3		4108
ACP	JMK	1932	October	From 10 to 13	Attributed	Keynes–King's	CAC/1/94	CWK XXI: 137–40	4109
ACP	JMK	1932	October	After 13	Attributed	Keynes–King's	GTE/1/86–7		4124

Table 5.1 continued

From	*To*	*Year*	*Month*	*Day*	*Date*	*Archive*		*Published in*	*Item*
JMK	ACP	1934			Attributed	Keynes–King's	CO/3/111–12		4150
JMK	ACP	1935	January	14	Dated letter	Keynes–King's	RES/1/2/57–8		4191
ACP	JMK	1935	January	After 14	Attributed	Keynes–King's	RES/1/2/60–1		4141
JMK	ACP	1937	April	11	Dated letter	Keynes–King's	CO/3/110		4192
ACP	JMK	1937	May		Attributed	Keynes–King's	CO/3/113–14	CWK XIV: 54	4151
JMK	ACP	1937	October	12	Dated letter	Keynes–King's	EJ/1/4/154–5	CWK XIV: 255–6	4193
ACP	JMK	1937	October	15	Inferred from other sources	Keynes–King's	EJ/1/4/156	CWK XIV: 256, (E)	4131
ACP	JMK	1937	October	18	Inferred from other sources	Keynes–King's	EJ/1/4/172–3	CWK XIV: 256–7	4132
JMK	ACP	1937	October	20	Dated letter	Keynes–King's	EJ/1/4/174–5	CWK XIV: 257, (E)	4194
ACP	JMK	1937	October	21	Inferred from other sources	Keynes–King's	EJ/1/4/179–80	CWK XIV: 257–8 (E)	4133
JMK	ACP	1937	October	25	Dated letter	Keynes–King's	EJ/1/4/181	CWK XIV: 258, (E)	4195
ACP	JMK	1937	December	14	Inferred from other sources	Keynes–King's	EJ/1/4/228–9	CWK XIV: 265	4134
JMK	ACP	1937	December	14	Dated letter	Keynes–King's	EJ/1/4/232–3	CWK XIV: 265, (E)	4196
ACP	JMK	1937	December	23	Inferred from other sources	Keynes–King's	EJ/1/4/230–1	CWK XIV: 266, (E)	4135
JMK	ACP	1938	January	3	Dated letter	Keynes–King's	EJ/1/5/1–2	CWK XIV: 267	4197
ACP	JMK	1938	January	4	Inferred from other sources	Not found in the archives		CWK XIV: 268, (E)	4172
JMK	ACP	1938	January	26	Dated letter	Keynes–King's	MM/5/21		4236
JMK	ACP	1938	March	5	Dated letter	Keynes–King's	UA/5/4/22		4198
ACP	JMK	1938	March	Before 8	Attributed	Keynes–King's	MM/5/27–8		4237
JMK	ACP	1938	March	8	Dated letter	Keynes–King's	MM/5/23		4238

ACP	JMK	1938	May	Before 28	Attributed	Keynes–King's	UA/5/4/123		4116
JMK	ACP	1938	May	28	Dated letter	Keynes–King's	UA/5/4/124		4199
JMK	ACP	1938	June	3	Dated letter	Keynes–King's	GTE/2/4/45	CWK XXIX: 173–4	4200
ACP	JMK	1938	June	10	Dated letter	Keynes–King's	GTE/2/4/46–7	CWK XXIX: 174–5	4201
JMK	ACP	1938	June	17	Dated letter	Keynes–King's	GTE/2/4/48–9	CWK XXIX: 175–6	4202
JMK	ACP	1938	June	27	Dated letter	Keynes–King's	GTE/2/4/58	CWK XXIX: 177, (E)	4203
ACP	JMK	1938	June	From 17 to 27	Attributed	Keynes–King's	GTE/2/4/50–3	CWK XXIX: 176, (E)	4106
JMK	ACP	1938	July	5	Dated letter	Keynes–King's	GTE/2/4/54–5	CWK XXIX: 178	4107
ACP	JMK	1938	August	Before 17	Attributed	Keynes–King's	UA/5/4/149–50	Aslanbeigui–Oakes 2002: 29, (E)	4117
JMK	ACP	1938	August	17	Dated letter	Keynes–King's	UA/5/4/151–3	Moggridge 1992: 601–2, (E)	4206
ACP	JMK	1938	August	18	Attributed	Keynes–King's	UA/5/4/154–5		4207
JMK	ACP	1938	August	20	Postmark	Keynes–King's	UA/5/4/156–7	Moggridge 1992: 602, (E)	4233
JMK	ACP	1938	August	30	Dated letter	Keynes–King's	UA/5/4/195–7	Aslanbeigui and Oakes 2002: 31, (E)	4208
						Keynes–King's	UA/5/4/167–9		
ACP	JMK	1938	August	31	Attributed	Keynes–King's	UA/5/4/190–1		4118
ACP	JMK	1938	September		Attributed	Keynes–King's	UA/5/4/115		4115
JMK	ACP	1938	September	5	Dated letter	Keynes–King's	UA/5/4/192		4210
ACP	JMK	1938	September	6	Attributed	Keynes–King's	UA/5/4/200–1	Aslanbeigui and Oakes 2002: 32. (E)	4119
ACP	JMK	1938	From 27 June to 5 July		Attributed	Keynes–King's	GTE/2/4/56–7	CWK XIV: 177, (E)	4205
ACP	JMK	1938	December	Before 10	Inferred from other sources	Keyes–King's	A/39/190–1	CWK XIV: 273, (E)	4146
JMK	ACP	1938	December	10	Dated letter	Keynes–King's	A/39/188–9	CWK XIV: 272	4211
ACP	JMK	1938	December	After 10	Attributed	Keynes–King's	A/39/186–7	CWK XIV: 271–2	4145
ACP	JMK	1939	June	Before 15	Inferred from other sources	Keynes–King's	EJ/1/6/3–4	CWK XIV: 320, (E)	4136

Table 5.1 continued

From	*To*	*Year*	*Month*	*Day*	*Date*	*Archive*		*Published in*	*Item*
JMK	ACP	1939	June	15	Dated letter	Keynes–King's	EJ/1/6/5–7		4212
JMK	ACP	1940	March	29	Dated letter	Keynes–King's	EJ/1/6/76–80		4213
ACP	JMK	1940	April	1	Attributed	Keynes–King's	EJ/1/6/81–2		4137
ACP	JMK	1940	June	12	Inferred from other sources	Keynes–King's	PP/45/254/44–5	Skidelsky 2000: 77, (E)	4214
ACP	JMK	1940	June	Before 18	Attributed	Keynes–King's	PP/45/254/46–7		4215
JMK	ACP	1940	June	18	Dated letter	Keynes–King's	PP/45/254/48–9	Moggridge 1992: 636, (E)	4217
ACP	JMK	1940	July	Before 3	Attributed	Keynes–King's	PP/45/254/51–2		4216
JMK	ACP	1940	July	3	Dated letter	Keynes–King's	PP/45/254/53–6	Skidelsky 2000: 78, (E)	4218
ACP	JMK	1940	September	2	Attributed	Keynes–King's	EJ/1/7/100–2		4138
JMK	ACP	1940	September	5	Dated letter	Keynes–King's	EJ/1/7/103–8		4219
ACP	JMK	1941	April	24 or after	Attributed	Keynes–King's	EJ/1/7/204–5		4139
ACP	JMK	1942	February		Attributed	Keynes–King's	BA/1/54–5		4152
ACP	JMK	1942	February		Attributed	Keynes–King's	BA/1/76–7		4153
JMK	ACP	1942	February	23	Dated letter	Keynes–King's	BA/1/97		4231
JMK	ACP	1942	May	28	Dated letter	Keynes–King's	MM/4/121		4239
ACP	JMK	1942	October	3	Attributed	Keynes–King's	CO/7/131		4113
JMK	ACP	1942	October	5	Dated letter	Keynes–King's	CO/7/132–3		4221
ACP	JMK	1942	October	7	Attributed	Keynes–King's	CO/7/134–6		4220
ACP	JMK	1942	December		Attributed	Keynes–King's	MM/5/212		4241
ACP	JMK	1943	early		Attributed	Keynes–King's	CO/7/137–8		4114
JMK	ACP	1943	January	13	Dated letter	Keynes–King's	MM/5/199–200		4242
ACP	JMK	1943	January	After 13	Attributed	Keynes–King's	MM/5/196–8		4243
ACP	JMK	1943	March	24	Attributed	Keynes–King's	CO/7/141–2		4222

JMK	ACP	1943	March	30	Dated letter	Keynes–King's	CO/7/143–4	4223
ACP	JMK	1943	April		Attributed	Keynes–King's	PP/45/254/57–8	4224
ACP	JMK	1943	April		Attributed	Keynes–King's	PP/45/254/59–60	4225
JMK	ACP	1943	April	8	Dated letter	Keynes–King's	CO/7/145	4227
JMK	ACP	1943	April	25	Dated letter	Keynes–King's	PP/45/254/63	4228
ACP	JMK	1943	April	11 or 18	Attributed	Keynes–King's	PP/45/254/61–2	4226
ACP	JMK	1943	August		Attributed	Keynes–King's	EJ/1/7/268–9	4140
JMK	ACP	1943	August	31	Dated letter	Keynes–King's	EJ/1/7/270–1	4229
ACP	JMK	1944			Attributed	Keynes–King's	EJ/6/12/48	4144
ACP	JMK	1944			Attributed	Keynes–King's	BA/1/145–6	4155
ACP	JMK	1944			Attributed	Keynes–King's	BA/1/157	4156
ACP	JMK	1944			Attributed	Keynes–King's	BA/1/158	4157
ACP	JMK	1944	February	4	Postmark	Keynes–King's	BA/1/132–3	4154
ACP	JMK	1945	January	Before 2	Attributed	Keynes–King's	MM/1/5/160	4240
JMK	ACP	1945	January	2	Dated letter	Keynes–King's	MM/1/5/162	4244
ACP	JMK	1945	March	Before 3	Attributed	Keynes–King's	UA/14/2/380–2	4120
JMK	ACP	1945	March	3	Dated letter	Keynes–King's	UA/14/2/383	4230

6 Fighting for Keynesian revolution

The correspondence between Keynes and J. Robinson

Maria Cristina Marcuzzo and Claudio Sardoni

An overview of the pre-war correspondence

There are 140 letters between J. Robinson and John Maynard Keynes, running from 1932 to 1945, 82 of which published, mostly in excerpts (see Table 6.1). The extant correspondence begins in April 1932 and ends in April 1945.

We do not know exactly when Keynes and Robinson met, but it is likely that they made acquaintance when she came back from India a few months ahead of Austin in October 1928 and was looking for somewhere for them to settle down in Cambridge. J. Robinson already had strong connections in Cambridge as a former Girton student and member of a family closely associated with Cambridge on both her mother's and her father's side.

Her involvement in academic life started when she was invited by the Faculty of Economics and Politics to give eight lectures in the Michaelmas Term of 1931 based on the book which would become *The Economics of Imperfect Competition*. In the previous two years she had attended Sraffa's lecture course, supervised a few pupils and strengthened her acquaintance with Kahn both personally and professionally.

She was a member of the Circus, the informal discussion group debating the issues presented by Keynes in his *Treatise on Money*; the group met between late 1930 and the spring of 1931, and proved very active in their deliberations. In fact, the correspondence between Keynes and J. Robinson began over an article of hers, 'A Parable on Saving and Investment' (J. Robinson 1933d), in which she challenged the assumption behind the argument in the *Treatise*, namely that an excess of savings over investment leads to a fall in the price of consumption goods. In May 1932, together with Kahn and Austin Robinson, she wrote a 'Manifesto'[1] debating a point raised by Keynes in his lectures about the mechanism leading to an increase in output following upon an increase in investment.

In October of the same year Keynes accepted an article by her for the *Economic Journal* (J. Robinson 1932a), praising it as 'excellent – most beautiful and lucid' (letter 1883, 16 October 1932); in contrast, her *Economics is a Serious Subject. The Apologia of an Economist to the Mathematician, the Scientist and the Plain Man* (J. Robinson 1932b) did not meet with much favour on the part of Keynes (letter 1783, 21 October 1932).

In her pamphlet she dealt with the questions raised in the discussions over the validity of the Marshallian theory with a more general scope in mind, defending the methodology of making irrealistic assumptions against the charge of the mathematician, who would defend logic against realism, and the charge of the plain man, who would do exactly the opposite (see Harcourt 1990). The pamphlet is dedicated to 'the fundamental pessimist'. In the original manuscript the place of the anonymous dedication was occupied by the following legend: 'To Piero Sraffa, whose introduction of pessimism into Cambridge has made Economics a Serious Subject'.[2] The pamphlet was in fact the methodological manifesto of the book J. Robinson had been writing since the spring of 1931 (letter 748 from JVR to RFK, 30 March 1931), and which was published in 1933 under the title of *The Economics of Imperfect Competition* (J. Robinson 1933a).

In November 1932 Keynes acted as reader of the manuscript of her book for Macmillan and, although his report was not entirely flattering (CWK XII: 865–8), he recommended publication. This opened up a new phase in the relationship between Keynes and J. Robinson, as a result of much manoeuvring by Kahn, who was equally involved in assisting Robinson in the writing of the *Economics of Imperfect Competition* and Keynes in what would become the *General Theory* (Marcuzzo 1996b, 2002; see Ch. 10).

Early in 1933, from America Kahn urged her to pursue her involvement in Keynes's work:

> Naturally, you cannot raise the point, but if Maynard hints that he would like you to look at his stuff, I do wish you would. I must confess that I am a bit appalled at the prospect of having the sole responsibility thrust on to me after my return.
>
> (letter 574 from RFK to JVR, 2 March 1933)

A few months later she was able to write 'a kind of interim report on how far the Keynesians had got by that time' (J. Robinson 1951a: viii); in that article – published in October 1933 under the title 'The Theory of Money and the Analysis of Output' – she repeated her criticism of the 'widow's cruse' reasoning in the *Treatise* as being valid only under the assumption that 'an increase in demand for consumption goods leads to no increase in their supply' (J. Robinson [1933b] 1951a: 55).

By 1934 J. Robinson was relying ever more on Keynes's advice:

> I am expecting to produce a baby in the Summer. I do not think myself that this ought to be considered relevant to the question of

> lecturing – but I quite see that there is another point of view. I haven't told any of our colleagues except Kahn and Piero. Do you think it might be left to dawn on the other gradually or ought it to be mentioned when my lectures are discussed?
>
> (letter 1787, 26 March 1934)

As far as the lectures were concerned, she wanted to present a 'grand scheme' (letter 1787, 26 March 1934) illustrating historical episodes and controversial theoretical issues. Keynes invited here to use caution (letter 1788, 29 March 1934), but supported her wholeheartedly, and later on even stepped in to prevent her proposal to give a course on Money for two terms from being turned down (JMK to C.R. Fay, 5 March 1935, JMK papers, UA/14.2). (See Chs 2: 69; 7: 208–9; 13: 339.)

When, during the summer of 1934, the building blocks of the *General Theory* were firmly laid out, J. Robinson was so confident in her role as one of Keynes's interlocutors that she could write to Kahn: '[. . .] of course I am absolutely full of views about the *Treatise.* Would Maynard like me to write him a Preface for the new work showing in what respects his ideas have altered?' (letter 645 from JVR to RFK, 5–6 September 1934).

It was in fact in 1934 that a change occurred in the personal relationship between J. Robinson and Keynes. She wrote to Kahn: 'I see Maynard signed 'yours faithfully' in type and crossed it out in ink so I can't really complain' (letter 630 from JVR to RFK, 15 August 1934).

In June 1935 J. Robinson was asked, together with Harrod, Hawtrey and Kahn, to read the second set of proofs of the *General Theory*, and Keynes held her comments in great consideration. In that same June of 1935 Keynes sent J. Robinson his correspondence with Hawtrey for her to read and offer him her advice; in October he praised a paper she presented at the Political Economy Club as 'crystal clear and extremely interesting' (letter 1800, 24 October 1935, CWK XII: 652).

By 1935 J. Robinson was anxious to explain, popularise and extend the results of the *General Theory*, as we shall see in more detail in the next section. She started with the concept of 'disguised unemployment', dedicating to the topic an article which Keynes accepted for the *Economic Journal* (J. Robinson 1936a). In correspondence with her, he pointed out that she had not clearly stated the conditions under which employment can be increased without 'any change in either the propensity to consume or the inducement to invest' (letter 1804, 3 March 1936). To which she replied:

> I am sure you are right that the formal treatment of disguised unemployment wants to be cleared up. I was trying not to be high brow in my paper, but I think with the assistance of your notes I can put this point fairly simply.
>
> (letter 1805, 4 March 1936)

In 1937 she published two books following in Keynes's footsteps. The first, *Essays in the Theory of Employment* (J. Robinson 1937a), drew 'riders from the main theory' (J. Robinson 1979b: 185–6), the second, *Introduction to the Theory of Employment* (J. Robinson 1937b), was meant to be 'a told to the children version of *The General Theory*', as she put it in a letter to him (letter 1825, 18 November 1936, CWK XXIX: 184–5).

As far as the *Essays in the Theory of Employment* were concerned, she later recalled that 'Keynes read the draft and I cut anything that I could not persuade him was correct' (J. Robinson 1973b: 174). In fact Keynes read the proofs during his trip to Russia, made detailed comments and raised doubts on the soundness of certain conclusions. In particular he was very critical of her article on the foreign exchanges, discussion of which – as we shall see – went on throughout November.

However, in the end he wrote to her: 'Your fierceness may quite possibly land you in trouble in some quarters [. . .] I consider the book as a whole a bit uneven [. . .] But the general effect is splendid, full of originality and interest' (letter 1822, 12 November 1936, CWK XIV: 147). To which she replied: 'I am more grateful than it would be decent to say for all the trouble you have taken, and I am most delighted to have your approval in general for the book' (letter 1824, 14 November 1936, CWK XIV: 148).

As for her second book, Keynes did not initially welcome the idea of a popular version of the *General Theory* with great enthusiasm, as he was 'against hurry and in favour of gestation' (letter 1827, 2 December 1936, CWK XXIX: 185–6). But his reaction did not dissuade her. In March 1937 (letter 1829, 6 March 1937) she announced to him that she was revising it and Keynes (letter 1830, 25 March 1937, CWK XIV: 149) again fought shy of the idea, letting her know that he was thinking of presenting the *General Theory* in a different way. She defended her project as a teaching device for non-first-class students, in a light-hearted tone:

> I do not regard my proposed book as of the smallest importance (either way) in the development of ideas. With your consent I will get on with it. I am having a baby in October, so this seems suitable light work for the summer.
>
> (letter 1832, 22 April 1937)

When the *Introduction to the Theory of Employment* came out Keynes seems to have welcomed it, writing to her: 'You have been very successful, I think, in simplifying and have skated round the complications beautifully' (letter 1842, 20 November 1937).

In August 1937 she was asked to comment on Keynes's reply to Pigou's article on real and money wages, which Robertson had accepted for the *Economic Journal* during Keynes's illness. (see Chs 2: 70; 8: 219–20; 15: 378–82). The autumn of the same year saw discussion of some import on innovations prompted by a note J. Robinson had written in response to criticism raised by Harrod (see below: 183). Another exchange started in March 1938 on an article by Abba Lerner that met with Keynes's liking (Lerner 1938). Since Robinson was working on similar topics she felt that there was no point in publishing her work, but Keynes wanted it for the *Economic Journal* and it eventually came out in June (J. Robinson 1938b) (letters 1843–1846, 6–30 March 1938).

The topic is interesting because it is connected with her strong feelings in the argument Keynes was having with Robertson regarding the issue of 'finance' constraint on investment. She wrote to him:

> D.H.R. seems to grow more and more perverse. I can't make any sense of this at all. He seems to be wandering vaguely about in a featureless wilderness. I think your reply would be more telling if you put in the working a bit more. Abandon D.H.R. as hopeless and write as tho' for a 2nd year man who is hoping to get a II.2. You want the reader, emerging dazed from D.H.R., to feel that you represent simplicity and commonsense.
>
> (letter 1845, 23 March 1938, CWK XXIX: 169)

The difficult situation between Keynes and his circle on the one hand and Robertson on the other is reflected in the exchange of the summer of 1938. In a letter J. Robinson complained about a sentence Robertson had included in an article of his – eventually published in the September issue of the *Economic Journal* – to the effect of accusing her of 'affirming without qualification that the desire to save does not promote investment' (letter 1847, 30 July 1938, CWK XXIX: 181–2). Keynes agreed with her

> that it would be much better if Dennis were to leave out that unprovoked reference to you. I do not see any possible object in attributing to you an opinion which you certainly do not hold. I will see what I can do about it.
>
> (letter 1849, 3 August 1938)

In the end Keynes succeeded in getting Robertson to withdraw his comment and for the time being the hostilities between Robertson and the 'Keynesians' came to a halt (see Ch. 2: 71–2).

Next we discuss in more detail some of the issues referred to above, with regard first to the making of the *General Theory* and then Robinson's endeavours to popularise and extend its main results.

Towards the *General Theory*

In the first exchange of this correspondence, in April 1932, Keynes defended himself from the charge brought against him in J. Robinson's article on saving and investment of having made the assumption of constant output in the *Treatise*, with the following argument:

> in my *Treatise* itself, I have long discussions with the effects of changes in output; it is only at a particular point in the preliminary theoretical argument that I assume constant output, and I am at pains to make this absolutely clear. Surely one must be allowed at a particular stage of one's argument to make simplifying assumptions of this kind; particularly when, as you agree, the assumption in question does not make a very vital difference to the whole character of the argument.
>
> (letter 1772, 14 April 1932, CWK XIII: 269–70)

A few months later, as a consequence of criticisms and comments coming from Kahn, Sraffa, Robertson and indeed J. Robinson, Keynes changed his mind on whether the assumption of constant output made 'a very vital difference', and his thoughts took a turn in that direction.

A crucial step in persuading Keynes to embrace a different approach was successfully made in May 1932. In the spring of 1932, Kahn and Austin and Joan Robinson had followed Keynes's lessons, eventually signing a 'Manifesto' on one aspect of Keynes's theory, presenting an 'alternative' (as Keynes put it) or 'complementary' (as J. Robinson had it in her subsequent correspondence) solution. The point under discussion was Keynes's 'proof' that the variation in investment (ΔI) had the same sign as the variation in output (ΔO). Keynes's proof rests on two initial hypotheses: (1) $\Delta E'$ (the variation in the entrepreneurs' earnings, i.e. the monetary value deriving from sales of the current output of goods and services) has the same sign as ΔO; (2) $\Delta E' - \Delta F$ (ΔF is the change in spending, and thus the difference between the change in the entrepreneurs' earnings and the change in spending accounts for the change in their savings) has the same sign as $\Delta E'$.

Since $\Delta E' - \Delta F = \Delta I$, it follows that ΔI and ΔO have the same sign.

The objection raised here by the Manifesto authors was that condition (2) – that spending does not rise as much as income – actually demonstrates not that the variation in investment has the same sign as the variation in output, but ensures

> that there shall be stable equilibrium. If expenditure were to increase by more than income, equilibrium would be unstable and any small increment in investment would cause output to rise either to infinity or to a point where condition (b) [i.e. (2)] came into operation, whichever happened first.
>
> (CWK XXIX: 43)

Moreover, the Manifesto authors went on, were an increase in spending to bring about a considerable increase in the costs of production, then output would fall instead of rising and condition (1) would no longer apply. It was at this point that an alternative to Keynes's proof was proposed:

> The problem seems to us to be susceptible to treatment by method of Supply and Demand. For the truth of the proposition that an increase in I will lead to an increase in *O*, the two following conditions appear to us to be sufficient, though not necessary:
>
> (a) That an increase in *I* will lead *per se* to a rise in the demand for consumption goods, i.e. that the demand for consumption goods on the part of the producers of capital goods will increase when the value of their output increases;
>
> (b) That the conditions of supply of consumption goods are not affected by change in *I*.
>
> When these conditions are fulfilled, an increase in *I* will lead to a rise in the demand curve for consumption goods without raising the supply curve, and so must lead to an increase of output of consumption goods, and *a fortiori* to an increase in total output.
>
> (letter 1774, May 1932, CWK XXIX: 43–4)

Keynes's resistance 'to scrap all my present half-forged weapons' (letter 1779, 9 May 1932, CWK XIII: 378), as he wrote to Robinson in the correspondence on the Manifesto, was short lived. In fact, the lectures of autumn 1932 showed Keynes taking up the 'method' of the Trumpington Street School, using the expression 'demand as a whole relatively to supply as a whole' (CWK XXIX: 53).

In the summer of 1933, Keynes informed J. Robinson that, after 'a pregnant conversation with Kahn', he was going to adopt a new technique of expression for the *General Theory* (letter 1785, 17 July 1933); in another he elaborated on what should be understood by the concepts of full employment and unemployment. There Keynes argued that

> there is full employment if employment is available to everyone wanting it at a wage equal in terms of product to the marginal efficiency in terms of product of the quantity of labour thus offering itself. In other words, on the normal assumption of the classical theory that real wages are equal to the marginal efficiency of labour in terms of product, then there is always full employment. Unemployment of the type we are considering occurs because it is not true, as Pigou, I think, assumes, that if a man can by his labour turn two grains of wheat into three over a production period, that it will therefore pay to employ him at a real wage of a grain of wheat.
>
> (letter 1786, 25 August 1933)

As we have seen, J. Robinson was involved in the proof-reading of *General Theory*. Keynes sent her the first batch between 6 and 12 June 1935. By the 16 June she had responded with detailed comments, mainly suggesting stylistic changes or calling for clarification of certain points. Three days later she sent him a note on liquidity 'which I take to be what you mean' (letter 1796, 19 June 1935, CWK XIII: 246–50), in which in fact she summarised his main point. In September Keynes sent a new set of proofs, informing her that Book I and most of Book II had been re-written during the summer. Once again, just four days later, she was ready to give him her comments, which unfortunately are not extant. Finally, in December, three days before the final version was delivered to the printer, he sent it to her with the following covering letter:

> I owe you a great deal of gratitude for taking so much trouble over my proofs. Even the last gleaning was very useful and you spotted several misprints which I had overlooked. Indeed I'd give you high percentage marks for that; for the number found by me that you missed was extremely small. The book is now finished, all but preliminary matter, last sheets are index which still have to be passed for press, and it is being printed off. I think that it should be published very early in February. As you guessed author's melancholy did come on at the last. In the final proof reading it seemed so flat and stale. But you have cheered me and so does Kahn, who has been here for Christmas.
>
> (letter 1803, 27 December 1935)

Extending the *General Theory*

In this section we will examine the extensions of the *General Theory* which Robinson was busy pursuing in 1935–37. They can be grouped under three main headings: the determination of the level of employment in the long period, in (1) an open economy and when the effects of (2) innovations and (3) technical progress are taken into account.

Her first attempt is contained in an article, completed before publication of the *General Theory*, originally published in *Zeitschrift für Nationalökonomie* (J. Robinson 1936b). Initially Keynes did not object to the exercise of extending his results to the long period, although he had some reservations about her use of elasticity of substitution, as we will see. However, when the issue of the long period came up again, in 1941, he commented on a manuscript she had sent to him with a sharp note:

> Broadly speaking, you are taking the view that profits, and indeed interest, generally, is, in the last analysis, an uncertainty phenomenon, – a view I share with you. But, if so, I do not clearly understand what you mean by a long-term theory of profits. Why should not the answer

> be that the long term ignores uncertain phenomena, and consequently it is a contradiction of terms to talk of the theory of profits in the long term? Is not that perhaps the answer to your difficulties? Each alternative you adopt to lead you to a conclusion seems to me unsatisfactory. But you start off with the assumption that there must be such a theory. Why?
>
> (letter 1860, 24 January 1941)

In the correspondence of autumn 1936 the main issue between them was whether there is such a thing as an equilibrium rate of exchange and whether the interest rate is equalised across countries. Initially her essay on the foreign exchanges (J. Robinson 1937c) was received by Keynes quite unfavourably: 'It seems to me that there is here a formal mistake in reasoning. The whole line of approach strikes me as unsafe and not likely to lead to reliable conclusions' (letter 1815, 4 November 1936, CWK XIV: 141). The point under scrutiny was Robinson's assumed relationship between saving (S) and investment (I) in an open economy. She claimed that:

> For an open system S = home I + foreign I, i.e. = home investment ± balance of trade. Home securities are being put on the market at a rate equal at home I. Home saving is forthcoming at a rate equal to home I ± balance of trade therefore the home demand for home securities exceeds or falls short of the supply according as the balance of trade is positive or negative.
>
> (letter 1816, 5 November 1936, CWK XIV: 141–2)

Keynes, however, pointed out that:

> The mistake comes in identifying the demand for home investment with the amount of home saving. There is also available the proceeds of disinvestment in foreign securities. Consequently the demand for home investment is equal to home saving minus or plus the balance of trade. In other words, the demand for home investments is equal to the amount of home investments, which is as it should be.
>
> (letter 1817, 6 November 1936, CWK XIV: 141–3)

In the end Robinson decided to cut 'all the controversial matter' and thanked him for preventing her 'from publishing a half-baked version' (letter 1823, 13 November 1936, CWK XIV: 147–8).

One year later a much more serious area of disagreement between them arose regarding Robinson's analysis of accumulation and technical progress. In her 1936 long-period article she had presented an analysis of employment on the basis of the elasticity of substitution between factors, defined as the proportionate change in the ratio of the quantities of factors employed divided by the proportionate change in the ratio of their prices, which she had originally presented in her *Economics of Imperfect Competition.*

According to her analysis, in the long period the amount of employment is the result of 'the contrary pulls of increased total output and increased output per head' (J. Robinson 1937a: 87). Therefore a fall in the rate of interest that has no direct effect on the amount of employment if savings are a function exclusively of the level of income, produces an indirect effect by the substitution of capital for labour and the subsequent change in the distribution of income (the share of labour will increase if the elasticity of substitution is less than one). This in turn affects the propensity to save and the multiplier, due to the different saving habits of rich and poor.

In the same article she also analysed the effects of inventions on the distribution of income, i.e. whether inventions reduce the share of labour (reducing the equilibrium level of income by increasing thriftiness) or whether they increase it (increasing the equilibrium level of income by decreasing thriftiness). She developed her analysis of inventions – for which she acknowledged Kalecki's assistance (J. Robinson 1937a: 95n) – on the basis of a classification centred on the distinction between neutral, capital-saving and capital-using inventions. In equilibrium, neutral inventions leave capital per unit of product and the relative shares of labour and capital in a given output unchanged, while capital-saving and capital-using inventions reduce/increase capital per unit of product and reduce/increase the relative shares of capital. The reason being that capital-saving inventions increase efficiency in producing capital goods more than in producing final goods, while the opposite occurs in the case of capital-using.

In his review of the book in which the article was published, Harrod challenged Robinson's definitions, and this occasioned an exchange with her which went on between May and June 1937 (see Ch. 12: 318–19). Keynes sided with Harrod's view of her 'elasticity substitution method' (letter 1246 from JMK to RFH, 12 April 1937, CWK XIV: 170–4) as being ambiguous without the provision of a precise measure of the quantity of capital.

As a consequence of her debate with Harrod, she decided to write an article on the nature of inventions (J. Robinson 1938a) and asked Keynes to comment on it. He was not convinced by her method of analysing the 'once-ever' effect of technology changes on distribution and wrote to her: 'you are introducing inventions into the debris of the static, one-at-the-time economics where inventions do not properly belong' (letter 1834, 27 September 1937). Moreover he objected to her use of the elasticity of substitution in the aggregate, since 'a great difficulty arises' in her use of cost units to measure capital.

Robinson retorted that as far as the measurement of capital was concerned she was not 'any worse than the others', adding that 'Piero is devoting his life to the question, and we cannot expect an answer quickly' (letter 1835, 28 September 1937). Keynes reacted by pointing out that his 'difficulty about measuring capital has nothing to do with Piero's problem, but it is concerned with the effect of inventions in lowering the cost of capital just as much as a product' (letter 1836, 29 September 1937). Moreover, he had a serious reservation as to whether there was 'any sense at all in elasticity of substitution between capital and labour in response to new inventions'. He maintained that 'With a given state of invention and a given rate of interest, there is as a rule only one proportion in which capital and labour can be combined, subject only to the exception of using the plant more intensively and this is an element in the situation on which invention may have little or no bearing' (ibid.).

Robinson was unshaken by this criticism and retorted that she was not talking of the 'elasticity of substitution in response to an invention', but of the value of that elasticity *after* an invention has occurred'. Keynes, too, remained adamant:

> I cannot see how the elasticity of substitution between capital and labour, after adjustment has been made to the new situation, has any bearing at all upon whether, in the usual sense of the term, an invention is capital-saving or labour-saving.
>
> (letter 1839, 6 October 1937)

The topic of elasticity of substitution was considered again some years later, in 1941, in a letter from Keynes, in which he praised Robinson's article on 'Rising supply price' (J. Robinson 1941a) (letter 1861, 20 April 1941).

An overview of the correspondence during and in the aftermath of the war

As war loomed ominously close, in October 1938, Robinson fell into an extreme emotional state, which was diagnosed as a manic-depressive crisis, and she was confined to hospital for a few months. Of that period, we have only two letters by Keynes (who was still ailing from his heart failure) to her witnessing the warmth and closeness of their friendship (letters 1852 and 1853, 28 December 1938 and 12 January 1939).

From 1939–40 on, Keynes, like most of his friends and colleagues, was personally involved in the war effort. J. Robinson, Sraffa and Kaldor – albeit for different reasons – were excluded and remained in Cambridge, carrying out most of the academic duties. The ensuing correspondence reflects the different occupations in which Keynes and J. Robinson were engaged. Although totally involved in many war-related activities, Keynes retained his habit of asking his closest friends their opinion on what he was writing or doing. Thus we have J. Robinson's comments on Keynes's

How to Pay for the War (letter 1855, 28 February 1940), a discussion on war policies and statistics in December 1940, and, in 1944, on the Bretton Woods agreements (letters 1872–1874, 9–16 September 1944, CWK XXVI: 129–33).

In turn, Keynes was very appreciative of her currency proposal paper (J. Robinson 1943), writing to her:

> It is first-class and I have no significant comments or criticisms. Just what is wanted for the purpose. It is excellently dry, in the sense of a good, dry sherry, not of Quaker Oats. I am sending it to the printer at once and am getting him to supply some extra proofs, since I may find it useful to circulate internally before the date of publication.
>
> (letter 1905, 6 June 1943)

Robinson was as usual involved in academic writing and activity. In 1940 'as a distraction from the news' (J. Robinson 1973c: 10) she began to read Marx. There is an amusing story about her first involvement with Marx and Marxism, which she later told in an unpublished paper:

> In 1936 I published a review of a book by John Strachey (brother of the more famous Lytton), who had set up as a popularizer of Marx – *The Nature of Capitalist Crisis* – I accused him of presenting the labour theory of value in terms of Say's Law, ignoring Keynes and treating Hayek as the representative of academic economics. He replied that it was absurd for someone who had never read Marx to talk about him. We each felt that the other had made a fair point. He began to read Keynes and I read Marx.
>
> (JVR papers, i/10/1)

Later she claimed that she 'began to read *Capital*, just as one reads any book, to see what was in it' (J. Robinson 1966: vi). M. Dobb was one of her 'tutors',[3] but Kalecki was the main influence. She wrote that Piero Sraffa used to tease her, saying that she 'treated Marx as a little-known forerunner of Kalecki' (ibid.). In a couple of years she produced a slim volume on Marx, *An Essay on Marxian Economics*, which raised a dust in academic and non-academic circles. Kalecki's comment on her book was very appreciative:

> I think that your analysis of Marx is very valuable: it has shown that one conception in his writing is quite consistent; while Marxists who wanted to show that everything is right and consistent failed to show even that.
>
> (Michal Kalecki to JVR, 30 July 1942, JVR papers, vii)

Keynes, too, expressed a favourable opinion of the book, but was not persuaded. As he saw it, J. Robinson was trying to make sense of what in fact was nonsense, that is to say Marx's economics (letter 1864, 20 August 1942). In the discussion that followed, Robinson conceded to Keynes that perhaps Marx was not a great thinker (letter 1865, 21 August 1942); this obviously contrasts with what she came to believe in the years to follow (see Marcuzzo 2001d).

Keynes was not involved in academic matters during wartime, but he was often consulted on them: in the correspondence we find, for instance, a report by J. Robinson of Sraffa's progress in the preparation of the much overdue edition of Ricardo's works (letter 1859, 1941); a request to Keynes to support an application to the National Research Institute (letter 1882, 3 September 1941). Another interesting exchange on academic topics occurs in 1942 (letters 1867 and 1868, 7 and 9 December 1942). Robinson informed Keynes that there was a proposal for him to succeed Pigou in Marshall's chair of political economy in Cambridge; Keynes refused to take such a possibility into consideration, judging that he would not be able to stay in Cambridge permanently after the war.

Finally, in 1944, we have an exchange concerning the creation of a fund to support Erwin Rothbarth's widow. Rothbarth was a German refugee who was killed in action over Holland; he was associated with the 'Cambridge Research Scheme' (see below) and was very close to Kalecki. And in fact the Kalecki *affair* is the last important issue to review in this correspondence.

Kalecki

In 1936 J. Robinson received a letter from Kalecki, who at the time was visiting the London School of Economics, commenting on one of her articles (J. Robinson 1936a), published in the *Economic Journal* in June 1936. Later she gave a lively account of their first encounter:

> He told me that he had taken a year's leave from the institute where he was working in Warsaw to write the *General Theory*. In Stockholm someone gave him Keynes's book. He began to read it – and it was the book that he had intended to write. He thought that perhaps further on there would be something different. But no, all the way it was his book. He said: 'I confess, I was ill. Three days I lay in bed. Then I thought: Keynes is more known than I am. These ideas will get across much quicker with him and then we can get on to the interesting question, which is their application. Then I got up.'
>
> (J. Robinson 1979b: 186)

She said she had very soon realised that Kalecki's analysis was indeed as important as Keynes's, and took upon herself the task of 'playing the trumpet for him' (ibid.). She even indulged in some wishful thinking and wrote to Kahn: 'Do you think that Kalecki will induce Piero to take the General Theory seriously?' (letter 679 from JVR to RFK, 20 March 1937).

Kalecki moved to Cambridge in 1937 and for the first six months of 1938 he was given a grant. In the meanwhile steps were taken to set up a research project to provide him with a permanent job. At the end of 1938, the 'Cambridge Research Scheme of the National Institute of Economic and Social Research into Prime Costs and Proceeds and Output' was launched, managed by a Board consisting of Austin Robinson, Kahn, Kalecki and Sraffa and chaired by Keynes.

Early in 1939 Keynes made a very favourable comment on Kalecki's book (Kalecki 1939) to J. Robinson:

> I have been reading Kalecki's proofs. Perhaps as a result of your proof readings, I find it remarkably lucid and very agreeable, and almost easy, reading. I have not compared these articles he is reprinting to see how much he has changed them and it may be that it is familiarity with his ideas that is helping me. At any rate I find the new version enormously easier. His device of making bold, and perhaps precarious, simplifications in his assumptions on the basis of alleged statistics and *there* beginning his theory (instead of working a theory on generalities and making simplifying assumptions afterwards) is very interesting and, if one minds one's step and remembers where one is, useful and illuminating. The flavour of him is most peculiar – very subtle, very aesthetic and complete within its own field, yet all the same light weight I can't help feeling. But it is an important book, so individual and original that it throws light in new courses.
>
> (letter 1853, 12 January 1939)

A few months later Kalecki presented the main findings of his research work with the Cambridge Scheme, in the form of reports on individual industries and an 'Interim Summary of Results'. Contrary to expectations, these reports were received with scepticism by J. Robinson, Kahn and Keynes, who objected to the methodology employed. Kalecki resigned from his Cambridge job, at the end of 1939 moving to Oxford, where he joined the University Institute of Statistics. Initially Robinson reported to Kahn that 'Kalecki has swallowed the Oxford job without a murmur' (letter 1462 from JVR to RFK, 14 January 1940); however, six months later she noted: 'I get a short and bitter letter from Kalecki from time to time. Anyway he seems well dug in at Oxford' (letter 1546 from JVR to RFK, 27 July 1940).

However, a year later, another incident occurred in relation to an article Kalecki had sent to Keynes (Kalecki 1940), which Robinson vigorously defended against Keynes's attack. In this article Kalecki set out to study the effects of technical progress, without assuming long-run equilibrium, and envisaged a 'reference system' to compare with the system under consideration. He assumed that the reference system

> is endowed with the features of technical progress as regards the tendency to raise the degree of oligopoly, the pressure of the raising productivity of labour on the price level, and the influence of inventions upon investment; but it is not subject to the rise in productivity of labour and to the fall in the ratio of productive capacity to capital.
>
> (Kalecki [1941] 1991: 111)

Moreover, for both the actual and the reference system he assumed constant marginal costs, imperfect competition and undercapacity utilisation. The result of the comparison was that the effect of technical progress is not to increase output, but to save labour; output is influenced only through the channels of investment, oligopoly and the general price level.

Keynes was thoroughly unhappy with the approach and wrote to J. Robinson in a very negative key: 'after a highly rational introduction of a couple of pages my first impression is that it becomes high, almost delirious nonsense' (letter 1893, 4 February 1941, CWK XII: 830). He complained that many of Kalecki's assumptions were 'latent and tacit', if not probably 'self-contradictory' and in particular that of undercapacity utilisation 'rather odd'. Robinson reacted firmly: 'I am prepared to stick up for Kalecki' and explained that there is another meaning of long-period – besides the classical one – and that in imperfect competition underutilization of capacity is a normal situation (letter 1892, 4 February 1941, CWK XII: 830).

The exchange continued in the following days in a fairly tense mode, Keynes accusing Kalecki of writing 'subject to a whole contraption of secrete knowledge, atmosphere and assumption' (letter 1895, 18 February 1941, CWK XII: 832) and Robinson insisting that 'Kalecki is explaining mysteries, not creating them' (letter 1896, 24 February 1941, CWK XII: 833); she attempted to persuade Keynes of the importance of Kalecki's results, in showing that 'capital-using inventions do not reduce the share of labour in the Nat. Div.' (CWK XII: 833), but to no avail.

At this point Robinson volunteered to help Kalecki revise his article, and as a result Keynes agreed that it was 'enormously improved in its present form and is not open to my previous criticisms, at any rate of presentation' (letter 1897, 4 March 1941, CWK XII: 833). However, he remained unconvinced of the argument and decided to send the article to Kaldor for another opinion. Kaldor's reaction was equally negative: 'The method of proof adopted in the 'reference system' makes the analysis unnecessarily cumbrous and lengthy' (letter 1716 from NK to JMK, 9 March 1941). Eventually, Keynes made it final that the article 'is pretentious, misleading, inconclusive and perhaps wrong' (letter 1899, 12 March 1941, CWK XII: 836). Robinson was forced to retreat: 'As you still do not get the point about inventions and relative shares, and Kaldor also failed to see it, I have to confess that Kalecki's article is not a success' (letter 1900, 13 March 1941, CWK XII: 836). According to the extant correspondence they never discussed Kalecki's work again.

Conclusions

The correspondence between J. Robinson and Keynes examined here shows that, although not always in agreement with her, Keynes trusted Robinson's judgement, was appreciative of her work and took account of her opinion. For her part, J. Robinson, always respectful of Keynes's authority, was rarely intimidated by him and often held her own position without giving ground. The correspondence also witnesses J. Robinson's effort to bring new elements into the Keynesian revolution and to induce Keynes to follow an approach to problems that she regarded as better suited to convey the fundamental ideas of his 'revolution'.

At times she would try to lead him to a line other than the one he had chosen, and on several occasions attempted to get Keynes to change his mind on specific issues, as we have seen. After Keynes's death, especially under the influence of Kalecki and Sraffa, she sought to bridge the Keynesian revolution with other non-mainstream lines of approach from the classical and Marxian tradition. In later works she implied that in the 1930s and 1940s she and Kahn had grasped the true revolutionary implications of Keynes's theory while Keynes was more reluctant to break radically and definitively with the past tradition. By contrast, the correspondence between Keynes and Robinson shows that, with the possible exception of the 1932–33 period, the roles were quite the reverse, with J. Robinson trying to develop analysis along more traditional lines, while Keynes appears to have been bolder in defending a radically alternative approach to orthodoxy. Such is the case with J. Robinson's attempt to extend Keynes's *General Theory* to the long period, or her and Kahn's allegiance to the Marshallian apparatus, as shown by their reliance on the elasticity of substitution among factors, marginal and average curves, and so forth.

It is true that, after Keynes's death, J. Robinson tried to bridge Keynes's theory with other non-neoclassical strands of thought, while Keynes had failed to appreciate contributions coming from different frameworks of thought, as the Kalecki affair amply demonstrates. Perhaps it is fair to conclude that each succeeded in being independent, original and stubborn both in their relationship and in their endeavours.

Notes

1 They signed it as 'The Manifesto of the Trumpington Street School' from the name of the street where Austin and Joan lived in Cambridge.
2 Sraffa reacted with some uneasiness; see Ch. 12: 313.
3 See the exchange of letters with Dobb between January and May 1941 in JVR papers, vii.

Table 6.1 Keynes–J. Robinson correspondence

From	*To*	*Year*	*Month*	*Day*	*Date*	*Archive*		*Published in*	*Item*
JVR	JMK	1932	April	9	Attributed	Keynes–King's	L/32/77–8	CWK XIII: 268–9	1771
JMK	JVR	1932	April	14	Dated letter	Robinson–King's Keynes–King's	JVR/vii/240/1–2 L/32/79–81	CWK XIII: 269–70	1772
JVR	JMK	1932	May		Attributed	Keynes–King's	GTE/1/42–4	CWK XIII: 376	1773
JVR	JMK	1932	May		Attributed	Keynes–King's	GTE/1/45–9	CWK XXIX: 42–5	1774
JVR	JMK	1932	May		Attributed	Keynes–King's	GTE/1/56–9	CWK XXIX: 47	1775
JVR	JMK	1932	May		Attributed	Keynes–King's	GTE/1/60–1	CWK XIII: 376–7	1776
JVR	JMK	1932	May		Attributed	Keynes–King's	GTE/1/62–3	CWK XIII: 377	1777
JMK	JVR	1932	May		Attributed	Keynes–King's	GTE/1/64–6	CWK XXIX: 46	1778
JMK	JVR	1932	May	9	Dated letter	Keynes–King's	GTE/1/50–1	CWK XIII: 377–8	1779
JVR	JMK	1932	May	10	Attributed	Keynes–King's	GTE/1/52–5	CWK XIII: 378	1780
JVR	JMK	1932	May	11	Attributed	Keynes–King's	GTE/1/67–8	CWK XIII: 379	1781
JMK	JVR	1932	May	12	Dated letter	Keynes–King's Keynes–King's	GTE/1/70–1 GTE/1/72–3	CWK XIII: 379–80	1782
JMK	JVR	1932	August	14	Dated letter	EAGR Archives, Marshall Library			1886
JMK	JVR	1932	October	16	Inferred from other sources	Not found in the archives		Marcuzzo 2003: 551, (E)	1883
JMK	JVR	1932	October	21	Dated letter	Robinson–King's Robinson–King's	JVR/vii/240/3 JVR/i/2.3/33	Turner 1989: 21, (E)	1783
JVR	JMK	1932	December	5	Attributed	Keynes–King's	CO/8/226		1784
JMK	JVR	1933	May	8	Dated letter	Not found in the archives		CWK XIII: 419	1887
JMK	JVR	1933	July	17	Dated letter	Robinson–King's	JVR/vii/240/4–5	Moggridge 1992: 565, (E)	1785
JMK	JVR	1933	August	25	Dated letter	Robinson–King's	JVR/vii/240/6–7		1786
JVR	JMK	1934	March	26	Attributed	Keynes–King's	UA/5/3/124–30		1787
JMK	JVR	1934	March	29	Dated letter	Keynes–King's	UA/5/3/131	CWK XIII: 422 (E)	1788
JMK	JVR	1934	April	17	Inferred from other sources	Not found in the archives			1884

JMK	JVR	1935	June	8	Dated letter	Keynes–King's	GTE/1/215	CWK XIII: 638	1791
JMK	JVR	1935	June	12	Dated letter	Keynes–King's	GTE/1/216	CWK XIII: 638	1792
JVR	JMK	1935	June	13	Attributed	Keynes–King's	GTE/1/217–8		1793
JVR	JMK	1935	June	16	Attributed	Keynes–King's	GTE/1/219–20 and L/R/144–5 and GTE/1/221–31 and GTE/1/234–7 and GTE/1/241–3	CWK XIII: 638–45	1794
JMK	JVR	1935	June	18	Dated letter	Keynes–King's	GTE/1/247	CWK XIII: 645	1795
JVR	JMK	1935	June	19	Attributed	Keynes–King's	GTE/1/248–52 and /232–3 and /238–40 and /244–6 GTE/2/4/218	CWK XIII: 646–50	1796
JMK	JVR	1935	September	3	Dated letter	Robinson–King's Keynes–King's	JVR/vii/240/8 GTE/1/277	CWK XIII: 650–1	1797
JVR	JMK	1935	September	7	Attributed	Keynes–King's	GTE/1/278–9	CWK XIII: 651	1798
JMK	JVR	1935	September	15	Dated letter	Keynes–King's	GTE/1/280–1	CWK XIII: 651	1799
JVR	JMK	1935	Autumn		Attributed	Keynes–King's	GTE/1/253–7	CWK XIII: 651–2	1789
JMK	JVR	1935	October	24	Dated letter	Keynes–King's	GTE/1/413	CWK XIII: 652	1800
JVR	JMK	1935	November	7–20	Attributed	Keynes–King's	GTE/1/421		1790
JMK	JVR	1935	November	29	Dated letter	Keynes–King's Keynes–King's	GTE/1/417 GTE/1/418	CWK XIII: 612	1801
JVR	JMK	1935	December	2	Attributed	Keynes–King's	GTE/1/419–20	CWK XIII: 612–13	1802
JMK	JVR	1935	December	27	Dated letter	Robinson–King's	JVR/vii/240/9–10		1803
JMK	JVR	1936	March	3	Dated letter	Keynes–King's	EJ/1/1/367–70		1804
JVR	JMK	1936	March	4	Attributed	Keynes–King's	EJ/1/3/371–3		1805
JVR	JMK	1936	March	29	Attributed	Keynes–King's	EJ/1/3/374–5		1806
JVR	JMK	1936	May	29	Attributed	Keynes–King's	GTE/2/4/216–7	CWK XIV: 34–5	1807
JMK	JVR	1936	September	8	Dated letter	Not found in the archives		CWK XIV: 134	1888

Table 6.1 continued

From	*To*	*Year*	*Month*	*Day*	*Date*	*Archive*		*Published in*	*Item*
JMK	JVR	1936	September	11	Dated letter	Not found in the archives		CWK XIV: 134	1889
JVR	JMK	1936	September	16	Attributed	Keynes–King's	L/36/60–3	CWK XIV: 135	1808
JMK	JVR	1936	September	17	Dated letter	Keynes–King's	L/36/64–6	CWK XIV: 136–7	1809
JMK	JVR	1936	October	5	Dated letter	Not found in the archives		CWK XIV: 137–8	1890
JMK	JVR	1936	October	15	Dated letter	Keynes–King's	L/36/67–8	CWK XIV: 138	1810
JMK	JVR	1936	October	16	Postmark	Robinson–King's	JVR/vii/240/11–12		1811
JVR	JMK	1936	October	16	Attributed	Keynes–King's	L/36/69–71	CWK XIV: 139	1812
JVR	JMK	1936	October	16–20	Attributed	Keynes–King's	L/36/72–3	CWK XIV: 140	1814
JVR	JMK	1936	October	20	Attributed	Keynes–King's	L/36/74–5	CWK XIV: 140	1813
JMK	JVR	1936	October	28	Dated letter	Not found in the archives		CWK XIV: 140–1	1891
JMK	JVR	1936	November	4	Dated letter	Keynes–King's	L/36/76–7	CWK XIV: 141	1815
JVR	JMK	1936	November	5	Attributed	Keynes–King's	L/36/78–80	CWK XIV: 141–2	1816
JMK	JVR	1936	November	5	Dated letter	Not found in the archives		CWK XIV: 142	1997
JMK	JVR	1936	November	6	Dated letter	Keynes–King's	EJ/1/4/213	CWK XIV: 143	1817
JVR	JMK	1936	November	6	Attributed	Keynes–King's	L/36/81–2	CWK XIV: 143	1818
JVR	JMK	1936	November	7	Attributed	Keynes–King's	L/36/83–4	CWK XIV: 144	1819
JMK	JVR	1936	November	8	Dated letter	Not found in the archives		CWK XIV: 144–5	1998
JVR	JMK	1936	November	9	Attributed	Keynes–King's	L/36/85–7	CWK XIV: 145–6	1820
JMK	JVR	1936	November	9	Dated letter	Not found in the archives		CWK XIV: 146	1999
JVR	JMK	1936	November	10	Attributed	Keynes–King's	L/36/88–9	CWK XIV: 147	1821
JMK	JVR	1936	November	12	Dated letter	Keynes–King's	L/36/90	CWK XIV: 147	1822
JVR	JMK	1936	November	13	Attributed	Keynes–King's	L/36/91–2	CWK XIV: 147–8	1823

JVR	JMK	1936	November	14	Attributed	Keynes–King's	L/36/93	CWK XIV: 148	1824
JVR	JMK	1936	November	18	Attributed	Keynes–King's	GTE/2/4/200–1	CWK XXIX: 184–5	1825
JVR	JMK	1936	November	25	Attributed	Keynes–King's	GTE/2/4/202–3	CWK XXIX: 185	1826
JMK	JVR	1936	December	2	Dated letter	Robinson–King's Keynes–King's	JVR/vii/240/13 GTE/2/4/204	CWK XXIX: 185–6	1827
JVR	JMK	1936	December	3	Attributed	Keynes–King's	GTE/2/4/205–6	CWK XXIX: 186	1828
JVR	JMK	1937	March	6	Attributed	Keynes–King's	GTE/2/4/207–9	CWK XIV: 148–9	1829
JMK	JVR	1937	March	25	Dated letter	Keynes–King's	GTE/2/4/210–11	CWK XIV: 149	1830
JMK	JVR	1937	April	20	Dated letter	Keynes–King's	GTE/2/4/212–13	CWK XIV: 150	1831
JVR	JMK	1937	April	22	Attributed	Keynes–King's	GTE/2/4/214–15		1832
JVR	JMK	1937	August	10	Attributed	Keynes–King's	EJ/1/4/61–2	CWK XIV: 239–40	1833
JMK	JVR	1937	September	27	Dated letter	Keynes–King's	CO/8/228–31		1834
JVR	JMK	1937	September	28	Attributed	Keynes–King's	CO/8/232–5		1835
JMK	JVR	1937	September	29	Dated letter	Keynes–King's	CO/8/236–7		1836
JVR	JMK	1937	September	30	Attributed	Keynes–King's	CO/8/238–42		1837
JVR	JMK	1937	October	1	Attributed	Keynes–King's	CO/8/243		1838
JMK	JVR	1937	October	6	Dated letter	Keynes–King's	CO/8/244–5		1839
JMK	JVR	1937	October	6	Dated letter	Keynes–King's	EJ/1/4/131–2		1840
JVR	JMK	1937	October	8	Attributed	Keynes–King's	EJ/1/4/133–5		1841
JMK	JVR	1937	November	20	Dated letter	Robinson–King's	JVR/vii/240/14–15	Marcuzzo 2003: 552, (E)	1842
JVR	JMK	1938	March	6	Attributed	Keynes–King's	EJ/1/5/74–5		1843
JMK	JVR	1938	March	22	Dated letter	Keynes–King's	EJ/1/5/76		1844
JVR	JMK	1938	March	23	Attributed	Keynes–King's	GTE/2/4/159–62	CWK XXIX: 169	1845
JMK	JVR	1938	March	30	Dated letter	Keynes–King's	GTE/2/4/163	CWK XXIX: 170	1846
JVR	JMK	1938	July	30	Attributed	Keynes–King's	GTE/2/4/188–9	CWK XXIX: 181–2	1847
JVR	JMK	1938	August		Attributed	Keynes–King's	GTE/2/4/191–2		1848
JMK	JVR	1938	August	3	Dated letter	Robinson–King's	JVR/vii/240/16		1849
JVR	JMK	1938	August	4	Postmark	Keynes–King's	GTE/2/4/195	CWK XXIX: 183	1850
JVR	JMK	1938	September	21	Attributed	Keynes–King's	A/39/159–60		1851
JMK	JVR	1938	December	28	Dated letter	Robinson–King's	JVR/vii/240/17–18		1852
JMK	JVR	1939	January	12	Dated letter	Robinson–King's	JVR/vii/240/19–20		1853
JMK	JVR	1939	December	19	Dated letter	Robinson–King's	JVR/vii/240/21		1854

Table 6.1 continued

From	*To*	*Year*	*Month*	*Day*	*Date*	*Archive*		*Published in*	*Item*
JVR	JMK	1940			Attributed	Keynes–King's	W/1/49		1881
JVR	JMK	1940	February	28	Attributed	Keynes–King's	HP/4/79–80		1855
JMK	JVR	1940	May	7	Dated letter	Keynes–King's	W/1/48		1856
JMK	JVR	1940	November	28	Dated letter	Keynes–King's	EJ/1/6/57		1857
JMK	JVR	1940	December	5	Dated letter	Keynes–King's	L/40/139		1858
JVR	JMK	1941			Attributed	Keynes–King's	MM/4/285–6		1907
JVR	JMK	1941	January	16	Attributed	Keynes–King's	MM/1/5/71		1906
JMK	JVR	1941	January	24	Dated letter	Keynes–King's	EJ/1/7/163–4		1860
JVR	JMK	1941	February	4	Dated letter	Keynes–King's	MM/4/147–8	CWK XII: 830	1892
JMK	JVR	1941	February	4	Dated letter	Keynes–King's	MM/4/149–50	CWK XII: 829–30	1893
JMK	JVR	1941	February	12	Dated letter	Keynes–King's	MM/4/145–6	CWK XII: 830–1	1903
JVR	JMK	1941	February	14	Inferred from other sources	Keynes–King's	MM/4/143–4	CWK XII: 831–2	1895
JMK	JVR	1941	February	18	Dated letter	Keynes–King's	MM/4/141–2	CWK XII: 832	1894
JVR	JMK	1941	February	24	Inferred from other sources	Keynes–King's	MM/4/139–40	CWK XII: 832–3	1896
JMK	JVR	1941	March	4	Dated letter	Keynes–King's	MM/4/137–8	CWK XII: 833	1897
JVR	JMK	1941	March	6	Inferred from other sources	Keynes–King's	MM/4/134–5	CWK XII: 834–5	1898
JMK	JVR	1941	March	12	Dated letter	Keynes–King's	MM/4/132–3	CWK XII: 835–6	1899
JVR	JMK	1941	March	13	Inferred from other sources	Keynes–King's	MM/4/131	CWK XII: 836	1900
JMK	JVR	1941	April	20	Dated letter	Keynes–King's	L/41/14–15		1861
JMK	JVR	1941	May	16	Dated letter	Robinson–King's	JVR/vii/240/22		1862
JVR	JMK	1941			Attributed	Keynes–King's	L/41/13		1859
JMK	JVR	1941	September	3	Dated letter	Kaldor–King's	NK/3/30/118/30–1		1882
JVR	JMK	1941	September	19	Attributed	Keynes–King's	BE/1/15	CWK XXII: 409	1863

JMK	JVR	1941	September	24	Dated letter	Not found in the archives		CWK XXII: 409	1901
JMK	JVR	1942	March	24	Inferred from other sources	Not found in the archives			1885
JMK	JVR	1942	August	20	Dated letter	Keynes–King's	L/42/102–3	Moggridge 1992: 470, (E)	1864
JVR	JMK	1942	August	21	Attributed	Keynes–King's	CO/8/246–8		1865
JMK	JVR	1942	August	27	Dated letter	Keynes–King's	CO/8/249–50		1866
JVR	JMK	1942	December	7	Attributed	Keynes–King's	UA/5/6/17–18		1867
JMK	JVR	1942	December	9	Dated letter	Keynes–King's	UA/5/6/19–20		1868
JMK	JVR	1943	June	4	Dated letter	Keynes–King's	MM/4/232–3		1904
JVR	JMK	1943	June	6	Attributed	Keynes–King's	MM/4/230–1		1905
JVR	JMK	1943	November		Attributed	Keynes–King's	EJ/1/7/263–4		1869
JMK	JVR	1943	December	1	Dated letter	Keynes–King's	EJ/1/7/265–6		1870
JVR	JMK	1944	September	7	Attributed	Keynes–King's	GTE/3/240–1		1871
JMK	JVR	1944	September	9	Dated letter	Robinson–King's Keynes–King's	JVR/vii/240/23–8 W/10/114–19	CWK XXVI: 129–32	1872
JVR	JMK	1944	September	14	Inferred from other sources	Keynes–King's Robinson–King's	W/10/120–1 JVR/vii/31–3	CWK XXVI: 132	1873
JMK	JVR	1944	September	16	Dated letter	Robinson–King's Keynes–King's	JVR/vii/240/29–30 W/10/122–3; W/10/124–5.	CWK XXVI: 133	1874
JMK	JVR	1944	October	9	Dated letter	Keynes–King's	W/10/126–7		1875
JMK	JVR	1945			Attributed	Keynes–King's	G/1/82		1876
JVR	JMK	1945	February	1	Attributed	Keynes–King's	G/1/76–7		1877
JMK	JVR	1945	February	5	Dated letter	Keynes–King's	G/1/78–9		1878
JVR	JMK	1945	February	15	Attributed	Keynes–King's	G/1/80–2		1879
JMK	JVR	1945	March	24	Dated letter	Keynes–King's	G/1/84		1902
JVR	JMK	1945	April	7	Attributed	Keynes–King's	G/1/87		1880

7 A lifelong friendship

The correspondence between Keynes and Shove

Anna Carabelli

Keynes and Shove: their personal relationship

The correspondence between Shove and Keynes counts 85 letters, 70 from Shove to Keynes and 15 from Keynes to Shove (mainly carbon copy letters), only 10 of which were published in the *Collected Writings of J. M. Keynes* (see Table 7.1). Six letters are undated. Shove 'left instructions in his Will that all manuscripts were to be destroyed' (Kahn 1987: 327), so what remains are mainly Shove's letters to Keynes. The correspondence adds very interesting insights into Shove's personal relationship with Keynes during the years of their youth in Cambridge, shedding light on the homosexual friendship they shared with other close friends, and their early political discussions. As one might expect, a sizeable part of the correspondence (although we could have hoped for more) deals with later debate on economic theory and academic affairs.

Gerald Shove, who was born in 1887, entered King's College, Cambridge, in 1907 and became an Apostle in 1909. He entered as a classicist, but then switched to economics having been deprived of his scholarship by the College Council. He took the economics part II Tripos in 1911. In 1923 he was appointed university lecturer, to become a fellow of King's in 1926 and reader in the faculty of economics in 1945. He died 'prematurely without having published much, but is remembered as a very good teacher' (Kahn 1987: 327). Skidelsky (1983: 430) describes him as 'generally silent and taciturn, but with flashes of ebullience (as when he proposed the toast of 'The King, God damn him' at the Carbonari[1] dinner of 1909), and moral passion'. Shove had been at Cambridge since December 1906, when he met Keynes in 1907. In 1911 Keynes was his supervisor; but for Gerald he was much more than that. Although Kahn (1987: 327) portrayed him as 'a shy, studious boy', his personality was complex. He was 'a man subject to black moods but with a vehement, biting edge and a blasphemous, dare-devil side which Maynard found attractive' (Skidelsky 1983: 265).

The significant exchange concerning Shove's personal relationship with Keynes consists of 24 letters (19 of the 1909–13 period and five of the

1928–43 period). All but three of the letters are dated (letters 3702, 3703 and 3704 remained undated).[2] An interesting group of letters (11 letters, from 1909 to 1943) is particularly relevant to Shove's psychological and mental state, while all the letters offer sidelights on Shove's personal attitude to life, research and academic career. They also add details to Keynes's biography, only partially covered by his biographers.

The early letters show Shove in conflict with his family conventions (letter 3706, 25 December 1909; letter 3709, 17 August 1910). Referring to his family problems Shove, who was at Studland, wrote:

> You would hardly believe the misery that I've been in for the last week: I'm in the middle of a beastly *bourgeois* family quarrel: – all the ravings of respectability and snobbery poured out by the hour against one of my unfortunate brothers who's supposed to have offended against their filthy conventions.
>
> (letter 3714, 7 January 1911)

Problems with his health and mental state dogged Shove throughout his life, waxing acute during the 1909–13 period, while the winter of 1910–11 saw his negative psychological attitude and depression growing particularly black (letters 3710 and 3707). He wrote:

> There seems nothing to be done except to abandon academic gewgaws. I'm not brilliant enough for the '*dolce far niente*' line so much in vogue with our modern brothers, and the beginning of an active career will be hell with no prestige behind me. Altogether I'm more depressed than you can well believe.
>
> (letter 3715, 28 February 1911)

Young Gerald had serious difficulties in answering the Tripos exam questions and writing his dissertation. In the surviving letters, from August 1910 to February 1911, he devoted paranoiac attention to the timing and quality of his answers (letters 3709, 3711, 3713 and 3715). In 1910–11 Keynes, as his supervisor for the Tripos, offered him some encouragement. Writing his dissertation was a serious ordeal for him given his psychological problems and his total lack of self-confidence. He began writing the dissertation in 1911 (letter 3719, 31 October 1911), sending Keynes the first chapter and part of another. The topic of this draft is unknown since he eventually submitted two dissertations for a King's College Fellowship – one on the application of Moore's Ethics to political theory, the other on local taxation (Kahn 1987: 327; Shove MSS, Marshall Library). Shove being a classicist, we conjecture that it was the one on Moore's ethics. In October he was critical of the draft and reached the conclusion that 'it's absolute balderdash'; he had 'only just been restrained from burning the whole thing' and had 'actually destroyed a few pages concluding the first section of chapter two' (letter 3719). On 26 December, he also wrote about 'Goldie's worries' on his dissertation (letter 3721).[3] On 15 August 1913, he told Keynes that his 'dissertation isn't begun' (letter 3724).

Neither his psychological problems nor his health improved with age. In 1933, when reading Pigou's book, he feared that his difficulty in understanding the fundamental assumptions therein was due to his 'own stupidity and lack of education'; he suspended judgement until he had 'gone through it again more carefully and in detail' and it was 'a comfort' to learn from Keynes that the fault probably did 'partly lie in the book and not altogether' in him (letter 3742, 11 September 1933; letter 3767, 9 February 1940).

Friendship, Bloomsbury and homosexuality

A group of early letters show the importance of friendship and intellectual relations. Friendship was *good in itself*, for Keynes's Moorean speculative ethics – i.e. for his 'religion', as he called it in his 1938 'My Early Beliefs' (CWK X: 433–50). Friendship was central to both the Cambridge Apostles and the Bloomsbury Circle. Within the Apostles and the Bloomsbury group, intellectual relations were cultivated through discussion and conversation, ranging from Christianity, modern civilisations and metaphysics to politics and mathematics, notably between Bertie (Bertrand Russell) and Ralph Hawtrey (letter 3708, 5 April 1910).

Shove belonged to both the Apostles and the broad Bloomsbury circle. His close friends – apart from Maynard Keynes – were Rupert Brooke (the poet) and James Strachey (the younger brother of Lytton). According to Hale (1998: 39), Brooke probably met Shove in the Fabians and it was Brooke who pushed through Shove's election to the Apostles in 1909, exactly one year after he himself had been elected.

The correspondence of Keynes and Duncan Grant, and of Rupert Brooke and James Strachey (now published, see Hale 1998) respectively, show that Shove was not, however, greatly appreciated by his Apostle and Bloomsbury friends for his intellectual qualities. Keynes considered him 'very charming, though not very clever I dare say, and quite nice to look at' (letter to Duncan Grant on 26 July 1908, quoted in Skidelsky 1983: 195). Rupert Brooke wrote to James Strachey on 11 July 1908, 'I admit that Mr. Shove begins to pall: he's really *too* much of a coarse-feeder – Mr Schloss appears refinement itself in comparison' (Hale 1998: 39). Rupert and James used to nickname him 'his Lordship', 'poor dear Gerald' and 'Shovel'. In addition, his two beloved friends would often make fun of his family, in particular targeting his mother Bertha's affair with her son's friend Hugh Popham and, later, the *naiveté* of his wife, Fredegond (Hale 1998: 151, 256–7).

Shove's homosexual penchant emerges quite clearly from the exchange, but in the surviving letters there is no further evidence suggesting there might have been an intimate relationship between him and Keynes in 1912, when they went together to the French Riviera on Easter vacation (Skidelsky 1983: 265; Hession 1984: 85).

Skidelsky (1983) and Moggridge (1992) provided ample information on the subject of Keynes's homosexuality, in contrast with the reticence of Keynes's first biographer, Roy Harrod (1951). The relevant, unpublished[4] correspondence between Shove and Keynes adds new details, eleven letters, from April 1910 to August 1913, including open discussion of homosexuality, some long and lavish in details, names and references.[5]

The first letter in this group, dated 1910, made Shove's homosexuality evident.

> Perhaps my greatest moment was on the last night when the 'practical poet' – as we must now call him – and I were left alone. We talked for three solemn hours about sodomy and Christians. He rather diffidently disapproved of sodomy and faintly admired Christians: at last he was driven to saying that copulation with people of one's own sex was unnatural and that, if I knew more history, I should see how much modern civilization owed to the Church!
>
> (letter 3708, 5 April 1910)

On 15 September (letter 3710), Shove noted that Compton-Burnett, then living in a family at Göttingen, had written that 'one of his fellow-guests (who is a theology student) greeted him on his arrival thus: "*Ich liebe nicht Madchen* [sic] *aber Knaben*"'.[6] Later that year, Shove was concerned about Keynes's adventures with street boys and the risk of being caught. Shove asked him whether his 'passion for low life isn't vicious: but perhaps you keep it within bounds' (letter 3712, 29 December 1910) (see Moggridge 1992: 214). He then proceeded in writing that his 'own life' had, as usual, been 'extraordinarily dull' and 'gloomy', and he had not 'the courage or the energy for adventures'. As to the Founder's Feast, he supposed that 'there were no rapes; just blithering sottish drunkenness, a little groping and a cock-stand or two'.

When Shove was at Studland, he mentioned a 'scandal' and some 'prurient facts' about Rupert's school career, adding that 'Frankie is not the only person who heard scandal: I got hold of some interesting facts about Rupert's school career the other day. I'll tell you when we meet' (letter 3714, 7 January 1911).[7] On 28 February 1911 (letter 3715), Shove evinced his passion for Phil,[8] and the same letter also contained references to other friends of Shove's.

> It'll be a comfort, however, to kiss Robin's photograph sometimes, when I'm not immersed in dreams of Phil. [. . .] At present the chief object of my return is a scheme to sit next to Phil at the Liberal Club

> Dinner. I'm afraid he may want to sit with the women, but I'm writing him a pathetic appeal which may move him.
>
> (letter 3715, 28 February 1911)

In 1911 the exchange on homosexuality continued with a letter rich in details. There were references again to Phil and also to Reggie Davies as a possible substitute. Pigou, 'the Prof.', was mentioned as a possible rival to Shove as far as Phil was concerned. Shove's language was open and his pen was bright. He attributed 'Pigou's illness' to love problems.

> The explanation of the Prof.'s illness would appear painfully obvious to a German. I told you (didn't I?) Compton-Burnett's tale of the Austrian count at Gottingen? He was a very passionate creature, and when he's paroxysms came on him used to fall down senseless. On recovering he would shout for hours at a time 'Bring me a boy! Bring me a boy!' adding in a quieter voice, 'Or if you can't find one, a girl.' The Germans, C-B tells me, hold it as one of their cardinal article of faith that all buggers have fainting fits when they're in love. I'm afraid the Prof. is still my rival. Next time such a thing happens you must hurry off for Phil, 'or – if you can't find him' – Reggie Davies.
>
> (letter 3716, 6 March 1911)

In March and April 1911 Keynes was on a trip to Tunisia, Sicily and Turkey with Duncan Grant. Shove wrote him another long letter (letter 3717, 26 March 1911), again mixing homosexuality, mental problems and psychological difficulties in his relationship with his family. Later that same year (letter 3718, 5 April 1911) Shove was again worried about Keynes's propensity to pick up boys in the street, and thanked him for his recent prudence. The text was again an intricate mixture of comments on homosexuality, his mental state and his inability to concentrate on Tripos papers ('I haven't done a single paper').

Discussing politics: the Liberal Party, socialism and conscientious objection

The period from 1909 to 1916 saw correspondence (seven letters) turning to politics, the liberal party, socialism and conscientious objection. Shove was a Fabian and an active member of the Liberal Party, for which he electioneered in 1909 (letter 3706, 25 December 1909). In these letters we find discussion of the nature of belief, be it political or religious, the Liberal Party, socialism, Christianity and free trade. These were themes that interested Keynes, too. Rational belief, in particular, was central to his 1907–08 dissertation on probability (CWK VIII). In one of these (letter 3710, 15 September 1910) Shove recalled the period spent in Burford, the town in Oxfordshire where Keynes invited his friends to the Little House during the summers of 1909 and 1910 (Moggridge 1992: 187).

A few letters deal with conscientious objection and Shove's hearing at the tribunal. Many of Keynes's friends were pacifists – Lytton and James Strachey, Duncan Grant, Bertrand Russell, David Garnett and Francis Birrell among his Bloomsbury friends and, at Cambridge, Pigou. Shove had been a pacifist all his life: during the First World War he was an active member of the National Council for conscientious objection to war; in the thirties he organised the New Peace Movement.

On 5 January 1916, the Military Bill, stating that all single men between 18 and 41 should render themselves available for military service, was introduced. Conscientious objectors to military service would be allowed to state their case before a local tribunal, which could grant absolute or conditional exemption. Keynes played an active role in helping all his Bloomsbury friends to obtain either exemption or non-combatant service (in the army but not fighting) or work of national importance. On 18 June 1916, Keynes wrote to Dennis Robertson that 'The Tribunal crisis is getting over now, as concessions to the C.[onscientious] O.[bjector]s are impending. But it has been a foul business, and I spend half of my time on the boring business of testifying to the sincerity, virtue and truthfulness of my friends' (letter 3067 from JMK to DHR).

Shove was one of those friends. Keynes was then working for the Treasury, dealing with problems of war finance. At the beginning of 1916, he formulated amendments, within the Treasury, to protect the rights and interests of conscientious objectors. He had strong feelings about conscription, but there was also great pressure on him from his pacifist friends, especially Lytton Strachey and Bertrand Russell, to resign from the Treasury. Keynes made a special application to be exempted, writing a declaration of conscientious objection, but his application for exemption was dismissed on 29 March 1916.

To appreciate Keynes's correspondence with Shove on conscientious objection, it is useful to understand Keynes's own attitude, comparing it with Shove's life-long attitude to war, and the more opportunistic reasons Shove manifested in his 1916 letters. Shove was a pacifist, but Keynes was not. A pacifist thinks that any war is immoral. Keynes expressed objection to being conscripted rather than objection to war; he was against conscription as it limited the liberty of individuals, in particular the liberty of judgement and choice.[9] His own attitude was closer to the Liberal principles of his acquaintance Sir John Simon, who resigned from the Cabinet in opposition to the state taking over the right of individual decision (CWK XVI: 157).[10] On war, Keynes thought that 'War resembles matters of faith and belief and differs from most other objects of public policy in that one may reasonably doubt whether even a large majority has a right to enforce a minority' (CWK XXVIII: 77).

The correspondence concerning the National Council for

conscientious objection and Shove's hearing and written evidence to the Tribunal consists of five letters, written between January and June 1916. All the letters are dated, apart from undated letter 3705, written in 1916 (perhaps in June), as Shove referred to his appeal at the Tribunal as 'coming on next Thursday'. Keynes appeared before the Tribunal in June on behalf of Gerald Shove (Skidelsky 1983: 327).

In January 1916, Shove – who was then editing the monthly pacifist *War and Peace* – noted that as the 'bloody bill is going through', he was going 'to make the backbone of the next number a demand for the conscription of wealth' (letter 3726). On 17 and 21 February, he informed Keynes about the organisation of the National Council for conscientious objection and discussed the peace campaign (letter 3727 and 3728). The letter (3729) dated 13 June 1916 is the most significant of this exchange as it deals with Shove's reasons for exemption on conscientious grounds. It is crucial to understanding both his general attitude as a pacifist and his tactical reasons. Shove asked Keynes's advice on the reasons to be adduced at the hearing in the Tribunal, and in particular whether it was 'a wise move to apply for exemption on two grounds (1) conscience and (2) work of national importance', or whether he 'had better apply on conscience grounds alone and try to get the conditional exemption'. In the former case, he would try for 'exemption on conscientious grounds' conditional on his continuing to edit *War and Peace.* His aim was to show that his work was 'of sufficient national importance to be a reasonable form of alternative service' if his 'conscience' was established, by arguing that *War and Peace* made 'a valuable contribution to the political thought of the country'. To this effect he would produce letters from Graham Wallas, J.A. Hobson, Edwin Cannan and Charles Buxton. He also asked Keynes for a written 'statement testifying to any or all of these points'. Later on he again asked Keynes for 'a written testimonial' to his qualifications 'as an economist' (undated letter 3705 after 13 June 1916). As a result of the appeal, Shove was sent to work on a farm near Cheltenham (Gloucester); from there he went to Oxfordshire, and finally moved to a farm run by 'a mental specialist, Irishman and crank', 'the Kentish farm at Tatsfield, where those who worked the farm were the Doctor's patients' (F. Shove 1952: 32–4).

A few considerations are to be added on Keynes's anonymous text, 'How to Pay for the War', which Shove referred to in these letters in 1916. In January, he asked Keynes for a short article (1800 words) 'on the need for some such drastic measure on practical patriotic grounds' (letter 3726). In February, he again asked him for an anonymous contribution of 1600–1800 words to the forthcoming number of *War and Peace* on 'How to Pay for the War' (letter 3727). This seems to be the same contribution already asked for in January. An anonymous article with this title does not figure in Keynes's writings (CWK XVI: 179).[11]

Many years later Shove invited Keynes to give a talk to the New Peace Movement (letter 3750, 8 December 1934). We have Keynes's reply, suggesting the subject: 'What is likely to be the value of economic sanctions as a means of keeping the peace?' (letter 3751, 10 December 1934).

Debates on economic theory: Marshall, Pigou and decreasing and increasing returns

The surviving correspondence has little to show in terms of discussion of economic theory. Early exchanges were on Pigou and Bastable's theory of international trade (letter 3717, 26 March 1911) and on 'a piece-wage' (letter 3703, attributed 1910). Few, also, were Shove's remarks on Keynes's own writings and achievements, including some observations on his article on Karl Pearson and alcoholism statistics (letter 3707, 3 October 1910).

An interesting group of letters (13 letters, from July 1925 to October 1933), only two of which are published, dealt with discussion of increasing and decreasing returns. As Kahn noted, 'Marshall had fudged' the problem of decreasing and increasing returns by his famous analogy, with the 'trees in the forest', 'by the fear of spoiling the market' and by the 'representative firm'. Pigou exacerbated the confusion'. Pigou's 'successive editions of his *Economics of Welfare* resulted in great confusion over the subject of increasing and diminishing returns, involving distinction between internal and external economies, a confusion resulting in part from Pigou's loyalty to Marshall' (Kahn 1987: 328). In the history of economic thought, the story goes that Shove made no lasting contribution to economics and that when he did eventually write something it was 'in collaboration with' or 'at suggestion of' somebody else: his main contribution, 'Increasing returns and the representative firm', was 'made in collaboration with Dennis Robertson and Piero Sraffa' in the 1930 *Symposium* (Kahn 1987: 328); his 1928 article 'Varying costs and marginal net products' was 'essentially a restatement of Allyn Young's criticism of Pigou's construction of Marshall's treatment of increasing and decreasing returns', and the emphasis he placed on 'the importance of time and rates of growth' in Marshall's theory of industry was in response to a 'suggestion' by Austin Robinson (Collard 1981: 178–9).

Shove's attitude to the classical approaches of Marshall and Pigou was controversial. It seems to have been a love and hate relationship: love of Marshall and hate of Pigou. One explanation for this duality can be found within the Cambridge tradition. As Groenewegen (1995: 757) pointed out, Marshall's methodological approach to economics differed from Pigou's. Shove and Keynes sided with Marshall's methodological approach rather than Pigou's. In his 'Introduction for the *Cambridge Handbooks*' Keynes's emphasis on the virtue of economics' relative imprecision contrasts sharply with the formal mathematisation that Pigou liked to indulge in when writing theory. Keynes himself implicitly made this distinction between Marshall and Pigou in his preface to the Japanese edition of the *General Theory*: 'But his immediate successors and followers have certainly dispensed with it and have not, apparently, felt the lack of it [the need of a theory of output and consumption as a whole]' (CWK VII: xxix).[12]

The correspondence makes it evident that Shove's defence of Marshall was a constant in his life. It also supports the view that his defence was methodological, and that his approach to economics was original and more in line with Keynes's own approach than with that of the other thinkers of the Cambridge tradition (Sardoni 2004), so Shove's love and hate may have had *methodological* and *rational* grounds. Shove's criticism of Pigou's theoretical approach was severe and it was essentially *methodological*, as was Keynes's in 1933. Oddly enough, when Pigou came under Keynes's fire in 1933, Shove sided staunchly – for a while, at least – with his 'enemy', attempting an extreme defence of Pigou purely on methodological grounds. After strenuous methodological discussion he surrendered to Keynes's critique and sided with him against Pigou.

The story of Shove's criticism of Pigou began earlier than had previously been thought.[13] On 31 July 1925, after congratulating Keynes on the official announcement of his marriage with Lydia, Shove referred to a manuscript for the *Economic Journal*:

> I don't know whether the enclosed M.S. ought to be sent to you or to Edgeworth. Although I have cut it countless times – at great expense of time, patience, literary quality, and vanity – it is about half as long again as it ought to be (Edgeworth said 400 words), but it can be brought nearly into the specified size by leaving out the last paragraph.
>
> (letter 3730, 31 July 1925)

We do not know the content of this manuscript. No article by Shove was published in the *Economic Journal* either in 1925 or 1926. However, in 1925 Shove presented a memoir on the foundations of the Marshallian supply curve at the annual meeting of the British Association for the Advancement of Sciences (letter sent to RFK in October 1931 – letter 3903; see also Ch. 14: 352). We might plausibly infer that the manuscript referred to was a draft of the Memoir.

The exchange regarding the 1928 article on Pigou consists of six letters, from 24 March to 9 August 1928. This correspondence makes it clear that Ramsey helped Pigou to bring in some modifications to the increasing supply price in what would become the third edition of his *Economics of Welfare*. It also shows that Shove attempted to write another article for the September issue of the *Economic Journal*, but was too late. The article never appeared, but the contents may well have eventually found their way, together with the 1925 Memoir, into his main theoretical contribution to the 1930 *Symposium* (Shove 1930).

The first two letters were related to the publication of Shove's article

'Varying costs and marginal net products', published in the 1928 June issue of the *Economic Journal* (Shove 1928: 258–66). On 24 March 1928 (letter 3731), referring either to a draft or to the submitted version of his article, Shove stressed that the 'principal addition is right at the end – an outline of the alternative way of stating Marshall's point about D.[ecreasing] R.[eturns] and I.[ncreasing] R.[eturns]' and mentioned Pigou's revisions in answer to his criticisms. Shove's attitude to Pigou was hostile, calling him 'the wicked Professor'. On 7 April (letter 3732), while Keynes was in Russia, Shove thanked him for printing his 'stuff' (he was 'excited at this prospect of appearing in print – but rather alarmed too') and for the proof of Pigou's article (where Pigou – in Shove's opinion – answered to his criticisms). Criticising Pigou's methodological approach to economic theory and his use of algebra and diagrams, Shove wrote of Pigou's inability 'to think in concrete terms'. He did not believe Pigou had 'any clear concrete image of what he is talking about in this article and at several points he seems to me to be all astray'.

After the publication of Shove's article in the June issue of the *Economic Journal*, Shove announced that he had 'just finished a commentary on Pigou's latest revision of his doctrine about I.[ncreasing] R.[eturns] and D.[ecreasing] R.[eturns] (June Journal)' and asked for Keynes's advice about sending it with a view to publishing it in the September issue of the *Economic Journal*:

> It tries to show (1) that ACP's position now is different from that taken up in Economics of Welfare: (2) how his *new* position differs from mine: (3) why he is wrong where it does so. If it is to be published at all, it must be in the September number because (a) people will have forgotten the whole thing otherwise and (b) I gather that A.C.P. is going, – as a result of representations from me supported by Ramsey, – to alter his position *again* in the 3rd edition of E. of W. (which will appear in the autumn) and I don't want to pursue him any further into his labyrinth. I am afraid, however, you may by now have no space left (I should judge my thing to be about as long as my last effort).
>
> (letter 3733, 18 July 1928)

The commentary on Pigou's article was also a review of what would become the third edition of Pigou's *Economics of Welfare*, which – according to Shove's specifications – would have to appear in the autumn of the same year; the source of the information about Pigou's revision of his book was Ramsey. The commentary-review never appeared in the *Economic Journal*, the reason being, as usual, his mental state. His attempt was already showing the first signs of aborting on 26 July: 'the difficulty about reviewing edition 3 is that the point I am on is dealt with in a single chapter and if I went beyond it I should never get the review finished'(letter 3734). By 3 August there was no longer time to publish it in the September issue: 'Too late, I know. Also too long and probably in other ways unsuitable. The crudity is partly due to my efforts to condense – partly to my intellectual shortcomings' (letter 3735). On 9 August, Shove thanked Keynes for his comments and criticisms, writing that he had an answer to his major criticism but he wanted 'to turn it over rather more' in his mind and concluded that 'Ramsey told me some time ago that in edition 3 the Professor is going to retract from – or 'hedge' about – his view on increasing supply price as inverted for transfers [. . .] I could not budge him but Ramsey succeeded' (letter 3736).

No letters – to or from Keynes – survive (if indeed there were any) on the 1930 *Symposium.*

Commenting on Keynes's activities: before and after the Keynesian revolution

The subsequent exchange refers to the 1933 controversy between Keynes and Pigou. It consists of five letters, already published, from 11 September to 22 October 1933, all from Shove to Keynes. On 11 September (letter 3742, in CWK XIII: 321–2), Shove wrote that Pigou's book struck him 'as the worst book on economics' that he had read 'for a very long time – a good deal worse than Hicks'. He found it difficult to make out what exactly Pigou was saying and 'in particular what the fundamental assumptions' were. To defend Pigou from Keynes's criticism from a methodological point of view, he investigated Pigou's tacit assumptions, their logical conclusion and their generality. Pigou's tacit hypotheses were that currency consists of wage-goods, that all payments are in wage-goods, that wage-goods are *produced* (as well as consumed) in uniform and constant 'packets' and that there is the 'Edible Currency'. He also searched for logical flaws or fallacies in Pigou's arguments, and tried to spot inconsistencies in his text: 'A.C.P. does not *consistently* adhere to the assumption that P/π [i.e. the price of output in terms of wage-goods] is constant'. He then compared Pigou's with Keynes's assumptions, evaluating their generality. His conclusion was that Keynes's 'hypothesis goes deeper and explains more'.

The discussion went on in a detailed letter on 19 September (letter 3744). Shove re-read some of the relevant passages in Pigou's book. Again, discussion focused mainly on his hypotheses. Sifting for logical fallacies in Pigou's argumentation, Shove wrote:

> the exposition still strikes me as obscure and elliptic and I do not feel inclined to spend a vast amount of time puzzling it out. Also, as you know, I have absolutely no mathematics, so that in any case my opinion would not be worth much.
>
> (letter 3744, 19 September 1933, CWK XIII: 322–4)

He thought there was confusion 'between the elasticity of demand for labour in an individual *firm* and in an *industry*', that 'the assumption of constant price-ratios was not required', and that the assumption that '*the wage-rate ruling in the industry does not affect prices* [or price-ratios or the relevant price-ratios] *except indirectly through its effect upon (the quantity of labour employed in, and consequently) the output of the industry*' was required. Further, he discussed the assumption of independence of the wage-rate from prices, deeming that it deprived 'the conclusion of any pretension to generality' and made it 'inapplicable to many of the most important problems encountered in practice' (letter 3744).

On 23 September Shove seems finally to have surrendered to Keynes's criticism of Pigou:

> I realized that the defence with which I had tried to provide the Professor was rubbish. [. . .] I wish I could get out of the habit of thinking that there *must* be some defence for anything which the Prof. says. I have spent so much time in the course of my life in abortive attempts to invent defences for him.
>
> (letter 3745, 23 September 1933, CWK XIII: 326)

However, on 27 September (letter 3746, CWK XXIX: 33–4) he was still investigating Pigou's tacit assumption that 'wage-goods are money for all purposes', concluding that Pigou had not had 'any idea that he is making such an assumption or that it affects his conclusions'. In his last letter, he admitted that he tried to see whether he 'could knock a hole' in Keynes's refutation of Pigou but his conclusion was that he could not 'find a chink anywhere'. It was 'unanswerable' (letter 3749, 22 October 1933, CWK XIII: 326).

The main topic of the 1936 exchange on the classical analysis and the *General Theory* (two letters, one from Shove, the other from Keynes, both already published), in striking continuity with the 1933 exchange, was the role of tacit assumptions in economic theory (Carabelli 1991). In 1933, it was in Pigou's economic theory; in 1936, in classical theory. On 15 April (letter 3760, CWK XIV: 1–2), commenting on the *General Theory*, Shove opined that Keynes was 'too kind to the "classical" analysis as applied to the individual industry and firm. Unless very artificial assumptions (e.g. perfect and instantaneous fluidity of resources)' were made, it seemed to him 'either wrong or completely jejeune'. He found 'liquidity preference' and its relation to the rate of interest the least clear part of Keynes's book and suspected that 'Marshall's failure to produce a theory of the credit cycle may have been due to his seeing more or less clearly that treatment on "classical" lines didn't do'. In Keynes's reply on 21 April, we find the well-known methodological passage on the limitation of 'formally exact' in economics.

> What you say about the classical analysis as applied to the individual industry and firm is probably right. I have been concentrating on the other problem, and have not, like you, thought very much about the elements of the system. But you ought not to feel inhibited by a difficulty in making solution precise. It may be that a part of the error in the classical analysis is due to that attempt. As soon as one is dealing with the influence of expectations and of transitory experience, one is, in the nature of things, outside the realm of the formally exact.
>
> (letter 3761, 21 April 1936, CWK XIV: 2)

Finally, in 1938 Keynes asked Shove to read a paper on buffer stocks for him at a meeting of Section F of the British Association in Cambridge on 19 August 1938, given his poor health after his 1937 stroke. On the following day Shove informed him of his own presentation and the ensuing discussion (letter 3762, 20 August 1938). In his reply Keynes commented: 'The trouble is not that we are governed by conservatives – I am a conservative myself – but that we are governed by boobies' (letter 3763, 23 August 1938).[14]

Faculty life and the veto on Joan Robinson

Nineteen letters, from 1929 to 1945, have to do with the faculty bureaucracy, Gerald Shove being the Secretary of the Faculty Board of Economics and Politics when Keynes and Shove discussed a variety of faculty matters over the years. Three letters, from 1939 to 1946, dealt with the establishment and financing of the department: funds were to be raised through the National Institute of Economic and Social Research, and the Rockefeller Foundation (letters 3764 and 3776). Another exchange (three letters in 1940) concerned procedures for the appointments and re-appointments of Assistant Directors of Research: Saunders was in charge of the procedure and Piero Sraffa was involved (letter 3766, 31 January 1940; letter 3767, 9 February 1940; letter 3768, 24 February 1940). Two other letters dealt with the financial aspects and the announcement of and applications for the Montague Burton chair in 1930 (letter 3738 and 3740). On a few occasions (three letters) they discussed the Reform of Part I and II of the Economic Tripos (letter 3737, 8 November 1929; letter 3769, 15 May 1940; letter 3775, 6 August 1945).

In 1935 the main issue was the veto on J. Robinson's lectures see Chs 2: 69; 6: 176 and 13: 339–40). This correspondence shows Shove siding with R. Fay against her. On 2 March, Fay had informed Pigou, Keynes and Shove about his thought that 'a full course of two terms by Mrs Robinson on Money, supplemented in the Easter Term by Keynes or Plumptre', meant 'a big second year course'. This course 'pre-judged, or warned in advance against, the conclusions of Robertson in his third year course'. His solution was that Joan Robinson was to be informed that they wanted from her 'a course in Money of one term only and in the Lent Term of each year'. This meant that she would not qualify as a full-time lecturer. Fay pointed out that Keynes's view that 'most things' were to be 'included under Money' was questionable. There was the danger of 'producing a dichotomy, on the one hand the central theorists, and on the other hand all the rest of us counting as frills'. When Keynes himself lectured, there was no 'danger of this because of his vast experience in affairs', but he felt it was altogether wrong to suggest to J. Robinson that she was capable of acting 'as his substitute'.

In his answer to Fay, on the same day, Keynes hoped that Fay would not reopen the question of J. Robinson's lectures. It would have been 'very strong measures, almost unprecedented' to veto a course which 'a lecturer greatly wanted to give' and J. Robinson's lectures were 'exceedingly good and successful'. He agreed with Fay that 'the question of her qualifying as a full-time lecturer should not depreciably prejudice the other issue' but she was 'rather unlucky in not getting a University lectureship'. On monetary theory, he thought that it was 'inevitable' that 'more than one point of view' should be expounded. The subject was 'in precisely the sort of condition' that made 'some measure of duplication and even a possible overweighing practically inevitable and not really undesirable'.

On 5 March, Keynes informed Shove that Fay had sent him a letter, also sent to Shove and Pigou. He enclosed a copy of it and his answer, explaining to Shove what he had in mind on Fay's position. There was 'a possibility of serious rift between the older and younger lecturers', if 'the lectures of Joan Robinson's had to be vetoed' (letter 3752, 5 March 1935). Shove answered on 8 March, agreeing with him that it would be difficult to raise the question of Robinson's lectures '*in isolation*'. However, he thought that 'there ought to be a systematic overhaul of the *whole* lecture list' and that 'the possibility of modifying the arrangement provisionally agreed to in her case ought not, in that event, to be ruled out' (letter 3755).

Shove's opposition to J. Robinson can be traced back to their discussion while the *Economics of Imperfect Competition* was being written. It resurfed again in the criticism of her 1942 essay on Marxian economics. On 23 November 1943, Keynes wrote that he had heard from Austin Robinson that Shove had written 'a large-scale criticism of Joan on Marx'. Rather abruptly, Keynes asked Shove to let him have 'just as it is, without any curtailment', 'the manuscript at once'. The *Economic Journal* had 'room in March for a revue article', which allowed him all the space he wanted (letter 3773). Shove replied on 24 November (letter 3774), thanking him, but stating that he could not let his review go in its actual form. He had shown the manuscript to Piero Sraffa and from his comments it was evident that he had not made his 'meaning clear on some of the more important issues', mainly, he thought, because of his '(ineffective) attempts to condense'. The letter ended with 'a *solemn vow*' to hand it in not later than 15 December. The review appeared in the April issue of the *Economic Journal* in 1944.

A major topic of academic correspondence were students and research students. This group of letters from 1931 to 1936 concerned Shove's organisation of the coaching and acceptance of research students by the faculty. The professors involved were Keynes, Kahn and Shove and, among the students, Reddaway, Champernowne and Cuthbertson were listed.[15]

In this exchange, two letters dated 1936 are especially relevant as they dealt with individual judgement and freedom of choice. Shove was worried about Champernowne's research project about the distribution of incomes and with the fact that Pigou and Keynes had told him that he had to drop it and work on something else: 'In spite of what you and Pigou have said, I think he will go on working at it unless I tell him that, in view of your advice, it would be folly. Ought I to do this?' (letter 3758, 24 March 1936). Keynes replied that he had told Champernowne that he should choose another subject, but went on to point out that if he was quite sure that he wanted to develop the subject he had chosen, 'not too much pressure' should be put on him to the contrary. It was a matter on which he should be 'his own judge' (letter 3759, 29 March 1936).

In all the letters of the 1909–43 period, it is evident how great Shove's psychological dependence on Keynes was, and how well aware he was of his generosity and effective help (letter 3734, 26 July 1928; letter 3772, 5 June 1943). In theses letters there is no further evidence of an intimate relationship between the two. The exchange adds further relevant details on Bloomsbury's sentimental relationships and Shove's homosexual penchant.

The only relevant discussion on economic theory is present in the letters already published in Keynes's *Collected Writings*, on the role of tacit assumptions, especially of independence of wage-rate from prices in Pigou's theory and of independence of investment and saving from output as a whole in the classical theory in general. It also shows clearly that there are two lines in the Cambridge Marshallian traditions of economic method, a Pigouvian methodological approach based on precision and formalisation (which deprives 'the conclusion of any pretension to generality') and another approach, which Shove and Keynes shared, based on the generality of hypotheses ('Keynes's hypothesis goes deeper and explains more') and on the organic interdependence of economic variables which occurs when we move from the individual, to the industry and aggregate level.

Notes

1 The radical society of King's College founded by Rupert Brooke.
2 The first was probably written in 1910; the second (3702) should fall between October 1912 and September 1914. As for the third (3704), it was surely sent after September 1914: perhaps in 1915–16.
3 Goldie was Dickinson Goldsworthy Lowes, a humanist and philosopher, and also a Fellow of King's and an Apostle.
4 Only two passages from the 29 December 1910 and 26 December 1911 letters are published (Moggridge 1992: 214).

5 From the correspondence of Rupert Brooke and James Strachey, we know that there was 'an understanding between Rupert and Gerald', who 'had fallen in love with Steuart Wilson', and that he was 'violently jealous of Rupert'. Shove was also interested in James Strachey, and in a note written to him on 8 April 1911 Shove confided that during his second year at Cambridge he had a 'lust for' Rupert. The same note suggests an affair with Strachey during Shove's first year at Cambridge (Hale 1998: 33, 35, 39). However, according to Hale, Shove's primary romantic interests at Cambridge were Francis Birrell and Ferenc Békássy. On 11 February 1909, Keynes wrote to Duncan Grant that 'Rupert and Gerald spend their time imagining copulations between every possible pair of people' (quoted by Hale 1998: 39). Shove was also intimate with 'Daddy' Dalton, later a Labour member of parliament and Chancellor of the Exchequer, in the academic year 1907–08 (Hale 1998: 61). Rosenbaum (1998: 168) mentioned a letter of Saxon Sydney-Turner to James Strachey in December 1912, referring to Wittgenstein's admiration for Shove. For the Founder's Feast at King's College in 1909, Keynes wrote to Duncan Grant that Alfred Brooke (Rupert's younger brother), Frankie Birrell, Gerald Shove, Freddy Hardman, Jack Sheppard and himself were all kissing in public at the event (quoted in Skidelsky 1983: 235).

6 'I do not like girls but boys'.

7 Frankie was Francis Frederick Birrell, one of Keynes's lovers in the years 1910–15, according to Keynes's own list, cited by Moggridge (1992: 838). Birrell read history at Cambridge, then in 1920 started a bookshop in London with Keynes's financial assistance.

8 Phil was Philip John Noel-Baker (later Lord), educated at King's College and later Labour MP, Minister of State, Minister of Fuel and Power, and winner of the Nobel Peace Price in 1959 (Moggridge 1992: 895).

9 These were the reasons he gave in his anonymous letter to the Editor of the *Daily Chronicle* on 6 January 1916, signed *Politicus* (CWK XVI: 157–61). They were reiterated in his letter on 28 February 1916, when he made a special application to be exempted (CW XVI: 178).

10 Skidelsky opposed this interpretation. In particular, he affirmed that Keynes's Bloomsbury friends, apart from Shove, were not pacifists. They would not have volunteered under the circumstances because they no longer approved of the war. For him, this was exactly Keynes's position (Skidelsky 1983: 325).

11 Elisabeth Johnson pointed out that, in April 1916, *War and Peace* published a short essay entitled 'Face the Facts' under the pseudonym *Politicus* (CWK XVI: 179–84), which 'has some of the earmarks of Keynes's literary style, but no manuscript could be found'. According to her, this was the second time Keynes used the pseudonym *Politicus* after having used it in the letter to the *Daily Chronicle* mentioned above, fn. 9.

12 The story of Keynes's method is, however, long and complex and had various roots, some independent of Marshall's approach (Carabelli 1988).

13 Unfortunately, no letters between Shove and Pigou are extant.

14 In the thirties Shove also sent Keynes two comments on *A Treatise on Money* (letters 3739, 9 November 1930 and 3740, 21 December 1930). He also commented on the announcement of Keynes's appointment as director of the Bank of England on 18 September 1941 and on 'Keynes Plan' (letter 3770, 20 September 1941; letter 3771, 8 April 1943).

15 See letter 3741, 8 October 1931; letter 3747, 6 October 1933; letter 3748, 13 October 1933; letter 3756, 7 October 1935 with a reference to Piero Sraffa; letter 3760, 15 April 1936, this part was not published in CWK XIV: 1–2; letter 3761, 21 April 1936, this part was not published in CWK XIV: 2.

Table 7.1 Keynes–Shove correspondence

From	*To*	*Year*	*Month*	*Day*	*Date*	*Archive*		*Published in*	*Item*
GFS	JMK	1909	December	25	Dated letter	Keynes–King's	PP/45/296/2–3		3706
GFS	JMK	1910			Attributed	Keynes–King's	PP/45/296/1		3702
GFS	JMK	1910			Attributed	Keynes–King's	PP/45/296/10–11		3703
GFS	JMK	1910	April	5	Dated letter	Keynes–King's	PP/45/296/4–7		3708
GFS	JMK	1910	August	17	Dated letter	Keynes–King's	PP/45/296/8–9		3709
GFS	JMK	1910	September	15	Dated letter	Keynes–King's	PP/45/296/12–14		3710
GFS	JMK	1910	October	3	Dated letter	Keynes–King's	PP/45/296/15–16		3707
GFS	JMK	1910	December	21	Dated letter	Keynes–King's	PP/45/296/17		3711
GFS	JMK	1910	December	29	Dated letter	Keynes–King's	PP/45/296/18–19	Moggridge 1992: 214, (E)	3712
GFS	JMK	1911	January	2	Dated letter	Keynes–King's	PP/45/296/20		3713
GFS	JMK	1911	January	7	Dated letter	Keynes–King's	PP/45/296/21–2		3714
GFS	JMK	1911	February	28	Dated letter	Keynes–King's	PP/45/296/23–4		3715
GFS	JMK	1911	March	6	Dated letter	Keynes–King's	PP/45/296/25–8		3716
GFS	JMK	1911	March	26	Dated letter	Keynes–King's	PP/45/296/29–34		3717
GFS	JMK	1911	April	5	Dated letter	Keynes–King's	PP/45/296/35–6		3718
GFS	JMK	1911	October	31	Dated letter	Keynes–King's	PP/45/296/37		3719
GFS	JMK	1911	December	18	Dated letter	Keynes–King's	PP/45/296/38–9		3720
GFS	JMK	1911	December	26	Dated letter	Keynes–King's	PP/45/296/40–1	Moggridge 1992: 214, (E)	3721
GFS	JMK	1912			Attributed	Keynes–King's	PP/45/296/44		3722
GFS	JMK	1912	July	2	Dated letter	Keynes–King's	PP/45/296/42–3		3723
GFS	JMK		Between October 1912 and September 1914		Attributed	Keynes–King's	PP/45/296/49–50		3704
GFS	JMK	1913	August	15	Dated letter	Keynes–King's	PP/45/296/45–6		3724
GFS	JMK	1915	September	29	Dated letter	Keynes–King's	PP/45/296/47–8		3725
GFS	JMK	1916	January		Attributed	Keynes–King's	PP/45/296/51–2		3726
GFS	JMK	1916	February	17	Dated letter	Keynes–King's	PP/45/296/53–6		3727

GFS	JMK	1916	February	21	Dated letter	Keynes–King's	PP/45/296/57–60		3728
GFS	JMK	1916	June		Attributed	Keynes–King's	PP/45/296/66–7		3705
GFS	JMK	1916	June	13	Dated letter	Keynes–King's	PP/45/296/61–5		3729
GFS	JMK	1925	July	31	Dated letter	Keynes–King's	PP/45/296/70–1		3730
GFS	JMK	1928			Attributed	Keynes–King's Kahn–King's	EJ/1/3/30 RFK/14/75/55		3700
GFS	JMK	1928			Attributed	Keynes–King's Kahn–King's	EJ/1/3/44 RFK/14/75/75		3701
GFS	JMK	1928	March	24	Dated letter	Keynes–King's Kahn–King's	EJ/1/3/31–2 RFK/14/75/57–6		3731
GFS	JMK	1928	April	7	Dated letter	Keynes–King's Kahn–King's	EJ/1/3/33–4 RFK/14/75/59–8		3732
GFS	JMK	1928	July	18	Dated letter	Keynes–King's Kahn–King's	EJ/1/3/35–7 RFK/14/75/53–4		3733
GFS	JMK	1928	July	26	Dated letter	Keynes–King's	EJ/1/3/38–9		3734
GFS	JMK	1928	August	3	Dated letter	Keynes–King's Kahn–King's	EJ/1/3/40–1 RFK/14/75/80–1		3735
GFS	JMK	1928	August	9	Dated letter	Keynes–King's Kahn–King's	EJ/1/3/42–3 RFK/14/75/78–9		3736
GFS	JMK	1929	November	8	Dated letter	Keynes–King's	UA/5/2/113		3737
GFS	JMK	1930	March	17	Dated letter	Keynes–King's	UA/5/2/109		3738
GFS	JMK	1930	November	9	Dated letter	Keynes–King's	TM/1/4/88–9		3739
GFS	JMK	1930	December	21	Dated letter	Keynes–King's	TM/1/4/90–1		3740
GFS	JMK	1931	October	8	Dated letter	Keynes–King's	UA/5/3/1–3		3741
GFS	JMK	1933	September	11	Dated letter	Keynes–King's	GTE/1/173–5	CWK XIII: 321–2	3742
GFS	JMK	1933	September	12	Postmark	Keynes–King's	GTE/1/176–77	CWK XIII: 322	3743
GFS	JMK	1933	September	19	Dated letter	Keynes–King's	GTE/1/178–86	CWK XIII: 322–5	3744
GFS	JMK	1933	September	23	Dated letter	Keynes–King's	GTE/1/187–8	CWK XIII: 326	3745
GFS	JMK	1933	September	27	Dated letter	Keynes–King's	GTE/1/189–90	CWK XXIX: 33–4	3746
GFS	JMK	1933	October	6	Dated letter	Keynes–King's	UA/5/3/40–2		3747
GFS	JMK	1933	October	13	Dated letter	Keynes–King's	UA/5/3/43–4		3748
GFS	JMK	1933	October	22	Dated letter	Keynes–King's	CO/8/211	CWK XIII: 326	3749

Table 7.1 continued

From	*To*	*Year*	*Month*	*Day*	*Date*	*Archive*		*Published in*	*Item*
GFS	JMK	1934	December	8	Dated letter	Keynes–King's	PS/6/8–9		3750
JMK	GFS	1934	December	10	Dated letter	Keynes–King's	PS/6/10		3751
JMK	GFS	1935	March	5	Dated letter	Kahn–King's Keynes–King's	RFK/14/99/209–14 UA/5/3/139		3752
GFS	JMK	1935	March	8 or 18	Dated letter	Keynes–King's	UA/5/3/143–4		3755
GFS	JMK	1935	October	6	Dated letter	Keynes–King's	UA/5/3/149–50		3754
JMK	GFS	1935	October	7	Dated letter	Keynes–King's	UA/5/3/151		3756
GFS	JMK	1936	March	24	Dated letter	Keynes–King's	UA/14/2/194–5		3758
JMK	GFS	1936	March	25	Dated letter	Keynes–King's	UA/14/2/196–7		3759
GFS	JMK	1936	April	15	Dated letter	Keynes–King's	UA/5/4/1–5	CWK XIV: 1–2, (E)	3760
JMK	GFS	1936	April	21	Dated letter	Keynes–King's	UA/5/4/6–8	CWK XIV: 2, (E)	3761
GFS	JMK	1938	August	20	Dated letter	Keynes–King's	PS/6/247–8		3762
JMK	GFS	1938	August	23	Dated letter	Keynes–King's	PS/6/249–50		3763
JMK	GFS	1939	July	22	Dated letter	Keynes–King's	UA/5/4/443–7		3764
GFS	JMK	1939	July	24	Dated letter	Keynes–King's	UA/5/4/448		3765
GFS	JMK	1939	August	2	Dated letter	Keynes–King's	MM/1/4/44–5		3753
JMK	GFS	1939	August	4	Dated letter	Keynes–King's	MM/1/4/43		3757
JMK	GFS	1940	January	31	Dated letter	Keynes–King's	UA/5/5/34		3766
GFS	JMK	1940	February	9	Dated letter	Keynes–King's	UA/5/5/41–2		3767
GFS	JMK	1940	February	24	Dated letter	Keynes–King's	UA/5/5/51		3768
GFS	JMK	1940	May	15	Dated letter	Keynes–King's	UA/5/5/63–4		3769
GFS	JMK	1941	September	20	Dated letter	Keynes–King's	BE/1/17	CWK XXII: 409	3770
JMK	GFS	1942	April	30	Dated letter	Keynes–King's	MM/4/266–7		3777
GFS	JMK	1942	May	1	Dated letter	Keynes–King's	MM/4/264		3778

JMK	GFS	1942	May	12	Dated letter	Keynes–King's	MM/4/263		3779
GFS	JMK	1942	October	20	Dated letter	Keynes–King's	MM/4/262		3780
JMK	GFS	1942	October	24	Dated letter	Keynes–King's	MM/4/261		3781
GFS	JMK	1942	October	26	Dated letter	Keynes–King's	MM/4/259–60		3782
GFS	JMK	1943	April	8	Dated letter	Keynes–King's	PP/45/296/72	CWK XXV: 236	3771
GFS	JMK	1943	June	5	Dated letter	Keynes–King's	PP/45/296/73–4		3772
JMK	GFS	1943	November	23	Dated letter	Keynes–King's	MM/3/28		3773
GFS	JMK	1943	November	24	Dated letter	Keynes–King's	MM/3/26–7		3774
GFS	JMK	1943	December	22	Dated letter	Keynes–King's	MM/5/271–2		3783
JMK	GFS	1944	January	12	Dated letter	Keynes–King's	MM/5/269–70		3784
GFS	JMK	1945	August	6	Dated letter	Keynes–King's	UA/5/6/42–4		3775
JMK	GFS	1946	January	1	Dated letter	Keynes–King's	UA/5/6/80–1		3776

8 Employment, the trade cycle and the war effort

The correspondence between Keynes and Kaldor

Claudio Sardoni

Nicholas Kaldor, born in Hungary in 1908, began his study of economics in Germany and then moved to the London School of Economics, where he graduated in 1930. After his graduation, Kaldor stayed at LSE first as a research student and then as a teacher until the school was evacuated to Cambridge during the war. He became a member of the Cambridge Faculty of Economics and Fellow of King's College only in 1949, where he spent the rest of his academic career (see Thirlwall 1987 and Harcourt 1988). Kaldor began his career under the influence of the Austrian tradition, which was quite far from, if not altogether hostile to, the Cambridge tradition. He became a convinced Keynesian later on in the 1930s and therefore played no part in the early phases of the 'Keynesian revolution' at Cambridge, remaining outside the small circle of people closest to Keynes during that period.

Harcourt (1988) sees three stages in Kaldor's intellectual biography: the young Austrian economist at LSE; the Keynesian of the pre-war period; and the Kaldor of the post-war period, involved in theoretical as well as empirical and policy issues and increasingly critical of orthodox economics and its methodological approach. The correspondence between Kaldor and Keynes began in 1931, soon after Kaldor's graduation, and then continued until 1945. There are 77 letters; 43 from Keynes and the remaining 34 from Kaldor (see Table 8.1). Fourteen of these letters are published in Keynes's *Collected Writings*. For obvious reasons, the correspondence covers only aspects of the first two stages of Kaldor's intellectual development, but clues as to how Kaldor approached empirical and policy problems can be gleaned from reading his correspondence with Keynes on matters related to the war during the years 1939–45. This chapter concentrates mainly on their exchanges on theoretical issues and matters related to the war effort.

Economic theory: criticism and defence of Keynesian theory

Kaldor's extraneousness to the Cambridge circle shows up in his early correspondence with Keynes. Though Keynes and Kaldor eventually came to a basic agreement on the issue at hand (in various cases), they often retained points of disagreement deriving mainly from their different theoretical backgrounds and the different paths they took to reach their conclusions. However, some of their differences were probably also the consequence of their different styles in the approach to economic problems and debates. Keynes always tried to get straight to the heart of the issue at hand and was very little, if at all, interested in the more technical and formal aspects of the problem; on the other hand, Kaldor usually tackled the issue under discussion paying far more attention to its analytical aspects. As a result, their correspondence is usually characterised by asymmetry: very short and straightforward letters from Keynes and much longer, detailed letters from Kaldor. Only later on in his life did Kaldor take an attitude toward economics that was more similar to Keynes's. He became increasingly impatient with the detailed analytical aspects of an argument and more interested in grasping its essence and implications (Harcourt 1988).

The first letter from Kaldor to Keynes (letter 1150, 19 November 1931) was occasioned by a debate between Robertson and Keynes on the *Treatise on Money*. In the *Economic Journal* of September 1931, Robertson had published an article on several issues dealt with by Keynes in his *Treatise* (Robertson 1931a); in the same number of the journal, Keynes wrote a rejoinder where he paid particular attention to the problem of the determination of the prices of capital (non-liquid) assets[1] and their relationship with changes in the prices of consumer goods (Keynes [1931b] in CWK XIII: 219–36, see Ch. 2: 65). In considering the effects of an excess of savings over investment, Robertson had argued that the two prices move in the opposite direction. For Robertson, excess saving would bring about a decrease in the price of consumer goods, accompanied by an equal increase in the price of capital assets, unless the excess savings were totally diverted to inactive deposits. In other words, excess savings imply an increase in purchases of investment goods and, at the same time, a loss of the same amount for the producers of consumer goods. Keynes rejected Robertson's position and argued that excess savings do not necessarily imply an increase in the price of capital assets, due to the excess demand for them. More in particular, Keynes argued that the prices of capital goods would temporarily increase only in some particular cases, which he regarded very unlikely. Moreover, Keynes criticised Robertson for considering only the price of newly produced capital assets, which meant misunderstanding the nature of the capital market (see CWK XIII: 227–30). In fact, for Keynes, the prices of all investment goods, 'old and new alike', would be affected by the existence of excess savings. Keynes concluded:

> The essential point, which I maintain and Mr Robertson resists, is the fact that an increase of saving which is not associated with an increase of investment does not change in any way either the quantity of assets

> or the quantity of purchasing power, but merely transfers command over cash in the first instance, and the ownership of assets after there has been time to reduce individual cash holdings to a normal level, between one set of persons and another set, i.e. between the saving public and the disappointed entrepreneurs. Since the total amount of non-liquid assets is unchanged and the total amount of liquid assets is unchanged, nothing has happened so far [. . .] to cause a change in the valuation of the one in terms of the other, i.e. in the price of non-liquid assets.
>
> (CWK XIII: 230)

In his letter Kaldor considered several aspects of Keynes's rejoinder, but his main point was that the processes discussed by Keynes and Robertson could take place even though there was no discrepancy between saving and investment. He considered a case of a decrease in the demand for a consumer good (boots) accompanied by a corresponding increase in the demand for another consumer good (hats). This would give rise to a loss for the producers of boots, exactly compensated for by the increased profits of the producers of hats. If the producers of boots (the 'losers') do not adjust their expenditures to their lower income and sell securities (i.e. they consume part of their capital), they bring about a loss also for the producers of capital goods. If the producers of capital goods behave in the same way as the producers of boots by selling part of their securities, the negative effects of the initial loss will spread and enlarge.[2] This process was not started by a discrepancy between saving and investment, but by 'the determination of some entrepreneurs [...] *to counterbalance the falling-off of their current income* [. . .] *by consuming their capital*' (letter 1150, 19 November 1930).

In a letter of 27 November, Keynes replied to Kaldor's observations and tried to clarify his position. As to the problem of the discrepancy between saving and investment, Keynes argued that there must be 'some change in saving in the sense in which I define that. For if some part of the public were to decide, for any reason, to consume their capital, this would in itself mean a change in the rate of saving' (letter 1677, 27 November 1931). Keynes's reply was short and clearly showed his intention to put an end to the discussion with Kaldor, who nevertheless sent another long letter a few days later (letter 1678, 3 December 1931), arguing that, precisely because consuming capital implies a change in the rate of saving, the case considered by Keynes in the rejoinder to Robertson had nothing to do with excess saving. Keynes concluded the exchange on these topics with his letter of 9 December by restating his disagreement with Kaldor and announcing that he was planning to reconsider the whole issue in a different way in two years time.[3] Keynes had already decided to proceed to a revision of his *Treatise*, the project that eventually led him to the *General Theory* five years later.

For several years, the correspondence between Keynes and Kaldor was not concerned with theoretical or analytical issues. They returned to discuss analytical problems in 1937, on the occasion of an article by Pigou on the effects of a reduction of money wages on employment and output. Keynes's and Kaldor's letters on this topic have already been published (CWK XIV: 240–50) and their positions illustrated in Thirlwall (1987: 64–9).

Pigou's analytical conclusion was that a reduction in wages would bring about an increase in both employment and output (Pigou 1937). Pigou, using a simple model, considered both short-period and long-period equilibria as well as conditions of perfect and imperfect competition. In particular, he considered a case of short-period equilibrium under perfect competition, in which investment is zero, so that also saving is zero; the money supply is an increasing function of the rate of interest (which is equal to the public's rate of time-preference) and there is no credit rationing.[4] In this framework, if money-wages were reduced, equilibrium could remain at its initial state only if money income decreased in the same proportion as wages. But this, for Pigou, was impossible: if the level of employment does not change, saving must remain unchanged as well (nothing has happened to the rate of interest); therefore, the supply of money also remains unchanged, as does the velocity of circulation of money, so that money income remains unchanged too. If money income does not change when there is a wage cut, employment must necessarily increase (Pigou 1937: 410).

For Pigou, when wages were reduced the rate of interest did not change. However, he also contemplated a case in which the rate of interest temporarily decreases. Such a reduction in the interest rate could lead one to believe that a wage cut can make employment rise only because the rate of interest falls, so that the same result could be obtained through monetary policy. This was not the case according to Pigou: an increase in employment due to a fall in the interest rate would last until the rate remained below its initial level; instead, a decrease in money wages would give rise to a permanent increase in employment, as it led to a fall in real wages.

In the December 1937 issue of the *Economic Journal*, both Keynes and Kaldor published a note on Pigou's article. Both concentrated on paragraphs 7 and 8 of Pigou's article. Kaldor's main criticism was that Pigou had made saving depend only on the rate of interest and not also on income, the fundamental innovation introduced by Keynes in the *General Theory* (Kaldor 1937: 748). Kaldor, therefore, introduced real income in Pigou's saving function to obtain

$$S = \varphi(r, x) \text{ with } \frac{\partial S}{\partial x} > 0$$

(where r is the rate of interest and x is real income).

In this new framework, an increase in real income makes savings increase; prices must fall and real balances increase. Therefore, the rate of interest must decrease to the point at which $S=0$ again. This means that there exists a rate of interest that ensures $S=0$ for any level of employment and that 'the actual equilibrium level of employment at any given level of money wages will be determined by the additional "Keynesian" condition that the rate of interest must also equate the demand for money with its supply' (Kaldor 1937: 749). Thus Pigou was wrong in thinking that 'his result does not depend on the reduction of the rate of interest' (Kaldor 1937: 749). In substance, Kaldor tried to 'adjust' Pigou's analysis in such a way as to bring it to the same conclusions as Keynes's in Chapter 19 of the *General Theory*.

In his note Keynes entered far less into the analytical details of Pigou's article than did Kaldor. Keynes criticised Pigou for assuming that the demand for money is independent of money income and for his implicit assumption that when employment and real income change, the rate of interest remains unchanged. In other words, for Keynes, Pigou assumed that the interest rate and saving are independent of real income, so that

> Professor Pigou rejects my fundamental assumption that the amount of real saving is, in part, a function of real income. If he were right in this, it would follow that the amount of employment in the system would be in neutral equilibrium, in the sense that *any* level of employment would be compatible with equilibrium.
>
> (CWK XIV: 264–5)

Keynes's and Kaldor's published version of their notes were the result of quite a long exchange between them on the topic.[5] Soon after the publication of Pigou's article, Kaldor wrote a comment on it and sent it to Keynes (letter 1685, 27 September 1937), who in turn informed Kaldor that he himself had written a note on Pigou (letter 1686, 30 September 1937). Kaldor read the draft of the note that Keynes sent to him and reacted with a number of comments and observations.[6] Kaldor thought that his own 'charitable' interpretation of Pigou had the merit of making Pigou's analysis logically consistent and coherent with his earlier writings. More in general, Kaldor believed that Pigou's analysis could be made consistent with Keynes's own analysis of the effects of a wage reduction on employment.[7] But Keynes was never convinced of Kaldor's interpretation of Pigou. Keynes argued that, in Pigou's framework, it was impossible to give account of an even temporary fall in the interest rate (see Keynes's letter 1692, 1 November 1937).[8] It was because of their differences that Keynes decided to publish both his note and Kaldor's (letter 1693, 15 November 1937).

A year later Keynes and Kaldor started a new exchange on another interesting analytical issue. Once again, the exchange was started by Kaldor, who sent two papers to Keynes. In September 1938, Kaldor sent Keynes a paper on the trade cycle and another on stability and full employment. He wanted to submit only the first for publication in the *Eco-*

nomic Journal (letter 1380, 3 September 1938). Keynes, however, liked the article on stability better and wanted it for the journal (letter 1694, 19 September 1938). For Keynes, Kaldor's paper on the trade cycle was 'half-baked and not likely to be intelligible to more than a very small number of readers', even though Kaldor had probably 'got a really interesting point in the background' (letter 1694). Kaldor regarded the article on the cycle as more important and, on the other hand, he had 'half-promised' the article on stability to Lionel Robbins for *Economica* (letter 1381, 22 September 1938).[9]

In the end, Kaldor published the article on stability and full employment in the *Economic Journal* (Kaldor 1938c), while the article on the trade cycle was eventually published in *Economica* (Kaldor 1939a). But, some time in April or May 1939, Kaldor sent Keynes another paper on the trade cycle, which Keynes found interesting and was willing to publish in the *Economic Journal*. There is no record of Kaldor's letter to Keynes accompanying his paper. Kaldor's paper was published in 1940 (Kaldor 1940). Keynes, however, made some criticisms of Kaldor's analysis. In particular he concentrated on the accelerator principle and the investment function. In his letter of 27 May 1939, Keynes wrote:

> it is dangerous to assume that the credit cycle is wholly determined by the multiplier and the acceleration principle, and that I [investment] is a function only of x [output]. I still prefer, when one is dealing with the general problem to have regard to the relation between the marginal efficiency of capital and the rate of interest rather than to the acceleration principle taken in isolation. The acceleration principle is, of course, a very important determinant of the marginal efficiency of capital. But even if we regard the rate of interest as constant, which is in itself a considerable abstraction, it remains unsafe to omit other possible influences on the m. e. of c. [marginal efficiency of capital].
>
> (letter 1696)

Kaldor replied to Keynes in the following terms:

> I would agree that it is dangerous to assume the trade cycle entirely governed by the multiplier and the acceleration principles. I did not mean to put it forward as *the* explanation, but rather as a model which gives a *possible* explanation.
>
> I agree also that it is a far-reaching abstraction to treat the rate of interest as *constant*. But there is no necessity to do so, even under my method. For insofar as the rate of interest is itself some function of the level of activity – and in a first approximation, in a community such as ours, it could be regarded so – its influence could be incorporated in the $I(x)$ and $S(x)$ functions.
>
> (letter 1698, 19 June 1939)

Keynes's reply to Kaldor came only a month later. He thought he had found a contradiction between Kaldor's argument and its symbolic representation,

> there is an important discrepancy between the real nature of your argument and its symbolic expression. According to the acceleration principle, the demand for new investment is a function of the *rate* of growth of output and not simply of output itself. That is to say I is a function of dx/dt, not of x itself. In your argument, this is really what you are doing. You seem to me to be thinking all the times in terms of dx/dt, but this is not the way in which you have expressed yourself in the symbolism.
>
> (letter 1699, 22 July 1939)

But Kaldor did not agree and proposed a different definition of the accelerator principle:

> I do not agree with your interpretation, though the use of the term 'acceleration principle' may be slightly misleading. In the literature it is used to denote both the assumption $I=f(x)$ and $I=f(dx/dt)$. My model only requires the former assumption, not the latter.
>
> (letter 1700, 1 August 1939)

For Keynes, however, if investment is a function of output and not of its variation, also the rate of interest and the marginal efficiency of capital should be arguments of the investment function (letter 1701, 14 August 1939).

The aversion to consider investment as a function of current output that Keynes conveyed to Kaldor recalls a similar exchange between Keynes and Hicks two years earlier, on the occasion of the publication of 'Mr. Keynes and the "classics"' (Hicks 1937). As is well known, Keynes criticised Hicks for considering investment as dependent on current income:

> In the case of the inducement to invest, expected income for the period of the investment is the relevant variable. This I have attempted to take account of in the definition of the marginal efficiency of capital. As soon as the prospective yields have been determined, account has been implicitly taken of income, actual and expected. But, whilst it may be true that entrepreneurs are over-influenced by present income, far too much stress is laid on this psychological influence, if present income is brought into such prominence.
>
> (letter from JMK to Hicks, 31 March 1937, CWK XIV: 80–1)

In the light of Keynes's observation on Hicks's model, it is easier to understand his reluctance to accept Kaldor's way of defining the investment function. The correspondence on Kaldor's article on the trade cycle continued until October 1939, when it was sent to the printer.

With the outbreak of war in 1939 both Keynes and Kaldor became deeply interested in the problem of how to finance the war and from then on most of their correspondence dealt with such issues, although they still corresponded on certain theoretical and analytical issues too. In December 1939, Kaldor sent Keynes an off-print of his article on speculation (Kaldor 1939b) with an appendix that was not published at the time but only in 1960 (Kaldor 1960: 59–74) (letter 1382, 28 December 1939). In this article Kaldor criticised Keynes's notion of liquidity preference and proposed a partially alternative way to look at speculation and its effects on income and employment. It would be interesting to know Keynes's reaction to Kaldor's work but, unfortunately, Keynes did not have enough time to concentrate on these topics as he was working on issues related to war finance.[10] Kaldor held that in conversation Keynes admitted that Kaldor's approach could be more satisfactory (see Kaldor 1986a: 23n). In the following years, Kaldor continued to give Keynes's notion of liquidity preference a secondary role in the explanation of the working of market economies (see, for example, Kaldor 1981). On the other hand, other Keynesian economists, like J. Robinson and Kahn, strongly criticised Kaldor's 1939 article (see J. Robinson 1951b; Kahn 1954).[11]

In 1941 there was an exchange on technical progress and its effects on output and employment. This exchange was occasioned by a letter from Keynes (letter 1715, 4 March 1941) with some criticisms of an article by Kalecki (Kalecki 1940). Kaldor also came up with some critical comments on Kalecki's paper. In particular, he argued that technical progress reduces output and employment only in the unlikely case in which the factors determining national income are given. Kaldor also criticised Kalecki's hypothesis that technical progress raises the degree of oligopoly (letter 1716, March 9 1941).[12] Finally, in 1942, Kaldor sent Keynes some comments on Pigou's rejoinder to Kaldor's review of his *Employment and Equilibrium* (Pigou 1941) (letter 1732, 23 May 1942).[13]

1939–1945: the war and the reconstruction[14]

The correspondence between Keynes and Kaldor on matters related to the war or plans for the post-war period can be divided into three groups: the correspondence on fiscal issues; the correspondence on the measurement of the national output; and a short exchange on the Beveridge plan.

On 14 and 15 November 1939, Keynes published an article in *The Times* (Keynes [1939a] CWK XXII: 41–51) on taxation and forced saving for the war. Kaldor, in November (letter 1704, 15 November 1939), wrote a long letter to Keynes with various comments on the scheme that Keynes had proposed. In *The Times*, Keynes had argued that the most equitable way to avoid the risk of inflation[15] and ensure the availability of resources to finance the war was a system of 'compulsory saving'. His scheme was based on the idea that all incomes in excess of a stipulated minimum level should accrue to the government either in the form of taxes or compulsory saving.[16] In such a way people would be subject only to certain constraints on how to use their wealth and not to its confiscation, so that the inducement to work and produce would remain adequately strong. Kaldor found Keynes's scheme 'extremely ingenious and commendable' (letter 1704), but was worried about possible practical objections to it in terms of difficulties in collection and evasion. Kaldor elaborated on Keynes's scheme to improve it. Keynes replied a few days later (letter 1706, 19 November 1939), appreciating Kaldor's comments and suggestions. Keynes, however, pointed out that the objections to his scheme had not been concerned with practical aspects but with its more general aspects.[17]

The next group of letters related to the war deal with the notions of gross and net income. The exchange began in February 1940, triggered by a conversation between Keynes and Kaldor some time in early February. In the course of the discussion Clark's work on national accounting was often cited.

In December 1939, Keynes had already published an article on the measurement of income in relation to the war effort (Keynes [1939c] in CWK XXII: 52–66). He returned to the topic in the *Economic Journal* of March 1940 with a supplementary note in which he criticised Clark's definition of gross national income in several respects. After providing his own definitions of national output and taxable income,[18] Keynes criticised Clark's definition of gross national income, because it was sensitive to changes in the type of taxation. Another aspect that, for Keynes, made Clark's notion misleading had to do with the measurement of potential consumption. Keynes argued that Clark's way of measuring the potential rate of consumption amounted to estimating it

> not over an annual or any other substantial period, but only over the instantaneous or very brief period in which *no* replacement of wastage is necessary to maintain the current rate of output. When, therefore, Mr Clark proceeds (as he does) to speak of an *annual* gross national income thus defined, he has fallen into the pit he has himself dug and is clearly in error. For the amount of making good wastage which can be avoided without detriment to the rate of output depends on the length of time in view.
>
> (Keynes [1940a] in CWK XXII: 71)[19]

The final version of Keynes's note was the result of the correspondence with Kaldor. Kaldor's first letter on the topic (letter 1709, 6 February 1940) started from his definitions of net and gross income. While the definition of net income is straightforward (Net Income = Consumption + Net Investment), the definition of gross income is more problematical. To define net income, it is necessary to deduct from the total value created in a period all the firms' expenditures on output produced by other firms. Gross income is calculated by not deducting all such expenditures, but what to deduct can be chosen according to different criteria and, therefore, different concepts and estimates of gross income are possible. Kaldor argued that all the firms' expenditures on the output of other firms indispensable for their own production should be deducted; but there are other expenditures that, at least in the short period, are not indispensable in the same sense and therefore should not be deducted. In this way there would be double accounting, but it is justified because it allows a more correct estimate of the extent to which the economy can expand war production without reducing consumption. Kaldor observed,

> We can assume that the shoe output could be maintained, for a certain period at any rate, without the firms spending anything on the purchase of new shoe-making machines. In so far as it is possible to turn the firms producing shoe-making machinery to the manufacture of armaments, *without thereby automatically reducing the output of shoes,* we are justified in adding to the value of the total shoe output the value of the whole machine output; since this gives the true pictures of how much we can spend on armaments (or anything else) without (in the short period) having to reduce the output of shoes.
>
> (letter 1709, 6 February 1940)

Kaldor called 'equipment goods' the kind of things that are not indispensable for the current production of consumer goods and gave the following definition of gross income (inclusive of government spending):

> Gross Income = Value of Consumption + Value of Equipment goods produced + Value of net increase in the stock of raw materials + Value of government expenditure (net of transfers) = Sum of personal incomes + Indirect taxation + Depreciation

Therefore, net income is

> Consumption + Equipment goods produced + Net increase in Stocks + Government expenditure (net of transfers) − Depreciation = Sum of personal incomes + Indirect taxes

These definitions, for Kaldor, were the same as those given by Colin Clark. Keynes's reply came on 25 February, when he sent Kaldor a draft of his forthcoming note on national income in the *Economic Journal* (Keynes [1940a] in CWK XXII: 66–73). Keynes thanked Kaldor for his comments, which had improved his exposition of the topic, but he remained 'hostile' to the concept of gross national income and critical of Clark's definition of gross income (letter 1712, 25 February 1940).

In his letter of 1 March 1940, Kaldor returned to the notion of gross income and argued in favour of his own definition:

> the concept of gross income is – analytically and statistically – prior to net income i.e., net income can only be arrived at by estimating depreciation per annum and then *deducting* it from gross income. The total value of capital outlay can be reasonably well calculated on the basis of objective data. But current capital depreciation has to be determined more or less arbitrarily; its magnitude depends on accounting procedures, on expectations, etc., all of which lend to the measure of net income a vagueness from which the concept of gross income is free. E.g. we can estimate reasonably clearly (from census figures, etc.) the value of the total output of houses. But is there any corresponding unambiguous measure of the value of the annual depreciation of houses?
>
> (letter 1713)

Moreover, from the point of view of the determination of current activity and its fluctuations – that is, from the trade-cycle point of view – gross income is the key concept rather than net income.[20]

Kaldor concluded his letter by proposing three definitions of national income, as an alternative to Keynes's two definitions. Kaldor's three definitions were:

> *Taxable income*, which was the same as Keynes's notion;
>
> *National output* = (Taxable income + Indirect taxes + Depreciation), which corresponded to Clark's definition;
>
> *National output from the point of view of war potential*, which was obtained as (National output − Depreciation that cannot be avoided + Stocks than can be depleted − Indirect taxes − Monopoly earnings − Rents of specific factors).[21]

According to Kaldor, Keynes's definition of national output included both definitions 2 and 3 above, so that it was 'a half-way-house between the two'. Keynes took account of Kaldor's comments in writing the final version of his note but, as we saw above, he did not change his mind on Clark (letter 1714, 12 March 1940).

The exchange between Keynes and Kaldor on matters related to the war effort continued in 1941, when Kaldor published an article with some estimates of war finance (Kaldor 1941b) and sent a copy of it to Keynes. In his reply, Keynes concentrated on the problem of the so-called *inflationary gap*, which he defined as follows:

> I prefer a different definition of the inflationary gap. I am now using for my own purposes the term 'primary saving', corresponding to

what in another context one calls primary employment. I measure the inflationary gap by the amount of purchasing power which has to be withdrawn, either by taxation or primary savings, in order that the remaining purchasing power should be equal to the available supplies on the market at the existing level of prices.

(letter 1719, 19 April 1941)

In relation to the inflationary effect of the war, Keynes observed:

On the whole it is astonishing with how little inflation we have got through, so much of the rise of the price being properly attributable to the higher prices of imports and the repercussions of that. It looks to me as if the experience in U.S.A. is going to be entirely different. Germany will be at one pole with no rise of prices worth mentioning, and U.S.A., I should not be surprised, at the opposite extreme with a good old-fashioned rise in wages and prices alike.[22]

(ibidem)

In the following years, Keynes and Kaldor continued to address the problem of measuring national output in relation to the war effort, exchanging letters on the estimation of several aggregates and the availability of data.[23] The discussion between Kaldor and Keynes on war finance in 1942–43 was also occasioned by a paper by Pigou on taxes and elasticity of demand, which he had submitted for publication in the *Economic Journal.* Keynes asked for Kaldor's help on the paper (letter 1725, 23 December 1942). Kaldor read the article and expressed the opinion that it did not contain anything particularly new (letter 1726, 31 December 1942).[24]

As from 1942, Kaldor was involved with the Beveridge plan, contributing statistical estimates of its impact on the economy. Kaldor's involvement and Keynes's interest in Beveridge's proposal is reflected in their correspondence in the years 1943–44. One of the topics discussed in relation to Beveridge's scheme and Kaldor's estimates was the possible negative effects of the scheme on British exports. In December 1942, Kaldor had written a letter to *The Times* in which he expressed concern over the possible negative effects of the Beveridge scheme on British exports. Keynes made some criticisms of Kaldor's position, to which Kaldor replied in a letter to Keynes of 29 December 1942 (letter 1733). Kaldor held that Keynes had misunderstood him with respect to the effects of depreciation on exports. He also argued that the Beveridge plan was feasible even in the case of a very large reduction in income due to post-war difficulties. In January 1943 (letter 1727, 15 January 1943), Keynes replied to Kaldor and argued, in particular, that the plan would not be feasible if there was a significant post-war reduction in income (by 10 per cent). Keynes, on the other hand, was not too worried about the effects of the plan on exports. In his reply four days later (letter 1386, 19 January 1943), Kaldor essentially restated his position.

Keynes reiterated his opinion in another letter ten days later. Here, in considering the possible trade implications of the Beveridge scheme, Keynes made some interesting considerations about the likely evolution of terms of trade after the war:

> During the ten years before the war we were gaining through the disorganisation of primary producers and their inability to handle surplus production. There is every evidence that, after the war, there will be more concerted action by primary producers than by manufacturing interests. Moreover, if, as one hopes, there is an increase in the volume of consumption as a whole, I should expect that to raise the prices of primary products relatively to manufactures.
>
> (letter 1728, 25 January 1943)

Other issues

As we saw above, much of the correspondence between Keynes and Kaldor on theoretical and analytical issues was prompted by Kaldor when he submitted one of his papers for publication in the *Economic Journal*. We also have some letters dealing with more mundane aspects of the papers, Keynes often showing concern about the excessive length of Kaldor's papers and his delay in submitting the revised version. In particular, it is worth mentioning a group of letters, all dated 1932,[25] concerning a paper by Kaldor on the economic situation in Austria that he sent to Keynes. After reading the first version of Kaldor's paper, Keynes suggested a shorter and more updated version of it; Kaldor accepted Keynes's suggestions and sent a revised version. This second version, however, did not satisfy Keynes, who rejected the article. We have a long reply from Kaldor, who defended his paper.[26] Finally, we have one letter from Keynes (letter 1684, 22 November 1933), in which he communicates to Kaldor that an article of his has been accepted for publication in the *Economic Journal* of March 1934; it was 'The equilibrium of the firm', one of Kaldor's fundamental theoretical contributions.

Other letters between Keynes and Kaldor were about academic activities. When Kaldor moved to Cambridge with LSE because of the war, he planned to give some lectures on dynamic economics. Keynes inquired about the nature of these lectures and asked Kaldor whether he was also interested in giving other lectures on more general topics (letter 1384, 12 February 1940). Kaldor sent Keynes the syllabus of his LSE lectures on dynamics and proposed a course on the theory of distribution (letter 1710, 13 February 1940). Keynes accepted Kaldor's proposal, but invited him not to give too advanced lectures.[27]

Conclusion

The correspondence between Keynes and Kaldor, already studied by others and partly published, does not contain material that could shed fundamental new light on the two economists' positions. Nonetheless, examination of their exchange is helpful for a better understanding of Keynes's and Kaldor's ideas. In particular, it is useful for a better understanding of Kaldor's theoretical evolution.

We start from the young economist who addresses himself to the well established and famous economist. Kaldor, though respectful, was not too intimidated by Keynes, and never hesitated to express his own ideas and criticise Keynes's. In the early years this is quite evident, given Kaldor's closeness to the Austrian tradition. But also in the following years, when he espoused Keynes's theory, Kaldor never played a passive role of uncritical acceptance of Keynes's ideas. The correspondence concerning Pigou and the trade cycle is particularly indicative of Kaldor's autonomous position within the circle of Keynesian economists in the 1930s.

From this point of view, it is unfortunate that the 1939 correspondence between Keynes and Kaldor on the notion of liquidity preference and Chapter 17 of the *General Theory* is so slim. Because of lack of time, Keynes did not read and comment on Kaldor's work, so that we do not have direct evidence of his reactions to Kaldor on a topic that, as is well known, placed Kaldor in quite a different position with respect to other Keynesian economists who followed Keynes's ideas more closely.

Acknowledgements

I would like to thank Geoff Harcourt for his valuable comments and suggestions to an earlier version of the present chapter. I would also like to thank all the participants in the research group on Cambridge economists, who helped me improve this chapter with their comments and observations.

Notes

1 After stating that the demand for hoards (inactive bank deposits) depends on the public's propensity to hoard and the price of non-liquid assets, Keynes held that, given the quantity of inactive deposits offered by the banking sector and the public's propensity to hoard, the price of non-liquid assets sets at the level required to equate demand and supply of hoards.

2 It is a process that 'is cumulative and might lead, under certain assumptions, to the destruction of the total stock of existing capital' (letter 1150, 19 November 1931).

3 Keynes wrote: 'in two years' time I may feel able to publish a revised and completer version' (letter 1679, 9 December 1931). For more details on Keynes's rejoinder, Kahn's comments on it and Robertson's reaction, see CWK XIII: 218ff, which contains also excerpts of the letters mentioned above.

4 Pigou described this situation as one characterised by 'normal banking policy'.

5 Over the period 27 September to 1 November 1937, Keynes and Kaldor exchanged eight letters on Pigou's article (letters 1685–1692).

6 Kaldor's letter of 20 October (letter 1689) contains his most detailed exposition of his criticisms of Keynes's note.

7 'For you would agree, I think, that on Pigou's assumptions, the fall in money wages will lead to a fall in interest; and *if it is assumed* that the fall in interest increases the propensity to consume, it must also, and to that extent, increase employment: even if investment is assumed to be zero (or constant). And this is all that Pigou's demonstration amounts to' (letter 1689, 20 October 1937).

In the end, however, Kaldor recognised that he had made 'too much concession to Pigou', so that he decided to revise his paper before publication (letter 1691, 27 October 1937).

8 Kaldor, however, convinced Keynes to change partly his original version of the note on Pigou. In particular, Keynes eliminated a paragraph on the stability of Pigou's equilibrium. See Kaldor's letters of 1 and 20 October (letters 1687 and 1689) and Keynes's letters of 14 and 25 October (letters 1688 and 1690).

9 Kaldor, in the same period, also discussed the problem of the trade cycle and capital intensity with Harrod; see Besomi 1999b for more details about their exchange.

10 Keynes wrote to Kaldor: 'When the article first came out, I read it through rather hastily, but sufficiently to see that it was of the highest interest. But it is a subject one has to work one's way back into a bit of a concentration, and I have not at the moment the leisure for that' (letter 1383, 3 January 1940).

11 In a letter to Kaldor (letter 881, 11 January 1940), J. Robinson mentions some of the points of disagreement between her (and Kahn) and Kaldor. The main point of disagreement was the determination of the long-term rate of interest (see Ch. 12).

12 In his reply (letter 1717, 18 March 1941), Keynes mentioned Joan Robinson's role in the presentation and diffusion of Kalecki's work by observing: 'I do not doubt that in the end she will write a good article for him' (see Ch. 6: 188).

13 Kaldor (1941a) had published a review article of Pigou's book, in which he criticised Pigou's hypothesis that investment depends only on the interest rate (and not also on the level of activity) and that Pigou did not distinguish between the short and the long term interest rates. Pigou wrote a rejoinder, which he sent to Keynes for publication in the *Economic Journal*; Keynes sent the rejoinder to Kaldor, who sent the comments mentioned above, which in turn he passed on to Pigou. Pigou's rejoinder was published (Pigou 1942) together with Kaldor's comments (Kaldor 1942a), as requested by Keynes in his letter to Pigou of May 28, 1942.

14 Thirlwall (1987) provides a detailed and interesting reconstruction of Kaldor's activities during the war. For Keynes's activities, see Skidelsky (2000).

15 Brought about by the increase in money wages due to the increased demand for labour.

16 The forced saving would have been ensured by the fact that a certain percentage of earned and unearned incomes had to be deposited in the Post Office Saving Bank.

17 Keynes replied to the critics of his scheme in a further article in *The Times* on 28 November 1939 (Keynes [1939b] in CWK XXII: 74–81).

18 National output, for Keynes, is given by current factor-cost of private consumption plus current outlay on buildings, plant, transport and stocks plus current cost of government operations (net of transfers); taxable income is the aggregate of individual incomes (Keynes [1940a] in CWK XXII: 67–8).

19 The final part of Keynes's note was devoted to the discussion of the fact that any sort of estimate of national resources available for the war was misleading 'when we contemplate diverting them from one use to another, for the reason

that their specific character is likely to lead to a loss on such diversion' (Keynes [1940a] in CWK XXII: 72). The basic point of Keynes's reasoning was that there is a loss of efficiency when specific resources are moved from one type of use to another.

20 Kaldor also pointed out that his conviction of the importance of gross income derived from his reading of Chapter 6 of the *General Theory*.

21 Kaldor also defined net national income as a variant of national output (Net national income = National output − Depreciation).

22 Keynes's letter of 19 April was followed by some others on issues related to Kaldor's article. Keynes returned to these topics in his letter of 30 September 1942 (letter 1723).

23 Keynes tried to help Kaldor obtain data from the Board of Inland Revenue (see letters 1387, 1391, 1392, 1393, which range from June 1943 to January 1944).

24 Pigou eventually decided to withdraw his paper (see Keynes's letter 1728, 25 January 1943).

25 Letters 1680, 1376, 1681, 1682, 1683, from 5 April to 18 May 1932.

26 The article on Austria was eventually published in the *Harvard Business Review* in 1932 (October).

27 'Do not be too difficult in the assumption of knowledge; your class will not be stupid, but they will be ignorant and are particularly ill-acquainted with modern controversial work. They will understand what you say so long as not too much previous knowledge is required'. In the same letter, Keynes also mentioned that, for administrative reasons, it was not possible for the University of Cambridge to pay Kaldor an honorarium for his teaching (see also Kaldor's letter of 28 February 1940; letter 1385). See Kahn (1988).

Table 8.1 Keynes–Kaldor correspondence

From	*To*	*Year*	*Month*	*Day*	*Date*	*Archive*		*Published in*	*Item*
NK	JMK	1931	November	19	Dated letter	Keynes–King's	TM/1/4/168–70	CWK XIII: 238–40	1150
						Kaldor–King's	NK/3/4/36–8		
						Kaldor–King's	NK/3/4/39–41		
						Kaldor–King's	NK/3/30/118/141–3		
						Kaldor–King's	NK/3/30/118/177–9		
JMK	NK	1931	November	27	Dated letter	Kaldor–King's	NK/3/30/118/144	CWK XIII: 241	1677
						Keynes–King's	TM/1/4/171		
						Kaldor–King's	NK/3/30/118/180		
						Kaldor–King's	NK/3/4/35		
NK	JMK	1931	December	3	Dated letter	Keynes–King's	TM/1/4/172–3	CWK XIII: 241–2	1678
						Kaldor–King's	NK/3/30/118/145–6		
						Kaldor–King's	NK/3/30/118/175–6		
JMK	NK	1931	December	9	Dated letter	Kaldor–King's	NK/3/30/118/147	CWK XIII: 243	1679
						Kaldor–King's	NK/3/30/118/174		
						Keynes–King's	TM/1/4/174		
JMK	NK	1932	April	5	Dated letter	Kaldor–King's	NK/3/30/118/138–9		1680
NK	JMK	1932	April	30	Dated letter	Kaldor–King's	NK/3/30/118/136–7		1376
NK	JMK	1932	May	5	Dated letter	Kaldor–King's	NK/3/30/118/135		1681
JMK	NK	1932	May	17	Dated letter	Kaldor–King's	NK/3/30/118/133–4	Turner 1993: 20, (E)	1682
NK	JMK	1932	May	18	Dated letter	Kaldor–King's	NK/3/30/118/130–2	Turner 1993: 21, (E)	1683
JMK	NK	1933	November	22	Dated letter	Kaldor–King's	NK/3/30/118/129		1684
NK	JMK	1937	September	27	Dated letter	Keynes–King's	EJ/1/4/123	CWK XIV: 240	1685
JMK	NK	1937	September	30	Dated letter	Kaldor–King's	NK/3/30/118/127–8	CWK XIV: 240–1	1686
						Kaldor–King's	EJ/1/4/124–5		
NK	JMK	1937	October	1	Dated letter	Kaldor–King's	EJ/1/4/126–7	CWK XIV: 241–2	1687
						Kaldor–King's	NK/3/30/118/125–6		
						Kaldor–King's	NK/3/30/118/125–6		
JMK	NK	1937	October	14	Dated letter	Kaldor–King's	NK/3/30/118/119–20	CWK XIV: 242–3	1688
						Kaldor–King's	EJ/1/4/128–9		

NK	JMK	1937	October	20	Dated letter	Keynes–King's Kaldor–King's	EJ/1/4/188–92 NK/3/30/118/115–18	CWK XIV: 243–7	1689
JMK	NK	1937	October	25	Dated letter	Kaldor–King's Keynes–King's	NK/3/30/118/101–3 EJ/1/4/193–5	CWK XIV: 247–8	1690
NK	JMK	1937	October	27	Dated letter	Keynes–King's Kaldor–King's	EJ/1/4/207–8 NK/3/30/118/99–100	CWK XIV: 248–9	1691
JMK	NK	1937	November	1	Dated letter	Kaldor–King's Keynes–King's	NK/3/30/118/97–8 EJ/1/4/209–10	CWK XIV: 249–50	1692
JMK	NK	1937	November	12	Postmark	Kaldor–King's	NK/3/30/118/95–6		1377
JMK	NK	1937	November	15	Postmark	Kaldor–King's	NK/3/30/118/93–4		1693
NK	JMK	1938	July	14	Dated letter	Keynes–King's	EJ/1/5/225		1378
JMK	NK	1938	July	15	Dated letter	Kaldor–King's	NK/1/11/1–2		1379
NK	JMK	1938	September	3	Dated letter	Keynes–King's	EJ/1/5/228		1380
JMK	NK	1938	September	19	Dated letter	Kaldor–King's Keynes–King's	NK/3/30/118/90–2 EJ/1/5/229–31	Thirlwall 1987: 48, (E)	1694
NK	JMK	1938	September	22	Dated letter	Keynes–King's	EJ/1/5/232–3		1381
JMK	NK	1939	April	25	Dated letter	Kaldor–King's	NK/3/30/118/89		1695
JMK	NK	1939	May	27	Dated letter	Kaldor–King's	NK/3/30/118/85–6		1696
NK	JMK	1939	June		Attributed	Kaldor–King's	NK/3/30/118/88		1697
NK	JMK	1939	June	19	Attributed	Kaldor–King's	NK/3/30/118/87		1698
JMK	NK	1939	July	22	Dated letter	Kaldor–King's	NK/3/30/118/73–5		1699
NK	JMK	1939	August	1	Dated letter	Kaldor–King's	NK/3/30/118/76–8		1700
JMK	NK	1939	August	14	Dated letter	Kaldor–King's	NK/3/30/118/79–80		1701
JMK	NK	1939	October	15	Dated letter	Kaldor–King's	NK/3/30/118/81–2		1702
JMK	NK	1939	October	27	Dated letter	Kaldor–King's	NK/3/30/118/83		1703
NK	JMK	1939	November	15	Dated letter	Keynes–King's Kaldor–King's	HP/2/34–7 NK/3/30/118/67–70		1704
JMK	NK	1939	November	15	Dated letter	Kaldor–King's	NK/3/30/118/84		1705
JMK	NK	1939	November	19	Dated letter	Kaldor–King's Keynes–King's	NK/3/30/118/71 HP/2/38		1706
NK	JMK	1939	December	28	Dated letter	Keynes–King's	L/39/143–64		1382
JMK	NK	1940	January	3	Dated letter	Keynes–King's	L/39/165		1383

Table 8.1 continued

From	*To*	*Year*	*Month*	*Day*	*Date*	*Archive*		*Published in*	*Item*
JMK	NK	1940	February	5	Dated letter	Kaldor–King's	NK/3/30/118/58–9		1708
NK	JMK	1940	February	6	Dated letter	Keynes–King's	W/4/139–44		1709
						Kaldor–King's	NK/3/30/118/165–70		
JMK	NK	1940	February	12	Dated letter	Keynes–King's	UA/5/5/5–6		1384
NK	JMK	1940	February	13	Dated letter	Keynes–King's	UA/5/5/9–12		1710
						Kaldor–King's	NK/3/30/118/66		
JMK	NK	1940	February	24	Dated letter	Kaldor–King's	NK/3/30/118/55–6		1711
						Keynes–King's	UA/5/5/25–6		
JMK	NK	1940	February	25	Dated letter	Kaldor–King's	NK/3/30/118/44–5		1712
						Keynes–King's	W/4/145–6		
						Kaldor–King's	NK/3/30/118/171–2		
NK	JMK	1940	February	28	Dated letter	Keynes–King's	UA/5/5/27		1385
NK	JMK	1940	March	1	Dated letter	Keynes–King's	W/4/147–52		1713
						Kaldor–King's	NK/3/30/118/46–51, NK/3/30/118/159–164		
JMK	NK	1940	March	12	Dated letter	Kaldor–King's	NK/3/30/118/52–4		1714
						Kaldor–King's	NK/3/30/118/156–8		
						Keynes–King's	W/4/153–5		
JMK	NK	1941	March	4	Dated letter	Kaldor–King's	NK/3/30/118/40	CWK XII: 834	1715
NK	JMK	1941	March	9	Dated letter	Kaldor–King's	NK/3/30/118/41–2		1716
JMK	NK	1941	March	18	Dated letter	Kaldor–King's	NK/3/30/118/43	CWK XII: 836	1717
						Keynes–King's	MM/4/120		
NK	JMK	1941	April	10	Dated letter	Kaldor–King's	NK/3/30/118/37		1718
JMK	NK	1941	April	19	Dated letter	Kaldor–King's	NK/3/30/118/33–6	Skidelsky 2000: 84, (E)	1719
NK	JMK	1941	April	29	Dated letter	Kaldor–King's	NK/3/30/118/32		1720
JMK	NK	1941	September	10	Dated letter	Kaldor–King's	NK/3/30/118/39		1721
NK	JMK	1942	May	23	Dated letter	Keynes–King's	MM/4/125		1732
JMK	NK	1942	June	18	Dated letter	Kaldor–King's	NK/3/30/118/29		1722

JMK	NK	1942	September	30	Dated letter	Kaldor–King's	NK/3/30/118/25–8	1723
JMK	NK	1942	November	11	Dated letter	Kaldor–King's	NK/3/30/118/24	1724
JMK	NK	1942	December	23	Dated letter	Kaldor–King's	NK/3/30/118/21–3	1725
NK	JMK	1942	December	29	Dated letter	Keynes–King's	MM/5/205–8	1733
NK	JMK	1942	December	31	Dated letter	Kaldor–King's	NK/3/30/118/16–20	1726
JMK	NK	1943	January	15	Dated letter	Kaldor–King's	NK/3/30/118/13–15	1727
NK	JMK	1943	January	19	Dated letter	Kaldor–King's	NK/3/30/118/10–12	1386
JMK	NK	1943	January	25	Dated letter	Kaldor–King's	NK/3/30/118/8–9	1728
NK	JMK	1943	June	23	Dated letter	Kaldor–King's Kaldor–King's	NK/3/10/40 NK/3/10/41	1387
JMK	NK	1943	July	28	Dated letter	Kaldor–King's	NK/3/30/118/5–7	1729
NK	JMK	1943	August	4	Dated letter	Kaldor–King's	NK/3/10/23	1388
JMK	NK	1943	August	12	Dated letter	Kaldor–King's	NK/3/30/118/3–4	1730
NK	JMK	1943	November	10	Dated letter	Kaldor–King's Kaldor–King's	NK/3/29/285 NK/3/29/286	1389
JMK	NK	1943	November	10	Dated letter	Kaldor–King's	NK/3/29/285	1390
NK	JMK	1943	December	16	Dated letter	Kaldor–King's	NK/3/29/436–7	1391
JMK	NK	1943	December	18	Dated letter	Kaldor–King's	NK/3/29/435	1392
JMK	NK	1944	January	19	Dated letter	Kaldor–King's	NK/3/29/423	1393
NK	JMK	1944	January	20	Dated letter	Kaldor–King's	NK/3/29/424	1394
NK	JMK	1944	June	14	Dated letter	Kaldor–King's	NK/3/29/167	1395
JMK	NK	1945	February	22	Dated letter	Kaldor–King's	NK/3/30/118/2	1731

9 When the abyss yawns and after

The correspondence between Keynes and Hayek

Bruna Ingrao

The early encounter: the first controversy

The correspondence conserved in the archives includes 66 letters, 22 of which by Hayek to Keynes and 44 by Keynes to Hayek (see Table 9.1). This correspondence has mixed contents and is only in part relevant to scientific comparison between the two authors. Of special interest are a group of letters in the Hayek archives at the Hoover Foundation, which have so far been neither published nor studied with the due attention. The correspondence illustrates various aspects of the scientific controversies between Hayek and Keynes, but also various phases in their personal relations.[1] The letters will be examined in groups, according to period considered and subject.

The first batch of letters (1927–29) are of mainly biographical interest, documenting the meeting of Keynes and Hayek at the end of the 1920s, when Hayek was still a young economist while Keynes was already a well-known scholar. Hayek later recalled their first meeting in an article recounting his personal recollections of Keynes (Hayek [1966] 1995: 240).

In 1927 a few lines by Keynes explained that the stock of Edgeworth's *Mathematical Psychics* was depleted; Hayek had clearly requested the volume (letter 801, 24 February 1927). On another card (letter 802, 9 July 1927) Keynes acknowledged the first issue of the publication by the Austrian Institute of Business Cycle Research, to which Hayek was appointed director a few years after his return from the United States (Ebenstein 2001: 43).[2] In 1928, after personally making the acquaintance of Keynes at the London conference where scholars from various institutions for the study of business cycles had met (Kresge and Wenar 1994: 89; Ebenstein 2001: 86), Hayek sent him a paper they had already talked about at the conference (letter 803, 12 July 1928). This was probably the article published in 1928, which would become well known to historians later on since it introduced the idea of intertemporal general equilibrium (Hayek 1928). Hayek asked for comments on his main thesis and also enclosed a report prepared for the *Vereins für Sozialpolitik*, where he discussed money and the business cycle.[3] In March 1929 Keynes thanked Hayek after receiving *Geldtheorie und Konjunkturtheorie* (Hayek 1929) in the original version published in German (letter 804, 26 March 1929). Keynes noted that the last chapter of the book interested him in particular, but complained that Hayek's German was quite difficult for him. The same letter announced the German edition of *A Treatise on Money*, to be published almost contemporaneously with the English one. In short, the young Austrian economist sent his work to Keynes, who was obliged but did not seem to pay much attention to it.[4]

A second group of letters (1931–32), already well known to scholars, is much more interesting from an analytical point of view. It has already been published both in the *Collected Writings* of Keynes (CWK XIII), and in *Contra Keynes and Cambridge* (Hayek 1995), and includes seven letters by Keynes and five letters by Hayek exchanged from July 1931 to February 1932.

In the first letter by Keynes, answering a previous letter by Hayek on 26 July (not found), Keynes expressed curiosity about the review of his *Treatise on Money* Hayek was writing ('I am looking forward very much to seeing your review in *Economica*', letter 805, 31 July 1931). When the review by Hayek was published in August 1931, Keynes was greatly disappointed and responded polemically in an article published in *Economica* in the November of the same year (Keynes 1931a).[5]

Since Keynes had attacked *Prices and Production* in that article, Hayek published a short rejoinder in the same issue of the journal (Hayek 1931d). Their private epistolary controversy opened in December 1931. The first letter by Keynes asked for elucidation on the definition of saving used by Hayek in his rejoinder (letter 806, 10 December 1931). The private controversy on monetary theory continued until February 1932, when Keynes kindly but firmly expressed the idea that the dialogue had gone on as far as it could in correspondence; further in-depth investigation would require a book by Hayek (letter 816, 11 February 1932).

In 1932 Keynes wrote to Kahn and Sraffa, referring to his own correspondence with Hayek: 'What is the next move? I feel that the abyss yawns – and so do I. Yet I can't help feeling that there *is* something interesting in it' (letter 264 from JMK to RFK, 1 February 1932). A mark was left, even if the abyss yawned.

The correspondence saw development after the publication of Sraffa's article attacking Hayek's theory of capital in the March issue of the *Economic Journal* (see Ch. 4: 125ff). Hayek had asked for the opportunity to answer in the same issue and Keynes responded promising to give him some space in the June issue provided Hayek kept his reply within the proper limits of length (letter 817, 29 March 1932).

Meanwhile, the second part of Hayek's review of the *Treatise* had been published in February 1932 in *Economica* (Hayek 1932a). In the same letter Keynes mentioned the review, explaining that he had not yet had time to read it carefully. In conclusion he explained that he was preoccupied with improving his argument, and thus preferred to work in that direction rather than go on with the controversy (letter 817, 29 March 1932).

Hayek's answer to Sraffa's article was published in the *Economic Journal* in the June 1932 issue (Hayek 1932b), together with Sraffa's rejoinder. At the beginning of May, receiving Hayek's text and mentioning the proofs, Keynes commented in a line in his own handwriting: 'I don't think that Sraffa has misunderstood *me*. May I add a footnote to that effect?' (letter 818, 4 May 1932). In the early 1930s Keynes referred to Hayek's theory scornfully on a number of occasions (Skidelsky 1992: 459).[6]

In September 1932 Keynes sent another letter to Hayek, but the issue was exclusively editorial: he was sorry, since all offprints had been sent to Sraffa. He then explained to Hayek that no payment was due for rejoinders in controversies (letter 819, 22 September 1932).

It is worth noting how well this correspondence highlights the difference in conceptual language and analytic approach between the two economists. The impression is as of a dialogue between people who have a very poor understanding of one another's language. Indeed, one reason for the asperity of argumentation was the difficulty in communicating and sharing a theoretical language. However, in the end some submerged communication between Keynes and Hayek came about, at least as a mutual signalling to each other of the dead ends or theoretical difficulties in their arguments. The further evolution of their thinking was partially marked by the controversy of the early 1930s, which at first sight might appear to have been totally barren.

In 1931 Keynes admitted the weakness of his analysis as regards the theory of capital, although decidedly asserting: 'But there is no such theory at present [. . .]' (Keynes [1931a] in Hayek 1995: 155).

In the *General Theory* he discussed the issues raised in the controversy and mentioned the Austrian theory of capital in various passages. While choosing the units of measurement Keynes carefully avoided the 'general price level' variable and the 'general level of production' variable, extensively motivating his choice in Chapter 4. He reflected on the concept of net income, admitting its ambiguity (CWK VII: 59–60) and, moreover, admitting confusion in the definitions of income and saving adopted in the *Treatise* (CWK VII: 60–1).

Chapter 16 of the *General Theory*, entirely devoted to discussing the nature of capital, contained an effort to settle the score with the Austrian approach, while avoiding the accusation of having forgotten the theory of capital. Keynes extensively discussed roundaboutness, criticising its link with the productivity of capital and rejecting its analytical relevance for the measurement of capital and the theory of interest.

In Chapter 20, however, Keynes introduced the concept of the 'period of production', although with a peculiar meaning, to discuss the elasticity of supply in a time dimension.[7] In these interesting pages he went so far as to examine the effects of additional demand on employment, adopting an almost Austrian approach, taking into account different stages in the production process, and considering consumption goods as the last stage (CWK VII: 287 ff.). Ambiguities and uncertainties remain.

Confronted with criticism from the Cambridge economists, Hayek was stimulated to rethink his own business cycle theory and better articulate it, endeavouring along these lines until the end of the 1930s.

Editorial correspondence in the 1930s

The third group of letters (1933–35) is of more limited interest to the historian of economic thought. All the letters in this group were written by Keynes to Hayek and have to do with social contacts or academic affairs. We know from J. Robinson's testimony that Hayek and Keynes met on friendly terms for lunch, but that after the acrimony of their dispute they still had to fully 'edge themselves out of their untenable position' (letter 579 from JVR to RFK, 5 March 1933). It seems that by the mid-1930s they had re-established a certain degree of scientific contact and cordial relations, although not real friendship.

Some of the correspondence is on editorial matters, with no scientific content. Five letters from 1933 to 1934 (letters 820–824, from 30 December 1933 to 6 April 1934) deal with the publication of an article by Hayek, presumably 'On the Relationship between Investment and Output', which came out in the *Economic Journal* in June 1934 (Hayek 1934).

In 1935 correspondence turned to the possibility of a rejoinder by Hayek to Knight, which Keynes might publish in the *Economic Journal*. Knight had submitted an article attacking the Austrian theory of capital and Hayek's theory in particular ('Professor Hayek and the Theory of Investment'). Keynes had accepted it for publication in the *Economic Journal* (Knight 1935). Hayek – so it seems – asked to reply (letter 825, 10 July 1935).

Keynes accepted, but invited him to be short, in accordance with the editorial policy on controversies to be published in the *Economic Journal* (letters 826 and 827, 10 and 17 July 1935). In a further letter, thanking Hayek for two offprints he had received, Keynes asked him whether his reply to Knight was ready (letter 829, 7 October 1935). A manuscript note was added at the end of the letter in answer to a successive letter by Hayek (not found). Keynes politely expressed his regret that Hayek had already sent his comment to the *Quarterly Journal of Economics* (letter 829). Eventually Hayek's rejoinder to Knight became a full article on 'The Mythology of Capital' (Hayek 1936a).

A short manuscript note by Keynes to Hayek in July 1935 made playful reference to bimetallism, asking whether bimetallism strangely affected the mind or if it was the other way round (letter 828, 19 July 1935).

In the crucial years before and shortly after the publication of the *General Theory*, when debate of Keynes's theory was being broached, the exchange between Keynes and Hayek seemed limited and poor in content. Between 1936 and 1938 Keynes's letters to Hayek included an invitation to lunch with Robertson, an invitation to a seminar, comments on a weak dissertation and editorial correspondence (letters 832–837, from 14 May 1936 to 9 December 1938). Part of the correspondence may have been lost when Hayek moved from London to Cambridge at the beginning of the war, or later, when he moved from London to Chicago on the occasion of his second marriage.

The truly surprising thing about the scant existing material is not what is said, but how little is said! Not a single letter deals with their thinking in years of intensive theoretical work for both, and dramatic events for Europe. We know the severe judgement Hayek later passed on an article by Keynes in 1933 on 'National Self-sufficiency', originally published in a German version (Hayek [1952] 1995: 230; Keynes 1933b). We also know he expressed particularly negative appraisal of the preface Keynes wrote for the German edition of the *General Theory* (Hayek [1983] 1995: 254). We do not know whether Hayek ever expressed these comments to Keynes, or at least we have no trace of this in their correspondence.

There are, however, a few elements of interest to the historian. In January 1936 (letter 830, 12 January 1936) Keynes read with great interest a text sent by Hayek and wrote: 'I find this article extremely interesting'. The article, entitled 'Utility Analysis and Interest', would later be published in the *Economic Journal* (Hayek 1936b). The letter gave a positive evaluation of Hayek's work, which sounded odd coming from Keynes but is understandable if we consider that the text was a criticism of interest theories based on time preference, and that it pointed out weaknesses in the static apparatus of utility functions and indifference curves.

In the same letter Keynes promised Hayek to send him a copy of the *General Theory*. Hayek thanked him in February after receiving the advance copy of the book (letter 831, 2 February 1936). In his letter he expressed agreement on the great relevance of the general theme of the book, but politely dissented from Keynes's assertion that the issue had been completely ignored. He wrote that he had already heard about the contents from Bryce and J. Robinson. Finally, he expressed some perplexity about the relationship between saving and investment and about liquidity preference, advancing a prudent proposal to write some comments in the *Economic Journal* once he had read the book more carefully. We know in fact that Hayek never reviewed Keynes's new book, deciding – for various reasons – to avoid further public controversy with the author.[8]

Dialogue continued on the themes that were favourite topics of conversation for them in the war years, when Keynes and Hayek had occasion to meet quite regularly in Cambridge, namely antique books, the history of ideas and discovering rare books on economics. In December 1938 Hayek brought Boisguillebert's 1707 essay to Keynes's attention. In his letter he explained why he considered the essay so important, although it did not make easy reading. He called attention to the themes he found most fascinating: discussion of the equilibrium in relative prices, how a local crisis spreads through the interdependence of monetary incomes, the uses of money, crises of confidence, money hoarding and credit squeezes (letter 839, 18 December 1938).

The letter shows that they were in the habit of discussing some of their intellectual pursuits together ('the reference I promised') and, in fact, in April 1939 Keynes wrote to thank him after receiving the reprint of Thornton's essay introduced by Hayek (Hayek 1939b). He warmly appreciated Hayek's 'fascinating' introduction and commented: 'you have told me a great deal new about it'; but he noted that Hayek might have attributed more to Thornton than he really said. According to Keynes, Thornton was primarily preoccupied with the quantity of money; the more innovative aspects of his thinking emerged as little more than hints, without great development (letter 840, 11 April 1939).

A private controversy in the late 1930s

In 1939, a collection of Hayek's essays was published under the title *Profits, Interest and Investment* (Hayek 1939a). The essays show the evolution of Hayek's research programme on the business cycle. The introductory essay, 'Profits, Interest and Investment', first published in 1939, introduced important innovations in the basic analytic model Hayek utilised to discuss how monetary influences generated the trade cycle (Hayek 1939a: 3–71). The model was built on the assumption of specialised labour and capital goods, with no mobility in the short run and the possibility of underemployment of resources, which the equilibrium model in *Prices and Production* had excluded.

Profits, Interest and Investment offered the opportunity to broach a new monetary controversy, which proved more polite and moderate in tone than the previous one, and again of considerable interest. Six letters were exchanged in September and October 1939; they cast light both on the final stage Hayek had reached in his thinking about the business cycle, and on the curiosity, doubts or dissent Keynes expressed when confronted with Hayek's new analytical effort.

The discussion was opened with a long letter by Keynes (letter 841, 20 September 1939), drawing attention to the most recent essay in the collection, the introductory one, where Hayek outlined his theory of fluctuations, with a few substantial revisions.

Keynes asked for detailed explanation above all of the assumptions regarding prices: whether 'the price' [increase] considered by Hayek was instantaneous ('instantaneous and once-for-all') or referred to a time period ('a rate over a period'); whether it referred to all goods, both final and instrumental; whether it was anticipated; whether, once effective, it was expected to be permanently established or tending to generate further reactions; and whether it was uniform for all goods regardless of the proportion of wages over costs.

Keynes, in short, asked why proportional changes in the prices of different goods (bread and rents), expected to be permanent, should have different effects on supply ('the supply of bread will expand faster than that of houses') and, if that was the case, how it could be conciliated with the initial assumption of a proportional variation in costs. He asked, moreover, how it is that a fall in real income can be associated with an increase in demand: 'If earners' real incomes per unit of output are falling, why does real demand increase?' (letter 841, 20 September 1939).

While Keynes was asking questions about the proportional changes of prices and supply of different goods (letters 841 and 843, 20 September and 9 October 1939), Hayek went on repeating that the effects were diverse and with different timing (letter 842, 24 September 1939). While Keynes was arguing in terms of real income *tout court*, Hayek was dealing with the real value of incomes in terms of available final consumption goods (letters 841 and 842). He emphasised the imbalances that would emerge over time between consumption expenditure and the allocation of productive resources to the production process of final consumption goods (letter 842). The supply of bread will increase more quickly than the supply of houses, but only as long as the rate of profit in the production of bread is higher than that in the production of houses.

Hayek affirmed that, excluding the case in section 5 of his essay,[9] he always and only considered an increase in the price of consumption goods that was not perfectly anticipated but was afterwards perceived as permanent. By assumption, only the price of consumption goods increased. The problem was to deduce if and how much all the other prices would increase as a consequence. In conclusion, Hayek was actually quite taken aback by Keynes's questions and comments. He wrote: 'But I am afraid the rest of your statement I do not understand. I speak nowhere of a 2% *cost* rise' (letter 842, 24 September 1939).

Keynes repeated again that he failed to understand why the same initial increase (permanent) by 2 per cent in the price of bread and rents should produce different effects (letter 843, 9 October 1939). He asked how it could be that these different effects prevailed if there was no change in the consumers' demand, or in other words in the consumers' preferences (letter 845, 16 October 1939).

Hayek answered the question with a long letter restating his overinvestment theory, to apply the expression used by Hicks, who well understood its spirit (Hicks 1967). It is perfectly clear that Hayek denied the possibility of a contemporaneous, direct multiplier effect of investment on the production of final consumption goods working through the increased volume of resources applied in the production of investment goods. It is worth quoting the central sentence of this letter (letter 844, 15 October 1939).

> if incomes are increased (by investment) without a simultaneous increase of output, it is impossible that the prices of all factors should rise in proportion to the rise in the price of the product. Whether investment is increased by employing people on the production of investment goods which were formerly unemployed, or by transferring people from the production of consumers' goods to the production of investment goods, so long as these people spend any considerable part of their income on consumers' goods it seems to me obvious that the price of consumers' goods in terms of factors must rise (or 'real wages' fall).
>
> (letter 844, 15 October 1939)

Keynes's diagnosis of unemployment pointed to an insufficient level of investment. Hayek's diagnosis pointed to a misdirected expansion of investment which, during the trade cycle, happened to block the production of consumption goods with respect to demand, creating a whole sequence of imbalances over time. As Hicks noted, the intertemporal imbalances Hayek was considering may be very significant in some historical conditions, but his diagnosis of the 1930s depression was faulty (Hicks 1967).

The debate died out inconclusively at the end of October with two final letters, much shorter than the previous ones (letters 845, 16 October 1939; 846, 20 October 1939) but both of some interest. In the letter of 16 October Keynes raised a question on the issue he thought to be really crucial ('the ultimate point'): was Hayek considering temporary disequilibrium ('momentary mal-adjustment') or a new long-term equilibrium position ('a new long-period equilibrium')? According to Keynes, Hayek always seemed to be referring to the latter (new long-term equilibrium), but argued as if he were discussing the former problem (momentary mal-adjustment).

Hayek answered on 20 October, referring to the time structure of the Wicksellian cumulative process ('But I am certainly not concerned with a question of merely long term equilibrium but with the same sort of period with which the usual analysis of the "cumulative" process of expansion is concerned'). He firmly denied, then, that he had analysed a mere problem of long-term equilibrium. In fact, in his essay Hayek had clearly and indeed repeatedly stated the intention to analyse the phases of a cyclical process. No doubt his analytical construction was built to such an end. He meant to deal with a problem of traverse, generating fluctuations along a time path before converging back to equilibrium.

The misunderstanding over dynamics and time structure was radical.

Equilibrium and the cycle: divergence in dynamic analysis

In the new controversy it is evident that Hayek had some difficulty in arguing about the Ricardo effect. Also evident, at the same time, is the importance of Hayek's effort to analyse variations in final demand taking into account the productive structure, examining changes in time, temporary rigidities in supply, specialised resources and labour in various industries, and the role of relative prices.

In Hayek's reasoning investment is a process that extends over more than one period. Capacity is built over a sequence of periods in time by a coherent flow of invested resources. Resources must accrue in proper sequence and the value of an investment project in time is only preserved by appropriate price ratios. In non-stationary conditions, the crucial problem was, then, to study whether existing intermediate products and durable capital goods or labour resources were constrained by the original time structure of past investment projects, and how the time structure of production adapted to changing relative prices in dynamic conditions.

Although it failed to account for the great depression, and for this reason was at the time discredited, Hayek's inquiry offered an array of pointers to analyse economic change over time. It was such a forceful lesson on the complexities of dynamic processes as to undermine the oversimplified model itself that Hayek had started from. The focus on the longer term nature of capacity building and the disequilibria which may result (or conversely the market mechanisms of adaptation to ongoing change) affords valuable insight in understanding economic development.

Theoretically, neither Hayek nor Keynes was able to link equilibrium and cycle in a sound, well-defined analytical model. In the 1930s their debate revolved on this unsolved theoretical problem, even more arduous in the Marshallian approach than in the Austrian one. Later on, commenting on the analytical structure of the *General Theory*, Lindahl accused Keynes of the same ambiguity between adjustment processes and equilibrium that Keynes had pointed out to Hayek in this correspondence (Lindahl 1954).[10] Again and again in the post-war years Keynesian literature came up against the same dilemma in the interpretation of Keynes's thinking.

The very critique of general equilibrium theory that Hayek advanced (Hayek 1937b) undermined his own research project on equilibrium and business cycle as structured in the early 1930s. In the programme to build a dynamic approach inspired by general equilibrium theory (such was the original intention and aspiration), reconciliation between equilibrium and cycle proved impossible, since there appeared to be no way to incorporate disappointed expectations and change into equilibrium models. The result was reached by Hayek himself as also by Lindahl and Hicks, while they were rethinking a common core of analytical questions about equilibrium left open by the Lausanne school. It turned out to be not the provisional weakness of an incomplete research project, but a substantial theoretical difficulty, which brought the project to a dead end. In 1937 Hayek's efforts to embody expectations and change in the structure of equilibrium models was not so much a solution to the insoluble problem as the beginning of new investigation, which brought Hayek practically to abandon the equilibrium scaffolding.

In the 1940s Hayek's research project ran aground due to difficulties in the theory of capital. *A Pure Theory of Capital* (Hayek 1941a) marked another critical point on the ambitious path to merging equilibrium and cycle, starting from the Austrian vision of capital as investment of resources in structured time sequences. Complexity prevailed and Hayek gave up the project to incorporate monetary theory into his capital theory (Kresge and Wenar 1994: 90–1, 141–2). Meanwhile Hayek was moving in other directions; new tasks absorbed him, leaving the earlier research programme to take second place in his mind. Actually, it was never resumed.

Keynes's general theory of employment was born devoid of analytic tools to study economic dynamics and change, since it was rooted in an ambiguous notion of the short period. In fact, Keynes wavered in his book between a very short period perspective (as when considering the given conditions in Chapter 18) to ideas of stagnation and chronic shortage of investment, which, on the contrary, imply a medium or long-term perspective and analysis of dynamic adjustment paths. In the *General Theory* we find side by side, with little effort at consistency, historical overviews on very long term processes and an analytical structure considering investment only on the demand side in a single, self-contained short period.

Keynes's strategic choice to adopt an analytical model based on the Marshallian short period, although reformulated in an aggregate context, was not without a heavy cost. Apparently motivated by the need to capture academic audience, the choice eased both presentation and assimilation of the new theory, but it stood in the way of in-depth investigation into economic realities where time structure and change play a crucial role (as in the case of processes of development or inflation). This basic weakness in Keynes's original theory gave rise to many of the controversies over interpretation. It also accounts for many of the difficulties Keynesian theory and policies have run into in the now close on seventy years following publication of the *General Theory*.

Convergence and debate in the 1940s

The correspondence of the 1940s (1940–46), although less rich than the 1939 exchange considered above, contains a few letters of great relevance to relations between Keynes and Hayek, the two scholars' paths occasionally converging although differences persist.

The first episode was Hayek's enthusiastic support for Keynes's plan to finance war expenditure, published in *How to Pay for the War* (Keynes 1940b). After the two articles by Keynes had been published in *The Times*, an article by Hayek was published in the *Spectator* on 24 November 1939

(Hayek 1939c), commenting favourably on the financing scheme advanced by Keynes with some further proposals to improve the plan.[11] When Keynes himself sent copies of the revised pamphlet to friends and colleagues (Moggridge 1992: 633), he pointed out to Hayek that he had 'bagged' his idea of 'a post-war capital levy' (letter 847, 27 February 1940). To express his warm agreement, Hayek wrote personally to Keynes soon after receiving it.

> I have now read it carefully and still find myself in practically complete agreement in so far as policy during the war is concerned. It is reassuring to know that we agree so completely on the economics of scarcity, even if we differ on when it applies.
>
> (letter 848, 3 March 1940)

Keynes answered that he was glad about their concordance and accepted the idea of a group of economists subscribing to the plan (letter 849, 6 March 1940).[12] He mentioned to Hayek Hicks's partial dissent on some aspects of his plan. Eventually Hayek wrote a very positive review of *How to Pay for the War* in the June–September issue of the *Economic Journal* in 1940 (Hayek 1940).

When Hayek moved to Cambridge in the same year, Keynes helped him to find proper accommodation (letters 850, 22 October 1940; 851, 26 October 1940). In April 1941 Keynes asked him if he would accept appointment on the Council of the Royal Economic Society (letter 852, 28 April 1941).

In 1943 they exchanged letters on Mill's correspondence (letters 853–855, 1 to 18 January 1943), since Hayek was working on a new critical edition, more complete than the previous one (Hayek 1943a, 1943b). Keynes approved of the project and expressed warm appreciation ('most fascinating and instructive') for Hayek's introduction to the reprint of Mill's *Spirit of the Age* (Hayek 1942a). Both read with great interest the *Journal of the History of Ideas*, which Keynes received and sent to Hayek (letters 856, 21 March 1943; 857, 24 April 1943; 863, 17 January 1946). Keynes being the only subscriber in Cambridge, Hayek had asked to read the issues he received (letter 797, 13 March 1943). Keynes kept Hayek informed on his antiquarian purchases, such as the Sterling side of the Mill–Sterling correspondence or the precious series of Hume letters collected by Lord Minto (letter 858, 4 April 1944).

On 13 March Hayek sent Keynes's a 'semi-popular exposition of the American commodity-currency scheme'; he wondered whether it could be published in *The Times* (letter 797, 13 March 1943). On 21 March 1943 Keynes wrote to Hayek (letter 856, 21 March 1943) commending his draft, the article 'A Commodity Reserve Currency', to be published in the *Economic Journal* (Hayek 1943c), which addressed the question of how to rebuild the international monetary system. Hayek was well aware of the risks for international stability created by totally unco-ordinated national policies, but also of the difficulties in international co-operation. He endorsed the proposals advanced by F. Graham and B. Graham, both American scholars. Hayek proposed a mechanism based on a basket of staple commodities, which should substitute gold as the basis of the international monetary system while, however, essentially retaining the same functions as the gold standard.

In his letter Keynes acknowledged the soundness of Hayek's argument ('Theoretically your points are sound'), but complained about the lack of realism in his plan given the political conditions of the period ('Practically I do not believe that the world is ripe for this sort of thing'). Keynes suggested, as more appropriate, testing schemes to stabilise the markets for staple goods ('buffer stock plans and the like'). Keynes's note accompanying the published article by Hayek was rather less favourable than the previous letter, although appreciative of the theoretical relevance of the proposal. Keynes criticised the viability of the scheme and insisted that stabilisation of internal prices should be an objective for domestic policy, fully dependent on national sovereignty (Keynes 1943). In December 1944 a controversy followed in the *Economic Journal* (F.D. Graham 1944). In a further note Keynes admitted a possible misconception in his reading of Hayek's proposal, but pointed to the vested interests of gold holders and producers, and doubted the political wisdom of imposing external constraints on national wage policies (Keynes 1944a).

Keynes recalled Hayek's proposal on a number of occasions. In the 1940s, along with his major involvement in reconstruction of the international monetary system, he was preoccupied with plans to stabilise the international commodities markets. Both scholars paid attention to institution building in the international scene, although from very different perspectives. Hayek had published *Monetary Nationalism and International Stability* in 1937 (Hayek 1937a). Keynes was very much in favour of schemes to stabilise commodities markets for the purpose of stabilising income in raw-material producing countries.

In May 1944, Keynes sent two short cards to Hayek. In the first he answered Hayek on the question of Tyrol, apologising for not being able to deal with the problem (letter 859, 20 May 1944); Hayek had presumably sent him one of his pamphlets on this vexed question (Hayek 1943d, 1943e). On this occasion it seems that Keynes was involved because of his seat in the House of Lords, but apologised for not being able to deal with all issues of importance. The second, very short card is unusually enthusiastic about an article by Hayek in the *Sunday Times*. Keynes wrote: 'Thank you for a splendid article in today's *Sunday Times*. Most helpful to good cause. *Ecrasez l'infame*' (letter 860, 21 May 1944). In the copy at the Hoover archive the article was identified as 'Good and bad unemployment'; but on that date the article by Hayek in the *Sunday Times* was devoted to a polemic against the advocates of bilateralism in foreign trade (Hayek

1944b). The title of the article was: 'To totalitarianism by the back door?' Keynes would later reject the economic isolationism and bilateralism option calling it sardonically the 'starvation corner' (Moggridge 1992: 784–5).

In 1945 Hayek, a new fellow of the British Academy thanks to Keynes's support, expressed his preferences for new nominations, as he did again in 1946, in doubt between J. Robinson and Harrod (letters 862, 9 February 1945; 864, 14 February 1946). He was not particularly keen on either of them, but his preference went to Harrod as a more promising scholar. This is his last letter to Keynes of which we have any knowledge.

Shared feelings and different visions of liberalism

The last letter by Keynes to Hayek contained positive comment on *The Road to Serfdom* (Hayek 1944a)(letter 861, 28 June 1944). The comment was preceded by a shorter letter (letter 858, 4 April 1944), which anticipated some of its contents (Shearmur 1997: 72–3). Both letters are known to scholars, and both have already been commented on (Shearmur 1997; Carabelli and De Vecchi 1999).

Keynes's first reaction was of some diffidence. He found the book (which he had only glanced at) 'fascinating' and 'in the nature of medicine with which I shall disagree, but which may agree with me in the sense of doing me good'. The medicine was doing good in keeping public opinion on the right track, but the main message on active economic policy would not do. Keynes added:

> Wholesome, and yet nevertheless to be rejected. Something to be kept at the back's of one's head rather than at the front of it. But it is just as serviceable a public act to get the right packings in the back of people's heads as the right impulse to action in the front of them.
>
> (letter 858, 4 April 1944)

On closer reading the book must indeed have proved wholesome, after all, since Keynes's later comment was quite flattering, while still retaining a peculiar mix of approval and dissent, showing how Keynes and Hayek viewed the contemporary world from different perspectives.

In the extended comment, significantly, Keynes admitted the superior efficiency of planning in economic matters in principle ('the very doubtful assumption that planning is not more efficient'). To understand this peculiar aspect of Keynes's comment, illustrating the difference in vision we have mentioned, we must consider the different lines Keynes and Hayek took on uncertainty about the future. The issue was crucial for both, admitting no compromise with the ideal assumption of perfect certainty or perfectly anticipated expectations (Carabelli and De Vecchi 1999).

In the *General Theory* uncertainty about the future is conceived as a kind of mist or darkness, dimming our rational sight and affecting the soundness of our present choices and actions. As far as possible, we must strive to overcome it, not with conventional judgement but with a real effort to achieve more far-sighted judgement. Uncertainty about the future impairs our rational mind. As a good rationalist and an acute critic of the pretty, polite techniques of Benthamite calculations, Keynes inevitably aspired to the clearer sight that a better knowledge of future might give us.

As from the mid-1930s Hayek attributed a maieutic role to future uncertainty. The unknown future incubates discovery of the new. Uncertainty about the future is the other face of the creative quality that the future may disclose, precisely because it cannot be fully anticipated *a priori*. This vision of uncertainty about the future is crucial in Hayek's liberalism. Innovative changes and novelties cannot be foreseen at present. If we could rationally and perfectly anticipate what the future will bring, there would be no progress in human history. We must allow due freedom to the future, opening a space where the new can be born. The pursuit of rational control, even if exercised by the best minds in a non-authoritarian regime (and Hayek distrusted the arbitrary restrictions even the best minds might impose), confounds the riches the future might disclose, and thus reduces the potential for human development. Social institutions should protect the maieutics of unforeseeable innovation. In the market place Hayek emphasised the effective, essential function of local knowledge, restricted and myopic as it may be, in co-ordination and efficiency.

The contrast between these two perceptions of uncertainty impinged on their different conceptions of the relationship between ethics and institutions.

The Road to Serfdom lacked the crude evolutionist approach that marked Hayek's later thought. The emphasis on values, human rights and the ethical foundation of politics was perfectly clear in the book, recurring in various passages. The book also contained an explicit definition of the proper scope and specific tasks of State intervention (Shearmur 1997). Keynes's objection that Hayek did not explain 'where to draw the line' was not sound, although of course much more might have been said on the functions of the State and its proper limits.

Hayek advanced the idea that people's ethical behaviour should not be considered as given independently of the context of social institutions. Lacking well-balanced control over arbitrary decisions, centralised social rule systematically produces totalitarian deviations, however good the initial intentions of those in power might have been. Hayek denounced the totalitarian bias deriving from the extreme centralisation of power, when authoritarian mechanisms of governance are institutionally put in place to control individual behaviour and the use of resources.

Totalitarianism and the arbitrary exercise of power will produce adverse selection in ethical behaviour: this is the leitmotif of the book.

Totalitarian systems systematically encourage the social advance of servile people, betrayers and informers, as well as of people prone to violence, lacking ethical restraint (Hayek 1944a: Ch. 10). Hayek pointed both to the degenerative process in ethical conduct at work when totalitarian rule prevails and to the erosion of ethical values produced by collectivist ideologies, no matter what good intentions might lie behind them.

On this aspect Hayek's analysis had illustrious antecedents in European political thought, such as Montesquieu's analysis of the consistency between ethical behaviour and the world of social values supporting various political systems and ensuring their survival (Aron 1967). Discussing passions and the stability of political institutions, a number of eighteenth-century authors had addressed the same issue from various viewpoints (Lovejoy 1961; Hirschmann 1977).

Historically, there is hardly any need to demonstrate how relevant the problem raised by Hayek was in the period when he was writing. Historical experience in Russian society (a society of extremely young and limited democracy, with little or no liberal tradition when the October revolution broke out, marked for centuries by autocratic State power, not far as yet from feudal serfdom) fully confirmed Hayek's warning.[13] A whole literature on totalitarian societies has flourished addressing themes which touch upon Hayek's insights (Todorov 1994).

Just how relevant the problem is in so many other circumstances is clear enough if we look at the closed societies constituting totalitarian microcosms (such as certain religious sects, jails or lunatic asylums). The totalitarian intention is not necessarily openly declared in the rules or values governing such closed societies, but authoritarian behaviour easily prevails, as do extreme forms of misbehaviour practised by those in power. In totalitarian institutions there is a high risk of the working mechanism generating horrendous ethical deviations in behaviour as an effect of the inherent nature of the governance system.

In his letter on Hayek's book, although well aware of the strong feelings motivating Hayek in the circumstances, Keynes was looking in another direction. He suggested that sound ethical sentiments rooted in individual minds – the collective control exercised by a society imbued with liberal values – would avoid the risk of totalitarian deviations when moderately centralised methods for the management of resources were put in place. Keynes suggested to Hayek that educated public opinion, committed to liberal values, would exercise sufficient restraint on the ruling class and governing bodies to protect society against any totalitarian bias. Hayek's book could have a most positive effect by helping to keep these liberal values alive in the hearts and minds of the people. In fact Keynes valued the book more for its educational value in reinforcing liberal thinking than because he believed in the political proposals the book advanced, on which he expressed moderate but clear dissent. The emphasis on the possibility to disjoin the matter of moulding public opinion to strengthen liberal sentiments on the one hand, and management of economic affairs with moderate centralisation, on the other, is characteristic of Keynes's dissent from Hayek's crucial argument.

There was something decidedly paternalistic in the idea that the wise administration of public affairs might be put into the hands of an enlightened ruling class, which could (up to a point) concentrate power since it was educated and trained not to abuse it. Keynes, as we know, stressed the 'vital importance of establishing certain central controls in matters which are now left in the main to individual initiative' and the expediency, if not indeed urgency, to promote an 'enlargement of the functions of government' (CWK VII: 377 ff.). There was a problem of where to draw the line in his own proposals, since he was crystal clear in defending individualism ('purged of its defects and its abuses') as 'the best safeguard of personal liberty' (CWK VII: 380).

We have, then, no reason to be surprised at Keynes's sincere approval of Hayek's book. What is more surprising is the confidence Keynes implicitly expressed in the men in power as intelligent, dedicated, far-sighted people, neither arbitrarily abusing their increased power of control nor misbehaving while exercising their extended government functions. At Versailles the young Keynes wrote a dramatic letter to Duncan Grant expressing total mistrust in the group of international politicians present at the peace conference (Moggridge 1992: 311–12). We might conjecture that he recovered confidence in the political world through his later experience, or thanks to his close contacts with top-ranking government executives who carried through public decisions and activities as a well-trained body of permanent officers. He seemed very confident in the loyalty of civil servants to democracy and their commitment to the public welfare.

Historical experience and national background influenced Hayek's and Keynes's different perceptions of totalitarian biases. Hayek himself pointed out that in his writing he was motivated by direct experience of the evolution of German culture and public opinion subsequent to the First World War. He denounced the illiberal nature of the State in Germany well before the Nazis took power, and complained of the frailty that had been displayed by liberal ideals in central Europe since the nineteenth century, before totalitarianism dominated the scene.[14] With this historical background in mind, public opinion could not be relied on to control authoritarian deviations. Indeed, Hayek argued that a change in public opinion fuelled by socialist ideologies lay behind the changing balance between liberalism and totalitarianism in Germany. Lacking were the social mechanisms Keynes would have preferred to rely on to combine moderate centralisation of economic decisions with the maintenance of a liberal society.

Historians may expect difficulties in reconstructing the atmosphere that prevailed at some point in history but has since melted away. The 'emotional atmosphere', as Hayek called it (Hayek [1944a] 1994: 203) must have been tangible to have deeply impressed two minds as diverse as Schumpeter's and Hayek's. Both pointed to the intellectuals' disaffection as a primary source of the serious risk for the survival of liberal societies. Hayek feared repetition of the German experience in more liberal societies. The precious heritage of moderate behaviour by the public authorities and strong liberal feelings on the part of public opinion, which Keynes found so reassuring, might rapidly dry up. The liberal heritage was to be kept alive as much in people's minds as in institutional rules if it were not to give out, leaving society deprived of any protection against totalitarianism.

The dissent between Hayek and Keynes was no simple matter of rigid opposition between State intervention and free market. Rather, they were meeting on crucial themes still very much alive in the contemporary debate on liberalism.

Notes

1 The biographers of both Keynes and Hayek have dealt quite extensively with their personal and scientific relations, although their accounts consist largely of various specific episodes (Moggridge 1992; Skidelsky 1992; Ebenstein 2001; Caldwell 2004). A wholly comprehensive account is still lacking.
2 Keynes was referring to the *Monatsberichte des österreichishen Instituts für Konjunkturforschung.*
3 Possibly *Einige Bemerkungen über das Geldtheorie zur Konjunkturtheorie* or *Discussionsbemerkungen über 'Kredit und Konjunktur'* both published in 1928 in *Vereins für Sozialpolitik.*
4 In the *Treatise* Keynes mentioned Hayek's book in passing, in the context of Austrian theory, pointing again to his difficulties with the German language. Significantly, he mentioned Austrian bank rate and credit cycle theory as 'fairly close to the theory of this treatise'(Keynes [1930a] CWK V: 178).
5 Hayek's critique was unusual for a young foreign scholar judging a famous economist, as indeed Keynes already was. In fact, some scholars have conjectured that it was calculated to attract attention (Mongiovi 1990: 135; Ebenstein 2001: 71) We have no evidence to support the conjecture, while it is worth considering Hayek's tendency to uncompromising expression of his ideas throughout his life.
6 On the relations between Hayek and Keynes in the early 1930s see Caldwell (1995). For a different evaluation of their theoretical debate, see Kurz (2000). Cochran and Glahe (1999) contains ample reference to the monetary controversy in 1931.
7 'A product, I should prefer to say, has a period of production n if n time-units of notice of changes in the demand for it have to be given if it is to offer its maximum elasticity of employment' (CWK VII: 287).
8 B. Caldwell looked carefully into the reasons why Hayek did not review the *General Theory*, advancing, obviously, only conjectural hypotheses (Caldwell 1998). The research effort absorbing him in the late 1930s may well explain why Hayek did not choose to concentrate on Keynes's theory. As he wrote to J. Robinson in 1941, he was aware of moving in a radically different perspective ('a consistent system of subjectivism') after publishing 'Economics and knowledge' (see Ch. 16: 408).

9 In section 5 Hayek briefly discussed various possibilities regarding the price expectations held by entrepreneurs.
10 On Lindahl's criticism of Keynes's model see Ingrao and Ranchetti (1996: 778–9). Hicks, too, would later criticise Keynes's model on account of weaknesses and ambiguities in analysis of processes in time (Hicks 1974).
11 Hayek proposed 'a post-war capital levy on old wealth, payable partly in shares of the industrial capital of the countries' to face the risk of post-war inflation (Hayek [1939c] 1997: 166–7).
12 The project of a joint letter by a group of well-known economists to subscribe the plan never materialised (Moggridge 1992: 631 ff.).
13 Note, however, that in the book Hayek was more preoccupied with Germany, both because of its alarmingly rapid transformation from democratic to totalitarian State, and because after the German invasion the Soviet Union had become an ally.
14 Hayek, for instance, recalled with distaste the servility shown to Hohenzollern by the rector of Berlin University (Hayek [1944a] (1994): 209).

Table 9.1 Keynes–Hayek correspondence

From	*To*	*Year*	*Month*	*Day*	*Date*	*Archive*		*Published in*	*Item*
JMK	FAH	1927	February	24	Dated letter	Hayek–Stanford	30/19		801
JMK	FAH	1927	July	9	Dated letter	Hayek–Stanford	30/19		802
FAH	JMK	1928	July	12	Attributed	Hayek–Stanford	30/19		803
JMK	FAH	1929	March	26	Dated letter	Hayek–Stanford	30/19		804
JMK	FAH	1931	July	31	Dated letter	Hayek–Stanford	30/19		805
JMK	FAH	1931	December	10	Dated letter	Hayek–Stanford Keynes–King's	30/19 CO/3/117	CWK XIII: 257	806
FAH	JMK	1931	December	15	Dated letter	Keynes–King's Hayek–Stanford	CO/3/118–9 30/19	CWK XIII: 257–8	807
JMK	FAH	1931	December	16	Dated letter	Hayek–Stanford Keynes–King's	30/19 CO/3/120	CWK XIII: 258	808
FAH	JMK	1931	December	19	Dated letter	Keynes–King's	CO/3/121	CWK XIII: 259	809
JMK	FAH	1931	December	23	Dated letter	Hayek–Stanford Keynes–King's	30/19 CO/3/122	CWK XIII: 259	810
JMK	FAH	1931	December	25	Dated letter	Hayek–Stanford Keynes–King's	30/19 CO/3/123	CWK XIII: 260	811
FAH	JMK	1931	December	25	Dated letter	Keynes–King's Hayek–Stanford	CO/3/123 30/19	CWK XIII: 259–60	812
FAH	JMK	1932	January	7	Dated letter	Keynes–King's Hayek–Stanford	CO/3/124–6 30/19	CWK XIII: 260–2	813
JMK	FAH	1932	January	12	Dated letter	Hayek–Stanford Keynes–King's	30/19 CO/3/127–8	CWK XIII: 262–3	814
FAH	JMK	1932	January	23	Dated letter	Keynes–King's Hayek–Stanford	CO/3/129–30 30/19	CWK XIII: 263–4	815
JMK	FAH	1932	February	11	Dated letter	Hayek–Stanford Keynes–King's	30/19 CO/3/132	CWK XIII: 265	816
JMK	FAH	1932	March	29	Dated letter	Hayek–Stanford	30/19	CWK XIII: 266	817
JMK	FAH	1932	May	4	Dated letter	Hayek–Stanford	30/19		818

JMK	FAH	1932	September	22	Dated letter	Hayek–Stanford	30/19		819
JMK	FAH	1933	December	30	Dated letter	Hayek–Stanford	30/19		820
JMK	FAH	1934	January	24	Dated letter	Hayek–Stanford	30/19		821
JMK	FAH	1934	February	6	Dated letter	Hayek–Stanford	30/19		822
JMK	FAH	1934	February	8	Dated letter	Hayek–Stanford	30/19		823
JMK	FAH	1934	April	6	Dated letter	Hayek–Stanford	30/19		824
JMK	FAH	1935	January	10	Dated letter	Hayek–Stanford	30/19		825
JMK	FAH	1935	July	10	Dated letter	Hayek–Stanford	30/19		826
JMK	FAH	1935	July	17	Dated letter	Hayek–Stanford	30/19		827
JMK	FAH	1935	July	19	Dated letter	Hayek–Stanford	30/19		828
JMK	FAH	1935	October	7	Dated letter	Hayek–Stanford	30/19		829
JMK	FAH	1936	January	12	Dated letter	Hayek–Stanford	30/19		830
FAH	JMK	1936	February	2	Dated letter	Keynes–King's	GTE/2/2/229–30	CWK XXIX: 207–8	831
JMK	FAH	1936	May	14	Dated letter	Hayek–Stanford	30/19		832
JMK	FAH	1936	November	19	Dated letter	Hayek–Stanford	30/19		833
FAH	JMK	1936	December	10	Dated letter	Keynes–King's	L/36/94		834
JMK	FAH	1938	December	6	Dated letter	Hayek–Stanford	30/19		835
						Keynes–King's	UA/14/2/256		
FAH	JMK	1938	December	8	Dated letter	Keynes–King's	UA/14/2/257		836
JMK	FAH	1938	December	9	Dated letter	Hayek–Stanford	30/19		837
						Keynes–King's	UA/14/2/258–9		
FAH	JMK	1938	December	10	Dated letter	Keynes–King's	UA/14/2/260		838
FAH	JMK	1938	December	18	Dated letter	Keynes–King's	L/38/102		839
						Hayek–Stanford	30/19		
JMK	FAH	1939	April	11	Dated letter	Hayek–Stanford	30/19		840
						Keynes–King's	CO/3/150–1		
JMK	FAH	1939	September	20	Dated letter	Hayek–Stanford	30/19		841
						Keynes–King's	CO/3/152–4		
FAH	JMK	1939	September	24	Dated letter	Keynes–King's	CO/3/155–7		842
JMK	FAH	1939	October	9	Dated letter	Hayek–Stanford	30/19		843
						Keynes–King's	CO/3/158–9		
FAH	JMK	1939	October	15	Dated letter	Keynes–King's	CO/3/160–1		844

Table 9.1 continued

From	*To*	*Year*	*Month*	*Day*	*Date*	*Archive*		*Published in*	*Item*
JMK	FAH	1939	October	16	Dated letter	Hayek–Stanford	30/19		845
						Keynes–King's	CO/3/162		
FAH	JMK	1939	October	20	Dated letter	Keynes–King's	CO/3/163		846
JMK	FAH	1940	February	27	Dated letter	Keynes–King's	HP/4/65		847
FAH	JMK	1940	March	3	Dated letter	Keynes–King's	HP/4/66	CWK XXII: 106, (E)	848
JMK	FAH	1940	March	6	Dated letter	Hayek–Stanford	30/19		849
						Keynes–King's	HP/4/67		
FAH	JMK	1940	October	22	Dated letter	Keynes–King's	PP/45/137/1–2		850
JMK	FAH	1940	October	26	Dated letter	Hayek–Stanford	30/19		851
						Keynes–King's	PP/45/137/3		
JMK	FAH	1941	April	28	Dated letter	Hayek–Stanford	30/19		852
JMK	FAH	1942	August	27	Dated letter	Keynes–King's	MM/5/160		761
FAH	JMK	1943	January	1	Dated letter	Keynes–King's	CO/3/164–5		853
JMK	FAH	1943	January	15	Dated letter	Keynes–King's	CO/3/170–1		854
FAH	JMK	1943	January	18	Dated letter	Keynes–King's	CO/3/172		855
FAH	JMK	1943	March	13	Dated letter	Keynes–King's	MM/5/223		797
JMK	FAH	1943	March	21	Dated letter	Hayek–Stanford	30/19		856
JMK	FAH	1943	April	24	Dated letter	Hayek–Stanford	30/19		857
JMK	FAH	1944	April	4	Dated letter	Keynes–King's	MM/4/14–16	Shearmur 1997: 68–82, (E)	858
JMK	FAH	1944	May	20	Dated letter	Hayek–Stanford	30/19		859
JMK	FAH	1944	May	21	Dated letter	Hayek–Stanford	30/19		860
JMK	FAH	1944	June	28	Dated letter	Hayek–Stanford	30/19	CWK XXVII: 385–8	861
						Keynes–King's	CO/3/173–7		
FAH	JMK	1945	February	9	Dated letter	Keynes–King's	BA/1/166		862
						Hayek–Stanford	30/19		
FAH	JMK	1946	January	17	Dated letter	Keynes–King's	BA/1/183		863
						Hayek–Stanford	30/19		
FAH	JMK	1946	February	14	Dated letter	Keynes–King's	BA/1/207		864

Part II

Keynes's disciples

10 An enduring partnership

The correspondence between Kahn and J. Robinson

Annalisa Rosselli

The correspondence between J. Robinson and Richard Kahn from 1930 to 1946 consists of 518 letters, 461 by Robinson and 57 by Kahn (see Table 10.1). Most of the letters by Kahn were written from 1930 to 1933. After this year, we have only four letters from Kahn plus a newspaper cutting in 1945 with a very short note by him.

The correspondence is very unevenly distributed over time, concentrating in the periods when one or both were away from Cambridge, which – in peacetime – was mainly during the summer vacation and the shorter Christmas or Easter holidays. At such times correspondence came thick and fast – close on a letter a day, and sometimes more than one.

Kahn carefully preserved the correspondence he received from Robinson: almost all the letters examined here were found among his papers, including some he had written himself and asked to have back for his meticulous files. We may therefore assume that only a few letters from Robinson to Kahn were destroyed, apart from a period between September 1941 and the summer of 1945, corresponding to the time Kahn spent in Egypt (until January 1943) and a crucial phase in the war. Of these years nothing remains, so that their correspondence for the period under consideration virtually ends in 1941.[1]

By contrast Robinson did not keep files, and only nine letters were found among her papers, containing notes by Kahn on analytic aspects of the theory of imperfect competition together with the letter Kahn sent her the day after her first daughter was born.

Kahn carefully dated all his letters and most of his notes, while Robinson often noted day and month but never the year, which was sometimes – possibly later – added by Kahn. The latter, however, had the habit of keeping most of Robinson's letters in their envelopes so that dating has often been possible from the postmarks. In four of the various cases in which even day and month are missing no attribution has been possible.

Kahn's contribution to the making of *Economics of Imperfect Competition*

The origin of *The Economics of Imperfect Competition* (EIC, thereafter) and, above all, of the concept of marginal revenue, has been recounted on various occasions, also by Robinson herself (J. Robinson 1933a: v; see also A. Robinson 1992: 210 and A. Robinson 1994: 7). The idea emerged from an essay by a brilliant young student of Austin Robinson – Charles Gifford – sometime in 1930. The usefulness of this analytic tool immediately struck Austin Robinson and he lost no time in discussing it with his wife and Kahn, who happened to be invited to lunch that very day. For some time all three applied the new tool to various problems with no precise research plan in mind, until J. Robinson decided to collect all the results achieved in a co-ordinated book project.

The surviving correspondence between J. Robinson and Kahn bears out this reconstruction. We know that Robinson and Kahn met in 1929[2], although their relations must have remained on a fairly formal level until Kahn gained a Fellowship at King's College. It was only after that that Robinson added at the end of a letter replying to thanks to both herself and her husband: 'Please, refer to us as Joan and Austin' (letter 502, 25 March 1930). July saw all three deep in critical discussion of an article by Henderson on a classical case of joint production, and in particular debating the effects of a variation in the price of mutton on the price of wool. (The debate also involved Gerald Shove who, when questioned by Kahn, remarked interestingly enough that the answer depended on the type of sheep!) (letter 736, undated and 737, 29 July 1930). A few months later closer collaboration between Robinson and Kahn seems to have developed. In November 1930 Robinson wrote: 'Does this correspondence bore you? It gives me so much pleasure to discuss with somebody more intelligent than myself – (modified arrogance)' (letter 503).

The problem they were focusing on in this period was comparison between output according as to whether the industry is monopolistic or characterised by perfect competition – an issue that was to constitute Chapter 11 of EIC. The subjects discussed were termed Paradoxes, a label that Robinson was later to drop, and which made no appearance in EIC. We do not know the exact formulation of these paradoxes, although one example might be this point raised by Kahn:

> Under pure i.r. [=increasing returns] monopoly output must be less than competitive output (for straight line curves the one is half the other). Under pure d.r. [=diminishing returns] monopoly output must be less than competitive output (though a greater proportion, in general, than under pure i.r). But if both i.r. and d.r. are present, monopoly output may be greater than competitive output: this is the

more likely to happen the greater the amount of i.r present (and, therefore, for a given supply curve, the greater the amount of i.r).

(letter 504, 11 November 1930)

This collaboration probably proved congenial to both from the outset. They both shared a method of analysis based on meticulous classification of all the possible combinations of two or more elements, the reasoning often going: if X can be A or B and Y can be C or D, let us examine all four combinations AC, AD, BC and BD. Behind this method of reasoning – 'hair-splitting' as Keynes defined it (letter 504, 11 November 1930) – there were, however, probably two different needs. Robinson had no other analytic tools at her disposal. She knew absolutely nothing of calculus,[3] and headway could only be made in a rigorous manner by breaking the problem down into simple cases which might be examined one by one. Kahn had been educated as a physicist and this method probably satisfied his need for order, as well as paving the way to pinpointing real cases corresponding to the theoretical cases examined.[4]

In April 1931 the book project got going, but Robinson still saw it as work for a team of three: 'I am now toying with the idea of producing a complete book of all this stuff. Austin will put in some letterpress to give it a realistic flavour, and give the reader a rest between theorems. Don't you think it would be fun?' (letter 748, 30 March 1931) and two days later, having jotted down a table of contents and the first draft of Chapter 2, she went on to explain: 'It is not I who am bringing out this book. It is a syndicate of you, A[ustin] and me.' (letter 752, 2 April 1931). Nevertheless, Kahn's preference was to turn down co-authorship, retaining for himself the role of attentive reader and critic: 'I shall have a good deal to say about individual passages when I think that there is undue compression or that the exposition might be made clearer in some other way.' (letter 505, 10 April 1931).

Few letters have come down to us from the period of the actual drafting of EIC, which took Robinson until November 1932, in general containing odd notes, graphs and calculations. Both Kahn and Robinson were in Cambridge and correspondence was limited to the short vacation periods when their – presumably very frequent and lengthy meetings[5] – could not take place. In the one brief epistolary exchange remaining, from September 1931, we find ample confirmation of what Robinson herself wrote in the first lines of EIC:

> I have had the constant assistance of Mr. R.F. Kahn. The whole technical apparatus was built up with his aid, and many of the major problems – notably the problems of Price Discrimination and Exploitation – were solved as much by him as by me.
>
> (J. Robinson 1933a: v)

The surviving correspondence, consisting of eight letters in 3 days, refers neither to price discrimination nor to exploitation, but to the change in the level of employment when the industry passes from perfect competition to monopoly – an issue that also interested Kahn at the aggregate level. A point emerging from these letters is that his contribution in the initial phase of drafting, when efforts concentrated on a rigorous result, was indeed enormous, and certainly greater than that of the others who, in accordance with the customary Cambridge practice of collaboration, contributed to EIC: Piero Sraffa and Austin Robinson. As Austin Robinson pointed out: 'he [Kahn] eliminated numerous initial mistakes' (A. Robinson 1994: 8). Kahn had mathematical demonstration at his command, although we cannot tell whether his choice to apply geometry rather than calculus,[6] which he was certainly grounded in, was dictated by a personal preference for the graphically representable or the decision to use only such tools (high-school geometry, trigonometry) as were accessible to Robinson and the average economist.

However, once the result was demonstrated, the exposition and the capacity to raise new questions lay entirely in the domain of J. Robinson, who acquired growing confidence *vis-à-vis* Kahn as the EIC was drafted. By the time the proofs were being read – by Kahn – it was a decidedly independent Robinson who could write, to the consternation of Kahn:

> It is a great comfort to feel that any errors which you fail to spot will take a long time to be discovered by anyone else. But some of your own corrections are wrong (this is also a comfort to me). I hope you won't be annoyed where I reject your advice.
>
> (letter 552, 8 February 1933)

It may also have been on account of this, and not only of the usual modesty, that Kahn expressed his reluctance to accept Robinson's acknowledgements:

> you are attributing to me very much more than I am responsible for. What I did was to read what you had written. Most of my attempts to do constructive work (e.g. in regard to Discrimination and Exploitation) ended in failure and it was almost invariably you who found the clue. Remember that there are plenty of footnote refs. to me. Apart from everything else I intensely dislike the way you start straight off with my name. Shouldn't you mention some of the others first?
>
> (letter 593, 30 March 1933)

Moreover, there was a reciprocal exchange of help. While preoccupied with her labours on the EIC Robinson does not seem to have taken much notice of the work Kahn was struggling with, but in 1934 she was more generous in her help to Kahn as he worked on the article 'Some Notes on

Ideal Output' for the *Economic Journal* (Kahn 1935) and it was her turn to decline excessive acknowledgements:

> It is terribly annoying not to be there to help but I am very much delighted that you are enjoying it and making an important thing of it. Of course it's my article in the sense that I ought to have done it and saved you all this delay in doing your own stuff. If it's mine in any other sense you know very well that I give it you with both hands.
>
> (letter 642, 4 September 1934)

Kahn's visit to the United States

At the end of 1932 Kahn set sail for the United States, where he stayed until mid-April 1933. He spent a few weeks in Chicago, took part in a conference of the American Statistical Association in Cincinnati, was subsequently the guest of Taussig and Schumpeter at Harvard, and concluded his stay in America with the last month spent in New York (see Ch. 1: 24–5). The correspondence between J. Robinson and Kahn from this period has probably survived in its entirety, carried ahead at the rate of several letters a week, although it could not have the immediate question-and-answer exchange characterising the English correspondence given the time taken by the postal service. Rather, it appears as a series of long accounts. From one side of the Atlantic Robinson sends Kahn packs of EIC galley proofs to correct, reports her successes and retails Cambridge chronicles and gossip, while from the other Kahn sends his final advice for the publication of EIC and gives his impressions of the population, academic life and state of economic science in the USA. In the background – but very much in the background – were the major events marking the period: the Reichstag fire, the persecution of the Jews in Germany, the crisis in the USA when Roosevelt took over from Hoover and the banks were closed for some days to stem panic and the run on the dollar.

Kahn's first impression of the United States was disastrous and did not change much during his stay: he found nothing there to his liking, at least until he arrived in New York. He did not like the food, the chlorine in the water, the men's ties, the women's looks, the predominance of the shower over the bath-tub, and above all he did not like the Americans: 'The trouble about all these places is that when one has been there a week one has learnt all there is to know. The people are so desperately dim, and far too frequently grubby into the bargain' (letter 558, 15 February 1933). 'The fact of the matter is, in respect to society, I have had to lower my standards considerably, in respect to both age, eminence, intelligence, and quality' (letter 526, 8 January 1933).

Kahn felt attuned only to two types of people: those who were not American – better still if they were English, and even better if they were educated at Oxford or Cambridge – and those of old families (in this, it seems, sharing an opinion of Keynes (letter 523, 4 January 1933)). England, and above all Cambridge, seem to him infinitely superior: 'After watching the struggle of these wretched people I shall for the first time realise my good fortune in being a member of the King's High Table, and take more pleasure in its society than I have in the past' (letter 571, 27 February 1933). The academic world struck him as particularly bleak and squalid, and returning to his opinions on American society as a whole he remarked: 'There is not the slightest doubt that the nicest Americans are the wealthiest (a lot of them Jewish.) [. . .] I believe that Americans being what they are, it is only the unfitted who are relegated to academic life' (letter 583, 14 March 1933).

Of the academic life he endorsed neither the research organisation nor the teaching methods. He felt that too much money went on providing professors with secretaries and research assistants (engaged in futile pursuit of data) and too little on creating an environment that would in both spirit and substance favour the exchange of ideas and a serene quest for knowledge. The material living conditions of the teaching staff struck him as shabby, especially in Chicago, where the professors worked in cramped rooms and had to gulp down quick meals in the canteen rather than relishing the leisure of the High Tables. Comparison with Cambridge, UK, reminded him of Virginia Woolf's comparison between the men's colleges and the mean conditions in the women's:

> But partly it is, I am sure, due to the grubbiness of their style of living. One would prefer not to be obliged to think in such terms, but as I swallow the revolting food that is served up in all their halls and clubs my mind turns insistently to the theme of A Room of One's Own.
>
> (letter 559, 17 February 1933)

Above all it was the didactic methods that failed to convince him, the students having no opportunity for discussion with their professors apart from the seminar Schumpeter held with his pupils at Harvard. Alternative didactic methods were only greeted with the sneer:

> They have introduced the use of the movie into the curriculum at the Business School. They showed À nous la liberté to demonstrate to the students that after all there was something to be said against mass production. They quite realised the importance of the ethical side. It is hard to take them seriously.
>
> (letter 571, 27 February 1933)

What aroused his greatest mistrust, however, was an intellectual climate characterised by work in isolation. There was no forum for debate like the Keynes Club or the Marshall Society, and each seemed utterly to ignore his neighbour:

> The pursuit of learning is regarded as a business, to be discussed with underlings at 'conferences', rather than as a social art which pervades one's whole life [. . .] Another trouble that holds up intellectual activity is the terrible business of career hunting and the fear of saying the wrong thing (even though genuinely believed). There are nasty undercurrents of bickering and professional jealousy.
>
> (letter 559, 17 February 1933)[7]

None of the economists encountered made much of an impression on him, particularly in Chicago, where he went no further than a handshake with Irving Fisher and the odd meeting with Viner and Schultz, initially favourably impressed by the intelligence of both the latter, but appalled at their manners and the superior attitude they took to Cambridge, UK:

> they both have quite good minds and if they had nicer characters they would be really good. They are neither of them very old. At the very outset they made it clear to me that nothing being done at Cambridge would be of any interest to them. Either they had done it all themselves long ago or it was done even longer ago by Cournot or somebody.[8]
>
> (letter 530, 15 January 1933)

Subsequently his assessment of Schultz changed, to the extent that he eventually defined him a 'charlatan', squandering money on collecting useless data. Knight struck him as a decidedly odd character who was going through a crisis over the very fundaments of the discipline. 'Knight is friendly in a forbidding kind of way. He is very disgruntled with economic theory – in fact he is disgruntled about most things but his cynicism is of the pleasanter variety' (letter 530, 15 January 1933). The only one to elicit any degree of liking was Douglas, who appeared to him as an isolated figure, regarded 'as a somewhat silly sort of communist politician' (ibid.).

At Harvard he was the guest of Schumpeter, with whom he was already acquainted, and who was in turn a guest of Taussig (Swedberg 1991: Ch. 6). Taussig, then 72 years old, made the greatest impression on him, although he rejected an article Kahn had submitted to the *Quarterly Journal of Economics* as excessively discursive and somewhat arrogant in tone. Of the younger generation – practically his own – it was the recently arrived Leontieff who aroused his admiration: 'Leontieff is very definitely a man to watch. I suspect that he is really brilliant' (letter 558, 15 February 1933). Once again, however, Leontieff seemed to him to confirm the rule that anyone worth his salt, but of European origin and culture ('he played me Bach on his gramophone'), was doomed to isolation: his lessons were deserted,[9] and he had hardly any friends.

In New York Kahn was incomparably happier, possibly because the end of his stay was near. It may also have been the multiethnic atmosphere that he appreciated, the nights in Harlem and meetings with the Wall Street personalities Keynes had recommended to him. Thus his impressions were far more agreeable: 'Wesley Mitchell had a lunch party for me at Columbia, and he struck me this time as a rather superior type of American professor, genial and moderately human! Hotelling is a perfect dear, which is just as it should be' (letter 589, 23–24 March 1933).[10]

At the same time, the state of economic science and in particular of monetary theory seemed hopeless to Kahn, fresh from the Circus debates and involved in the work on the future *General Theory* of Keynes. Few of the older generation of economists had read the *Treatise*, the Quantity Theory of Money reigned supreme and, now that the depression had reached its worst, the only remedies proposed were balancing the budget and reducing the gold content of the dollar to coax prices upwards:

> I see less hope than ever for this country. People in authority are divided into two classes (e.g. the Senate):- those who are in favour of balanced budgets and sound financial policy and those who are in favour of reducing the gold content of the dollar, demonetising silver, and the like. There is nobody, as I can see, who is prepared to advocate courageous spending.
>
> (letter 596, 4 April 1933)

Greater satisfaction came from his meetings with business people who he kept interviewing in the hope of finding a solution to the problem of price determination:

> My experience so far has been extremely limited, but I am now absolutely convinced that every business man is at a kink (a pretty kinky kink too) on his demand curve, or thinks he is. This creates a quandary. It is quite true that it does not pay either to raise or lower the price. But what on earth determines the position of the kink? This is going to be my main theoretical problem.
>
> (letter 571, 27 February 1933)

On the other side of the Atlantic, J. Robinson showed moderate sympathy for the lamenting Kahn. Her attention was now focusing on the events unfolding around publication in the *Economic Journal* of her article (J. Robinson 1932a) anticipating some of the findings of EIC. Pigou threw both Joan and Austin Robinson into panic announcing that he had found an error: when new firms enter a sector the demand curve can shift above and below the average cost curve in such a way as never to reach the point of tangency guaranteeing equilibrium for the monopolistic firm in the long period. After a long discussion that saw the couple in some difficulty ('when our case seemed to be going badly Austin remarked with fervour I wish we had Kahn here' wrote Robinson in letter 532, 14–16 January 1933) Pigou came round to positive appraisal of the results, actually offering a demonstration in terms of differential calculus that he wished to see included in EIC.[11] Far more complicated was the discussion with Shove, who required Keynes to publish in the *Economic Journal* a note protesting at what he interpreted as criticism of his ideas by Robinson (see Ch. 14: 361–2).

Apart from the documentary interest regarding facts, people and ideas to be found in this correspondence between Cambridge and the United States, however, there is the further interest in what it can tell us of the personalities of the two correspondents and the points that brought them together in this period. There can be no doubting their reciprocal respect, as indeed there can be no doubt about Kahn's very strong feelings towards Robinson at the time, although his expressions of admiration for Robinson's intellectual labours were independent of amorous sentiments. Robinson seems to have been greatly preoccupied with the difficulty of emerging in the Cambridge environment, winning the good opinion of Keynes and fostering the triumph of the new ideas she had helped deliver to the light of day. She was gratified by the respect and recognition she was beginning to receive from circles extending beyond that of her husband and a few friends: 'I seem to be springing into fame at a startling rate. But my goodness if my small article raises such a hornet's nest what will happen when the book comes out!' (letter 563, 15 February 1933). She needed the constant encouragement of Kahn and responded with fond, humorous indulgence to his manias and excessive worries. Kahn was full of protective attitudes towards her, worried that she might catch flu, preoccupied with her career, anxious that she send the offprints of her work to the US, and concerned about her absent-mindedness and carelessness ('By the way, you really are rather lucky that all the proofs turned up. Four of your large envelopes and one of your ordinary small ones arrived unstuck. Do be more careful' (letter 550, 7 February 1933). Nevertheless, he could not bring himself to give full vent to his disappointment and wounded pride when Taussig rejected his article, hiding behind his customary modesty. There is a basis of truth, besides her usual self-irony, to the playful way Robinson summed up their reciprocal attitudes: 'I notice that as you become more modest and restrained I become more arrogant and outrageous' (letter 577, 3 March 1933) and she drew a neat diagram with increasing and decreasing curves to illustrate the point.

Family life

All the correspondence between Robinson and Kahn abounds with references to family life, Cambridge and the people there and, indeed, this is virtually the only interest in the correspondence subsequent to Kahn's return from the United States.

Kahn's letters have not come down to us, with very few exceptions. One is the missive written two days after Robinson had given birth to her first-born child, Ann. Kahn reassures Robinson that she is missing nothing important, and allays her fears that maternity might remove her from academic life by discussing with her the examination papers of the Tripos in Economics then in progress (it was Robinson herself who raised the subject 24 hours after giving birth to her daughter). Ann often appears with brief, loving observations in the subsequent correspondence which, after the birth of her second child, Barbara, in 1937, transmits a picture of Robinson apparently at peace with her role as a mother:

> Barbara is trying to tear this up as I write which makes it difficult. She is a fascinating character. I enjoy being idle with them. I no longer suffer from wondering if I shall ever be able to start working again so please excuse me being silly for the time being. I am relying on you to be making up for it.
>
> (letter 705, 7 September 1938)

Just a few weeks later, however, the onset of a serious mental illness belied these easeful words (see Ch. 12: 320–1).

It was, however, in family life that Robinson seems to have found peace and quiet after nearly two years of physical and mental illness, in the long summer of 1940 spent in Cornwall – the first summer of war and air raids for Britain, with the fear of imminent invasion. It was the first time that Robinson had found herself alone with her daughters – A&B, as she fondly called them – and she was fascinated and amused by them, intrigued even by her own reactions: 'If it were not for the nightmare background, this is very enjoyable. I have hardly ever had the children really to myself before – always grand mothers and nurses hanging around, so it's quite an experience' (letter 1522, 21 June 1940). And again, somewhat taken aback at having become the object of such attachment: '[Barbara] is a bit clinging as Ann was when I came back from Booke House,[12] but I hope an orgy of my company will get her over it' (letter 1525, 25 June 1940). However, her reactions were much the same as those of many mothers to follow her in finding some of the gratification of life outside the family and being unwilling to forego it. Robinson was full of tender affection for her children, and enjoyed relating to Kahn the usual funny stories that are so much a part of childhood for all, but found it 'exhausting' to be taking constant care of them, and dreaded the idea that she might not find a babysitter who would give her time to get on with her customary pursuits.

In the meantime Austin Robinson was drawing away. His absences were many and long, and he would often take his own good time in reporting his movements. Robinson may not have been the conventional wife, but she always seemed concerned about her husband's moods and never neglected her tasks as the one person in charge of housekeeping and family life. The decisions – when and where to go on holiday, how to plan their days together – always fell to Austin Robinson, but the subsequent action – moves, journeys, finding domestic staff – was always up to Joan. Indeed, the only objection she had against the traditional role of the woman seems to have gone no further than claiming some living space free from the cares of the family, to dedicate to intellectual pursuits: 'I find intensive family life quite amusing, but I can see it wouldn't suit me for an occupation' (letter 697, 11 August 1936).[13] We find no criticism of the different social roles of men and women, even when the difference is striking. On the outbreak of war, one by one her peers and partners in academic debate were summoned to take on roles of considerable importance in the management of the war economy: Austin Robinson moved to Whitehall, then to the Cabinet Office and subsequently became chief economic adviser at the Ministry of Production; Kahn worked on the Board of Trade and later at the Ministry of Supply. They received first-hand news, took part in discussions of crucial importance for the country and made the personal acquaintance of governors and ministers. In contrast, J. Robinson's contribution to the war effort was to join the Cambridge fire-watching squads. Although transfer of the LSE to Cambridge livened things up, she still felt left alone with Piero Sraffa, excluded as a foreigner. Bitter feelings emerged when she wrote to Kahn: 'Piero is a great stand by. Though I don't really see a terrific lot of him we give each other the feeling of not being abandoned on a desert island' (letter 1470, 26 January 1940).

Robinson's unconventional attitudes and social criticism emerged in other contexts. She took part in the Labour Party meetings, without a great deal of enthusiasm, and in the socialist marches. Her ideas about bringing up children were also very advanced: 'I haven't any natural authority. Children never do what I tell them because I tell them. The trouble is I always see their point of view and get led into an argument. It has some practical drawbacks, but I don't really disapprove of it' (letter 1522, 21 June 1940). And then there set in those various eccentric habits that were to impress her on the memory of generations of economists attending Cambridge: she became a vegetarian, loved sleeping in the open air, even in wintertime, took no interest in her clothing, preferred trousers to skirts and made good-natured fun of Kahn who, although normally very tolerant, did not hide his concern over her wayward style of dress (letter 1539, 12 July 1940).

Academic life in Cambridge

Of all the figures in Cambridge academic life, the one both of them nourished an infinite respect for in intellectual and personal terms alike was J.M. Keynes. Having assessed the level of discussion the field of monetary theory inspired in the United States, Kahn wrote:

> I did think we are sometimes inclined to forget Maynard's greatness (after all, we are in a sense his valets and it cannot be expected that we should fully realise his heroism). It is a terrifying thought, but if Maynard had continued with probability would we all be content with the filthy kind of bilge I have to put up with so much of? I find it a terrifying problem.
>
> (letter 553, 10 February 1933)

After the Circus experience, both felt committed to disseminating and perfecting the new theory. However, Kahn felt weighed down by the responsibility of helping Keynes write his new book and tried to get Robinson involved in the task:

> Naturally you cannot raise the point, but if Maynard hints that he would like you to look at his stuff I do wish you would. I must confess that I am a bit appalled at the prospect of having the sole responsibility thrust on to me after my return.
>
> (letter 574, 2 March 1933)

Robinson would have liked to play a significant role in the revision of the *Treatise*, a work that she considered 'an extraordinary combination of genius, confusion and sophistry' (letter 637, 1934). The surviving correspondence between them, however, bears few traces of Robinson's contribution to the construction of the *General Theory*, apart from showing that it was she who supplied the quotation from Marshall appearing on p. 19 as exemplification of Say's Law. Nevertheless, some interest might be found in an exchange revealing just how in 1933 she was still struggling to grasp the new concept of effective demand:

> I am beginning to have doubts about Maynard's long period equilibrium with under-employment. Wouldn't it lead to a fall in money wages? I.e. it isn't really equilibrium. You can't be said to be in equilibrium, with the price level tending towards 0.
>
> (letter 547, 31 January 1933)

and Kahn answered:

> Then Maynard's long-period equilibrium. The simplest assumption is that there is a definite upward sloping supply curve for each factor. But unless the elasticity of supply of labour is due to trade-union actions (as of course it is, in practice) it is hard to see why people should be willing to accept less work than they want. (I wonder if it is possible to weave in here your point about a falling 'supply curve' of labour.) You have in mind the extreme case where the supply of labour is completely inelastic. The answer is of course that in such a

> situation wages and prices would fall to zero if investment were deficient. If they don't it is up to you, not Maynard, to explain why. Is there, as a matter of fact, a chronic tendency for wages and firms to sag, which is only overcome by violent jerks at times of exceptional prosperity? But if competition in buying labour is imperfect it is, I think, quite possible to have static equilibrium with unemployment and yet no trade-union. I have been thinking for some time that this would provide an awfully good subject for an article – rather an important one.
>
> (letter 561, 20 February 1933)

The other figure assuming the status of master was Gerald Shove who often appears in their correspondence at the beginning of their relationship. However, while admiration for Keynes mingled with awe, in the case of Shove the respect due to a teacher combined with affectionate indulgence for his touchiness and chronic incapacity to make up his mind and give definitive form to his ideas: '[Shove] has already written the review [of EIC] but is keeping it by him to reconsider. I suppose it will come out in a year or two' Robinson wrote (letter 610, 25 August 1933).

Comments on the other representatives of academic life are of minor importance: a few references to Pigou and Robertson, for whom in the early 1930s Robinson shows affection and admiration; a few comments about other economists calling at Cambridge on a short visit or for a lesson at the Marshall Society, and who, if not British, could hardly claim any respect: 'It is wonderful to see someone produce such an impressive facade with so little behind it' (letter 545, 28 January 1933) Robinson remarked after having listened to the presentation of an American visitor. The only exception seems to be Kalecki – 'my Pole' or 'my protegé' as Robinson called him[14] – a source of constant worries for Robinson who was somewhat relieved when she saw him finally – in 1940 – ensconced at Oxford, from where Kalecki sent her 'short and bitter' letters (letter 1546, 27 July 1940).

After Austin Robinson, however, the person most often mentioned by Robinson and Kahn in their correspondence is Piero Sraffa.

On other works by J. Robinson

After the publication of EIC we find relatively few references to the works of Robinson in the correspondence with Kahn, partly because many of the letters were written during rest and holiday times, and partly because Robinson and Kahn worked on their ideas jointly and discussed them together so often that further communication was superfluous. The unfailing advice of Kahn still remained important for Robinson when she had achieved fame and repute, to the extent that in one of the few periods when Kahn was absent during the war she wrote:

> I am working on my article,[15] which is coming out quite nicely. I make use of Piero and Kaldor and Kalecki as a synthetic substitute for your criticism. It is not so good but one has to put up with it in wartime.
>
> (letter 1610, 13 December 1940)

The news is mostly about the reception given her works, and in particular the 'baby book', *Essays on the Theory of Employment*, never raising issues of a theoretical nature, with just the odd reference to the study of Marx. In 1940 Robinson decided to set out on a more systematic study of Marx, at least as a 'holiday task.' (letter 1533, 5 July 1940). Her study, which was to lead to the publication of *An Essay on Marxian Economics* in 1942, soon developed into the book project, whose aims Robinson initially defined thus: 'My next project is to make a dictionary to Marx so that he can be read by economists. Value = man hours, Surplus value = product − real wages etc.' (letter 1614, 18 December 1940). Subsequently her aim grew more ambitious, and in addition to making Marx comprehensible to economists she set out to demonstrate the economic validity of his arguments to Marxists themselves: 'there is a lot of excellent stuff in Marx, e.g. that the quantity of money is determined by prices, not viceversa, but none of the Marxists seem to understand him' (letter 1627, 13 March 1941). So it was that Robinson began to seek out orthodox Marxists to see how they reacted to her ideas, having ascertained that Dobb would not be of any use to her: 'I had some conversation with Dobb but he is really useless: always running with the hare and hunting with the hounds' (letter 1614, 18 December 1940).

Finally, when the book Robinson was writing at her usual brisk pace was near the end, the aim became even more radical: 'I am working on my book on Marx. Its chief purpose is to show that economics is no good – either Marxist or ours – except for short period analysis. This ought to please Maynard' (letter 1638, 22 May 1941).

It is doubtful that it could have pleased anybody else.

Notes

1 The extant correspondence between Robinson and Kahn resumes in 1946 and continues copiously until Robinson's death.

2 According to A. Robinson (1994: 7), in an article penned just a few weeks before his death, J. Robinson and Kahn attended Sraffa's lessons during the same period. That she followed Sraffa's course is certain, and on many occasions recalled by her. However, we do not have archival evidence of when this happened – whether in 1928–29 or 1929–30. Sraffa's notes containing comments on the essays by his 1928–29 students mention Kahn, but not Robinson (Marcuzzo 2005; Ch. 6).

3 See letter 661, 8 July 1935: ' I did a bit of calculus but decided that it would be more painless to go through it all with you step by step. We might sit on the hillside in Austria and do it.'

4 Concern that his work should not appear a mere intellectual game is constant

in Kahn: 'I should rather like to suggest that you put in a spot of realism – just to show that it is not all a parlour game and nothing more' (letter 756, 16 September 1931).

5 'Can you spare me the whole of Tuesday? Come here in the morning and have lunch here anyway' asked Robinson 'in a damn awful mess' (letter 763, 19 September 1931).

6 Almost all the EIC demonstrations are geometrical. The few exceptions are expressly attributed to Kahn (see J. Robinson 1933a: 41).

7 Kahn's impression that work was conducted in isolation is borne out by a reconstruction of Harvard life provided by Edward Mason, a young professor at the time of Kahn's visit: 'I have the impression that at Cambridge (and perhaps also at Chicago) production frequently, if not usually, arises out of group discussion from which the author emerges, if not as an interpreter of group opinion, at least as one whose ideas have been shaped and reshaped in the give and take of discussion. Research at Harvard had not usually had the benefit of this process' (Mason 1982: 425).

8 The same criticisms are repeated to Sraffa: 'Viner has a good head, but is quite hopelessly conceited' (letter 462 from RFK to PS, 17 February 1933).

9 'A very young foreigner called Leontieff who was recently appointed here started last term with a class of twelve and now has two' (letter 553, 10 February 1933).

10 In fact, Robinson showed a certain scepticism in the face of such enthusiasm: 'I am so glad Hotelling is nice. I wonder how much of it you will be able to believe when you are back here' (letter 595, 2 April 1933).

11 The note by Pigou was in fact included in the March 1933 issue of the *Economic Journal* (Pigou 1933b). (See Ch. 13: 336.)

12 Booke House is the clinic where Robinson spent several months in 1938–39 during her nervous breakdown.

13 And a few days later she adds: 'Virginia Woolf is quite right about family life' (letter 733, 19 August 1936).

14 'My Pole is a really intelligent man (tho' lacking in charm). His claim to have anticipated a lot of the *General Theory* is substantiated by an article in *Econometrica* written in 1933. He is really possible to talk to. What a change. He is interested in the James-Roy business about investment inducing investment' (letter 674, 16 September 1936).

15 The article was 'The financial problem of 1941' (J. Robinson 1941b).

Table 10.1 Kahn–J. Robinson correspondence

From	*To*	*Year*	*Month*	*Day*	*Date*	*Archive*	*Published in*	*Item*
JVR	RFK				not yet attributed	Kahn–King's	RFK/13/90/1/21	518
JVR	RFK				not yet attributed	Kahn–King's	RFK/13/90/2/134	663
JVR	RFK				not yet attributed	Kahn–King's	RFK/13/90/2/110–1	671
JVR	RFK				not yet attributed	Kahn–King's	RFK/13/90/2/151	673
JVR	RFK	1930	March	15	Attributed	Kahn–King's	RFK/13/90/1/1–2	501
JVR	RFK	1930	March	25	Attributed	Kahn–King's	RFK/13/90/1/3–4	502
JVR	RFK	1930	July		Attributed	Kahn–King's	RFK/16/1/1	736
RFK	JVR	1930	July	29	Dated letter	Kahn–King's	RFK/16/1/2–4	737
JVR	RFK	1930	November		Attributed	Robinson–King's	JVR/vii/228/1/6–8	503
RFK	JVR	1930	November	9	Dated letter	Kahn–King's	RFK/16/1/22–3	739
JVR	RFK	1930	November	10	Attributed	Robinson–King's	JVR/vii/228/1/1–4	734
RFK	JVR	1930	November	10	Dated letter	Robinson–King's	JVR/vii/228/1/5–7	735
RFK	JVR	1930	November	11	Dated letter	Robinson–King's	JVR/vii/228/1/9–12	504
JVR	RFK	1930	December	26	Postmark	Kahn–King's	RFK/16/1/24–5	740
JVR	RFK	1931			Attributed	Kahn–King's	RFK/16/1/28	741
JVR	RFK	1931			Attributed	Kahn–King's	RFK/16/1/33–4	743
JVR	RFK	1931			Attributed	Kahn–King's	RFK/16/1/52	744
JVR	RFK	1931			Attributed	Kahn–King's	RFK/16/1/53–4	745
JVR	RFK	1931			Attributed	Kahn–King's	RFK/16/1/57–8	747
JVR	RFK	1931			Attributed	Kahn–King's	RFK/16/1/61–2	749
RFK	JVR	1931			Attributed	Kahn–King's	RFK/16/1/91	759
JVR	RFK	1931			Attributed	Kahn–King's	RFK/16/1/128	765
RFK	JVR	1931			Attributed	Kahn–King's	RFK/16/1/131–45	766
JVR	RFK	1931	January		Attributed	Kahn–King's	RFK/16/1/66–7	754
RFK	JVR	1931	February	14	Dated letter	Kahn–King's	RFK/16/1/29–31	742
JVR	RFK	1931	March	28	Attributed	Kahn–King's	RFK/16/1/55–6	746
JVR	RFK	1931	March	30	Attributed	Kahn–King's	RFK/16/1/59–60	748
JVR	RFK	1931	March	31	Attributed	Kahn–King's	RFK/16/1/68	750

JVR	RFK	1931	April	1	Attributed	Kahn–King's	RFK/16/1/69 and RFK/16/1/5 and RFK/16/1/100–5	751
RFK	JVR	1931	April	1	Dated letter	Kahn–King's	RFK/16/1/65	753
JVR	RFK	1931	April	2	Attributed	Kahn–King's	RFK/16/1/68–9	752
RFK	JVR	1931	April	10	Dated letter	Robinson–King's	JVR/vii/228/1/13–14	505
JVR	RFK	1931	September	15	Postmark	Kahn–King's	RFK/16/1/70–1	755
RFK	JVR	1931	September	16	Dated letter	Kahn–King's	RFK/16/1/72–5	756
RFK	JVR	1931	September	16	Dated letter	Kahn–King's	RFK/16/1/76–7	757
RFK	JVR	1931	September	16	Dated letter	Kahn–King's	RFK/16/1/78–80	758
JVR	RFK	1931	September	17	Attributed	Kahn–King's	RFK/16/1/94–9	760
JVR	RFK	1931	September	17	Attributed	Kahn–King's	RFK/16/1/106–8	762
RFK	JVR	1931	September	18	Attributed	Kahn–King's	RFK/16/1/116–27	764
JVR	RFK	1931	September	19	Attributed	Kahn–King's	RFK/16/1/109–15	763
RFK	JVR	1931	October		Attributed	Robinson–King's	JVR/vii/228/1/19	1676
RFK	JVR	1932			Attributed	Robinson–King's	JVR/vii/228/1/15–16	507
JVR	RFK	1932			Attributed	Kahn–King's	RFK/13/90/2/109	511
JVR	RFK	1932			Attributed	Kahn–King's	RFK/13/90/1/277–80	519
JVR	RFK	1932			Attributed	Kahn–King's	RFK/13/90/1/27	520
JVR	RFK	1932	January	25	Postmark	Kahn–King's	RFK/13/90/1/5–6	506
JVR	RFK	1932	March	25	Attributed	Kahn–King's	RFK/13/90/1/15	514
JVR	RFK	1932	March	31	Attributed	Kahn–King's	RFK/13/90/1/9–10	508
JVR	RFK	1932	March	31	Attributed	Kahn–King's	RFK/13/90/1/1/7–8	509
JVR	RFK	1932	April	1	Attributed	Kahn–King's	RFK/13/90/1/16	515
JVR	RFK	1932	April	6	Attributed	Kahn–King's	RFK/13/90/1/11–12	512
JVR	RFK	1932	April	7	Attributed	Kahn–King's	RFK/13/90/1/13–14	513
JVR	RFK	1932	April	9	Attributed	Kahn–King's	RFK/13/90/1/17–18	516
JVR	RFK	1932	April	15	Attributed	Kahn–King's	RFK/13/90/2/107–8	510
JVR	RFK	1932	July		Attributed	Kahn–King's	RFK/16/1/6–21	738
JVR	RFK	1932	November		Attributed	Kahn–King's	RFK/13/90/1/19–20	517

Table 10.1 continued

From	*To*	*Year*	*Month*	*Day*	*Date*	*Archive*	*Published in*	*Item*
JVR	RFK	1940	May	13	Postmark	Kahn–King's RFK/13/90/4/139–41		1508
JVR	RFK	1940	May	14	Postmark	Kahn–King's RFK/13/90/4/142–4		1509
JVR	RFK	1940	May	15	Postmark	Kahn–King's RFK/13/90/4/145–7		1510
JVR	RFK	1940	May	16	Postmark	Kahn–King's RFK/13/90/4/148–9		1511
JVR	RFK	1940	May	16	Postmark	Kahn–King's RFK/13/90/4/150–2		1512
JVR	RFK	1940	May	30	Postmark	Kahn–King's RFK/13/90/4/153–5		1513
JVR	RFK	1940	May	31	Postmark	Kahn–King's RFK/13/90/4/156–8		1514
JVR	RFK	1940	June	1	Postmark	Kahn–King's RFK/13/90/4/159–61		1515
JVR	RFK	1940	June	3	Postmark	Kahn–King's RFK/13/90/4/162–4		1516
JVR	RFK	1940	June	4	Postmark	Kahn–King's RFK/13/90/4/165–9		1517
JVR	RFK	1940	June	5	Postmark	Kahn–King's RFK/13/90/4/170–1		1518
JVR	RFK	1940	June	11	Postmark	Kahn–King's RFK/13/90/4/172–3		1519
JVR	RFK	1940	June	12	Postmark	Kahn–King's RFK/13/90/4/174–5		1520
JVR	RFK	1940	June	20	Attributed	Kahn–King's RFK/13/90/4/176–7		1521
JVR	RFK	1940	June	21	Attributed	Kahn–King's RFK/13/90/4/178–81		1522
JVR	RFK	1940	June	23	Attributed	Kahn–King's RFK/13/90/4/182–3		1523
JVR	RFK	1940	June	24	Attributed	Kahn–King's RFK/13/90/4/184–5		1524
JVR	RFK	1940	June	25	Attributed	Kahn–King's RFK/13/90/4/186–9		1525
JVR	RFK	1940	June	26	Attributed	Kahn–King's RFK/13/90/4/190–1		1526
JVR	RFK	1940	June	27	Attributed	Kahn–King's RFK/13/90/4/192–3		1527
JVR	RFK	1940	June	28	Attributed	Kahn–King's RFK/13/90/4/194–5		1528
JVR	RFK	1940	June	29	Attributed	Kahn–King's RFK/13/90/4/196–7		1529
JVR	RFK	1940	July	1	Attributed	Kahn–King's RFK/13/90/4/198–200		1530
JVR	RFK	1940	July	2	Attributed	Kahn–King's RFK/13/90/4/201–2		1531
JVR	RFK	1940	July	3	Attributed	Kahn–King's RFK/13/90/4/203–4		1532
JVR	RFK	1940	July	5	Attributed	Kahn–King's RFK/13/90/4/205–6		1533
JVR	RFK	1940	July	6	Attributed	Kahn–King's RFK/13/90/4/207–8		1534
JVR	RFK	1940	July	8	Attributed	Kahn–King's RFK/13/90/4/209–10		1535

RFK	JVR	1933	February	7	Dated letter	Kahn–King's	RFK/13/90/1/94		549
RFK	JVR	1933	February	7	Dated letter	Kahn–King's	RFK/13/90/1/95–6		550
JVR	RFK	1933	February	8	Attributed	Kahn–King's	RFK/13/90/1/101–4		552
RFK	JVR	1933	February	9	Dated letter	Kahn–King's	RFK/13/90/1/96–100		551
RFK	JVR	1933	February	10	Dated letter	Kahn–King's	RFK/13/90/1/105–7		553
JVR	RFK	1933	February	11	Attributed	Kahn–King's	RFK/13/90/1/115–18	Marcuzzo 2003: 441, (E)	556
RFK	JVR	1933	February	12	Dated letter	Kahn–King's	RFK/13/90/1/107–9		554
RFK	JVR	1933	February	13	Dated letter	Kahn–King's	RFK/13/90/1/109–14		555
JVR	RFK	1933	February	13	Attributed	Kahn–King's	RFK/13/90/1/118		557
RFK	JVR	1933	February	15	Dated letter	Kahn–King's	RFK/13/90/1/131–2		558
JVR	RFK	1933	February	15	Attributed	Kahn–King's	RFK/13/90/1/119–22		563
JVR	RFK	1933	February	16	Attributed	Kahn–King's	RFK/13/90/1/122		564
RFK	JVR	1933	February	17	Dated letter	Kahn–King's	RFK/13/90/1/132–4		559
JVR	RFK	1933	February	18	Attributed	Kahn–King's	RFK/13/90/1/123–6		565
RFK	JVR	1933	February	19	Dated letter	Kahn–King's	RFK/13/90/1/134–5		560
RFK	JVR	1933	February	20	Dated letter	Kahn–King's	RFK/13/90/1/135–8		561
JVR	RFK	1933	February	20	Attributed	Kahn–King's	RFK/13/90/1/127–30		567
RFK	JVR	1933	February	21	Dated letter	Kahn–King's	RFK/13/90/1/138		562
JVR	RFK	1933	February	23	Attributed	Kahn–King's	RFK/13/90/1/139–44		568
JVR	RFK	1933	February	24	Attributed	Kahn–King's	RFK/13/90/1/145–6		569
RFK	JVR	1933	February	24	Dated letter	Kahn–King's	RFK/13/90/1/147–8		570
RFK	JVR	1933	February	27	Dated letter	Kahn–King's	RFK/13/90/1/148–54		571
JVR	RFK	1933	March	1	Attributed	Kahn–King's	RFK/13/90/1/155–8		572
JVR	RFK	1933	March	2	Attributed	Kahn–King's	RFK/13/90/1/159–61		573
RFK	JVR	1933	March	2	Dated letter	Kahn–King's	RFK/13/90/1/162–4	Marcuzzo 2003: 551, (E)	574
JVR	RFK	1933	March	3	Attributed	Kahn–King's	RFK/13/90/1/168–9		577
RFK	JVR	1933	March	3	Dated letter	Kahn–King's	RFK/2/5/43–4		767
JVR	RFK	1933	March	4	Attributed	Kahn–King's	RFK/13/90/1/169		578
RFK	JVR	1933	March	5	Dated letter	Kahn–King's	RFK/13/90/1/164–6		575
JVR	RFK	1933	March	5	Attributed	Kahn–King's	RFK/13/90/1/170–2		579
RFK	JVR	1933	March	6	Dated letter	Kahn–King's	RFK/13/90/1/166–7		576

Table 10.1 continued

From	*To*	*Year*	*Month*	*Day*	*Date*	*Archive*		*Published in*	*Item*
JVR	RFK	1933	March	8	Attributed	Kahn–King's	RFK/13/90/1/173–9		580
JVR	RFK	1933	March	11	Attributed	Kahn–King's	RFK/13/90/1/180–1		581
RFK	JVR	1933	March	12	Dated letter	Kahn–King's	RFK/13/90/1/184–6		582
JVR	RFK	1933	March	13	Attributed	Kahn–King's	RFK/13/90/1/182–3		584
RFK	JVR	1933	March	14	Dated letter	Kahn–King's	RFK/13/90/1/186–7		583
RFK	JVR	1933	March	15	Dated letter	Kahn–King's	RFK/13/90/1/187–8		798
JVR	RFK	1933	March	16	Attributed	Kahn–King's	RFK/13/90/1/189–94		585
JVR	RFK	1933	March	18	Attributed	Kahn–King's	RFK/13/90/1/198–9		586
JVR	RFK	1933	March	18	Attributed	Kahn–King's	RFK/13/90/1/195–7		799
RFK	JVR	1933	March	20	Dated letter	Kahn–King's	RFK/13/90/1/200		587
RFK	JVR	1933	March	22	Dated letter	Kahn–King's	RFK/13/90/1/201–3		588
JVR	RFK	1933	March	23	Attributed	Kahn–King's	RFK/13/90/1/205–8		591
RFK	JVR	1933	March	23–24	Dated letter	Kahn–King's	RFK/13/90/1/203–4		589
RFK	JVR	1933	March	28	Dated letter	Kahn–King's	RFK/13/90/1/209–10		592
RFK	JVR	1933	March	30	Dated letter	Kahn–King's	RFK/13/90/1/210–12	Marcuzzo 2003: 546, (E)	593
JVR	RFK	1933	March	30	Attributed	Kahn–King's	RFK/13/90/1/215–16		594
RFK	JVR	1933	April		Dated letter	Kahn–King's	RFK/13/90/1/225–6		598
JVR	RFK	1933	April	2	Attributed	Kahn–King's	RFK/13/90/1/217–18		595
RFK	JVR	1933	April	4	Dated letter	Kahn–King's	RFK/13/90/1/219–20		596
JVR	RFK	1933	April	7	Attributed	Kahn–King's	RFK/13/90/1/221–4		597
RFK	JVR	1933	April	14	Dated letter	Kahn–King's	RFK/13/90/1/226		599
JVR	RFK	1933	April	16	Postmark	Kahn–King's	RFK/13/90/1/227		600
JVR	RFK	1933	April	17	Postmark	Kahn–King's	RFK/13/90/1/228		601
JVR	RFK	1933	April	22	Attributed	Kahn–King's	RFK/13/90/1/229		602
JVR	RFK	1933	April	24	Attributed	Kahn–King's	RFK/13/90/1/230–2		603
JVR	RFK	1933	May		Attributed	Kahn–King's	RFK/13/90/1/235–6		566
JVR	RFK	1933	May	1	Attributed	Kahn–King's	RFK/13/90/1/233–4		604
JVR	RFK	1933	June	22	Attributed	Kahn–King's	RFK/13/90/1/237–8		605

JVR	RFK	1933	June	26	Attributed	Kahn–King's	RFK/13/90/1/239		606
JVR	RFK	1933	June	28	Postmark	Kahn–King's	RFK/13/90/1/240–1		607
JVR	RFK	1933	July	4	Attributed	Kahn–King's	RFK/13/90/1/242–3		608
JVR	RFK	1933	July	19	Attributed	Kahn–King's	RFK/13/90/1/244–5		609
JVR	RFK	1933	August	25	Postmark	Kahn–King's	RFK/13/90/1/246–8		610
JVR	RFK	1933	September	12	Postmark	Kahn–King's	RFK/13/90/1/249–52		611
JVR	RFK	1933	September	13	Postmark	Kahn–King's	RFK/13/90/1/253–5		612
JVR	RFK	1933	September	16	Postmark	Kahn–King's	RFK/13/90/1/256–8		613
JVR	RFK	1933	September	19	Postmark	Kahn–King's	RFK/13/90/1/259–61		614
JVR	RFK	1933	September	21	Postmark	Kahn–King's	RFK/13/90/1/262–4		615
JVR	RFK	1933	December	25	Postmark	Kahn–King's	RFK/13/90/1/270–3		616
JVR	RFK	1934			Attributed	Kahn–King's	RFK/13/90/2/3–4		618
JVR	RFK	1934			Attributed	Kahn–King's	RFK/13/90/2/5–6		619
JVR	RFK	1934			Attributed	Kahn–King's	RFK/13/90/2/69–72		637
JVR	RFK	1934	March	29	Attributed	Kahn–King's	RFK/13/90/2/1–2 and 21–22		617
JVR	RFK	1934	May	27	Postmark	Kahn–King's	RFK/13/90/2/12–13		620
JVR	RFK	1934	May	29	Postmark	Kahn–King's	RFK/13/90/2/17–20		621
RFK	JVR	1934	May	30	Dated letter	Robinson–King's	JVR/vii/228/1/17–19		622
JVR	RFK	1934	June	27	Postmark	Kahn–King's	RFK/13/90/2/23–5		624
JVR	RFK	1934	July	10	Attributed	Kahn–King's	RFK/13/90/2/26		625
JVR	RFK	1934	August	2	Attributed	Kahn–King's	RFK/13/90/2/28–9		626
JVR	RFK	1934	August	7	Attributed	Kahn–King's	RFK/13/90/2/30		627
JVR	RFK	1934	August	13	Postmark	Kahn–King's	RFK/13/90/2/31–3		628
JVR	RFK	1934	August	14	Postmark	Kahn–King's	RFK/13/90/2/34–8		629
JVR	RFK	1934	August	15	Postmark	Kahn–King's	RFK/13/90/2/39–41	Marcuzzo 2003: 552, (E)	630
JVR	RFK	1934	August	16	Postmark	Kahn–King's	RFK/13/90/2/42–4		631
JVR	RFK	1934	August	17	Postmark	Kahn–King's	RFK/13/90/2/45–7		632
JVR	RFK	1934	August	18	Postmark	Kahn–King's	RFK/13/90/2/48–50		633
JVR	RFK	1934	August	23	Postmark	Kahn–King's	RFK/13/90/2/59–61		634
JVR	RFK	1934	August	27	Attributed	Kahn–King's	RFK/13/90/2/62–3 and 97–104		636

Table 10.1 continued

From	*To*	*Year*	*Month*	*Day*	*Date*	*Archive*		*Published in*	*Item*
JVR	RFK	1934	August	30	Postmark	Kahn–King's	RFK/13/90/2/64–70		638
JVR	RFK	1934	September	2	Postmark	Kahn–King's	RFK/13/90/2/76–84		640
JVR	RFK	1934	September	4	Attributed	Kahn–King's	RFK/13/90/2/85–8		642
JVR	RFK	1934	September	5	Postmark	Kahn–King's	RFK/13/90/2/73–5		643
JVR	RFK	1934	September	6	Postmark	Kahn–King's	RFK/13/90/2/89–93		646
JVR	RFK	1934	September	5–6	Attributed	Kahn–King's	RFK/13/90/2/94–6	Marcuzzo 2003: 551, (E)	645
JVR	RFK	1934	October	15	Postmark	Kahn–King's	RFK/13/90/2/105–6		647
JVR	RFK	1934	October	30	Attributed	Kahn–King's	RFK/13/90/2/112–13		648
JVR	RFK	1934	November		Attributed	Kahn–King's	RFK/13/90/1/269		652
JVR	RFK	1934	November	1	Postmark	Kahn–King's	RFK/13/90/2/114–16		649
JVR	RFK	1934	November	2	Attributed	Kahn–King's	RFK/13/90/1/265–6		650
JVR	RFK	1934	December	20	Attributed	Kahn–King's	RFK/13/90/1/282–3		653
JVR	RFK	1935	January	21	Attributed	Kahn–King's	RFK/13/90/1/284–5		654
JVR	RFK	1935	April		Attributed	Kahn–King's	RFK/13/90/2/7–8		1675
JVR	RFK	1935	April		Attributed	Kahn–King's	RFK/13/90/2/9		656
JVR	RFK	1935	April	15	Attributed	Kahn–King's	RFK/13/90/2/10–11		657
JVR	RFK	1935	June	30	Attributed	Kahn–King's	RFK/13/90/2/117–20		658
JVR	RFK	1935	July	4	Attributed	Kahn–King's	RFK/13/90/2/121–3		659
JVR	RFK	1935	July	6	Attributed	Kahn–King's	RFK/13/90/2/124–7		660
JVR	RFK	1935	July	8	Attributed	Kahn–King's	RFK/13/90/2/128–31		661
JVR	RFK	1935	July	15	Attributed	Kahn–King's	RFK/13/90/2/132–3		662
JVR	RFK	1935	August	9	Postmark	Kahn–King's	RFK/13/90/2/135–7		664
JVR	RFK	1935	August	17	Postmark	Kahn–King's	RFK/13/90/2/51–5		665
JVR	RFK	1935	August	20	Postmark	Kahn–King's	RFK/13/90/2/56–8		666
JVR	RFK	1936	January	4	Attributed	Kahn–King's	RFK/13/90/1/275–6		667
JVR	RFK	1936	March	17	Postmark	Kahn–King's	RFK/13/90/2/138–41		668
JVR	RFK	1936	March	19	Postmark	Kahn–King's	RFK/13/90/2/142–4		669
JVR	RFK	1936	March	20	Postmark	Kahn–King's	RFK/13/90/2/145–8		670

JVR	RFK	1936	June	15	Attributed	Kahn–King's	RFK/13/90/2/149–50	672
JVR	RFK	1936	August	11	Attributed	Kahn–King's	RFK/13/90/3/6–7	697
JVR	RFK	1936	August	19	Attributed	Kahn–King's	RFK/13/90/3/28–9	733
JVR	RFK	1936	September	16	Postmark	Kahn–King's	RFK/13/90/2/152–4	674
JVR	RFK	1936	September	30	Postmark	Kahn–King's	RFK/13/90/2/155–8	675
JVR	RFK	1937	March	12	Attributed	Kahn–King's	RFK/13/90/2/159–61	676
JVR	RFK	1937	March	12	Attributed	Kahn–King's	RFK/13/90/2/162–3	677
JVR	RFK	1937	March	17	Attributed	Kahn–King's	RFK/13/90/2/164	678
JVR	RFK	1937	March	20	Attributed	Kahn–King's	RFK/13/90/2/165–6	679
JVR	RFK	1937	March	26	Attributed	Kahn–King's	RFK/13/90/2/167–8	680
JVR	RFK	1937	March	31	Attributed	Kahn–King's	RFK/13/90/2/169–70	681
JVR	RFK	1937	April	5	Attributed	Kahn–King's	RFK/13/90/2/171–2	682
JVR	RFK	1937	April	7	Attributed	Kahn–King's	RFK/13/90/2/173–4	683
JVR	RFK	1937	July	22	Attributed	Kahn–King's	RFK/13/90/2/175–6	684
JVR	RFK	1937	July	25	Attributed	Kahn–King's	RFK/13/90/2/177–9	685
JVR	RFK	1937	July	30	Attributed	Kahn–King's	RFK/13/90/2/180–1	686
JVR	RFK	1937	August	3	Attributed	Kahn–King's	RFK/13/90/2/182–3	687
JVR	RFK	1937	August	4	Attributed	Kahn–King's	RFK/13/90/2/184–5	688
JVR	RFK	1937	August	7	Attributed	Kahn–King's	RFK/13/90/2/186–7	689
JVR	RFK	1937	August	10	Attributed	Kahn–King's	RFK/13/90/2/188–9	690
JVR	RFK	1937	September	20	Attributed	Kahn–King's	RFK/13/90/2/190–1	691
JVR	RFK	1937	December	8	Attributed	Kahn–King's	RFK/13/90/2/192–3	692
JVR	RFK	1937	December	8	Attributed	Kahn–King's	RFK/13/90/2/194–5	693
JVR	RFK	1937	December	25	Dated letter	Kahn–King's	RFK/13/90/2/196	694
JVR	RFK	1938			Attributed	Kahn–King's	RFK/13/90/3/45–8	707
JVR	RFK	1938			Attributed	Kahn–King's	RFK/13/90/3/49–52	708
JVR	RFK	1938			Attributed	Kahn–King's	RFK/13/90/3/53	709
JVR	RFK	1938			Attributed	Kahn–King's	RFK/13/90/3/72	714
JVR	RFK	1938			Attributed	Kahn–King's	RFK/13/90/3/73	715
JVR	RFK	1938			Attributed	Kahn–King's	RFK/13/90/3/74	716
JVR	RFK	1938			Attributed	Kahn–King's	RFK/13/90/3/75–7	717
JVR	RFK	1938			Attributed	Kahn–King's	RFK/13/90/3/82–4	719

Table 10.1 continued

From	*To*	*Year*	*Month*	*Day*	*Date*	*Archive*		*Published in*	*Item*
JVR	RFK	1938			Attributed	Kahn–King's	RFK/13/90/3/85–7		720
JVR	RFK	1938			Attributed	Kahn–King's	RFK/13/90/3/88–92		721
JVR	RFK	1938			Attributed	Kahn–King's	RFK/13/90/3/93–4		722
JVR	RFK	1938			Attributed	Kahn–King's	RFK/13/90/3/95		723
JVR	RFK	1938			Attributed	Kahn–King's	RFK/13/90/3/182–3		727
JVR	RFK	1938	April	7	Attributed	Kahn–King's	RFK/13/90/3/1–3		695
JVR	RFK	1938	April	10	Attributed	Kahn–King's	RFK/13/90/3/4–5		696
JVR	RFK	1938	August	16	Attributed	Kahn–King's	RFK/13/90/3/8–9		698
JVR	RFK	1938	August	18	Attributed	Kahn–King's	RFK/13/90/3/10–11		699
JVR	RFK	1938	August	19	Attributed	Kahn–King's	RFK/13/90/3/12–13		700
JVR	RFK	1938	August	22	Attributed	Kahn–King's	RFK/13/90/3/14–15		701
JVR	RFK	1938	August	29	Attributed	Kahn–King's	RFK/13/90/3/18–19		702
JVR	RFK	1938	August	30	Attributed	Kahn–King's	RFK/13/90/3/20–1		703
JVR	RFK	1938	September	5	Attributed	Kahn–King's	RFK/13/90/3/22–3		704
JVR	RFK	1938	September	7	Attributed	Kahn–King's	RFK/13/90/3/24–5		705
JVR	RFK	1938	September	11	Attributed	Kahn–King's	RFK/13/90/3/26–7		706
JVR	RFK	1938	September	28	Attributed	Kahn–King's	RFK/13/90/3/78–81		718
JVR	RFK	1938	October	1	Attributed	Kahn–King's	RFK/13/90/3/54–5		710
JVR	RFK	1938	October	2	Postmark	Kahn–King's	RFK/13/90/3/56–8		711
JVR	RFK	1938	October	3	Postmark	Kahn–King's	RFK/13/90/3/61–2		712
JVR	RFK	1938	October	3	Postmark	Kahn–King's	RFK/13/90/3/63–6		713
JVR	RFK	1938	December	13	Attributed	Kahn–King's	RFK/13/90/3/152–3		724
JVR	RFK	1938	December	17	Attributed	Kahn–King's	RFK/13/90/3/158–9		725
JVR	RFK	1938	December	22	Attributed	Kahn–King's	RFK/13/90/3/162–72		726
JVR	RFK	1938	December	26	Attributed	Kahn–King's	RFK/13/90/3/184–5		728
JVR	RFK	1938	December	26	Attributed	Kahn–King's	RFK/13/90/3/186–95		729
JVR	RFK	1938	December	27	Attributed	Kahn–King's	RFK/13/90/3/200–1		730
JVR	RFK	1938	December	29	Attributed	Kahn–King's	RFK/13/90/3/204–5		731

JVR	RFK	1938	December	30	Attributed	Kahn–King's	RFK/13/90/3/206–7	732
JVR	RFK	1939			Attributed	Kahn–King's	RFK/13/90/3/316–7	1674
JVR	RFK	1939	January	1	Attributed	Kahn–King's	RFK/13/90/3/208–9	768
JVR	RFK	1939	January	2	Attributed	Kahn–King's	RFK/13/90/3/210–5	769
JVR	RFK	1939	January	3	Postmark	Kahn–King's	RFK/13/90/3/216–7	770
JVR	RFK	1939	January	4	Attributed	Kahn–King's	RFK/13/90/3/225–8	771
JVR	RFK	1939	January	5	Attributed	Kahn–King's	RFK/13/90/3/229–30	772
JVR	RFK	1939	January	6	Attributed	Kahn–King's	RFK/13/90/3/231–2	773
JVR	RFK	1939	January	9	Attributed	Kahn–King's	RFK/13/90/3/236–7	774
JVR	RFK	1939	January	10	Attributed	Kahn–King's	RFK/13/90/3/238–41	775
JVR	RFK	1939	January	11	Attributed	Kahn–King's	RFK/13/90/3/242–3	776
JVR	RFK	1939	January	13	Attributed	Kahn–King's	RFK/13/90/3/252–3	777
JVR	RFK	1939	January	14	Postmark	Kahn–King's	RFK/13/90/3/254	778
JVR	RFK	1939	January	14	Attributed	Kahn–King's	RFK/13/90/3/255–8	779
JVR	RFK	1939	January	16	Attributed	Kahn–King's	RFK/13/90/3/259–60	780
JVR	RFK	1939	January	18	Attributed	Kahn–King's	RFK/13/90/3/264–71	781
JVR	RFK	1939	January	20	Attributed	Kahn–King's	RFK/13/90/3/272–6	782
JVR	RFK	1939	January	26	Attributed	Kahn–King's	RFK/13/90/3/279	783
JVR	RFK	1939	January	27	Attributed	Kahn–King's	RFK/13/90/3/280–1	784
JVR	RFK	1939	January	28	Attributed	Kahn–King's	RFK/13/90/3/282	785
JVR	RFK	1939	February	3	Attributed	Kahn–King's	RFK/13/90/3/289–90	786
JVR	RFK	1939	February	7	Attributed	Kahn–King's	RFK/13/90/3/291–2	787
JVR	RFK	1939	February	11	Attributed	Kahn–King's	RFK/13/90/3/293–4	788
JVR	RFK	1939	February	14	Postmark	Kahn–King's	RFK/13/90/3/295–6	789
JVR	RFK	1939	February	17	Attributed	Kahn–King's	RFK/13/90/3/297	790
JVR	RFK	1939	February	25	Attributed	Kahn–King's	RFK/13/90/3/298	791
JVR	RFK	1939	February	27	Attributed	Kahn–King's	RFK/13/90/3/299–300	792
JVR	RFK	1939	February	28	Attributed	Kahn–King's	RFK/13/90/3/301–2	793
JVR	RFK	1939	March	3	Attributed	Kahn–King's	RFK/13/90/3/303	794
JVR	RFK	1939	March	13	Attributed	Kahn–King's	RFK/13/90/3/306	795
JVR	RFK	1939	March	19	Attributed	Kahn–King's	RFK/13/90/3/307–8	796

Table 10.1 continued

From	*To*	*Year*	*Month*	*Day*	*Date*	*Archive*		*Published in*	*Item*
JVR	RFK	1939	April	7	Attributed	Kahn–King's	RFK/13/90/3/313–14		800
JVR	RFK	1939	June	5	Attributed	Kahn–King's	RFK/13/90/3/315		1653
JVR	RFK	1939	September	2	Attributed	Kahn–King's	RFK/13/90/3/322–3		1451
JVR	RFK	1939	September	2	Postmark	Kahn–King's	RFK/13/90/3/320–1		1655
JVR	RFK	1939	September	5	Attributed	Kahn–King's	RFK/13/90/3/325		1452
JVR	RFK	1939	September	7	Attributed	Kahn–King's	RFK/13/90/3/324		1453
JVR	RFK	1939	September	10	Attributed	Kahn–King's	RFK/13/90/3/326		1454
JVR	RFK	1939	December	15	Attributed	Kahn–King's	RFK/13/90/3/328–31		1455
JVR	RFK	1939	December	16	Attributed	Kahn–King's	RFK/13/90/3/332–3		1456
JVR	RFK	1939	December	24	Attributed	Kahn–King's	RFK/13/90/3/334–5		1457
JVR	RFK	1939	December	27	Attributed	Kahn–King's	RFK/13/90/3/336		1458
JVR	RFK	1940	January	1	Attributed	Kahn–King's	RFK/13/90/4/1–2		1459
JVR	RFK	1940	January	4	Attributed	Kahn–King's	RFK/13/90/4/3–6		1460
JVR	RFK	1940	January	9	Attributed	Kahn–King's	RFK/13/90/4/7–11		1461
JVR	RFK	1940	January	14	Postmark	Kahn–King's	RFK/13/90/4/12–14		1462
JVR	RFK	1940	January	15	Attributed	Kahn–King's	RFK/13/90/4/17		1463
JVR	RFK	1940	January	18	Postmark	Kahn–King's	RFK/13/90/4/15–16		1464
JVR	RFK	1940	January	19	Postmark	Kahn–King's	RFK/13/90/4/18–22		1465
JVR	RFK	1940	January	23	Postmark	Kahn–King's	RFK/13/90/4/23–8		1466
RFK	JVR	1940	January	23	Dated letter	Kahn–King's	RFK/13/90/4/29–30		1467
RFK	JVR	1940	January	24	Dated letter	Kahn–King's	RFK/13/90/4/31–3		1468
JVR	RFK	1940	January	25	Postmark	Kahn–King's	RFK/13/90/4/34–6		1469
JVR	RFK	1940	January	26	Postmark	Kahn–King's	RFK/13/90/4/37–8		1470
JVR	RFK	1940	January	27	Postmark	Kahn–King's	RFK/13/90/4/39–42		1471
JVR	RFK	1940	January	31	Postmark	Kahn–King's	RFK/13/90/4/43–5		1472
JVR	RFK	1940	February	1	Postmark	Kahn–King's	RFK/13/90/4/46–8		1473
JVR	RFK	1940	February	2	Postmark	Kahn–King's	RFK/13/90/4/49–51		1474
JVR	RFK	1940	February	8	Postmark	Kahn–King's	RFK/13/90/4/52–4		1475

JVR	RFK	1940	February	12	Postmark	Kahn–King's	RFK/13/90/4/55–7	1476
JVR	RFK	1940	February	13	Postmark	Kahn–King's	RFK/13/90/4/58–60	1477
JVR	RFK	1940	February	14	Postmark	Kahn–King's	RFK/13/90/4/61–3	1478
JVR	RFK	1940	February	21	Postmark	Kahn–King's	RFK/13/90/4/64–6	1479
JVR	RFK	1940	February	22	Postmark	Kahn–King's	RFK/13/90/4/67–9	1480
JVR	RFK	1940	February	23	Postmark	Kahn–King's	RFK/13/90/4/70–1	1481
JVR	RFK	1940	February	25	Postmark	Kahn–King's	RFK/13/90/4/72–3	1482
JVR	RFK	1940	February	26	Postmark	Kahn–King's	RFK/13/90/4/74–6	1483
JVR	RFK	1940	February	29	Postmark	Kahn–King's	RFK/13/90/4/77–9	1484
JVR	RFK	1940	March	4	Attributed	Kahn–King's	RFK/13/90/4/93–4	1490
JVR	RFK	1940	March	8	Postmark	Kahn–King's	RFK/13/90/4/80–2	1485
JVR	RFK	1940	March	11	Postmark	Kahn–King's	RFK/13/90/4/83–4	1486
RFK	JVR	1940	March	11	Dated letter	Kahn–King's	RFK/13/90/4/85–6	1487
JVR	RFK	1940	March	12	Postmark	Kahn–King's	RFK/13/90/4/87–9	1488
JVR	RFK	1940	March	13	Postmark	Kahn–King's	RFK/13/90/4/90–2	1489
JVR	RFK	1940	March	15	Postmark	Kahn–King's	RFK/13/90/4/95–7	1491
JVR	RFK	1940	March	17	Postmark	Kahn–King's	RFK/13/90/4/98–100	1492
JVR	RFK	1940	March	18	Postmark	Kahn–King's	RFK/13/90/4/101–4	1493
JVR	RFK	1940	April	8	Attributed	Kahn–King's	RFK/13/90/4/105–6	1494
JVR	RFK	1940	April	10	Attributed	Kahn–King's	RFK/13/90/4/107–8	1495
JVR	RFK	1940	April	13	Attributed	Kahn–King's	RFK/13/90/4/109–10	1496
JVR	RFK	1940	April	15	Attributed	Kahn–King's	RFK/13/90/4/111–12	1497
JVR	RFK	1940	April	16	Attributed	Kahn–King's	RFK/13/90/4/113–14	1498
JVR	RFK	1940	April	19	Postmark	Kahn–King's	RFK/13/90/4/115–16	1499
JVR	RFK	1940	April	22	Postmark	Kahn–King's	RFK/13/90/4/117–19	1500
JVR	RFK	1940	April	24	Attributed	Kahn–King's	RFK/13/90/4/120–1	1501
JVR	RFK	1940	April	27	Postmark	Kahn–King's	RFK/13/90/4/122–5	1502
JVR	RFK	1940	April	29	Postmark	Kahn–King's	RFK/13/90/4/126–8	1503
JVR	RFK	1940	April	30	Postmark	Kahn–King's	RFK/13/90/4/129–30	1504
JVR	RFK	1940	May	2	Postmark	Kahn–King's	RFK/13/90/4/131–3	1505
JVR	RFK	1940	May	6	Postmark	Kahn–King's	RFK/13/90/4/134–5	1506
JVR	RFK	1940	May	8	Postmark	Kahn–King's	RFK/13/90/4/136–8	1507

Table 10.1 continued

From	*To*	*Year*	*Month*	*Day*	*Date*	*Archive*	*Published in*	*Item*
JVR	RFK	1940	May	13	Postmark	Kahn–King's RFK/13/90/4/139–41		1508
JVR	RFK	1940	May	14	Postmark	Kahn–King's RFK/13/90/4/142–4		1509
JVR	RFK	1940	May	15	Postmark	Kahn–King's RFK/13/90/4/145–7		1510
JVR	RFK	1940	May	16	Postmark	Kahn–King's RFK/13/90/4/148–9		1511
JVR	RFK	1940	May	16	Postmark	Kahn–King's RFK/13/90/4/150–2		1512
JVR	RFK	1940	May	30	Postmark	Kahn–King's RFK/13/90/4/153–5		1513
JVR	RFK	1940	May	31	Postmark	Kahn–King's RFK/13/90/4/156–8		1514
JVR	RFK	1940	June	1	Postmark	Kahn–King's RFK/13/90/4/159–61		1515
JVR	RFK	1940	June	3	Postmark	Kahn–King's RFK/13/90/4/162–4		1516
JVR	RFK	1940	June	4	Postmark	Kahn–King's RFK/13/90/4/165–9		1517
JVR	RFK	1940	June	5	Postmark	Kahn–King's RFK/13/90/4/170–1		1518
JVR	RFK	1940	June	11	Postmark	Kahn–King's RFK/13/90/4/172–3		1519
JVR	RFK	1940	June	12	Postmark	Kahn–King's RFK/13/90/4/174–5		1520
JVR	RFK	1940	June	20	Attributed	Kahn–King's RFK/13/90/4/176–7		1521
JVR	RFK	1940	June	21	Attributed	Kahn–King's RFK/13/90/4/178–81		1522
JVR	RFK	1940	June	23	Attributed	Kahn–King's RFK/13/90/4/182–3		1523
JVR	RFK	1940	June	24	Attributed	Kahn–King's RFK/13/90/4/184–5		1524
JVR	RFK	1940	June	25	Attributed	Kahn–King's RFK/13/90/4/186–9		1525
JVR	RFK	1940	June	26	Attributed	Kahn–King's RFK/13/90/4/190–1		1526
JVR	RFK	1940	June	27	Attributed	Kahn–King's RFK/13/90/4/192–3		1527
JVR	RFK	1940	June	28	Attributed	Kahn–King's RFK/13/90/4/194–5		1528
JVR	RFK	1940	June	29	Attributed	Kahn–King's RFK/13/90/4/196–7		1529
JVR	RFK	1940	July	1	Attributed	Kahn–King's RFK/13/90/4/198–200		1530
JVR	RFK	1940	July	2	Attributed	Kahn–King's RFK/13/90/4/201–2		1531
JVR	RFK	1940	July	3	Attributed	Kahn–King's RFK/13/90/4/203–4		1532
JVR	RFK	1940	July	5	Attributed	Kahn–King's RFK/13/90/4/205–6		1533
JVR	RFK	1940	July	6	Attributed	Kahn–King's RFK/13/90/4/207–8		1534
JVR	RFK	1940	July	8	Attributed	Kahn–King's RFK/13/90/4/209–10		1535

JVR	RFK	1940	July	9	Attributed	Kahn–King's	RFK/13/90/4/211–12	1536
JVR	RFK	1940	July	10	Attributed	Kahn–King's	RFK/13/90/4/213–14	1537
JVR	RFK	1940	July	11	Attributed	Kahn–King's	RFK/13/90/4/215–16	1538
JVR	RFK	1940	July	12	Attributed	Kahn–King's	RFK/13/90/4/217–18	1539
JVR	RFK	1940	July	13	Attributed	Kahn–King's	RFK/13/90/4/219–21	1540
JVR	RFK	1940	July	16	Attributed	Kahn–King's	RFK/13/90/4/222–3	1541
JVR	RFK	1940	July	22	Attributed	Kahn–King's	RFK/13/90/4/224–5	1542
JVR	RFK	1940	July	23	Attributed	Kahn–King's	RFK/13/90/4/225	1543
JVR	RFK	1940	July	25	Attributed	Kahn–King's	RFK/13/90/4/226–7	1544
JVR	RFK	1940	July	26	Attributed	Kahn–King's	RFK/13/90/4/228–9	1545
JVR	RFK	1940	July	27	Attributed	Kahn–King's	RFK/13/90/4/230–1	1546
JVR	RFK	1940	July	29	Attributed	Kahn–King's	RFK/13/90/4/232–3	1547
JVR	RFK	1940	July	31	Attributed	Kahn–King's	RFK/13/90/4/234–5	1548
JVR	RFK	1940	July	31	Attributed	Kahn–King's	RFK/13/90/4/236–7	1549
JVR	RFK	1940	August		Attributed	Kahn–King's	RFK/13/90/4/252	1557
JVR	RFK	1940	August	1	Attributed	Kahn–King's	RFK/13/90/4/240–2	1550
JVR	RFK	1940	August	1	Attributed	Kahn–King's	RFK/13/90/4/238–9	1551
JVR	RFK	1940	August	3	Attributed	Kahn–King's	RFK/13/90/4/243	1552
JVR	RFK	1940	August	4	Attributed	Kahn–King's	RFK/13/90/4/244–5	1553
JVR	RFK	1940	August	6	Attributed	Kahn–King's	RFK/13/90/4/246–7	1554
JVR	RFK	1940	August	6	Attributed	Kahn–King's	RFK/13/90/4/248–9	1555
JVR	RFK	1940	August	8	Attributed	Kahn–King's	RFK/13/90/4/250–1	1556
JVR	RFK	1940	August	17	Attributed	Kahn–King's	RFK/13/90/4/253–4	1558
JVR	RFK	1940	August	18	Attributed	Kahn–King's	RFK/13/90/4/255–6	1559
JVR	RFK	1940	August	19	Attributed	Kahn–King's	RFK/13/90/4/257–8	1560
JVR	RFK	1940	August	20	Attributed	Kahn–King's	RFK/13/90/4/259–60	1561
JVR	RFK	1940	August	20	Attributed	Kahn–King's	RFK/13/90/4/261–4	1562
JVR	RFK	1940	August	21	Attributed	Kahn–King's	RFK/13/90/4/265	1563
JVR	RFK	1940	August	21	Attributed	Kahn–King's	RFK/13/90/4/266–9	1564
JVR	RFK	1940	August	22	Attributed	Kahn–King's	RFK/13/90/4/270–1	1565
JVR	RFK	1940	August	23	Attributed	Kahn–King's	RFK/13/90/4/272–3	1566
JVR	RFK	1940	August	24	Attributed	Kahn–King's	RFK/13/90/4/274–6	1567

Table 10.1 continued

From	*To*	*Year*	*Month*	*Day*	*Date*	*Archive*	*Published in*	*Item*
JVR	RFK	1940	August	24	Attributed	Kahn–King's RFK/13/90/4/277–8		1568
JVR	RFK	1940	August	26	Attributed	Kahn–King's RFK/13/90/4/279–80		1569
JVR	RFK	1940	August	26	Attributed	Kahn–King's RFK/13/90/4/281–6		1570
JVR	RFK	1940	August	27	Attributed	Kahn–King's RFK/13/90/4/287–8		1571
JVR	RFK	1940	August	27	Attributed	Kahn–King's RFK/13/90/4/289–90		1572
JVR	RFK	1940	August	28	Attributed	Kahn–King's RFK/13/90/4/291–2		1573
JVR	RFK	1940	August	29	Attributed	Kahn–King's RFK/13/90/4/293–6		1574
JVR	RFK	1940	August	30	Attributed	Kahn–King's RFK/13/90/4/297–8		1575
JVR	RFK	1940	August	31	Attributed	Kahn–King's RFK/13/90/4/299–300		1576
JVR	RFK	1940	September	2	Attributed	Kahn–King's RFK/13/90/4/301–2		1577
JVR	RFK	1940	September	3	Attributed	Kahn–King's RFK/13/90/4/303–4		1578
JVR	RFK	1940	September	4	Attributed	Kahn–King's RFK/13/90/4/305–6		1579
JVR	RFK	1940	September	5	Attributed	Kahn–King's RFK/13/90/4/307–8		1580
JVR	RFK	1940	September	6	Attributed	Kahn–King's RFK/13/90/4/309–11		1581
JVR	RFK	1940	September	24	Attributed	Kahn–King's RFK/13/90/4/312		1582
JVR	RFK	1940	September	25	Attributed	Kahn–King's RFK/13/90/4/313–14		1583
JVR	RFK	1940	September	26	Attributed	Kahn–King's RFK/13/90/4/315–16		1584
JVR	RFK	1940	September	29	Attributed	Kahn–King's RFK/13/90/4/317–18		1585
JVR	RFK	1940	September	30	Attributed	Kahn–King's RFK/13/90/4/319–20		1586
JVR	RFK	1940	October		Attributed	Kahn–King's RFK/13/90/4/373		1612
JVR	RFK	1940	October	1	Attributed	Kahn–King's RFK/13/90/4/321–2		1587
JVR	RFK	1940	October	1	Attributed	Kahn–King's RFK/13/90/4/323		1588
JVR	RFK	1940	October	3	Attributed	Kahn–King's RFK/13/90/4/324–5		1589
JVR	RFK	1940	October	4	Attributed	Kahn–King's RFK/13/90/4/326–7		1590
JVR	RFK	1940	October	4	Attributed	Kahn–King's RFK/13/90/4/372		1611
JVR	RFK	1940	October	7	Attributed	Kahn–King's RFK/13/90/4/328–9		1591
JVR	RFK	1940	October	8	Attributed	Kahn–King's RFK/13/90/4/330–1		1592
JVR	RFK	1940	October	10	Attributed	Kahn–King's RFK/13/90/4/332–3		1593

JVR	RFK	1940	October	11	Attributed	Kahn–King's	RFK/13/90/4/334–8	1594
JVR	RFK	1940	October	14	Attributed	Kahn–King's	RFK/13/90/4/339–40	1595
JVR	RFK	1940	October	25	Attributed	Kahn–King's	RFK/13/90/4/341–2	1596
JVR	RFK	1940	November	4	Attributed	Kahn–King's	RFK/13/90/4/343–4	1597
JVR	RFK	1940	November	5	Attributed	Kahn–King's	RFK/13/90/4/345–6	1598
JVR	RFK	1940	November	7	Attributed	Kahn–King's	RFK/13/90/4/347–8	1599
JVR	RFK	1940	November	8	Attributed	Kahn–King's	RFK/13/90/4/349–50	1600
JVR	RFK	1940	November	12	Attributed	Kahn–King's	RFK/13/90/4/351	1601
JVR	RFK	1940	November	13	Attributed	Kahn–King's	RFK/13/90/4/352–3	1602
JVR	RFK	1940	November	20	Attributed	Kahn–King's	RFK/13/90/4/354–5	1603
JVR	RFK	1940	November	22	Attributed	Kahn–King's	RFK/13/90/4/356–7	1604
JVR	RFK	1940	November	23	Attributed	Kahn–King's	RFK/13/90/4/358–9	1605
JVR	RFK	1940	December	3	Attributed	Kahn–King's	RFK/13/90/4/360–1	1606
JVR	RFK	1940	December	5	Attributed	Kahn–King's	RFK/13/90/4/362–5	1607
JVR	RFK	1940	December	8	Attributed	Kahn–King's	RFK/13/90/4/366–7	1608
JVR	RFK	1940	December	11	Attributed	Kahn–King's	RFK/13/90/4/368–9	1609
JVR	RFK	1940	December	13	Attributed	Kahn–King's	RFK/13/90/4/370–1	1610
JVR	RFK	1940	December	16	Attributed	Kahn–King's	RFK/13/90/4/374–5	1613
JVR	RFK	1940	December	18	Attributed	Kahn–King's	RFK/13/90/4/376–7	1614
JVR	RFK	1940	December	19	Attributed	Kahn–King's	RFK/13/90/4/378–9	1615
JVR	RFK	1941	January	3	Attributed	Kahn–King's	RFK/13/90/4/380–1	1616
JVR	RFK	1941	January	4	Attributed	Kahn–King's	RFK/13/90/4/382	1617
JVR	RFK	1941	January	8	Attributed	Kahn–King's	RFK/13/90/4/383–4	1618
JVR	RFK	1941	January	28	Attributed	Kahn–King's	RFK/13/90/4/385	1619
JVR	RFK	1941	January	30	Attributed	Kahn–King's	RFK/13/90/4/386–7	1620
JVR	RFK	1941	February		Attributed	Kahn–King's	RFK/13/90/4/390	1622
JVR	RFK	1941	February	10	Attributed	Kahn–King's	RFK/13/90/4/388–9	1621
JVR	RFK	1941	February	25	Attributed	Kahn–King's	RFK/13/90/4/391–2	1623
JVR	RFK	1941	March	3	Attributed	Kahn–King's	RFK/13/90/4/393–4	1624
JVR	RFK	1941	March	4	Attributed	Kahn–King's	RFK/13/90/4/395–6	1625
JVR	RFK	1941	March	5	Attributed	Kahn–King's	RFK/13/90/4/397–8	1626
JVR	RFK	1941	March	13	Attributed	Kahn–King's	RFK/13/90/4/399–400	1627

Table 10.1 continued

From	*To*	*Year*	*Month*	*Day*	*Date*	*Archive*		*Published in*	*Item*
JVR	RFK	1941	April	1	Attributed	Kahn–King's	RFK/13/90/4/401–4		1628
JVR	RFK	1941	April	1	Attributed	Kahn–King's	RFK/13/90/4/405–6		1629
JVR	RFK	1941	April	3	Attributed	Kahn–King's	RFK/13/90/4/407–8		1630
JVR	RFK	1941	April	7	Postmark	Kahn–King's	RFK/13/90/4/409–10		1631
JVR	RFK	1941	April	8	Attributed	Kahn–King's	RFK/13/90/4/411–2		1632
JVR	RFK	1941	April	17	Attributed	Kahn–King's	RFK/13/90/4/413–14		1633
JVR	RFK	1941	May	1	Attributed	Kahn–King's	RFK/13/90/4/415–16		1634
JVR	RFK	1941	May	5	Attributed	Kahn–King's	RFK/13/90/4/417–18		1635
JVR	RFK	1941	May	7	Attributed	Kahn–King's	RFK/13/90/4/419–20		1636
JVR	RFK	1941	May	13	Attributed	Kahn–King's	RFK/13/90/4/421–2		1637
JVR	RFK	1941	May	22	Attributed	Kahn–King's	RFK/13/90/4/423–4		1638
JVR	RFK	1941	May	27	Attributed	Kahn–King's	RFK/13/90/4/425–6		1639
JVR	RFK	1941	June	30	Attributed	Kahn–King's	RFK/13/90/4/427		1640
JVR	RFK	1941	June	30	Attributed	Kahn–King's	RFK/13/90/4/428–9		1641
JVR	RFK	1941	June	30	Attributed	Kahn–King's	RFK/13/90/4/430–1		1642
JVR	RFK	1941	September	26	Attributed	Kahn–King's	RFK/13/90/4/432–3		1643
RFK	JVR	1945	January	29	Dated letter	Robinson–King's	JVR/vii/228/2/29		1644
JVR	RFK	1945	August		Attributed	Kahn–King's	RFK/13/90/5/695–6		1647
JVR	RFK	1945	August	7	Postmark	Kahn–King's	RFK/13/90/5/701–3		1645
JVR	RFK	1945	August	11	Attributed	Kahn–King's	RFK/13/90/5/697–700		1646
JVR	RFK	1945	August	22	Attributed	Kahn–King's	RFK/13/90/5/691–4		1648
JVR	RFK	1945	August	23	Attributed	Kahn–King's	RFK/13/90/5/689–90		1649
JVR	RFK	1945	August	29	Attributed	Kahn–King's	RFK/13/90/5/688		1650
JVR	RFK	1945	September	13	Attributed	Kahn–King's	RFK/13/90/5/684–7		1651
JVR	RFK	1945	September	18	Attributed	Kahn–King's	RFK/13/90/5/682–3		1652
JVR	RFK	1946	July	31	Attributed	Kahn–King's	RFK/13/90/5/678–81		1087
JVR	RFK	1946	August	3	Attributed	Kahn–King's	RFK/13/90/5/674–7		1654
JVR	RFK	1946	August	6	Attributed	Kahn–King's	RFK/13/90/5/670–3		1088

JVR	RFK	1946	August	7	Attributed	Kahn–King's	RFK/13/90/5/666–9	1656
JVR	RFK	1946	August	8	Attributed	Kahn–King's	RFK/13/90/5/662–3	1657
JVR	RFK	1946	August	8	Attributed	Kahn–King's	RFK/13/90/5/664–5	1658
JVR	RFK	1946	August	12	Attributed	Kahn–King's	RFK/13/90/5/659–61	1659
JVR	RFK	1946	August	13	Attributed	Kahn–King's	RFK/13/90/5/655–8	1660
JVR	RFK	1946	August	14	Attributed	Kahn–King's	RFK/13/90/5/653–4	1661
JVR	RFK	1946	August	15	Attributed	Kahn–King's	RFK/13/90/5/651–2	1662
JVR	RFK	1946	August	17	Attributed	Kahn–King's	RFK/13/90/5/647–50	1663
JVR	RFK	1946	August	19	Attributed	Kahn–King's	RFK/13/90/5/645–6	1664
JVR	RFK	1946	August	20	Attributed	Kahn–King's	RFK/13/90/5/643–4	1665
JVR	RFK	1946	August	21	Attributed	Kahn–King's	RFK/13/90/5/640–2	1666
JVR	RFK	1946	August	24	Attributed	Kahn–King's	RFK/13/90/5/638–9	1667
JVR	RFK	1946	August	24	Attributed	Kahn–King's	RFK/13/90/5/634–7	1668
JVR	RFK	1946	August	25	Postmark	Kahn–King's	RFK/13/90/5/631–33	1669
JVR	RFK	1946	August	26	Attributed	Kahn–King's	RFK/13/90/5/627–30	1670
JVR	RFK	1946	August	28	Dated letter	Kahn–King's	RFK/13/90/5/625–6	1671
JVR	RFK	1946	September	9	Attributed	Kahn–King's	RFK/13/90/5/589–90	1672
JVR	RFK	1946	September	10	Attributed	Kahn–King's	RFK/13/90/5/585–88	1673

11 The Keynesian tutor

Kahn and the correspondence with Sraffa, Harrod and Kaldor

Maria Cristina Marcuzzo with Daniele Besomi and Fabio Ranchetti

In this chapter we review the correspondence between Kahn and Sraffa, Harrod and Kaldor and we will explore the personal relationships and the main issues debated among them. The purpose of this chapter is to highlight differences of approach, style and focus of those economists who were close to Keynes, in relation to his 'favourite pupil'[1] (see Ch. 1).

Kahn was 'Keynes's disciple' and the 'main pillar support' (Harrod 1951: 451) in the making of the *General Theory*. Sraffa was brought to Cambridge by Keynes and remained throughout personally very close to him, although from the mid-1930s onwards he was less and less involved in discussions around Keynes's work, and ceased to involve Keynes in the discussion of his own work (see Ch. 4). Harrod was geographically and intellectually more distant from Keynes than the other three authors we are considering here. However, he was one of the recipients of the proofs of the *General Theory*, succeeded Keynes as editor of the *Economic Journal* and eventually became his biographer (see Ch. 3). Kaldor was a latecomer to Keynes's circle; after the publication of the *General Theory* he became a convert to the Keynesian Revolution, distancing himself from the LSE-based intellectual circle of which he was part in the early 1930s. After Keynes's death he was given an official position at the University of Cambridge and was made Fellow of King's College (see Ch. 8).

The number of letters examined here amounts to 46: 20 letters and a set of notes, from 1929 to 1946 between Kahn and Sraffa; 25 letters between Kahn and Harrod from 1931 to 1946 and only two letters, both by Kahn and both written in 1935, in relation to Kaldor (see Tables 11.1 to 11.3).

We will review this correspondence under three headings, two of which are related to economic theory, the third to the personal sides of their relationships.

Arguing about imperfect competition

The missing letter

Kahn was seven years younger than Sraffa and a pupil of his, since he attended Sraffa's lectures in the academic year 1928–29;[2] he was supervised by Keynes and got a First in the economics Tripos in 1928. Soon afterwards he began to write his Fellowship Dissertation[3] on the *Economics of the Short Period*, and in the choice of the topic he acknowledged Sraffa's (and Shove's) influence, rather than Keynes's (Kahn 1989: viii, xi) (see Ch. 1: 21–2).

We saw that Kahn's Dissertation was an investigation into the behaviour of firms in the cotton and coal industries during the 1920s depression. He described the actual cost structure of those firms, and by introducing the assumption of imperfect competition explained the apparent paradox that they worked at full capacity for some days of the week and closed down their plants for the remaining days. However, in the course of his analysis he came across a result which contradicted the conclusions reached by Sraffa in his 1926 article. There Sraffa argued that, when the market is imperfect, under the assumption of uniformity among firms, 'the imperfection is irrelevant to the equilibrium price' (Sraffa 1926: 529; Kahn 1989: 94). On the contrary, Kahn claimed that 'a reduction of the amount of imperfection causes – in the short run at any rate – a fall in price and in profits' (Kahn 1989: 86).

Kahn had reached his conclusion on the basis of the assumption that the demand curves facing each individual firm indicate what the entrepreneur *imagined* to be the relation between his price and his output. The assumptions – 'that are in the mind of the business man when he maximises his profit' (Kahn 1989: 100) – are that when he alters his price or output, either prices or outputs of the other firms remain constant or they will react by varying both prices and output. In all these cases, Kahn argued, the slope of the demand curve facing each firm in an oligopolistic industry is greater than the aggregate demand curve of an industry in the hands of a single monopolist. It follows therefore that 'under conditions of polypoly the equilibrium price is less than under conditions of monopoly' (Kahn 1989: 117), contrary to Sraffa's assertion.

Moreover, Kahn claimed that Sraffa had acknowledged 'the force of my [Kahn's] objection to his argument' (Kahn 1989: 95), adding that 'An unpublished letter from Sraffa to Keynes (King's College, Cambridge) is of interest' (Kahn 1989: xv). The extant evidence is not, however, to this effect; in fact there is no trace of this discussion in the correspondence and the letter has never been found. However, in Sraffa's *Lecture Notes* there is a passage related to this issue:

> To say that in imperfect competition price is always less than in monopoly, it means to fall [into] error, which is based on assumption that

> problem is independent of the relation between individual and collective elasticity of D[emand]. The point is that I assume a slight, but finite, degree of imperfection (elasticity of demand not infinite). But in this case, with the rise in prices, the elasticity decreases all the time, without limit.
>
> (PS papers, D 2/4/10 verso)

The issue can be interpreted as follows.

Kahn based his analysis on conjectural demand curves whose slopes embody various assumptions made by each firm about the behaviour of other firms within the industry. A change in price by any one firm does not leave the slope of the demand curves of all the other firms unchanged, because account is taken of the reactions of competitors. In general, when there is only one producer (as in monopoly), his demand curve is steeper than when there are many producers (as in oligopoly), because in that case there is no behaviour of other firms to be taken into account. Since the equilibrium price, for a given supply curve, is determined by the slope of the demand curve, it follows that price is higher in monopoly than in oligopoly.

On the contrary, Sraffa's argument is based on the degree of consumer preferences as shown by the value of the elasticity of demand, which is the expression of consumers' tastes, rather than producers' conjectures. Following an increase in price by one firm, demands for all firms are raised. When prices of substitutes go up, each buyer is willing to pay a higher price for the product of the firm from which he prefers to buy (Sraffa 1926: 547); so buyers will return to their preferred firm when the other firms have also raised their prices. Thus, limit to the price increase is given by the loss of customers to the market, not to the individual firm. Therefore, for Sraffa, unlike Kahn, 'for an industry consisting of firms which are all similar and similarly situated' (Sraffa 1926: 547) there is no reason why the equilibrium price should be different in monopoly than in oligopoly.

According to Dardi (2001: 130), Sraffa's position is 'a non sequitur', because his 'conclusion needs precise assumptions concerning the strategies that each entrepreneur expects from his rivals, and the latter from him'. Dardi argues that the point at stake is the relationship between the elasticity of the market demand and that of the particular demand facing each firm; since that relationship 'depends in fact on the conjectures of each agent regarding the correlation between his own price and those of the others' (ibid.), Kahn's approach and conclusion are the correct ones.

It seems, rather, that it is Dardi's position that is 'a non sequitur', since the relationship between the individual and the market demand curves need not be expression of 'conjectures', but simply of consumers' preferences. Since demand curves are a function of the price of the individual commodity, the price of substitutes and of income, when the prices of substitutes go up demand curves are all raised. In the final position of equilibrium when all firms have raised their price, the level of demand will be exactly the same, regardless of the number of firms in the industry.

Marketing expenses

The other issue between Kahn and Sraffa in the correspondence is related to the role of marketing expenses. In fact, the correspondence, as we have it, begins with a letter by Sraffa on the issue of 'inefficient' firms having a higher demand curve for their product, because of their marketing advantages (letter 455, 13 March 1929). This letter is possibly a follow-up of a point raised by Kahn in one of Sraffa's lectures (which he attended). There is a record of this in Sraffa's *Lecture Notes* in a passage where Sraffa mentions a question posed by Kahn on whether the demand price curve 'is always raised by an amount equal to the expenses made in advertisement' (PS papers, D 2/4/13 (e)).

In his Dissertation, Kahn argued that if the simplifying assumption is made that the only way in which a producer can increase his output is by reducing his price rather than increasing his selling and advertising expenses, [those expenses] 'are to be regarded as completely determined, being unambiguously dependent on the output' (Kahn 1989: 89). This 'simplifying assumption' would make it possible to disregard Sraffa's objection that 'the inclusion of *marketing* expenses in costs of production renders the expression "cost of production" dependent upon elements quite extraneous to the conditions under which the production of a given undertaking takes place' (ibid.: 90; Sraffa 1926: 544).

In a set of notes found among Kahn's papers, Sraffa objects to Kahn's solution on the ground that:

> a reference to the price at which it must be sold is required, since a firm could sell practically any amount, without any marketing costs, at a price sufficiently near to zero; just as it could produce any amount, without any marketing costs, if it hoards the product. Nothing is said about this price in §8 [of Kahn's Dissertation]: and therefore marketing expenses are not unambiguously dependent upon output [as Kahn had stated].
>
> (RFK papers, 3/13/153)

The issue between Sraffa and Kahn on marketing expenses can be summarised as follows. Kahn postulated that once marketing expenses are made a function of output and price, they can be added to the cost function to find the maximum level of profit. Following Kahn's route, we get the familiar solution for the equilibrium price corresponding to the maximum profit, as a function of the elasticity of demand, with the only difference that the elasticity of demand is also a function of the level of marketing expenses (Dardi 2001).

Sraffa's point was that marketing expenses affect the demand curve and therefore 'there is no demand curve that can be used with a supply curve that includes them'(PS papers, D3/7/23). For any level of marketing expenses there is no longer an independently determined curve of demand, and those expenses are to be regarded as the 'costs of producing the profits' (ibid.). So that the

> price that covers all kind of costs and gives the maximum profit enables us to draw, not a curve, but a point – the maximum to be sought: in solving the problem we start from a single datum – and it is the solution itself.
>
> (RFK papers, 3/13/153)

This point was made by Sraffa on several occasions: in the *Economic Journal* article (1926: 543), in his comments to the point raised by Kahn in Sraffa's course and in a comment to Shove, following a discussion meeting of the Political Economy Club held in February 1930 between Robertson, Shove and Sraffa on the issue of 'Increasing Returns and the Representative Firm', the topic of the *Symposium* published in the *Economic Journal* in March of the same year (see Ch. 14: 352–6).

It seems to me, therefore, that the issue between them is not whether the inclusion of marketing expenses in the profit function to be maximised is possible, but whether the independence of demand and supply curve in the determination of price and output is violated, emptying the meaning of the Marshallian explanation of value on the basis of both blades of the scissors.

Oddly enough, there is no discussion on the issue of imperfect competition in correspondence with Harrod, nor with Kaldor but for a related matter, as we shall see in the next section.

Welfare implications

In the first letter Kahn wrote to Kaldor, he expressed concern that the article 'Some Notes on Ideal Output' he was about to publish in the March issue of the *Economic Journal* (Kahn 1935) might cover the same ground as something Kaldor was also working on: 'your review of Mrs. Robinson's book *The Economics of Imperfect Competition* indicated to me that you were thinking on very analogous lines' (letter 499, 8 February 1935).[4]

In fact, in his *Review* of J. Robinson's book Kaldor showed a full grasp of the theory of imperfect competition, well beyond the simplifications made in Robinson's book, namely strategic interaction between producers, the 'imagined' demand curve and its discontinuity and the problems with the marginal productivity theory in conditions of imperfect competition.

In that article Kahn shows that it is possible to measure the social benefit deriving from a re-allocation of resources reached in *laissez-faire* conditions through the instruments of taxation and subsidies. He extends the Marshallian–Pigouvian apparatus (external and internal economies, various measures of marginal productivity of factors) to cover the case of imperfect competition with the aim of showing how resource allocation by the market may be inefficient and why there is scope for intervention. On announcing to Keynes that he might send him an article for his consideration, Kahn explained that he wanted to demonstrate what a narrow field of application Pigou's results had, especially as far as the unemployment problem was concerned. 'There might possibly also be a short article on the sense in which unemployment invalidates the methods of the *Economics of Welfare*, i.e. in what sense the existence of unemployed labour differs from the existence of unemployed land' (letter 245 from RFK to JMK, 9 August 1934).

We do not have the answer by Kaldor, but the second letter by Kahn reveals that he was pleased with the exchange. Kaldor had read Kahn's article and extensively commented upon it. There was some disagreement about the general applicability of the concept of marginal utility and the definition of industry, but Kahn's response was very obliging:

> I must thank you for your extraordinarily interesting letter, it was really very good of you to take so much trouble and I appreciate it all the more inasmuch as all the evidence suggests that you are the only person in the world who has read my article (I do not even except myself).
>
> (letter 500, 25 March 1935)

Arguing out Keynesian economics

Sraffa's role in the Circus

Possibly the most important 'event' in Cambridge economics was the making of the *General Theory*, whose beginnings are related to the dust raised by the *Treatise on Money*, especially within the Circus. Two very short and scrappy handwritten notes (letters 458 and 459, 1931), the first by Kahn, the second by Sraffa, provide us with evidence of the points in the *Treatise* disputed in the Circus, and in particular by Sraffa.

In early April 1931, in one of his many attempts that year[5] Kahn sought to persuade Keynes that variations in the price level of consumption goods (P) and investment goods (P'), contrary to Keynes's observation in the *Treatise* (CWK V: 123), are not independent, and that Keynes's statement, therefore, had little ground to stand on in the face of criticism raised also by Robertson, Pigou and Sraffa.[6]

Kahn argued his case imagining – as he wrote in a letter to Keynes on 17 April 1931 – drawing 'a cordon' (CWK XIII: 206) to separate the sector producing consumption goods from the rest of the economy and doing the same for the sector producing investment goods. The value of monetary expenditure channelled into the consumption goods sector is equal to the value of the monetary expenditure channelled into the rest of the economy by the consumption goods sector. Similarly, the value of monetary expenditure going into the investment goods sector equals the value of the monetary expenditure flowing from the investment goods sector into the rest of the economy. So the two price levels, unless special assumptions are made, are not independent, since expenditure in each sector is influenced by that in the other sector (see Marcuzzo 2002). Kahn's argument here was the logical consequence of the reasoning underlying the multiplier principle which appeared in the article which he published in June 1931.

In Kahn's note (letter 458, 1931), undated but clearly written in these months, one of the special assumptions is spelt out, i.e. that the demand for consumption goods be perfectly inelastic. In this case, even if the demand for investment good is perfectly elastic, the price level of consumption goods is independently determined from the price of investment goods and 'Maynard [is] quite right'.

In Sraffa's note, also undated, the same point is being made. He writes:

> Formally he [Keynes] is right in saying that P is determined by $I' - S$[7] but $I' - S$ depends on P' – only on extreme assumptions is P independent of P'. On the opposite extreme assumptions, P' is independent of P. In general P' is connected with P.
>
> (letter 459, 1931)

It seems that Sraffa is here summarising Kahn's argument, since his own is more general and is contained in a note of April 15, following an earlier note by Kahn, of April 5. In this note, Sraffa commented extensively on the implicit assumption made in the *Treatise* according to which 'the process of making profits and spending them (an infinite number of steps) takes no time to happen', stressing the point that 'profits made by the sale of given goods cannot be spent in purchasing the same goods' (PS papers, D1/8/1–2).[8]

Sraffa's argument is that the income generated by the production of goods represented by the cost of production cannot determine the price at which those goods will be sold. Expenditure takes place after earnings are paid out, and therefore the decision on how to allocate consumption and saving out of a given income occurs after consumption and investment goods have been produced. Profits or losses made on goods produced and sold can only be influential on the output of the next period. The role of profits therefore is to influence what the level of output will be in the next period, rather than the level of prices in the current period.

'Coaching' Harrod on saving and investment

The main subversive idea of the *General Theory* was reversing the direction of causality between saving and investment. This was a difficult point to accept, not only by those imbued with the classical tradition (like Robertson and Pigou), but also by someone like Harrod who, not having been part of the Circus, had some way to catch up on the latest developments.

The first extant letter in the correspondence with Harrod (letter 1351, 25 June 1931, Harrod 2003: 134–5) is Kahn's reply to a query about Keynes's *Treatise* which Harrod originally addressed to Robertson, who then passed it on to Kahn. Interestingly – as it anticipates the subject discussed in 1934 – Kahn pointed out the difference between the 'simple-minded' definition of saving and Keynes's special definition, which was the result of discussion within the Circus.

In his letter Kahn points out that in the *Treatise* savings depend on the price of consumption goods (P) and of investment goods (P'), as a consequence of Keynes's definition of income, which excludes windfall profits and losses. On the contrary, Kahn argues, on the basis of a simple-minded definition of savings as the difference between net receipts and expenditure it is immediately apparent that '"savings" are necessarily and always equal to I, the value of investment' (letter 1351, 25 June 1931, Harrod 2003: 134–5).

The second interesting point raised in this letter is the condition which has to be introduced in order to determine the pair values of P and P' uniquely among the infinite series of possible ones:

> Such a condition – Kahn writes – is afforded by the speculative demand curve for securities. The fundamental importance of this demand curve in the logical scheme of things was gradually brought home to some of us in the wrangles that preceded some public discussions that we held on the *Treatise* during the Term.
>
> (ibid.)

In the *Treatise*, entrepreneurs in the investment sector make up for losses (resulting from the value of the new investment goods being less than current savings) either by selling securities or reducing their bank deposits. Keynes wrote: 'The bank deposits thus released and the securities thus sold are available from, and are exactly equal to, the excess of current savings over the value of new investment' (CWK V: 131). Savings are again brought in line with the value of new investment goods, with no necessary change in the price of investment goods, assuming accommodating behaviour on the part of the banking system.[9]

Harrod apparently did not see the point: in a letter written almost a year later, Kahn had once again to complain that 'You still refrain from distinguishing between the effects of a reduction of expenditure on goods and the effects of a reduction of expenditure on securities' (letter 1353, 18 April 1932, Harrod 2003: 153).

Meanwhile another exchange took place when Harrod started working on his *International Economics* (Harrod 1933c; letter 1352, 24 March and letter 1353, 18 April 1932). This exchange was prompted by discussion of a paper (not extant) on the 'Theory of Balance of Foreign Payments' read by Harrod before the Marshall Society in Cambridge. Harrod (his letters have not been preserved), apparently inspired by Kahn's multiplier article (Kahn 1931: 190 fn.), seems to have put forward a preliminary version of his foreign trade multiplier – a mechanism, that is, of equalisation of the balance of current accounts based on the induced effect on home income of a change in the volume of exports, which in turn causes a variation in expenditure and imports. Kahn commented that Harrod's 'geometrical progression' was based on rather unrealistic assumptions and failed to account for the leakage of savings. In spite of its incompleteness (only Kahn's letters are extant), this exchange is interesting as it indicates that Harrod was an early experimenter with the new multiplier approach. One would therefore expect that he would be quick to grasp the implications of the investment multiplier. The following exchange with Kahn, however, proves that the 'conversion' was a difficult one.

When, two years later, Harrod entered the debate with Hayek and the Hayekians with letters to *The Economist* and an article in *Economica* (Harrod 1934a, 1934b, 1934c), Kahn perceived that Harrod was unaware of the latest developments in Keynes's thought. The ensuing correspondence, focusing in particular on the multiplier and the saving-investment relationship (letters 1357–1370, 15 October 1934 to 11 January 1935), is of some interest as it shows Harrod's resistance to accepting the main ideas (Besomi 2000b). Harrod admitted he was still thinking in terms of the *Treatise* argument, and that he was 'impatient for the new book' (letter 1360, 25 October 1934, Harrod 2003: 299–301; similarly in letter 1357, 15 October 1934, Harrod 2003: 302). As soon as Kahn had grasped the real state of Harrod's knowledge of the evolution of Keynes's thought, he set about tutoring him, beginning from the truism that saving = investment and abandoning arguments in terms of prices:

> In short, I do not think in terms of money and prices. In the view of Keynes and his followers the Theory of Money has ceased to exist. Of course, that is an exaggeration (it is the quantity of money which determines the rate of interest), but the exaggeration is a pardonable one.
>
> (letter 1359, 22 October 1934, Harrod 2003: 309)

Harrod failed to appreciate the implications of these points, as he was still thinking in terms of Keynes's definition of saving as in the *Treatise*, where the trade cycle theory was based on the divergence of saving and investment (letter 1360, 25 October 1934, Harrod 2003: 310).

Kahn retorted that:

> There is no sense, as I see it, in which 'investment>savings', even in a boom. In fact, in my philosophy there is no such thing as a boom – not what you mean by a boom. The great point to get clear is that investment is always equal to savings; and that is the whole of the matter.
> (letter 1361, 28 October 1934, Harrod 2003: 318)

This was too much for Harrod:

> when you say that 'there is no such thing as a boom' my heart shrinks. When you say that Investment is always equal to Saving and that is the whole of the matter, I think it may be the whole of the matter so far as the Hayekian arguments are concerned; but this tautology does not contain the secret of the trade cycle!
> (letter 1362, 29 October 1934, Harrod 2003: 320)

After a further explanation of the reasons why the new definition, making saving = investment, was adopted (letter 1363, 1 November 1934), Harrod found the argument 'paradoxical', and commented: 'this is simply frightening' (letter 1364, 2 November 1934 and letter 1367, 17 November 1934) (see Besomi 2000b).

The stability of equilibrium

Harrod and Kahn also discussed the effect of technological progress on the operation of the acceleration principle (letters 1371–1373, 6 March to 6 April 1935). Unfortunately only three short letters from Kahn are extant; these, however, coupled with Keynes's contemporaneous letters to Harrod on the same topic (see Ch. 3: 99–100), show Harrod for the first time experimenting with the acceleration principle and seeking the conditions for the 'neutrality' of technological progress in terms of its effect on roundaboutness. Harrod's attempt to disentangle the effects on total investment of a change in technical methods and of a change in demand was marred, according to Kahn, by the failure to recognise:

> the fact that investment can take place even in the absence of inventions. How does your equation apply in such a case? Investment is designed not merely to add new equipment when there was no equipment before, but also to replace old equipment by better equipment.
> (letter 1372, 23 March 1935, Harrod 2003: 389–90)

From Kahn's next letter in the exchange it is difficult to work out how Harrod reacted to this criticism. However, discussion now turned to the conditions of the stability of the full employment equilibrium. Harrod seems to have been interested in determining how the rate of interest should move to compensate for an increase in the rate of savings as income increases, and to have understood Keynes as maintaining that 'in the absence of inventions the rate of interest must fall continuously in order to maintain full employment'. Kahn, however, rejected this interpretation, and explained that the role of the assumptions regarding the relationship between rate of savings and income had to do with the stability of equilibrium:

> JMK's assumption that saving increases with income is the assumption which has to be made in order to ensure stability of equilibrium. If saving is independent of income equilibrium is neutral (as you pointed out at the Marshall Society) and if saving diminishes as income increases, equilibrium is unstable.
>
> (letter 1373, 6 April 1935, Harrod 2003: 391–2)

Harrod seems to have pursued his research on this topic without further help from Kahn or Keynes.[10]

Relationships

Kahn and Sraffa

Both Kahn and Sraffa played the Stock Market and we have a short handwritten note by Sraffa (letter 469, October 1937) on the behaviour behind sales and purchases of future contracts, which is related to another note by Sraffa with a marginal annotation by Kahn to Keynes dated 29 October 1937 (CWK XII: 23–4).

Kahn had little to do with the preparation of the Ricardo edition, except for help in collating the various editions of the *Principles* (letter 1926 from PS to JMK, 22 March 1930). In the same letter he told Kahn he has just had a letter from Keynes (about Sraffa's reply to Hollander)[11] who 'has taken away even the mild sting you had left and makes a very good suggestion'.[12] In another (letter 461, 18 May 1932) Sraffa asked for Kahn's help in checking over the manuscript of a letter of Isaac Lyon Goldsmid to Ricardo, published in the *Transactions of the Jewish Historical Society*.

We have a very interesting letter (462, 17 February 1933) sent to Sraffa when Kahn was in the United States, where he described his encounters with American economists and criticised various aspects of American culture (see Chs 1: 24 and 10: 263–6). For example, of Viner, Kahn remarked to Sraffa that he 'has a good head, but he is quite hopelessly conceited'. Of Knight, that he would amuse Sraffa because 'he believes in nothing, but he is not an agnostic in the sense that he enjoys having nothing to believe. It is quite pitiful to watch him striving to find a resting-place'. Kahn then added: 'the man I liked was Paul Douglas, but I scarcely saw him'. He remarked that the

American economists 'are all jealous of one another in a petty kind of way. Knight's colleagues are said never to have read his book, and the Douglas-Cobb article is despised and mistrusted'. In Chicago he said he 'searched for gangsters but failed to find any. And I saw nobody killed, and kept my money in my socks, but was not ever held up. Altogether a disappointing place'. The whole letter is rich in telling and significant observations. On Hayek, he said: 'One blessing is that I do not have to argue much about Hayek. They have looked into the thing [. . .] but they seem to have lost heart. [. . .] His replies to you and Maynard do not cut any ice'.

Finally, eight letters are on matters related to the flat Sraffa was renting from King's College, of which Kahn was the Bursar. Seven (the first being letter 463, 5 March 1937, the last one being letter 473, 20 September 1946) are from Kahn, and one from Sraffa (letter 464, 28 May 1937). The subject is obviously boring, and the two friends try their best to make it less so: 'The College fully recognise that the attitude that you are adopting is in no way dictated by self interest but purely and simply provoked by a desire to cause the Bursar as much annoyance as possible' (letter 467, 1 June 1937).

Kahn and Kaldor

Kaldor was a late-comer in the circle of Keynes supporters, while at the LSE pursuing a more traditional line of research, and becoming converted to the Keynesian revolution after the book was published (see Ch. 8: 216). Moreover, he really got to know Cambridge people only when the LSE was evacuated from London at the end of 1939 (Dahrendorf 1995: 343). Kaldor and Kahn shared the economics teaching, and their professional and personal relationship became close. Later Kahn was instrumental in Kaldor's appointment to a fellowship at King's in 1949, after the deaths of Keynes and Shove (Thirlwall 1987).

Of their pre-war acquaintance we know of two episodes in which they were both implicated: one was Kahn's reaction to Keynes's choice of Kaldor as the author of a Reply to Pigou's article (Kaldor 1937; see Chs 2: 70, 6: 177, 8: 219–20 and 15: 378–82); 'I have not seen Kaldor's article but I am sure that the publication of it will darken council. After all, we could all of us write replies to Pigou if you wanted them and I do not see why Kaldor should be thus favoured' (letter 393 from RFK to JMK, 22 October 1937).[13] The other episode is of 1938, when Kahn commented on a paper by Kaldor for Keynes.

Their relationship evolved during the years and at times it became very strained. They closely collaborated in the running of the Faculty and College business, but the mid-1950s saw a crisis in their relationship. They disagreed on appointments to a Fellowship at King's and a lectureship at the University and above all they disagreed about J. Robinson. While Kahn was a staunch defender of J. Robinson and her work, Kaldor felt bullied and annoyed by their alliance. These developments could have hardly been anticipated in the period which concerns us here.

Kahn and Harrod

Harrod, not having taken direct part in the discussion leading to the *General Theory* until he was sent the proofs in June 1935, was largely an outsider. Open-minded and eager to learn the most recent developments, but detached enough to maintain a critical eye, Harrod seems to have been chosen as a reference point for experimenting the impact of the progress in Keynes's doctrine upon a sympathetic but not well-informed reader (see Ch. 3: 92–4).

Harrod's surviving exchanges with Kahn are mostly occasional in origin; their relationship was certainly cordial but not intimate – sometimes '[bordering] on the formalistic' (letter 1373, 6 April 1935). The correspondence indicates that Harrod understood the role of Kahn as the best informed among Keynes's disciples, while Kahn's attitude towards Harrod is not so clear (and sometimes even puzzling). In particular, during the 'coaching' period in late 1934, when it must have been fairly obvious to Kahn that Harrod had failed to understand the basic principles of the new doctrine and was not actually changing his mind, Kahn wrote that 'we [Maynard's supporters] do very much look to you as a leader in what must after all be described as a fight' (letter 1366, 13 November 1934). Whether Kahn was just joking, or whether this statement indicates that a strategy for the diffusion and the defence of Keynes's ideas was explicitly drawn up, the correspondence does not tell.

Conclusions

During their lifetime, both Keynes and J. Robinson constantly turned to Kahn for help and reassurance on the logic and soundness of their argument while drafting their books, adding a further obstacle to the difficulty Kahn faced in writing his own work. His natural fastidiousness and obsession with precision were accompanied by apprehensions about the risk of invading somebody else's territory. On these aspects of Kahn's personality we have the testimony of Keynes and J. Robinson. At one point Keynes urged Kahn to publish part of his Fellowship Dissertation with these prophetic words:

> you *must not* get with the habit of never doing your own work but always someone else's for them. In the first place you will get subconsciously (or consciously) badly irked by it yourself; and in the second place you will end up by getting the credit for everything of any merit published by anyone during your lifetime!
>
> (letter 228 from JMK to RFK, 13 August 1934)

And J. Robinson, in her *Introduction* to the Italian edition of the only collection of essays published by Kahn (1972), wrote: 'He [Kahn] had a great repugnance to the thought that there might be an error attached to his name' (JVR papers, i/8/7).

These traits of Kahn's personality did not emerge in the relationships he had with the authors examined here. At times he played the mentor role with Harrod, but never with Sraffa nor with Kaldor, although the correspondence with them highlights other sides of their relationship.

Notes

1 In an interview which Kahn gave to one of the present authors at the end of his life he still considered himself as such, and chose the title of 'Keynes's disciple' for its publication (Kahn 1988).
2 We have the notes taken by Kahn and his essays written for the course (RFK papers, 3/3/359–84) and the answers given by Sraffa to a question raised by Kahn in one of the lectures (PS papers, D 2/4/13 (2)).
3 The Dissertation was actually written between October 1928 and December 1929. On the Dissertation see Kahn (1984, 1988, 1989: 10–11). See also Marcuzzo (1994, 1996b).
4 An offprint of Kaldor's review of *The Economics of Imperfect Competition* (Kaldor 1934b) inscribed 'with the compliments of NK' is among RFK papers. There are two footnotes to Kahn's article referring to Kaldor's review (Kahn 1935: 23n).
5 See letters 405, 380 and 271 from RFK to JMK on 5 and 17 April and 7 May 1931; see Chapter 1.
6 Eventually Keynes had to acknowledge the point and revised his formulation (CWK XIII: 225–6).
7 According to *Treatise* terminology, I' is the cost of production of investment goods. S is saving, being defined as the difference between earnings and expenditure on consumer goods.
8 Sraffa adds: 'As this point is overlooked in several arguments of the *Treatise*, it will probably have to be raised often in our discussions.'
9 The speculative demand for securities is indeed the topic of a long letter by Sraffa to Keynes of 9 May 1931 (CWK XIII: 207–9), answered by Keynes on 15 May 1931 (ibid., 209–11) and was mentioned in one of the exchanges between Sraffa and Kahn in 1931 (letters 458 and 459) (see Ch. 4).
10 This led him to work out, in his *Trade Cycle*, the condition for the neutrality of inventions which led him first to an argument with Joan Robinson in 1937, and later to a number of comparisons with the alternative definition proposed by Hicks (on these developments see Besomi 1999b; Ch. 12: 318–19).
11 While Sraffa was preparing the Ricardo edition, Jacob Hollander behaved very badly, refusing to hand over or even reveal the contents of letters by Ricardo in his possession. There followed a long exchange, involving others besides Hollander and Sraffa (see Gehrke and Kurz 2002).
12 In a letter Sraffa explained to Keynes, who was at the time still ill and recovering from his heart attack, that his reply to Hollander 'has been, in your absence, entirely rewritten by the Second Bursar [Kahn]. It is a little too polite for my taste; my own version was full of abuse' (letter 1942 from PS to JMK, 20 October 1937).
13 Kahn reported that Sraffa also had reservations: 'Piero confirms that Kaldor is thoroughly muddled and merely fogs the issue' (letter 394 from RFK to JMK, 20 October 1937).

Table 11.1 Kahn–Sraffa correspondence

From	*To*	*Year*	*Month*	*Day*	*Date*	*Archive*		*Published in*	*Item*
PS	RFK	1929			Attributed	Kahn–King's	RFK/3/13/151–5		454
PS	RFK	1929	March	13	Dated letter	Kahn–King's	RFK/3/13/149–50		455
RFK	PS	1930	February	12	Dated letter	Sraffa–Trinity	Sraffa/D3/11/65/12		456
RFK	PS	1930	December	19	Dated letter	Sraffa–Trinity	Sraffa/D3/11/72/56		457
RFK	PS	1931			Attributed	Sraffa–Trinity	Sraffa/D1/83/1		458
PS	RFK	1931			Attributed	Sraffa–Trinity	Sraffa/D1/83/2		459
PS	RFK	1931			Attributed	Kahn–King's	RFK/13/57/255		460
PS	RFK	1932	May	18	Dated letter	Sraffa–Trinity	Sraffa/D3/11/64/37		461
RFK	PS	1933	February	17	Dated letter	Sraffa–Trinity	Sraffa/C/150/1–2		462
RFK	PS	1937	March	5	Dated letter	Sraffa–Trinity	Sraffa/B/10/2/6		463
PS	RFK	1937	May	28	Dated letter	Sraffa–Trinity	Sraffa/B/10/2/5		464
RFK	PS	1937	May	28	Dated letter	Sraffa–Trinity	Sraffa/B/10/2/7		465
RFK	PS	1937	June	1	Dated letter	Sraffa–Trinity	Sraffa/B/10/2/3	Marcuzzo 2004: 146, fn. 74 (E)	467
RFK	PS	1937	June	18	Dated letter	Sraffa–Trinity	Sraffa/B/10/2/4		468
PS	RFK	1937	October		Attributed	Kahn–King's	RFK/13/57/256	CWK XII: 23–4	469
RFK	PS	1937	December	21	Dated letter	Kahn–King's	RFK/13/57/386–7		470
RFK	PS	1938	September	1	Dated letter	Kahn–King's	RFK/13/57/338		466
RFK	PS	1946	August	28	Dated letter	Sraffa–Trinity	Sraffa/B/10/2/2		471
RFK	PS	1946	August	31	Dated letter	Marshall Library Archives			472
RFK	PS	1946	September	20	Dated letter	Sraffa–Trinity	Sraffa/B/10/2/1		473

Table 11.2 Kahn–Harrod correspondence

From	*To*	*Year*	*Month*	*Day*	*Date*	*Archive*		*Published in*	*Item*
RFK	RFH	1931	June	25	Dated letter	Harrod–Chiba	IV/586–638	Besomi 1999a: 46, (E)	1351
RFK	RFH	1932	March	24	Dated letter	Harrod–Chiba	IV/586–638b	Besomi 1999a: 46, (E)	1352
RFK	RFH	1932	April	18	Dated letter	Harrod–Chiba	IV/586–638b	Besomi 2000b: 357, (E)	1353
RFK	RFH	1933	November	12	Dated letter	Harrod–Chiba	IV/586–638	Harrod 2003: 230–1, (S)	1354
RFK	RFH	1933	November	15	Dated letter	Harrod–Chiba	IV/586–638	Harrod 2003: 233 (S)	1355
RFK	RFH	1933	November	18	Dated letter	Harrod–Chiba	IV/586–638	Harrod 2003: 235–6	1356
RFH	RFK	1934	October	15	Dated letter	Kahn–King's	RFK/13/57/87–94	Harrod 2003: 299–302	1357
RFH	RFK	1934	October	15	Dated letter	Kahn–King's	RFK/13/57/95	Harrod 2003: 302	1358
RFK	RFH	1934	October	22	Dated letter	Harrod–Chiba Kahn–King's	IV/586–658b RFK/13/57/83–6	Besomi 1999: 46, (E)	1359
RFH	RFK	1934	October	25	Dated letter	Kahn–King's	RFK/13/57/80–2	Besomi 1999: 46, 223, (E)	1360
RFK	RFH	1934	October	28	Dated letter	Harrod–Chiba	IV/586–658b	Besomi 1999: 46, (E)	1361
RFH	RFK	1934	October	29	Dated letter	Kahn–King's	RFK/13/57/77–9	Besomi 1999: 47, 223–4, (E)	1362
RFK	RFH	1934	November	1	Dated letter	Harrod–Chiba	IV/586–658b	Besomi 1999: 47–8, (E)	1363
RFH	RFK	1934	November	2	Dated letter	Kahn–King's	RFK/13/57/72–6	Harrod 2003: 325–7	1364
RFK	RFH	1934	November	10	Dated letter	Harrod–Chiba	IV/586–668b	Harrod 2003: 340–1	1365
RFK	RFH	1934	November	13	Dated letter	Harrod–Chiba Kahn–King's	IV/586–668b RFK/13/57/69–71	Harrod 2003: 341–2	1366
RFH	RFK	1934	November	17	Dated letter	Kahn–King's Kahn–King's	RFK/13/57/67–8 RFK/13/57/65–6	Besomi 1999: 5–6, 48, (E)	1367
RFK	RFH	1934	November	24	Dated letter	Harrod–Chiba	IV/586–668b	Harrod 2003: 353–4	1368
RFK	RFH	1935	January	8	Dated letter	Harrod–Chiba	IV/586–668b	Besomi 1999: 224, (E)	1369
RFK	RFH	1935	January	11	Dated letter	Harrod–Chiba	IV/586–668b	Harrod 2003: 365	1370
RFK	RFH	1935	March	6	Dated letter	Harrod–Chiba	IV/586–668b	Harrod 2003: 387	1371
RFK	RFH	1935	March	23	Dated letter	Harrod–Chiba	IV/586–668b	Harrod 2003: 389–90	1372
RFK	RFH	1935	April	6	Dated letter	Harrod–Chiba	IV/586–668b	Harrod 2003: 391–2	1373
RFK	RFH	1938	March	22	Dated letter	Harrod–Tokyo	174	Harrod 2003: 764 (S)	1374
RFH	RFK	1946	June	13	Dated letter	Kahn–King's	RFK/13/2/8		1375

Table 11.3 Kahn–Kaldor correspondence

From	*To*	*Year*	*Month*	*Day*	*Date*	*Archive*		*Published in*	*Item*
RFK	NK	1935	February	8	Dated letter	Kaldor–King's	NK/3/5/88–9		499
RFK	NK	1935	March	25	Dated letter	Kaldor–King's	NK/3/5/90–2		500

12 The unlooked for proselytiser

J. Robinson and the correspondence with Sraffa, Harrod and Kaldor

Annalisa Rosselli with Daniele Besomi

The correspondence of J. Robinson with Sraffa, Harrod and Kaldor is not numerous, consisting of 25, 40 and 24 letters respectively (see Tables 12.1 to 12.3). However limited, this correspondence well reflects the different relationships Robinson had with these economists in the period under examination.

Her relationship with Sraffa was the oldest, and the only one that developed into a true friendship in the early 1930s. It began when Robinson attended some of Sraffa's lectures in 1929 (see Ch. 10: 272 fn2) and was strengthened when they both took part in the Circus discussing Keynes's *Treatise* in 1930–31. Although a closer relationship began only a few years later, from the outset it benefited from the fact that they both lived in Cambridge and shared academic life in the Faculty.

On the contrary, Robinson's relationship with Kaldor and Harrod began very formally, and with Kaldor it remained so until 1939. In that year the LSE, where Kaldor had held a post since 1932, moved out to Cambridge. At the time of the first extant letter, in 1934, they had already met. Robinson acknowledged the acquaintance with Kaldor in a letter to Kahn of 2 April 1933: 'I have been invited by Miss Joseph (who was here the other day with Ruth Cohen) to meet Kaldor who has, it seems, a desire to make my acquaintance'(letter 595). The impression he gave, Robinson commented to Kahn in a following letter, was mixed '[he] is intelligent, but very much in the silly tradition. [...] He is quite nice to argue with'(letter 597, 7 April 1933). Further contacts must have been fostered by the meetings of the Consultative Board of the *Review of Economic Studies,* the first issue of which was published in the Autumn 1933, and by occasional seminars at the LSE or in Cambridge. However, geographical separation and differences in approach to economic theory kept their relationship on very formal terms until 1939, when we see them getting onto first-name terms.

Harrod had been a frequent visitor at Cambridge since 1922, when he was at King's College for the Michaelmas term, and where he returned from time to time. He was certainly well acquainted with Austin Robinson and, after the first exchange in 1931, the tone of his correspondence with Joan Robinson shows greater familiarity.

Not surprisingly, Robinson's correspondence with each of them begins with some problem related to the theory of imperfect competition. In fact, in the early 1930s Robinson, Harrod and Kaldor were all actively engaged on this topic, while Sraffa had provided the inspiration for this new line in research.

The first section of this chapter will review the correspondence over *The Economics of Imperfect Competition* (henceforth EIC), while the following sections will examine the successive letters distinguishing those about theoretical issues and those on personal matters.

The debate over *The Economics of Imperfect Competition* with Sraffa, Harrod and Kaldor

The correspondence of Robinson with Sraffa over the making of EIC runs from 5 May 1931 to 16 January 1933. Let us remember that Robinson began to formulate some of her ideas which then became part of EIC in the summer of 1930, although the decision to write a book containing all the results achieved in analysis of the firm, based on the principle of the marginal revenue, dates from April 1931 (see Ch. 10: 260–1).

Sraffa's contribution appears concentrated in two phases. The first was at the beginning of the work, in May 1931, when a provisional draft of Chapter 8 of EIC ('A digression on rent') was submitted to him. In fact, according to the table of contents Robinson jotted down as soon as she decided to write her book, the chapter on rent was meant to be the second, and thus probably was one of the first to be written (letter 751 from JVR to RFK, 1 April 1931). The second contribution by Sraffa that we find in the correspondence came during the correction of the final proofs, in 1933, when Sraffa commented on Book III of EIC, which includes the chapter on rent with several remarks on the article he had written in the *Economic Journal* in 1926 (Sraffa 1926). Robinson's impression that 'Piero has sent back the proof of Book III which I sent him. He can't swallow the modern demand curve, but otherwise makes no big point – some useful minor ones' (letter 534 from JVR to RFK, 18 January 1933) is borne out in the covering letter Sraffa sent her with the corrected proofs: 'I have scribbled remarks on small points on the proofs [. . .] I have avoided raising "broad issues" – it would be of no use to you at this stage, or indeed at any stage' (letter 1982, 12 January 1933).

Robinson had always acknowledged her debt to Sraffa for her own interest in a theory alternative to Marshall's perfect competition (see, for example, her introduction to the first edition of EIC where she admits her 'chief debt' towards Sraffa (J. Robinson 1933a: v). She had followed at least some of Sraffa's lectures, which gave ample space to the themes of both of Sraffa's 1925 and 1926 articles. It was therefore only natural that she should submit to Sraffa some of her findings regarding the elements that can make it possible to draw an upward sloping supply curve for a single industry, showing costs that vary with output. Robinson's aim was to show that there are cases that Sraffa had not considered which made Sraffa's critique of Marshall's theory of value less forceful.

The content of Sraffa's critique is well known: increasing costs are confined to the rare case of an industry in which there is a 'specialised factor' employed exclusively by that industry. This factor, being available in a fixed quantity, causes recourse to less and less efficient combinations with other variable factors. In all other cases where the factor is shared with other industries, either an industry uses that factor only in a negligible percentage of the amount available, which means that an increase in the industry's demand for the factor cannot determine a rise in its price (thus the supply of the factor, although fixed for the system as a whole, may be considered infinitely elastic for that industry), or the industry uses a substantial proportion of the factor, so that an increase in demand for the factor leads to rising prices for all the industries using it. The result is an increase in costs for the other industries with a rise in the price of their products, which are often substitutes for the output of the industry under consideration, whose demand curve shifts. This violates the *ceteris paribus* rule for the determination of partial equilibrium, which states that supply must be independent of demand. Therefore, according to Sraffa, the supply curve of a factor for an industry is either perfectly elastic and costs do not vary with output or, if increasing, causes irremediable damage to Marshall's theory of prices.

Robinson's attempt to save Marshall's theory (although she denies any intention of defending it) seems to have focused on the likelihood of finding cases in which an industry faces increasing costs. Behind the increasing costs lie two causes: decreasing productivity and/or increasing price of the factors. The former case was discussed by Sraffa in his criticism of Marshall, which seems to have been accepted by Robinson; she therefore had recourse to the latter and tried to demonstrate that, allowing for the possibility of heterogeneity of a factor from the point of view of its uses in one industry and/or in alternative uses, its supply curve could be rising for one single industry. She writes to Sraffa

> You only seem to allow for two cases: (1) a perfectly elastic supply of the factor; (2) a perfectly inelastic supply [. . .]. Why am I not right in taking the view that as land (and to some extent labour or management) are not homogeneous there are likely to be a lot of cases in between?
>
> (letter 1064, 1931)

She must have provided a classification of these cases, probably similar to the one which appears in EIC (J. Robinson 1933a: 110–14), where she discusses the cases which lead to an upward sloping supply of a factor. She writes to Sraffa: 'it seems to me that my four types do increase the likelihood of finding cases, as your kind of specialized factor would all come under my first head and leave the other to be filled up with additional cases' (ibid.). Sraffa was not convinced: 'Your subdivision of the "specialized factor" cases into groups [...] is an interesting piece of analysis, but it does not in the least help to increase their number' (letter 1978, 31 May 1931). In fact, in the same letter he remarks that she was unable to cite any other example of 'specialized factor' but the usual one of the 'mineral which no other industry uses'. However, we do not know what stage her reasoning had reached at the time she discussed this issue with Sraffa. The text submitted to him in 1931 has not survived, which also makes it impossible to understand some of Sraffa's comments. What is certain is that Robinson failed to convince Sraffa, who concluded:

> On the whole, in the question of the *a priori* reasoning, as far as it goes, you accept the criticism; and in the question of fact you have not produced the evidence. I am therefore unable, in the name of whichever school I am supposed to be identified with, to acknowledge defeat.
>
> (letter 1978, 31 May 1931)

The basic disagreement therefore remained, as they both recognised. For Sraffa it was of prime importance to have demonstrated that Marshall had based his analysis of the relationship between cost and quantity on extremely restrictive hypotheses, since this showed up the artificiality of the demand and supply symmetry and demonstrated that Marshall had drawn supply curves 'based on the sort of Diminishing Returns that is appropriate for distribution' (ibid.). For her part, while appreciating Sraffa's position, Robinson never showed an inclination to follow him at the level of radical criticism of Marshall's theory of perfect competition, retaining a highly ambiguous stance in this respect. She argues in EIC that with the necessary adjustment, difficult as it may be in practice, Marshall's theory was in principle emendable (J. Robinson 1933a: 117–18). Behind her attitude there might have been a certain anxiety to defend, more than Marshall, the results of her own work. As she writes to Sraffa: 'I am not trying to defend Marshall and his knife-handles[1] – I don't mind how few the cases of I.C. [increasing costs] are as long as there are some on which I can use my ingenious analysis of monopoly under I.C.' (letter 1064, 1931).

Robinson's position is explained and justified in her *Economics is a Serious Subject* (J. Robinson 1932b), pleading the optimism of the analytic economist who, for lack of anything better, will even accept heroic hypotheses provided that the problem remains within the bounds of formal treatment: 'I see that all you want is that Diminishing Returns should be very rare and I don't mind at all if it is' (letter 1063, 1931). In contrast, Robinson saw Sraffa as the 'Continental fundamental pessimist' who highlights the hypotheses underlying the analytic procedure, shows how restrictive they are, but thus condemns himself to making economics a science that is 'not serious'.

Sraffa replies to Robinson's accusation of pessimism with a joke: 'who is the idiotic continental economist on p. 6? anyhow he had no right to disgrace a whole Continent' (letter 1979, October 1932) and, more seriously, rejects the accusation of denying the 'possibility of having a serious subject dealing with human beings'. He writes:

> Economics [. . .] has taken in modern society to a large extent the place that theology had in the Middle Ages; and there has never been anything as serious as that [. . .] It is just because one thinks that theology cannot stand rational criticism that one regards as possible a scientific study of the objects of theology (e.g. the origin of man, physical cosmogony, etc.). I mean to say that the fog is not outside, in the air or in human society, but inside the heads of theologians (and economists).
>
> (letter 1981, 31 October 1932)

This was also the reason why the comments on the proofs of EIC that Sraffa sent to Robinson from Italy in January 1933 keep well away from the 'broad issues' (letter 1982, 12 January 1933), as indeed Sraffa had decided they should. Explaining that he has written a few remarks directly on the proofs, Sraffa limits himself to expressing his dissatisfaction with what Robinson calls the 'modern demand curves' (letter 534 from JVR to RFK, 18 January 1933) which, in Sraffa's definition, 'include in the individual demand curve the reaction in demand due to change in price of other firms due to change in price of the first firm' (letter 1057, 16 January 1933). It is the idea itself of a conjectural not observable demand curve, that at first seems to trouble Sraffa. As he wrote: 'why should the entry of new firms lower the dem[and] curves of old firms? But the entry is due to the old firms having raised their prices, and their curves should show all effects without being shifted about'. Robinson commented to Kahn: 'I fear he has a vested interest in demand curves that require other prices to be constant' (letter 534 from JVR to RFK, 18 January 1933).

The discussion with Robinson continued face-to-face when Sraffa returned to Cambridge after the Christmas vacation. Robinson reported her progress to Kahn: 'Afterwards we continued to debate about demand curves. He now admits that he doesn't know what his objection is but he's sure there is one' (letter 543 from JVR to RFK, 25 January 1933). Yet her efforts were not quite successful: 'I have succeeded in budging him a bit, but he will not concede the point until he has thought some more' (letter 541 from JVR to RFK, 23 January 1933).

At the end of the discussion Sraffa promised Robinson a few footnotes. We do not know whether they were ever written, but a couple of months later a much worried Robinson reported to Kahn the doubts Sraffa had raised before leaving for the vacation:

> The trouble about duopoly is this. Firm A says to himself if I fix price y_1, B will have such and such a demand curve. Then he will find it profitable to sell x_2 at y_2 and I will sell x_1. So he draws up a demand curve for himself and sets a price. B accommodates himself accordingly and the position is stable. But suppose B went thro' the same process. He could fix a different price and expect A to accommodate himself. A second stable position is reached. Or suppose each simultaneously fixes his price by this process. Then two prices are reached which are not compatible. They crash about, and reach a third position. It all seems most queer. If there is really a bad snag here it is rather serious as it affects the validity of our method of doing demand curves.
>
> (letter 591 from JVR to RFK, 23 March 1933)

If Robinson reported Sraffa's objections correctly, he was well aware of how difficult it could be to prove the existence of equilibrium in a duopoly when both players rationally pursue a strategy of profit maximisation; in any case, he knew that the solution could not be found while preserving a partial equilibrium approach that takes into consideration one firm at a time. Whether it was this analytical problem that troubled Sraffa or the fact that conjectural demand curves are relations that have no objective or empirical foundations, we do not know. Be that as it may, from then on we find no more references to imperfect competition in the correspondence between Robinson and Sraffa.

The limitations of the method of partial equilibrium are also the focus of the first exchange of Robinson with Kaldor. Robinson praised Kaldor's article on 'The equilibrium of the firm' (Kaldor 1934a) (letter 865, 29 March 1934), a conception that she regards as crucial to both the Paretian and the Marshallian method. In his reply (letter 866, 10 April 1934) Kaldor points out that the introduction of demand curves for the individual firms in imperfect competition makes the concept of supply curve of a single industry untenable since 'it will not be possible to formulate any functional relationship between price and the amount produced, since a whole series of output can be associated with any particular price'. He reiterates the same critique – which obviously stems from his general equilibrium approach – in his review of EIC, which he defines 'the ultimate logical outcome of Marshallian method' (Kaldor 1934b). Robinson's comments on the review are not extant, but she does not seem to have been displeased by it. Nowhere, in fact, did Robinson show any intention of abandoning Marshall's method of partial equilibrium.

However, a few years later Kaldor and Robinson appear on the same side against Chamberlin and his article about the differences between his monopolistic and Robinson's imperfect competition (Chamberlin 1937). Kaldor was prone to react and take sides. He wrote to Robinson that 'he would take the liberty to defend you and Kahn and Pigou as well' (letter 874, 7 October 1937). Soon after he published a rebuttal of Chamberlin (Kaldor 1938b) and volunteered to write another one in response to Chamberlin's Reply, but Robinson dissuaded him (letter 876, 27 May 1938). They seem to have shared the view that Chamberlin was 'alarmed at finding out the anti *laissez-faire* implications of his own analysis' (letter 875, 17 November 1937), thus anticipating their future alliance in the anti-*laissez-faire* battles.

While Sraffa and Kaldor show a fundamental disagreement with Robinson's book, although from different standpoints, Harrod appears to be perfectly in tune with Robinson's effort. Their discussion deals exclusively with technical points. The first exchange took place in December 1931 (letters 1101 and 1102, 10 and 13 December 1931). It was occasioned by a mistake in Harrod's 'The Law of Decreasing Costs' (1931), which Robinson pointed out (letter 1101) and Harrod acknowledged (letter 1102 and Harrod 1932b: 492).

The second exchange (letters 1106–1110, 1147 and 1148, 4–23 March 1933) regarded excess capacity and the notion of normal profit to be included in the average cost curve. Harrod opened the correspondence by criticising the definition of normal rate of profit given by Robinson in her 1932 article in the *Economic Journal* (J. Robinson 1932a) which was not very clear – a point also raised by Shove. Harrod thus summarises the main difference between them:

> The difference between us is that in drawing a total cost curve, you assumed that fixed plant is reckoned as earning that rate of profit which it does earn on the average, I that rate of profit which in the long period it does earn at the margin.
>
> (letter 1106, March 1933)

Robinson, who found the letter 'a bit silly' (letter 799 from JVR to RFK, 18 March 1933) explained that the choice of the relevant profit rate to be included in the long-period average cost curve depended on the problem under examination: 'I do not think there is a Platonic Ideal Average which one must find, and use for all purposes. The definitions must be made in each case which are appropriate to the problem in hand' (letter 1107, 18 March 1933). And she added that when the problem was to determine the number of firms in an industry, her choice was correct. When the number of firms was fixed, average cost had no role to play in determining the output the firm must produce, although it might still have one in determining the optimum size of the firm.

Harrod however was not convinced:

> There are 2 conditions for long period equilibrium. 1. Profit must not be so high as to attract new firms. 2. Profit on marginal fixed equipment must be equal to the firm's own supply price of fixed equipment. In your article you certainly seemed to say that normal profits are those at which new firms are just not tempted to enter in and to say that in long period equilibrium firms must be earning a normal profit. I hold that in long period equilibrium a firm may be earning less than normal profit in this sense; but it must be earning normal profit at the margin in my sense.
>
> (letter 1110, 23 March 1933)[2]

The following exchange (letters 1111–1114, 1 July to 19 August 1933) is significant in that it contains Harrod's first complaint that the discovery of 'marginal revenue' was not attributed to him (see Ch. 3).

Further correspondence on theoretical issues

After the publication of EIC and until the war, Robinson's interest lay in the dissemination of the new ideas of the *General Theory* and their generalisation to an open economy, to the long period and to when technical progress occurs (see Ch. 6: 183–4).

However, the relation between these issues and the extant correspondence with Sraffa is not evident. Two letters by Sraffa of 9 and 11 December 1935 (letters 1983 and 1984) are not easy to understand as we lack the other side of the correspondence. Their subject seems to be whether the rate of interest can be overdetermined or negative (Sraffa denies the former but admits the latter, although only in principle). The 1936 letter (letter 1985, 27 October 1936) is of much greater interest, since it anticipates with extraordinary clarity the problem underlying the famous capital controversy of the 1950s, namely that – unlike land and labour – capital is not a factor susceptible to physical measurement. Sraffa's position here is that we must indeed speak of measurable quantities ('Sidgwick [. . .] after lecturing Ricardo on how meaningless it is to talk of a quantity of labour, goes on cheerfully himself to talk of quantities of utility'). However, capital is not subject to measurement: 'How many tons is, e.g., a railway tunnel?' The problem of the measurement of capital was not new in Cambridge and it had already been discussed by Shove in his review of Hicks (Shove 1933c). What is interesting here is the comparison between the soundness of two alternative theories of value, a subject that Sraffa had investigated while preparing his lectures in the late 1920s (Rosselli 2004).

On the other hand, Robinson's role as propagator of the new Keynesian doctrine is clear in her correspondence with Kaldor on the wage subsidies 'Plan' (Kaldor 1936). He had published it in the autumn of 1935 and 'circulated [it] privately to colleagues including Hugh Gaitskell,

Sraffa and Robinson' (Thirlwall 1987: 61). Kaldor argued that wage subsidies were a possible alternative to a cut in money wages to alleviate unemployment. His argument was that 'a scheme of wage-subsidies, in contradistinction to a reduction of money wages, does not reduce the price level of a given output; since it does not reduce the effective money-demand for commodities' (letter 869, 29 May 1935).

Robinson's immediate objection on seeing a draft of the plan was obvious from a Keynesian point of view: when there is a decrease in costs, 'Why do not prices fall?' (letter 868, 28 May 1935). And she insisted in a further letter:

> Your statement that price of a given output depends not upon cost but upon effective demand (in money terms) also seems to be flawed. Effective demand depends upon money incomes and money incomes depend in part upon prices. And (I should have said) prices depend in part upon costs. You cannot so easily throw away the whole of the Principles of Economics.
>
> (letter 870, 1 June 1935)

Clearly, while Robinson was already arguing in terms which would become clear with the publication of the *General Theory*, Kaldor's reasoning follows different lines. 'I fear that Cambridge economics is beyond me' he comments despairingly. And he goes on: 'I thought that economists since Senior were generally agreed that costs can only affect price by influencing supply. Or are we returning to a naive costs-of-production theory of value?' (letter 871, 3 June 1935). Robinson suggests interrupting their exchange until 'agreement about fundamentals' is reached and urges him to provide a statement of his views regarding the determination of 'employment, prices, real wages the rate of interest etc.' (letter 872, 3 June 1935). Then, obviously anticipating with pleasure the confrontations that the *General Theory* was to arouse, she adds: 'I hope you will not be too much discouraged at a first set-back. There's bound to be a lot of trouble for some time yet'. She was implicitly proposing herself as tutor of the new Keynesian ideas, but Kaldor withdrew from the role of pupil.

Their exchange was to resume, on a more equal footing, when Kaldor was 'converted' to Keynesianism. Kaldor asked for Robinson's opinion on his article on capital intensity and the trade cycle (Kaldor 1939a), written with the aim of drawing attention to the role played by the methods of production in determining the trade cycle. The article concluded that, contrary to the views of the Austrian School, failure of the capital intensity to increase and not excessive increase was the cause of the end of a boom. Robinson had a methodological objection (letter 878, 18 April 1939), as the method of the representative firm adopted by Kaldor did not appear to her the best suited since the number of firms must be taken into account and it is not clear whether the rate of new firms entering the market is the same with a boom as with a depression. She seems to have abandoned some of the certainties of the past: 'the question of what one means by a firm, and in respect to what the commodity demand curve is falling is always awkward'. All in all, she seems to favour an empirical approach to the problem: 'Is boom investment actually less capitalistic?' (ibid.).

Two long letters (letter 879, November 1939 and letter 881, 11 January 1940) of detailed comments by Robinson on Kaldor's article on speculation (Kaldor 1939b), discussing the relationship between short and long term rates, conclude the theoretical exchange. Later correspondence between them relates only to occasional matters connected with the activities they shared in the war years such as the Committee on the Profit Margin (King 2000a) and BBC programmes.

Apart from a few occasional letters, prompted by the publication of some of the authors' writings (among which *Economics is a Serious Subject*, letters 1103 and 1104, 27 and 29 October 1932), Harrod's collective letter to *The Times* on 'More Money in Circulation' (letter 1105, 25 February 1933) and the Oxford Economists' Research group inquiry on the rate of interest (letters 1137 and 1138, 11 and 14 March 1938) (see Besomi 1998), the correspondence between Robinson and Harrod centres on technological progress.

In June 1937, Harrod reviewed Robinson's *Essays in the Theory of Employment* for the *Economic Journal*. This occasioned a very interesting exchange, of which unfortunately only Robinson's letters are extant, on the classification of technological progress (letters 1119–1125, 7 May to 16 June 1937).

In her book, Robinson had adopted Hicks's classification of inventions and defined a neutral invention as one that leaves the ratio of marginal productivity of capital to that of labour unchanged when the relative amounts of the factors are unchanged (J. Robinson 1937a: 132). Harrod criticised some aspects of the production function approach and proposed the alternative classification implied in the argument of the *Trade Cycle*. In particular, Harrod attacked Robinson's use of the concept of elasticity of substitution (see Ch. 6: 183–4), and proposed as an alternative definition of neutral inventions 'to divide inventions into those which at a given rate of interest, and an infinitely elastic supply of capital at that rate, increase, leave unchanged or diminish the length of the productive process' (Harrod 1937a: 329).

Robinson was intrigued by Harrod's alternative classification, and endeavoured to express the conditions under which the two notions coincide with respect to the problem of the effect of inventions on the distribution of income. The difficulty began with the very first step, as Robinson rightly observed that Harrod claimed both that neutral inventions raise 'the m[arginal] p[roductivity] of labour and capital in the same proportions' and that '(with constant rate of interest) [leave] the period of production unchanged'. Moreover, she raised some doubts 'about measuring capital by the period of production' (letter 1119, 7 May 1937). From Robinson's next letter it would seem that Harrod explained that he measured roundaboutness in terms of capital per head, while she refers to the total stock of capital (letter 1120, 13 May 1937).

Having cleared up the terminological difficulties, Robinson sought to compare the domains of application of Harrod's, Hicks's and Pigou's definitions by mapping the respective regions along a unidimensional line (the dimension was not specified, but was presumably the relative shares of capital and labour of the national dividend) (letter 1121, 30 May 1937). Such an attempt was doomed to failure (admitted in letter 1123, 8 June 1937), for Harrod's notion left out a fundamental ingredient for determining the distribution of income along the lines dictated by the production function approach: in fact, the production function itself was missing, or at least some assumption regarding either the elasticity of substitution between capital and labour or variations in the relationship between prices and productivity. The success of Robinson's further attempt therefore required consideration of the induced variations of the relative productivities of capital and labour, which led to the conclusion that Harrod's neutral case

> would correspond to a case where, in my language the invention is neutral (Hicks) and $\eta = 1$. But equally it would correspond to a whole range of cases in which the invention is capital or labour saving (Hicks) and η correspondingly greater or less than 1.
>
> (letter 1123, 8 June 1937)[3]

The last extensive exchange between Robinson and Harrod in the period under consideration is more political than theoretical. It regarded the population problem and was occasioned by Harrod's collective letter to *The Times* (21 January 1938) in favour of the Population (Statistics) bill, debated in the House of Commons in 1937–38. The discussion went far beyond the point of the letter, with Harrod airing all his worries on declining population and Robinson being more preoccupied with abortion, family planning and family allowances (letters 1126–1136, 12 January to 3 March 1938). Harrod argued, in fact, that 'there seems hardly any chance of saving the British race from more or less complete extinction' (letter 1126, 12 January 1938). He was pursuing the argument that individual women can be sacrificed 'to save our posterity'. He was worried that

> natural selection will get to work again and cause the survival of those races whose ideals and social institutions are adapted to large families. And in that process of survival I foresee a return of a dark age, the persecution of women, purdah rigidly enforced, violent intolerance, a recrudescence of crude religious superstition and probably a glorification of war.
>
> (ibid.)

In contrast, Robinson

> was thinking of the human rather than the statistical aspect of the question. There are still plenty of women who have children when they don't want to, and the campaign in which you are taking part is already hampering efforts to give birth control facilities to those who need them most, and I fear will help to put off all hope of legalising abortion.
>
> (letter 1127, 13 January 1938)

The whole debate came nowhere near agreement, probably because, as Robinson commented, the discussion 'involves one's whole philosophy of life and on such points it is useless to argue' (ibid.) This is one of the few examples in Robinson's correspondence in which gender really matters.

Friendship with Sraffa

After the short exchange on the measurement of capital, the remaining letters, both by Sraffa and by Robinson, do not touch on theoretical aspects but only on personal matters and they reveal the deep friendship and mutual respect that bound Robinson and Sraffa together in those years.

Six letters by Robinson conserved in the archives of Kahn – whom Sraffa probably entrusted them to – and sent between September and October 1938 are practically unintelligible, the handwriting notably changed, a number of corrections, insertions and references introduced: 'Sorry, I think so much faster than I write at this moment I leave out half my sentences' (letter 1065, 27 September 1938). They bring evidence of the serious bout of mental illness that saw Robinson hospitalised from October 1938 to March 1939. In the first letter she sent to Kahn after recovery from the worst crisis, Robinson wrote:

> I think it is best to write off altogether the queer week end of 1–3 October – but in dreams I have cleared out whatever grit there was in the machinery – so no one need worry about how or what or why this sad accident occurred. Please give my love to Piero.
>
> (letter 724 from JVR to RFK, 13 December 1938)

The letters do not shed light either on what the 'sad accident' was, or on the possible causes of such a serious crisis. Robinson had given birth to two daughters in 1934 and 1937 and published three books and a number of articles in less than six years. According to Keynes, 'The strain of combining babies with so much intellectual work is at the bottom of it' (letter 2209 from JMK to RFK, 4 October 1938). However, the whole crisis had in fact occurred immediately before the Munich Pact which saw the triumph of Chamberlain's appeasement policy and defeat for those who saw agreements with Hitler as not only indecorous but also quite useless. In one of the two letters that she sent to Sraffa on the same day (letter 1065, 27 September 1938), a greatly agitated Robinson insistently urges Sraffa – then in Italy – to come back to England immediately and points out that she had felt closely involved in the events through two members of her family. Her father 'has in all innocence bless his incredible simple heart been used to play a crucial part in Chamberlain scheme',[4] while her sister with a group of Conservative members of parliament had taken the alternative, hard line in favour of presenting Hitler with an ultimatum after his invasion of Czechoslovakia. Emotional turmoil, complex relations with Sraffa and Kahn and family conflict may well have combined with political conflict and the spectre of war to form a devastating mixture. No clear evidence emerges in the correspondence with Sraffa or indeed with anyone else.

The letters by Sraffa from December 1937 to February 1939 – while Robinson was recovering from her illness – have an interest that lies in the light they cast on Sraffa's personality and his attitudes towards the other figures at Cambridge.

They also testify of the real reciprocal understanding and respect that existed between Robinson and Sraffa in those years. While intense intellectual dialogue rapidly developed between them, their relations seem to have been kept to a rather formal level until 1933, one reason probably being a certain coyness on the part of Sraffa and the difficulty he had in talking about himself. In January 1933 Robinson, together with Kahn, still seems to have been trying to make out Sraffa's personality: 'I think he is very pleased at my references to him in Chapter I, which is rather an unexpected trait. I might add it to my Analysis'(letter 543 from JVR to RFK, 25 January 1933) and 'I went round to Piero at 11. A.M. and woke him up. He took it very well – he really is a very good natured type. I wasn't at all sure he would like it' (letter 547 from JVR to RFK, 31 January 1933). It was in fact during the absence of Kahn, in the United States from January to April 1933, that their friendship seems to have taken on new depth.

The tone of Sraffa's letters is humorous and affectionate, especially during the period of Robinson's nervous breakdown. Robinson was frequently consulted on academic decisions:

> Piero says he has now got to decide before the week-end whether he accepts the job designed for him. He says that after not thinking about it for two years he can't see how to decide so quickly. But it doesn't look as if there would be any trouble. He's definitely to be paid for not sitting in the library so it ought to suit him nicely.
>
> (letter 649 from JVR to RFK, 1 November 1934)

Other aspects emerging from the correspondence include Sraffa's real feelings of friendship for Dobb (Sraffa explains he would be ready to forego the offer of a Fellowship at Trinity if it were offered to Dobb), no great respect for the work of Champernowne who has written a paper 'to prove that the multiplier does not multiply' (letter 1989, 10 January 1939) and a clear liking for Dennis Robertson, to the extent that he declares he is 'rather sad' about his abandonment of Cambridge ('but Kahn thinks this is a disgraceful feeling', letter 1988, 28 December 1938). We also note Sraffa's concern for Kalecki and commitment to finding him a post at Cambridge, while some affectionate leg-pulling is reserved for the singularly scrupulous Kahn (who, on Keynes's advice, went to see 'why the death rate of the College pigs is so much higher than that of Maynard's private ones'(letter 1989, 10 January 1939). In particular, the long letter in which Sraffa spells out to Robinson the reasons for and against deciding to accept the Fellowship at Trinity left vacant by Robertson is extremely revealing with regard to Sraffa's feelings about the Cambridge environment (Marcuzzo 2004), including a mixture of vindictiveness and superiority that induced him to turn down something he knew many avidly aspired to

> a sort of disgust at the attitude of some people in Cambridge to a Fellowship: the immoderate desire to get one, and the absurd conceit of some who have it. This is similar to the attitude of other people to titles etc which is one of my horrors.
>
> (letter 1991, 15 February 1939)

The last extant letter of the correspondence in this period was sent by Sraffa to Robinson in 1940, in the days preceding his internment as an enemy alien, from the hospital where he had on the advice of Keynes (letter 1516 from JVR to RFK, 3 June 1940) gone to, both to have his shingles treated and in the hope of delaying his arrest.

Sraffa had for some time been prepared for this eventuality, ever since Italy's entry into the war became imminent (letter 1511 from JVR to RFK, 16 May 1940) and the news spread about life in the camps where the Germans and Austrians had already been interned. While sharing in the apprehensive expectation, Robinson could not help remarking with her usual ready wit: 'Piero has been thinking about the camp life so much I really believe now he will be quite disappointed if he weren't taken'(letter 1520 from JVR to RFK, 12 June 1940). Nevertheless, Robinson's concern was real, and when she arrived in Cornwall at the end of June seeking refuge from the air raids with her children, she never failed to ask after Sraffa in her letters to Kahn. She also wrote to Sraffa's mother (Mrs Piero, as she called her), urging her to keep her informed.

In this letter of 27 June 1940 (letter 1992), Sraffa showed concern over his imminent arrest, not only on account of the hard living conditions and the thought of how much the prisoners in the camps were deprived of, but above all at the prospect of having no newspapers or information in a crucial phase of the war: 'the real horror is not to be allowed to see any newspapers; no doubt they wish to put the whole population on that diet'.

A few days later Sraffa was arrested, and it was Robinson who spread the news, writing to Kahn: 'Letter from Mrs. S.[raffa] Piero was carried off on Thursday. I hope that won't send him to Canada and drown him. Mrs S. promises to write as soon as she knows anything more. Will you tell Maynard' (letter 1534 from JVR to RFK, 6 July 1940).

There are no letters from Sraffa to Robinson during his internment on the Isle of Man. Robinson wrote to him twice, but the correspondence did not get through – nor did a Fortnum and Mason parcel and the cigarettes she and Kahn sent him. Keynes immediately set about doing what he could for Sraffa and the other friends interned, but results were slow in coming and, vexed by the injustice her friend had to endure, Robinson remarked: 'I wonder if the authorities also have forgotten that there are antifascist Italians' (letter 1550 from JVR to RFK, 1 August 1940). It still took over a month before Robinson was able triumphantly to proclaim Keynes's success in having Sraffa released. Physically Sraffa was weakened, but his spirits must have been quite high if Robinson could write to Kahn: 'Piero is really appreciating being out and finds it delightful to be allowed to help himself to bread and jam. He says he will eat too much and get horribly fat' (letter 1595 from JVR to RFK, 14 October 1940).

Fondness, concern, self-irony and an indulgent attitude to the other's weaknesses at a time when their theoretical positions were at their most distant thus characterise relations in the 1930s between Robinson and Sraffa, the latter being the only one who seems to have been able to stem the impetus of Robinson's proselytising spirit, which she profused lavishly on Kaldor and Harrod.

Notes

1 The case when the supply price of a product is increasing because it is the sum of the increasing supply prices of its factors is referred to by Sraffa, J. Robinson and Kahn as the 'knife-handles' case, quoting the example in Marshall's *Principles* (Marshall 1920: 384).

2 This view was eventually incorporated in (Harrod 1933d); see for context Sardoni (1999).

3 This conclusion was resumed in J. Robinson (1938a), which indirectly gave rise to prolonged debate in the 1960s. See, for an assessment of this and the following debates, Besomi (1999a).

4 Her father had signed a petition to give the British Legion to Hitler (letter from Austin Robinson to JMK, 4 October 1938, JMK papers, L/K/100).

Table 12.1 J. Robinson–Sraffa correspondence

From	*To*	*Year*	*Month*	*Day*	*Date*	*Archive*		*Published in*	*Item*
JVR	PS	1931			Attributed	Sraffa–Trinity	Sraffa/D1/86/1		1063
JVR	PS	1931			Attributed	Sraffa–Trinity	Sraffa/D1/86/2		1064
PS	JVR	1931	May	31	Dated letter	Robinson–King's	JVR/vii/431/1–3		1978
						Sraffa–Trinity	Sraffa/D1/87		
PS	JVR	1932	October	Thursday	Attributed	Robinson–King's	JVR/vii/431/5	Harcourt 1990: 421, (E)	1979
						Robinson–King's	JVR/i/2.3/24		
PS	JVR	1932	October	14	Dated letter	Robinson–King's	JVR/vii/431/4		1980
PS	JVR	1932	October	31	Dated letter	Robinson–King's	JVR/vii/431/6–7	Harcourt 1990: 421, (S)	1981
PS	JVR	1933	January	12	Dated letter	Robinson–King's	JVR/vii/431/8		1982
PS	JVR	1933	January	16	Dated letter	Robinson–King's	JVR/vii/431/8–9		1057
PS	JVR	1935	December	9	Dated letter	Robinson–King's	JVR/vii/431/10–11		1983
PS	JVR	1935	December	11	Dated letter	Robinson–King's	JVR/vii/431/12–13		1984
PS	JVR	1936	October	27	Dated letter	Robinson–King's	JVR/vii/431/14–15	Bradford and Harcourt 1997: 131, (E)	1985
PS	JVR	1937	December	30	Dated letter	Robinson–King's	JVR/vii/431/16		1986
PS	JVR	1938	August	4	Dated letter	Robinson–King's	JVR/vii/431/17–18		1987
JVR	PS	1938	September		Attributed	Sraffa–Trinity	Sraffa/J/8/1–8		1055
JVR	PS	1938	September	27	Postmark	Kahn–King's	RFK/13/90/3/30–2		1065
JVR	PS	1938	September	27	Postmark	Kahn–King's	RFK/13/90/3/33–7		1066
JVR	PS	1938	October		Attributed	Kahn–King's	RFK/13/90/3/38–9		1058
JVR	PS	1938	October		Attributed	Kahn–King's	RFK/13/90/3/40		1059
JVR	PS	1938	October		Attributed	Kahn–King's	RFK/13/90/3/41		1060
JVR	PS	1938	October	2	Postmark	Kahn–King's	RFK/13/90/3/42–3		1056
PS	JVR	1938	December	28	Dated letter	Robinson–King's	JVR/vii/431/19–22		1988
PS	JVR	1939	January	10	Dated letter	Robinson–King's	JVR/vii/431/23–4		1989
PS	JVR	1939	January	31	Dated letter	Robinson–King's	JVR/vii/431/25–6	Marcuzzo 2004: 141, fn. 54 (E)	1990
PS	JVR	1939	February	15	Dated letter	Robinson–King's	JVR/vii/431/27–32	Marcuzzo 2004: 153, fn. 89, (E)	1991
PS	JVR	1940	June	27	Dated letter	Robinson–King's	JVR/vii/431/33–4	Naldi 2004: 115–16 and fn. 57, (E)	1992

Table 12.2 J. Robinson–Harrod correspondence

From	To	Year	Month	Day	Date	Archive		Published in	Item
JVR	RFH	1931	December	10	Attributed	Harrod–Chiba	IV/1089–107	Harrod 2003: 139–40	1101
RFH	JVR	1931	December	13	Dated letter	Robinson–King's	JVR vii/191/1	Harrod 2003: 140–1	1102
RFH	JVR	1932	October	27	Dated letter	Robinson–King's	JVR vii/191/2	Harrod 2003: 183	1103
JVR	RFH	1932	October	29	Attributed	Harrod–Tokyo	216	Harrod 2003: 183–4	1104
JVR	RFH	1933	February	25	Postmark	Harrod–Chiba	IV/1270–1303/9	Harrod 2003: 204 (E)	1105
RFH	JVR	1933	March		Attributed	Robinson–King's	JVR vii/191/3–4	Harrod 2003: 207–9	1106
JVR	RFH	1933	March	4	Dated letter	Harrod–Chiba	IV/1270–1303/25	Harrod 2003: 207	1147
JVR	RFH	1933	March	10	Attributed	Harrod–Chiba	IV/1270–1303/9		1148
JVR	RFH	1933	March	18	Attributed	Harrod–Chiba	IV/1089–107	Harrod 2003: 209–11	1107
RFH	JVR	1933	March	21	Dated letter	Robinson–King's	JVR vii/191/5–6	Harrod 2003: 211–12	1108
RFH	JVR	1933	March	23	Dated letter	Robinson–King's	JVR vii/191/7–8	Harrod 2003: 213–15	1110
JVR	RFH	1933	March	21–23	Inferred from other sources	Harrod–Chiba	IV/1089–107	Harrod 2003: 212	1109
RFH	JVR	1933	July	1	Dated letter	Robinson–King's	JVR vii/191/9–10	Besomi 2003: 222–3	1111
JVR	RFH	1933	July	10	Attributed	Harrod–Chiba	IV/963–73	Harrod 2003: 223	1112
RFH	JVR	1933	August	16	Dated letter	Robinson–King's	JVR vii/191/11–12	Harrod 2003: 223–4	1113
JVR	RFH	1933	August	19	Attributed	Harrod–Chiba	IV/1089–107	Harrod 2003: 224–5	1114
RFH	JVR	1933	October	6	Dated letter	Robinson–King's	JVR vii/191/13	Harrod 2003: 226	1115
RFH	JVR	1934	March	5	Dated letter	Robinson–King's	JVR vii/191/14	Harrod 2003: 267	1116
JVR	RFH	1934	March	10	Postmark	Harrod–Chiba	IV/1089–107	Harrod 2003: 269–70	1117
RFH	JVR	1934	October	16	Dated letter	Robinson–King's	JVR vii/191/15	Harrod 2003: 302	1118
JVR	RFH	1937	May	7	Attributed	Harrod–Chiba	IV/1089–107	Harrod 2003: 690–1	1119
JVR	RFH	1937	May	13	Attributed	Harrod–Chiba	IV/1089–107	Harrod 2003: 692–3	1120
JVR	RFH	1937	May	30	Attributed	Harrod–Chiba	IV/1089–107	Harrod 2003: 695–6	1121
JVR	RFH	1937	June	3	Attributed	Harrod–Chiba	IV/1089–107	Harrod 2003: 696	1122
JVR	RFH	1937	June	8	Attributed	Harrod–Chiba	IV/1089–107	Harrod 2003: 697–9	1123
JVR	RFH	1937	June	12	Attributed	Harrod–Chiba	IV/1089–107	Harrod 2003: 700	1124

Table 12.2 continued

From	*To*	*Year*	*Month*	*Day*	*Date*	*Archive*		*Published in*	*Item*
JVR	RFH	1937	June	16	Attributed	Harrod–Chiba	IV/1089–107	Harrod 2003: 703–4	1125
RFH	JVR	1938	January	12	Dated letter	Robinson–King's	JVR vii/191/16–19	Harrod 2003: 745–6	1126
JVR	RFH	1938	January	13	Postmark	Harrod–British Library	72737/1–2	Harrod 2003: 748–9	1127
RFH	JVR	1938	January	18	Dated letter	Robinson–King's	JVR vii/191/20–3	Harrod 2003: 749–50	1128
JVR	RFH	1938	January	19	Postmark	Harrod–British Library	72737/3–5	Harrod 2003: 750–1	1129
JVR	RFH	1938	January	20	Postmark	Harrod–British Library	72737/6–7	Harrod 2003: 751–2	1131
RFH	JVR	1938	January	20	Dated letter	Robinson–King's	JVR vii/191/24–7	Harrod 2003: 753	1130
RFH	JVR	1938	January	22	Attributed	Robinson–King's	JVR vii/191/28–31	Harrod 2003: 754–5	1132
JVR	RFH	1938	January	24	Postmark	Harrod–British Library	72737/8–11	Harrod 2003: 757–8	1133
RFH	JVR	1938	January	25	Dated letter	Robinson–King's	JVR vii/191/32–6	Harrod 2003: 758–9	1134
RFH	JVR	1938	January	27	Dated letter	Robinson–King's	JVR vii/191/37–8	Harrod 2003: 759–60	1135
JVR	RFH	1938	March	3	Postmark	Harrod–Tokyo	217	Harrod 2003: 761–2	1136
JVR	RFH	1938	March	11	Postmark	Harrod–Chiba	IV/1089–107	Harrod 2003: 762–3	1137
RFH	JVR	1938	March	14	Dated letter	Robinson–King's	JVR vii/191/39–40	Harrod 2003: 763	1138

Table 12.3 J. Robinson–Kaldor correspondence

From	*To*	*Year*	*Month*	*Day*	*Date*	*Archive*	*Published in*	*Item*
JVR	NK	1934	March	29	Attributed	Kaldor–King's	NK/3/5/45–7	865
NK	JVR	1934	April	10	Dated letter	Robinson–King's	JVR/vii/230/1–4	866
NK	JVR	1934	August	17	Dated letter	Robinson–King's	JVR/vii/230/11–14	867
JVR	NK	1935	May	28	Attributed	Kaldor–King's	NK/1/9/11–12	868
NK	JVR	1935	May	29	Dated letter	Robinson–King's	JVR/vii/230/5–8	869
JVR	NK	1935	June	1	Attributed	Kaldor–King's	NK/1/9/13–15	870
NK	JVR	1935	June	3	Attributed	Robinson–King's	JVR/vii/230/9–10	871
JVR	NK	1935	June	3	Attributed	Kaldor–King's	NK/1/9/16–8	872
NK	JVR	1937	September	7	Dated letter	Robinson–King's	JVR/vii/230/15–18	873
NK	JVR	1937	October	7	Dated letter	Robinson–King's	JVR/vii/230/19–20	874
JVR	NK	1937	November	17	Attributed	Kaldor–King's	NK/3/30/177/5–8	875
JVR	NK	1938	May	27	Attributed	Kaldor–King's	NK/3/30/177/3–4	876
JVR	NK	1938	September	22	Attributed	Kaldor–King's	NK/3/30/177/11–14	877
JVR	NK	1939	April	18	Attributed	Kaldor–King's	NK/3/6/29–30	878
JVR	NK	1939	November		Attributed	Kaldor–King's	NK/1/13/49–50	879
JVR	NK	1940			Attributed	Kaldor–King's	NK/1/13/51–4	880
JVR	NK	1940	January	11	Attributed	Kaldor–King's	NK/3/30/177/9–10	881
JVR	NK	1940	December	16	Attributed	Kaldor–King's	NK/3/9/1/150–1	882
JVR	NK	1941	September	3	Dated letter	Kaldor–King's	NK/3/30/118/31	883
JVR	NK	1942	March	7	Attributed	Kaldor–King's	NK/3/30/177/15–16	884
JVR	NK	1943	August	4	Postmark	Kaldor–King's	NK/3/10/12–13	885
NK	JVR	1944	February	15	Dated letter	Kaldor–King's	NK/3/29/234	886
NK	JVR	1945	February	6	Dated letter	Kaldor–King's	NK/3/29/219	887
NK	JVR	1946	June	27	Dated letter	Kaldor–King's	NK/3/12/2/149	888

Part III

The old versus the young generation

13 The Prof and his younger colleagues

Pigou and the correspondence with Kahn, Kaldor, J. Robinson and Sraffa

Nerio Naldi

The correspondence reviewed in this chapter consists of 31 letters sent by Pigou and of only two letters sent by his correspondents – neither of the latter being available in its original but both as draft copies kept by the sender (which, in both cases, was Sraffa) (see Tables 13.1 to 13.4). Most probably this is a result of the fact that, as generally accepted in Cambridge oral tradition, Pigou ordered all his papers to be destroyed after his death.

By far the majority of the extant letters deal with economic theory. Nineteen letters (which are all part of Pigou's correspondence with Robinson and Kahn) have to do with the development of the theory of the firm and Robinson's and Kahn's approach to imperfect competition. A letter to Sraffa shows Pigou's reaction to an early draft of what was to become Sraffa's 1960 book. The letters to Kaldor (only two) are part of the discussion which followed the publication of Pigou's article 'Real and money wage rates in relation to unemployment' (Pigou 1937). Five of the remaining letters deal with questions connected to teaching in the Cambridge Faculty of Economics and Politics and provide some information on the difficult progress of J. Robinson's career as an academic lecturer and on the difficulties faced (or raised) by Sraffa on various occasions during his stay in Cambridge.

The earliest of the letters that we are to consider dates to 1928, the latest to 1939. In general, the characteristics of the extant documents suggest dividing this chapter into three main sections, respectively focused on Sraffa's correspondence, on the development of the theory of imperfect competition, and on the correspondence subsequent to 1933.

It is not unlikely that Pigou made acquaintance first with J. Robinson, who studied economics in Cambridge between 1922 and 1925; then with Sraffa and Kahn at approximately the same time, in 1927, when Sraffa was appointed to a lectureship in Cambridge and Kahn, after a degree in Natural Sciences (mathematics and physics), became a student in the Faculty of Economics and Politics; and only later with Kaldor, who was the youngest: he had been a student at the LSE, after which he went on to teach there in 1932 (Thirlwall 1987: 27, 335).

Pigou's correspondence with Sraffa

The extant correspondence between Pigou and Sraffa consists of seven letters: five from Pigou and two from Sraffa. As was generally the case with Pigou, his letters are undated.

Pigou's letters are generally quite brief and only one deals with economic questions: it is a letter of great interest, for at least two reasons. First of all, since Sraffa dated it 'January 1928', we can pinpoint the moment when Sraffa circulated a document illustrating the content of the research he had just started and an early version of the equations that would not be published until 1960. Moreover, it contains Pigou's comments on those propositions and equations. Most probably Sraffa had shown such a document (apparently not extant) to Pigou, just as he had done with Keynes (Sraffa 1960: vi). On an earlier occasion Keynes had already judged Sraffa's work interesting and original, but wondered if 'his class will understand it when he lectures' (JMK to Lydia Lopokova Keynes, 28 November 1927, JMK papers, PP/45/190/3/268–9). Probably reading the same document shown to Pigou, he gave Sraffa some suggestions on how to present his arguments (Sraffa 1960: vi). Pigou, on the contrary, although stressing twice that he did not suppose he had really understood the nature of the problem Sraffa was tackling, did not show much appreciation for this particular piece of his work.[1] In fact, in Sraffa's equations he could see only a special case of demand and supply analysis where constant returns to scale were assumed (a criticism which anticipated an important aspect of the actual reception of Sraffa's book):

> I don't expect I've really understood the nature of your value problem. But here, for what it is worth, is what occurs to me about it: (1) It seems to me that, even if we assume capital etc. to be a fixed stock, the ordinary demand and supply analysis is still applicable. If, for example, people's taste for one commodity increases, resources are drawn to producing it from the margin of all other lines of production. The effect *on satisfaction* in respect of all other commodities is of the second order of smalls, as argued by Marshall in relation to consumers' surplus. (2) Your equations seem to me to be capable of being subsumed as a special case of the general analysis. You in effect are simply supposing that each of the three (or n) commodities is being produced under conditions of constant returns. Of course an elaborate scheme of demand and supply is not needed in this case: but this case can be treated as a limiting case of the more general theory. I don't suppose for a moment that I've really got your point, but may as well send this along on the off chance.
>
> (letter 4454, January 1928)

Two other letters (one from Sraffa and one from Pigou) deal with

Sraffa's request to postpone for a second time the start of his 1927–28 lectures on the theory of value (letter 4455, 14 January 1928; letter 4453, January 1928), while a third letter (from Sraffa) deals with his appointment to the post of Assistant Director of Research (letter 4456, 10 March 1935). These letters are interesting in several respects. From the former, dated 14 January 1928, we gather that at the time Sraffa was determined to remain at Cambridge and that to this end he was prepared to lecture also on subjects other than the theory of value:

> With reference to our conversation yesterday [sic], I should like to state say [sic] that, if the General Board were to grant me leave of absence for the present academic year, I would undertake definitely to lecture in October. This would be quite independent of the progress of the work which I mentioned to you. Should lecture [sic], if possible on the theory of value, or else if I could not in the near future overcome the difficulties which have prevented my lecturing on that subject at present, on some subject unconnected with it, which I should be able to prepare and put in writing in the meantime.[2]
>
> (letter 4455, 14 January 1928)

In this context it is interesting to note how deeply Sraffa's attitude towards his life permanence and teaching in Cambridge was to change during the three following years. In fact, between 1930 and 1931 Sraffa grew quite determined to resign from his Cambridge position. Sraffa's determination can be appreciated by reading how the episode was related by Paul Rosenstein Rodan to Luigi Einaudi on 5 February 1932 (these pieces of information are consistent with documents kept among the Sraffa Papers): 'the sensational news here is that Sraffa resigned from Cambridge, nobody knows why; they know that after his resignation was announced they immediately offered him a position "for life" with a higher salary, but he wrote directly to the Chancellor of the University in order to avoid any argument, and did not change his mind' (Archivio Fondazione Luigi Einaudi; my translation from the Italian original).

The letter dealing with Sraffa's appointment to the post of Assistant Director of Research reveals (see Ch. 15: 373–4) how strongly Sraffa disliked tying his work down to a precise timetable. In fact, stating that he would be glad to accept the post of Assistant Director of Research and that he would like to combine the duties of this position with the office of Marshall Librarian, he made the limits he would set to this engagement quite clear:

> I should be ready to advise any undergraduates (and not only research students) on their reading and on sources (in so far as I am competent to do so), whenever I happen to be in the library or

> whenever it might suit them to come and see me for that purpose (the Assistant Librarian would be able to tell enquirers where and when they would probably be able to find me). But I had not conceived myself as sharing the duties of the Under Librarian in the sense of being on duty in the library at fixed hours. My main attention would be directed to research and, without distraction from this, I should be able to perform the duties of Marshall Librarian, as I have understood them hitherto, in intervals and odd times. But to be regularly on duty at fixed hours would be irksome and distracting to me and I would not willingly undertake it.
>
> (letter 4456, 10 March 1935)

Considering that Pigou ordered all his papers to be destroyed after his death, it is hardly surprising that the two letters from Sraffa to Pigou are draft copies kept among Sraffa's papers. Oddly enough, however, neither of them is in Sraffa's hand. The first, dealing with Sraffa's lectureship, is in the hand of his mother (letter 4455); the second, dealing with his appointment to the post of Assistant Director of Research, is in Keynes's hand (letter 4456). In the second case we may reasonably guess that Keynes drafted the letter because he knew better how to address Pigou, and how to overcome the difficulties Sraffa was raising against the offer and the conditions that the General Board of the University was presenting him. In the first case we may wonder if his mother had acted merely as an amanuensis or if she had played a role comparable with Keynes's in 1935.

In what is probably the last letter of the period Pigou asked Sraffa to look through a book that he was going to publish with Macmillan (most probably *Employment and Equilibrium*) (letter 4452, 19 November 1939).

Imperfect competition

The extant letters sent by Pigou to Kahn and Robinson between 1929 and 1933 are all concerned with the research which led the two young scholars to develop Sraffa's suggestions, as contained in his 1926 article, into a theory of imperfect competition. The letters are all undated, all from Pigou (ten to Kahn and nine to Robinson) and may be divided into five small groups.

Two letters were addressed by Pigou to Kahn, probably in late March or April 1930, shortly after the approval of the latter's dissertation and election to a fellowship to King's College.[3] In the first letter (letter 4503) Pigou suggested to Kahn that his dissertation should be published as a book, albeit after some rearrangement of the material. The second letter reveals that Kahn was hesitating and considering the possibility of adding 'further stuff'. Pigou's opinion, however, was different:

> It is a unity as it stands, and I think to make it a bigger thing and still a unity, you would have to do a *lot* more. I wouldn't just add bits,

because that might only throw the general plan out of shape: e.g. I don't think you improved your duopoly chapter by inserting the bit about Chamberlin. But I think some rearranging is wanted.[4]

(letter 4502, spring 1930)

Most probably, Kahn himself had also shown some dissatisfaction with parts of his own analysis, but in spite of this Pigou repeated his advice (letter 4502, spring 1930). In 1983, recalling that many years before he had abandoned the idea of publishing his dissertation, Kahn implicitly acknowledged the soundness of Pigou's early suggestion: 'I now strongly advise a young author of a striking but incomplete piece of work to publish it, or at least sections of it, after seeking advice, without delay'(Kahn 1989: xii). In the first letter Pigou also asked Kahn to check 'that elasticity theory of mine' (letter 4503, spring 1930) – most probably as developed in the article 'The statistical derivation of demand curves' (Pigou 1930) – and later described Kahn's comments as extremely useful (letter 4502).

The letters in the second group were also from Pigou to Kahn. There are six of them and they clearly form a coherent series. Since one of them contains a reference to a newspaper article where Lionel Robbins had put forward 'some remarks on our committee' (letter 4505, November 1930), we may date them to the weeks following the conclusion of the activity of the Committee of Economists; i.e. to the weeks following 24 October 1930. In fact, Pigou was a member of that Committee, Kahn was one of its joint secretaries, and Robbins had signed a report as a minority of one (see Robbins 1971: 150–2; Keynes CWK XX: 402–4). This dating is also consistent with Pigou's reference to the fact that he had to 'review Keynes' (letter 4505, November 1930).[5]

The discussion reflected in these letters started, as it seems, after Kahn had asked Pigou to read a paper where some special cases relating to the analysis of perfect competition and monopoly were discussed. Pigou answered: 'I expect this is all right, but the things don't seem to me to be paradoxes e.g. all that paradox 3 says really is that, if a landlord farms his land and *doesn't sell his corn*, it won't pay him to restrict output!'(letter 4510, November 1930).

Pigou's reference to *paradoxes* suggests that the paper he had received from Kahn might have been a result of discussions between Kahn and Robinson. In fact, in the correspondence between Kahn and Robinson we find that some *paradoxes* (labelled *I*, *II* and *III*) are frequently mentioned (but not expounded) between November 1930 and January 1931 (letters 503, 504, 734, 739, 749, 754; see Ch. 10). *Paradox III*, in particular, seems to have been abandoned by the two young economists in December 1930 (letter 740 from JVR to RFK, 26 December 1930); i.e. after the exchange with Pigou that we are considering.

The difficulty of deciphering Pigou's handwriting and the lack of Kahn's letters make it particularly difficult to follow the development of the exchange, but we may certainly gather that it centred on discussion of a case in which a number of firms consolidate into a monopoly and there are large external economies (letter 4510; see letters 4505 and 4507, November 1930). The discussion developed as a challenge that Pigou threw down to Kahn. Most probably, the paper shown by Kahn to Pigou contained a geometrical analysis framed in terms of linear curves (letter 4510), but Pigou believed that: 'the analytic method will work out simpler than the curves – assuming of course linear functions which you also do' (letter 4507), and wrote he was ready to bet on it. Two letters later he declared: 'I win my bet', and presented his analytical argument (letter 4508, November 1930). In the following letter (letter 4509, November 1930) he admitted his argument had to be corrected and in the last letter (letter 4506, November 1930), if our deciphering can be relied upon, he reasserted its validity.[6]

Five letters addressed by Pigou to Robinson may be dated to the weeks between the publication of her December 1932 article 'Imperfect Competition and the Falling Supply Price' and mid-January 1933. The earliest letter was written by Pigou immediately after reading Robinson's article. In this letter he suggested that, if she wished to use that analysis in her book, she should explicitly explain why a general rise in demand for the commodity would call new firms into the industry and consider the precise conditions under which this would realistically happen or not happen (letter 4351, December 1932). In other letters Pigou spotted and discussed a weakness in Robinson's article in that it did not show that, when firms were not identical, all firms would be in equilibrium with the average cost curve tangent to the demand curve after new firms had entered the industry (letters 4357, 4358, 4363 and 4359, January 1933).[7] Pigou elaborated his criticism in various ways, provided a counter-criticism, and finally said he had found proof that Robinson's result was correct even in the more general case (letters 4363 and 4359). As we may infer from Pigou's letters, Robinson had answered him that considering the case in the continuum (Pigou's example considered finite changes) the problem would disappear. But Pigou replied that the question he was pointing out was different, that it was necessary to show that the number of unknowns was equal to the number of equations, and that on these grounds he had actually found a way to solve the problem (letter 4363). The proof provided by Pigou was published in the March 1933 issue of the *Economic Journal* as 'A Note on Imperfect Competition', probably because it could not be included in Robinson's book (which by that time had already been printed), as Pigou would have preferred (letter 4363) (see Ch. 10: 267).

Five other letters had been sent by Pigou to Robinson shortly after the publication of her 1933 book, but only two contain a discussion of some parts of it (letters 4356, and 4362, spring 1933); the other three letters (letters 4361, 4355 and 4360, spring 1933) only refer to discussions that Pigou and Robinson had already had or were to have. The first of the two most interesting letters was written by Pigou when he had read about two-thirds of Robinson's book; the note attached to this letter is also extant and it contains some general comments and some specific remarks extending to Ch. 19 of that book. The second letter consists of a further note relating to the book in general and to its final part. All in all, some criticisms notwithstanding ('Of course there are some things I don't much like'), Pigou expressed a favourable judgement: 'I think [your book is] a very fine effort, containing any amount of stuff, and should give you a very strong claim to the next lectureship that we have going'[8] (letter 4356).

In the same letter, against the geometric approach adopted by Robinson, Pigou reasserted his preference for an algebraical approach, as he had already done in his correspondence with Kahn in 1930; nevertheless, he also stated that 'the thing that matters is results and you've got a whole lot in organized coherent form' (letter 4356). The same points are stated in a letter to Kahn most probably dating to spring 1933:

> I think Mrs R's book's a very fine concentrated intellectual effort: though I think it would have *saved time* for most people if the main proposition had been set out in an appendix in algebra, which would have been very much shorter. But that's a matter of taste.
>
> (letter 4504, spring 1933)

According to Pigou, the description of the conditions for the equilibrium of the firm in terms of marginal revenue and marginal cost or in terms of demand price, elasticity of demand and marginal cost adopted by Robinson were equivalent to that based on Marshall's monopoly revenue curve and he stressed that this 'analytical background should be set out somewhere' (letter 4356). He praised Robinson's work on some specific points, including the discussion of cases where curves were concave or convex and not simply straight lines, and defended Marshall on several scores: against Robinson's claim that he had not perceived the continuity between the extreme cases of monopoly and competition;[9] against the charge of postulating no substitution;[10] in connection with the way Robinson had treated increasing returns in the case of monopoly.[11] Pigou's second letter concluded with a suggestion distinctly Marshallian in tone and confirmed that, although deeply aware of the importance of theoretical analysis, he was also always keen to see that analysis applied to real economic problems (something which he did himself as well as asking the younger scholars to do):

> Suggestion for next opus. This one having been all about machinery, opus II shall be about some substantial real problem, in the handling of which the machinery, while kept in the background, should prove its worth in doing the job!
>
> (letter 4362, spring 1933)

The last group of documents dealing with imperfect competition consists of two letters (letters 4504 and 4501) sent by Pigou to Kahn which may be dated to spring 1933, since one of them contains a reference to Robinson's *Economics of Imperfect Competition.* The focus of the exchange, however, is not that book but, most probably, a paper on Euler's Theorem written by Kahn. In fact (assuming that, as in Wicksteed's *Essay on the Co-ordination of the Laws of Distribution*, *O*, *C* and *L* stand for *output*, *capital + labour*, and *land*; *p* for *price of output* and *c* and *l* for the *rental price* of *capital + labour* and *land*), the opening sentence of the letter immediately directs us towards an attempt to elaborate upon the so-called 'adding up' or 'exhaustion problem' on the assumption that a variation of output does not imply variations of the price of the output and of the factors of production:

> Many thanks. But this doesn't seem to me right, I don't see that your final string $p\Delta O = c\Delta C + l\Delta L$ is warranted. What this means is that [. . .] the addition to output multiplied by the old price = the addition to C multiplied by *its* old wage rate and the addition to *L* multiplied by *its* old wage rate.
>
> (letter 4504, spring 1933)

In the following letter, however, Pigou changed his verdict: 'Yes, thanks; I'd made a mistake in my checking. It's a surprisingly neat formula, which might have important applications' (letter 4501).

This favourable judgement notwithstanding, Kahn did not publish any paper on Euler's Theorem, nor do we find any trace of his 'surprisingly neat formula' in his published works. However, in June 1933, Robinson published a review of a reprint of Wicksteed's *Essay on the Co-ordination of the Laws of Distribution* (J. Robinson 1933c) and in the following 1934 a paper on Euler's Theorem (J. Robinson 1934); and Kahn himself in his articles 'The Elasticity of Substitution and the Relative Share of a Factor' (Kahn 1933: 78) and 'Some Notes on Ideal Output' (Kahn 1935: 22–3) touched upon questions related to the use of marginal productivity as the magnitude which regulates the reward of a factor of production. Unfortunately, the progress of Kahn's work on this subject is also unclear: his correspondence with Robinson suggests that in February 1933 he was extremely dissatisfied with it:

> my article on Euler's theorem [ought to be rather fun]. I now see that the whole thing is complete bilge. If profits *are* normal, then *by the definition of normal profits* the product is just sufficient to go round whether the factors are rewarded on the basis of marginal productivity or on the number of false teeth of their grandmothers. And that is all there is to it.
>
> (letter 553 from RFK to JVR, 10 February 1933)

But in spring 1933 (provided our dating is correct), as we have indirectly seen, Kahn successfully defended at least part of his paper against Pigou's criticisms. Yet, in the end, he did not publish it.

After 1933

Except for two letters, already considered, which are part of Pigou's correspondence with Sraffa, the only extant correspondence exchanged after 1933 between Pigou and his young colleagues are two letters he sent to Kaldor in October 1937 and four letters he sent to J. Robinson in February 1934, in February 1935, in spring 1939, and, probably, in summer 1939. The two letters sent to Kaldor are part of the discussion on Pigou's September 1937 article 'Real and Money Wage Rates in Relation to Unemployment' (Pigou 1937). In these letters Pigou first suggested that the differences between his results and Kaldor's results might lie 'in certain differences of assumption' (letter 4401, October 1937), but then acknowledged that one of the basic assumptions of his article read as singled out by Kaldor and not as he had thought.[12]

In a letter postmarked 28 February 1935 Pigou acknowledged receipt of a typescript from Robinson: most probably a document she had prepared for the Faculty Board to illustrate the content of the lectures on monetary theory she wished to deliver (letter 4353). On that occasion, the decision to appoint Robinson to teach a two-term course on money was to prove very controversial: on 2 March 1935 C.R. Fay wrote to Keynes, Shove and Pigou stating that Robinson's course 'may pre-judge, or warn in advance against, the conclusions of Robertson in his third year course', he added that this 'would be a disaster for him and us' and that he thought 'the solution might be that Mrs Robinson should be definitely informed that we desire from her a course in Money of one term only, and that in the Lent Term of each year' (letter from C.R. Fay to JMK, 2 March 1935 in JMK papers, UA/5/3/137–9). But Keynes sided most decidedly in favour of Robinson (see Chs 1: 35 fn 14, 2: 69–70, 6: 176, 7: 208–9), and in the end she taught a two-term course: 'Applications of Monetary Theory' (two hours per week in Michaelmas and Lent Terms followed in Easter Term by a course on 'Some Problems of Economic Theory'). The courses taught by Robinson, however, were included in the list of lectures for Part II of the Economic Tripos so that neither of them appeared as *preliminary* to Robertson's course on 'Money' (two hours per week for three terms).[13]

Another letter was written by Pigou in spring 1939 (letter 4364) when Robinson was recovering from her nervous breakdown. He wrote he was delighted to hear of her recovery, adding that Fay, who had also suffered from a similar problem, was recovering more slowly, and offering her his own house in the Lake District to spend some weeks there during the last part of Easter Term or in Summer Term. In the last extant letter, probably written in summer 1939, Pigou informed Robinson that she was to be asked by the Lecture-List Committee 'to give lectures on Monetary Theories preliminary to Keynes's lectures on his own stuff' (letter 4354). This letter most probably refers to the arrangement of the lectures planned for the year 1939–40, when Keynes was expected to lecture on 'Theory of Fluctuations of Output' in Lent Term,[14] and J. Robinson was to lecture on 'Monetary Theories' in Michaelmas Term, on 'Applications of Monetary Theory' in Lent Term, and on 'Some Problems of Economic Theory' (plus a Discussion Class) in Easter Term.[15] This dating of the letter is also consistent with the fact that in it Pigou mentioned the time 'when Denis was here', which suggests that it must have been written during the years Robertson spent in London (i.e. 1939–44). Turning again to the content of this letter, we may see that Pigou felt he had to express his opinion to Robinson on her teaching:

> I think that in recent years the men have been put into a terrible muddle by having controversies, largely, in my opinion, about minor more or less verbal differences, emphasized to them, and it will be good, for their side, to have monetary lectures given by people more in agreement with one another than was the case when Denis was here. On the other hand, I think it would be a great pity if they got the impression that everybody who wrote about money before Keynes was an imbecile and that his way was a sort of sacred gospel of which every word was inspired. My hesitancy was that you, being so very much a Keynesian, might unconsciously treat other people's theories as merely stepping stones to his. I hope very much that you will treat them objectively of course. I don't suggest that you shouldn't criticize them or should suppress your own views. It's really a matter of degree; but I'm sure you will see my point. Here's an illustration. Keynes said incidentally in the course of our talk (I don't suppose he would really stick to it) that Marshall regarded money merely *as a veil* of all points of view. When one remembers Marshall's express statement that the Principles is based on the assumption that stable prices are maintained, together with the immense trouble he took to clarify a stable price-scheme (he told me once, if I remember rightly, that he kept a draft of the article by him for 10 years before publishing it), the idea that he thought money unimportant and *nothing but* a veil seems to me fantastic. What I'm really getting at is to express a hope that you will not use other theories just as illustrations of Keynes, but will treat them on their merits. Please forgive this. It's really rather an impertinence for me to write it. But, as it's all in very friendly spirit, I hope you won't mind.
>
> (letter 4354, Summer 1939)

We do not know how far Pigou was ready to go in order to keep Robinson's Keynesian enthusiasm within boundaries. Certainly, in November

1939, when the Michaelmas Term lectures had already started, the Faculty Board oddly asked Robinson 'to adapt her half course of lectures or preferably her discussion class in Easter Term so as to deal with general monetary theory' (Faculty Board Minutes). On the other hand, in January 1940 Keynes's course on 'Theory of Fluctuations of Output' disappeared from the Cambridge University Reporter's list of lectures, and on the 26 February Keynes was asked by the Faculty Board to lecture on 'A Commentary on Problems of War Economics' (a subject closely related to the focus of his activity in that period, as he had just published his pamphlet *How to Pay for the War*) (Faculty Board Minutes).[16] We may wonder if such changes were an effect of Pigou's preoccupations (see Ch. 5: 154), but the latter were certainly greatly reinforced by the results of the exams and by the impression he had that the students had been 'stuffed like sausages' with Keynes's 'stuff':

> My own guess – because there is no direct evidence – is that the parrot-like treatment of your stuff is due to the lectures and supervision of the beautiful Mrs. R. – a magpie breeding innumerable parrots! I gather that she puts in the Truth, with an enormous T, with such Prussian efficiency that the wretched men become identical sausages without any minds of their own! Obviously there is nothing we can do about this at present, but, I think, if peace ever comes, we ought to introduce some counter-irritant in their territory. Even the muddle into which they all got when Denis and the beautiful lady were lecturing against one another seems better than this drill sergeant business.
>
> (letter 4214 from ACP to JMK, 12 June 1940)

Compared with the 1930s, Pigou's attitude towards Robinson had changed dramatically. And things did not improve with time. In fact, in 1944 he would write to Keynes: 'As to Mrs. R. for next year [elections to the British Academy], I'm in a weak position to have a view because the dogmatism and arrogance, when equipped with a pen, irritate me so much that I can't read her' (letter 4156 from ACP to JMK, 1944).

Nevertheless, he also added: 'But, she has, no doubt, produced a more substantial body of stuff than anyone else of her standing except Hicks. So she certainly ought to be seriously considered' (letter 4156 from ACP to JMK, 1944).

Conclusions

In general, Pigou's attitude towards this group of young economists, as shown by his correspondence, seems to have been very supportive. He was not hostile to being the object of direct or indirect criticism but was indeed open to discussion. He was always ready to put forth his opinions, yet disposed to change them if persuaded he had been wrong or if his own train of thought altered direction. This attitude, which emerges particularly well in his correspondence with Kahn and J. Robinson, is exemplified by the first paragraph of the short paper, where Pigou put forward a generalisation of the results reached by Robinson in 1932:

> I should certainly never have thought of [this way to discuss the problem] if Mrs. Robinson had not first blazed the trail. This note attempts only the subordinate task of improving, on a rather bleak ice-wall, a staircase which has already been made and ascended.
>
> (Pigou 1933b: 108)

The same attitude was probably important also in the case of Sraffa's appointment to a lectureship in 1927. In fact, shortly after the publication of his 1926 article, Keynes wrote to Sraffa:

> Your article in the December Journal has been very much liked over here. Everyone I have spoken to agrees that it puts you in the front rank of the younger economists. Pigou is extremely interested, and has been looking up your Italian article. You may be interested to know that he feels he must, in the light of it, reconsider his whole position.
>
> (letter 1005 from JMK to PS, 25 January 1927)

It is clear that Pigou did not oppose the appointment of a young economist whose stance was critical of his own approach.

Pigou's supportive attitude towards these younger scholars, and his positive reactions to the criticisms they were levelling at his own analysis, was most probably rooted in the intellectual environment he belonged to; but it could also reflect a personal detachment from the heat of economic debate. In this sense, his approach seems to be aptly described as that attitude that Robinson, after a discussion with Gerald Shove, came to think that only women could possess:

> I feel badly vis a vis [sic] poor old Gerald, who takes it all so much to heart when it only makes me laugh. I begin to think that the conventional view is all wrong and that only women can take an impersonal interest in things because they have no ambition or public spirit.
>
> (letter 567 from JVR to RFK, 20 February 1933)

In fact, when, in 1937, his paper on wages and unemployment (Pigou 1937) came under attack from several fronts, his correspondence with Keynes and with Kaldor revealed great calmness.

The only occasions when his letters showed signs of impatience were, apparently, when he thought his correspondents were breaking the rules of the academic and intellectual game, as played at the University of Cambridge. His answer to Sraffa's request to postpone the beginning of his lectures for a second time, and to the following academic year, was negative. Although encouraging Sraffa to start his course, he made it clear that in his opinion 'it would [not] be possible to allow you to postpone your lectures a second time and continue your lectureship' (letter 4453, January 1928).[17] Correspondingly stronger was his reaction, when he felt that Robinson's teaching might have posed an obstacle to the intellectual development of the students.

The words Sraffa used several years later, in 1955, in commenting on the news that the Italian Accademia dei Lincei had awarded Pigou its Feltrinelli Prize, well reflected the position Pigou had occupied in Cambridge and his relationship with the younger economists as it emerges from the correspondence we have studied: 'Pigou has always been so modest and shy that as a result he has never received the honour he deserves: this great prize is a great act of justice' (letter from PS to Gustavo Del Vecchio, 26 May 1955, Archivio A. Zanni and Centro Sraffa; my translation from the Italian original).[18]

Notes

1 This could explain why Sraffa in the preface to his 1960 book mentioned Keynes's comments on his early draft but not Pigou's.

2 The allusion to the 'programme of the work' that Sraffa had mentioned to Pigou the day before suggests that if Sraffa showed Pigou a paper illustrating his work in January 1928, this must have happened after the 14th.

3 The dissertation was published in Italian in 1983 and only in 1989 in English (Kahn 1983, 1989). The original typescript of Kahn's dissertation is conserved in RFK papers, (RFK 2/7–9) as are the referees' reports (RFK 2/8/1–15; see Ch. 1)

4 The reference to Kahn's discussion of Chamberlin's article on duopoly suggests that Pigou had seen or discussed a draft of the Dissertation before the final text was submitted to the College.

5 Most probably Pigou was preparing the review of Keynes's *Treatise on Money* that was published in *The Nation and Athenaeum* in January 1931 (Pigou 1931).

6 From the writing paper used by Pigou it may be gathered that he wrote some of these letters while he was resting in a Cambridge clinic.

7 Robinson referred to these criticisms in a letter to Kahn written on 16 January 1933 (letter 532). See Ch. 10: 266–7.

8 In fact, Robinson, who had already taught a short course on *Pure Theory of Monopoly* in Michaelmas 1931, taught a course entitled *Economics of Imperfect Competition* in the Michaelmas and Lent Terms of the academic years 1933–34 and 1934–35, but she was to become a Faculty Lecturer only in 1938, while in 1934 she became Probationary Faculty Lecturer.

9 'No doubt it is worth while stressing [to] your literary readers the fact that monopolies are not an entirely different sort of thing from competition. But mathematically, of course, nobody ever supposed it was. Under competition you have a maximum and minimum problem [. . .] Under monopoly another kindred one [. . .] Then [. . .] I can't credit that [Marshall] really made the sort of elementary mistakes that you attribute to him' (letter 4356, spring 1933).

10 'I think the concept of elasticity of substitution, which you and Hicks seem to

have hit on independently, is important and should be developed. But Marshall wasn't making "errors". He knew perfectly well – indeed it's explicit in his algebra – that he was postulating no substitution. This is natural enough as he was thinking of such things as workpeople cooperating with materials' (letter 4362, spring 1933).

11 'In the whole of this I think you have unduly neglected Marshall's account of substitution between entrepreneurs and managers and so on. If your monopoly world were set up, there would be an enormous inducement to managers etc to borrow capital and start firms of their own' (letter 4362, spring 1933).

12 As we have already seen, reconsidering and revising his own position as expressed in correspondence was not unusual for Pigou. But in this case we may presume that the clarity of his thought had been somewhat impaired by the precariousness of his health. In fact, in his second letter Pigou concluded: 'I have been much preoccupied lately and not really compos [mentis] to understand my own article!' (letter 4402, late October 1937). The assumption referred to concerned the possibility of producing capital equipment in the period considered.

13 Cambridge University Reporter. During the following year, however, Robinson's course on 'Applications of Monetary Theory' was to be attended also by students sitting the Preliminary Examination (which happened again during the 1940s, when the name of the course became 'Money'). It was certainly in this context that Robertson wrote to Keynes: 'I *don't* think it good that people coming over from other subjects should get their first introduction to this whole range of very controversial topics from someone who seems to think that everything that has been said and thought about it is "moth-eaten" rubbish except one book, – and that, whatever its merits, a very difficult one! And I *do* feel that over this business there is an atmosphere of dogmatism and proselytisation about into which our Socialists and Communist[s] have never landed on, and which is new and un-Cambridge-y. However I realise it's no use at present our trying to get eye to eye about this: and also that the position is complicated by my inability, after years of effort for Austin's sake, to preserve personally cordial relations with Mrs. R' (letter 3154 from DHR to JMK, 28 August 1936, Moggridge, 1992: 600; see Chs 1: 35 fn 4, 6: 176, 7: 208–9). As we shall see, in 1940 Pigou referred to this period as that in which 'Denis and the beautiful lady were lecturing against one another' (letter 4214 from ACP to JMK, June 1940) (see Ch. 5; Pigou, in his correspondence, generally referred to Robertson as 'Denis').

14 Since 1936–37, this was the first year in which Keynes's name appeared in the Lecture List of the University of Cambridge; it appeared again in 1940–41, but no course title was put beside his name.

15 Cambridge University Reporter.

16 This course was announced for Easter Term in April 1940 (Cambridge University Reporter).

17 In the end, however, most probably through Keynes's intervention, Sraffa was granted his request.

18 The first part of the letter gives us some first-hand information on Pigou's life in the mid-1950s (at that time he was 78): 'Dear Del Vecchio [...] I went immediately to Pigou to tell him the news. And even though he told me, as usual, that he was more dead than alive, and that he had totally lost his intelligence, and who knows if he'll even make it to the middle of June, I am certain that it brought him great pleasure, indeed he was quite moved. The truth is that he isn't doing so badly, despite his melancholy: he's working on a new

book (Income Revisited) and in a few days he will be leaving for the country and later for Switzerland. I reassured him, however, that he won't have to attend any ceremonies (an idea which had scared him a little). He wanted to write you a personal letter immediately (making a tremendous effort to write relatively legibly)' (my translation from the Italian original).

Table 13.1 Pigou–Kahn correspondence

From	*To*	*Year*	*Month*	*Day*	*Date*	*Archive*		*Published in*	*Item*
ACP	RFK	1930	Spring		Attributed	Kahn–King's	RFK/2/8/16–17		4503
ACP	RFK	1930	Spring		Attributed	Kahn–King's	RFK/2/8/18–19		4502
ACP	RFK	1930	November		Attributed	Kahn–King's	RFK/16/1/50–1		4510
ACP	RFK	1930	November		Attributed	Kahn–King's	RFK/16/1/43–4		4507
ACP	RFK	1930	November		Attributed	Kahn–King's	RFK/16/1/39–40		4505
ACP	RFK	1930	November		Attributed	Kahn–King's	RFK/16/1/45–7		4508
ACP	RFK	1930	November		Attributed	Kahn–King's	RFK/16/1/48–9		4509
ACP	RFK	1930	November		Attributed	Kahn–King's	RFK/16/1/41–2		4506
ACP	RFK	1933	Spring		Attributed	Robinson–King's	JVR/vii/347/42–3		4504
ACP	RFK	1933	Spring		Attributed	Robinson–King's	JVR/vii/347/44		4501

Table 13.2 Pigou–Kaldor correspondence

From	*To*	*Year*	*Month*	*Day*	*Date*	*Archive*		*Published in*	*Item*
ACP	NK	1937	October		Attributed	Kaldor–King's	NK/3/30/118/112–13		4401
ACP	NK	1937	October		Attributed	Kaldor–King's	NK/3/30/118/114		4402

Table 13.3 Pigou–J. Robinson correspondence

From	*To*	*Year*	*Month*	*Day*	*Date*	*Archive*	*Published in*	*Item*
ACP	JVR	1932	December		Attributed	Robinson–King's JVR/vii/347/16–17		4351
ACP	JVR	1933	January		Attributed	Robinson–King's JVR/vii/347/8–9		4357
ACP	JVR	1933	January		Attributed	Robinson–King's JVR/vii/347/10–12		4358
ACP	JVR	1933	January		Attributed	Robinson–King's JVR/vii/347/13		4363
ACP	JVR	1933	January		Attributed	Robinson–King's JVR/vii/347/14–15		4359
ACP	JVR	1933	Spring		Attributed	Robinson–King's JVR/vii/347/20–1		4361
ACP	JVR	1933	Spring		Attributed	Robinson–King's JVR/vii/347/6–7, 29–35		4356
ACP	JVR	1933	Spring		Attributed	Robinson–King's JVR/vii/347/18–19		4360
ACP	JVR	1933	Spring		Attributed	Robinson–King's JVR/vii/347/26–8		4362
ACP	JVR	1933	Spring		Attributed	Robinson–King's JVR/vii/347/5		4355
ACP	JVR	1934	February		Attributed	Robinson–King's JVR/vii/347/1		4352
ACP	JVR	1935	February	28	Postmark	Robinson–King's JVR/vii/347/22–3		4353
ACP	JVR	1939	Spring		Attributed	Robinson–King's JVR/vii/347/24–5		4364
ACP	JVR	1939	Summer		Attributed	Robinson–King's JVR/vii/347/2–4		4354

Table 13.4 Pigou–Sraffa correspondence

From	*To*	*Year*	*Month*	*Day*	*Date*	*Archive*		*Published in*	*Item*
ACP	PS				not yet attributed	Sraffa–Trinity	Sraffa C1/20		4457
PS	ACP	1928	January	14	Dated letter	Sraffa–Trinity	Sraffa B9/1/11	Marcuzzo 2004: 127 fn. 14, (E)	4455
ACP	PS	1928	January		Attributed	Sraffa–Trinity	Sraffa C 239/2	Marcuzzo 2004: 127, fn. 13, (E)	4453
ACP	PS	1928	January		Attributed	Sraffa–Trinity	Sraffa C 239/1	Naldi 1998: 514	4454
PS	ACP	1935	March	10	Dated letter	Sraffa–Trinity	Sraffa B9/3/10–15		4456
ACP	PS	1937			Attributed	Kahn–King's	RFK/19/3/186–7		4451
ACP	PS	1939	November	19	Attributed	Sraffa–Trinity	Sraffa C 239/8		4452

14 The defender of the Marshallian tradition

Shove and the correspondence with Kahn, J. Robinson and Sraffa

Annalisa Rosselli

The extant correspondence between Gerald Shove and the younger economists at the Cambridge Faculty of Economics in the 1930s and 1940s – Sraffa, Kahn and J. Robinson – is not particularly voluminous (see Tables 14.1 to 14.3). Only 27 letters exchanged between Shove and J. Robinson have come down to us, four with Kahn and four with Sraffa (two of which, however, are of no real importance). One obvious explanation for this lies in Shove's disposition by will that his 'professional' papers should be destroyed on his decease (Kahn 1987: 327), which occurred in 1947. Another possible explanation lies in the particular position occupied by Shove, hierarchically intermediate between Keynes and the younger generation.

Shove belonged to the 'senior' generation in terms of age, institutional role and theoretical framework. The year of his birth, 1887[1], places him in the group of Cambridge Faculty members including Robertson, Pigou and, of course, Keynes who had taken the Tripos in economics before the 1914–18 War and had studied before or immediately after Marshall's retirement. He had been supervisor and teacher of Austin Robinson, who had followed his 'Labour' course in 1921–22, and, together with Keynes, supervisor to Kahn in 1927–28 (Kahn 1987: 328). It seems fairly certain that J. Robinson must have followed his lectures when preparing the Tripos, and she may well have been among the 56 students that Shove, lacking a fellowship, gave lessons to in the early 1920s to rake together a decent remuneration.[2] From the point of view of theoretical approach, too, Shove was an exponent of the 'old guard' who found in Marshall's *Principles* not only an essential source of suggestions useful in dealing with any economic problem ('It is all in Marshall', as they used to say at Cambridge in the early 1920s) but, indeed, a method to be assimilated by the economist, to become an integral part of the person. As Shove wrote to the young Kahn, who complained about the difficulty of them, the *Principles* are 'more a matter of inward meditation and contemplation than of reading' (letter 3901, 29 June 1928).

Shove was therefore too closely identified with the previous generation to have more confidential relations in correspondence, but at the same time he probably did not seem to his younger colleagues sufficiently authoritative at the scientific or academic level[3] for his approval to be felt necessary when embarking on new work. In fact, in 1928 Sraffa submitted the initial equations of *Production of Commodities* to Pigou and Keynes, but we do not have evidence that he showed them to Shove. J. Robinson sent an outline of the *Economics of Imperfect Competition* to Robertson (letter 3406 from JVR to DHR, September 1931) requesting an opinion and a preface, but not to Shove, although he had written and lectured on the subject matter. Once they had abandoned their role as students, none seemed to make a point of keeping up the scientific exchange with Shove. This probably reflected no lack of respect, but rather the off-putting impact of an awkward personality. Indeed, while the praise heaped on him by his most important pupils many years later[4] might have been dictated by affection and nostalgia, the correspondence examined in this volume offers ample evidence of the genuine respect and consideration that Shove's opinions were held in.[5]

It also shows time and time again just how difficult it must have been to maintain scientific relations with Shove. In the first place, there was what Shove himself called his 'complex about putting pen to paper' (letter 3968, from GFS to JVR, 8 May 1938), which led him to publish very little while at the same time being obsessed by the fear that others might steal his ideas without due acknowledgement (see, for example, below, the problems arising on various occasions with J. Robinson), and then, having a positive aversion to conflict, he would defer to his interlocutor, only to change his mind the following day (see letter 3904, from GFS to RFK, 11 October 1931 and 3852, from GFS to PS, 25 February 1930). Behind all this was a proverbial insecurity and an incurable tendency to fight shy of any final word, which saw him often withdrawing work that had already been handed over to the printer (letter 3851, from GFS to PS, February 1930), and which emerged in his writings in frequent references to the exhaustive treatment that would be appearing in some future work (Shove 1928: 258 and 265; Shove 1930: 114; Shove 1933a: 124).

In Gerald Shove there coexisted the meticulous teacher,[6] generous with the time and attention he dedicated to his pupils, who for their part cherished fond memories of him (Plumptre 1975: 250; Kahn 1989: xi), and the scholar prone to resentment, who would at times vent on his colleagues (ever more famous, ever more brilliant) what was essentially frustration with his own limitations. As J. Robinson wrote to Kahn: '[Gerald] is so very nice when he is not being mad' (letter 580 from JVR to RFK, 8 March 1933). Eventually, however, the relational difficulties seem to have prevailed; we have no evidence of a deterioration in his personal relations, but not much of the correspondence that has come down to us dates any later than the early 1930s.

The correspondence with Sraffa in 1930

In any case, most of Shove's scant production is concentrated between the late 1920s and the early 1930s when, as Austin Robinson recalled, Shove returned from a sabbatical leave in 1929–30 a new man, some at least of his shyness shed (A. Robinson 1977: 28). For some years Shove had been dedicating himself to study of the foundations of the Marshallian supply curve, and had presented a memoir on the subject – since lost – at the annual meeting of the British Association for the Advancement of Sciences in Southampton in 1925 (letter 3903 from GFS to RFK, October 1931).[7] He was a firm follower of Marshall, and it was therefore natural that when the Marshallian theory of value came under fire from Sraffa in the *Economic Journal* of 1926 (Sraffa 1926) Shove felt the need to intervene.

The opportunity arose when Robertson submitted an article to the *Economic Journal* in reply both to Lionel Robbins, who had questioned the relevance of the Representative Firm, and to Sraffa, who had questioned the possibility of reconciling competitive equilibrium with increasing returns arising from internal economies. Shove, who had written a note 'pleading for a change in the classification and labelling of the "external and internal economies of large-scale production"' was asked by Keynes, then editor of the *Journal*, to make it into a comment on Robertson's essay, as Shove himself recalls (Shove 1930: 94). In this new form, Shove's article was published as a contribution to the *Symposium on Increasing Returns and the Representative Firm*, which appeared in the March 1930 issue of the *Economic Journal*. The correspondence with Sraffa that has come down to us is related to this publication.

Shove's defence of Marshall against Sraffa is based on new definitions for what Marshall had labelled 'external' and 'internal' economies, and on a distinction between the decrease in costs for an individual firm deriving from concentrating a given output of an industry on a smaller number of firms and the reduced costs obtained with general enlargement of the scale of production of the whole industry to which the firm belongs. Shove suggests calling the former change in costs for the individual firm 'economies (or diseconomies) of individual expansion' and the latter 'economies (or diseconomies) of large scale industry' (Shove 1930: 104). The relevance of the distinction for Shove is that in both cases the firm may benefit from a reduction in costs following an increase in its own output, but if the increase in output and sales is carried out by 'invading' the market of the rivals, the advantages of the larger volume of production will be offset by the additional marketing and/or transport expenses which the firm must face. This particular problem does not arise if the firm can simply expand its production, while the other firms may be doing the same, and sell the additional output on its own market.

Shove therefore argues that increasing returns accompanied by expansion of the output of the industry are compatible with equilibrium and competitive conditions in the industry, as Sraffa had admitted when he allowed for economies external from the point of view of the individual firm but internal to the industry as a whole (although he regarded them as very rare).[8] However, increasing returns not accompanied by expansion of the output of the industry do not imply transformation of the competitive firm into a monopoly since, sooner or later, expansion of the firm will inevitably be frustrated by the increase in marketing expenses and transport costs, or by the need to fall back on price cuts in order to draw customers away from the competitors. In keeping with the Marshallian tradition, Shove believed that a 'perfect' market does not imply that a firm can sell any amount of output at the prevailing price, because each firm may have a 'private market' that makes it difficult and costly for other firms to increase the number of their customers.

Sraffa did not comment on Shove's article in writing, and his contribution to the *Symposium* deals only with Robertson's criticisms. It is likely that Shove's article was not available until the last possible moment and Sraffa may not have had the time to comment on it without falling short of his usual standards of accuracy. (A brief note from Shove was found among Sraffa's paper related to the *Symposium* that could confirm this supposition.[9]) However, we know that the whole *Symposium*, still at the proof stage, was discussed in a meeting of the Political Economy Club held on 24 February 1930.[10] In preparation for the discussion, Sraffa jotted down a few pages of notes and added his comments on the margins of the proofs (PS papers, D3/7), which, together with the brief exchange of correspondence following the discussion, give us an idea of his reactions.

Sraffa found the distinction Shove had introduced between addition of output by a firm to its own market or its competitor's market 'confusing' and confessed himself unable 'to disentangle altogether the contradictions'. He did not see how a firm could know *a priori* the destination of its additional output, and wrote: 'Mr S[hove] speaks as if a firm had a choice and selected the most profitable. But he never explains how it is to be done'. He accused Shove of misunderstanding a similar distinction suggested by Pigou (Pigou 1928: 242) between 'marginal additive cost', which is the difference made to the total cost of the Pigouvian equilibrium firm when its output is increased while the output of other firms is kept constant, and 'marginal substitute cost', which is the change in costs when the increase in output of the equilibrium firm is balanced by an equal decrease in the outputs of some other firms. Pigou had introduced the distinction with the aim of allowing for external economies in the former case, and of excluding them in the latter, taking into account the conditions of production only. As Sraffa notes:

> [Pigou] refers to differences not in sales but in outputs: he considers external economies, not marketing difficulties [...]. In P[igou] case

> the difference (whether ind[ividual] increment is or is not accompanied by expansion of industry) is that in one case external economies are brought about, in the other they are not: whereas in Shove case the difference is that in one case a price cut, in the other advert[sing] expenses are required – but in both cases expenses of production are the same, being independent of who buys the product.
>
> (PS papers, D3/7/23)

The brief exchange of correspondence between Sraffa and Shove is a sort of follow-up to the discussion at the Political Economy Club. On the following day, 25 February, Shove continued in his efforts to convince Sraffa of the relevance of his distinction, defending himself against the accusation of having misinterpreted Pigou's thought. In a peevish and resentful tone, he wrote to Sraffa: 'My distinction is not based on his [Pigou's] at all: it was arrived at many years ago and it is based on Marshall' (letter 3852, 25 February 1930). He then explained that marginal substitute cost is an ambiguous term that can have two meanings, since a firm can increase its output and leave the output of the industry constant either when a rival firm spontaneously decreases its production by the same amount or when it is compelled to do so by a policy of aggressive marketing.

In his reply on the following day (letter 3853, 26 February 1930),[11] Sraffa does not sound particularly impressed by this new attempt at clarification. He apologises for misunderstanding what Shove himself had said in a footnote (Shove 1930: 106) about the similarity between his and Pigou's distinction, but reiterates what he had already noted in preparation for the discussion, when he remarked:

> The chief objection is that he [Shove] fails to keep distinct 'forces on supply side' and 'forces on demand side'. The result is that any supply curve constructed on the basis of S[hove]'s 'economies of production' cannot be used in conjunction with a D[emand] curve, since it is not independent of it.
>
> (PS papers, D3/7/23)

This remark is similar to what Sraffa had noted in his 1926 article, where he rejected the method of including into the cost curve the marketing expenses necessary to sell the product at the prevailing price since 'it misrepresents the manner in which the actual process of determining the price and the quantity produced by each undertaking is affected' (Sraffa 1926: 544).[12]

Given that the debate on marketing expenses went on for quite a while at Cambridge (see J. Robinson 1933a: 21 and Shove 1933a: 116), it is worth quoting Sraffa's reply to Shove on this issue in full. The issue at stake is the independence of the demand and supply curves:

> My point, which I did not succeed in explaining properly in Monday's discussion, is this:
>
> The cost of producing an additional unit is a definite sum of money which depends only upon the quantity produced.
>
> But the cost of marketing is different: the 'cost of marketing 100 pairs of boots' is indeterminate until we know at what price the boots have to be sold.
>
> You can always find a sufficiently low price at which you can sell your 100 p. of boots without incurring into any marketing expenses; and, on the other hand, if you spend a sufficiently large sum in advert. etc., you can sell your boots at any desired price, however high.
>
> Therefore, when you speak of the cost (including marketing expenses) of putting an additional unit on your competitor's market, I do not know what you mean until you tell me at what price it has to be sold.
>
> (letter 3853, 26 February 1930)

It is interesting to note that the correspondence does not touch on the second argument put forward by Shove to reconcile competitive equilibrium with internal economies (or 'economies of individual expansion'). Shove was aware that when marketing expenses or transport costs are involved, a market can be defined more correctly as 'monopolistic' rather than 'competitive' (Shove 1930: 109). Therefore, for the sake of the argument, in the last part of his contribution to the *Symposium*, he ruled out any difference among firms, assumed that all of them faced a horizontal demand curve and resorted to the argument that changes take time, holding that by the time a firm has adjusted its scale of production to a new level of output implying lower average costs, it may well have run into other problems. He mentioned 'fluctuations in luck, ability and other factors' or, as he had explained in his lectures,[13] the 'natural decrepitude' of the firm that could offset the advantages of a larger scale of production. This does not happen if the output of the industry is also increasing in reaction to an increase in demand, since the enlargement of the whole industry would speed up the growth of new and more efficient firms able to produce at lower costs and drive the less efficient firms out of the market. In this way Shove was able to retain the distinction he set so much store by between increase in the output of the firm accompanied or not by an increase in the output of the whole industry.

We know from his notes that Sraffa found this second argument totally unconvincing. He could not see why the change in the circumstances during the adjustment period should always be for the worse, or why firms should grow faster when the demand increases for the whole industry:

> What was the obstacle to more rapid growth of firms? Lack of demand, or physiological reasons? If the first, then the increase of demand will be effective – but we fall back in the private markets and the effect will be due to these and not to the time trouble; if the second, the increase in demand will have no effect. The increase in demand for tall men for the police will not cause the children to grow faster.
>
> (PS papers, D3/7/47)

Above all, Sraffa objected to the introduction of time into a purely theoretical analysis. Time cannot be *one* of the independent variables, as Shove suggested, but, if introduced, it is the *only* independent variable. Theoretical analysis and historical description cannot be mixed together.

It is a great pity that no evidence has survived of further discussion on this point, since the fundamental difference between Sraffa and Shove seems to lie precisely here.

The correspondence with J. Robinson and Kahn on the cost curves

As we have seen, Shove was a difficult person to deal with. In the correspondence examined in this volume we find ample evidence of his problems in relating with his colleagues, but the difficulties in his relations with J. Robinson seem to have been second to none. For two years, from 1931 to 1933, the 17 letters that Shove sent to Robinson alternate between accusations and apologies, apparently inspired above all by the fear that her book – *The Economics of Imperfect Competition* – and the lecture course that Robinson was working on might anticipate the ideas that Shove was struggling to give satisfactory form to, depriving them of their originality.

It is hard to see why there should have been such animosity against Robinson: perhaps there was envy of this younger colleague – a woman, moreover – who succeeded in a year and a half in writing a book that Shove would never have been able to finish; perhaps it was a matter of the attitude Robinson showed, very indulgent, never taking Shove's often highly offensive insinuations too seriously.[14]

The ideas Shove was afraid that might be 'stolen' from him by Robinson are listed in a letter he sends her – the first of those extant – on 24 October 1931, at a time when she had been working at her book for only a few months and had just begun her first short course of lectures on Monopoly. The letter was inspired by a discussion Shove had with Kahn on the definition of aggregate costs, which took place at the beginning of

October (see letter 3904 from GFS to RFK, 11 October 1931 and 3903, October 1931; letter 3902 from RFK to GFS, October 1931). During this discussion Kahn, who was following the progress of Robinson's book day by day, had probably informed Shove of the outline of the book, arousing his fears and exciting an irritated reaction:

> dear Joan, from conversation with Kahn, I gathered that, though the theorems in your book about monopoly are new and original, a good deal of the fundamental apparatus or line of approach (e.g. the treatment of 'costs' and 'rents', heterogeneity of resources, I[increasing] R[eturns] and D[iminishing] R[eturns] and so on) is derived, directly or indirectly, from suggestions which I have put forward at various times in teaching, lectures etc.
>
> I am delighted that any of my ideas or methods of exposition should bear fruit in this way, but may I say that I think some acknowledgement should be made of their source?
>
> (letter 3951, 24 October 1931)

The list of ideas, which Shove obviously regarded as his main contribution and hoped to develop into a publishable form, was repeated and presented in more detail in a note attached to a letter of two months later (letter 3953, 2 December 1931).[15] Shove informed Robinson of the topics he intended to expound in his course in the following term and inquired, somewhat anxiously, whether she had already dealt with any of them. The selected topics were:

1. The definition of supply price of a resource and its relationship with the concept of rent both from the standpoint of the owner of the resource and from the standpoint of the industry or firm that employs the factor (or producer's surplus).
2. The heterogeneity of the productive factors expressed by the different 'suitability' of the resources, measured by the supply price of the resource in relation to its productivity.
3. The distinction between several types of costs, and the three possible alternatives for each of them (constant, diminishing and increasing).
4. The causes of diminishing and increasing returns.

Robinson was probably puzzled by the classification of costs suggested by Shove in this letter and must have asked for further explanations. In fact, while Robinson was certainly familiar with the definitions of marginal cost and final trade cost (which had appeared for the first time in Shove 1928: 264), the other definitions were new and required better clarification. However, this clarification was neither provided by Shove in his confused reply (letter 3954, 8 December 1931) nor ever since, and we must conclude that the suggested classification was another – and unsuccessful – attempt by Shove at solving a problem that he had long been wrestling with.

The problem can be expressed thus: Shove defines marginal cost – which is equal to the supply price of the product – as the cost 'at which the "least suitable" unit of resources contributes to output (i.e. its supply price / its (private) product)' (letter 3953, 2 December 1931) and final trade cost as the change in aggregate costs when the output of the industry is increased by one unit. The two types of cost differ if the increase in output modifies the price and/or the productivity of the factors engaged in the production of the inframarginal units. In other words, if the aggregate cost of producing y is $C(y)$ and $p_i(y)$ is the price of factor i, $a_i\,(y)$ is the reciprocal of the average productivity of factor i, then

$$C(y) = \Sigma p_i(y) \,.\, a_i(y) \,.\, y$$

and

$$\begin{aligned} dC &= \text{final trade cost} \\ &= \Sigma dp_i(y) \,.\, a_i(y) \,.\, y + \Sigma p_i(y) \,.\, da_i(y) \,.\, y + \Sigma p_i(y) \,.\, a_i(y)\, dy \end{aligned}$$

which is equal to the cost of producing dy (marginal cost) if and only if $dp_i = da_i = 0$, i.e. if neither the prices of the factors nor their productivities are affected by the amount of the factor employed. The particular case when the productivity of the factors is independent of the amount employed but their prices can vary was discussed with Kahn in a brief exchange of letters in October 1931, of which Kahn informed Joan Robinson (see letter 3904 from GFS to RFK, 11 October 1931 and letter 3903, October 1931; letter 3902 from RFK to GFS, October 1931). The case under consideration was the decrease in price of machines due to economies of large scale in the capital goods industry. Shove was, however, set on investigating all the possible situations in which dp_i and/or da_i proved different from zero.

A similar problem is satisfactorily dealt with by Robinson in Ch. 10 of *The Economics of Imperfect Competition* ('A digression on the four cost curves'), where she examines the curves of marginal and average costs, including or excluding rent, under perfect competition. She might have shown Shove a draft of the chapter, which she probably wrote with the collaboration of Kahn, since Shove refers to 'your 4 curves' and also to 'Kahn's curves' (and says that he had already dealt with 3 of them) (letter 3954, 8 December 1931). In her book Robinson acknowledges her debt to Shove but she also adds that 'her exposition differs considerably from his own' (J. Robinson 1933a: 133).

The real difference lies not so much in the conclusions of the analysis as in the methodology followed. Robinson is excellent at dealing with one problem at a time. She makes strong simplifying assumptions and then releases them one by one. She focuses on the most relevant cases, and these are presented exhaustively, all the assumptions clearly stated. Shove, instead, aims at a presentation that embraces all cases; he tries to take into account even the slightest detail and to find a definition for each different type of cost; he continually refers to possible exceptions and complications, thus confirming what J. Robinson once said of him: 'whatever point I accused him of overlooking he showed that he had mentioned somewhere – for he mentions every damn thing, that's just the trouble' (letter 567 from JVR to RFK, 20 February 1933). The end result is that Shove gets entangled with all his definitions and possible cases and the picture, instead of becoming clearer, grows ever cloudier.

This difference in the approach to economic theory was clear to Joan Robinson who, a few months later, in her pamphlet *Economics is a serious subject* makes Shove the prototype of the Pessimistic economists, who are interested in all the problems that economic realities suggest to them, as opposed to the Optimists (of whom she regarded herself as a champion), who deal only with those problems that can be treated with the available techniques. She wrote, in what she intended as praise of Shove:

> the pure-English pessimists who like Nothing but facts are apt to damp the spirits of the optimists to an undesirable extent. But the logical English pessimists of whom Mr. Shove is the prototype have only a beneficial effect on them. They challenge the optimists by proposing new sets of assumptions just too hard for the existing technique, and meanwhile evolve by their own methods techniques adapted to realistic problems.
>
> (JVR papers, i/2.1/9)

The pamphlet was sent to Shove who thanked Robinson rather coldly. However, he did not deny having different opinions on what the task of the economists should be:

> My view is that they [the economists] can and should set to work *now* to develop a technique capable of dealing with assumptions which are at present untreatable but rather nearer to reality: (which need not of course prevent their using the existing technique at the same time for the problems to which it is suited).
>
> This is, indeed, what I have been trying to do for several years now. I believe the thing to be perfectly possible and, though I am diffident about my own capacity to contribute to it, I can't help feeling a little – shall I say? – hurt at being publicly relegated to the duty of suggesting 'fresh problems' for you to solve.
>
> (letter 3962, 19 October 1932)

The correspondence with J. Robinson on diminishing returns and equilibrium

If Shove feared an overlapping between his treatment of the cost curves and that in Robinson's book, he grew even more anxious when he realised that Robinson intended to invade one of his favourite fields of research – the causes underlying diminishing returns – and had probably already done so in her short course in the Michaelmas Term of 1931. Shove asked Robinson for an urgent meeting in order that 'this business should not cause any misunderstanding between us' and wrote to her, referring to the subject of his next course:

> It would help me very much in deciding how full to make my treatment if you could tell me whether you did this [=diminishing returns] in my way (i.e. by pointing to the heterogeneity of land – and other resources –, the consequent possible differences in its (their) 'suitability' for any particular industry and so on).
>
> (letter 3955, 9 December 1931)

What Shove called 'my way' is a treatment of diminishing returns (and rent) based on increasing supply price of factors and/or their different 'suitability' to a given industry or firm, 'suitability' being defined by the relationship between supply price and productivity of the factor. The supply price of a factor was defined as the minimum payment required to prevent its transfer to another firm or industry which, in its turn, is determined mainly[16] by the income that the factor could earn in the best available alternative. If factors are heterogeneous, a difference arises between the actual earnings of a resource and its supply price, and this difference represents a rent for the owner of the resource.

Robinson accepted the invitation to discuss the matter in a meeting which took place at Christmas time, on which occasion Shove probably also gave her some notes. It seems[17] that Robinson assuaged Shove's anxiety by telling him that she intended to deal with diminishing returns by 'assuming the factors to be homogeneous within each industry and measuring them by productivity' (i.e. measuring them in terms of efficiency units), while Shove's treatment of the same problem was different in both respects. Indeed, he assumed factors to be heterogeneous, and that they could not be aggregated so as to generate a supply curve of the factor, but each of them was to be considered individually. This was what Robinson called in her book 'Mr. Shove's jig-saw puzzle' (J. Robinson 1933a: 107), referring to a definition of the economic problem given by Shove himself in the *Symposium*: 'a question of sorting out and fitting each into its appropriate niche a vast number of heterogeneous individuals and activities [...] a jigsaw-puzzle rather than a problem of hydrodynamics' (Shove 1930: 99).

However, in June 1932, Shove heard from Kahn that Robinson was revising the first draft of her work extensively and this, again, aroused his suspicion. He wrote to her to enquire whether she had changed her mind since their talk at Christmas. The letter was far from diplomatic:

> I am assuming that you have not altered your treatment so as to make it still more like mine either in these matters or as regards the various elaboration I have been putting into my lectures. Is this all right?
>
> (letter 3958, 9 June 1932)

This time Robinson reacted angrily. We do not have her letters (she must have sent three at least) but the tone of Shove's replies (letters 3959, 3960 and 3961, 17, 23 and 24 June 1932) becomes ever humbler and more apologetic. After further reassurances that Robinson had not changed her mind significantly, he concluded that 'we have got everything straight between us now', although he was still convinced that Robinson had wronged him when she began 'preparing for publication and lectures a treatment of Diminishing Returns very similar to mine', without informing him. At any rate, he was aware of his own limitations and rejected Robinson's offer to wait for the publication of his book: 'It is very kind and generous of you to offer to postpone publication, but please don't. I shall probably never publish and anyhow I should hate to keep you back' (letter 3959, 17 June 1932).

However, he should not have been so worried about too many similarities with Robinson's work. They shared the interest in the same problems, but not the approach to them, as became apparent when Robinson published her first article in the *Economic Journal* in December 1932. The article (J. Robinson 1932a) is famous since it contains for the first time what is known as Kahn's theorem, i.e. the double condition for the equilibrium of the firm and of the industry in an imperfect market: marginal cost equal to marginal revenue and average cost equal to price. Robinson wrote it, somewhat provocatively, to prove that, unlike the case under perfect competition, as had been assumed by Marshallian economists until then, if markets are imperfect, diminishing costs in the individual firms may not lead to diminishing supply price of the product of the industry. This conclusion was probably discussed with Shove as early as March 1932, since, in a letter of 22 March 1932, he is careful to restate thus his position, quoting in part from his contribution to the *Symposium*:

> where there is diminishing cost in individual firm as well as market imperfection, an increase in the output of the industry will often (though *not always or necessarily*) be accompanied by a fall in costs.
>
> (letter 3957)

When the article appeared, Shove again interpreted Robinson's words as criticism of himself and wrote a reply which was published in the

Economic Journal (Shove 1933a), thanks to the efforts of Keynes who 'finally got it out of him by saying that if he withdrew it he would encourage everyone to pinch all Gerald's ideas and never make any acknowledgement' (letter 565 from JVR to RFK, 18 February 1933). Robinson saw the article when it was already in proof and the *Journal* was behind time for the printer; thus, she was given only 24 hours and 400 words by Keynes to reply (letter 563 from JVR to RFK, 15 February 1933). In spite of the shortage of time and space, she succeeded in drafting a rejoinder with the help of her husband, but this was not the end of the story. When Shove saw it, he rushed to Keynes, complained that Robinson had misunderstood him and asked for some more space to explain himself. In the end it was Robinson who had to give in and modify her note. This is how she described the episode to Kahn, then in the US:

> I had to sit in a corner and draft my version while G[erald] and M[aynard] chatted away – and Gerald complains of the nervous strain. Then of course when I had done he began to say that he had behaved unfairly and bullied me into withdrawing criticisms which were probably after all quite right and so forth. Maynard was an angel chaffing Gerald to prevent him from getting hysterical, and telling me that anyway I ought to be pleased to get so much 'reaction' to my article. I think Gerald has made a fool of me, but it is all in a good cause.
>
> (letter 567 from JVR to RFK, 20 February 1933)

The 'good cause' was having convinced Shove to overcome his hesitations in putting his thoughts into print. Robinson was ready to accept Shove's criticisms about the imprecision surrounding her definition of normal profit[18] and she even admitted that she had strained the conclusions of the article, by overstating the case against a falling supply price.[19] However, she was not ready to substitute her neat definition of the equilibrium of the industry, based on a set of equations that gave precise value to the variables, for the vague definitions suggested by Shove, based on intervals of variations, disequalities and stopping rules for the movements of the productive factors. Robinson finds that Shove 'makes everything so confusing and uses words in such odd senses' (letter 567 from JVR to RFK, 20 February 1933); she is sorry that Shove 'refuses to admit that the 'full equilibrium' idea is in any way an advance upon what he says in the Symposium' (letter 580 from JVR to RFK, 8 March 1933); but she is also aware that behind any single point of disagreement there might be a fundamental difference of approach. As she wrote to James Meade:

> You will see in the E.[Economic] J.[Journal] some back chat between me and Gerald. When I talked to him I found a far more deep and subtle difference in our methods than could be put into print at the

> last moment. In spite of appearances to the contrary I don't think there is any difference in results, but I am not sure till I have had another go at him.
>
> (letter 21 February 1933, James Meade papers, 2/4)

Robinson was indeed annoyed by the tone of the article and of the footnotes, which contrasts with that of the letters that Shove sent her to thank her warmly for taking his criticisms so well. The letters are full of understanding for the difficult position he had got her into, and play down any disagreement. He wrote to Robinson: 'I was not (and am not) *consciously* controverting or rejecting any of your conclusions. I supposed myself merely to be interpreting them and expressing them in another way' (letter 3963, 15 February 1933) and 'I think the explanation of the apparent difference between us (I don't believe there is a real one) is that we are talking about different kinds of "cost"' (letter 3964, 16 February 1933). Robinson, understandably, comments: 'He really is as mad as a hatter' (letter 564 from JVR to RFK, 16 February 1933).

The same schizophrenic attitude was to be found a few months later when Shove at last brought himself to read the *Economics of Imperfect Competition*. He wrote to Robinson:

> Did I make clear to you at lunch the other day how much I admire 'Imperfect Competition'?[20] What I like particularly about it is the refreshing precision and accuracy of statement. The points I should rate highest are, I think, 'Price Discrimination' and the 'Comparison of Monopoly and Competition Output'. In both of these you seem to me to have carried things a stage further than they have been carried hitherto – which is a big achievement in this field.
>
> (letter 3967, 10 August 1933)

However, when the review came out, it was not exactly enthusiastic. Again, it was her 'technique' that he did not like, her recourse to heroic assumptions in order to make the problems manageable in mathematical terms; 'an essay in geometrical political economy' (Shove 1933b: 660), as he called the book.

In any case, the lack of enthusiasm was reciprocated. While Shove was working on his review, Robinson wrote to Kahn: 'I re-read the Symposium and find that a lot of Gerald's stuff is really hopeless. I shall write an attack on it in the Children's Magazine' (letter 612 from JVR to RFK, 13 September 1933).[21] The attack was never written, but the differences do not seem to have lessened in the course of time.

The correspondence with J. Robinson on Marx and Marshall

The last exchange of letters between Shove and J. Robinson that has come down to us has to do with the book on Marxian economics that Robinson published in 1942. Shove began to work on a review of the book in August 1942,[22] but it appeared only in April 1944. Robinson started the exchange with a letter of thanks for the review and a request for some clarifications (letter 3971, 1 May 1944). Five more letters from Robinson followed but, after receiving ten pages from Shove all at once, she suggested continuing the debate in person (letter 3977, 18 June 1944).

It is not easy to reconstruct the whole discussion since, with the exception of that long letter from Shove, we have only Robinson's side of the correspondence, the interest of which lies in the old and new aspects of their difficult scientific and personal relationship that it reveals.

One of the old aspects is the contrast between the meticulous care over the correct interpretation of past authors exhibited by Shove and Robinson's somewhat cavalier attitude. The first part of Shove's review was devoted to showing that Robinson had misinterpreted both classical and neo-classical economists. But, as Robinson replied to him:

> we are playing quite different games. I admit I am a bit slap dash with my quotations – what I try to do is to find a coherent system of ideas that seems to fit and what I say a man 'really meant' is often something he never says at all [. . .]. You are playing quite a different game – of 'exact scholarship'.
>
> (letter 3972, 5 May 1944)

Another old aspect is Shove's devotion to Marshall. As so often before,[23] he was eager to point out that Marshall had not overlooked any difficulty. He even suggested that Marshall's theory of the rate of interest could be reconciled with that of Keynes, but his attempt was cut short by Robinson (letter 3973, 10 May 1944), who, at that time, was much more critical of the Marshallian tradition, and remarked: 'What I cannot fathom is why you feel obliged to defend him [Marshall]. You ought to be writing to expose his inadequacy. (Of course we all agree that he was a great man, but that's not the point)' (letter 3975, 30 May 1944).

The new aspects are the problems they discuss, under the obvious influence of the Keynesian revolution and the new ideological position taken by Robinson.

In her book Robinson criticises the Marshallian notion of the rate of interest as the supply price of capital and its justification as the reward for 'deferring gratification' or 'waiting'. In a letter she makes her point even clearer:

> I agree that for society investment and maintaining capital that might be physically consumed represents waiting e.g. under the 5 year plan

> USSR was waiting like mad [. . .] It is Marshall's attempt to justify the actual reward that actual chaps get as corresponding to the real cost to society that causes all the trouble.
>
> (letter 3972, 5 May 1944)

She then goes on to ask who provides the waiting in a joint-stock company, the managers or the shareholders?

Shove, as was his wont, tried to rescue Marshall and deny any real difference:

> Whereas you maintain that Marshall, in his first edition at any rate, explained, (and justified) interest primarily, if not exclusively, on the ground that it is necessary in order to induce people to abstain from *selling* their capital [. . .] I maintain that he does so primarily on the ground that it is necessary to induce people to *replace* or *add* to capital.
>
> (letter 3974, 12 May 1944, italics are mine)

Subsequently, the focus of the discussion moved to the problem of whether the expected rate of profit must be higher than the supply price of capital if there is accumulation. Shove stated thus his position in a letter to Maurice Dobb, with whom he continued the discussion when Robinson had tired of it:

> if Joan had said only that, in an expanding system with the stock of capital growing, the rate of profit may be above normal, I should have had no quarrel with her. What I object to is her claim that it must be: my point being that there is no logical inconsistency between an expanding system and the maintenance of an equilibrium rate of profit.
>
> (letter from GFS to Maurice Dobb, 22 June 1944, Dobb papers, CA200.2)

Shove suggested a framework of analysis where the demand and supply of capital are two curves which are a function of time – an old idea of his that would become the foundation of theory of growth in equilibrium. But the times were not ripe for that. And Robinson commented: 'I think the whole trouble arises from stepping from a static to a dynamic system without working out the problems involved' (letter from JVR to Maurice Dobb, 12 August 1944, JVR papers, vii/120).

Conclusions

Shove's correspondence with the younger Cambridge economists casts some light on his complex personality. It helps us to understand how many of the references to Shove that we find in the works of Robinson, Kahn and others in the early 1930s may have been dictated by the wish not to arouse Shove's susceptibility. However, the correspondence also shows quite clearly that Shove was the object of real respect and affection, as borne out by numerous episodes.

Sraffa, who shared Shove's concern for precision in historical reconstruction, proposed Shove's promotion to reader. Robinson seems to have cherished the idea of making Shove the third member of a team working on reformulation of the theory of Marshallian prices.[24] In 1989 Kahn was still speaking of his debt towards the person whom he considered his real economics teacher, and who had guided him in drafting his dissertation. Unfortunately, in the case of Kahn above all there remains hardly any evidence of a long friendship accompanied by cultural exchange, and cemented by membership of the same college and unstinting admiration of Keynes.

The correspondence highlights some of the qualities that endeared Shove to his younger colleagues – his generous dedication of time to discussing the work of others, his refusal to speak of things where his knowledge was in any way limited, and his fear that the written word could never give full expression to his thought. It also makes it clear that Shove's contribution to the economic debate lay more in the problems he raised than in the answers he provided. The best assessment is probably the one he gave of himself:

> the Awful Truth is that I know in my heart that my work in theory will never amount to anything of real value. I never feel really on top of the subject in that field. I must be content to be a teacher and perhaps to throw out a few suggestions which others may follow up and make something of it. And after all that will be worth while, if I can do it.
>
> (letter from GFS to DHR, 15 March 1938)

Notes

1 1888 has often mistakenly been indicated as the year of Shove's birth, an error that can be traced back to Kahn 1987. I wish to thank Gordon Fletcher who kindly found Shove's birth certificate for me.

2 Obituary, King's College Annual Report, 1947 (the author is almost certainly Kahn, since some passages in Kahn 1987 are identical). J. Robinson never stated that she had had Shove as supervisor, but Shove, in a letter to her (letter 3952, 27 October 1931), refers to ideas expounded 'on various occasions in supervision'. However, the phrase is ambiguous, and may not refer to supervision of Robinson herself.

3 For most of his professional life Shove held only the lectureship he was awarded in 1923, obtaining a readership only in 1945, two years before his death.

4 Kahn recognised his 'originality as dauntless thinker' (1987: 327) and Austin Robinson regretted that his contribution had yet to receive just recognition (A. Robinson 1977).

5 J. Robinson wrote to Kahn with reference to a meeting of the Political Economy Club: 'Piero opened and mainly conducted the discussion, and the

main value of the paper lay in the things that it led Piero and Gerald to say' (letter 569 from JVR to RFK, 24 February 1933) and also: 'They tell me that Gerald's essay was extremely good. Various plots are on foot for getting it published' (letter 552 from JVR to RFK, 8 February 1933).

6 Austin Robinson had found his lectures 'inordinately dull' (A. Robinson 1977: 28), possibly because Shove's qualities as a teacher emerged not in public, given his shyness, but at the level of individual supervision.

7 An abstract of Shove's memoir is preserved in the Bodleian Library, Oxford, Dep. BAAS 252. The title was 'Various interpretations of the Laws of Diminishing Returns, with special reference to their bearing on the problem of Population'. It purported to deal with 'those senses of "diminishing returns" which do and those which do not imply an increasing supply-price for commodities in question'.

8 Shove also seems to agree with Sraffa's view that external economies shared by the industry with other industries employing the same factors of production must be ruled out, but he is not explicit on this point.

9 The note says 'On looking through my stuff last night, I decided it will not do in its present form, and have therefore withdrawn it' (letter 3851, February 1930).

10 See the card of invitation sent by Kahn, then secretary of the Club, in PS papers, D3/7.13.

11 A draft of the letter is kept among Sraffa's papers. We cannot be sure that the letter was actually sent.

12 The problem of independence of the supply and demand curves when marketing expenses are taken into account had been raised by Kahn at one of Sraffa's lectures and discussed again during the drafting of Kahn's dissertation. See Marcuzzo (2001b: 90–2) and Dardi (2001: 128–35).

13 The notes on Shove's lectures in the year 1928–29 taken by one of his students, John Saltmarch, are among RFK papers.

14 As Robinson writes to Kahn: 'I fear my failure to take offence will only make him feel badly and break out afresh in some way' (letter 564, 16 February 1933).

15 The note is in JVR papers, VII/412: 48–50, but it is not kept together with the letter to which it was originally attached.

16 Shove also takes into account the 'preferences' for a particular employment (Shove 1930: 97).

17 This is how Shove recalls their meeting in letter 3958, 9 June 1932.

18 She writes to Kahn: 'He has scored one point against me as you will see' (letter 563 from JVR to RFK, 15 February 1933) and three days later she admits her mistake in a letter to Harrod (letter 1107, 18 March 1933) (Ch. 12: 315).

19 'I think he [Gerald] and Piero should be given the point about falling supply price being due to internal economies. After all I wrote my article rather to show that it wasn't' (letter 580 from JVR to RFK, 8 March 1933).

20 It is interesting to note that Shove even seems unable to remember the title of the book correctly. In another letter he calls it 'economics of an imperfect market' (letter 3966, July 1933).

21 This is how the *Review of Economic Studies* was nicknamed.

22 See Robinson's remarks to Keynes: 'Gerald is supposed reviewing me for E.[conomic] J.[ournal]. It will be interesting to see his views (assuming he gets it done)' (letter 1865, 21 August 1942).

23 See, for example, letter 3968 from GFS to JVR, 8 May 1938 on Marshall's assumption that entrepreneurs maximise profit.

24 J. Robinson wrote to Kahn, 23 February 1933: 'If only he weren't subject to these fits of mania we really could work with him (do you remember our ancient plot?) He is far more sensible than Prof [Pigou] or Dennis' (letter 568 from JVR to RFK, 23 February 1933).

Table 14.1 Shove–Kahn correspondence

From	*To*	*Year*	*Month*	*Day*	*Date*	*Archive*		*Published in*	*Item*
GFS	RFK	1928	June	29	Dated letter	Kahn–King's	RFK/13/100/1–2		3901
RFK	GFS	1931	October		Attributed	Robinson–King's	JVR/vii/228/1/20		3902
GFS	RFK	1931	October		Attributed	Robinson–King's	JVR/vii/228/1/21		3903
GFS	RFK	1931	October	11	Dated letter	Robinson–King's	JVR/vii/412/1–2		3904

Table 14.2 Shove–J. Robinson correspondence

From	*To*	*Year*	*Month*	*Day*	*Date*	*Archive*	*Published in*	*Item*
GFS	JVR	1931	October	24	Dated letter	Robinson–King's JVR/vii/412/3–4		3951
GFS	JVR	1931	October	27	Dated letter	Robinson–King's JVR/vii/412/5–7		3952
GFS	JVR	1931	December	2	Dated letter	Robinson–King's JVR/vii/412/8–9 and 48–50		3953
GFS	JVR	1931	December	8	Dated letter	Robinson–King's JVR/vii/412/10–13		3954
GFS	JVR	1931	December	9	Dated letter	Robinson–King's JVR/vii/412/14–15		3955
GFS	JVR	1931	December	19	Dated letter	Robinson–King's JVR/vii/412/16–17		3956
GFS	JVR	1932	March	22	Dated letter	Robinson–King's JVR/vii/412/18–19		3957
GFS	JVR	1932	June	9	Dated letter	Robinson–King's JVR/vii/412/20–1		3958
GFS	JVR	1932	June	17	Dated letter	Robinson–King's JVR/vii/412/22–5		3959
GFS	JVR	1932	June	23	Dated letter	Robinson–King's JVR/vii/412/26–8		3960
GFS	JVR	1932	June	24	Dated letter	Robinson–King's JVR/vii/412/29		3961
GFS	JVR	1932	October	19	Dated letter	Robinson–King's JVR/vii/412/30–1		3962
GFS	JVR	1933	February	15	Dated letter	Robinson–King's JVR/vii/412/32–3		3963
GFS	JVR	1933	February	16	Dated letter	Robinson–King's JVR/vii/412/34		3964
GFS	JVR	1933	May	24	Dated letter	Robinson–King's JVR/vii/412/35–7		3965
GFS	JVR	1933	July		Dated letter	Robinson–King's JVR/vii/412/38–9		3966
GFS	JVR	1933	August	10	Dated letter	Robinson–King's JVR/vii/412/40–41		3967
GFS	JVR	1938	May	8	Dated letter	Robinson–King's JVR/vii/412/42–3		3968
GFS	JVR	1938	May	9	Dated letter	Robinson–King's JVR/vii/412/44–45		3969
GFS	JVR	1938	May	11	Dated letter	Robinson–King's JVR/VII/412/46–47		3970
JVR	GFS	1944	May	1	Attributed	Keynes–King's L/44/19–20		3971
JVR	GFS	1944	May	5	Attributed	Keynes–King's L/44/21–4		3972
JVR	GFS	1944	May	10	Attributed	Keynes–King's L/44/25–6		3973
GFS	JVR	1944	May	12	Dated letter	Keynes–King's L/44/27–37		3974
JVR	GFS	1944	May	30	Attributed	Keynes–King's L/44/38–9		3975
JVR	GFS	1944	June	2	Attributed	Keynes–King's L/44/40–1		3976
JVR	GFS	1944	June	18	Attributed	Keynes–King's L/44/42		3977

Table 14.3 Shove–Sraffa correspondence

From	*To*	*Year*	*Month*	*Day*	*Date*	*Archive*		*Published in*	*Item*
GFS	PS	1930	February		Attributed	Sraffa–Trinity	Sraffa D3/7/40		3851
GFS	PS	1930	February	25	Dated letter	Sraffa–Trinity	Sraffa D3/7/9		3852
PS	GFS	1930	February	26	Dated letter	Sraffa–Trinity	Sraffa D3/7/8	Marcuzzo 2001b: 90, (E)	3853
PS	GFS	1930	May	31	Dated letter	Sraffa–Trinity	Sraffa B9/1/10	Naldi 2004: 109–10, fn. 48, (E)	3854

15 Robertson and the great divide

The correspondence with Kahn, Kaldor, J. Robinson and Sraffa

Nerio Naldi

The letters we are to consider number 59, 42 from Robertson and 17 from his correspondents (see Tables 15.1 to 15.4). The predominance of letters sent by Robertson is explained by the fact that he did not always keep the correspondence he received, that he himself and his literary executor destroyed many of his papers, and that several of Robertson's papers have been dispersed among scholars interested in his work.[1]

The earliest of the extant letters we are to consider dates to 1928; the latest to 1946. Most probably Robertson made his acquaintance first with Robinson, then with Sraffa and Kahn and, in 1930–31, with Kaldor, when Robertson was teaching 'Principles of Currency' at the London School of Economics and Kaldor was a research student there (Thirlwall 1987: 23–5, 335). Like Pigou, Robertson also had a fruitful intellectual exchange with the young economists we are considering. However, from the 1930s onward, when he found himself in the position of an opponent to an intellectual front pivoting on Keynes's theories, his letters reveal some difficulties and strain, mainly when Keynesian economists and Keynesian economics were involved. The correspondence was always quite warm and affectionate with Sraffa and Kaldor and rather formal with Kahn, while coming quite close to showing signs of animosity with Robinson (but the signs emerged much more clearly in the correspondence with Keynes).

Based on the characteristics of the extant correspondence this chapter is divided into three main sections, respectively focused on Robertson's correspondence with Piero Sraffa, on his correspondence dating to the late 1920s and early 1930s and mainly relating to the development of the theory of the firm and of imperfect competition, and on his correspondence relating to discussions which took place after the publication of Keynes's *General Theory*.

Robertson's correspondence with Sraffa

The extant correspondence between Robertson and Sraffa consists of fifteen letters: twelve sent by Robertson, three written by Sraffa.

A first group of documents contains five short undated letters (letters

3521–3523, 3525 and 3534) reflecting the discussion which took place between Robertson and Sraffa when they were preparing the *Symposium on increasing returns and the representative firm*. If we consider the deadline for publication in the *Economic Journal* and that some notes on Robertson's paper seem to have been written by Sraffa in Italy and in France (PS papers, D3/7/30, 34), where he had been during the 1929–30 Christmas vacations (PS papers, E3), we may infer that the group of letters we are considering was exchanged approximately between early–mid-December 1929 and mid-February 1930.

Four of the five extant letters mainly reflect Robertson's reactions to Sraffa's criticisms, but the lack of Sraffa's letters is a serious obstacle to reconstruction of their discussion. In any case, the tone of Robertson's letters is extremely friendly and shows that, despite the differences between their positions in the *Symposium*, their personal relations were very good. Such circumstances were by no means unusual among the economists considered in this book, but in this case the content and the tone of the correspondence also suggest that Robertson did not feel as if his views had been successfully attacked by Sraffa.[2] To this group of letters belongs one of the few extant letters from Sraffa to Robertson, but in this case it is most probable that the letter, kept among PS papers, was not sent. Here, quoting various passages from Marshall's published writings, Sraffa argued that the concept of representative firm could not be conceived as an *afterthought* – as Robbins had written in his 1928 article – because it already appeared in the first edition of the *Principles* and was referred to by Marshall himself as the main result of his work between 1870 and 1890 (3521, February 1930).

Two other letters reflect a discussion on Sraffa's 1932 article on Hayek's book *Prices and Production*, whose aim was that of explaining economic fluctuations through a combination of the traditional instruments of equilibrium analysis (in their Austrian version) with explicit attention to the effects of banking policies on relative prices of consumption and capital goods (Hayek 1931b). In the first letter Robertson wrote of Sraffa's paper: 'at first [it] made me think there was nothing left of Hayek: but on reflection I believe I am on his side on most of the main points of controversy' (letter 3528, 31 January 1932).[3]

The three points briefly developed by Robertson with the aim of presenting the reasons for his siding with Hayek touch upon crucial aspects of Sraffa's argument: his contention that Hayek's definition of money actually deprived it of its crucial features (and his results of any interest); his contention that an economy that has been led to an equilibrium by a 'non-neutral' banking policy could not revert to the 'neutral' or 'natural' equilibrium even if that policy reverts to 'neutrality'; his contention that the ambiguity of the concept of natural rate of interest, even in a non-monetary economy, has a crucial destructive effect on Hayek's reasoning. Given the way Robertson developed his argument, the second point, which he illustrated with an arithmetical example, was the most important to the discussion:

> I do not think you have disproved H[ayek]'s argument that after an inflation stops there will be decumulation of capital. For this to occur it is not necessary that those who have [been] spending their whole incomes on consumption all along should spend more on consumption, which as you rightly say is impossible. It is only necessary that those who have been dividing the expenditure of their receipts from the sale of goods in a certain proportion between expenditure on consumption goods and expenditure on keeping capital intact should go on acting as they have been doing. The cessation of the flow of new money from the banks will then mean that the total flow of expenditure on keeping capital intact is inadequate for its purpose, – i.e. decumulation occurs.
>
> (letter 3528, 31 January 1932)

Sraffa's reply, as far as we can tell from the draft he kept among his papers, focused precisely on that objection:

> No doubt you forget that *after* the inflation by means of loans to producers has come to an end, the Govt. (or Central Bank) *remain* the owners (or creditors) of the cash; and they are determined that it should remain a credit to producers and not one to consumers. This means that in your case II (inflation) they will not allow the entrepreneurs to whom they have lent this money to consume it for their own private pleasure – They will insist on their holding assets equivalent to their debts: when you suppose that these entrepreneurs will revert to the old proportions, and consume the capital, you forget that inflation money is issued as a credit, not as a gift.
>
> (letter 3535, 2 February 1932)

From this passage it is clear that in Sraffa's view Robertson – just as Hayek – had in mind an economy formed by atomistic and aspecific agents. Sraffa, on the contrary, attached great importance to the peculiar characteristics of the subjects supposed to act in the particular cases considered.

Two letters dated May 1935 document the final phase of the tiresome discussions which preceded Sraffa's appointment to the post of Assistant Director of Research (letters 3530, 1 May 1935; 3531, 3 May 1935). A previous phase of the same process is documented by three letters sent by Keynes to his wife in March 1935 (JMK papers, PP/45/190/7/28–9, 31–2, 33–4) and by a letter to Pigou drafted by Keynes on Sraffa's behalf in the same month (letter 4456 from PS to ACP, 10 March 1935) which we have already considered in Ch. 13: 333–4. The two letters sent by Robertson to

Sraffa confirm that, two months after Keynes's intervention, Sraffa's hostility to the idea of having to be available to students at fixed times was still the greatest obstacle to overcome.

In two letters Robertson asked Sraffa to read papers he was writing (or rather read a new draft of such papers). The titles of the papers are never explicitly stated, but they might have been drafts of Robertson's 1931 criticisms of Keynes's *Treatise on Money* and of Robertson's 1936 paper on Keynes's *General Theory*. In fact, the reference to L.P. [level of prices] in the first letter recalls a passage in his paper on the *Treatise on Money* where Robertson discussed the four ways in which the concept of price-level of 'investments' was used by Keynes: 'I have altered this damn thing again on p.19, having unearthed a *fourth* way of dressing up L.P. which I had overlooked, but which I think is really the one they have now settled down to. It's like trying to catch an eel!' (letter 3527, 6 March 1931; see Robertson 1931a: 399–400).

Robertson's review of the *General Theory*, on the other hand, appeared in the *Quarterly Journal of Economics* as part of a *Symposium* which is recalled in this letter:

> I have no right to ask you to waste any more time on this product, the sight of which you have probably come to hate as much as I have. But I'm rather dashed by HDH [Hubert Henderson]'s letter, and have in consequence wired to Taussig that, I can't promise to produce anything for his symposium!
>
> (letter 3532, 12 June 1936)

The same letter is also particularly interesting because it shows how closely knitted Robertson felt his research activity to be to his teaching:

> I think I'd better withdraw the thing if it's going to lay me open to smashing replies and ruin what is left of my scanty reputation as a theorist! Yet that seems cowardly if I'm going to find myself talking to pupils etc on these lines.[4]
>
> (letter 3532, 12 June 1936)

Not surprisingly, three of the extant letters touch upon questions related to teaching (letters 3526, 3 March 1931; 3529, 16 February 1932; 3533, 19 November 1946). In the last of them Robertson dealt with a difficulty with Shove which emerged in 1946, when he refused to supervise research students. Robertson associated this problem with the general problem of the way research in economics was directed, but the tenor of his letter does not seem to put any blame for this situation on Sraffa, who was Assistant Director of Research and worked with research students; on the contrary, Robertson asked Sraffa if he would raise the issue before the appropriate academic body.

When Sraffa heard that Robertson had accepted the offer of the Chair of Economics previously occupied by Pigou, he sent him a very warm letter, showing that his feelings were of deep and sincere friendship:

> you can imagine how happy I was last Saturday when the Vice Chancellor rang me up to announce your acceptance. Partly because you could imagine it, and partly because I didn't know how to write as beautiful a letter of congratulations as I should have wanted, or as those which you have no doubt been receiving in large numbers – well, I didn't. But I am sure that you do know [...] I hope you will soon come, you will *have* to come, at least for a day.
>
> (letter 3536, 24 February 1944)

Late 1920s and early 1930s: correspondence with Kahn, Kaldor and J. Robinson

An important part of Robertson's extant correspondence with his younger colleagues in the late 1920s and early 1930s has to do with analysis of the theory of the firm and of markets. Around the end of 1929 Robertson sent to Kahn notes containing observations and corrections to the text of the dissertation submitted by Kahn in December 1929 for a Fellowship of King's College (letter 3589).

Robertson was one of the referees and his official report is kept among Kahn's papers (RFK papers, 2/8/1–15). However, the document we are considering has nothing to do with that report, but simply suggests a number of minor alterations to the text of the dissertation. The document is not dated, but we may suppose that it was sent to Kahn shortly after submission, probably around the end of December 1929. In fact, having read the proofs of Keynes's *Treatise on Money*, on 8 January 1930 Robertson sent him his comments and wrote: 'I've been taking a holiday (from Kahn and lecture-notes) over the enclosed' (letter 3092 from DHR to JMK, 8 January 1930, CWK XIII: 121–2).[5] As we have already seen in Ch. 13, after the dissertation was accepted, for some time Kahn considered the possibility of publishing it or large parts of it. As a matter of fact, however, the dissertation was not published until sixty years later (Kahn 1983, 1989), and Robertson's suggestions were left aside.

We have an earlier instance (letter 3583, 17 January 1929) of interaction between the two: their engagement in a project of the Royal Institute of International Affairs aimed at preparing 'a return of the value of British economic interests in China' (RFK papers, 3/5/44). The project was supervised by Robertson and Gregory, and Kahn came to be involved in the preparation of the questionnaires to be used to collect the desired information (RFK papers, 3/5/38).

Another exchange between Robertson and Kahn took place in Autumn 1932. In the first of these letters Kahn briefly discussed two papers by

Robertson. The first is referred to by Kahn as a 'monetary paper' (evidently 'Some revised definitions of Saving & allied concepts' which Robertson had sent to Keynes in September 1932 – see letter 3117 from DHR to JMK, 2 September 1932, CWK XIII: 301–6; see Ch. 2). In his comment Kahn stressed his difficulty in disentangling Robertson's new definition of saving and that he considered the paper's disregard of wage movements as a serious deficiency (letter 3590, 5 October 1932). Robertson's reply on this point, undated but probably written on the same day, is particularly telling: 'Really, this is a little hard! Here am I trying to adapt my analysis to your fantastic world in which entrepreneurs' incomes are the only mobile ones, and you accuse me of neglecting wage movements!' (letter 3581, 5 October 1932).

We may well imagine that the reference to 'your fantastic world' was pointing to the world of the *Treatise on Money*, and that Robertson was trying to bridge the gap between himself on the one side and Keynes and his followers on the other. The second paper discussed by Kahn is Robertson's 'A note on the supply curve' (see Besomi 2004: 8–11), and in this context he mentioned an article that Robinson was 'contemplating' writing on one of the points dealt with by Robertson: the relation between total output and average cost in an imperfect market (unfortunately, no letter from Robinson to Robertson on this point seems to have survived but we may wonder whether the article mentioned by Kahn was her 1932 paper on 'Imperfect competition and falling supply price'). Robertson's reply on this aspect was very brief and mentioned Shove and Harrod, who had already been involved in a discussion on the same paper (letter 3581, 5 October 1932).

Another letter from Robertson to Kahn belonging to approximately the same period is also undated, but was probably written in mid-1933 (letter 3582). It contains some comments by Robertson on Kahn's article 'The elasticity of substitution and the relative share of a factor' published in October 1933 and, given that a typescript draft of the paper is enclosed with the letter, it seems likely that Kahn had asked Robertson to read it before publication. In the final text Kahn deleted a passage that had come in for unfavourable comment from Robertson ('The accusation on p. 14 that [Hicks] excludes backward-rising supply curves is surely an exaggeration' – letter 3582; see Kahn 1933: 77, n. 23), suggesting that the exchange between the two economists was not fruitless.

The rest of the correspondence between Robertson and Kahn relating to this period and to the theory of the firm consists of two documents (a note from Robertson and Kahn's reply) written in 1946. We include them in this section because the object of the exchange was a paper ('Some notes on ideal output') published by Kahn in 1935. As Kahn's paper contained an attack against Pigouvian analysis of unemployment based on the conceptions of external economies and diseconomies and imperfect competition (see Ch. 11: 296–7), we may suppose that Robertson approached it anew in the 1940s as part of an attempt to reconsider classical economics and the attacks it had suffered from Keynes and his followers. Discussions of works of the 1920s and 1930s also appear in letters that Robertson sent to Kaldor and J. Robinson in 1944–46, suggesting that such an attitude was typical of his train of thought at that time, when he was returning to academic life after having served at the Treasury. In any case, even though Kahn was probably better equipped than Robertson in terms of mathematical skills, the exchange, involving an underlying formalisation, was to benefit both parties: at least in one case Kahn acknowledged that he had made a mistake and that Robertson's criticism was appropriate. However, no crucial result seemed to follow from this or other parts of that discussion (letters 3585, 20 November 1946; 3586, 25 December 1946).

Robertson's correspondence with J. Robinson and Kaldor in the late 1920s and early 1930s consists of a single letter from Kaldor, one from J. Robinson, and a letter from Robertson to Robinson. The letter from Robinson concerns the preparation of the book *The Economics of Imperfect Competition*, is kept among RFK papers, and, although undated, seems to have been written during the summer of 1931 (letter 3406 from JVR to DHR, September 1931). In this letter Robinson asked Robertson to write a preface to the book that she was preparing, reproduced its index, and stated that she was attaching a draft of some chapters. We do not know if the letter was actually sent, but certainly Robertson's answer is not to be found among the papers known to us, and he does not seem ever to have written a preface to that book or comments on drafts of its chapters.

The first extant letter (3451, 14 July 1932) exchanged between Robertson and Kaldor dates to July 1932, when they had probably just made acquaintance, and contains Robertson's comment on the article 'A case against technical progress?' (Kaldor 1932) which Kaldor had sent him. Kaldor's article was developed as an extensive critique of a recent book where Emil Lederer had attacked the traditional optimistic stance on the relationship between technical progress and unemployment. Robertson declared his agreement with the 'analytical arguments' used by Kaldor, which were based on the distinction between three circumstances which may cause a change in technique: inventions; change in the relative scarcity of factors originated on the supply side; change in factor prices with no variation of their scarcity. However, he differed in his interpretation of 'the facts'. In particular, he listed three specific points of disagreement regarding the relationship between technical improvements and wage policy, the practicability of a wage reduction sufficient to put a brake on technical progress, and 'the strength of the forces making for obliteration of incomes as the result of an improvement occurring over a wide field' (letter 3451, 14 July 1932).

The last extant letter concerning the theory of the firm and the development of the analysis of imperfect competition, dated 15 August 1933, was sent by Robertson to Robinson with considerations on a document she had sent him (letter 3401). The tenor of the letter suggests that the document might have been an outline of the course she was to give during the following academic year.[6] The main point raised by Robertson suggested that Robinson's decision of 'starting from the monopoly end and keeping pure competition in the background' might not be such an improvement with respect to the traditional approach which placed more emphasis on the case of pure competition. In the same letter Robertson also touched very briefly upon a point in Robinson's 1933 book which they had probably already discussed; in fact he declared that he still thought that a specific passage in that book was 'somewhat lacking in clarity' (the passage referred to by Robertson is in Chapter VIII, in the last part of Section 5 of the 'Digression on rent').

After the *General Theory*

Robertson's correspondence with Kaldor, Kahn and Robinson concerning Keynes's *General Theory* and the development of a Keynesian front in economics consists of thirty letters, which may be divided into four groups. The first group consists mainly of letters exchanged between Robertson and Kaldor, and may be taken to reflect Robertson's position in the debate on Pigou's 1937 article 'Real and money wage rates in relation to unemployment'. The second group contains eleven letters exchanged between Robertson and Kahn between June and July 1938 as part of 'an attempt [. . .] to persuade Kahn that the efficacy of 'Keynesian' action to stimulate output does, on ordinary competition short period theory, depend on real wages being reduced' (DHR papers, C18/35/1).[7] The third group contains letters exchanged with Kaldor shortly after Robertson had decided to accept a professorship in London and in the months immediately following his return to Cambridge. The letters in the fourth group are all part of Robertson's correspondence with J. Robinson.

Correspondence on Pigou's paper on wages and unemployment

Two letters sent by Kaldor and three letters from Robertson were written in October 1937 and relate to the paper published by Pigou in the September 1937 issue of the *Economic Journal.* Although the content of this article and the events which followed its publication have already been considered in some of the previous chapters (see Chs 2: 70, 6: 177, 8: 219–20; CWK XIV: 234–68; Thirlwall 1987: 64–9), we shall recall them briefly here. In 1937, during Keynes's illness, Robertson decided to publish Pigou's paper in the *Economic Journal.* The main contention in this paper was that a reduction in money wages would cause an increase of employment. The paper had been presented by Pigou 'in atonement' for his failure to produce a presidential address to the Royal Economic Society (Pigou 1937: 405): a failure evidently due to the fact that in that period, just like Keynes, he had suffered from heart trouble. But when Keynes saw it he was very critical of Robertson's decision and described Pigou's paper as 'the work of a sick man, which no one would print who was in his right mind' (JMK to A. Robinson, 7 August 1937, CWK XIV: 234). Keynes's deep scepticism notwithstanding the paper was published (A. Robinson stated that Pigou was determined to publish it either in the *Economic Journal* or in the *Quarterly Journal of Economics*, and that Robertson had made clear to him that the paper accurately represented Pigou's thought – letter from A. Robinson to JMK, 11 August 1937, CWK XIV: 239). In August 1937 Keynes had already prepared and circulated a short comment on Pigou's paper but soon after it was published Kaldor pinpointed certain weaknesses in it which he felt called for attention (notably, the fact that it did not consider the role of income in the determination of savings), and sent Keynes a detailed analytical comment (letter 1685 from NK to JMK, 27 September 1937, CWK XIV: 240). Kaldor, in turn, received from Keynes the note Keynes himself was preparing on the same article, and some correspondence ensued.

At the same time, or shortly thereafter, correspondence on Pigou's article also started between Kaldor and Robertson, and between Pigou and Kaldor (letters 4401, 4402; see Ch. 13). The correspondence involving Pigou, Robertson and Kaldor and that between Keynes and Kaldor was mainly concerned with identification of the hypotheses underlying Pigou's paper. The assumptions under consideration concerned the possibility of producing capital equipment in the period considered and the possibility that Pigou's argument required the additional assumption that saving was independent of real income (Keynes [1937d] in CWK XIV: 264; Kaldor 1937: 749). Robertson and Kaldor, on the other hand, seemed to agree that Keynes, too, had failed to understand Pigou's hypotheses properly: 'I had another letter from Keynes, who still seems to misunderstand Pigou on one important point. I have tried to explain this in my reply; so perhaps this point might get cleared up too' (letter 3456 from NK to DHR, 29 October 1937).[8] Robertson was particularly clear: 'I'm very glad your article is to appear, for I do think it helps the matter forward, – I can't say the same of Keynes's note!' (letter 3455, 29 October 1937).

The correspondence between Keynes and Kahn reveals that Pigou's paper was – as one may well imagine – also being discussed by the other economists in Cambridge and that at least some of the younger economists bore Keynes some resentment, as if he had chosen Kaldor, instead of one of them, to reply to Pigou's article (letter 393, 22 October 1937, CWK XIV: 260). The feeling shows how dependent they were on Keynes, but it was most probably ill placed: Keynes did not *choose* Kaldor for this job; it was Kaldor who had on his own initiative sent him a paper most probably very different from any that could have been written by the young

Cambridge followers of Keynes. In particular, it seems that those young followers and Keynes himself considered that no other reply was needed once he had prepared his own comment. Peculiarly enough, however, Robertson and Kaldor were not the only ones among Keynes's correspondents who tried to persuade him to delete or modify a specific section of his comment because it misinterpreted Pigou's hypotheses. Kahn also did so, although touching upon a different note:

> As I expected, Pigou has seized on your last paragraph (which I am still opposed to your printing) and declared triumphantly that you have misunderstood him. Why not force him (and your readers) to concentrate on what is important by agreeing to omit the final paragraph?
>
> (letter 393 from RFK to JMK, 22 October 1937, CWK XIV: 260)[9]

In the end, Keynes and Kaldor published their two notes in the December 1937 issue of the *Economic Journal*; Robertson published no note;[10] Pigou did not write a reply for the same issue of the *Economic Journal* but decided to reconsider the matter (letter 3455 from DHR to NK, 29 October 1937; letter 4402 from ACP to NK, late October 1937; see CWK XIV: 255–8) and published his reply in March 1938. The correspondence between Robertson and Kaldor touched upon the same discussion again in 1939 (letter 3462, 2 June 1939) in connection with a subsequent paper written by Kaldor (1939c). While these discussions were going on, correspondence was evidently also taking place between Pigou and Keynes; in this case, however, either correspondent was at least as worried about the health of the other as he was of their theoretical disagreement (see Ch. 5; CWK XIV: 255–68).

As we have seen, a letter from Kahn to Keynes shows that discussion on Pigou's article was not confined to the people considered so far. In particular, Kahn stated that 'Gerald [Shove] says that without exception this is the worst article he has ever read' (letter 399 from RFK to JMK, 18 October 1937, CWK XIV: 258); that 'Piero [Sraffa] is studying this with his research students [and] agrees with Gerald's verdict' (letter 400 from RFK to JMK, 18 October 1937, CWK XIV: 259); and that 'Piero confirms that Kaldor is thoroughly muddled and merely fogs the issue' (letter 394 from RFK to JMK, 20 October 1937, CWK XIV: 260). In this connection, we may mention the position that Sraffa had expressed on the core issue of this discussion (i.e. the effects of wage reductions on unemployment) a few month before, in June 1937, when Dobb asked him, Robertson and Hicks to read a note on 'The Effect of Cost Reduction on Employment' (Dobb papers, CC3/5: 1–3).[11] In this note Dobb had argued that a wage reduction would produce some incentives to increase employment and that this would happen because cost reduction and the subsequent price reduction would stimulate entrepreneurs to consume more. His conclusion was:

True, cost-reduction may be much weaker in its influence than has traditionally been supposed [...] But it will not be true that *no* internal restorative tendencies have existed hitherto under 'laissez-faire'; and long-trend interpretations based on the assumption of *permanent* equilibrium at less than full-employment become dubious.

(Dobb papers, CC3/5: 3)

Sraffa's response, as expressed in a letter to Dobb kept among the latter's papers, seems worth quoting (our insertions are intended to clarify the context of the discussion which involved Dobb, Robertson and Sraffa):

I agree of course with you that, in equilibrium, the statement [that, in general, wage reductions do not lead to expansions of output and employment] is all wrong. I have often argued against it, but have never obtained any satisfactory answer. I am pretty sure, however, that your rationalization does not represent what is in the back of their mind: in particular, I don't think that saving has anything to do with it [[12]], and I don't believe therefore that Dennis's No 1 is what they would answer [[13]] [...] My impression is that the following is nearer to their views. When wages are cut, profits do not rise: the money which remains in the employers' hands is simply a part of their working capital which has been rendered idle – it forms no part of their incomes and therefore of course they do not spend it on consumption: since only the reduced wages are forthcoming to purchase the output of goods, which is unchanged, of course their prices fall in proportion with wages. As to the idle working capital, this is used to pay off loans or to add to idle balances: the schedule of liquidity preference being unchanged, the rate of interest falls – and the other consequences follow; but, mind you, only as an effect of the fall in the rate of interest (as is shown by the fact that if liq. pref. were infinitely elastic, the rate of int. would not fall, prices and wages would stay at the lower level, and so would investment and employment).

(from PS to Maurice Dobb, undated, Dobb papers, CC3/4)

The latter point, which relates to the causal relation between wages and employment, was at the very core of the discussion on Pigou's article between Robertson and Kaldor. In fact, according to Kaldor: 'a reduction of money wages is merely an alternative method for lowering the rate of interest' (letter 3453, 20 October 1937); but Robertson was loath to accept it:

that the cut in wages affects employment 'through the rate of interest' [...] still seems to me a mis-statement. The cut in wages affects employment directly, and is (on the agreed assumption) associated with a fall in the rate of interest.

(letter 3454, 21 October 1937)

June 1938: Correspondence with Richard Kahn

Less than a year later, in June 1938, Robertson started discussion with Kahn on the relationship between government measures aimed at increasing aggregate demand and real wage movements. This discussion developed through at least eleven letters (four from Robertson and seven from Kahn; letters 3591–3594 and 3596–3602, June–July 1938), beginning with a note (letter 3591, June 1938) in which Robertson considered the case of a government deciding to pay dole to the unemployed, and studied the effects on output under the alternative assumptions that real wages were reduced or remained constant. According to Robertson, output would be increased only if real wages were reduced – a result which followed from the fact that his analysis hinged upon the traditional theory of the firm. In fact, he assumed 'short period competitive equilibrium, under conditions of short period increasing cost' (letter 3591, June 1938). But Robertson did not succeed in bringing Kahn to tackle his main point; i.e. the relationship between the principle of effective demand (to which Kahn consistently adhered) and what Keynes called the first postulate of classical theory, whose validity he had accepted in his *General Theory*. In this respect, they proved unable to understand one another, which was a pity, because the point raised by Robertson was relevant and clarification of it was to remain important to the debate on Keynesian theory in the decades to come.

1938 to 1945: correspondence with Nicholas Kaldor

Following on with the chronological development of Robertson's correspondence, we come to six letters from Robertson to Kaldor between September 1938 and February 1939 and a letter from Kaldor to Robertson in March 1939. This is the period when Robertson moved from Cambridge to London.[14]

The letter sent by Kaldor discusses a paper Robertson had written on Hicks' *Value and Capital* (letter 3468, 7 March 1939). Three letters deal with Kaldor's paper 'Stability and full employment' (Kaldor 1938c) (letters 3457, 11 September 1938; 3458, 6 October 1938; 3460, 21 December 1938). Another letter deals with Kaldor's paper 'Capital intensity and the trade cycle'. In this case, Robertson's observations reveal once more what he saw to underlie the difference separating him from Keynes and the Keynesians: 'I have all my usual difficulties about your apparatus, e.g. that it is expressed in terms of stable equilibrium positions, while what we are discussing is processes of cumulative and reversible change!' (letter 3461, 16 February 1939).

He then went on to an equally characteristic note which reveals his feeling of isolation:

> It is evident that if people of the calibre of Hicks, Harrod, yourself (as

> well as the stricter sect of disciples) have got so much out of the GTE, there must be great merits in it! It is perhaps inevitable that I should have been unduly sensitive to its distortions and exaggerations! Let us hope that in time what is fruitful in it will have been absorbed into the corpus of economic theory and what is not, discarded
>
> (letter 3461, 16 February 1939)

and concluded recalling his concern with teaching: 'Meanwhile the existence of the book does, I think, create a different *pedagogical* problem' (letter 3461, 16 February 1939).

The same themes emerge more forcefully in five other letters (letters 3463–3467) sent by Robertson to Kaldor in 1944–45, where he also stressed that the general lay interpretation of the state of economic science and of its struggle to cope with real world problems was highly irrational.

1937 to 1946: correspondence with Joan Robinson

The extant correspondence between Robertson and Robinson subsequent to the publication of Keynes's *General Theory* consists of three letters from Robertson and one from Robinson dating to 1937 and 1946.

The first letter, dated 17 December 1937, is part of a longer exchange and what we may gather is that, in answering a letter from Robinson, Robertson tried to make clear that his position was not that as she seemed to have assumed:

> you pose two conundrums, phrased in terms (i) of a concept ('forced saving') which for many years I have avoided using (ii) of concepts (identity of 'saving' and 'investment', 'propensity to save' defined in particular manner) which I haven't used at all.
>
> (letter 3402, 17 December 1937)[15]

From the correspondence between Keynes and Robinson (see Ch. 6 above and, in particular, letters 1845, 1847 and 1849) it is clear that the discussion continued and that the contrast between Robertson and Robinson had become quite strong by 1938, when they published three articles on monetary theory in the *Economic Journal* (Robertson 1938a, 1938b; J. Robinson 1938b).

The second letter, written almost ten years later (letter 3403, 20 May 1946), seems to be part of a discussion closely connected to Robinson's lectures.[16] The letter opens with a crucial sentence: 'Dear Joan, I see great difficulties about announcements that this or that piece of mechanism is "non-controversial"' (letter 3403, 20 May 1946),[17] and continues on a similar note:

> Isn't it better [that the students] should try to form their own conclusions as to how far all their various lectures, with their various mental make-ups and intellectual histories, are or are not saying substantially the same thing, – on this or any other topic?
>
> (letter 3403, 20 May 1946)

It appears that Robinson had submitted to Robertson a list of points she meant to present to her students as generally shared and agreed upon by economists. The core of the controversy was Keynesian economics and its analytical framework, and a note in Robertson's hand apparently added later (the letter is conserved among DHR papers and there is no telling if it was actually sent to Robinson) recalls an argument which was at the bottom of his disagreement with Keynes and Keynes's followers:

> The above remarks are of quite general application; but personally I feel that all these questions involving lags, processes, disequilibrium positions are so difficult, and so much in embryo, that they are among the least rather than the most suitable points of economics for attempting to draw a hard and fast line between the controversial and the not.
>
> (letter 3403, 20 May 1946)

The last two letters that we are to consider were written in November 1946. They contain a comment by Robertson, who had probably been asked by Robinson to read a paper she had written, and her reply. Robertson's letter confirms the difficulties he was experiencing in his relationship with Robinson. His comment on the paper is very brief: after raising a point which appears to be rather marginal, he continued with a sentence which shows how deep was the more general gap he perceived between them:

> I don't think I have any holes to pick in the enclosed. It being remembered, of course, that we are still on the hyper-simplified model in which we assume (a) infinite instantaneous elasticity of supply, so that we needn't bother to distinguish between real and money income (b) unchanging income-consumption function: thereby impounding much of the real difficulties of the whole subject
>
> (letter 3404, 3 November 1946)

But after this comment Robertson felt he had to add 'a retrospective postscript' and reconsider past discussions on the concepts of savings and hoarding between Keynes, Keynesians and other economists – including himself. Robertson seems to have been eager to reassert the worth of his own work against the sense of humiliation he probably felt from the second half of the 1930s, but, like so many various other documents, this letter again shows the importance Robertson attributed to teaching as part of his intellectual activity and achievements:

> The more the young can honestly come to the conclusion that in our lectures etc we are all now really saying the same thing the better pleased I shall be. (It was Maynard, not me, who insisted that his 'stock of money' way of looking at the role of interest was 'radically opposed' to Ohlin's and my 'stream of loanable funds' way – see EMT pp. 9–10). But *littera scripta manet.* They all read the 'General Theory', and your 'Introduction', and some of them read the Journal interchanges. And one must be free, if occasion presents itself, to comment on those sacred texts as they are, and not as they might have been if their distinguished authors had been a little less determined to maintain that they were saying something utterly different not only from the 'classics' but from their own contemporaries!
>
> (letter 3404, 3 November 1946)

Robinson replied that she did not understand why he had mentioned 'hoarding' and that she did not understand the way he talked of savings 'getting lost in the banking system', but, most probably, she was just refusing to follow Robertson on his own grounds (letter 3405, 5 November 1946). In fact, in her June 1938 article she really had used the sentences mentioned by Robertson and she really had attacked the conceptions of saving and investment mentioned by Robertson in his letter.[18]

Conclusions

The correspondence that we have been able to study is not in itself sufficient to draw a complete picture of the relationship between Robertson and Kahn, Kaldor, J. Robinson and Sraffa in the two decades between the end of the 1920s and 1946. Nevertheless, several interesting points have emerged. The subjects treated in the correspondence are, in general, strictly academic, mainly reflecting discussions on theoretical works or on questions relating to teaching. From the theoretical point of view, the discussions centred on two main points: the theory of the firm and its developments after the critique advanced by Sraffa in his 1926 paper, and the development of a Keynesian front after the publication of Keynes's *General Theory*. Other important debates of the period are also touched upon, but the most conspicuous absence concerns the debate on Keynes's *Treatise on Money*, which surfaces in only two letters (one to Sraffa and one to Kahn). This probably reflects the fact that on that occasion Robertson found himself outside of the group that was co-operating on critique of the *Treatise on Money* and on preparation of the *General Theory*. After the latter book was published, Robertson's attempts to discuss it could not bridge the gap between himself and Keynes's young followers, just as had happened after the publication of the former. A failure which, in this case, may well be exemplified by the fact that a few months after Robertson's attempt to reach common ground in discussion with Kahn on the relationship between real wage rate and output in Keynes's system had proved unsuccessful, Kahn said to Sraffa that Sraffa's sadness for Robertson's departure for London was 'a disgraceful feeling' (letter 1988 from PS to JVR, 28 December 1938; see Ch. 12: 321–2). This episode also reflected a sharp division within the younger economists considered in this chapter: from a purely personal point of view, Kaldor and Sraffa appeared to have been much closer to Robertson than Kahn and Robinson. Nevertheless, after Pigou's retirement, no one in Cambridge seems to have opposed the idea of offering Robertson the Chair of Political Economy.

Notes

1 We owe the latter information to professor D.E. Moggridge (see also Mizen, Moggridge and Presley 1997; Fletcher 2000). It is also to be noted that, at least in the 1950s, Robertson re-read his papers and put them in order, adding comments on some of them (see below: fn7).

2 In this context, it is also worth mentioning a short note, kept among the PS papers, on Robertson's book *Banking Policy and the Price Level*. Sraffa probably wrote it in Italy in 1926–27 criticising the book on the ground that it applied 'the apparatus of supply and demand, as had been constructed for the analysis of the equilibrium of a single commodity when all the other conditions remain unchanged [...], to analysis of the simultaneous equilibrium of all commodities [...] Such reasoning implies a great number of arbitrary and entirely unacceptable hypotheses' (PS papers, I 75/1; my translation from the Italian original).

3 The date of the letter suggests that Sraffa gave Robertson a copy of the typescript sent to the printer.

4 In the end, Robertson published a sceptical review of Keynes's *General Theory*, and stated that his paper 'should, at the least, be peppered with footnotes containing [Sraffa's] name' (Robertson 1936: 168).

5 This dating of the document would explain why it covers less than a quarter of Kahn's dissertation.

6 According to the Cambridge University Reporter, the title of the lectures she actually delivered – one hour per week in Michelmas Term 1933 and Lent Terms 1934 – was 'Economics of Imperfect Competition'.

7 These words were written by Robertson when, in 1959, he summarised the content of the discussion for his own archive.

8 In this case the hypothesis had to do with the modelling of money demand and banking policy (letter 1691 from NK to JMK, 27 October 1937, CWK XIV: 248–9).

9 In this case the hypothesis in question was most probably the one concerning the possibility of producing capital equipment (CWK XIV: 237–8) implicitly referred to in Pigou's letters to Kaldor. As Pigou came to acknowledge the correctness of Kaldor's view on this point, we may infer that Pigou's second letter to Kaldor was written after 22 October.

10 He had circulated a short paper (see letter 3166 from DHR to JMK, 17 October 1937, CWK XIV: 252–4; and letter 3452 from DHR to NK, 19 October 1937), but he had also stated that 'having endeavoured to fill the function of

an honest broker, whose only concern is to persuade the protagonists (a) to remember their own assumptions (b) to try to understand each others', I now retire from the controversy: only hoping that the matter will have been cleared up for good by the time I reach it in my lecture course in March!' (letter 3455 from DHR to NK, 29 October 1937).

11 We may also note that a draft paper written by Khan on *The Effect on Employment of a Reduction of Wages in a Closed System* is kept among RFK papers, 2/3–4.

12 Dobb had argued against Keynes's view, as expressed in pp. 260–2 of the *General Theory*, that only if the community's marginal propensity to consume were equal to one would an attempt to increase production after a wage reduction not end up in profits below expectation.

13 Robertson had argued that, according to them, i.e. Keynes and his followers, what prevented a wage reduction from resulting in more employment was not savings made out of wages, but savings made out of increased profits.

14 On 26 October he thanked Kaldor for his note of welcome 'it is a great pleasure to feel that one is not coming among strangers' (letter 3459, 26 October 1938) and on 21 December he announced he was to move on the 28th of that month (letter 3460, 21 December 1938).

15 It does not seem that Robertson's position on the concept of forced savings was an effect of his discussion with Sraffa on Hayek's *Prices and Production* considered in the section 'Robertson's correspondence with Sraffa' above. In fact, in his 1933 paper 'Saving and Hoarding' he had written: 'Until there is a greater measure of agreement as to what "Forced Saving" really consists in, I do not feel able to abandon my own inelegant terminology!' (Robertson 1933b: 412–13).

16 In the year 1946–47, as she had done from 1940–41, Robinson was to teach a course on 'Money' in Michaelmas and Lent terms and a course on 'Some problems of economic theory' in Lent Term. Robertson, on the other hand, since his return to Cambridge had been teaching a course on 'Principles of Economics' (Cambridge University Reporter).

17 Note how this and the following sentences resembles what Robertson had written to Keynes about ten years before: 'I *don't* think it good that people coming over from other subjects should get their first introduction to this whole range of very controversial topics from someone who seems to think that everything that has been said and thought about it is "moth-eaten" rubbish except one book – and that, whatever its merits, a very difficult one!' (letter 3154, 28 August 1936).

18 It may be noted that this discussion between Robertson and Robinson echoes another which, as we have already seen, had taken place in 1938 (see Ch. 6: 177–8).

Table 15.1 Robertson–Kahn correspondence

From	*To*	*Year*	*Month*	*Day*	*Date*	*Archive*	*Published in*	*Item*
RFK	DHR	1929	January	17	Dated letter	Kahn–King's	RFK/3/5/48–51	3583
DHR	RFK	1929	December		Attributed	Kahn–King's	RFK/2/8/20–5	3589
RFK	DHR	1932	October	5	Dated letter	Robertson–Trinity	C18/10/1–3	3590
DHR	RFK	1932	October	5	Attributed	Robinson–King's	JVR/vii/376/7–8	3581
DHR	RFK	1933	Spring		Attributed	Kahn–King's	RFK/13/57/25–6	3582
DHR	RFK	1938	June		Attributed	Robertson–Trinity	C18/35/2	3591
RFK	DHR	1938	June	7	Dated letter	Robertson–Trinity	C18/35/3	3592
DHR	RFK	1938	June	7	Attributed	Robertson–Trinity	C18/35/3	3593
RFK	DHR	1938	June	8	Dated letter	Robertson–Trinity	C18/35/4	3594
DHR	RFK	1938	June	10	Dated letter	Robertson–Trinity	C18/35/5	3596
RFK	DHR	1938	June	12	Dated letter	Robertson–Trinity	C18/35/5	3597
DHR	RFK	1938	June	13	Dated letter	Robertson–Trinity	C18/35/6	3598
RFK	DHR	1938	June	20	Dated letter	Robertson–Trinity	C18/35/6	3599
DHR	RFK	1938	June	21	Dated letter	Robertson–Trinity	C18/35/7	3600
RFK	DHR	1938	June	26	Dated letter	Robertson–Trinity	C18/35/8–9	3601
RFK	DHR	1938	July	14	Dated letter	Robertson–Trinity	C18/35/10	3602
DHR	RFK	1944	February	11	Dated letter	Kahn–King's	RFK/13/88/1	3584
DHR	RFK	1946	November	20	Dated letter	Robertson–Trinity	C9/1/1–3	3585
RFK	DHR	1946	December	25	Dated letter	Robertson–Trinity	C9/1/4–9	3586

Table 15.2 Robertson–Kaldor correspondence

From	*To*	*Year*	*Month*	*Day*	*Date*	*Archive*	*Published in*	*Item*
DHR	NK	1932	July	14	Dated letter	Kaldor–King's NK/3/30/179/3–4		3451
DHR	NK	1937	October	19	Dated letter	Kaldor–King's NK/3/30/179/5–11		3452
NK	DHR	1937	October	20	Dated letter	Kaldor–King's NK/3/30/179/12–15		3453
DHR	NK	1937	October	21	Dated letter	Kaldor–King's NK/3/30/118/104–5		3454
DHR	NK	1937	October	29	Dated letter	Kaldor–King's NK/3/30/118/106–7		3455
NK	DHR	1937	October	29	Dated letter	Kaldor–King's NK/3/30/118/108–11		3456
DHR	NK	1938	September	11	Dated letter	Kaldor–King's NK/3/30/179/16		3457
DHR	NK	1938	October	6	Dated letter	Kaldor–King's NK/3/30/179/17–18		3458
DHR	NK	1938	October	26	Dated letter	Kaldor–King's NK/3/30/179/19		3459
DHR	NK	1938	December	21	Dated letter	Kaldor–King's NK/3/30/179/21–2		3460
DHR	NK	1939	February	16	Dated letter	Kaldor–King's NK/3/30/179/23–4		3461
NK	DHR	1939	March	7	Dated letter	D. Moggridge's private archive		3468
DHR	NK	1939	June	2	Dated letter	Kaldor–King's NK/3/30/179/25–6		3462
DHR	NK	1944	November	28	Dated letter	Kaldor–King's NK/3/30/179/27–8		3463
DHR	NK	1944	December	4	Dated letter	Kaldor–King's NK/3/30/179/29–30		3464
DHR	NK	1944	December	6	Dated letter	Kaldor–King's NK/3/30/179/31–2		3465
DHR	NK	1944	December	19	Dated letter	Kaldor–King's NK/3/30/179/33–4		3466
DHR	NK	1945	February	1	Dated letter	Kaldor–King's NK/3/30/179/35		3467

Table 15.3 Robertson–J. Robinson correspondence

From	*To*	*Year*	*Month*	*Day*	*Date*	*Archive*	*Published in*	*Item*
DHR	JVR	1928	November	15	Dated letter	D. Moggridge's private archive		3407
JVR	DHR	1931	September		Attributed	Kahn–King's RFK/16/1/92–3		3406
DHR	JVR	1933	August	15	Dated letter	Robinson–King's JVR/vii/376/1–2		3401
DHR	JVR	1937	December	17	Dated letter	Robinson–King's JVR/vii/376/3		3402
DHR	JVR	1946	May	20	Dated letter	Robertson–Trinity C8/1/1		3403
DHR	JVR	1946	November	3	Dated letter	Robertson–Trinity C8/1/5–6		3404
JVR	DHR	1946	November	5	Dated letter	Robertson–Trinity C8/1/2		3405

Table 15.4 Robertson–Sraffa correspondence

From	*To*	*Year*	*Month*	*Day*	*Date*	*Archive*		*Published in*	*Item*
DHR	PS	1930	January		Attributed	Sraffa–Trinity	Sraffa D3/7/10		3522
DHR	PS	1930	January		Attributed	Sraffa–Trinity	Sraffa D3/7/29, 32		3523
PS	DHR	1930	February		Attributed	Sraffa–Trinity	Sraffa D3/7/13A		3521
DHR	PS	1930	February		Attributed	Sraffa–Trinity	Sraffa D3/7/43		3525
DHR	PS	1930	February		Attributed	Sraffa–Trinity	Sraffa D3/7/44		3534
DHR	PS	1931	March	3	Dated letter	Sraffa–Trinity	Sraffa C 264/1		3526
DHR	PS	1931	March	6	Dated letter	Sraffa–Trinity	Sraffa C 264/2		3527
DHR	PS	1932	January	31	Dated letter	Sraffa–Trinity	Sraffa D3/9/130–1		3528
PS	DHR	1932	February	2	Dated letter	Sraffa–Trinity	Sraffa D3/9/134		3535
DHR	PS	1932	February	16	Dated letter	Sraffa–Trinity	Sraffa C 264/3		3529
DHR	PS	1935	May	1	Dated letter	Sraffa–Trinity	Sraffa B9/3/2–3	Marcuzzo 2004: 135, fn. 34, (E)	3530
DHR	PS	1935	May	3	Dated letter	Sraffa–Trinity	Sraffa B9/3/1		3531
DHR	PS	1936	June	12	Dated letter	Sraffa–Trinity	Sraffa C 264/4		3532
PS	DHR	1944	February	24	Dated letter	Robertson–Trinity	C18/49/12		3536
DHR	PS	1946	November	19	Dated letter	Sraffa–Trinity	Sraffa C 264/5		3533

16 Hayek and Cambridge: dialogue and contention

The correspondence with Kahn, Kaldor, J. Robinson and Sraffa

Bruna Ingrao and Fabio Ranchetti

The extant correspondence

Sifting through the Cambridge archives (Trinity College Library and King's College) turned up some surprises as regards the letters Hayek exchanged with the Cambridge economists (see Tables 16.1 to 16.4). The surviving correspondence is not as numerous as that between Hayek and Keynes, already dealt with in Ch. 9. We have evidence of just one episode of scientific correspondence with both Kahn and J. Robinson. The same is true of Kaldor, with whom Hayek also clashed in one particular academic confrontation. More varied was the correspondence with Sraffa. A summary overview of the first encounters between Hayek and these Cambridge economists will help to introduce their epistolary controversies.

Hayek probably first met Kahn and J. Robinson in 1931, when he gave a seminar at Cambridge soon after his arrival in Great Britain. Both Kahn and J. Robinson left sarcastic accounts of the seminar (J. Robinson 1978a; Kahn 1984).[1] We have evidence that after their first meeting at Cambridge they met in London, both at the regular meetings between Cambridge economists and London School economists (Ebenstein 2001: 86), and on various other occasions. We know that Hayek and Keynes met in amiable circumstances to have lunch together, and J. Robinson joined them.[2] In 1936, writing to Keynes to thank him for the copy of the *General Theory*, Hayek recalled that he had already had some idea of what Keynes's theory was about from J. Robinson (letter 831 from FAH to JMK, 2 February 1936). Their relationship was, however, marked by mutually low opinions. J. Robinson's judgement of Hayek's theory was especially harsh.[3] When the London School moved to Cambridge during the war, she went to Hayek's seminar, taking pleasure in provoking him (as she used to do with Robertson as well).[4]

In the post-war years, Hayek expressed severe judgement on Keynes's younger pupils. He maintained that Keynes's 'disciples' had a more fanatical approach than their master did, being totally blind to the harm caused by monetary disturbances (Hayek [1983] 1995: 252). He also recalled that he had warned Keynes against the version of his theory that his disciples were divulging (Hayek [1952] 1995: 232; Hayek [1966] 1995: 244).

Hayek's scant correspondence with Keynes's most militant pupils records two episodes of debate: with Kahn after the *Treatise* was published, in 1931, and with J. Robinson ten years later, after the *General Theory* had already been widely discussed.

No exchange of letters with Hayek is available in the Kahn archives, but two letters by Kahn to Hayek have come to light in the Hayek archives at the Hoover Foundation at Stanford (letters 1140 and 1139, 23 June and 8 October 1931). We do not know the precise occasion that gave rise to their correspondence in June 1931. Keynes's private correspondence with Hayek on monetary issues started in December 1931, and continued until February 1932, when Keynes firmly brought it to an end, declaring that his interest was waning. Thus Kahn's letter in June 1931 seems to be the first epistolary exchange we have evidence of in the keen controversy over the *Treatise.*

The issues discussed in the letter closely resemble those discussed in the first part of Hayek's review of the *Treatise,* published in August 1931. Reference is made to a diagram which, given the perfect correspondence of symbols, seems to be the one published in Hayek's review (Hayek [1931a] 1995: 134). The manuscript note that followed in October 1931 – just a few lines – attests to continued dialogue, but no further correspondence has been discovered.

Kahn wrote to Hayek in respectful tones. While defending the analytical structure of the *Treatise,* the budding scholar recognised that some of Hayek's points were legitimate, nor did he deny a certain ambiguity in some concepts applied in the *Treatise.* Politeness was due in a letter addressed by a younger scholar to another young but already well-known professor. However, it might well be that the accents of the debate changed, waxing ruder when Hayek published his harsh critique of the *Treatise* and Keynes decided to answer.

The documents in J. Robinson's archives show that there was a short dialogue between the two scholars, with little success in advancing their mutual understanding. The archives contain nine letters sent by Hayek to Robinson between 14 February and 26 March 1941. Robinson's letters to Hayek have not been found. The letters confirm their conflict. Hayek went on answering the questions Robinson proposed, although he found her tone exasperating. The exchange came to a close, as far as we know, soon after a letter by Hayek that was still polite, but betrayed evident irritation. He wrote: 'I want neither to induce you to continue a controversy when you feel is useless, nor am I particularly anxious to have the last word' (letter 1758, 24 March 1941).

The letters testify to the detachment Hayek had already developed from his research agenda of the 1930s by the early 1940s. Robinson, deeply involved in the Keynesian revolution, seemed neither to be curious nor, perhaps, to perceive Hayek's change of mind. On 1 April 1941 she wrote to Kahn: 'I have wound up my correspondence with Hayek. He is quite hopeless' (letter 1629, 1 April 1941).

Sraffa was of course an outstanding figure in the controversy between Hayek and Cambridge in the early 1930s. Keynes decided not to reply to the second part of Hayek's review-article of his *Treatise on Money*, which was published in February 1932 (Hayek 1932a). In the meanwhile, Keynes had invited Sraffa to join in the debate. In a few months of hard work, Sraffa duly produced for the March 1932 issue of the *Economic Journal* (Sraffa 1932a) an attack on Hayek's theory as presented in *Prices and Production.* Hayek replied in the June issue of the same *Economic Journal* (Hayek 1932b); in turn, Sraffa then added a brief Rejoinder (Sraffa 1932b). Despite a degree of acrimony in their theoretical controversy, Hayek and Sraffa maintained a polite and even quite friendly relationship. Over the years they exchanged information about their shared passion for antique books, history of economics and antiquaria, as their correspondence testifies.

The Cambridge archives record eighteen letters in the period running from 1931 to 1946; except for six letters from Sraffa, all are from Hayek. Sraffa and Hayek exchanged messages on different occasions and on various subjects, which did not seem to have been the case with Kahn and Robinson. The eighteen letters can be conveniently arranged into three groups, according to the subject dealt with: economic theory, Ricardiana, and varia academica.

The first group comprises six letters, three from Hayek and three from Sraffa. They date to the end of 1931 and the beginning of 1932, and touch on the controversy on money and capital. Four letters in this group are directly related to Sraffa's devastating article on Hayek's theory in March 1932 (Sraffa 1932a).

Ten letters (letters 1072–1078 and 1084–1086, 4 November 1932 to 26 November 1946) have to do with their common interest in Ricardo and Ricardiana. In the margin of Hayek's letters 1072, 1073 and 1075, we have, in Sraffa's handwriting, indication that he had replied to those letters, and in two cases (letters 1072 and 1075) we also have the dates and summary contents of his replies.

As we know, Sraffa was engaged in editing Ricardo's *Works*, whilst Hayek was on the Committee set up at University College, London, for the publication of Bentham's *Works.* The tone of the correspondence was friendly, with exchange of both information and favours. Only a few months after their vehement controversy in the *Economic Journal*, Hayek wrote to Sraffa: 'I hear about a most marvellous discovery of a manuscript by J. Bentham on Money with annotations by Ricardo which you have made in Geneva. In the first place my sincerest congratulations [...]' (letter 1072, 4 November 1932). For his part, Sraffa readily placed the Bentham manuscript at Hayek's disposal, inviting him to spend a weekend in Cambridge and read it. In another letter (letter 1077, 19 December 1945), Hayek wrote to Sraffa telling him he had just returned from Dublin, bringing with him the copies of the Ricardo letters to Mill, which he was going to send to Sraffa.

The last group includes two letters of minor importance (letters 1082 and 1083, 2 and 10 March 1944). In the first Hayek asks for permission for Mr Eshag to consult Marshall's copies of some books by Giffen, Cairnes, Pigou, D. Hume, Thornton and Senior; replying in his capacity as librarian of the Marshall Library, Sraffa gives his consent. Eventually, twenty years later, Eshag published a book on Cambridge monetary theory (Eshag 1963) with a Preface where both Hayek's and Sraffa's advice and help are acknowledged.

More conflictive were Hayek's relations with Kaldor. They met at the London School of Economics, where Kaldor studied between 1927 and 1930 and Hayek arrived in 1931. Kaldor began his studies with Allyn Young, who died prematurely. Robbins and Hayek then began to exert a certain fascination over him (Thirlwall 1987: 23). In the early 1930s Kaldor matured as a scholar, basing his reasoning on the combination of equilibrium theory and Austrian theory peculiar to both Hayek's early writings and the parallel reflections by the young Hicks (Kaldor 1934c). He worked on the English translation of *Geldtheorie und Konjunkturtheorie* (Hayek 1929) published in 1933, edited by Kaldor and Croome, under the title *Monetary Theory and the Trade Cycle* (Hayek [1933a] (1966)).

Kaldor's break with Hayekian theory began when he was translating Hayek's article 'The Paradox of Saving' in 1931 (Kaldor 1980: X). Dialogue with Hicks helped him to perceive the limits of Mises's and Hayek's monetarist approach, opening his mind to Keynesian ideas (Kaldor 1986a: 7). Through Hicks he learnt of the German translation of Myrdal's essay in the book edited by Hayek in 1933 (Hayek 1933b). As from 1934, Brinley Thomas's lectures on Swedish thought left their mark in the development of his ideas, as was also the case with Hicks and Shackle (Shehadi 1991: 383–4).

Once he had lost his enthusiasm for Austrian theories, Kaldor proved one of the sternest critics of Hayek's work (Kaldor 1939a, 1942b; Hayek 1942b), while conflict also found its way into their personal relations, given Kaldor's low opinion of Hayek and hostile attitude towards him. Kaldor recounted that at the London School of Economics he often contradicted Hayek in seminars and even took pleasure in making him look ridiculous when the opportunity to provoke him arose (Ebenstein 2001: 63–4).

Kaldor's and Hayek's archives contain four rounds of correspondence between the two scholars: a letter by Hayek to Kaldor in 1930; a scientific controversy in 1935 (one letter and two notes); an academic controversy in 1942 (four letters); and, finally, an exchange of letters in 1981 (two letters) which are not being considered here. In addition, in August 1943 a short note by Kaldor contains thanks for bibliographic material (letter 498, 13 August 1943). The correspondence is scant, but interesting in terms of both scientific controversy and biography.

The first letter, written in German (letter 490, 1 December 1930), was sent about two months before Hayek's journey to London. Hayek thanked

Kaldor for his willingness to translate his book into English and made arrangements for the translation, which Kaldor was to carry out under the supervision of Robbins (Hayek [1933a] (1966)).

In 1935 Hayek and Kaldor exchanged two typescript notes in a controversy on imperfect competition. Both notes, neither signed nor dated, are attributed to February 1935 on the basis of the short cover letter by Kaldor with the second one (letter 493, 19 February 1935). The debate was about Kaldor's article 'Market Imperfection and Excess Capacity' published in *Economica* in 1935 (Kaldor 1935) and the tone was unfriendly.

The correspondence of January 1942 dealt with an academic dispute. Kaldor resentfully asked Hayek why he had been excluded from the role of examiner, as Laski informed him, 'on the ground that you regard my work as a colleague and teacher as unsatisfactory' (letter 494, 23 January 1942). Hayek accused Kaldor of systematically evading his academic duties (letters 495, 25 January 1942 and 497, 29 January 1942). On this sharp judgement the correspondence closed.

The episode may well have left its mark, fostering mutual distrust between the two scholars. Years later, in a dispute over Austria's economic outlook, answering Hayek Kaldor added a wicked manuscript note, saying: 'If you talk about the "lost generations of Keynesians", what about the (even older) "lost generations of Hayekians" who believed in *Prices and Production*?' The phrase 'lost generations of Hayekians' was asterisked, and the asterisk read: 'Like myself!'

In these exchanges, whose content has been briefly summarised, the remarkable episodes are three: in chronological order, the monetary debates in the early 1930s; the dispute on imperfect competition in the mid-1930s; the clash on macroeconomic theory and policy in the early 1940s. The letters testify that both dialogue and keen contention continued well after the first clash in the early 1930s, involving a variety of theoretical issues (competition, theory of capital, portfolio theory, public finance).

The early 1930s – discussion with Kahn and Sraffa on money and capital

Early in 1931 Kahn was busy rewriting his paper on the multiplier. He was critically commenting on Keynes's fundamental equations and discussing with Keynes the weak points in the *Treatise* (Marcuzzo 2002; Ch. 1: 23ff). He remained involved in Keynes's controversy with Hayek, perhaps reluctantly, as he wrote to J. Robinson in September 1931, while at Tilton with the Keyneses (letter 757, 16 September 1931).

In June 1931 Kahn belatedly answered a letter from Hayek, now lost, apologising for the delay (letter 1140, 23 June 1931). We can form some idea of its content reading through Kahn's reply. Kahn took all the questions raised by Hayek one by one: the definition of profits and losses, the definition of savings, the legitimacy of using aggregate variables, and in particular the price level, the various and contradictory definitions of consumption and the theory of capital. The letter offers the opportunity to review the issues of dissent which, almost obsessively, emerge over and again in all exchanges between Hayek and the Cambridge economists in the early 1930s.

The first difficulty arose over the definition of profits, which was crucial to the analytical structure of Keynes's theory in the *Treatise.* For Hayek, windfall profits or unexpected losses depend on the capital gains or losses that emerge from the variability of relative prices, given the time structure which characterises existing capital (Hayek [1931a] 1995: 126–7). Profits and losses cannot be ascertained with mere comparison of current receipts and current expenditures. He wrote in his review:

> Not only is it possible for the changes which Mr. Keynes attributes only to changes in 'total profits' to occur when 'total profits' in his sense are absent. It is also possible for 'total profits' to emerge for causes other than those contemplated in his analysis. It is by no means necessary for 'total profits' to be the effect of a difference between *current* receipts and *current* expenditure. Nor need every difference between current receipts and current expenditure lead to the emergence of 'total profits'.
>
> (Hayek [1931a] 1995: 126)

Kahn argued that the entrepreneurs making losses might cover them by selling bonds, or with bank credit, or drawing upon saving deposits. He asked whether Hayek was including this in his diagram, and whether he considered the entrepreneurs making losses as proprietors of the existing capital.

On the second point of difficulty raised by Hayek, he admitted the legitimacy of the criticism but denied the significance of the problem. Actually, Hayek's dynamic approach did not treat the costs of production of consumption goods and the receipts from sales of consumption goods as identical; in his review, he stated that the identities Keynes postulated were valid only under an assumption of stationarity, while Keynes aimed at analysing a dynamic economy (Hayek [1931a] 1995: 135). In dynamic conditions costs of production of current output may not be equal to monetary income distributed to the factors of production, since the economy changes over time. Hayek rejected the atemporal analysis of monetary variables, be they income or cost variables, and required a precise time index for all variables in the dynamic process.

Kahn found this criticism 'quite immaterial', since the important variable was '*R*, the volume of consumption'. He mentioned the idea of a period of production, apparently admitting a possible divergence in the length of the production period for investment goods and consumption goods. According to Kahn, however, working capital in the production of consumption goods would react as a buffer absorbing disequilibria. ('But the difference will be made good by disinvestment in working capital in the production of consumption goods, so that *C* remains the same as before.')

In the second part of the letter, Kahn dealt with the problem of index numbers and the definition of saving in Keynes's approach as compared with the more usual one. The question of the time dimension of variables returned as a central issue once again.

Kahn admitted some confusion in the definition of consumption in the *Treatise*, recognising a plurality of definitions, as Hayek had critically suggested (Hayek [1931a] 1995: 133). However, he considered only one of the three definitions really relevant, namely the amount effectively consumed, whether taken from stocks of consumption goods already produced or from flows of new productions.

Kahn emphatically maintained that savings in the usual definition must necessarily adapt to the volume of the current production of investment goods: 'savings_u = value of investment'. In Kahn's notation, savings_u was saving defined in the usual way, as excess of receipts over expenditure, as opposed to Keynes's peculiar sense. Kahn came to the conclusion that 'unless the volume of the current output of investment goods alters, savings_u cannot alter'. It was an early recognition of the idea that investment controls the level of saving.

The role of Sraffa in the capital controversy in the early 1930s has been extensively studied (Caldwell 1995; Kurz 1995, 2000; Ingrao and Ranchetti 1996; Ranchetti 2001; Zappia 2001). The Hayek–Sraffa correspondence in 1931, although of some interest, does not add substantially to what is already known. Considering the importance of their controversy, and in the light of the rich material on the subject contained in the unpublished PS papers, it is quite revealing that the letters Sraffa and Hayek exchanged have so little to offer from the theoretical point of view. In fact, they do not add any elements contributing to a better understanding of the questions involved. They confirm that Sraffa was very reluctant to be drawn into a theoretical discussion in a private correspondence, except with the people he felt to be closest (at that time, possibly only Keynes and, to a lesser extent, Richard Kahn). The overall tone of the first exchange between Hayek and Sraffa was friendly:

> Since I hear that you are just reading my *Prices and Production* and are experiencing difficulties with certain parts, I take pleasure in sending you a copy of the recently published German edition [Hayek 1931c] in which I have added certain explanations. I have taken the liberty to mark the main additions with pencil for your convenience.[5]
>
> (letter 1079, 10 November 1931)

Hayek mentioned a letter he had received from Sraffa the previous spring on Böhm-Bawerk (which we were unable to find) and invited Sraffa to stay with him and his wife in their London flat: 'We live just around the corner from Robbins'. Sraffa thanked Hayek for the German edition of *Prices and Production*, 'which' – he adds – 'comes particularly welcome, since I have undertaken to review it for the *Economic Journal*' (letter 1080, 12 November 1931). He politely turned down the invitation, 'as I very seldom come to town, except for the day [...] I hope however to have soon an opportunity to meet you and have a long discussion'.

Four letters contain explicit reference to Sraffa's article (Sraffa 1932a). The first (letter 1081, 19 February 1932) is a covering letter: 'Dear Hayek, I enclose a proof of my review, for your tearing it to pieces. Before physically doing so, will you please show it to Robbins [...]'. In the second letter to Hayek (letter 1993, 22 February 1932), Sraffa wrote that he was 'looking forward to read' the second part of Hayek's review of Keynes's *Treatise*. Significantly, he added: 'As regards my suggestion of your agreeing with Keynes, I am sure that, in view of your recent controversies, there is little danger of its being taken too literally!' The last letter is from Hayek to Sraffa (letter 1071, 24 March 1932), just after publication of Sraffa's critique of Hayek's theory in the March issue of the *Economic Journal*. It is mostly on 'some Bentham-stuff', testifying to their common interest in the history of economics. Only the last paragraph referred to Sraffa's article: 'I think I shall answer your *Economic Journal* article at some length and shall try to meet your objections'. Hayek then concluded: 'I hope that you will not mind if I am quite as outspoken in it as you were.' In the subsequent correspondence between the two economists, questions of economic theory were never again touched upon.

It is generally recognised (although with varying emphasis) that Sraffa's criticisms had a destructive impact on Hayek's theoretical construction, as built up in *Prices and Production*. During the 1930s Hayek went on revising his research project on capital theory and the trade cycle, both as a matter of internal development and under the pressure of his critics in and outside the Cambridge school (Donzelli 1988; Birner 1999; Zappia 2001). Although his efforts failed in terms of producing a coherent theory of fluctuations maintaining the core research programme, Hayek reached critical insights into equilibrium theory and a new perspective as regards the analysis of dynamic processes of change in time. Less recognised is the mark Hayek's criticism left on Keynesian theory. Once open polemics had come to an end, a more covert debate with Hayek's dynamic approach continued.

The mid-1930s – Kaldor and Hayek on competition

In the mid-1930s the London School offered a breeding ground for the cross-fertilisation of ideas, although not without disputes and conflict. In this conflicting environment, Kaldor and Hayek clashed on the theory of imperfect competition in 1935. Kaldor had argued, qualifying Chamberlain's theory, that strategic interactions between firms in an environment of free entry, market imperfection and increasing returns might lead to excess capacity (Kaldor 1935). Fragmentation of demand among producers of close substitutes might lead single firms to opt for sub-optimal scale, losing in efficiency.

In the note opening the controversy (letter 491, February 1935), Hayek criticised the approach Kaldor adopted, both for its consequences in terms of economic policy and for its fallacious conceptual foundations. While devoting hardly any attention to firms' strategies in an environment of strategic interaction, Hayek criticised Kaldor for adopting a purely 'technical' view of the concept of excess capacity, which obscured the role of consumers' preferences.

> the criteria on which the definition of over capacity is based are simply quantities of a particular product and are in no way related to the preferences shown by the consumers [. . .].
>
> (letter 491, February 1935)

According to Hayek this view of imperfect competition led to biased evaluation of product standardisation, giving the impression that the market was not spontaneously conducive to the optimal degree of standardisation in terms of welfare, imposing excessive costs on the consumer.

> Mr. Kaldor's argument, and indeed the argument of all planners, is however, that competition left to itself will not secure the degree of standardisation which in some sense can be regarded as desirable, and that in consequence compulsory standardisation might increase economic welfare in general.
>
> (letter 491, February 1935)

Hayek recognised that the variety of products might impose additional costs, but he argued that variety did not make consumer's choices less effective, even in conditions of declining cost curves. He emphasised the importance of incomplete information, taking a line in sharp contrast with Kaldor's, since he denied the informational advantage of the public authorities, should they wish to intervene authoritatively to reduce the assumed social cost of excess capacity.

> The case for interference here, as in so many other cases, is therefore based on the assumption that the interfering authority would know more about the shape of the cost and demand curves than the entrepreneurs. But although this is not an impossible case, I doubt whether Mr. Kaldor would wish to base his argument on this assumption.
>
> (letter 491, February 1935)

This typescript is particularly interesting for the light it casts on the evolution of Hayek's thought. In 1944 Hayek discussed standardisation in *The Road to Serfdom*, with similar arguments. In the fourth chapter of the book ('The "Inevitability" of Planning') he vehemently criticised the idea that central planning is needed because of the advantages offered by scale economies associated with technological advance. The loss in the variety of opportunities would lead to major welfare losses in the future.

> Though in the short run the price we have to pay for variety and freedom of choice may sometimes be high, in the long run even material progress will depend on this very variety, because we can never predict from which of the many forms in which a good or service can be provided something better may develop. [. . .] we ought to leave room for the unforeseeable free growth.
>
> (Hayek [1944] 1994: 58)

In 'The Meaning of Competition' (Hayek 1948) there is no direct reference to the 1935 controversy, but the criticism of the theory of imperfect competition as developed at Cambridge is evident. In the article Hayek elaborated innovative ideas, insisting on the variety of goods conceived as an essential aspect of real markets. According to his criticism, the idea of an economic system split into well defined markets where single standardised goods are produced and traded is sheer fiction, a fancy dreamed up by economists. Investigation of competitive conditions should be conducted considering, more realistically, markets in which buyers choose in a *continuum* of close substitutes, exploring the opportunities which emerge. In Hayek's thought, variety of opportunities and the possibility to exploit them are crucial to the competitive process, and all the more so in markets where the abstract theoretical conditions of perfect competition cannot apply.

Kaldor's answer to Hayek's criticism (letter 492, February 1935), on the contrary, underlined the identical quality of products in terms of utility functions, although an apparent differentiation exists induced by separate trademarks ('brands') or consumers' inertia. Reducing the number of produced 'varieties' does not imply a substantial standardisation and loss of variety, Kaldor argued, since brands or varieties do not necessarily bring about true product differentiation.

> The criterion of market imperfection is the presence of *finite magnitudes* for the cross-elasticities of demand for each particular 'product'; but this criterion cannot be regarded as being necessarily equivalent to the concept of different 'goods' in the sense required by the theory of value: without reducing this latter theory to a meaningless tautology. The presence of some buyers' inertia, for example, is sufficient to make these products 'imperfect substitutes' in the market theory

> sense (and thus 'different products') but not in the sense required by the theory of value; since the presence of 'inertia' cannot in turn be explained away in terms of the individual's utility function.
>
> (letter 492, February 1935)

According to Kaldor, however, the issue did not affect the central point of his exposition in the article. In dynamic terms, the free entry of new competitors prevented each single firm from reaching the critical dimension necessary to take advantage of scale economies. The deficiency in far-sightedness by individual entrepreneurs hampered their chances of appreciating opportunities for long run profit ('the degree of foresight required to produce the output most profitable *in the long run*') deriving from expanded output.

> *The degree of foresight* (on behalf of entrepreneurs) necessary to escape the conclusion of this theory includes such things as knowledge of the hypothetical demand curves for a 'product' under varying numbers of competitors; the amounts of losses competitors are willing to bear, before they go out of existence, etc., the true shape of the entrepreneurs' 'true' long-run demand curve and the amount of his own loss necessary before he can 'get onto it', – all things which are completely unnecessary under conditions of perfect competition.
>
> (letter 492, February 1935)

The argument presented by Kaldor was a variation on the theme of short-sightedness, or lack of transparent information in market economies. Implicitly, by contrast, the theoretical reference model was still the perfectly transparent market, which Jevons had established as the ideal competitive one in the *Theory of Political Economy.* Hayek's analysis had a critical impact both on the ideal model of perfect competition from Cournot to Marshall and on the vision of imperfect or monopolistic competition forged in the economic literature in the mid-1930s. Variety of goods – the continuum of imperfect substitutes that such literature associated with deviations from optimality (as valid for perfectly competitive conditions) – was shown to be a basic aspect of competition 'as discovery procedure', and a fruit of its advantages in terms of welfare (Hayek 1948, 1978).

The early 1940s – Hayek and J. Robinson on liquidity preference and portfolio theory

After the *General Theory,* private controversy arose between J. Robinson and Hayek on the very conception of the basic macroeconomic model. Since Robinson's letters are missing, a balanced evaluation of the debate is impossible. We hear only Hayek's voice. Nevertheless, the topics under discussion emerge quite clearly.

The correspondence dealt mostly with saving behaviour and the effects of changes in the quantity of money. Discussion centred especially on the effects of a variation in the quantity of money and liquidity preference. Public deficit financing (money versus bonds) was also at issue. For Hayek the debate represented a taxing effort to design ideal cases, addressing the controversial points with no ambiguities in the causal links and the timing of effects. Since he was focusing on the theory of economic fluctuations, Hayek argued in terms of complex processes of reaction to change, referring to dynamic paths of relevant variables and adjustment processes converging to equilibrium or moving from equilibrium. Hayek's argument dealt with the end of a boom, the recovery of investment, the behaviour of wages during the business cycle, and so forth. Often he indicated the possible directions of evolution, with no clearly defined conclusion.

The questions raised by Robinson, as we may infer from the answers, dealt always with the *final* effect via direct or indirect effects of changes in the value of a crucial variable. She seemed to suggest reasoning in terms of comparative statics, as would become the norm in most post-war Keynesian theory.

The correspondence began with a cordial letter (letter 1751, 14 February 1941) by Hayek, accepting Robinson's invitation to open discussion between them on 'what is really the central issue between us – the significance of thrift for the formation of capital'. Hayek signalled to Robinson his first essay in *Profits, Interest and Investment* (Hayek 1939a) and suggested she might review the book in *Economica* as an opportunity to open the debate. He also mentioned the last chapter of *The Pure Theory of Capital* (Hayek 1941a) as a further source to elucidate the issue.

The review was not mentioned again. The second letter (letter 1752, 15 February 1941) answered Robinson's question: 'when there is general unemployment, an increase in the rate of investment can occur without any decline in consumption?' Hayek argued that he had clearly explained in his 1939 essay that in such a case consumption is not necessarily reduced.[6] Since Robinson had approvingly mentioned an article by Wilson, Hayek reacted by saying that he had read it in manuscript and pointed out various mistakes or cases of confusion to the author.[7]

Thus the debate began. Robinson listed their points of divergence. As summarised by Hayek, they were: (1) the elasticity of saving to income; (2) the elasticity of saving to the rate of interest; (3) the velocity of reaction of investment to changes in the rate of interest; and (4) the effects of changes in the quantity of money on the level of income (letter 1753, 6 March 1941). It is worth noting that these are issues that would become dominant in post-war macroeconomic debates.

Hayek admitted a considerable income elasticity of saving, as compared with a low (although positive) elasticity of saving to the rate of interest. On investment behaviour his answer was more guarded: the reaction of fixed capital to a change in the rate of interest will be slow, but the reaction in stocks might be faster (letter 1753, 6 March 1941).

Hayek summed up his view of their divergence, mentioning their differences on the very definition of unemployment as opposed to full employment of resources (letter 1753, 6 March 1941). According to Hayek, changes in demand will bring about changes in relative prices with unbalanced effects crucially depending on time, or in other words on the velocity of adaptation of supply as regards the specialised means of production in different productive processes.[8] Investment opportunities run out at the end of a boom almost entirely on account of a price phenomenon. Hayek maintained that the phenomenon had nothing to do with a reduction in the marginal productivity of capital due to an increased quantity of capital: '[. . .] the marginal productivity of capital at unchanged prices would not have been very much lowered by the comparatively small additions to the stock of capital made by the investments during the boom'. He concluded: 'Hence the crucial importance to me of the connection between relative prices and the profitability of investment' (letter 1753, 6 March 1941). He also noted the high specificity of investment in fixed capital and of the related flows of specialised labour. Both extreme cases – excess resources for all goods or scarce resources for all goods – failed to prove truly relevant.

Robinson raised a new series of questions. The main issue was liquidity preference, a term Hayek disliked (letter 1754, 8 March 1941). It seems that she distinguished between a direct effect of the increased quantity of money on the rate of interest, reducing it, and an indirect effect on income, following the first one. Hayek emphasised, by way of contrast, the direct link between the increase in credit and the increase in the propensity to spend.

> The main reason why I dislike it [i.e. the notion of liquidity preference] is that the original borrower (or seller of securities) may have been willing to borrow (or sell) only because he means to spend the proceeds, so that the increase in income would be a necessary effect of the increase in the quantity of money, although, like the latter, only possible with a fall in interest.
>
> (letter 1754, 8 March 1941)

Moreover, he asserted the potential inflationary effect on monetary income of the recurrent, monetary financing of public deficit. When discussing recurrent deficit spending financed by money, Hayek appears to have been taken aback by a remark made by Robinson, possibly pointing to the liquidity trap.

> Are you suggesting that in this case there is a definite maximum beyond which money income will not rise and that once this maximum is reached, all the new money is immediately absorbed without inducing people to increase their expenditure?
>
> (letter 1754, 8 March 1941)

The discussion focused on investment demand and liquidity preference (letter 1755, 14 March 1941). Hayek raised criticism about introducing assumptions regarding the *aggregate* propensities to spend. The aggregate propensity to save should not be assumed from the very beginning as an exogenous datum, since it depended on the distribution of income and individual behaviour. 'You seem to me often inclined to treat the p[ropensity].t[o].s[ave]. of the community (and similar concepts) as constants or as 'given' when from the nature of your assumption they must change [...]' (letter 1755, 14 March 1941).

Further criticism touched on the inelastic behaviour of consumption not only as regards the rate of interest, but also as regards the value of wealth ('the amounts of assets which individuals possess'). Hayek associated this assumption, which he judged to be totally misconceived, with the liquidity trap, namely a situation where people were willing to hold any quantity of money without increasing consumption expenditure: '[...] a rate of interest low enough to induce people to hold any quantity of money, however large, without increasing their expenditure on consumption' (letter 1755, 14 March 1941). According to Hayek, a considerable increase in liquidity will undoubtedly stimulate an increase in consumption expenditure: '[...] as the cash holdings of the different individuals increase relatively to what they expect to be able promptly to invest, their propensity to save is certain to fall off.' (letter 1755, 14 March 1941).

Moreover, Hayek made a clear distinction between the effects on monetary income of recurrent public deficits continually financed with money or by the issuance of debt. In the former case, he saw no limits to the growth of monetary income given the direct stimulating effects on expenditure caused by the additional, permanent flow of liquidity. In the latter case, he seemed to suggest – while admitting a considerable inflationary effect even here – a prevailing crowding out effect on private spending.

The following letter (letter 1756, 17 March 1941) seems to have prompted a piqued reply from Robinson. Soon after, on 20 March, Hayek admitted both a delay in answering and a confused formulation. He addressed the point which, to his surprise, would emerge as crucial in their controversy, namely portfolio choices and the substitution between real and financial assets. The issue was discussed in the last three letters of their correspondence.

On 24 March, four days later, the tone of the discussion grew sharper. 'It would be easier to clear up differences if you could believe that one could differ from you without being a complete fool', wrote Hayek, although declaring he did not feel offended (letter 1758, 24 March 1941). In this short letter, the last but one in the group, Hayek focused on what he took to be the basic divergence emerging from the discussion, namely a divergent conception of wealth.

For Hayek wealth was a vector of assets, each of which had its own price. He was surprised to discover that in Robinson's approach wealth was reduced to one remunerative activity (with just one price, the rate of interest), opposed to which was liquidity. 'My quarrel with you is rather that you lump together the effect on the prices of all existing wealth under the term rate of interest. This seems to me a highly misleading use of the term [. . .]' (letter 1758, 24 March 1941). Hayek could not understand Robinson's insistence on the difference between stocks and flows, or the relevance of her remarks on this point.

> To the entrepreneurs in question the stock is not given and they have to choose between the stream of services they will derive over a given period from holding more money and the stream of services which would result from investing it (in any of the various meanings of this term). Stocks and flows are incommensurable only because the first usually relates to a moment of time. But holding a quantity of anything, whether it be money or a pet-dog, involves as much a decision about a flow over a period of time as spending at a certain rate.
>
> (letter 1758, 24 March 1941)

In the letter closing the correspondence, Hayek once again clarified the divergence (letter 1759, 26 March 1941).

> If again the different types of assets are *a*, bonds, *b*, *c*, *d*, . . . other types of securities and existing real assets, *k*, consumers' goods, and *m*, money, the question is: what is the difference of an increase of *a* or *M* by the same amounts. I denied your proposition that the only difference is with respect to the effect on the rate of interest, because I understood this as the price of *a*.
>
> (letter 1759, 26 March 1941)

Hayek underlined a direct wealth effect on consumption, working through substitution when wealth increased. He thought Robinson had mistakenly cancelled this wealth effect, simply by considering it empirically irrelevant. In the restricted context designed by Robinson's assumptions, Hayek seemed to accept the reduction in the rate of interest, which should follow the monetary financing of deficit spending, but he insisted on arguing against the peculiar assumptions and the irrelevance of the theoretical procedure adopted by his correspondent. And, in any case, he refused to accept the full equivalence of deficit financing by money or debt, because of long term viability conditions: '[. . .] not every deficit financed by the creation of money can be financed by borrowing' (letter 1759, 26 March 1941).

Almost all the crucial issues in post-war macroeconomic debates were on the table.

Conclusions

These exchanges of correspondence show just how much toil had to go into the effort to build a common language to discuss the issues of divergence or the occasional points of agreement. In these, as in many other scientific controversies, the first problem was to establish a common ground, translating into a shared language the diverse conceptual languages used to structure problems and answers. Once again, these letters call our attention to the divergent analytic approach between Hayek and Keynes's disciples (not to mention Sraffa's peculiar position).

Hayek insisted on adjustment processes over time, and on the sequence of periods over which choices were made and economic actions performed. He reasoned on the complex dynamic paths over a sequence of periods in the business cycle, after the initial change. The difference in analytic structure created considerable difficulty in the dialogue, as an observation on Wilson's approach well illustrates.

> [. . .] I believe that W., in comparing alternative states of equilibrium, leaves out important traditional effects (the sort of things that happen *while* more expensive or durable machinery is replaced by less expensive etc.).
>
> (letter 1753, 6 March 1941)

Misunderstanding prevailed. Hayek's view did not fit in with the Keynesian dual decision hypothesis, which insisted on the dichotomy between current income choice (to consume or to save) and portfolio choices, as independent choices. According to Hayek, on the contrary, there must be consistency in time between the two groups of decisions. They are part of a unified process of choice about how to allocate resources and spending, considering the whole set of relative prices, and thus the opportunity costs of substituting between all potential flows of future services.

We can see something of the difficulty the dialogue was fraught with in Hayek's remarks to J. Robinson:

> When I said with respect to Wilson that I did not know yet how to answer the central part of his article *briefly*, I meant exactly what I said. The 'minor points' on which I am fairly sure he is wrong, is all that he offers in direct criticism of my argument. The other, far more interesting part, is an alternative argument, using a different set of concepts and leading to different conclusions. What I cannot do at present is refuting it without examining the whole approach to the theory of capital on which it is based, and that must wait for an opportunity when I can devote more time to it.
>
> (letter 1754, 8 March 1941)

Discussion with Robinson, as indeed with Kahn, Kaldor or Sraffa, implied comparing alternative theoretical approaches that were not directly communicating, being construed on different systems of concepts and diverse analytic scaffoldings and assumptions. From the methodological perspective, the failure to establish a common ground to settle the controversy is the most interesting point in this mass of correspondence.

While the Keynesian revolution was in full swing, Hayek was elaborating his innovative conception of the competitive market, struggling to free his theorising from received tradition. His Cambridge correspondents failed to latch on to the evolution in his thinking. On the contrary, indeed, the Keynesian revolution spread all the more vigorously being rehashed as a palatable vulgata, safely couched in Marshallian language. The linguistic advantage was offered by short period comparative statics of Marshallian descent. Its analytic simplicity and apparent solidity facilitated assimilation, although they also brought about pitfalls and ambiguities which emerged clearly in post-war macroeconomic debate, and perhaps also betrayed some of the more innovative aspects of Keynes's own thought.

As from the mid-1930s Hayek set out on a different road, with some self-criticism and keen perception of analytic deadlocks in the Austrian apparatus, as clearly emerged in *The Pure Theory of Capital* (Hayek 1941a). A note – almost a second, independent letter – dated 10 March 1941, was added to his letter to J. Robinson on 8 March 1941. Ready to admit some perplexity in his argumentation, Hayek underlined that his difference with almost all 'modern' economists on such diverse issues as monetary theory, the theory of competition, the use of aggregate concepts and socialism stemmed from one single root. He recalled *Economics and Knowledge* (Hayek 1937b) as the only published result, so far, of his painstaking effort to build 'a consistent system of "subjectivism"'. He wrote: 'But I feel that to elaborate these fundamental problems is more important than to go on with the work on particular problems where one comes up all the time against the same difficulties' (letter 1754, 8 March 1941).

Notes

1 'So I got up and asked: "It is your view that if I went out tomorrow and bought a new overcoat, that would increase unemployment?" "Yes", said Hayek. "But", pointing to his triangles on the board, "it would take a very long mathematical argument to explain why"' (Kahn 1984: 182). Joan Robinson accused Hayek of confusing current investment with the stock of capital (J. Robinson 1978a: 2–3).

2 She wrote to Kahn in 1933: 'I had lunch today with Piero, Hayek and Maynard (Austin is away). Hayek was rather nice and very sensible on every topic except "capital consumption" which he brought into the conversation about the American situation (if he were Hoover his remedy would be to "declare a return to *Laissez Faire*"). Maynard was very sweet with him. He seems a bit uneasy about his theory. I dare say they will edge themselves out of their untenable position as time goes by' (letter 579, 5 March 1933).

3 She wrote to Kahn in 1934: 'Hayek is even more of a fraud than we thought. The theory of Capital Consumption (depletion of stocks of raw materials) is

all here. But it occurs in a slump, and prevents a boom, instead of occurring in a boom and causing a slump' (letter 640, 2 September 1934).

4 She wrote to Kahn: 'I went to Hayek's seminar today, found it much diminished. They have got no one who is any good. Kaldor happened to be away. They are discussing Pigou's *Economics of Welfare.* I tried to have some fun saying it was socialist propaganda' (letter 1598, 5 November 1940).

5 The volume with Hayek's (as well as Sraffa's and Keynes's) annotations is conserved in the Wren Library of Trinity College under S2258.

6 In fact, Hayek examined the initial positive impact of demand on the production of consumption goods in unemployment (Hayek 1939a: 42–4 ff.).

7 Wilson's article was published in June 1940 in the *Review of Economic Studies* (Wilson 1940). It originated from Kaldor's earlier criticism of Hayek's theory (Kaldor 1939a).

8 '[. . .] because it takes time, and often very considerable time, till the particular kinds of tools, semifinished products, etc. needed will be available in the requisite quantities' (letter 1753, 6 March 1941).

Table 16.1 Hayek–Kahn correspondence

From	*To*	*Year*	*Month*	*Day*	*Date*	*Archive*		*Published in*	*Item*
RFK	FAH	1931	June	23	Dated letter	Hayek–Stanford	30/19		1140
RFK	FAH	1931	October	8	Dated letter	Hayek–Stanford	30/19		1139

Table 16.2 Hayek–Kaldor correspondence

From	*To*	*Year*	*Month*	*Day*	*Date*	*Archive*		*Published in*	*Item*
FAH	NK	1930	December	1	Dated letter	Kaldor–King's	NK/3/4/5–6		490
FAH	NK	1935	February		Attributed	Hayek–Stanford	105/18		491
						Kaldor–King's	NK/2/3/75–80		
NK	FAH	1935	February		Attributed	Hayek–Stanford	105/18		492
						Kaldor–King's	NK/2/3/81–6		
NK	FAH	1935	February	19	Dated letter	Hayek–Stanford	105/18		493
NK	FAH	1942	January	23	Dated letter	Kaldor–King's	NK/3/30/85/3		494
FAH	NK	1942	January	25	Dated letter	Kaldor–King's	NK/3/30/85/5		495
NK	FAH	1942	January	28	Dated letter	Kaldor–King's	NK/3/30/85/8		496
FAH	NK	1942	January	29	Dated letter	Kaldor–King's	NK/3/30/85/9		497
NK	FAH	1943	August	13	Dated letter	Kaldor–King's	NK/3/10/30		498

Table 16.3 Hayek–J. Robinson correspondence

From	*To*	*Year*	*Month*	*Day*	*Date*	*Archive*	*Published in*	*Item*
FAH	JVR	1941	February	14	Dated letter	Robinson–King's JVR/vii/194/1–2		1751
FAH	JVR	1941	February	15	Dated letter	Robinson–King's JVR/vii/194/3–4		1752
FAH	JVR	1941	March	6	Dated letter	Robinson–King's JVR/vii/194/5–8		1753
FAH	JVR	1941	March	8	Dated letter	Robinson–King's JVR/vii/194/9–11		1754
FAH	JVR	1941	March	14	Dated letter	Robinson–King's JVR/vii/194/12–13		1755
FAH	JVR	1941	March	17	Dated letter	Robinson–King's JVR/vii/194/14–15		1756
FAH	JVR	1941	March	20	Dated letter	Robinson–King's JVR/vii/194/16–18		1757
FAH	JVR	1941	March	24	Dated letter	Robinson–King's JVR/vii/194/19–20		1758
FAH	JVR	1941	March	26	Dated letter	Robinson–King's JVR/vii/194/21–2		1759

Table 16.4 Hayek–Sraffa correspondence

From	*To*	*Year*	*Month*	*Day*	*Date*	*Archive*		*Published in*	*Item*
FAH	PS	1931	November	10	Dated letter	Sraffa–Trinity	Sraffa/D3/9/153		1079
PS	FAH	1931	November	12	Dated letter	Sraffa–Trinity	Sraffa/D3/9/149		1080
PS	FAH	1932	February	19	Dated letter	Sraffa–Trinity	Sraffa/D3/9/150		1081
FAH	PS	1932	February	21	Dated letter	Sraffa–Trinity	Sraffa/I/77/11		1994
PS	FAH	1932	February	22	Dated letter	Sraffa–Trinity	Sraffa/I/77/10		1993
FAH	PS	1932	March	24	Dated letter	Sraffa–Trinity	Sraffa/D3/11/63/86		1071
FAH	PS	1932	November	4	Dated letter	Sraffa–Trinity	Sraffa/D3/11/63/73		1072
FAH	PS	1932	November	18	Dated letter	Sraffa–Trinity	Sraffa/D3/11/63/74		1073
FAH	PS	1933	February	11	Dated letter	Sraffa–Trinity	Sraffa/D3/11/63/97		1074
FAH	PS	1938	October	26	Dated letter	Sraffa–Trinity	Sraffa/D3/11/63/75		1075
FAH	PS	1943	March	23	Dated letter	Sraffa–Trinity	Sraffa/D3/11/63/94		1076
FAH	PS	1944	March	2	Dated letter	Marshall Library Archives			1082
PS	FAH	1944	March	10	Dated letter	Marshall Library Archives			1083
FAH	PS	1945	December	19	Dated letter	Sraffa–Trinity	Sraffa/D3/11/67/99		1077
FAH	PS	1946	November	11	Dated letter	Sraffa–Trinity	Sraffa/C/131/2		1078
FAH	PS	1946	November	18	Dated letter	Marshall Library Archives			1084
PS	FAH	1946	November	26	Dated letter	Marshall Library Archives			1085
PS	FAH	1946	November	26	Dated letter	Marshall Library Archives			1086

References

Ahiakpor, J.C.W. (ed.) (1998) *Keynes and the Classics Reconsidered*, Norwell Mass.: Kluwer Academic Publisher.

Ahiakpor, J.C.W. (1999) 'The genesis of the only diagram in the *General Theory*. A Comment', *Journal of the History of Economic Thought*, 21: 39–41.

Amendola, M. and Gaffard, J.L. (1998) *Out of Equilibrium*, Oxford: Oxford University Press.

Anyadike-Danes, M.K. (1985) 'Dennis Robertson and Keynes's *General Theory*', in G.C. Harcourt (ed.) (1985).

Aron, R. (1967) *Les étapes de la pensée sociologique*, Paris: Gallimard.

Aslanbeigui, N. (1992) 'Pigou's inconsistencies or Keynes's misconceptions?', *History of Political Economy*, 24: 413–33.

Aslanbeigui, N. (1996) 'The cost controversy: Pigouvian economics in disequilibrium', *European Journal of the History of Economic Thought*, 3: 275–95.

Aslanbeigui, N. and Oakes, G. (2002) 'The theory arsenal: the Cambridge Circus and the origins of the Keynesian revolution', *Journal of the History of Economic Thought*, 24: 5–37.

Beherens, C.B.A. (1955) *Merchant Shipping and the Demands of War*, London: HMSO.

Besomi, D. (1995) 'From the trade cycle to the essay in dynamic theory. The Harrod–Keynes correspondence, 1937–1938', *History of Political Economy*, 27: 309–43.

Besomi, D. (1996a) 'Introduction to "An Essay in Dynamic Theory": 1938 draft by Roy F. Harrod', *History of Political Economy*, 28: 245–51.

Besomi, D. (1996b) 'An additional note on the Harrod–Keynes correspondence', *History of Political Economy*, 28: 281–94.

Besomi, D. (1997) 'Roy Harrod and traditional theory', *European Journal for the History of Economic Thought*, 4: 92–115.

Besomi, D. (1998) 'Harrod and the Oxford Economists' Research Group's Inquiry on Prices and Interest, 1936–1939', *Oxford Economic Papers*, 50: 534–62.

Besomi, D. (1999a) *The Making of Harrod's Dynamics*, London: Macmillan.

Besomi, D. (1999b) 'Harrod on the Classification of Technological Progress. The origin of a wild-goose chase', *Banca Nazionale del Lavoro Quarterly Review*, 52: 95–118.

Besomi, D. (2000a) 'Keynes and Harrod on the classical theory of investment. More on the origin of the only diagram in the General Theory', *Journal of the History of Economic Thought*, 22: 367–76.

Besomi, D. (2000b) 'On the spreading of an idea: the strange case of Mr. Harrod and the multiplier', *History of Political Economy*, 31: 347–79.

Besomi, D. (2004) 'Dynamics, trade and money in the correspondence between Roy Harrod and Dennis Robertson', *Research in the History of Economic Thought and Methodology*, 22: 1–64.

Birner, J. (1999) 'The place of the Ricardo Effect in Hayek's Economic Research Programme', *Revue d'économie politique*, 109: 803–16.

Borutti, S. (1985) 'Le virtù ermeneutiche dei modelli', *Materiali Filosofici*, 15: 62–88.

Bradford, W. and Harcourt, G.C. (1997) 'Units and definitions', in G.C. Harcourt and D.A. Riach (eds), *A Second Edition of the General Theory*, vol. 1, London: Routledge, pp. 107–131.

Brady, M.E. (1994) 'A note on the Keynes-Pigou controversy', *History of Political Economy*, 26: 697–706.

Bridel, P. (1987) *Cambridge Monetary Thought: The Development of Saving–Investment Analysis from Marshall to Keynes*, Basingstoke: Macmillan.

Brown, H. Phelps (1980) 'Sir Roy Harrod: a memoir', *Economic Journal*, 90: 1–33.

Caldwell, B. (1995) 'Introduction', in *The Collected Works of F.A. Hayek*, vol. 9, *Contra Keynes and Cambridge*, London: Routledge.

Caldwell, B. (1997) 'Introduction', in *The Collected Works of F.A. Hayek*, vol. 10, *Socialism and War*, London: Routledge.

Caldwell, B. (1998) 'Why didn't Hayek review Keynes's *General Theory*?', *History of Political Economy*, 30: 545–69.

Caldwell, B. (2004) *Hayek's Challenge. An Intellectual Biography of F.A. Hayek*, Chicago and London: The University of Chicago Press.

Carabelli, A. (1988) *On Keynes's Method*, London: Macmillan.

Carabelli, A. (1991) 'The methodology of the critique of the classical theory: Keynes on organic interdependence', in B. Bateman and J. Davis (eds), *Keynes and Philosophy, Essays on the Origin of Keynes's Thought*, Aldershot: Elgar.

Carabelli, A. (1995) 'Uncertainty and measurement in Keynes: probability and organicness', in J. Hillard and S. Dow (eds), *Keynes, Knowledge and Uncertainty*, Aldershot: Elgar.

Carabelli, A. and De Vecchi, N. (1999) '"Where to draw the line?" Keynes versus Hayek on knowledge, ethics and economics', *The European Journal of the History of Economic Thought*, 6: 271–96.

Chamberlin, E. (1937) 'Monopolistic or imperfect competition?', *Quarterly Journal of Economics*, 51: 557–80.

Champernowne, D. (1959) 'Obituary: Arthur Cecil Pigou', *Journal of Royal Statistical Society*, Series A, 122: 263–5.

Cochran, J.P. and Glahe F.R. (1999) *The Hayek–Keynes Debate. Lessons for Current Business Cycle Research*, Lewinston, Queenston, Lampeter: The Edwin Mellen Press.

Collard, D. (1981) 'A.C. Pigou, 1877–1959', in D.P. O'Brien and J.R. Presley (eds), *Pioneers of Modern Economics in Britain*, London: Macmillan.

Collard, D. (1996) 'Pigou and modern business cycle theory', *Economic Journal*, 106: 912–24.

Collard, D. (1999) 'Introduction', in A.C. Pigou (1999).

Costabile, L. (1997) 'Robertson and the post-Keynesian approach to growth and cycles', in P. Arestis, G. Palma and M. Sawyer (eds), *Essays in Honour of Geoff*

Harcourt. Volume 1. Capital Controversy, Post-Keynesian Economics and the History of Economic Thought, London: Routledge.

Cottrell, A. (1994) 'Brady on Pigou and Keynes', *History of Political Economy*, 26: 697–706.

Cozzi, T. and Marchionatti, R. (eds) (2001) *Piero Sraffa's Political Economy. A Centenary Estimate*, London: Routledge.

Dahrendorf, R. (1995) *A History of the London School of Economics and Political Science, 1895–95*, Oxford: Oxford University Press.

Dardi, M. (2001) 'Why did Sraffa lose interest in imperfect competition? A comment on Marcuzzo', in T. Cozzi and R. Marchionatti (eds) (2001).

Dennison, S.R. (1968) 'Robertson Dennis Holme', in David L. Sills (ed.), *International Encyclopedia of the Social Sciences*, 13: 529–33, New York: The Macmillan Company and The Free Press.

Dennison, S.R. and Presley, J.R. (1992) *Robertson on Economic Policy*, London: Macmillan.

De Vivo, G. (2000) 'Produzione di merci a mezzo di merci: note sul percorso intellettuale di Sraffa', in M. Pivetti (ed.), *Piero Sraffa. Contributi per una biografia intellettuale*, Roma: Carocci.

Dimand, R.W. (1988) *The Origins of the Keynesian Revolution*, Aldershot: Elgar.

Dobb, M. (1928) *Wages*, Welwyin: Nisbet.

Dobb, M. (1978) 'Random biographical notes', *Cambridge Journal of Economics*, 3: 115–20.

Donzelli, F. (1988) 'Introduzione', in F.A. Hayek, *Conoscenza, mercato, pianificazione. Saggi di economia e di epistemologia*, Bologna: Il Mulino.

Ebenstein, A. (2001) *Friedrich Hayek. A Biography*, New York: Palgrave.

Eshag, E. (1963) *From Marshall to Keynes. An Essay on the Monetary Theory of the Cambridge School*, Oxford: Blackwell.

Fitzgibbons, A. (1988) *Keynes's Vision*, Oxford: Clarendon Press.

Fletcher, G.A. (1987) *The Keynesian Revolution and its Critics: Issues of Theory and Policy for the Monetary Production Economy*, 2nd edn, London: Macmillan.

Fletcher, G.A. (2000) *Understanding Dennis Robertson*, Cheltenham: Edward Elgar.

Gehrke, C. (2003) 'More on the Sraffa–Dobb collaboration in Piero Sraffa's edition of *The Works and Correspondence of David Ricardo*', mimeo.

Gehrke, C. and Kurz, H.D. (2002) 'Keynes and Sraffa's "Difficulties with J.H. Hollander"', *European Journal of the History of Economic Thought*, 9: 644–71.

Gifford, C.H.P. (1933) 'The concept of the length of the period of production', *Economic Journal*, 43: 611–18.

Gilboy, E.W. (1938) 'The propensity to consume', *Quarterly Journal of Economics*, 53: 120–40.

Goodhart, C. and Presley, J. (1994) 'Real business cycle theory: a restatement of Robertsonian economics?', *Economic Notes*, 23: 275–91.

Graham, F.D. (1944) 'Keynes vs Hayek on a commodity reserve currency', *Economic Journal*, 54: 422–9.

Groenewegen, P. (1995) *A Soaring Eagle: A. Marshall 1842–1924*, Aldershot: Elgar.

Hale, K. (ed.) (1998) *Friends and Apostles. The Correspondence of Rupert Brooke and James Strachey 1905–1914*, New Haven: Yale University Press.

Hansen, A. (1941) *Fiscal Policy and Business Cycles*, New York: Norton.

Harcourt, G.C. (1984) 'Harcourt on Robinson', in H.W. Spiegel and W.J. Samuels (eds), *Contemporary Economists in Perspective*, Stanford: JAI Press.

Harcourt, G.C. (ed.) (1985) *Keynes and His Contemporaries*, London: Macmillan.
Harcourt, G.C. (1988) 'Nicholas Kaldor, 12 May 1908–30 September 1986', *Economica*, 55: 159–70; reprinted in C. Sardoni (ed.) (1992) *On Political Economists and Modern Political Economy, Selected Essays of G.C. Harcourt*, London: Routledge.
Harcourt, G.C. (1990) 'Joan Robinson's early view on method', *History of Political Economy*, 22: 411–27.
Harcourt, G.C. (1995) 'Joan Robinson, 1903–1983', *Economic Journal*, 105: 1228–41.
Harcourt, G.C. (1996) 'Some reflections on Joan Robinson's changes of mind and their relationship to post-Keynesianism and the economics profession', in M.C. Marcuzzo, L.L. Pasinetti and A. Roncaglia (eds) (1996).
Harrod, R.F. (1927) '*Banking*, by Walter Leaf', *Economic Journal*, 37: 76–81.
Harrod, R.F. (1930) 'Notes on supply', *Economic Journal*, 40 : 233–41.
Harrod, R.F. (1931) 'The law of decreasing costs', *Economic Journal*, 41: 566–76.
Harrod, R.F. (1932a) 'The dilemma in the economy. How to restore demand. A case for limited reflation', *The Times*, 4 November: 15–16 (anonymous); reprinted in Harrod (2003), vol. 3: 1244–9.
Harrod, R.F. (1932b) 'Decreasing costs: an addendum', *Economic Journal*, 42: 337–41.
Harrod, R.F. (1932c) 'Monetary policy', letter to the Editor of *The Economist*, CXIV, 4 June: 1238–41; reprinted in Harrod (2003), vol. 3: 1238–40.
Harrod, R.F. (1933a) 'More money in circulation. Spending on capital account. Provision in the budget', collective letter to *The Times*, 10 March: 15; reprinted in Harrod (2003), vol. 3: 1249–52.
Harrod, R.F. (1933b) 'Trade of the world. British policy of expansion. Financing increased imports', letter to *The Times*, 21 April: 8; reprinted in Harrod (2003), vol. 3: 1257–8.
Harrod, R.F. (1933c) *International Economics*. London: Nisbet; Cambridge: Cambridge University Press; New York: Harcourt and Brace.
Harrod, R.F. (1933d) 'A further note on decreasing costs', *Economic Journal*, 43: 337–41.
Harrod, R.F. (1933e) 'Britain's lead in currency policy. "The time is ripe for action; the opportunity now is ours"', *The Daily Telegraph*, 31 March: 12; reprinted in Harrod (2003), vol. 3: 1252–7.
Harrod, R.F. (1934a) 'The expansion of credit in an advancing community', *Economica*, 1: 287–99.
Harrod, R.F. (1934b) 'Banking policy and stable prices', letter to the Editor of *The Economist*, Monthly Banking Supplement, October 6: 8; reprinted in Harrod (2003), vol. 3: 1258–61.
Harrod, R.F. (1934c) 'Banking policy and stable prices', letter to the Editor of *The Economist*, Monthly Banking Supplement, November 10: 8; reprinted in Harrod (2003), vol. 3: 1261–4.
Harrod, R.F. (1934d) 'Professor Pigou's Theory of Unemployment', *Economic Journal*, 44: 19–32.
Harrod, R.F. (1935) 'A comment on the questions for discussion', in *Report of the Proceedings of the Meeting of economists, held at the Antwerp Chamber of Commerce, on July the 11th, 12th, and 13th, 1935*, Brecht-Anvers: Typ. Braeckmans.
Harrod, R.F. (1936a) 'Another fundamental objection to *laissez-faire*', *Economic Journal*, 46: 163–8.
Harrod, R.F. (1936b) *The Trade Cycle. An Essay*, Oxford: Clarendon Press.

Harrod, R.F. (1937a) 'Review of Joan Robinson's *Essays in the Theory of Employment*', *Economic Journal*, 47: 326–30.
Harrod, R.F. (1937b) 'Lord Nuffield's Foundation in Oxford', *Economic Journal*, 47: 757–61.
Harrod, R.F. (1937c) 'Mr. Keynes and traditional theory', *Econometrica*, 5: 74–86.
Harrod, R.F (1938) 'Scope and method of economics', *Economic Journal*, 48: 383–412.
Harrod, R.F. (1939) 'An essay in dynamic theory', *Economic Journal*, 49: 14–33.
Harrod, R.F. (1951) *The Life of John Maynard Keynes*, London: Macmillan.
Harrod, R.F. (1959) *The Prof. A Personal Memoir of Lord Cherwell*, London: Macmillan.
Harrod, R.F. (1996) 'An essay in dynamic theory (1938 draft)', D. Besomi (ed.), *History of Political Economy*, 28: 253–80.
Harrod, R.F. (2003) *The Interwar Papers and Correspondence of Roy Harrod*, D. Besomi (ed.), 3 vols, Cheltenham: Edward Elgar.
Hawtrey, R. (1937) *Capital and Employment*, Longmans: London.
Hayek, F.A. (1928) 'Das intertemporale Gleichgewichtssystem der Preise und die bewegungen des "Geldwertes"', *Weltwirtschaftliches Archiv*, 28: 33–76, English transl. 'Intertemporal price equilibrium and movements in the value of money', in F.A. Hayek (1999): 186–227.
Hayek, F.A. (1929) *Geldtheorie und Konjunkturtheorie*, Wien: Hölder-Pichler-Tempsky.
Hayek, F.A. (1931a) 'Reflections on the pure theory of money of Mr. J.M. Keynes'. Part I, *Economica*, 11: 270–95; reprinted in F.A. Hayek (1995): 121–46.
Hayek, F.A. (1931b) *Prices and Production*, London: Routledge & Sons.
Hayek, F.A. (1931c) *Preise und Produktion*, Wien: Springer.
Hayek, F.A. (1931d) 'A rejoinder to Mr. Keynes', *Economica*, 11: 398–403; reprinted in F.A. Hayek (1995): 159–64.
Hayek, F.A. (1932a) 'Reflections on the pure theory of money of Mr J.M. Keynes'. Part II, *Economica*, 12: 22–44; reprinted in F.A. Hayek (1995): 174–97.
Hayek, F.A. (1932b) 'Money and capital: a reply', *Economic Journal*, 42: 237–49.
Hayek, F.A. [1933a] (1966) *Monetary Theory and the Trade Cycle*, N. Kaldor and H.M. Croome (eds), New York: Kelley.
Hayek, F.A. (ed.) (1933b) *Beiträge zur geldtheorie*, Wien: Springer.
Hayek, F.A. (1934) 'On the relationship between investment and output', *Economic Journal*, 44: 207–31.
Hayek, F.A. (1936a) 'The mithology of capital', *Quarterly Journal of Economics*, 50: 199–228.
Hayek, F.A. (1936b) 'Utility analysis and interest', *Economic Journal*, 46: 44–60.
Hayek, F.A. (1937a) *Monetary Nationalism and International Stability*, London: Longmans.
Hayek, F.A. (1937b) 'Economics and knowledge', *Economica*, 4: 33–54.
Hayek, F.A. (1939a) *Profits, Interest and Investment*, London: Routledge.
Hayek, F.A. (1939b) 'Introduction' *to Henry Thornton, An Enquiry into the Nature and Effects of the Paper Credit of Great Britain*, London: Allen and Unwin.
Hayek, F.A. (1939c) 'Mr. Keynes and war costs', *The Spectator*, 24 November 1939; reprinted in F.A. Hayek (1997): 164–7.
Hayek, F.A. (1940) 'Review of John Maynard Keynes: *How to Pay for the War*', *Economic Journal*, 50: 321–6; reprinted in F.A. Hayek (1997): 167–72.
Hayek F.A (1941a) *The Pure Theory of Capital*, Routledge: London.
Hayek, F.A. (1941b) 'Maintaining capital intact: a reply', *Economica*, 8: 276–80.

Hayek, F.A. (1942a) 'John Stuart Mill at the age of twenty-five', in *John Stuart Mill, Spirit of the Age,* Chicago: University of Chicago Press.
Hayek, F.A. (1942b) 'A comment', *Economica,* 9: 383–5.
Hayek, F.A. (1943a) 'John Rae and John Stuart Mill: a correspondence', *Economica,* 10: 253–5.
Hayek, F.A. (1943b) 'John Stuart Mill's correspondence', *The Times Literary Supplement,* 13 February.
Hayek, F.A. (1943c) 'A commodity reserve currency', *Economic Journal,* 53: 176–84.
Hayek, F.A. (1943d) 'The economic position of South Tyrol', in *Committee on Justice for South Tyrol,* London.
Hayek, F.A. (1943e) 'The case of the Tyrol', in *Committee on Justice for South Tyrol,* London.
Hayek, F.A. (1944a) *The Road to Serfdom,* London: Routledge; reprint (1994), Chicago: Chicago University Press.
Hayek, F.A. (1944b) 'To totalitarianism by the back door?', *The Sunday Times,* May 21.
Hayek, F.A. (1948) 'The meaning of competition', in *Individualism and Economic Order,* London: Routledge.
Hayek, F.A. (1952) 'Review of Harrod's *Life of J.M. Keynes*', *The Journal of Modern History,* 24: 195–8; reprinted in F.A. Hayek (1995): 227–32.
Hayek, F.A. (1966) 'Personal recollections of Keynes and the Keynesian revolution', *The Oriental Economist,* 34: 78–80; reprinted in F.A. Hayek (1995): 240–6.
Hayek F.A. (1978) *New Studies in Philosophy, Politics, Economics and the History of Ideas,* London: Routledge.
Hayek, F.A. (1983) 'The Keynes centenary: The Austrian critique', *The Economist,* June 11: 45–8; reprinted in F.A. Hayek (1995): 247–55.
Hayek, F.A. (1995) *The Collected Works of F.A. Hayek. Contra Keynes and Cambridge,* vol. 9, B. Caldwell (ed.), London: Routledge.
Hayek, F.A. (1997) *The Collected Works of F.A. Hayek. Socialism and War,* vol. 10, B. Caldwell (ed.), London: Routledge.
Hayek, F.A. (1999) *The Collected Works of F.A. Hayek. Good Money,* vol. 5, S. Kresge (ed.), London: Routledge.
Hession, C.H. (1984) *J.M. Keynes,* London: Macmillan.
Hicks, J.R. (1936) 'Mr. Keynes's Theory of Employment', *Economic Journal,* 46: 138–252.
Hicks, J.R. (1937) 'Mr. Keynes and the "classics"', *Econometrica*; reprinted in J. Hicks (1967) *Critical Essays in Monetary Theory,* Oxford: Clarendon Press.
Hicks, J.R. (1964) 'Dennis Holme Robertson', *Proceedings of the British Academy,* 50: 305–16.
Hicks, J.R. (ed.) (1966) *Essays in Money and Interest,* London: Fontana Library.
Hicks, J.R. (1967) 'The Hayek story', in *Critical Essays in Monetary Theory,* Oxford: Clarendon Press.
Hicks, J.R. (1974) *The Crisis in Keynesian Economics,* Oxford: Blackwell.
Hill, M. (1933) 'The period of production and industrial fluctuations', *Economic Journal,* 43: 599–610.
Hirai, T. (1997–99) 'A study of Keynes's economics', *Sophia Economic Review,* I–IV.
Hirai, T. (2003) *Keynes's Economics from Multiple Points of View,* Tokyo: University of Tokyo Press.
Hirschmann, A.O. (1977) *The Passions and the Interests. Political Arguments for Capitalism before its Triumph,* Princeton: Princeton University Press.
Ingrao, B. and Ranchetti, F. (1996) *Il mercato nel pensiero economico,* Milano: Hoepli.

Johnson, E. and Johnson H.C. (1978) *The Shadow of Keynes*, Chicago: University of Chicago Press.
Johnson, H. (1960) 'Arthur Cecil Pigou', *Canadian Journal of Economics*, 26: 150–5.
Kahn, R.F. (1931) 'The relation of home investment to unemployment', *Economic Journal*, 41: 173–98.
Kahn, R.F. (1933) 'The elasticity of substitution and the relative share of a factor' *Review of Economic Studies*, 1: 72–8.
Kahn, R.F. (1935) 'Some notes on ideal output', *Economic Journal*, 45: 1–35.
Kahn, R.F. (1954) 'Some notes on liquidity preference', *Manchester School of Economics and Social Studies*, 24: 229–57; reprinted in R.F. Kahn (1972).
Kahn, R.F. (1972) *Selected Essays on Employment and Growth*, Cambridge: Cambridge University Press.
Kahn, R.F. (1976) 'Historical origins of the International Monetary Fund', in A.P. Thirlwall (ed.), *Keynes and International Monetary Relations*, London: Macmillan.
Kahn, R.F. (1983) *L'economia del breve periodo*, Torino: Boringhieri.
Kahn, R.F. (1984) *The Making of Keynes's General Theory*, Cambridge: Cambridge University Press.
Kahn, R.F (1987) 'Shove, Gerald Frank', in J. Eatwell, M. Milgate and P. Newman (eds), *The New Palgrave*, London: Macmillan.
Kahn, R.F. (1988) *A Disciple of Keynes*, M.C. Marcuzzo (ed.), University of Modena: Working paper n. 29; ital. trans., *Un discepolo di Keynes*, Milano: Garzanti.
Kahn, R.F. (1989) *The Economics of the Short Period*, London: Macmillan.
Kaldor, N. (1932) 'A case against technical progress?', *Economica*, 12: 180–96.
Kaldor, N. (1934a) 'The equilibrium of the firm', *Economic Journal*, 44: 60–74.
Kaldor, N. (1934b) 'Mrs. Robinson's "Economics of Imperfect Competition"', *Economica*, 1: 335–41.
Kaldor, N. (1934c) 'A classificatory note on the determinateness of equilibrium', *Review of Economic Studies*, 1: 122–36.
Kaldor, N. (1935) 'Market imperfection and excess capacity', *Economica*, 2: 33–50.
Kaldor, N. (1936) 'Wage subsidies as a remedy for unemployment', *Journal of Political Economy*, 44: 721–42.
Kaldor, N. (1937) 'Professor Pigou on money wages in relation to unemployment', *Economic Journal*, 47: 745–53.
Kaldor, N. (1938a) 'A rejoinder to Professor Knight', *Econometrica*, 6: 163–76.
Kaldor, N. (1938b) 'Professor Chamberlin on monopolistic and imperfect competition', *Quarterly Journal of Economics*, 52: 513–29.
Kaldor, N. (1938c) 'Stability and full employment', *Economic Journal*, 48: 642–57; reprinted in N. Kaldor (1960): 103–19.
Kaldor, N. (1939a) 'Capital intensity and the trade cycle', *Economica*, 6: 40–66; reprinted in N. Kaldor (1960): 120–47.
Kaldor, N. (1939b) 'Speculation and economic stability', *Review of Economic Studies*, 7: 1–27; reprinted in N. Kaldor (1960): 17–58.
Kaldor, N. (1939c) 'Money wage cuts in relation to unemployment: a reply to Mr. Somers', *Review of Economic Studies*, 6: 232–5.
Kaldor, N. (1939d) 'Principles of emergency finance', *The Banker*, 51: 149–56.
Kaldor, N. (1940) 'A model of the trade cycle', *Economic Journal*, 50: 78–95; reprinted in N. Kaldor (1960): 177–92.
Kaldor, N. (1941a) 'Employment and equilibrium. A theoretical discussion', *Economic Journal*, 51: 458–73; reprinted in N. Kaldor (1960): 83–100.

Kaldor, N. (1941b) 'The White Paper on national income and expenditure', *Economic Journal*, 51: 181–91.

Kaldor, N. (1942a) 'Models of short-period equilibrium', *Economic Journal*, 52: 250–8.

Kaldor, N. (1942b) 'Prof. Hayek and the Concertina Effect', *Economica*, 9: 359–82.

Kaldor, N. (1943) 'The 1943 White Paper on National Income and Expenditure' (with T. Barna), *Economic Journal*, 53: 259–74.

Kaldor, N. (1960) *Essays on Economic Stability and Growth*, London: Duckworth.

Kaldor, N. (1980) 'General introduction', in *Collected Economic Essays*, vol. I, London: Duckworth.

Kaldor, N. (1981) 'Origins of the new monetarism', The Page Fund Lecture; reprinted in N. Kaldor (1989): 160–77.

Kaldor, N. (1985) 'Piero Sraffa 1898–1983', *Proceedings of the British Academy*, 71: 615–40.

Kaldor, N. (1986a) 'Recollections of an economist', *Banca Nazionale del Lavoro Quarterly Review*, 156: 3–26; reprinted in N. Kaldor (1989): 13–37.

Kaldor, N. (1986b) *Ricordi di un economista*, M.C. Marcuzzo (ed.), Milano: Garzanti.

Kaldor, N. (1989) *Further Essays on Economic Theory and Policy*, New York: Holmes & Meier.

Kalecki, M. (1938) 'The determinants of distribution of national income', *Econometrica*, 6: 97–112.

Kalecki, M. (1939) *Essays in the Theory of Economic Fluctuations*, London: Allen and Unwin.

Kalecki, M. (1941) 'A theorem on technical progress', *Review of Economic Studies*, 8: 178–84; reprinted in M. Kalecki (1991): 107–16.

Kalecki, M. (1991) *Collected Works of Michal Kalecki. Capitalism: Economic Dynamics*, vol. 2, J. Osiatynski (ed.), Oxford: Clarendon Press.

Keynes, J.M. (1919) *The Economic Consequences of the Peace*, London: Macmillan; reprinted in CWK II.

Keynes, J.M. (1921) *A Treatise on Probability*, London: Macmillan; reprinted in CWK VIII.

Keynes, J.M. (1922) 'The Theory of the Exchanges and "Purchasing Power Parity"', Reconstruction Supplements to the *Manchester Guardian Commercial*; reprinted in CWK IV: 70–80; 164–9.

Keynes, J.M. (1923) *A Tract on Monetary Reform*, London: Macmillan; reprinted in CWK IV.

Keynes, J.M. (1924) 'Alfred Marshall, 1842–1924', *Economic Journal*, 34: 311–72; reprinted in CWK X: 161–231.

Keynes, J.M. (1925a) *La riforma monetaria*, trans. by P. Sraffa, Milano: Treves.

Keynes, J.M. (1925b) *The Economic Consequences of Mr. Churchill*, London: Hogarth Press; reprinted in CWK XIX: 357–453.

Keynes, J.M. (1928) 'The amalgamation of the British note issues', *Economic Journal*, 38: 321–8.

Keynes, J.M. (1930a) *A Treatise on Money*, London: Macmillan; reprinted in CWK V and VI.

Keynes, J.M. (1930b) 'Editor's introduction', Symposium on Increasing Returns and the Representative Firm, *Economic Journal*, 40: 79.

Keynes, J.M. (1931a) 'The Pure Theory of Money. A reply to Dr. Hayek', *Economica*, 11: 387–97; reprinted in F.A. Hayek (1995): 147–58.

Keynes, J.M. (1931b) 'A rejoinder to Mr. D.H. Robertson', *Economic Journal*, 41: 412–23; reprinted (with changes) in CWK XIII: 219–36.

Keynes, J.M. (1933a) 'The means to prosperity', *The Times*, 13–16 March; reprinted in CWK IX: 335–66.

Keynes, J.M. (1933b) 'National self sufficiency', *The New Statesman* and *The Nation*, 8 July and 15 July; reprinted in CWK XI: 233–46.

Keynes, J.M. (1933c), 'Mr. Robertson on Saving and Hoarding', *Economic Journal*, 43: 699–701; reprinted in CWK XIII: 327–30.

Keynes, J.M. (1937a) 'The General Theory of Employment', *Quarterly Journal of Economics*, 51: 209–23; reprinted in CWK XIV: 109–23.

Keynes, J.M. (1937b) 'Alternative theories of the rates of interest', *Economic Journal*, 47: 241–52; reprinted in CWK XIV: 201–15.

Keynes, J.M. (1937c) 'The "ex-ante" theory of the rate of interest', *Economic Journal*, 47: 663–9; reprinted in CWK XIV: 215–23.

Keynes, J.M. (1937d) 'Professor Pigou on money wages in relation to unemployment', *Economic Journal*, 47: 743–5; reprinted in CWK XIV: 262–5.

Keynes, J.M. (1938a) 'Mr. Keynes and "finance". Comment', *Economic Journal*, 48: 318–22; reprinted in CWK XIV: 229–33.

Keynes, J.M. (1938b) 'My early beliefs', in *Two Memoirs: Dr Melchior: a Defeated Enemy and My Early Beliefs*, London: Rupert Hart-Davis, 1949; reprinted in CWK X: 433–50.

Keynes, J.M. (1939a) 'The control of consumption' and 'Compulsory savings', *The Times*, November 14 and 15; reprinted in CWK XXII: 41–51.

Keynes, J.M. (1939b) 'The alternative to inflation', *The Times*, November 28, 1939; reprinted in CWK XXII: 74–81.

Keynes, J.M. (1939c) 'The income and fiscal potential of Great Britain', *Economic Journal*, 49: 626–35; reprinted in CWK XXII: 52–66.

Keynes, J.M. (1939d) 'Professor Tinbergen's method', *Economic Journal*, 49: 558–68; reprinted in CWK XIV: 306–18.

Keynes, J.M. (1940a) 'The concept of national income: a supplementary note', *Economic Journal*, 50: 60–5; reprinted in CWK XXII: 66–73.

Keynes, J.M. (1940b) *How to Pay for the War*, London: Macmillan; reprinted in CWK IX: 367–439.

Keynes, J.M. (1943) 'The objective of international price stability', *Economic Journal*, 53: 185–7; reprinted in CWK XXVI: 30–3.

Keynes, J.M. (1944a) 'Notes by Lord Keynes', *Economic Journal*, 54: 429–30; reprinted in CWK XXVI: 39–40.

Keynes, J.M. (1944b) 'Obituary. Mary Paley Marshall (1850–1944)', *Economic Journal*, 54: 268–86; reprinted in CWK X: 232–50.

Keynes, J.M. (1946) 'The balance of payments of the United States', *Economic Journal*, 56: 172–87; reprinted in CWK XXVII: 427–46.

Keynes, J.M. (1971–89) *The Collected Writings* (CWK), D. Moggridge (ed.), London: Macmillan.

CWK II, *The Economic Consequences of the Peace.*

CWK IV, *A Tract on Monetary Reform.*

CWK V, *A Treatise on Money. The Pure Theory of Money.*

CWK VI, *A Treatise on Money. The Applied Theory of Money.*

CWK VII, *The General Theory of Employment, Interest, and Money.*

CWK VIII, *A Treatise on Probability.*

CWK IX, *Essays in Persuasion.*

CWK X, *Essays in Biography.*

CWK XII, *Economic Articles and Correspondence. Investment and Editorial.*

CWK XIII, *The General Theory and After: Preparation.*

CWK XIV, *The General Theory and After: Defence and Development.*

CWK XVI, *Activities 1914–1919. The Treasury and Versailles.*

CWK XVII, *Activities 1920–22. Treaty Revision and Reconstruction.*

CWK XIX, *Activities 1922–29. The Return to Gold and Industrial Policy.*

CWK XX, *Activities 1929–1931. Rethinking Employment and Unemployment Policies.*

CWK XXI, *Activities 1931–1939. World Crisis and Policies in Britain and America.*

CWK XXII, *Activities 1939–1945. Internal War Finance.*

CWK XXIII, *Activities 1940–1943. External War Finance.*

CWK XXV, *Activities 1940–1944. Shaping the Post-War World. The Clearing Union.*

CWK XXVI, *Activities 1941–1946. Shaping the Post-War World. Bretton Woods and Reparations.*

CWK XXVII, *Activities 1940–1946. Shaping the Post-War World. Employment and Commodities.*

CWK XXVIII, *Social, Political and Literary Writings.*

CWK XXIX, *The General Theory and After. A Supplement.*

Keynes, J.M. and Sraffa, P. (1938) 'Introduction' to D. Hume *An Abstract of A Treatise of Human Nature* [1740]; Cambridge: Cambridge University Press.

King, J.E. (2000a) 'Introduction to an unpublished note by Nicholas Kaldor and Joan Robinson', *Review of Political Economy*, 12: 261–5.

King, J.E. (ed.) (2000b) 'Note on alternative hypothesis as to the determination of profit margins' by N. Kaldor and J.V. Robinson, *Review of Political Economy*, 12: 267–71.

Knight, F. (1935) 'Professor Hayek and the Theory of Investment', *Economic Journal*, 45: 77–94.

Kresge, S. and Wenar, L. (eds) (1994) *Hayek on Hayek*, London: Routledge.

Kregel, J.A. (1980) 'Economic dynamics and the theory of steady growth: an historical essay on Harrod's "Knife-edge"', *History of Political Economy*, 12: 97–123.

Kregel, J.A. (1985) 'Harrod and Keynes: increasing returns, the theory of employment and dynamic economics', in G.C. Harcourt (ed.) (1985).

Kurz, H.D. (1995) 'Sulle perturbazioni 'naturali' e 'artificiali' dell'equilibrio economico generale. La teoria monetaria del sovrainvestimento di Friedrich August Hayek in *Prices and Production*', *Studi Economici*, 56: 5–61.

Kurz, H.D. (2000) 'The Hayek–Keynes–Sraffa controversy reconsidered', in H. Kurz (ed.), *Critical Essays on Piero Sraffa's Legacy in Economics*, Cambridge: Cambridge University Press.

Laidler, D. (1991) 'The Austrians and the Stockholm School: two failures in the development of modern macroeconomics', in L. Jonung (ed.), *The Stockholm School of Economics Revisited*, Cambridge: Cambridge University Press.

Laidler, D. (1995) 'Robertson in the 1920s', *European Journal of the History of Economic Thought*, 2: 151–74.

Lerner, A. (1938) 'Alternative formulations of the theory of interest', *Economic Journal*, 48: 211–30.

Lindahl E. (1954) 'On Keynes's economic system', *Economic Record*, 30: Pt. I–II 30: 19–32, 159–71.

Lovejoy, A.O. (1961) *Reflections on Human Nature*, Baltimore: Johns Hopkins.

MacDougall, G.D.A. (1936) 'The definition of prime and supplementary costs', *Economic Journal*, 46: 443–61.

Marchionatti, R. (2001) 'Sraffa and the criticism of Marshall in the 1920s and 1930s', in T. Cozzi and R. Marchionatti (eds) (2001).

Marcuzzo, M.C. (1991) 'Introduzione: Joan Robinson e la formazione della Scuola di Cambridge', in J. Robinson, *Occupazione, distribuzione e crescita,* Bologna: Il Mulino.

Marcuzzo, M.C. (1993) 'La relazione salari-occupazione tra rigidità reali e rigidità nominali', *Economia Politica,* 10: 439–63.

Marcuzzo, M.C. (1994) 'R.F. Kahn and imperfect competition', *Cambridge Journal of Economics,* 18: 25–40.

Marcuzzo, M.C. (1996a) 'Alternative microeconomic foundations for macroeconomics: the controversy over the L-shaped cost curve revisited', *Review of Political Economy,* 8: 7–22.

Marcuzzo, M.C. (1996b) 'Joan Robinson and Richard Kahn. The origin of the short period analysis', in M.C. Marcuzzo, L. Pasinetti and A. Roncaglia (eds) (1996).

Marcuzzo, M.C. (1997) 'Joan Robinson e le tre "rivoluzioni" di Cambridge', *Storia del pensiero economico* , 33–4: 19–39.

Marcuzzo, M.C. (1998) 'La collaborazione tra Keynes e Kahn dal *Treatise* alla *General Theory*', in N. De Vecchi and M.C. Marcuzzo (eds), *A Cinquant'anni da Keynes: teorie dell' occupazione, interesse e crescita,* Milano: Unicopli

Marcuzzo, M.C. (ed.) (2001a) *Economists in Cambridge. The letters between Kahn, Keynes, Harrod, J. Robinson, Sraffa, Kaldor and Hayek, 1921–1946,* Dipartimento di Scienze Economiche, Università degli Studi di Roma, La Sapienza, Discussion Papers, 37.

Marcuzzo, M.C. (2001b) 'Sraffa and Cambridge Economics, 1928–1931', in T. Cozzi and R. Marchionatti (eds) (2001).

Marcuzzo, M.C. (2001c) 'From the fundamental equations to effective demand: "natural evolution" or "change of view"?', in P. Arestis, M. Desai and S. Dow (eds) (2001) *Methodology, Microeconomics and Keynes. Essays in Honour of Victoria Chick,* vol. 2, London: Taylor and Francis.

Marcuzzo, M.C. (2001d) 'Joan Robinson: une quête passionnée de la rationalité', in G.C. Harcourt (ed.), *L'économie rebelle de Joan Robinson,* Paris: L'Harmattan.

Marcuzzo, M.C. (2002) 'The collaboration between J.M. Keynes and R.F. Kahn from the *Treatise* to the *General Theory', History of Political Economy,* 34: 421–47 (revised and expanded version of Marcuzzo 1998).

Marcuzzo, M.C. (2003) 'Joan Robinson and the Three Cambridge Revolutions', *Review of Political Economy,* 15: 545–60 (revised version of Marcuzzo 1997).

Marcuzzo, M.C. (2004) 'Sraffa all'Università di Cambridge', Roma: Accademia Nazionale dei Lincei (English version forthcoming in *European Journal for the History of Economic Thought* (2005)).

Marcuzzo, M.C. (2005) *Robinson and Sraffa,* in B. Gibson (ed.), *The Economics of Joan Robinson: A Centennial Celebration,* Cheltenham: Elgar.

Marcuzzo, M.C., Pasinetti, L. and Roncaglia, A. (eds) (1996) *The Economics of Joan Robinson,* London: Routledge.

Marshall, A. (1920) *Principles of Economics,* 8th edn, London: Macmillan.

Mason, E. (1982) 'The Harvard Department of Economics from the beginning to World War II', *Quarterly Journal of Economics,* 97: 384–433.

Mizen, P., Moggridge, D. and Presley, J. (1997) 'The papers of Dennis Robertson: the discovery of unexpected riches', *History of Political Economy,* 29: 573–92.

Mizen, P. and Presley, J.R. (1998) 'Keynes, Hicks and the Cambridge School', *History of Political Economy*, 30: 1–16.

Moggridge, D.E. (1992) *Maynard Keynes. An Economist's Biography*, London: Routledge.

Moggridge, D.E. (2001) 'Maynard would not have wished? Second-guessing the author of 'The balance of payments of the United States'', *History of Political Economy*, 33: 815–24.

Moggridge, D. (2002) 'Review of Fletcher's *Understanding Dennis Robertson*', *Journal of History of Economic Thought*, 24: 371–3.

Mongiovi, G. (1990) 'Keynes, Hayek and Sraffa: on the origins of Chapter 17 of the *General Theory*', *Economie Appliquée*, 43(2): 131–56.

Mongiovi, G. (1996) 'Sraffa's critique of Marshall: a reassessment', *Cambridge Journal of Economics*, 20: 207–24.

Naldi, N. (1998) 'Some notes on Piero Sraffa's biography, 1917–1927', *Review of Political Economy*, 10: 493–515.

Naldi, N. (2000a) 'Keynes on the nature of capital: an interpretation of the *General Theory* Chapter 16', *Review of Political Economy*, 12: 157–69.

Naldi, N. (2000b) 'The friendship between Piero Sraffa and Antonio Gramsci in the years 1919–1927', *The European Journal of the History of Economic Thought*, 7: 79–114.

Naldi, N. (2004) *Piero Sraffa: emigrazione e attività scientifica fra gli anni Venti e gli anni Quaranta*, Roma: Accademia Nazionale dei Lincei.

O'Donnell, R. (1999a) 'The genesis of the only diagram in the *General Theory*', *Journal of the History of Economic Thought*, 21: 27–37.

O'Donnell, R. (1999b) 'On reading and arguing: a reply to Ahiakpor', *Journal of the History of Economic Thought*, 21: 43–51.

Panico, C. (2001) 'Monetary analysis in Sraffa's writings', in T. Cozzi and R. Marchionatti (eds) (2001).

Patinkin, D. and Leith, J. C. (eds) (1977) *Keynes, Cambridge and the General Theory*, London: Macmillan.

Pigou, A.C. (1912) *Wealth and Welfare*, Macmillan: London.

Pigou, A.C. (1913) *Unemployment*, London: Williams and Norgate.

Pigou, A.C. (1927a) *Industrial Fluctuations*, London: Macmillan, reprinted in A.C. Pigou (1999), vol. 6.

Pigou, A.C. (1927b) 'The law of diminishing returns and increasing cost', *Economic Journal*, 37: 188–97.

Pigou, A.C. (1928) 'An analysis of supply', *Economic Journal*, 38: 238–57.

Pigou, A.C. (1930) 'The statistical derivation of demand curves', *Economic Journal*, 40: 384–400.

Pigou, A.C. (1931) 'Mr. Keynes on money', *The Nation and Athenaeum*, 24 January 1931: 544–5

Pigou, A.C. (1933a) *The Theory of Unemployment*, London: Macmillan; reprint in A.C. Pigou (1999), vol. 8.

Pigou, A.C. (1933b), 'A note on imperfect competition', *Economic Journal*, 43: 108–12.

Pigou, A.C. (1936) 'Mr J.M. Keynes' *General Theory of Employment, Interest and Money*', *Economica*, 3: 115–32.

Pigou, A.C. (1937) 'Real and money wage rates in relation to unemployment', *Economic Journal*, 47: 405–22.

Pigou, A.C. (1938) 'Money wages in relation to unemployment', *Economic Journal*, 48: 134–8.

Pigou, A.C. (1941) *Employment and Equilibrium*, London: Macmillan; reprinted in A.C. Pigou (1999), vol. 10.

Pigou, A.C. (1942) 'Models of short-period equilibrium', *Economic Journal*, 52: 250–7.

Pigou, A.C. (1943) 'The classical stationary state', *Economic Journal*, 53: 343–51.

Pigou, A.C. (1944) 'Employment policy and Sir William Beveridge', *Agenda*, August 1944; reprinted in A.C. Pigou (1999), vol. 14: 85–107.

Pigou, A.C. (1947) *Aspects of British Economic History*, London: Macmillan; reprinted in A.C. Pigou (1999), vol. 12.

Pigou, A.C. (1950) *Keynes's 'General Theory': A Retrospective View*, London: Macmillan; reprinted in A.C. Pigou (1999), vol. 13.

Pigou, A.C. (1999) *Collected Economic Writings*, D. Collard (ed.), vols 1–14, Basingstoke: Macmillan.

Pigou, A.C. and Robertson, D.H. (1931) *Economic Essays and Addresses*, London: P.S. King.

Plumptre, A.F.W. (1975) 'Maynard Keynes as a teacher', in M. Keynes (ed.) *Essays on John Maynard Keynes*, Cambridge: Cambridge University Press.

Porta, P.L. (1986) 'How Piero Sraffa took up the editorship of David Ricardo's *Works and Correspondence*', in *History of Economics Society Bulletin*, 8: 35–57.

Potier, J.P. (1991) *Piero Sraffa. Unorthodox economist 1898–1983*, London: Routledge.

Presley, J.R. (1978) *Robertsonian Economics*, London: Macmillan.

Presley, J.R. (ed.) (1992a) *Essays on Robertsonian Economics*, London: Macmillan.

Presley, J.R. (1992b) 'J.M. Keynes and D.H. Robertson: three phases of collaboration', in J.R. Presley (ed.) (1992a).

Pressnell, L.S. (1987) *External Economic Policy Since the War, I, The Post-War Financial Settlement*, London: Her Majesty's Stationery Office.

Ramsey, F.P. (1927) 'A contribution to the theory of taxation', *Economic Journal*, 37: 47–61.

Ranchetti, F. (1998) 'Sul rapporto tra Sraffa e Keynes', Conference on Piero Sraffa, Torino: Fondazione Luigi Einaudi.

Ranchetti, F. (1999) 'Introduzione' to P. Sraffa *Produzione di merci a mezzo di merci*, new edition, F. Ranchetti (ed.), Torino: Einaudi.

Ranchetti, F. (2001) 'On the relationship between Sraffa and Keynes', in T. Cozzi and R. Marchionatti (eds) (2001).

Robbins, L. (1928) 'The representative firm', *Economic Journal*, 38: 387–404.

Robbins, L. (1971) *Autobiography of an Economist*, London: Macmillan.

Robertson, D.H. (1915) *A Study of Industrial Fluctuation*, London: P.S. King; reprinted with a New Introduction in 1948, in *Reprints of Scarce Works on Political Economy*, London: London School of Economics and Political Sciences.

Robertson, D.H. (1920) 'Review of Mr. Keynes's *The Economic Consequences of the Peace*', *Economic Journal*, 30: 77–84.

Robertson, D.H. (1922) *Money*, Cambridge Economic Handbooks II, London: Nisbet.

Robertson, D.H. (1923) *The Control of Industry*, Cambridge Economic Handbooks IV, London: Nisbet.

Robertson, D.H. (1926) *Banking Policy and the Price Level*, London: P.S. King, Reprinted with a New Preface in 1949, New York: Augustus M. Kelley, Publishers.

Robertson, D.H. (1928a) *Money*, Cambridge Economic Handbooks II, revised edition, London: Nisbet.

Robertson, D.H. (1928b) 'Theories of banking policy', *Economica*, 7: 131–46; reprinted in J.R. Hicks (ed.) (1966).

Robertson, D.H. (1930) 'The trees of the forest', Symposium on Increasing Returns and the Representative Firm, *Economic Journal*, 40: 80–9.

Robertson, D.H. (1931a) 'Mr. Keynes's Theory of Money', *Economic Journal*, 41: 395–411.

Robertson, D.H. (1931b) *Economic Fragments*, London: P.S. King.

Robertson, D.H. (1933a) 'A note on the theory of money', *Economica*, 41: 243–7.

Robertson, D.H. (1933b) 'Saving and hoarding', *Economic Journal*, 43: 399–413.

Robertson, D.H. (1933c) 'A reply to J.M. Keynes and R.G. Hawtrey on saving and hoarding', *Economic Journal*, 43: 709–12.

Robertson, D.H. (1934) 'Industrial fluctuation and the natural rate of interest', *Economic Journal*, 44: 650–6.

Robertson, D.H. (1936) 'Some notes on Mr. Keynes' General Theory of Employment', *Quarterly Journal of Economics*, 51: 168–91.

Robertson, D.H. (1937) 'A rejoinder to Mr. Keynes's Alternative Theories of the Rates of Interest', *Economic Journal*, 47: 428–36.

Robertson, D.H. (1938a) 'Mr. Keynes and "Finance"', *Economic Journal*, 48: 314–18.

Robertson, D.H. (1938b) 'A reply to Keynes's comment on 'Mr. Keynes and "finance"', *Economic Journal*, 48: 555–6.

Robertson, D.H. (1940) *Essays in Monetary Theory*, London: P.S. King.

Robinson, E.A.G. (1947) 'John Maynard Keynes 1883–1946', *Economic Journal*, 57: 1–68.

Robinson, E.A.G.(1968) 'Pigou, Arthur Cecil', *International Encyclopedia of the Social Sciences*, 12: 90–7.

Robinson, E.A.G. (1971) 'Pigou, Arthur Cecil', in E.T. Williams and H.M. Palmer (eds), *Dictionary of National Biography*, Oxford: Oxford University Press.

Robinson, E.A.G. (1975) 'A personal view', in M. Keynes (ed.) (1975) *Essays on John Maynard Keynes*, Cambridge: Cambridge University Press.

Robinson, E.A.G. (1977) 'Keynes and his Cambridge colleagues', in D. Patinkin and J.C. Leith (eds), *Keynes, Cambridge and the General Theory*, London: Macmillan.

Robinson, E.A.G. (1985) 'The Cambridge "Circus"', in G.C. Harcourt (ed.) (1985).

Robinson, E.A.G. (1992) 'My apprenticeship as an economist', in M. Ezemberg (ed.), *Eminent Economists. Their Life Philosophies*, Cambridge: Cambridge University Press.

Robinson, E.A.G. (1994) 'Richard Kahn in the 1930s', *Cambridge Journal of Economics*, 18: 7–10.

Robinson, J. (1932a) 'Imperfect competition and falling supply price', *Economic Journal*, 42: 544–54; reprinted in J. Robinson (1951a).

Robinson, J. (1932b) *Economics is a Serious Subject. The Apologia of an Economist to the Mathematician, the Scientist and the Plain Man*, Cambridge: Heffers.

Robinson, J. (1933a) *The Economics of Imperfect Competition*, London: Macmillan.

Robinson, J. (1933b) 'The theory of money and the analysis of output', *Review of Economic Studies*, 1: 22–6; reprinted in J. Robinson (1951a).

Robinson, J. (1933c) 'Review of P.H. Wicksteed, *The Coordination of the Laws of Distribution*', *Economic Journal*, 43: 301–4.

Robinson, J. (1933d) 'A parable on saving and investment', *Economica*, 13: 75–84.
Robinson, J. (1934) 'Euler's theorem and the problem of distribution', *Economic Journal*, 44: 398–414.
Robinson, J. (1936a) 'Disguised unemployment', *Economic Journal*, 46: 225–37; reprinted in J. Robinson (1937a).
Robinson, J. (1936b) 'The long period theory of employment', *Zeitschrift für Nationalökonomie*, 7: 74–93, in J. Robinson (1937a).
Robinson, J. (1937a) *Essays in the Theory of Employment*, London: Macmillan.
Robinson, J. (1937b) *Introduction to the Theory of Employment*, London: Macmillan.
Robinson, J. (1937c) 'The foreign exchanges', in J. Robinson (1937a).
Robinson, J. (1938a) 'The classification of inventions', *Review of Economic Studies*, 5: 139–42.
Robinson, J. (1938b) 'The concept of hoarding', *Economic Journal*, 48: 231–6; reprinted in J. Robinson (1951a).
Robinson, J. (1941a) 'Rising supply price', *Economica*, 8: 1–8, in J. Robinson (1951a).
Robinson, J. (1941b) 'The financial problem of 1941', *The Banker*, 57: 8–13.
Robinson, J. (1942) *An Essay on Marxian Economics*, London: Macmillan.
Robinson, J. (1943) 'The international currency proposals', *Economic Journal*, 53: 161–75.
Robinson, J. (1951a) *Collected Economic Papers*, vol. I, Oxford: Blackwell.
Robinson, J. (1951b), 'The rate of interest', *Econometrica*; reprinted in J. Robinson (1979), *The Generalisation of The General Theory and Other Essays*, London: Macmillan.
Robinson, J. (1951c) 'Introduction', in J. Robinson (1951a).
Robinson, J. (1952) *The Rate of Interest and Other Essays*, London: Macmillan.
Robinson, J. (1966) 'Introduction', in J. Robinson, *An Essay on Marxian Economics*, 2nd edn, London: Macmillan.
Robinson, J. (1973a) *Collected Economic Papers*, vol. IV, Oxford: Blackwell.
Robinson, J. (1973b) 'Essays 1935. Introduction', in J. Robinson (1973a).
Robinson, J. (1973c) 'Preface', to J.A. Kregel, *The Reconstruction of Political Economy: an Introduction to Post-Keynesian Economics*, London: Macmillan
Robinson, J. (1976) 'Introduzione', in R. F. Kahn *L'occupazione e la crescita*, Torino: Einaudi.
Robinson, J. (1978a) *Contributions to Modern Economics*, Oxford: Blackwell.
Robinson, J. (1978b) 'The second crisis of economic theory', in *Contributions to Modern Economics*, New York: Academic Press.
Robinson, J. (1979a) *Collected Economic Papers*, vol. V, Oxford: Blackwell.
Robinson, J. (1979b) 'Michal Kalecki', in J. Robinson (1979a).
Roncaglia, A. (1975) *Sraffa e la teoria dei prezzi*, Roma: Laterza.
Roncaglia, A. (1978) *Sraffa and the Theory of Price*, London: Wiley.
Rosenbaum, S.P. (1998) *Aspects of Bloomsbury*, London: Macmillan.
Rosselli, A. (2001) 'Sraffa's edition of Ricardo's *Works*: reconstruction of a reconstruction', in T. Cozzi and R. Marchionatti (eds) (2001).
Rosselli, A. (2004) *Sraffa e la tradizione marshalliana*, Roma: Accademia Nazionale dei Lincei (English version forthcoming in *European Journal for the History of Economic Thought* (2005)).
Rymes, T.K. (1989) *Keynes's Lectures, 1932–1935*, Ann Arbor: University of Michigan Press.

Saltmarsh, J. and Wilkinson, P. (1960) *Arthur Cecil Pigou, 1877–1959*, printed for King's College Cambridge.

Samuelson, P. (1963) 'Sir D.H. Robertson (1890–1963)', *Quarterly Journal of Economics*, 77: 517–36.

Sanfilippo, E. (2003) 'Period analysis and ceteris paribus assumption in Marshall and Keynes', *International Journal of Applied Economics and Econometrics*, 11: 109–32.

Sardoni, C. (1999) 'The debate on excess capacity in the 1930s', in C. Sardoni and P. Kriesler (eds), *Themes in Political Economy. Essays in Honour of Geoff Harcourt*, vol. III, London: Routledge.

Sardoni, C. (2004) 'The contribution of Gerald Shove to the development of Cambridge Economics', *Review of Political Economy*, 16: 361–75.

Schumpeter, J.A. (1954) *History of Economic Analysis*, New York: Oxford University Press.

Shearmur, J. (1997) 'Hayek, Keynes and the State', *History of Economics Review*, 26: 68–82.

Shehadi, N. (1991) 'The London School of Economics and the Stockholm School in the 1930s', in L. Jonung (ed.), *The Stockholm School of Economics Revisited*, Cambridge: Cambridge University Press.

Shove, F. (1952) *Fredegond and Gerald Shove*, Cambridge: Cambridge University Press.

Shove, G.F. (1928) 'Varying costs and marginal net products', *Economic Journal*, 38: 258–66.

Shove, G.F. (1930) 'The representative firm and increasing returns', *Economic Journal*, 40: 94–116.

Shove, G.F. (1933a) 'The imperfection of the market'. *Economic Journal*, 43: 113–24.

Shove, G.F. (1933b) 'The economics of imperfect competition by Joan Robinson. Review', *Economic Journal*, 43: 657–61.

Shove, G.F.(1933c) 'Review of Hicks' *The Theory of Wages*', *Economic Journal*, 43: 460–72.

Shove, G.F. (1942) 'The place of Marshall's Principles in the development of economic theory', *Economic Journal*, 52: 294–329.

Shove, G.F. (1944) 'Mrs. Robinson on Marxian economics', *Economic Journal*, 54: 47–61.

Skidelsky, R. (1983) *John Maynard Keynes. Hopes Betrayed 1883–1920*, London: Macmillan.

Skidelsky, R. (1986) 'Keynes e Sraffa: un caso di non-comunicazione', in R. Bellofiore (ed.), *Piero Sraffa: tra teoria economica e grande cultura europea*, Milano: Franco Angeli.

Skidelsky, R. (1992) *John Maynard Keynes. The Economist as Saviour 1920–1937*, London: Macmillan.

Skidelsky, R. (2000) *John Maynard Keynes. Fighting for Britain 1937–1946*, London: Macmillan.

Sraffa, P. (1922) 'The bank crisis in Italy', *Economic Journal*, 32: 178–97.

Sraffa, P. (1925) 'Sulle relazioni tra costo e quantità prodotta', *Annali di Economia*, 2: 277–38; reprinted in P. Sraffa (1986); English translation in L. Pasmetti (ed.), *Italian Economic Papers*, vol III, Bologna: Il Mulino and Oxford University Press: 326–63.

Sraffa, P. (1926) 'The laws of returns under competitive conditions', *Economic Journal*, 36: 535–50.

Sraffa, P. (1930) 'A criticism', *Economic Journal*, 40: 89–92.
Sraffa, P. (1930) 'Rejoinder', *Economic Journal*, 40: 93.
Sraffa, P. (1932a) 'Dr. Hayek on money and capital', *Economic Journal*, 42: 42–53.
Sraffa, P. (1932b) 'A rejoinder', *Economic Journal*, 42: 249–51.
Sraffa, P. (1960) *Production of Commodities by Means of Commodities. Prelude to a Critique of Economic Theory*, Cambridge: Cambridge University Press.
Sraffa, P. (1986) *Saggi*, Bologna: Il Mulino.
Sraffa, P. (1991) *Lettere a Tania per Gramsci*, Roma: Editori Riuniti.
Swedberg, R. (1991) *Schumpeter. A Biography*, Princeton: Princeton University Press.
Targetti, F. (1984) 'Una biografia intellettuale', in N. Kaldor, *Equilibrio, distribuzione e crescita*, Torino: Einaudi.
Thirlwall, A.P. (ed.) (1976) *Keynes and International Monetary Relations*, London: Macmillan.
Thirlwall, A.P. (1987) *Nicholas Kaldor*, Brighton: Wheatsheaf Books.
Thirlwall, A.P. (1996) 'Nicholas Kaldor. A biography', in N. Kaldor, *Causes of Growth and Stagnation in the World Economy*, Cambridge: Cambridge University Press.
Tinbergen, J. (1939) *Statistical Testing of Business Cycles Theories. I: A Method and its Applications to Investment Activity*, Geneva: League of Nations.
Tinbergen, J. (1940) 'On a method of statistical business-cycle research. A reply', *Economic Journal*, 50: 141–54.
Todorov , T. (1994) *Face a l'extrême*, Paris: Éditions du Seuil.
Tonveronachi, M. (1983) *J.M. Keynes: dall'instabilità ciclica all'equilibrio di sottoccupazione*, Roma: La Nuova Italia Scientifica.
Tsiang, S.C. (1990) 'Keynes's "finance" demand for liquidity, Robertson's loanable funds theory, and Friedman's monetarism', in J.C. Wood and R.N. Woods (eds), *Milton Friedman: Critical Assessments*, vol. 3, London: Routledge.
Turner, M.S. (1989) *Joan Robinson and the Americans*, Armonk: Sharpe.
Turner, M.S. (1993) *Nicholas Kaldor and the Real World*, Armonk: Sharpe.
Waterman, A.M.C. (2003) 'Joan Robinson as a teacher', *Review of Political Economy*, 15: 589–96.
Wilson, T. (1940) 'Capital theory and the trade cycle', *Review of Economic Studies*, 7: 169–79.
Young, A.A. (1928) 'Increasing returns and economic progress', *Economic Journal*, 38: 527–42.
Young, W. (1987) *Interpreting Mr. Keynes. The IS-LM Enigma*, Cambridge: Polity Press.
Young, W. (1989) *Harrod and his Trade Cycle Group. The Origins and Development of the Growth Research Programme*, London: Macmillan.
Young, W. and Lee, F.S. (1993) *Oxford Economics and Oxford Economists*, London: Macmillan.
Zappia, C. (2001) 'Sraffa on Hayek: unexpected influences', in T. Cozzi and R. Marchionatti (eds) (2001).

Index

Printed in the United Kingdom
by Lightning Source UK Ltd.
110356UKS00006B/46-48